PERSONNEL MANAGEMENT

3rd Edition / **HERBERT J. CHRUDEN**
Professor of Business Administration
Sacramento State College

ARTHUR W. SHERMAN, JR.
Professor of Psychology
Sacramento State College

Published By

SOUTH-WESTERN PUBLISHING COMPANY

Cincinnati   Chicago   Burlingame, Calif.   Dallas   New Rochelle, N.Y.

P12

Preface

Since the first edition of this book was published, the body of knowledge relating to personnel management has continued to expand and to change as a result of research and developments that have occurred within the field. Furthermore, technological and social progress together with changing economic conditions and governmental regulations also have had influential effects upon the organizational environment within which people work. It has been the primary objective of the authors to consider these changes in the third edition. The many helpful suggestions that have been received from readers of the previous two editions have also been utilized in an effort to improve the organization and presentation of the material in this edition.

Greater recognition is given to the systems concept of personnel management and to the role and impact of computers in personnel work in this edition. The influence that modern organizational theory and the behavioral sciences have had upon the management of personnel has been given increased emphasis. More recent information pertaining to such topics as performance evaluation, morale, and employee adjustment has been introduced, and the material relating to the work group and its effect upon individual behavior has been expanded significantly. In several of the chapters, attention has been given to the impact that the civil rights movement and the federal manpower development programs are having upon personnel programs. The latest amendments to the Fair Labor Standards Act and to the Social Security Act, and data pertaining to manpower and occupational trends, are also included.

In order that students may continue to have the opportunity to apply the principles and theories of personnel management, a number of new cases, discussion problems, and questions have been included at the end of the chapters. These discussion materials are intended to encourage and to help the student integrate the information presented in the various chapters of the text and to apply it to the solution of current management problems.

A major purpose of this book is one of increasing the reader's knowledge of those theories and practices relating to the management of personnel which, in the light of current research and company experiences, appear to be most sound. Although the role of the personnel department and its program is emphasized, attention throughout the book also is focused upon the important role of department supervisors and executives with respect to personnel management. Wherever possible, the responsibilities of these individuals in the performance of the various personnel functions are considered. This book, thus, continues to support the view that while a personnel department must provide leadership for the personnel program, each executive and supervisor within an organization is to some extent a personnel manager. Consequently, it is the desire of the authors to provide a background of useful information for those persons who may have any responsibilities for the management of others within their organization as well as for those individuals who are members of a personnel department staff.

In preparing the manuscript for this edition, the authors have drawn not only upon the current literature in the personnel field but also upon the current practices of companies that have furnished materials relating to their personnel programs. The authors are indebted to the leaders in the field who have developed the available heritage of information and practices of personnel management and who have influenced the authors through their writings and personal associations. The authors have also been aided, particularly in the preparation of discussion problems and cases, by students in their classes, by former students, and by the participants in the management development programs with which they have been associated. The authors would like to recognize the following of their former students who have furnished materials that have been incorporated in some of the cases: Mike Bonham, Jim Quaschnick, Richard W. Corman, L. C. McClure, Jim Hanks, and Don Martine. In particular the authors also would like to express their appreciation to Mr. Earl Warner, Mr. Richard J. Jacinto, Mr. Frank Cathcart, Mr. Walter Halset, Professor Chester Healy, Col. Carroll S. Geddes, USAF Ret., Mr. Francis Stoffels, and Dr. Robert F. Mager for their contributions. Certainly this book would not have been possible without the understanding and cooperation of our wives, Marie Chruden and Leneve Sherman. Their many contributions are gratefully acknowledged.

Herbert J. Chruden

Arthur W. Sherman, Jr.

Contents

v

The Role of Personnel Management

The efficiency with which any organization can be operated will depend to a considerable measure upon how effectively its personnel can be managed and utilized. Every manager, therefore, must be able to work effectively with people and to resolve satisfactorily the many and varied problems that the management of these people may entail. Effective personnel management also requires the development of a program that will permit employees to be selected and trained for those jobs that are most appropriate to their developed abilities. Moreover, it requires that each employee be motivated to exert his maximum effort, that his performance be evaluated properly for results, and that he be remunerated on the basis of his contribution to the organization.

Although managers and supervisors in the past often tended to be arbitrary and autocratic in their relations with subordinates, today they are less able to have these tendencies. Neither are they able to force people to work harder by threatening them with the loss of their jobs or by subjecting them to physical or verbal abuse. The present generation of employees tends to be more enlightened and better educated than were their predecessors. They demand more considerate treatment and a more sophisticated form of leadership. Furthermore, because of the protection

1

that is afforded to them by their unions and by government legislation or because their skills are in short supply, many groups of employees are in a position to demand and obtain very favorable employment conditions and treatment.

Since the activities of most enterprises today are becoming more and more complex in nature, the managers in these enterprises are required to have greater technical competency than was formerly the case. In addition, they must have a better understanding of human behavior and of the processes by which personnel can be managed effectively. Fortunately, a growing body of knowledge relating to human behavior and to management systems and processes is being accumulated from experience and research which can be of assistance to the manager in developing good relations with subordinates. As an area of knowledge, personnel management is able to borrow from many of the more basic disciplines and to apply the contributions of these disciplines to the improvement of the personnel program. The contributions that have been derived from these disciplines will be covered in the discussion of the various processes of personnel management in this and the chapters that follow.

The purpose of this chapter is to acquaint the reader with the field of personnel management, the contributions that it can render to the enterprise, and the progress that has been made in the field and that may be expected to be achieved in the future. The discussion will be divided into the following topics:

- Contributions of personnel management.
- The nature and development of the personnel field.
- Personnel management as a field of study.

Contributions of Personnel Management

Since the early 1900's and particularly since the 1930's, a growing amount of attention has been given to personnel management by members of top management who have increasingly recognized the important contributions that it renders to the successful operation and, at times, to the survival of their organizations. The recognition being given to personnel management is the result of many factors some of which are: the growing enlightenment of management; the compelling pressures being exerted by economic competition, by organized labor, and by legislation; the effects that modern scientific and technological advancements have had upon the qualifications of and the composition of the labor force; and the growing body of knowledge relating to personnel management principles and methods that has been derived from experience and research.

Meeting Economic Competition

Both governmental and business enterprises are required by competitive pressures to keep their operating costs under control. Governmental agencies must compete with one another for the limited amount of revenue that is available and must keep their operating costs within the budgets that are established for them. Private enterprises must control their costs to the point that they can sell their product or service at a price that will meet domestic and/or foreign competition and still permit stockholders to earn a return on their investment.

Controlling labor costs. One of the principal costs in any organization is the cost of labor that is required to produce the goods or services that it supplies. The cost of this labor is determined not only by the amount of wages that a company pays to its personnel but also by the productivity that it receives from them in return. The labor costs of those employees who are paid a high wage rate but who are high producers, therefore, often may be less than the comparable cost of less efficient personnel who are paid a lower wage rate. Since labor costs are a function of individual productivity as well as remuneration, effective personnel management must insure that employees are selected, trained, and placed in those jobs where they can render the greatest contributions. Such management must also insure that each employee is motivated to exert his maximum effort and that he is remunerated in accordance with his worth to the company.

Increasing productivity. One of the major problems confronting employers today is that of increasing employee productivity in order to offset the cost of wage increases that must be granted to them. The trend lines in Figure 1-1 on page 4 indicate, however, that the wage rates for workers have tended to increase more rapidly than their output. Were it not for the constant efforts by management to increase employee output through the introduction of more effective personnel practices and production methods and through the installation of laborsaving equipment, the discrepancy between productivity and wage rates probably would be even greater. As employers continue to pay higher wage rates to their employees and to invest greater amounts of capital in laborsaving equipment, it is essential that they achieve corresponding improvements in efficiency. This achievement requires that management utilize the most scientific and most modern

Figure 1-1
WORKER PRODUCTIVITY

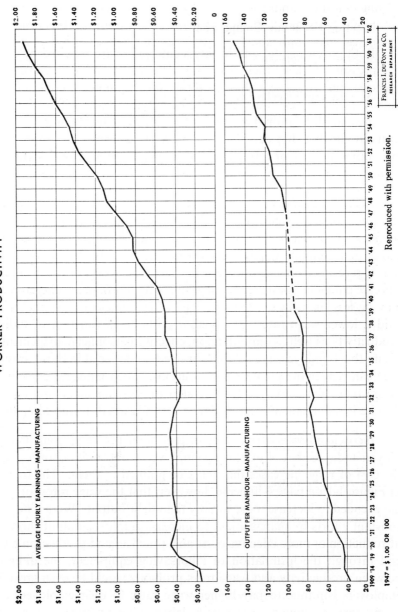

AVERAGE HOURLY EARNINGS—MANUFACTURING

OUTPUT PER MANHOUR—MANUFACTURING

1947 = $ 1.00 OR 100

Reproduced with permission.

methods and techniques of personnel management that existing experience and research in the field have been able to develop. Employers, thus, are finding that they can no longer manage their personnel on an arbitrary and emotional basis, nor can they staff the jobs within an organization with whomever may apply and still hope to compete effectively with companies that maintain progressive personnnel programs.

Maintaining Effective Relations with Unions

The fact that employers must now bargain collectively with their employees whenever the employees are unionized also has helped to increase the importance of the personnel program. Since union relations and collective bargaining require highly developed professional skills, competent management personnel as well as appropriate machinery and data must be developed for handling this phase of personnel management. The presence of a union also tends to make it more necessary for a company to conduct its program on an objective basis and to maintain more detailed records to substantiate management decisions affecting each employee.

An effective personnel program then is essential not only for the prevention of strife with the union but also for holding the union responsible for observing the terms of the labor agreement. While the unionization of a company's employees is not necessarily the result of poor personnel management, poor personnel management is likely to make the union seek protection for its members by forcing the addition of provisions to the labor agreement that may tend to restrict management's freedom of action or to increase its operating costs. Conversely, an effective personnel program can facilitate a feeling of mutual trust in which a "give and take" relationship reduces the need for having detailed provisions written into the agreement in order to protect the interests of both sides. The avoidance of such detailed provisions in the labor agreement results in an agreement which may prove to be more flexible and easier to administer.

Impact of Government Regulations

Since the 1930's personnel policies and practices increasingly have become the subject of federal and state regulation as have most phases of business activity in general. Prior to this time government regulations were limited largely to matters relating to the health and safety of workers and to the employment of women and children in industry. Since that time, however, the federal government has enacted numerous other laws. Examples of such laws are the Fair Labor Standards Act which affects minimum wage rates, overtime payments, and child labor and the Social Security Act which helps to provide a form of social insurance due to loss of income that an employee's family might suffer because of his unemployment, death, disability, or retirement. The Civil Rights Act which forbids discrimination based upon race, religion, color, and sex has had a significant impact upon employment, promotion, and other company personnel decisions.

Companies doing business with the government or engaged in transportation activities are subject to further regulations that may affect their personnel programs. Companies are also subject to laws affecting their relations with unions and unionizing efforts through such laws as the Taft-Hartley Act and the Landrum-Griffin Act.

Each state also provides certain regulations affecting the personnel program; and many states, such as New York, California, and Wisconsin, have enacted a considerable amount of legislation in this field. Laws affecting working conditions, workmen's compensation (for disability accidents), hours of employment, paydays, fair employment practices, and relations with unions are among the more common laws enacted by state governments.

As new laws affecting the personnel program are enacted, a greater responsibility is placed upon those individuals who are in charge of the personnel program to insure that the personnel actions of supervisors and managers throughout the organization are in compliance with these laws. Some state and federal laws also require that certain records be kept and reports submitted to appropriate agencies at specified intervals. The necessity for observing all applicable regulations and for keeping abreast of changes which continually occur in these regulations has increased considerably the responsibilities and the work load of the personnel program and has forced increases to be made in company personnel department staffs. While the primary objective of a personnel program should be to improve employee cooperation and efficiency rather than to keep the company out of trouble with the government, the latter objective is sometimes the one that stimulates the interest and support of top management for the program.

Contributing to Technological Progress

Industrial society today is characterized by technological and scientific advancements that are occurring at an ever-increasing rate. Achievements are now being realized that would have been impossible merely a few decades ago. The result is that new products, new production methods, and new equipment are continually emerging. These achievements have had their impact upon jobs being performed within a company and upon the individuals performing these jobs. In one survey of jobs in a large aircraft and missile company, for example, it was found that only a janitor's job and a few assembly jobs had remained basically unchanged since World War II.[1] While job conditions in this company may not necessarily be typical of industry as a whole, they do illustrate the types of changes that have been occurring to some degree in nearly every company.

The changes in the content of certain jobs, the creation of new jobs, and the elimination of existing jobs have created certain staffing problems for many companies. It has necessitated that more emphasis be placed either upon training personnel to meet the increased demands of their jobs or upon retraining them to fill other jobs where their former jobs have grown beyond their capacity or have been eliminated. Scientific and technological progress also has had the effect of increasing the proportionate number of jobs that require personnel with a greater degree of ability and education. Thus, as one article notes:

> Rosie the Riveter has long since been replaced by Andrew the Assembler, who must know riveting, drilling, countersinking, and a mixed batch of other techniques.[2]

This article also points out that:

> In industry after industry, jobs requiring some degree of judgment and flexibility have replaced the old one-operation tasks and the old continuous runs. Materials are costlier, tolerances closer, production lines more varied. Technician level jobs multiply like fruit flies as production line jobs decrease. This is especially true in research and development industries that do the most hiring.[3]

Technological progress has resulted in the more rapid growth of white-collar jobs in comparison with the blue-collar jobs. Figure 1-2 illustrates this growth trend and the fact that, since 1956, there have been more white-collar than blue-collar workers employed within the labor force. In view of this trend, it can be anticipated that jobs for professional, technical, service, and clerical workers will have the greatest rate of growth in the future.

Since there are proportionately fewer individuals in the labor market who possess the superior qualifications that are needed to meet the projected occupational growth trends, company personnel programs will be

---

[1] "Only High School Grads' Need Apply," *Business Week* (August 11, 1962), p. 50.
[2] *Ibid.*
[3] *Ibid.*, p. 51.

Figure 1-2

COMPARISON OF GROWTH TRENDS BETWEEN
WHITE-COLLAR AND BLUE-COLLAR OCCUPATIONS

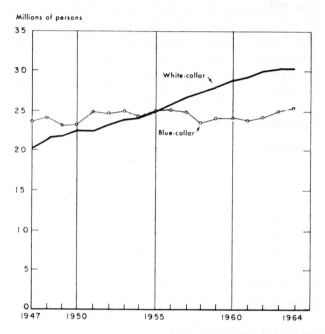

Source: U.S. Department of Labor, *Occupational Outlook Handbook*, 1966–1967 Edition, p. 6.

required to devote more attention to employee recruitment, selection, and training and to adapt their methods of motivation, supervision, and remuneration to meet these trends.

On the other hand a company, through its personnel program, must also cope with the problem of minimizing hardships for those employees who are displaced by technological progress. When it is not possible to reassign displaced employees to jobs within the organization, the company should assist them in obtaining employment with other companies. To ease their financial hardship, companies may grant employees who are nearing retirement-age pension benefits and may give others separation bonuses.

One of the major problems that many companies encounter as the result of technological progress is the demand of the union for provisions in the labor agreement that will help to protect its members against the loss of their jobs. In particular, unions may demand and, if they have the economic power, force the company to agree to certain work rules that may prescribe the size of work crews, the limits of the work load, and the employment of personnel on a standby basis. Grievances, slowdowns, and strikes also may reflect union displeasure over what it considers to be the company's failure to protect the employment rights of its members during periods of technological change. The problems created by technological progress, therefore, demand that personnel managers develop a program for solving these problems in a manner that will minimize personal hardships for employees and loss of efficiency for the company.

Overcoming the Cultural Lag

The progress in science and technology, unfortunately, has not been accompanied by comparable developments in the social sciences where personnel management has its roots. The widening gap between the physical and the social sciences has been cited frequently by scholars and is often referred to as *cultural lag*. While we are at present acquiring vast amounts of knowledge in such areas as nuclear energy and space technology, we are not making comparable progress in learning more about human behavior. Advancements in the physical sciences, furthermore, have created many new problems affecting behavior through the changes that have been brought about in the work environment. Increases in monotony and in emotional tensions have often been the by-product of improvements in production methods.

To reduce the cultural lag and the human problems created by technology, more money and emphasis must be devoted to research in the personnel field. Unfortunately, of the billions of dollars that government and industry are spending each year on research, only a very small proportion has been spent on research which relates directly to the personnel field.

Most companies also tend to devote most of their attention and budgets to their sales, production, and technical research programs rather than to their personnel program. The reason for this condition may be due to the fact that the results and benefits to be gained through efforts devoted to improved production and sales are more immediate and more tangible in nature. While improved selection and training procedures may result in an employee performing his job more effectively, the financial return that is realized over the years is difficult to measure with accuracy. When objective data can be compiled from personnel records and from research activities, however, these data can help to provide tangible evidence regarding the benefits to be gained from the personnel program and can serve as a basis for convincing top management of this fact.

As technological advancements create more personnel problems, it becomes increasingly important for a company to have an effective personnel program for resolving these problems. An effective program, however, can only be developed with the support of top management including the granting of sufficient funds for its operation and for the conduct of research which permits the program to keep abreast of technological progress. Future progress in the field also requires more coordination and exchange of information in the field through such professional organizations as the Society for Advancement of Management, the American Management Association, the Society for Personnel Administration, the Public Personnel Association, the American Psychological Association as well as various local personnel organizations and government agencies. These organizations and agencies, thus, are contributing much to the development of personnel management as a profession in fact rather than in name only.

The Nature and Development of the Personnel Field

While personnel management has become the subject of formal and specialized study and practice in comparatively recent times, the roots of the field go deep into the past. Although the existence of a personnel department is also fairly new, personnel management in some form has been necessary as long as formal organizations have been in existence. The policies and procedures governing the performance of personnel functions as well as the knowledge and tools that have been accumulated relative to their use, however, are advancing rapidly as the result of experience and research. Changes are occurring in the personnel field not only as the result of technological advancements and the accumulation of new knowledge but also as the result of the changing composition of the work force and the developing concepts concerning human behavior. The discussion of these changes which have characterized the evolutionary development of personnel management and the functions that it entails follows.

Processes of Personnel Management

Regardless of its size certain personnel management functions or processes must be performed within any company. These processes contribute to the procurement, development, utilization, and maintenance of the work force that is to be managed.

Procurement. This process includes the recruitment and selection of qualified individuals for employment with the company. The recruitment phase of this function may range from merely waiting for individuals to apply who happen to be looking for work to aggressively conducting a nationwide search for qualified candidates. Selection includes choosing from those who apply the candidate who is most qualified for a particular opening. The resulting selection decision may be based upon an extensive amount of data about each candidate or it may merely reflect a preference of an employer for blue eyes or for all-conference athletes.

Development. The development process is one of educating and training employees to meet the requirements of their jobs and to keep abreast of changes in these requirements. It may include the development of skill and knowledge as well as attitudes and personality traits. Employee development may occur as the result of extensive and carefully organized programs, or it may be left to occur informally and incidentally as the result of trial-and-error learning.

Personnel utilization. The utilization of personnel includes the initial placement of employees in those jobs that they can perform most effectively and in which the need is greatest for their services. It also entails the evaluation of their performance and of their work loads for the purpose of making required changes in placement by means of transfers, promotions, and demotions. The functions of motivation, supervision, leadership, and discipline all contribute to the effective utilization of personnel, as do those functions that contribute to their health and safety.

Remuneration. The desire of employees for income provides an important means of motivating them to exert greater effort. In order that employees may be paid fairly with respect to the demands of their jobs and the wages that are paid to other employees, job evaluations can be utilized to determine the rates for each job more objectively. Financial incentives based upon time standards provide another means of relating the remuneration of employees to their contributions and of motivating them to exert extra effort. Remuneration normally also includes the payment of certain fringe benefits such as paid holidays, vacations, health insurance, life insurance, and pensions which serve to supplement the wages that are paid to employees directly.

While some managers may not be aware that they are involved to some extent with each of these processes that have been mentioned, they nevertheless are involved to some extent, if only on an informal basis. This fact is equally true for those who are managing subordinate managers as it is for those who are managing operative personnel. Although some of these managers may tend to neglect or to ignore their share of responsibility for performing personnel functions, these functions generally have become the subject of increasing attention in most companies. As the body of knowledge within the personnel field continues to expand through the accumulation of information from experience and research, there is every reason to assume that the contributions of the field to the improvement of management will continue to grow.

Development of the Field

Although personnel management did not become a field of specialization until about World War I, certain developments from which the field has emerged may be traced back to the Middle Ages and to the Industrial Revolution. The growth of an industrial economy with large-scale manufacturing coupled with the scientific management movement and periods of economic and military crises in this country all have contributed to the evolutionary development of the personnel field.

The influence of the Middle Ages. It was during the Middle Ages that free employment relationships upon which contemporary personnel relations are based began to emerge. The growth of towns and villages provided a new demand for goods and services as well as employment for those seeking to escape their positions as serfs within the feudal system. Skilled artisans banded together to form guilds which established controls and regulations pertaining to their respective trades, and most important, the right of individuals to enter and practice the trade.[4] These guilds were the forerunner of today's employer associations and helped to provide standards of craftmanship and the foundation for apprenticeship training that many craft unions still require of individuals seeking to enter a trade. Since the opportunity for journeymen to establish their own shops was limited, many of them were forced to continue to work for other master craftsmen and, as a result, began to form yeomanry guilds which resembled the contemporary trade union.

Industrial Revolution. Until the Industrial Revolution most goods were manufactured in small shops or in the worker's home by handicraft methods of production. The Industrial Revolution stimulated the growth

---

[4]Cyril Curtis Ling, *The Management of Personnel Relations* (Homewood, Illinois: Richard D. Irwin, Inc., 1965), pp. 21–23.

of factories as the result of the availability of capital, free labor, power-driven equipment, improved production techniques, as well as the growing demand for manufactured goods. The factory system thus permitted goods to be manufactured more cheaply than had been possible in homes and small shops. The system with its specialization of work, however, brought about new problems in the area of human relations through the creation of many unskilled and repetitive jobs in which the work often tended to be monotonous and unchallenging as well as unhealthy and hazardous. Unlike the craftsman, who enjoyed some degree of economic security by virtue of having a marketable skill, the factory worker lacked security because he could be replaced easily by other individuals who could be trained quickly to perform his job. For this same reason he had very little bargaining power with which to improve his situation.

From the standpoint of personnel management, the Industrial Revolution represented the beginning of many problems which managers continue to face. While significant progress has been made in resolving the problems of how to organize, coordinate, motivate, and control the activities of large numbers of personnel who are working in a particular area and how to provide for their health, safety, and morale, further research and improvement is needed.

Early developments in America. During the early period of this country, the factory workers usually had to accept whatever conditions of employment were offered to them. The conditions that existed are typified by Figure 1-3. The need of employees for income and their fear of being unable to find other jobs usually ruled out the alternative of quitting. Even when workers were able to find other employment they were likely to receive equally poor conditions and treatment from the new employer. Their only outlet was to turn to the opportunities that were provided by the Western Frontier.

Prior to the middle of the last century workers had very little legal protection. There were no laws to guarantee their individual or collective bargaining rights and, until the Commonwealth v. Hunt decision of 1842, attempts of employees to organize and to bargain collectively with employers was considered, under the existing common law, to constitute a criminal act of conspiracy.

The gradual extension of voting privileges and free education to all citizens helped workers to become more effectual politically. Through their ability to muster public support for their cause, workers gradually were able to gain the passage of certain legislation that offered them some degree

Figure 1-3

RULES & REGULATIONS
To Be Observed By All Persons
Employed In The Factory Of
AMASA WHITNEY

FIRST : The Mill will be put into operation 10 minutes before sunrise at all seasons of the year. The gate will be shut 10 minutes past sunset from the 20th of March to the 20th of September, at 30 minutes past 8 from the 20th of September to the 20th of March. Saturdays at sunset.

SECOND : It will be required of every person employed, that they be in the room in which they are employed, at the time mentioned above for the mill to be in operation.

THIRD : Hands are not allowed to leave the factory in working hours without the consent of their Overseer. If they do, they will be liable to have their time set off.

FOURTH : Anyone who by negligence or misconduct causes damage to the machinery, or impedes the progress of the work, will be liable to make good the damage for the same.

FIFTH : Anyone employed for a certain length of time, will be expected to make up their lost time, if required, before they will be entitled to their pay.

SIXTH : Any person employed for no certain length of time, will be required to give at least 4 weeks notice of their intention to leave (sickness excepted) or forfeit 4 weeks pay, unless by particular agreement.

SEVENTH : Anyone wishing to be absent any length of time, must get permisison of the Overseer.

EIGHTH : All who have leave of absence for any length of time will be expected to return in that time; and, in case they do not return in that time and do not give satisfactory reason, they will be liable to forfeit one week's work or less, if they commence work again. If they do not, they will be considered as one who leaves without giving any notice.

NINTH : Anything tending to impede the progress of manufacturing in working hours, such as unnecessary conversation, reading, eating fruit, &c.&c., must be avoided.

TENTH : While I shall endeavor to employ a judicious Overseer, the help will follow his direction in all cases.

ELEVENTH : No smoking will be allowed in the factory, as it is considered very unsafe, and particularly specified in the Insurance.

TWELFTH : In order to forward the work, job hands will follow the above regulations as well as those otherwise employed.

THIRTEENTH : It is intended that the bell be rung 5 minutes before the gate is hoisted, so that all persons may be ready to start their machines precisely at the time mentioned.

FOURTEENTH : All persons who cause damage to the machinery, break glass out of the windows, &c., will immediately inform the Overseer of the same.

FIFTEENTH : The hands will take breakfast, from the 1st of November to the last of March, before going to work—they will take supper from the 1st of May to the last of August, 30 minutes past 5 o'clock P.M.—from the 20th of September to the 20th of March between sundown and dark—25 minutes will be allowed for breakfast, 30 minutes for dinner, and 25 minutes for supper, and no more from the time the gate is shut till started again.

SIXTEENTH : The hands will leave the Factory so that the doors may be fastened within 10 minutes from the time of leaving off work.

AMASA WHITNEY

Winchendon, Mass. July 5, 1830.

of protection. State laws regulating hours of work for women and children were among the earliest forms of labor legislation to be enacted in this country. As time passed protective legislation was extended to cover hours of work for male labor, working conditions affecting employee health and safety, and compensation payments for injuries suffered through industrial accidents. This legislation, together with the worker's collective bargaining achievements, eventually helped to bring about substantial improvements in employment conditions.

Growth of large-scale enterprise. It was not until the introduction of mass production methods that full advantage was to be gained from the developments that had been introduced by the Industrial Revolution. Mass production was made possible through the production and assembly of standardized parts and by the development of the corporate form of enterprise in which ownership was vested among many individual stock-holders. Thus, instead of taking an active hand in the management of the enterprise, this function was delegated by the stockholders to the new and expanding group of professional managers.

The growth of large-scale manufacturing operations also was made possible through the further improvement of production techniques and laborsaving machinery and equipment. Although these developments increased worker productivity, they also increased the overhead costs in relationship to total production costs. As a result of this situation, more attention had to be devoted to the problem of utilizing the production equipment and facilities efficiently. In addition to becoming more mechanized, many jobs were simplified to the point that the same work cycle was repeated by a worker hundreds of times a day. These repetitive type operations, however, permitted any time savings resulting from increased effort or improved work methods on the part of a worker to multiply very rapidly.

The scientific management movement. By the beginning of this century, rising labor and overhead costs had forced management to devote more effort to achieving greater production efficiency through the improvement of work methods and the development of standards by which employee efficiency could be judged. Such efforts led to the scientific management movement during the early part of this century, which had a definite impact upon personnel management. The movement helped to stimulate the use of new personnel management tools with which to appraise and stimulate efforts of employees. However, it also created new human relations problems for personnel managers to solve.

The scientific management movement to a considerable extent was stimulated by the contributions of Frederick W. Taylor. Taylor believed that work could be systematically analyzed and studied by using the same scientific approach as that followed by the researchers in the laboratory.[5] In his words, scientific management constituted "the substitution of exact scientific investigation and knowledge for the old individual judgment or opinion, either of the workman or the boss, in all matters relating to the work done in the establishment."[6] Thus, Taylor relied upon time studies as a basis for establishing the proper methods and standards for performing a job, for training and supervising employees in the use of the proper methods, and for evaluating their work.

Taylor believed also that scientific management offered the best means for increasing the productivity and the earnings of the workers and for providing higher profits for owners and lower prices for customers. He regarded accurate performance standards, based upon objective data gathered from time studies and other sources, as constituting an important personnel management tool for rewarding the superior workers and for eliminating the inefficient ones. Furthermore, he believed that financial incentives, which permit workers to earn more by working harder and more efficiently, represented the best form of employee motivation. This concept was in sharp contrast to the prevailing practice, that has never disappeared completely, of attempting to gain more work from employees by threatening them with punishment including the loss of their jobs.

Perhaps most important was Taylor's recognition that efficiency was dependent upon good planning as well as proper performance. However, as contrasted to today's prevailing philosophy which advocates enlarging the worker's job by allowing him to participate in planning and decision making, Taylor felt that the planning function was primarily the responsibility of management.

Taylor's contributions to personnel management. There probably has never been a leader in the field of management whose contributions and philosophies have been the subject of more review, analysis, and interpretation than those of Frederick W. Taylor.[7] While it has been suggested that Taylor, in placing primary emphasis upon work standards, methods improvements, and financial incentive systems may have neglected to consider the nonfinancial sources of motivation or the influence of the informal group, he did seek to improve the economic well-being of the factory

---

[5]See Chapter 26 for a detailed résumé of the scientific approach to problem solving.

[6]Frederick W. Taylor, "What Is Scientific Management?" as reprinted in Harwood F. Merrill (Editor), *Classics in Management* (New York: American Management Association, 1960), p. 80.

[7]See J. Boddewyn, "Frederick Winslow Taylor Revisited," *Journal of the Academy of Management*, Vol. 4, No. 2 (August, 1961), pp. 100–107.

worker. Taylor was convinced that scientific management afforded workers with the best opportunity for such improvement by offering them the means by which they could increase their productivity and share in the resulting benefits. Although his approach may have been somewhat autocratic in comparison with today's emphasis upon soliciting employee participation and contributions in connection with work measurement and methods improvement, it was progressive in terms of the practices used by management at the time. Furthermore, in the area of personnel management, Taylor helped management to recognize the fact that employees differ in their abilities and that many of them through lack of proper job placement and training do not have the opportunity to make maximum use of their abilities to the detriment of themselves and the company. Taylor's contributions were augmented by such contemporaries as the Gilbreths and Gantt whose approaches tended to place more emphasis upon the human as well as the technical problems of engineering.

Growth of Specialization in Personnel

It was not until about the beginning of this century that personnel management had evolved into a field of specialization. The influence of scientific management upon the development of functional specialization undoubtedly helped to stimulate the growth of personnel management as an area of study.

Functional specialization. Until about 1900 the functions of personnel management, which were limited largely to hiring, firing, and timekeeping, were handled by each supervisor as part of his job as a "boss." As production methods became more complicated and the work load of the supervisor increased, his responsibility relating to the keeping of time and payroll records was often assigned to a clerk, who was in effect one of the first "personnel specialists." This initial record-keeping function in some instances was enlarged to include certain responsibilities for employment and eventually to include other functions that were assigned to the personnel department.

Personnel as a welfare function. Employee welfare also had become the subject of attention by the beginning of this century, and the position of welfare secretary had been established within some companies by this time. The creation of this position resulted from the influence of religion and philanthropy, and in some instances was the result of management's desire to discourage unionization. Regardless of the underlying motives, the creation of the position of welfare secretary represented one of the beginnings of the personnel department and focused attention upon providing cultural, educational, or recreational facilities for employees and upon providing financial, medical, housing, and similar forms of assistance.[8] Many of the persons who were appointed as welfare secretaries, as might be expected, had backgrounds in philanthropic or social work. Some agencies such as the Y.M.C.A., furthermore, established programs for the purpose of training people to become welfare secretaries.[9] The influence of the welfare secretary approach to personnel management continued to exist to some degree until the depression of the 1930's and probably was a factor in attracting, among others, certain individuals to the field who "liked people and wanted to help them."

The personnel department. Although it existed earlier in the form of an employment or welfare department, 1912 has been established as the approximate date when the personnel department first came into being in the modern sense. By 1915 the first college personnel course consisting of a training program for employment managers was offered by the Tuck School at Dartmouth College, and by 1919 at least a dozen colleges were offering training programs in personnel management.[10] By the beginning of the 1920's, therefore, the field of personnel management had become fairly well established as had personnel departments in many of the larger companies and governmental organizations. These departments were established for the purpose of coordinating personnel activities and assisting managers and supervisors in the management of their personnel.

Development of the Functions of Personnel Management

Although the evolution of the personnel field progressed slowly at first, it began to accelerate during certain periods of history. War periods, in particular, forced significant developments to take place and special emphasis to be given to particular functional areas to meet the needs of the emergency. Periods of depression and prosperity also brought about new developments within the personnel program and as a result there were changes in the employment market and in the funds that were available to support the program.

_____

[8]Henry Eilbirt, "The Development of Personnel Management in the United States," *Business History Review*, Vol. 33, No. 3 (Autumn, 1959), pp. 345–364.

[9]Ling, *op. cit.*, p. 80.

[10]Eilbirt, *op. cit.*, pp. 10–11.

Employee selection. While employee selection was one of the personnel functions which was given early consideration, it was not until the need was created by World War I that significant progress began to be achieved in the development of selection tools. As a part of the contributions rendered by the field of psychology at that time, the Army Alpha and Beta tests were constructed for the purpose of selecting personnel for military assignments. Experience with the use of these tests for measuring intelligence encouraged the construction of various other tests for measuring such factors as trade knowledge, aptitude, interest, and personality, and these tests began to be used increasingly by government and industry. The use of psychological tests received a similar emphasis during World War II and more recent periods of military conflict.

Training. Another personnel function that was the subject of considerable emphasis by both industry and government during the two wars was training. Experience and knowledge gained in the field of training during these wars did much to make companies aware of its potential contributions with the result that training has become an important division of the personnel department. The influence of the Training Within Industry (T.W.I.) program which was developed to train supervisors during World War II is still experienced in many companies today.

Fringe benefits. By the 1920's certain benefits and services began to be provided for employees by some companies as a part of their personnel programs. One of these services, employee counseling, made use of the growing body of knowledge being acquired from the fields of psychology and psychiatry. Other benefits that were initiated included those relating to employee health and recreation, paid holidays, vacation, sick leave, and paid life insurance policies. However, many of these benefits, which often were installed in a spirit of benevolent paternalism, were eliminated during the 1930's. As the result of employee and union demands rather than employer generosity, most of these benefits were reintroduced on an even larger scale starting with World War II.

Other developments. During the 1920's efforts were made to develop a more effective system of wage and salary administration which led to the development of job evaluation. One of the first plans for evaluating jobs on the basis of their work characteristics was developed by Merrill R. Lott in 1924. While job evaluation has never received the attention accorded certain other functions of personnel management, systems utilized have been continually reinforced and improved. By the late 1920's the need for greater knowledge concerning human behavior based upon objective evidence rather than upon mere opinion was reflected in an emphasis upon personnel research. One of the most significant studies ever to be conducted was the Hawthorne Study which took place at the Chicago plant of the Western Electric Company beginning in the late 1920's. Several sociological studies, including the *Yankee City Study* of a New England industrial community, were also conducted during this period. While the depression severely limited funds for research in the social sciences, subsidies by the government during and following World War II directly and indirectly helped revitalize research efforts. The availability of funds from various educational foundations since World War II has also helped to stimulate greater research efforts.

Personnel Management in the Postwar Era

By the end of World War II personnel management as a field had come of age, and its contributions to production efficiency had become more widely accepted. No longer was personnel management a function that was being performed by a payroll clerk or a welfare secretary. Instead, the responsibility for the coordination of this function had been assigned to a member of management who might occupy a position in the company as high as that of vice-president.

The number of persons engaged in personnel work has continued to increase and today there are about 100,000 persons in this field, according to the *Occupational Outlook Handbook*.[11] Well over half of this number, according to the handbook, are employed by private firms. The next largest number is employed by federal, state, and local government agencies.

The functions performed by the personnel program and the benefits and services that are provided by it no longer are considered to be "frills" or acts of benevolence or paternalism; rather, they are the result of company efforts to improve employee efficiency and morale and/or the result of collective bargaining with the union. Due to the high level of economic prosperity, the increased emphasis upon personnel research, and the growing strength of organized labor, developments have continued at a rather rapid rate in the personnel field following World War II.

---

[11]U.S. Department of Labor, *Occupational Outlook Handbook*, 1966–1967 Edition (Washington, D.C.: U.S. Government Printing Office), p. 39.

Areas of emphasis. Following World War II management development became one of the first personnel functions to receive special attention
as a result of company efforts to rebuild their management staffs which had
become depleted and often inefficient during the competition-free period of
World War II. The existence of labor strife as well as a level of low morale
and efficiency in many companies also stimulated efforts to improve employee cooperation and to promote better mutual understanding. It also
caused a greater emphasis, and sometimes overemphasis, to be placed upon
employee communication and participation programs and upon the improvement of human relations. The organization of training programs to
help managers and supervisors better understand their subordinates as
individuals and as members of a work group tended to characterize company efforts to improve personnel relations. These programs generally
placed considerable emphasis upon the use of participative leadership
techniques in the supervision of personnel and upon helping the manager to
acquire greater insight into the causes of his subordinates' behavior and the
reaction of these subordinates to his personality. Managers also have been
aided in developing a greater awareness of the reactions of others to them
by participating in sensitivity training courses. This type of training which
was pioneered by the National Training Laboratory for Group Development is now being provided by a number of university centers throughout
the nation.

Current emphasis. In recent years the trend has been to broaden the
study of human behavior and to augment the basic contributions derived
from the field of psychology with those being provided by the fields of
sociology and anthropology to constitute what is termed _behavioral
science_. As the term science would imply, the study of human behavior is
approached through the use of the scientific method in which tests of
statistical and clinical significance are applied to the data that are collected.
Psychologists and others doing research in the behavioral sciences thus
attempt to resolve human relations problems in much the same way as the
physical scientists would study physical phenomena by formulating hypotheses and by measuring, counting, and observing behavioral phenomena
that will serve to test these hypotheses.[12]

Efforts to get employees to cooperate and to exert their maximum
efforts also have helped to renew company interest in financial incentive
plans. Unlike the original incentive plans of a few decades ago, the present

---

[12]See Harold M. F. Rush, "What Is Behavioral Science?" *The Conference Board Record,*
September, 1965.

ones devote greater emphasis to giving employees the opportunity to become more involved with decisions affecting their work as well as the opportunity to earn more money. Some of the present plans, such as profit sharing, have permitted the incentive payments to be deferred until retirement, thus providing funds for this purpose as well as savings in income tax to be realized. In addition to those pension plans that have been developed in connection with a financial incentive system, there are many more that have been integrated with company retirement programs. Private pension plans began to increase rapidly in number about 1950 following a 1948 Supreme Court ruling that they were a legitimate subject for collective bargaining. The vast majority of the larger companies now provide a pension plan for their employees, and the small enterprises, as the result of union pressure and the competition for good personnel, are rapidly being forced to do likewise.

Changing Conditions and Concepts

Employees today tend to be better educated and more enlightened. The proportion of males between the ages of 25 and 29 in the labor force who had completed 12 or more years of schooling, for example, rose from 38.8 percent in 1940 to 50.6 percent in 1950 and to 60 percent in 1960.[13] There is every reason to believe that this trend will continue in the decades ahead. If their cooperation is to be obtained, employees must be treated in a manner that recognizes their varied needs as well as their sense of dignity and self-respect as participants in a common organizational endeavor. As this trend has progressed and as employees have become more enlightened and accustomed to higher living standards, they have also demanded more sophisticated leadership from management. In order to provide such leadership, managers and supervisors are forced to have the intelligence, education, and training necessary to cope with the problems confronting them. With the body of knowledge pertaining to personnel management being expanded continually as the result of research and experience, the responsibility of the personnel department in getting the line managers and supervisors to translate this knowledge into practice is continuing to increase.

Personnel Management as a Field of Study

As noted earlier, the field of personnel management borrows heavily from the research and knowledge of other disciplines, particularly the social

[13]*Monthly Labor Review*, Vol. 88, No. 6 (June, 1965), p. 626.

sciences. The trend in personnel management, therefore, has been to make greater use of an interdisciplinary approach in personnel research efforts and in the analysis of personnel problems.

Disciplines Contributing to the Field

Psychology is probably the discipline that has contributed the most to the field of personnel management. In addition to psychology, personnel management also has drawn heavily upon the contributions rendered by the fields of economics, law, statistics, engineering as well as the field of management, which is developing into a discipline in its own right.

Psychology. Personnel management has relied heavily upon the contributions rendered by the field of psychology. One of the best known of the pioneers in industrial psychology was Hugo Münsterberg whose book, *Psychology and Industrial Efficiency*, published in 1913, called attention to the contributions that psychology as a field of study could render in the areas of employment testing, training, and efficiency improvement. Many other psychologists who followed his example made notable contributions to personnel management. Among them are Walter Dill Scott, recognized for his early work in the selection of salesmen and for his classic book in personnel management with Clothier and Spriegel; J. McKeen Cattell, noted for his test development activities and efforts in establishing The Psychological Corporation (1921); and Walter Van Dyke Bingham, author of books in interviewing and aptitude testing and later chief psychologist for the War Department. Professors and researchers in American universities whose early work has contributed substantially to the present efforts include Poffenberger of Columbia, Burtt of Ohio State, Kornhauser of Chicago, and Viteles of Pennsylvania.

G. Stanley Hall, the first president of the American Psychological Association (1892), was among those who recognized the need for a journal that would focus on the applications of psychology to industry. He founded the *Journal of Applied Psychology* in 1917 that shortly was taken over by J. P. Porter. The *Journal of Applied Psychology* and *Personnel Psychology*, which largely grew out of the early efforts of Bingham, are the leading psychological journals devoted to the dissemination of literature in the personnel and industrial fields. Psychological research stimulated by World War I and again in World War II has helped to bring about further advances in psychological testing, in performance appraisal techniques, and in learning theory. In more recent years research and training centers have

made significant progress in the areas of sensitivity training, group dynamics, and organizational behavior.   Currently, in government and
industry the contributions of industrial psychology are being utilized to
achieve more effective results in connection with job analysis, opinion surveys, vocational guidance, counseling, interviewer training, and the
reduction of fatigue and accidents.

Economics. Personnel recruitment, wage and salary administration,
fringe benefits, and collective bargaining are but a few of the areas of
personnel management which involve the subject of economics. Many of
the factors that affect the behavior and efficiency of employees, either
individually or collectively, are also economic in nature. The personnel
program, on the other hand, has an important influence upon labor costs
which in turn affect the cost, selling price, and demand for a company's
product and, ultimately, the profits that it earns. All of these factors which
are economic in nature are important to the development and maintenance
of a sound personnel program.

Law. The fact that personnel management more and more is the subject of government regulation and is itself contributing to a growing body
of industrial jurisprudence has increased the importance of law to personnel management.   Contract negotiation and administration, as well as
arbitration, is increasingly being handled by persons with legal training.
While the technical problems of law should be reserved for the legal
specialists, at least some basic understanding of law relating to employment
and labor relations is desirable for all persons who are engaged in personnel
management.

Mathematics and statistics. The growing use of computers and of
quantitative approaches to decision making, including those involving
personnel, has increased the importance and the use of mathematics and
statistics in business. Mathematical models are being used increasingly to
depict organizational and human relationships and to solve management
problems.   In personnel work, statistics is an important tool for use in
connection with testing, morale surveys, job evaluation, wage and salary
programs, and interpretations of various personnel data such as those
relating to turnover, absenteeism, and accidents. While the more complicated statistical work is handled by trained statisticians, all persons
working in the personnel field should have sufficient background to understand and interpret the statistical concepts and data and the quantitative
approaches that are being used to make personnel management decisions.

Industrial engineering. The field of industrial engineering has helped to provide a basis for establishing standards that can be used in judging performance and in developing financial incentives. It has helped to contribute also to the improvement of production methods and working conditions. Close coordination between industrial engineering and personnel activities, therefore, is essential to the maintenance of good employee morale and efficiency. If the personnel manager has some familiarity with industrial engineering, he is in a better position to utilize the contributions of that field for improving his relations with employees.

Management. The subject of management is rapidly becoming a field of study in its own right with a developing body of knowledge and principles. A knowledge of the processes that are involved in the management of personnel and of the organizational structures and principles that facilitate this process is just as important in personnel work as is a knowledge of human behavior. Increasingly it is recognized that development of the proper organizational environment, which is an important responsibility of management, can be just as vital to building good personnel relations as the face-to-face relations that supervisors have with their subordinates.

Criticism of the Field

Personnel functions and programs, like certain types of merchandise, are the subject of fashion cycles. As new tools and techniques prove successful in the performance of certain personnel functions and receive favorable publicity, there is usually a rush among companies to adopt them. Thus, when one company achieves a new development in the field, "everybody," to quote a famous comedian's punch line, "wants to get into the act." This situation has been true in the case of testing, training, performance evaluation, and every other function of personnel management with the result that expectations not infrequently tend to exceed the contributions that can be achieved by the function. People who lack the required understanding and experience tend to perform certain personnel functions improperly and tend to place too much stress on the extent of the results which can be achieved by expanded or changed efforts in a given area of personnel management. Such actions have generated criticisms of the personnel field as a whole and of particular personnel functions. Human relations, for example, has been the subject of misunderstandings, misuse, and gimmicks with the result that there has been a considerable amount of negative reaction to the emphasis being given to it.

In an article that received widespread attention, McNair says that the attempt of some people to "practice" human relations on others has led to undesirable consequences.[14] The practice of human relations, he feels, often constitutes an attempt to manipulate others in order to achieve selfish aims. Overemphasis upon human relations, McNair feels, tends to create rather than to solve human relations problems or, as he expresses it, tends to "encourage people to pick at the scabs of their psychic wounds."[15]

Peter Drucker is another author who has taken the field of personnel management to task on the grounds that it is often based on the philosophy that people do not want to work.[16] He is of the opinion that modern personnel management, to an unnecessary extent, is now looked upon as being the job of a personnel specialist rather than the job of a line manager. He is also critical of personnel management for being unduly preoccupied with "fire-fighting" and for being concerned primarily with the problems and headaches that threaten an otherwise smooth operation.

While the viewpoints of McNair, Drucker, and others who hold a similar opinion may be somewhat extreme, these views serve to challenge certain concepts and practices in the field that may tend to be accepted without question. Just as research in medicine and science has proved certain practices of long standing to be in error, so will research in the personnel field. It is important, therefore, for students and practitioners in the field to maintain a questioning attitude and not to accept practices or methods as being correct merely because they have been in existence for a period of time.

Professionalization of the Field

In spite of the improvements that still must be accomplished in the field, there is considerable evidence that personnel work is becoming more professional in nature.[17] Among the evidence to support this conclusion is the fact that those persons who are engaged in this field are demonstrating a greater sense of responsibility to society and to employees as individual beings. More emphasis, for example, is being given to the placement of employees in jobs that will utilize their talents as well as to the development of their potentials through the use of more democratic and

---

[14]Malcolm P. McNair, "Thinking Ahead: What Price Human Relations," *Harvard Business Review*, Vol. 35, No. 2 (March–April, 1957), pp. 15–39.

[15]*Ibid.*

[16]Peter F. Drucker, *The Practice of Management* (New York: Harper & Brothers, 1954), pp. 276–277.

[17]*Professional Standards for Personnel Work*, Pamphlet No. 13 (Washington, D.C.: The Society for Personnel Administration, 1962), pp. 2–8.

participative management. Greater concern also is being shown for the effect such personnel practices as layoffs and retirements may have upon employees and upon the community. The demonstration of improved attitudes toward union relations and of a greater sensitivity to employees and to public opinion are evidence of the sense of social responsibility that personnel managers are developing.

Another characteristic of this field's increasing professionalization is the growth in the emphasis that is being placed upon research in the field and upon the development and exchange of the growing body of knowledge relating to personnel management. The need for higher levels of intelligence and education and other personnel qualifications on the part of those who engage in personnel work also is becoming recognized more widely. Various personnel societies, furthermore, are assuming more active roles in contributing to the professional growth of those working in the field and to the development of ethical standards of conduct and performance.

Perhaps most significant is the fact that professional organizations in the field are aware of the need for raising the level of professional competency among personnel workers and are striving to achieve this improvement. Toward this end, continuing efforts are being made to improve the educational preparation for the field so as to insure an adequate supply of personnel workers. Hopefully the growing opportunity for both general and professional education at the college level will contribute to this end.

Personnel Management as a Course of Study

Personnel management as a college course also has received a share of criticism. In a report of one study of collegiate business education, the statement was made that "there is certainly no need to require a separate course in personnel if the core[18] also includes a course in human relations."[19] The authors of the report also indicated that personnel as a field is concerned primarily with human relations and that courses in this field too often involve little more than a description of routine administrative procedures. They are willing to concede, however, that if a core course concentrating on industrial relations were to be offered, "some material on personnel management might be included."[20]

Undoubtedly some criticism of personnel management courses in terms of the emphasis and the methods of instruction that are utilized is

---

[18]The core refers to those subjects that are required of all majors in business, regardless of their area of specialization.

[19]Robert Aaron Gordon and James Edwin Howell, *Higher Education for Business* (New York: Columbia University Press, 1959), p. 189.

[20]*Ibid.*

warranted. It should be recognized, however, that a college course in any subject can consist of a description of facts, events, or procedures if taught in such a manner. Furthermore, personnel management as a course need not and should not concern itself exclusively with human relations or behavior since this subject constitutes but a part of the total field. Human relations is merely a part of the subject of personnel management just as algebra is merely a part of the field of mathematics. The subject of personnel management is concerned also with the organizational structure and environment and the management processes that affect human behavior. Its purpose, therefore, is to integrate the various disciplines and areas of knowledge upon which the subject is based.

Some of the criticism of personnel management probably results from a misunderstanding concerning the nature of the jobs within an organization to which the subject matter is intended to apply. There are some who look upon the subject matter in a personnel course as being of importance and benefit primarily to those persons who are or will become personnel specialists. Actually, however, the personnel specialist does very little managing of personnel. Instead, this function is performed by the supervisors and managers who are in a position of direct authority over personnel. It is this latter group, therefore, who must translate personnel theory into practice and who must apply the principles and utilize the tools with which personnel management as a subject of study is concerned. The nature of management processes and the structure within which they are performed are discussed in the next two chapters.

Résumé

Since an organization must be operated by and through people, the degree to which it is able to achieve its objectives is contingent upon how efficiently its personnel perform individually and collectively. Efficient performance, however, does not occur automatically but, rather, is the result of good personnel management. The need for efficient performance in all types of organizations is becoming increasingly important because of the rising labor costs, the growth of the capital investment per worker, and the rapidly changing content of the jobs within the organization that has been necessitated by technological advancements.

In spite of its importance, personnel management as a field of functional specialization is relatively new; its beginnings date back to the period just before World War I. In its development the personnel field has relied heavily upon the contributions of other disciplines, particularly the social sciences, and it has applied the knowledges contributed by these disciplines to the solution of personnel problems. As new personnel functions have become the subject of attention within the personnel program, they have at times tended to be subject to overemphasis and misuse and have, therefore, been criticized. Testing, training, performance rating, executive development, and communication programs have on occasion been looked to for solutions that these programs were incapable of rendering. The fact that certain personnel functions have been subject to fads and gimmicks should not divert attention from the important contributions that can be achieved through effective personnel management.

Although the growth of the personnel field has led to the development of personnel departments and specialists to assist with and to coordinate the personnel activities throughout the organization, the responsibility for the actual management of personnel still rests with the department managers and supervisors. While the title "personnel manager" is reserved for the head of the personnel department, everyone within an organization who has responsibility and authority for the activities of other persons is in effect a manager of personnel. It is important that the latter managers have some knowledge and understanding as to how the various personnel functions should be performed as well as knowledge of the tools and methods relating to the performance of these functions. For this reason discussion of these personnel functions in the remaining chapters of this book is intended to be pertinent to all persons acting in a managerial capacity and not just to personnel specialists.

DISCUSSION QUESTIONS AND PROBLEMS

1. Will the trend toward further automation tend to make increases in employee efficiency more or less necessary? Why?
2. Is the fact that an organization appears to be functioning smoothly and to be free of personnel problems evidence that it has effective personnel management?
3. What is meant by the term "paternalism"? Why is it much less acceptable in personnel management than was once the case?
4. Assuming that Taylor in the practice of scientific management had the interests of the workers at heart, what may have been some of the causes for the widespread opposition by labor to these practices?
5. What contributions has scientific management rendered to the field of personnel?
6. Why is personnel management usually one of the first functions to bear the brunt of company economy drives?
7. Why is it that many tools and practices of personnel management tend to go through a fad period in their usage?

8. Does the position of welfare secretary or its equivalent have a counterpart in modern personnel departments?

9. Do you feel that by working in direct contact with his employer an employee is able to secure better treatment than he would receive if the employee had no contact with him at all? Discuss.

SUGGESTED READINGS

Baritz, Loren. *The Servants of Power: A History of the Use of Social Science in American Industry.* Middletown, Connecticut: Wesleyan University Press, 1960.

Chruden, Herbert J., and Arthur W. Sherman, Jr. *Readings in Personnel Management,* Second Edition. Cincinnati: South-Western Publishing Company, Inc., 1966. Pp. 1–58.

Landsberger, Henry A. *Hawthorne Revisited.* Ithaca, New York: Cornell University Press, 1958.

Ling, Cyril Curtis. *The Management of Personnel Relations, History and Origins.* Homewood, Illinois: Richard D. Irwin, Inc., 1966.

Mayo, Elton. *The Social Problems of an Industrial Civilization.* Cambridge: Harvard University Press, 1945.

Merrill, Harwood F. *Classics in Management.* New York: American Management Association, 1960.

Rathe, Alex W. (Editor). *Gantt on Management.* New York: American Management Association and American Society of Medical Engineers.

Spriegel, William R., and Clark E. Myers. *The Writings of the Gilbreths.* Homewood, Illinois: Richard D. Irwin, Inc., 1953.

Taylor, Frederick W. *Scientific Management.* New York: Harper & Brothers, 1947.

The Personnel Program

The extent to which an enterprise is able to achieve its objectives is dependent in a large measure upon the performance of its personnel. Efficient performance can best be achieved through good management which contributes to the procurement and development of personnel with the required qualifications that will permit each of them to render his maximum contributions. Effective personnel management should help a company to anticipate and to prevent personnel problems from developing and thereby reduce the time and energy that otherwise would be dissipated in resolving these problems.

Management, by simple definition, is the process of accomplishing results with and through the efforts of others. It involves the development of the necessary program of action for achieving the objectives of the company. This program should provide the policies, procedures, and other guidelines to govern the decisions to be made and the functions to be performed in order for these objectives to be achieved. In the management of personnel, a program can be an invaluable aid to managers in directing the work and in making decisions that affect the enterprise and the welfare of their subordinates. The personnel program, thus, constitutes the foundation for the management of personnel.

The discussion of the personnel program in this chapter covers the following topics:

- The management processes.
- The nature of the personnel program.
- Developing and administering the personnel program.
- Translating the personnel program into practice.

The Management Processes

The management of people involves the performance of certain basic *processes*, which include planning, organizing (and staffing), directing, and controlling. As the term would imply, processes are dynamic, interrelated, and interacting activities that must be performed in the achievement of the goals of the enterprise. These processes of management are referred to by some authorities as the *functions* of management. In this book the terms processes and functions will be used interchangeably.

The Process System

The processes of management may be linked together to form what is referred to as a management system. A *system*, according to one definition, is "an assemblage of objects or functions united by some interaction or interdependence."[1] Thus, since each of the management processes is a part of a larger system, any action involving one of the processes will have some effect on each of the other processes. Accomplishments in the process of planning, for example, will have some effect upon the organizing, directing, and controlling processes.

The growth of the "systems" concept of management can be attributed in part to its use by the aerospace industries. Because of the increasing complexity of the products being manufactured by these industries, it became necessary for them to design and produce their products as single, integrated component units rather than as a fabricated unit of separate parts. Developments in the field of operations research in which advanced mathematical techniques have been used to solve problems involving a number of interrelated variables also have helped to promote the systems concept of management. Thus, since it consists of performing a number of interrelated processes as well as making decisions that involve the considerations of many variables, it is appropriate to consider management as a system. The systems approach helps the manager to focus his attention on all of the processes rather than to become occupied with some of them to the neglect of others.

---

[1]Harold Koontz and Cyril O'Donnell, *Principles of Management* (Third Edition; New York: McGraw-Hill Book Company, 1964), p. 35.

One way of representing more clearly the complex relationships of a management system is through the construction of a management model. In the same way that a model may be developed to represent the structure of a building or a machine, a mathematical model may be used to illustrate the structure of relationships that exist within a system. Instead of being constructed from physical material, however, the management model is developed from mathematical formulas and symbols.

Nature of the Management Processes

Regardless of the level of the position that he occupies within the organizational structure, every manager from the chief executive to the first line supervisor is involved to some degree in performing each of the management processes. While those managers at the higher levels within an organization normally should devote proportionately more time to the planning and organizing processes than their colleagues at the lower levels, every individual in a managerial capacity must give some degree of attention to each of the following processes of management.

Planning. This is the process of forecasting and anticipating and of preparing to meet those conditions that may affect the enterprise and its operations. More important, it is the process of attempting to make those conditions occur that are favorable to the enterprise. Planning involves determining the objectives that are to be achieved and the processes that must be performed to insure their achievement. It includes *decision making*, which is the process of determining and evaluating the alternative courses of action that may be taken and of selecting the course that is considered to be the most feasible. Although planning is concerned primarily with the future, it requires the use of data from the past as the basis for projecting future trends and events. The development of computers and more advanced mathematical (or operations research) techniques for studying the many variable forces affecting a decision have made possible significant improvements in forecasting and planning.

Effective planning should stimulate and utilize the creative talents of personnel from all levels within an enterprise through "brainstorming" as well as other participation techniques which can help a company to originate new courses of action. Planning should not be just a forward projection of the past but should create new paths of action for the future.

Personnel planning provides the foundation for organizing, staffing, directing, and controlling those activities of employees that must be performed in order for established objectives to be achieved. It is only by being able to anticipate what work is to be accomplished and how it is to be accomplished that managers can develop, staff, and direct the organization that is required for this purpose.

The advantages of effective personnel planning to an organization are numerous. Plans that are formulated carefully and understood fully can serve as a foundation for organizing and coordinating the activities of employees and for clarifying their interpersonal relationships. Such plans also can make employees more aware of what to expect from management and what management expects of them. Plans thus help to provide employees with a basis for engaging in a greater degree of self-direction by setting forth certain standards or criteria against which they can measure the results of their endeavors.

Effective planning also contributes to the development of a more favorable human relations climate. As the result of careful personnel planning, employees are more likely to be placed in those jobs where they can render the greatest contributions and gain the most satisfaction from their work. Effective planning can contribute to the more orderly flow, distribution, and assignment of work and thus result in more efficient performance by employees and in the achievement of greater work satisfaction by them. Many personnel problems that might otherwise develop into major grievances or disciplinary issues can be avoided, or at least minimized, if anticipated by means of personnel planning.

Personnel planning probably will become even more important in the years that lie ahead. Continuing advancements in science and technology, coupled with the increased use of automation and data processing, will cause continual change in the number of and qualifications of personnel required within an enterprise. By using forecasting techniques these changes can be anticipated and planned for so that a minimum of adjustment of physical and human resources will be required. Planning for such changes may require the training or retraining of employees and helping them to prepare for the various adjustments that may be necessitated by the changes in the requirements of their jobs.

Organizing and staffing. According to one authority, *organization* is "the process of identifying and grouping the work to be performed, defining and delegating responsibility and authority, and establishing relationships for the purpose of enabling people to work most effectively together in accomplishing objectives."[2] It entails the building of a structure within which the functions to be performed may be divided and

---

[2]Louis A. Allen, *Management and Organization* (New York: McGraw-Hill Book Company, 1958), p. 57.

assigned to the appropriate departments, divisions, jobs, and positions. Organizing also includes *staffing* each unit and defining the duties, responsibilities, and relationships of the managers and the personnel within their units. The effectiveness with which the work can be organized and assigned to the individuals who are the most qualified can have a substantial effect upon the efficiency with which they are able to do the work and gain satisfaction from it.

Directing. This process consists of overseeing and supervising the activities and personnel within the enterprise. It provides the guidance for translating organizational plans into action and for insuring that established organizational relationships are observed. Directing includes training, motivating, counseling, and disciplining employees for the purpose of gaining their maximum contributions.

The direction of personnel can be facilitated if their duties, responsibilities, and organizational relationships have been properly planned, organized, and communicated to them. It therefore relates closely to the other processes of management. Since there is evidence to indicate that many, if not most, employees want to do a good job if conditions will permit them to do so, it is desirable that such individuals be given as much freedom as possible to engage in self-direction. By affording them a greater opportunity for independence and self-direction, a manager can contribute to the motivation of his subordinates. It must be recognized however, that the degree of freedom that a manager is able to provide subordinates will, in a large measure, be determined by the controls that he has developed to insure that they will perform their assigned responsibilities effectively.

Controlling. Controlling is the process of reviewing and measuring performance in order to determine the extent to which organizational plans and objectives are being achieved. Controls provide managers with a basis for detecting and correcting deviations from these plans, for correcting errors in the plans, and for improving the plans. Controls within an enterprise provide a source of valuable information to aid managers in making decisions and provide them with a means of stimulating and evaluating performance. In the management of personnel, controls are essential for the delegation of authority. Controls in the form of performance standards are especially helpful in making individuals more aware of the results of their performance and in providing them with a source of motivation for improvement.

The Nature of the Personnel Program

A *program*, which is an overall plan, serves to establish and define the objectives, policies, procedures, and budgets covering the functions that must be performed in the management of personnel. Personnel functions such as selection, training, and performance evaluation may also be covered by more detailed programs which are developed to govern their performance. As programs pertaining to each of these personnel functions are developed, the personnel program can coordinate and direct the programs for the various functions.

Objectives

Objectives constitute the goals of an organization toward which the endeavors of its members are directed. The objectives of an enterprise provide the purpose and the justification for its existence and serve to indicate the means by which it expects to realize an advantage over its competitors. Because a business enterprise is obligated to observe a sense of responsibility toward society, it must not attempt to gain its competitive advantage by sacrificing the interests of its employees, customers, or the public in general. It is recognized, of course, that any commercial enterprise must earn a profit over a period of time in order for its stockholders to realize a return on their investments and be willing to perpetuate the enterprise and the jobs that it provides. A company, however, should expect to earn a profit as a reward for the services that it provides to its customers and to society; it should not expect to receive a profit merely by virtue of its existence.

One of the nation's outstanding business leaders has expressed this concept very effectively as follows:

> The primary goal of any industry to be successful continuously must be to make a better and better product to be sold to more and more people at a lower and lower price. Profit, therefore, will and must be a by-product of service only.[3]

The credo of Johnson & Johnson in Figure 2-1 illustrates a statement of objectives that also recognizes the fact that company responsibilities go beyond those of earning a return for stockholders.

The objectives of a personnel program should augment those established for the company as a whole by providing the goals to guide in the performance of the various personnel functions. The objectives of a personnel program must of necessity be rather broad in nature as is illustrated by the following statement:

---

[3]James F. Lincoln, *Incentive Management* (Cleveland, Ohio: The Lincoln Electric Company, 1951), p. 14.

Figure 2-1

Our Credo

WE BELIEVE THAT OUR FIRST RESPONSIBILITY IS TO OUR CUSTOMERS
OUR PRODUCTS MUST ALWAYS BE GOOD, AND
WE MUST STRIVE TO MAKE THEM BETTER AT LOWER COSTS.
OUR ORDERS MUST BE PROMPTLY AND ACCURATELY FILLED.
OUR DEALERS MUST MAKE A FAIR PROFIT.

OUR SECOND RESPONSIBILITY IS TO THOSE WHO WORK WITH US —
THE MEN AND WOMEN IN OUR FACTORIES AND OFFICES.
THEY MUST HAVE A SENSE OF SECURITY IN THEIR JOBS.
WAGES MUST BE FAIR AND ADEQUATE.
MANAGEMENT JUST, HOURS SHORT, AND WORKING CONDITIONS CLEAN AND ORDERLY.
WORKERS SHOULD HAVE AN ORGANIZED SYSTEM FOR SUGGESTIONS AND COMPLAINTS.
FOREMEN AND DEPARTMENT HEADS MUST BE QUALIFIED AND FAIR MINDED.
THERE MUST BE OPPORTUNITY FOR ADVANCEMENT — FOR THOSE QUALIFIED
AND EACH PERSON MUST BE CONSIDERED AN INDIVIDUAL
STANDING ON HIS OWN DIGNITY AND MERIT.

OUR THIRD RESPONSIBILITY IS TO OUR MANAGEMENT
OUR EXECUTIVES MUST BE PERSONS OF TALENT, EDUCATION, EXPERIENCE AND ABILITY.
THEY MUST BE PERSONS OF COMMON SENSE AND FULL UNDERSTANDING.

OUR FOURTH RESPONSIBILITY IS TO THE COMMUNITIES IN WHICH WE LIVE.
WE MUST BE A GOOD CITIZEN — SUPPORT GOOD WORKS AND CHARITY,
AND BEAR OUR FAIR SHARE OF TAXES.
WE MUST MAINTAIN IN GOOD ORDER THE PROPERTY WE ARE PRIVILEGED TO USE.
WE MUST PARTICIPATE IN PROMOTION OF CIVIC IMPROVEMENT,
HEALTH, EDUCATION AND GOOD GOVERNMENT,
AND ACQUAINT THE COMMUNITY WITH OUR ACTIVITIES.

OUR FIFTH AND LAST RESPONSIBILITY IS TO OUR STOCKHOLDERS
BUSINESS MUST MAKE A SOUND PROFIT.
RESERVES MUST BE CREATED, RESEARCH MUST BE CARRIED ON,
ADVENTUROUS PROGRAMS DEVELOPED, AND MISTAKES MADE AND PAID FOR.
BAD TIMES MUST BE PROVIDED FOR, HIGH TAXES PAID, NEW MACHINES PURCHASED,
NEW FACTORIES BUILT, NEW PRODUCTS LAUNCHED, AND NEW SALES PLANS DEVELOPED.
WE MUST EXPERIMENT WITH NEW IDEAS.
WHEN THESE THINGS HAVE BEEN DONE THE STOCKHOLDER SHOULD RECEIVE A FAIR RETURN.
WE ARE DETERMINED WITH THE HELP OF GOD'S GRACE,
TO FULFILL THESE OBLIGATIONS TO THE BEST OF OUR ABILITY.

Johnson & Johnson

Reproduced by permission of Johnson & Johnson.

A soundly conceived and well-administered personnel program can contribute to the efficiency, teamwork, and morale of people working together.

Simply put, the main purpose of such a program is to select, place, train, and motivate people to work with understanding, cooperation, trust, and confidence in each other.

The principle of the square deal in daily practice for all people — on all levels — from top to bottom — plus decent, considerate, and understanding treatment, also on a daily basis and for a long pull, is the very bedrock of a good people's program.[4]

If the objectives of a personnel program are to be achieved, they must be supplemented with appropriate policies. Such policies, together with procedures, help to assist managers and supervisors in making those decisions that may arise in the management of personnel and their work.

Policies

Policies provide the guidelines to be followed in performing the functions to which they apply. As an aid to decision making, policies permit the more consistent solution to recurring problems. In making decisions, moreover, they help to reduce the range and the number of alternatives that a manager is required to consider.

Need for policies. Carefully developed policies are vital to the management of personnel because each person is sensitive to any differences in the treatment, no matter how slight, that he may receive as compared with other persons. One thing that will impair employee efficiency and morale most quickly is for the boss to display favoritism when making decisions, such as those relating to promotions, vacations, schedules, wage increases, assignment of overtime, or infractions of rules. Decisions, therefore, can be made more rapidly and more consistently if policies relating to these subjects have already been formulated. Personnel policies permit employees to enjoy a greater sense of security by enabling them to know what treatment to expect. Managers and supervisors also can act with a greater degree of confidence in resolving problems since they have a more objective basis upon which to make and to defend their decisions.

Policy formulation. Since personnel policies affect all segments of an organization, it is essential that these policies receive the approval and support of top management. Top management, however, should rely heavily upon the experience of its managers and supervisors and upon the professional competency of its personnel staff to formulate and to enforce

---

[4]Statement from "The Personnel Program at Owens-Illinois — Its Aims and Functions" (Toledo, Ohio: Owens-Illinois Glass Company).

those policies that it may approve. In the formulation of personnel policies, the personnel manager and his staff have the responsibility for exercising leadership to insure that these policies are desirable in terms of current research and industrial practices. They also ascertain that such policies are compatible with current business conditions, collective bargaining trends, and government regulations.

The leadership ability of the personnel staff is perhaps put to its greatest test in gaining the cooperation and support of managers and supervisors in each department of the organization in observing established personnel policies. Unless policies are interpreted and enforced uniformly within and between departments, the basic purpose of the policies — namely, to promote consistency of action — is not likely to be realized. The personnel department's education and communication programs can be used to familiarize managers, supervisors, and operative personnel with the personnel policies and thereby aid in achieving a uniform understanding and interpretation of these policies. As a result of such efforts, managers and supervisors are more likely to view policies as a source of help rather than as an infringement upon their freedom of action. Cooperation in the administration of personnel policies can be enhanced considerably if the personnel staff is able and willing at all times to assist supervisors and managers with the interpretation and enforcement of personnel policies.

Policy statements. In order that they may be made more authoritative, it is desirable that policies be formalized into written statements. Such statements permit policies to be communicated more rapidly and accurately to each individual within the company. Written policies also can serve as invaluable aids in orienting and training new personnel, in administering disciplinary action, and in resolving grievance issues with individuals and with unions. When distributed to employees, these statements can provide answers to many questions that might otherwise have to be referred to supervisors. Written statements also enable continuity of policy to be maintained within an organization even though changes occur in company management. In addition, organizational expansion and the decentralization of authority can be facilitated by formalized policies.

Administration of policies. Since policies should aid rather than hinder decision making, they must not be permitted to impair greatly freedom of action or to discourage the use of initiative by managers in searching for better courses of action. Furthermore, policies must never serve as an excuse for not taking action or for not approving a request; rather, they should serve as a guide for determining how to grant a request and how to satisfy employee desires. Personnel policies, like the objectives that they should help to achieve, must be dynamic in nature and change in accordance with the conditions affecting them. It was once the policy of most airlines, for example, to employ only registered nurses as flight stewardesses in order to provide maximum care for passengers. As a shortage of nurses developed, this selection policy had to be changed in order to maintain a sufficient supply of stewardesses.

Personnel policies must be integrated closely with policies relating to other functional areas. The policy of providing stabilized employment, for example, could not be accomplished without considering policies pertaining to sales, production, and inventory control. A policy of expanding manufacturing operations into foreign countries, on the other hand, might necessitate the review and change of certain personnel policies, such as those relating to employee selection, training, transfer, and remuneration.

Fair and consistent treatment of employees does not mean that they must receive identical treatment. Some degree of flexibility in administering policy must be permitted in order to allow for the particular conditions or circumstances surrounding the problem that is the subject of decision. An employee who previously had established a good work record and had demonstrated a cooperative attitude, for example, probably would not be disciplined as severely for violating a work rule as should another employee with a poor personnel record. Policies, therefore, should merely provide the tolerance limits within which some range of discretion can be permitted. A certain degree of flexibility in the administration of disciplinary action need not be inconsistent with the fair treatment of employees provided that they understand the basis upon which variations are made and to be expected.[5]

While there may be a temptation for managers to seek refuge behind established policies when making a decision, the need to exercise some degree of judgment and discretion in applying policies to specific situations constitutes the primary justification for the manager's existence. If the answer to each personnel problem could be obtained by referring to established rules and policies, the responsibility for personnel management could be delegated to a clerk who might be even better qualified to "look up the answer in a book."

---

[5]For a more detailed discussion on the subject, see John W. Seybold, "How Personal Can a Personnel Policy Be?" *Personnel Journal*, Vol. 37, No. 8 (January, 1959), pp. 285–287.

Procedures

Procedures serve to implement policies by prescribing the course of action to be taken in the administration of these policies. Personnel procedures thus indicate the chronological sequence of steps to be followed in observing established policies. Procedures relating to employee selection, for example, might provide that individuals first be required to complete an application blank and be interviewed by a personnel office representative after which they would complete other prescribed steps. Grievances, promotions, transfers, or wage adjustments likewise must be administered according to established procedures in order to prevent oversights from occurring that might be detrimental to the best interests of either the employee or the company. As an example, the failure to give written warning of a violation to the employee, as a step in the disciplinary procedure, might prevent the company from discharging the employee for a second violation since no formal record of the first violation exists.

In spite of their importance to the program, personnel procedures like policies must be treated as means to an end and not as ends in themselves or as excuses for failure to take needed action. It is not uncommon in many organizations to hear complaints about the presence of excessive "red tape." Unfortunately, when procedures become too detailed or numerous, they may impair rather than contribute to the interests of the company and its employees. In order that this hazard may be avoided, procedures need to be reviewed periodically and modified to meet changes in the conditions that may affect them.[6]

Budgets

Statements relating to objectives, policies, procedures, or to a program as a whole can be meaningful only if they are supported financially through the budget. A *budget* constitutes both a financial plan as well as a control for the expenditure of funds necessary to support the program. As such, it provides one of the best indicators of management's real attitude toward the program.

Thus, while a company's selection policy may be to hire only fully qualified applicants to fill vacancies, its ability to observe this policy will be contingent upon the expenditure of sufficient funds to permit applicants to be screened carefully. Similarly, a policy of paying a "fair wage" can be

---

[6]See *Personnel Procedure Manuals*, Studies in Personnel Policy, No. 180 (New York: National Industrial Conference Board, 1961). Also consult the labor services of the Bureau of National Affairs, Prentice-Hall, Inc., and the Commerce Clearing House for sample statements of personnel policy and procedure and their interpretation.

realized only if the company is willing to establish a sound wage structure and provide in the budget funds that are necessary to support it. In order to gain adequate funds for the personnel budget, however, the personnel staff must be able to convince top management, as well as managers of other departments who are competing for a share of available funds, that the personnel program is producing results.

Developing and Administering the Personnel Program

Most personnel management processes, including selection, training, and wage administration, must be performed by the managers of an enterprise regardless of its size or the nature of its operations. A greater degree of formal and specialized attention is likely to be devoted to the performance of these functions, however, if a formal personnel program has been established.

Even if it appears to be a successful one, the personnel program can never be considered as constituting the ultimate. Systematic appraisals of a program's performance should be conducted to reveal improvements as well as changes that are needed to make it even more effective.

Basis for Development

A personnel program that might prove successful for one company might not necessarily be successful in some other company. For this reason the personnel program should be tailored to achieve a specific set of objectives as determined by company needs. The type of program that is developed and the emphasis that is placed upon each of the personnel functions will be contingent upon such factors as the size of the enterprise, the number and qualifications of the persons that it employs, the location of its facilities, and whether or not the employees are unionized. As the enterprise and its work force grow in size, the size of the personnel staff can be increased, and more specialized attention can be devoted to specific personnel functions. The qualifications of the personnel staff, their ambition and drive, and the degree of support that they are able to enlist from the various departments and levels within the organization will also affect the extent to which the personnel program may be developed.

Gaining Support for the Personnel Program

The support of department managers and supervisors is essential to the successful operation of the personnel program since it is they who must interpret and follow the policies and procedures of the program and make them work. They are the individuals who are directly responsible for such activities as instructing employees to perform their jobs, motivating and evaluating their performance, handling grievance and disciplinary problems, and performing any other personnel functions that are necessary in order to translate the program into action.

Top management support. Support for the personnel program by top management is particularly essential to its success. Since individuals at the higher levels of management are interested in reducing costs and increasing revenues, their support for the program is likely to be contingent upon the contributions that they feel the program may offer in this regard. While the contributions of the personnel program to the morale, work satisfaction, and happiness of employees may be of interest to top-level managers, they are likely to be more concerned with how the program contributes to their enterprise's primary objective of producing a better product for a lower price. If the personnel staff is able to provide tangible evidence that the program is contributing to the achievement of this and other organizational objectives, their task of gaining top management's support can be made much easier.

Lower management support. In order for the middle and lower levels of management to support the program, they must be convinced that the personnel program is contributing to their self-interests by enabling them to manage their personnel more effectively and to achieve higher productivity from them. Educational and communication efforts by the personnel department which can help to make managers more aware of benefits and assistance that the program offers them will contribute to the enlistment of their support. Staff specialists, through the help they are able to provide, must also be able to demonstrate the professional competency necessary to gain the respect of these managers. Support for the personnel program, or any other program for that matter, also will be encouraged if those who are subject to its provisions are given the opportunity to participate in its development, to voice their complaints, and to suggest ways for improving it.

Maintaining a Dynamic Program

A company's personnel program should be sufficiently dynamic to meet changing conditions. Therefore, it must be reviewed periodically to determine if its objectives are being satisfactorily realized and if each of the existing personnel policies or procedures is still required. Reviewing the program regularly may also help to reveal whether or not any of its functions is receiving too much emphasis, is being neglected, or is not contributing adequately to the program. An examination of the training programs, for example, might disclose that the training function is being neglected by some departments. Similarly, a study of the results being achieved from psychological tests might indicate that changes in the testing program should be made.

A dynamic program should permit changes to be made in the objectives, policies, procedures, and budgets of the program whenever they are necessitated by changing conditions. The shortage of engineers, for example, has forced many companies to modify their selection policies by hiring technicians without college degrees for certain duties that engineering graduates were once hired to perform. In other instances, the automation of production processes has made it necessary for some companies to provide more retraining activities and to modify their retirement policies to permit an earlier retirement of those workers displaced by machines.

In maintaining the program it is important for management to recognize the need for preserving a balance within the program. There is often a temptation for management to become overly occupied with certain problem areas of personnel management to the neglect of other areas. The time consumed in handling grievance, disciplinary, and labor relations problems, for example, may consume time which could otherwise be devoted to such other functions as training or communication. Certain areas of a personnel program, furthermore, may receive disproportionate attention because of the interest and publicity that has been given to these areas by the professional literature or at professional meetings. The personnel manager for this reason must be able to evaluate critically what he reads and hears in order that he and other managers will not create an imbalance among the activities of the personnel program.

If the personnel program is to be maintained in accordance with the aims mentioned in the preceding paragraphs, suitable controls must be developed to insure this achievement. The personnel budget offers one of the most effective forms of control by establishing the financial limits within which the program must operate. Statistical records of employee turnover, absenteeism, accidents, grievances, and disciplinary action, as well as performance ratings and production records, provide some of the other sources of control information that may be utilized in the administration of the personnel program. Information can be gained through these sources by means of periodic audits or appraisals. Considerable information also can be obtained through personal observation. While the latter source of information may be subject to certain limitations, the intuitive judgments of experienced staff specialists can be most useful as a basis for developing more objective surveys and audits of the personnel processes.

Translating the Personnel Program into Practice

The real measure of a personnel program's value to a company is determined not by its appearance on paper but by how well it works in practice. The effectiveness of a company program, therefore, should not be judged on the basis of a glowing and enthusiastic description that managers may make of the program in journal articles or at professional meetings. Instead, the worth of the program should be judged in terms of how well it conforms to those practices that have proven to be sound on the basis of research and experience in the field. Some of the practices that characterize good personnel management are discussed in the remainder of this section.

Provide Job Satisfaction and Recognition

The desire of employees to gain satisfaction and recognition from their work may be as important, if not more, to them than financial benefits. Because employees may find their desires for job satisfaction and recognition difficult to define and embarrassing to admit, such desires may not be vocalized. Nevertheless, the failure of employees to gain satisfaction from their job or to feel unappreciated are common causes of industrial unrest.

Satisfaction and recognition are functions of both the individual and the job. Thus, satisfaction and recognition are contingent upon the proper placement and training which enable the individual to perform the type of work for which he has the necessary qualifications and interest. Job satisfaction also is a product of management processes which permit work to be performed in an orderly manner and with a minimum amount of disruption and close supervision. Job satisfaction and morale also result from having an organizational climate which generates a favorable and cooperative attitude among employees at all levels.

Maintain Good Communication

Many personnel problems arise from poor communication which causes employees to misinterpret expressions or actions of management.

Because of poor communication, moreover, management may not be able to recognize or interpret reactions of employees correctly nor to gain a true picture of their attitudes and feelings. Effective two-way communication, therefore, is essential in order for management to translate the personnel program into action and to recognize the effect that the program may be having on performance and upon the attitude and morale of its employees.

Provide an Objective System of Remuneration

While the remuneration usually is not the only return that the employee seeks from his job, it is, of course, important to him. Besides helping to determine his living standards, his remuneration also affects his status within the organization because it provides a tangible indication of his worth in comparison with fellow employees. Remuneration, therefore, can serve as a source of motivation and satisfaction for employees or as a source of discouragement and discontent, depending upon how effectively the program relating to it is developed and administered. For these reasons, it is important that every enterprise have an objective basis for determining the wages and salaries paid to employees that reflects differences in the demands of their jobs and the quality of their performance.

Cultivate Good Union Relations

If a company is unionized, its personnel program will, to a large extent, be determined by negotiation rather than by the unilateral action of its management. In order to maintain the type of program that it considers to be desirable, a company must through the use of persuasion, economic pressures, and bargaining skill gain the union's support for the program. If the company is able to develop a spirit of mutual trust and cooperation in its relations with the union, there is greater likelihood that it will be able to develop the type of personnel program that will serve the interests of both parties.

Build Employee Confidence and Loyalty

The presence of a union does not necessarily indicate failure on the part of management to provide for the welfare of its employees, nor need it indicate that the employees are disloyal to the company. Even though its employees are members of a union, management can and should attempt to cultivate their loyalty and their support as individuals. Management can help to achieve this objective by demonstrating consideration and empathy for their feelings and problems. It must be aware also of the fact that the confidence of employees, although slow to develop, can be lost overnight.

The fact that many companies have been successful in spite of their failure to observe many of the practices that have been mentioned does not mean that these practices are unsound or impractical. Instead, the explanation may lie in the fact that these companies have been successful because they have been able to enjoy certain competitive advantages. In the long run, however, if a company does not provide a sound personnel program, it may experience government controls, union opposition, and the loss of key personnel to other companies. The development of a good personnel program, therefore, represents one of the best means by which a company can fulfill its obligations to society, which includes the community, its customers, its stockholders, and its employees.

Résumé

The management of personnel includes the processes of planning, organizing, staffing, directing, and controlling their activities toward those company objectives that are to be achieved. These processes, which are interrelated and interdependent, are linked together to form a management system. The effective operation of a system, however, requires the establishment of objectives, policies, procedures, and budgets that can serve to guide in the performance of the various personnel functions and decision making relating to these functions. The personnel program thus provides a sense of direction and purpose to the performance of personnel functions and contributes to the fair and consistent treatment of personnel.

If the personnel program is to be operated with consistency and continuity, a written description of it should be prepared and maintained in current form. A formalized program will contribute to the performance of the functions; it will also provide personnel with a basis for evaluating as to whether they are being treated fairly and will permit them to anticipate any actions that may affect them. Although the quality of a personnel program may be evidenced by the formal records that describe it, the real measure of the program's worth is determined by the personnel practices that it generates. The soundness of such practices is, in large part, determined by how well the program has been adapted to the need of the organization. Personnel management under current conditions cannot be left to chance or be based upon imitating programs that have proved to be successful in another company. Personnel management has developed into an art and a science which requires skill, knowledge, and experience on the part of those who perform its functions.

DISCUSSION QUESTIONS AND PROBLEMS

1. Distinguish between an art and a science. To what extent does management involve each of them?

2. What interrelationships, if any, are there between the planning and controlling processes of management?

3. Are profits more correctly termed a motive or an objective of the business manager?

4. In the enforcement of personnel policies, managers are frequently asked to make exceptions. How far can a manager go in making exceptions? Will not such exceptions tend to invalidate the policies for which they are made?

5. It has been stated that when the personnel manager becomes involved in a conflict with the manager of an operating department, he is likely to be the loser. Do you agree with this statement?

6. The president of the Zero Company is opposed to the establishment of formal statements of personnel policies on the grounds that such action would restrict management's flexibility in resolving different types of problem situations. Discuss.

7. Because of the presence of combustible materials, smoking is forbidden in the shipping department of a large company. Although notice of this fact is stated in the employee's handbook and is posted on signs throughout the departmental areas, the regulation was not enforced until the company was required by fire insurance inspectors to do so. As a result of this development, notice was issued that any future violations would result in a three-day layoff without pay for the first offense and a discharge for a second offense.

   a. Comment on the reactions and problems that this approach might create.

   b. What other approach, if any, might prove to be more desirable?

8. In spite of the efforts of the personnel manager to correct the situation, the manager and his supervisors in the manufacturing department persist in the violation of certain personnel policies within their department.

   a. What action can and should the personnel manager take to correct this situation, and what human relations problems may be encountered?

   b. What effect may such human relations problems have upon the future role of the personnel department?

9. How do you account for the fact that some business enterprises earn a substantial profit while apparently not demonstrating any particular sense of social responsibility? What can happen to companies which continually neglect their social responsibilities and fail to recognize the need for having service objectives?

CASE 2-1

THE DISCOURTEOUS CASHIER

Mrs. Clara Norton, an attractive woman in her late thirties, was employed as a cashier and gift wrapper by the Vogue Department Store. The store had occupied the same building for several decades and was typical of the department stores found in many small communities. The store was managed by Mr. Armstrong and his assistant Mr. Cline, and it employed about 30 persons most of whom were married women of about Mrs. Norton's age or older.   Mrs. Norton had worked at the cashier gift-wrapping counter during the entire 2½ year period of employment with the store and apparently had taken care of both money and customers to the satisfaction of management. Most of the time she had been able to handle the work load at the counter by herself, but she did require an assistant during rush hours, particularly during the Christmas and back-to-school periods.   During these peak hours she would often find herself without any assistance and unable to handle the growing line of customers waiting to pay for their purchases or to have them gift wrapped. As these situations continued Mrs. Norton began to grow irritated with her superiors because of the pressures which she was forced to endure at work. Sometimes her irritation caused her to become rather curt in her relations with the saleswomen and their customers.

At the close of one particularly hectic afternoon in August, during which she had been unable to keep abreast of the gift wrapping requests, she bluntly informed her immediate superior, Mr. Cline, that she was going to quit if she could not receive assistance when needed. For a while, thereafter, she was able to obtain assistance, but gradually she began to find herself again with a growing line of customers waiting impatiently at her counter to be served. Consequently, Mrs. Norton on the evening of August 30 again threatened to quit. This time it was Mr. Armstrong who discussed the problem with her personally and solicited her suggestion on how procedures for getting relief help might be handled better. He promised specifically to provide extra help every day during the rush period from 5–5:30 p.m. and at other times when she called for it. As a result of this promise Clara Norton agreed not to quit. It was not long, however, before the relief help at times failed to report to her desk as Mr. Armstrong had promised.

Because she was quite intelligent and articulate, Mrs. Norton, in the meantime, had been elected to the executive committee of her local union. In this capacity she became an outspoken critic of the policies and the management at union meetings. Among other things, she condemned her superiors for allowing their daughters to work part-time in the store without being union members. As might be expected, it did not take long for management to learn about the criticism that Mrs. Norton had voiced about them at the union meetings.

As his difficulties with Mrs. Norton increased, Mr. Armstrong observed that many employees were tending to be less courteous in their relations with customers and with each other. In an effort to counteract this trend and remind them of the need to treat customers properly, Mr. Armstrong posted on the employees' bulletin board the notice and memo shown on page 50.

Although Mrs. Norton, along with the other employees, read and initialed this memo, it apparently had little effect upon her attitude or behavior. After closing time on September 14, Mr. Perkins, the store display and advertising manager, approached Mr. Armstrong with the suggestion that something should be done about Clara's temper and her relations with other people on the sales floor. Acting on the basis of this information, Mr. Armstrong made it a point to contact each of the saleswomen on the main floor during the next morning to ask them if they had noted during the preceding day any situations involving discourtesies on the part of store personnel in their relations with customers.

THE ELEVEN COMMANDMENTS OF GOOD BUSINESS

A CUSTOMER....is the most important person in any business.

A CUSTOMER....is not dependent on us — we are dependent on him.

A CUSTOMER....is not an interruption of our work — he is the purpose of it.

A CUSTOMER....does us a favor when he calls — we are not doing him a favor by serving him.

A CUSTOMER....is a part of our business — not an outsider.

A CUSTOMER....is not a cold statistic — he is a flesh and blood human being with feelings and emotions like our own.

A CUSTOMER....is not someone to argue or match wits with.

A CUSTOMER....is a person who brings us his wants — it is our job to fill those wants.

A CUSTOMER....is deserving of the most courteous and attentive treatment we can give him.

A CUSTOMER....is the fellow that makes it possible to pay your salary.

A CUSTOMER....is the life-blood of this and every other business.

I AM

I AM A LITTLE THING WITH A BIG MEANING.
I HELP EVERYBODY.
I UNLOCK DOORS, OPEN HEARTS, DISPEL PREJUDICE.
I CREATE FRIENDSHIP AND GOODWILL.
I INSPIRE RESPECT AND ADMIRATION.
EVERYBODY LOVES ME.

I BORE NOBODY.
I VIOLATE NO LAW.
I COST NOTHING.
MANY HAVE PRAISED ME, NONE HAVE CONDEMNED ME.
I AM PLEASING TO THOSE OF HIGH AND LOW DEGREE.
I AM USEFUL EVERY MOMENT OF THE DAY.

I AM COURTESY.

(Only if you wish. . .
You may initial. . .)   .. and I'll try. . .

About six of the saleswomen reported incidents in which they said that they felt Clara Norton had treated them or their customers in a rude manner.

Typical of the reports was the statement given by Milda Pine:

Yesterday, while I was writing up a sale at the cashier's desk, Mrs. Norton discourteously interrupted me in the presence of my customer to point out an error that I had made on a previous sales tag. It was a minor error that could have been pointed out later and not in front of the customer. Frankly, I was embarrassed to have this interruption occur in the presence of a customer, and I felt that it was discourteous and out of place.

Ruby Kale, another saleswoman, volunteered the following statement:

I was writing up a transaction for a customer at the end of the cashier's desk where the gifts are wrapped when Mrs. Norton approached from the other end of the desk and rudely remarked, "I almost hate to come down to this end of the desk where so many gifts have to be wrapped. This job is getting me down."

Mr. Armstrong's interviews with the office personnel who worked in the mezzanine area just above the sales floor brought the following comment from a bookkeeper named Sara Gray:

Yesterday, Clara Norton made several trips up here between 12 and 1 o'clock — each time with a complaint. On one trip she stopped at my desk and said, "I suppose Mr. Armstrong is out to lunch. I hope he gets back soon, I want to quit this job and go home. I don't want this damn job anyhow." Her face was red and she seemed angry.

After interviewing all personnel who might have had contacts with Mrs. Norton and making notes of their statements, Mr. Armstrong sent word to her to report to his desk at the end of the day. When Mrs. Norton arrived at his desk, Mr. Armstrong confronted her with a list of the statements that the other employees had made about her behavior. With a flushed face and trembling hands he held his written notes up to her face. Neither party could recall with any accuracy after this point in the meeting whether it had been before or after Mr. Armstrong shouted "you're fired" that Mrs. Norton "blew her stack," as she described her reaction later. Regardless of which event happened first, Mrs. Norton was fired before the ensuing verbal battle ended.

Shortly after Mrs. Norton was fired, the union filed a grievance demanding that she be reinstated with full back pay on the grounds that she had been fired without just cause. As evidence to support its demand, the union pointed out that Mrs. Norton had worked more than 2½ years without receiving any written reprimands from her superiors and that she had never been warned before that she was being discourteous. The union further claimed that management had merely searched for an excuse to fire her because it resented her criticism of store policy during union meetings.

    a. What are the implications of this case in terms of personnel management, and what personnel functions are involved?

    b. How do you account for the behavior exhibited by Mrs. Norton and for the statements made about her by her co-workers?

    c. Do you feel the bulletin board notices constituted sufficient warning to Mrs. Norton?

    d. If you were the manager of the store, would you yield to the demands of the union? (The union contract contains provisions for arbitration.)

CASE 2-2

THE VACATION CONFLICT

Around April 1 of each year, it had been the policy of Mr. Cain, the southern district manager of the Standard Supply Company, to finalize the summer vacation schedule for all district personnel. Mr. Cain always tried, as far as was possible, to accommodate the preferences of the employees in their choices of vacation dates. Sometimes he had even gone so far as to arrange his own vacation for the period that remained, after the preferences of other management personnel had been granted. In order to maintain the efficiency of his office, he had tried to limit the number of employees who were on vacation at any given time and had avoided taking his own vacation at the same time as his assistant manager, Mr. Allen, who preferred to take the first two weeks in June.

Vacation scheduling had never created any particular problem until one year when Mr. Cain found it necessary to schedule his vacation during the second week in June in order that he and his wife might attend their daughter's college graduation exercises in New England. When Cain informed Mr. Allen about the vacation period that he was reserving for himself, the latter became quite disturbed. The source of Allen's concern stemmed from the fact that he had reserved space on a chartered cruise to Bermuda for the first two weeks in June and had made a deposit for the trip that was not refundable. Allen defended his actions on the grounds that he had been taking his vacation during this period and that he had assumed that he was perfectly safe in making reservations for the cruise. Cain expressed sympathy with his predicament but informed Allen that he had no intention of missing his daughter's graduation exercises. Cain added that since he had previously always given Allen first choice of dates for his vacation, it was not unreasonable now for Allen to let him have first choice. Allen retorted that Cain should have announced earlier that he intended to take the vacation period that he (Allen) had previously used. Cain replied that he felt that the first of April constituted sufficient notice and that personnel in the office should not formalize their plans before this date without consulting him. The ensuing discussion tended to produce more heat than light with little progress being made toward a solution.

- a. What recommendations do you have for resolving this disagreement between the two parties?
- b. What effect, if any, is this incident likely to have upon future relationships between these two men?
- c. What bearing does this case have upon personnel policies and procedures?

SUGGESTED READINGS

Barnard, Chester I. *The Functions of the Executive.* Cambridge: Harvard University Press, 1954.

Chruden, Herbert J., and Arthur W. Sherman, Jr. *Readings in Personnel Management,* Second Edition. Cincinnati: South-Western Publishing Company, Inc., 1966. Articles 4–5.

Dale, Ernest. *Management: Theory and Practice.* New York: McGraw-Hill Book Company, 1965. Chapters 1–2.

"Essentials of Effective Personnel Administration; Case Studies of Successful Company Experience," *Personnel Series, No. 154.* New York: American Management Association, 1953.

Johnson, Richard A., *et al. The Theory and Management of Systems.* New York: McGraw-Hill Book Company, 1965. Chapters 1–3.

Koontz, Harold, and Cyril O'Donnell. *Principles of Management,* Third Edition. New York: McGraw-Hill Book Company, 1964.

McFarland, Dalton E. *Company Officers Assess the Personnel Function.* New York: American Management Association, 1967.

Schleh, Edward C. *Management by Results.* New York: McGraw-Hill Book Company, 1961.

3

The Organization
of Personnel

Sound management of an enterprise requires, in addition to the personnel program, the development of the organizational structure or framework that is necessary in order for the activities of the enterprise to be performed and its goals realized most effectively. The organizational structure provides the basis for the division of work among the personnel within the organization, for establishing their authority and responsibility, and for coordinating, directing, and controlling their activities. It serves to distinguish the relationships between the different departments and jobs in which the work is performed and between the personnel who are assigned to these units. The organization, therefore, can have an important effect upon efficiency as well as upon human relations within an enterprise. For this reason, its development should be governed by those considerations that relate to human behavior as well as those that relate to organizational and technological efficiency.

This chapter will discuss some of the considerations relating to the organization of company activities and personnel in terms of their effect upon employee behavior and efficiency as follows:

- The nature and function of organization.
- The organization structure.

- Line and staff relations.
- Impact of organization upon human relations.

The Nature and Function of Organization

The term organization, unfortunately, has been confused somewhat by the different meanings that are associated with it. According to the definition given in the last chapter, organization is the process of identifying and grouping the work to be performed, defining and delegating responsibility and authority, and establishing relationships for the purpose of enabling people to work most effectively in accomplishing objectives.[1] Rather than accept this concept of organization, some students of the subject regard an organization to be primarily a social structure. Members of this more behavior-oriented school of organization would consider any system of social behaviors involving human relationships in some form of group activity as constituting an organization. The term organization is used by still other individuals to refer to an enterprise, company, or institution.[2] In the discussion that follows in this and the other chapters of this book, however, the word organization will be used in the more traditional sense to mean a structural framework which establishes the basis for determining the responsibility, authority, and relationships of the enterprise's members.

Approaches to Organization

Classical or traditional organization was concerned primarily with achieving that type of structure which would maximize efficiency. Early pioneers of management such as Taylor, for example, approached the subject of organization with the view of achieving greater efficiency through the division of work and functional specialization. The classical approach to organization also recognized the need for coordination among the divisions of the organization into which the work was divided. The establishment of a hierarchy of authority as well as channels through which authority for decision making might be delegated were considered to be necessary. The limits in the span of control that a manager could exercise effectively was another subject of consideration and study.

---

[1]Louis A. Allen, *Management and Organization* (New York: McGraw-Hill Book Company, 1958), p. 57.

[2]See Harold Koontz, "Management Theory Jungle," *Journal of the Academy of Management*, Vol. 4, No. 3 (December, 1961), pp. 182–183. Also, Lyndall F. Urwick, "Have We Lost Our Way in the Jungle of Management Theory?", *Personnel*, Vol. 42, No. 3 (May-June, 1965), pp. 8–18.

Limitation of classical theories.   Unfortunately, in concentrating on the structural considerations in organization and on the principles and procedures pertaining to its operation, the classical approach tended to neglect the human factor. It tended to overlook the effect that employees may have upon organization as well as the effect that organization may have upon the behavior of employees. As a result of the more recent research being accomplished in the field of behavioral science, the interrelationships between organization and human behavior increasingly is recognized. This research, which began with the Hawthorne Study,[3] has caused managers to become more aware of the impact that human actions and relations — particularly within informal groups — can have upon the formal organization. Many contemporary practitioners of management, therefore, are taking the more middle-of-the-road approach to organization. While they accept much of the basic theory that comprises the classical approach, they tend to recognize the fact that the formal organization must be interpreted in the context of the people who comprise it and in terms of the organization that these people develop among themselves.[4]

Modern theory.   The influence of behavioral science has come to be felt and to be identified with what is referred to as *modern organization theory.* Students of modern organization theory tend to view organization as a system of mutually interdependent and interacting parts which are studied in terms of their relationship to each other and to the system as a whole. They view the basic part of the system as being the individual — his attitudes, feelings, motives, and other elements of his personality that may affect his participation in the system. The other parts of the system are considered to be the formal organization, the informal organization, the status and role patterns resulting from the interaction of the individuals with the formal and informal organizations, and the physical work setting. These parts or variables, thus, are woven together into a configuration called the organizational system.[5]

Modern organization theorists are somewhat critical of classical organization theory. They feel that classical theory places too much stress upon "tight controls, a very formal structure, tightly defined and definite policies and procedures and what they feel is a non-human approach or lack

---

[3]F. J. Roethlisberger and William J. Dickson, *Management and the Worker* (Cambridge: Harvard University Press, 1939).

[4]See William G. Scott, "Organization Theory: An Overview and an Appraisal," *Journal of the Academy of Management*, Vol. 4, No. 1 (April, 1961) pp. 7–26.

[5]*Ibid.*, pp. 19–20.

of concern about differences between people."[6] Classical theory has been criticized as being derived from the military or church models of organization which are considered by some modern theorists to be inappropriate for contemporary enterprises. It has been accused, also, of supporting the concept that people do not enjoy working. Classical theory, furthermore, has been criticized for relying upon authority as the central and indispensable means of management control and for viewing the employee as an inert instrument simply performing a task assigned to him.[7] One of the strongest criticisms of formal organization based upon classical theory is offered by Chris Argyris. On the basis of his research he concludes that, "if it is to obtain ideal expression, the formal organization may tend to place employees in work situations where they are dependent, subordinate, and submissive."[8] He also concludes that, "to the extent that the requirements of the individual and of the formal organization are not congruent, the individual will tend to experience frustration, conflict, and feelings of failure."[9]

Criticisms of modern theory.

Some of the criticisms that have been leveled against the classical organization theory by behavioral scientists and modern organization theorists have in turn been challenged by contemporary scholars in the field of management. One of them points out that a certain criticism of classical organization theory is the result of either a misstatement or misapplication by the critics of certain principles underlying this theory. He also believes that the criticism is due to the fact that the boundary lines of management (including organization) are not clearly defined, that other disciplines contributing to management have not been integrated fully with it, and that the terms used in the discussion of management are not clearly understood or interpreted uniformly.[10]

Urwick challenges some of the contemporary critics of organization theory, particularly with regard to their interpretation and use of the term "organization." He also points out that the bureaucratic rules and lack of humane leadership which might characterize the operation of certain institutions cannot be construed as a valid criticism of organization per se.[11]

---

[6]Marvin D. Dunnette and Wayne K. Kirchner, *Psychology Applied to Industry* (New York: Appleton-Century-Crofts, 1965), p. 161.

[7]*Ibid.*, pp. 162–163.

[8]Chris Argyris, *Personality and Organization* (New York: Harper & Row, Publishers, 1957), p. 119.

[9]*Ibid.*

[10]Koontz, *op. cit.*, pp. 184–187.

[11]Urwick, *op. cit.*, pp. 8–18.

   **Resolving the opposing concepts.** Organization theory undoubtedly will be debated for some time to come. In practice, however, both the classical and the modern theories have a contribution to make to the development of an effective enterprise. If an enterprise is to achieve its goal, a sound structure must be developed with which to facilitate the division and coordination of the work to be performed. In developing this structure it would be unwise to ignore the vast amount of experience that has been embodied in the more classical approach. Since it is people as well as work that are the subject of organization, however, consideration must also be given to the effect that their behavior may have upon the organizational structure that is developed and to the effect that the structure may have upon their behavior. Research in the field of the behavioral sciences which throws more light upon the behavior of people as individuals and as members of a group, moreover, can serve to augment the very valuable knowledge that practitioners of management have been able to acquire from their research and experience.

Organizational Growth

   As internal and external conditions affecting the operation of an enterprise change, the organization of the enterprise must be adjusted to cope with this change. One of the most common forms of change is that which results from the growth of an enterprise. Continued growth within an enterprise usually must be accompanied by further division and specialization of the activities within the enterprise. Specialization may lead to the creation of new jobs and eventually of departments within a company whose sole function is to provide counsel and assistance to other departments in matters pertaining to a particular area of specialization. One of the first such departments to develop is likely to be personnel whose responsibility is to assist other departments in performing personnel functions.

   It is important that organizational growth be anticipated and that effort be exerted to achieve the type of growth that is desired. Unfortunately, many organizations today have not expanded on the basis of any plan, but rather, have grown on the basis of expediency and impulse as problems affecting the enterprise have arisen. Often, the responsibility for resolving new problems or for performing new functions created by expansion has been assigned to those departments and managers who seem best able or most willing to shoulder the additional load. It often is a result of such practice that the personnel department is assigned the responsibility for performing functions that are not directly related to the personnel program. Such functions as plant protection, safety, community fund drives, and supervision of recreational areas are among those that may fall into this category. This system of organization has been termed the "trashcan pattern of organization"[12] and perhaps explains why critics charge that the personnel program "puts together and calls personnel management all of those things that do not deal with the work of people and that are not management."[13]

Responsibility and Authority in Organization

The organization structure, it has been indicated, provides the basis for dividing those activities that the enterprise is to perform into appropriate departments, divisions, jobs, or other units. It, thus, serves to determine the duties and responsibilities of each job and of the employees who are assigned to the jobs. The organization structure should make it possible for each employee to receive through the process of delegation the authority that he requires to carry out his duties and responsibilities. It also should make it possible for him to maintain those relationships with other people on his level that are necessary in order for him to perform, in a cooperative manner, those duties and processes relating to his work.

Nature of responsibility. Responsibility is the obligation that an employee has to his superior to perform those duties that comprise his job. The responsibility for the performance of each function within a company rests ultimately with the board of directors. This responsibility, however, is assigned by the board to the chief executive. The latter, in turn, divides and assigns portions of this responsibility to his subordinates, and so on downward through the various levels in the organization. A manager, regardless of his level, however, cannot escape the responsibility which is assigned to him even though he may reassign most of it to subordinates. Thus, although the chief executive may reassign the responsibility for the operation of the personnel program to his personnel manager, the chief executive is still the one who must answer directly to the board of directors for any difficulties that may arise in connection with the program. Since the major portion of a manager's responsibilities is carried out through subordinates, the success of his performance is determined in a large measure by how effectively he can develop and motivate subordinates to assume those responsibilities that he assigns to them. The manager in Figure 3-1 obviously has not been very successful in this regard.

---

[12]Dalton E. McFarland, *Cooperation and Conflict in Personnel Administration* (New York: American Foundation for Management Research), Chapter 3.
[13]Peter F. Drucker, *The Practice of Management* (New York: Harper & Brothers, 1954), p. 275.

Figure 3-1

"YOU call it passing the buck — I call it delegating
responsibility."

Reproduced with permission.

Personnel department very little authority

Nature of authority. *Authority* in the management context is a form of power or influence that is sometimes defined as the "supreme coordinating power."[14] It is the power to perform a responsibility . . . the right to take action or to direct others to do so.[15] It gives managers the power to direct and enlist the cooperation of subordinates and to achieve the coordination of their efforts.

Authority, like responsibility, in a company originates with the governing board. It is passed downward and divided among subordinate personnel through the process of delegation. Each individual can rightfully exercise only that authority which has been delegated to him. In the interests of good management and human relations, it is essential that each individual be delegated authority equal to his assigned responsibility and,

[14]Harold Koontz and Cyril O'Donnell, *Principles of Management* (Third Edition; New York: McGraw-Hill Book Company, 1964), p. 49.
[15]Brown, *op. cit.*, p. 37.

conversely, that he be held responsible for exercising properly the authority that has been delegated to him.

It is only by developing subordinates and delegating to them the authority that they require to make decisions that a manager can multiply his contributions to the enterprise. The delegation of authority permits decisions to be made more rapidly by those who are in more direct contact with the problem. It also demonstrates the manager's confidence in his subordinates and provides them with a greater feeling of recognition and a sense of participation.

Types of authority. The authority that is exercised within an organization may be classified into three types: *line, staff,* and *functional. Line authority* consists of the right or power to issue orders to subordinate personnel and to take disciplinary action against them for the violations of these orders or for other just causes. Line authority can be exercised only over subordinates in the chain of command and not horizontally over persons in other departments of the structure. *Staff authority* actually is not authority at all in the strict sense of the word because it does not provide any specific right to direct, issue orders, or to discipline others. Instead, it involves merely the capacity to provide assistance, advice, counsel, or service to others. As Anderson points out, the staff officer is one who deals merely with information and advice as his major activity. His responsibility is to supply authoritative information to all members who are entitled to receive it and his authority is that of getting information within his special field from those who may have it.[16] Individuals whose jobs involve staff authority, therefore, must rely upon their power of persuasion and upon their reputation for competency and expertness in their field of specialization in order to have their advice and recommendations accepted. Such positions as those bearing the title of "assistant to" or positions in staff departments are examples of those which involve staff authority. Staff authority, also, is the type that generally is exercised by a committee.

What frequently is termed staff authority might be more correctly classified as *functional authority.* The distinction between functional and staff authority, however, is largely one of degree. Functional authority involves the right to issue orders that pertain to the performance of a particular function. It is not as binding as line authority since it does not carry the right to discipline others in order to enforce compliance.[17]

---

[16]E. H. Anderson, "The Functional Concept in Organization," *Advanced Management,* Vol. 25, No. 10 (October, 1960), pp. 16–19.

[17]Hall H. Logan, "Line and Staff: An Obsolete Concept?" *Personnel,* Vol. 43, No. 1 (January–February, 1966), pp. 28–29.

Whether or not the authority that a manager can exercise over another individual is line or functional in nature is determined by his relationship to that individual. Functional authority, thus, may be exercised over individuals in other departments throughout the organizational structure, whereas line authority can be exercised only over subordinates within the chain of command. The personnel manager, for example, exercises functional authority over other managers, supervisors, and their subordinates with respect to the performance of personnel activities, but he exercises line authority over subordinates within his own department. Since it does entail the right to coordinate and enforce the policies and procedures governing the performance of a particular function, however, functional authority carries more power than staff authority.

The exercise of functional authority can be facilitated through the existence of the policies and procedures that govern the performance of a particular function. Personnel policies and procedures, for example, can help to assist the personnel manager in the exercise of functional authority as it relates to the operation of the personnel program throughout the enterprise. His knowledge and skill in the field of personnel management can serve to strengthen further the power that he may exert in exercising this functional authority.

Procedural relationships. The relationships that probably are the most prevalent within an organization are those of a procedural or cooperative nature. Such relationships usually occur laterally within the organization and do not involve the use of either line or functional authority. They occur between individuals as they perform their assigned duties in carrying out the work activities.

Procedural relationships are a potential source of confusion and conflict because their nature often is not well defined or understood by members of an enterprise and because neither party to such relationships is in a position of authority over the other. Thus, friction and resentment may result if either party to the relationship attempts to exert pressure or attempts to exercise initiative over the other. William F. Whyte, in one of his studies, for example, concluded that friction, tension, and accompanying emotional complications frequently were the result of one employee attempting to initiate action for another who considered himself to occupy an equal or higher status position.[18]

Since someone must exercise initiative in carrying out a particular procedure within the organization, it is inevitable that procedural or

---

[18]William Foote Whyte, *Men at Work* (Homewood, Illinois: The Dorsey Press, Inc., 1961), pp. 125–135.

crosswise relationships may at times result in conflict rather than cooperation. One of the most important requirements for a smooth-functioning organization, therefore, is the development of procedures that will permit each individual to understand better the nature of his relationships to others. Furthermore, managers must be alert to those relationships that precipitate conflict and attempt to correct them.

Considerations Relating to Organization

Experience and study in the field of management and organization has made possible the accumulation of a body of knowledge relating to the practice of management. This knowledge has provided a theoretical foundation for the development of certain principles of organization which, if applied under the conditions for which they are appropriate, can contribute to the more effective organization and management of personnel. Some of the more important principles of organization are:

Principle of division of work. The primary purpose for organizing work is to permit it to be divided into units that can be performed more effectively by those to whom it is assigned. The division of work, therefore, should be accomplished in such a way as to facilitate its performance and the achievement of the objectives of the enterprise.

Principle of responsibility. An individual cannot escape the responsibility that has been assigned to him merely by passing it on to a subordinate. It remains his obligation to see that his subordinates observe this responsibility.

Principle of parity of authority and responsibility. The authority that is delegated to an individual should be equal to his responsibility and not more or less than it.

Principle of unity of objective. According to this principle, the objectives of each department and other units within the organizational structure should be integrated with and contribute to the achievement of the objectives for the organization as a whole.

Principle of organizational balance. This principle requires that the relative size and budget of each department be consistent with the contribution to the enterprise that is desired from the department.

Principle of span of management. This principle recognizes that there are limits to the number of people that can be directly supervised by a manager. It usually is possible for the span of management (or span of control as it also is called) to be greater for managers at the lower organizational levels than for those at the upper levels. Span of management, thus, cannot be translated into any "magic" numbers but, rather, is contingent upon such factors as the nature of the activities being supervised, the number and frequency of the supervisor's contacts with others, the training and capacity of the supervisor and his subordinates, and the extent to which the supervisor is able to delegate authority.

Principle of delegation. A manager can increase his span of management by delegating more of his authority to subordinates. While the delegation of authority is essential to the growth of an enterprise and the capacities of its members, it cannot be accomplished merely by recognizing the need for it. Effective delegation requires that a manager plan and organize his own work in order to determine what decisions to delegate. It also requires the training of subordinates to assume authority and the establishment of controls to insure that the delegated authority is being exercised properly by subordinates.

Principle of unity of command. The exercise of authority requires that subordinates report directly to only one boss. An unbroken channel of authority should exist through the intermediate levels of management from the chief executive to the operative employees. Directions and other communications should be transmitted to subordinates and control exercised over them through these channels.

Principles of flexibility and stability. Changes that take place within an enterprise should be planned and directed toward the achievement of established objectives and should not be influenced unduly by short-term conditions. An enterprise should be capable of coping with such problems as those resulting from sharp changes in business activity or the loss of personnel.

The principle of stability can be implemented by developing versatile qualifications among subordinates, by decentralizing authority, and by effecting long-range planning and variable budgets that permit changing conditions to be met with a minimum of adjustment by the enterprise.

The Organization Structure

There are three basic types of structures into which the functions of an enterprise may be organized. These three types include the functional, the line, and the line-and-staff structures. The characteristic that distinguishes one type from another is the difference in the nature and pattern of the authority relationships that exists within the structure.

Functional Type of Organization Structure

The *functional type* of structure, of which Frederick W. Taylor was a strong advocate, is intended to provide personnel with the opportunity to achieve maximum functional specialization. In this type of structure, each manager has authority over the personnel within all other departments with respect to their performance of the function for which he is responsible. For example, in a functional type of structure, the personnel manager would have primary authority and responsibility for hiring, training, disciplining, and the handling of other functions relating to the management of personnel within all departments; the production manager would have authority and responsibility for the technical phases of production; and the quality control manager would have authority and responsibility for the maintenance of quality standards. Unfortunately, in a functional structure, the division of authority among a number of functional specialists requires employees to take orders from several bosses which leads to confusion and to inadequate control. This type of structure in its pure form, therefore, has little practical value.

Line Type of Organization Structure

The *line type* of organization structure, which is sometimes called the scalar structure, is the oldest and simplest type of structure. It permits a clear line of authority to be maintained from the highest to the lowest level within the structure. Each member of the organization is held directly responsible to only one superior.

The line type of structure is best suited to the needs of the small organization whose operations generally may be divided into the functions of production, sales, and finance. The managers of the departments that are responsible for each of these functions, as indicated by Figure 3-2, have complete authority and responsibility over the activities and personnel of their departments. Each manager is also responsible for personnel management, quality control, purchasing, or any other functions which contribute indirectly to the performance of his department's primary function. A department manager in a line organization, therefore, must have broad and diversified qualifications because he must be able to cope with a variety of problems without assistance from functional specialists.

As the activities of the line departments increase in scope and complexity, a straight line type of structure generally proves to be less satisfactory because a manager cannot keep abreast of all of the fields that relate to the operation of his department. Gradually, therefore, individuals must be employed to assist the line managers with the performance of the more specialized functions. Since the job of these individuals is to provide advice and assistance to other members of the organization, rather than to exercise authority over them, they often are referred to as staff specialists.

Figure 3-2

LINE TYPE OF ORGANIZATION STRUCTURE

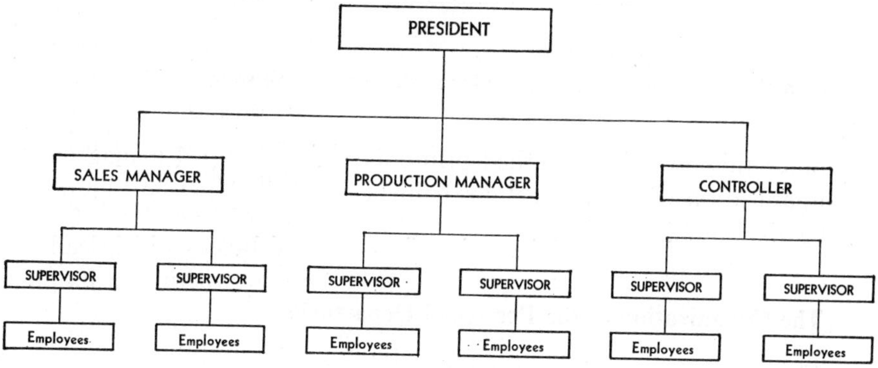

Line-and-Staff Type of Organization Structure

Staff advice and assistance may be provided within an organization by creating staff departments and positions or committees for this purpose. The line-and-staff type of structure has characteristics of both the line and the functional structures. The line departments are those that are concerned directly with the accomplishment of the objectives of the enterprise. The addition of staff departments provides assistance in those more specialized areas that the line managers do not have time to master. By utilizing staff assistance of this type, supervisors and managers are able to confine their attention to the primary work of their departments.

The chart in Figure 3-3 illustrates how a line-and-staff type of structure can be developed through the addition to the structure of staff departments whose functional authority is indicated by the broken lines. The staff departments that have been created on this chart include, on the same level as the line departments, those of engineering, personnel, and purchasing.

Figure 3-3

LINE-AND-STAFF TYPE OF ORGANIZATION STRUCTURE

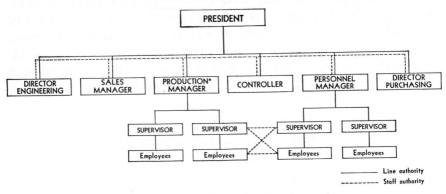

*For simplification, the structures for only two departments are given.

Since this book is concerned primarily with personnel management, the organization of a personnel department which is shown in Figure 3-4 will be discussed in detail.

The Organization of the Personnel Department

The organization of the personnel department should be determined by the needs and conditions within the company that it is to serve. The size of the company, the geographic location of its units, the nature of its operation, whether or not it is unionized, the caliber of its work force, and the importance that higher management attaches to personnel relations constitute some of the factors that may affect the department's organization. Figure 3-4 illustrates some of the divisions into which a department may be organized and the functions that each may perform.[19] If management feels that personnel relations are of considerable importance, the personnel department is likely to be accorded greater organizational status than otherwise would be the case. In some of the larger companies, the title of vice-president that is given to the personnel officer indicates the importance that these companies attach to the function. One study of personnel departments revealed that the head of the department in one out of every six companies had the title of vice-president.[20]

---

[19]See Bureau of National Affairs, Inc., *The Personnel Department*, Personnel Policies Forum Survey No. 73, 1964.

[20]*Ibid.*, p. 4.

Figure 3-4
PERSONNEL DEPARTMENT ORGANIZATION

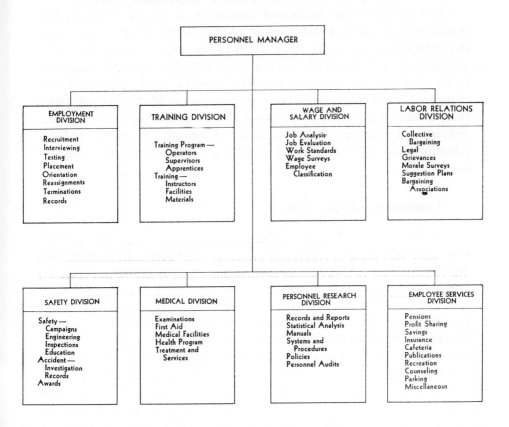

In another study, however, it was found that the influence of the personnel executive in some companies has tended to decrease as the importance of personnel relations has increased.[21] In these companies it would appear that top management has been prone to become involved directly in the performance of certain personnel functions, such as collective bargaining, rather than to elevate the personnel manager to a position of greater influence. When union relations is a matter of critical concern to the successful and continuous operation of the enterprise, the administration of the personnel program may be influenced heavily by the labor relations division. Personnel management in such instances, unfortunately, may

[21]McFarland, *op. cit.*, p. 11.

become more legalistically oriented to the neglect of the other phases of the personnel program which may become largely clerical in nature.

If a company has multiplant operations, a personnel department is usually established at each plant in addition to the company personnel department located at the main offices of the organization. With this arrangement, the personnel manager in each plant is responsible directly to the plant manager but is subject to functional control by the personnel manager for the company. The company personnel department under these conditions generally is concerned with the coordination of personnel policies and practices, the maintenance of centralized records, and the administration of that portion of the program that concerns the company as a whole.

Committees and Their Uses

Committees can be created within any type of organization to facilitate group communication, to secure group interaction, or to deal with specific problems. They may be utilized to plan, to coordinate, or to control the performance of various functions within the organization.[22]

The use of committees in the administration of the personnel program is quite widespread, for management must be knowledgeable as to employee reactions to the program and must secure employee support for the program. Committees in the personnel field may be used to appraise employee suggestions, to resolve grievances, to evaluate jobs and employee performance, and to select candidates for promotions. Committees can also enable employees to participate in the administration of programs in areas such as recreation, safety, methods improvement, and cost reduction. In managing personnel, the coordination of personnel policies, procedures, and practices can be facilitated through the use of committees composed of those managers and supervisors who must administer the personnel program within their respective departments.

Effective use of committees. The values to be derived from the use of committees to a large extent are contingent upon the willingness of top management to utilize the findings and recommendations of committees and upon the effectiveness with which committees can perform their assigned task. In forming a committee it is essential that those persons assigned to the committee have the qualifications necessary to discuss and

---

[22]An interesting discussion of committees is provided in the following article: Cyril O'Donnell, "Ground Rules for Using Committees," *Management Review* (October, 1961), pp. 63-67.

to act intelligently upon the task for which the committee was created. In a true committee, according to O'Donnell, the superior who forms the committee should not participate in its meetings and the subject matter to be considered should not be within the assigned duties of any of its members.[23] Committee chairmen, moreover, should have the ability to keep the discussion within the boundaries of the agenda, to control those members who otherwise might dominate the discussion, and to draw out those who are hesitant to express themselves.

Committees can make important contributions to a company as the result of enhancing the job satisfaction and improving the job performance of individuals on the committee. Working as a committee member provides the individual with a sense of participation in the organization and a feeling of having contributed to the organization. A committee assignment can also give a subordinate the feeling that his superior respects his intelligence and abilities. In addition, participating in the work of a committee gives the individual an opportunity to express his viewpoints and to gain a better understanding of the viewpoints of his associates. They can also help members to become more familiar with the operating problems of the enterprise and to gain experience in decision making. In this way committees can contribute to a member's growth and development. The experience obtained in being a member of a committee which has resolved an assigned problem is particularly fruitful in improving job performance when the performance involves coordination and cooperation with others.

Limitations of committees. While committees can serve many useful purposes within an organization, they do not always constitute the most appropriate approach to decision making. In a situation that requires individual executive action, for example, it may not be desirable to have a decision made and the responsibility for the results of it divided among the several members of a committee. In other instances, however, relieving an executive from the hostility of others when unpopular decisions are to be made could be a legitimate function of a committee.

In determining whether or not to utilize a committee, however, it is important to consider whether or not a group decision is superior to one that might be made by a capable individual. Committee action may require certain compromises which weaken the decision. Furthermore, unless the members have the required qualifications, the information, and the interest necessary for deliberating on a problem, committee meetings may waste time which the committee members could better utilize in performing their regular job assignments.

---

[23]*Ibid.*, pp. 63–67,

One of the unfortunate trends in many organizations has been to form committees of questionable need which, once established, have continued to exist even after the need for them has ceased. Some companies have attempted to reduce the drain of committee work upon executive time by providing certain controls to govern the formation and continuation of committees.

Line and Staff Relations

The development of an effective line-and-staff type of organization requires that the individuals within the line departments and the staff departments observe their respective line and staff roles and jobs. When a staff department such as personnel is established, for example, it is necessary for the supervisors and executives in the other departments to work with the personnel department in the performance of the personnel functions within their departments. They should rely upon the services and counsel of the personnel staff and must conform to the personnel policies and procedures over which the personnel department maintains functional control.

Achieving Cooperation Between Line and Staff

In the operation of a line-and-staff organization, the authority of a supervisor to hire, fire, discipline, and train personnel frequently has tended to be curtailed in comparison with the authority exercised by his counterpart in a straight line organization. It has been curtailed by the functional authority of the personnel department and by the more formal personnel policies, procedures, rules, and regulations that this department may help to create. In many instances the effect that all of this has had upon the supervisor has not been recognized fully by higher management. It is not surprising, therefore, that supervisors and executives may resent what they perceive to be unwarranted staff interference and encroachment upon their authority to operate their departments as they deem best. Such resentment is not reduced if the personnel department commits the error of attempting to compel compliance with the provisions of the personnel program should supervisors outside the personnel department refuse to do so voluntarily.

Whenever line supervisors are incapable of assuming responsibility for the performance of certain personnel functions, or are unwilling to do so, personnel specialists may be forced to take over the performance of these functions. The personnel staff sometimes is required, for example, to assume a direct role in conducting training programs, handling disciplinary problems, or in taking care of other personnel functions that are the primary responsibility of the line but which are being neglected by them. Whenever a staff department assumes the responsibilities that should be borne by the line departments, however, the authority of the line supervisor may be weakened in the process. Members of the personnel department, therefore, should attempt through educational and persuasive means rather than pressure tactics to get their advice and assistance accepted by the line departments. On the other hand, the personnel department cannot permit the line departments to neglect their responsibility for the management of the personnel in their departments. Line department personnel may have to be educated to recognize the value of staff assistance and be encouraged to utilize it. In order for cooperation between line personnel and staff personnel to be realized, therefore, the distinction and relationship between the two functions must be clearly established and communicated to line and staff personnel. It is only when each member of the organization understands his role and his relationships with the other members that cooperation and efficiency can be achieved.

Influence of Individual Personalities and Backgrounds

Even though the members of line departments and staff departments may be familiar with their prescribed roles, their personality traits and their qualifications may make it difficult for them to observe these roles precisely. A personnel manager who is a persuasive and articulate individual and who is sufficiently expert in his field may actually do more directing than advising in his relations with other departments. He may be able to impose his advice on others, for example, because of his greater familiarity with personnel policies and procedures. Such familiarity may give him an advantage over line executives when his views and objectives conflict with theirs.

Differences in background between executives in line positions and those in staff positions may, at times, create disharmonious relationships. Many line supervisors have risen to their positions as a result of practical operative experience rather than as the result of formal education. They, therefore, may tend to be somewhat apprehensive or resentful toward staff personnel who often have attained their positions with the help of a college education.

Qualification Requirements for Staff Personnel

If the members of personnel and other staff departments are to render their intended contribution to the organization, it is essential that they possess the technical competency necessary to win the respect and cooperation of the line personnel. In order to have line supervisors accept his services and assistance, the personnel or other staff specialist must be able to provide them with the type of help that they want and can understand. This help must be determined by what the line personnel actually want rather than what the staff specialist may think these personnel want. If the staff specialist is to provide this kind of service and assistance, he must have a high degree of empathy.

Sometimes line management personnel do not cooperate with the personnel or other staff departments because they view these departments and their programs as constituting a threat to their status and security. Supervisors, for example, may fear that the personnel department, as a result of its actions, is attempting to encroach upon their authority or to call the attention of higher management to their weaknesses in dealing with personnel. This feeling can become quite strong when such events as morale surveys, grievance hearings, or personnel audits bring to light poor personnel practices by a supervisor. When the personnel department is attempting to improve the personnel practices of line supervisors, it is important that procedures be followed which preserve the prestige and self-respect of the line supervisors and which permit them to receive credit for improvements that occur. Line supervisors are more likely to have desirable attitudes with respect to utilizing the services of the personnel staff, especially if higher management requires that they continually strive to obtain greater operating efficiency.

Impact of Organization Upon Human Relations

Organization is concerned both with functions and with the people who perform them. It is the people comprising the organization who play an important role in determining how effectively a particular organization structure is able to function. The organization structure, on the other hand, can have an important effect upon the efficiency with which employees are to perform their jobs, the extent to which they are able to work in harmony with others, and the degree of satisfaction that they are able to derive from their work. The nature of the structure and the position that an individual occupies within it, therefore, can exert a significant influence upon his status and role within the enterprise as well as upon his attitudes, feelings, and his behavior. Current research in the behavioral sciences, as indicated earlier, is seeking to uncover more information concerning the interrelationships between organizations and human behavior. New theories and concepts are emerging, and new insights are being gained as a result of this research that personnel managers should examine for possible application to their own enterprises. Some of the information and ideas pertaining to this subject will be discussed in the remainder of this section.

Influences of the Structure

The organization structure is pyramid shaped and provides for the arrangement of jobs in a series of levels to form a hierarchy. The number of jobs that may exist at each successively higher level in the structure, therefore, is less than it is at the level below. This fact means that not all of the individuals who occupy positions at a particular level will be able to advance to the next higher level.

Leavitt is of the opinion that this situation creates competition as well as a feeling of dependency among employees because their promotion is contingent upon favorable approval by their superior. He feels, also, that these conditions may lead to more intensified conflict and frustration and greater psychological pressures among employees.[24] Changes in the organization structure that bring about the decentralization of authority, that help to open up horizontal channels of communication, and that encourage greater use of committees are viewed as one way of reducing some of these particular causes of conflict, frustration, and pressure. The replacement of certain individuals by others who are less likely to be subject to pressures and conflict as well as the improvement of the climate within the structure might help to improve the situation.[25] Argyris, it was mentioned earlier, points out that the formal organization may create feelings of dependency, submissiveness, and frustration among employees for which he concludes the informal organization may serve as an outlet. He recommends more individual-centered leadership coupled with an enlargement of the job or role performed by the individual as a means of overcoming the antagonism between the individual and the formal organization.[26]

---

[24]Harold J. Leavitt, *Managerial Psychology* (Chicago: The University of Chicago Press, 1958), pp. 257–265.

[25]*Ibid.*, pp. 274–290.

[26]Chris Argyris, *Personality and Organization* (New York: Harper & Row, Publishers, 1957), pp. 230–237.

The Effect of the Size and Shape of the Structure

The growth within an enterprise can exert a significant influence upon human relations. As the enterprise increases in size, additional levels of management usually are created in order that the span of management of each manager and supervisor may be kept within satisfactory limits. As additional levels are created, the employee becomes further removed from top management and the lines of communication and supervision become lengthened. Managers at the top have greater difficulty in recognizing and understanding the feelings of employees at the lower levels. Employees under these conditions may have greater difficulty in identifying themselves with the goals and interests of the enterprise and consequently are likely to feel that they have become forgotten as individuals.

Organization structures that contain numerous levels of management are sometimes referred to as *tall* structures in contrast to the *flat* structures which have relatively few levels. Some large companies have made a concerted effort to achieve a flatter organization by eliminating some of the levels of management from what previously was a taller structure.[27] Figure 3-5 illustrates how some of the levels in the structure shown at the top can be eliminated to create the structure at the bottom which is flatter.

The elimination of some of the levels of management forces the span of management of each manager to be increased and authority to be decentralized. The authority to make decisions must be delegated downward as far as possible within the organization. Departments and other units within the structure are afforded greater autonomy. The personnel at each level are thus given greater responsibility as well as opportunity for self-development and for realizing their potential.[28]

While the flat organization may prove to be advantageous in certain situations, it may not necessarily prove to be effective for all types of enterprises. When it is necessary to achieve close coordination between the units of an enterprise, additional levels of authority may be required to provide more centralized control, thereby forcing the structure to become taller. The caliber of the management and subordinate personnel, the degree to which autonomy of the units within the organization is possible, as well as other factors may also help to determine how "flat" the structure can be made.

---

[27]The experiences of Sears, Roebuck and Company provide an example.

[28]For a study covering this subject, see Lyman W. Porter and Edward E. Lawler, III, "The Effect of 'Tall' versus 'Flat' Organization Structures on Managerial Satisfaction," *Personnel Psychology* (Summer, 1964), pp. 135–148.

Figure 3-5

"TALL" ORGANIZATION STRUCTURE

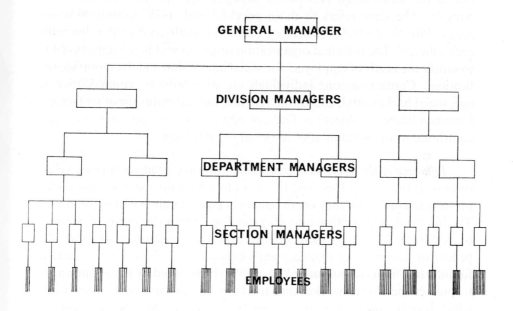

"FLAT" ORGANIZATION STRUCTURE

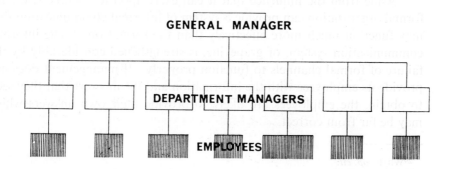

The Informal Organization

Research in the behavioral sciences has done much to make management more aware of the important role played by the informal organization. The term informal organization was first used by the Mayo Group during the well-known Hawthorne Study at the Western Electric Company.[29] The term refers to those personal and social relationships *not required by the formal organization* that individuals tend to develop with each other.[30] The informal organization or group within a company helps to satisfy the needs of employees for social interaction and for group identification. Contacts among individuals are stimulated by commonality of age, social background, education, religion, marital status, or other factors. Common interests, objectives, fears, or opposition to management also can contribute to the formation of informal organizations.

Influence of the informal organization. Informal groups tend to develop certain sentiments, values, and folkways to which the members are under pressure to conform if they are to remain in good standing within the group. The informal organization also may develop certain standards of conduct or performance that its members are expected to observe, to either the benefit or detriment of management's expectations. It is not uncommon for informal limits of output or "bogeys" to be adopted by the organization to protect the slower worker and to insure a constant backlog of work which is sufficient to guarantee the continued employment of the members. Attempts of superiors to counteract restrictions and resistances of the informal organization are likely to be frustrated, for the members usually are more anxious to please the members of their group than their superior; and rejection by the group can be more unpleasant for members than disciplinary action by a superior.

Aside from the influence that it can exert upon its members, the informal organization can provide a system of informal communication that may function much more effectively than the formal one. The informal communication system, or grapevine, is strengthened considerably by the failure of formal channels to function properly. If management does not provide its employees with the information and the answers that they seek to obtain, the employees are likely to provide their own answers which may be far from correct.

---

[29]Whyte, *op. cit.*

[30]Keith Davis, *Human Relations at Work* (New York: McGraw-Hill Book Company, 1962), p. 236.

The informal organization also provides an opportunity for persons with potential leadership abilities to make use of their talents. The informal leader may serve in the roles of policeman, spokesman, arbitrator, or counselor. It may be possible, furthermore, for more than one leader to emerge within an informal group, depending on whether group members at the moment are seeking to obstruct management action, are reacting to job boredom, or are soliciting favor and recognition from management.

If it exercises care, management can benefit from the presence of an informal organization by utilizing the leadership talent that the organization helps to develop. The use of informal leaders in some instances can permit management to gauge group reaction or to gain the support of the group for management goals. In other cases, informal leaders can be trained for supervisory positions. These leaders can be utilized to provide instruction and assistance to other employees and to aid in the orientation of new employees to the work situation. In utilizing informal leaders, however, management must recognize that some individuals may falsely convey the impression that they are group spokesmen. Instead, they may have group support only to the extent that they oppose management practices and not because they possess any real leadership qualities.

Coping with the informal organization. Regardless of whether informal groups prove to be beneficial or detrimental to the formal organization, they exist in every company. It is well for management to attempt to recognize these organizations and to develop them into a force that will be beneficial rather than harmful to the formal organization. Since informal group activities can serve to relieve the monotony of certain routine production work by facilitating social interaction and since these groups can help satisfy the need of employees for security and belongingness, management may at times find it desirable to create or strengthen these groups. The strengthening of informal groups may be achieved by modifying formal organizational relationships, by adjusting work procedures or layout, and by staffing the work groups with individuals who have a certain commonality of interest or background. Conversely, when the actions of a work group become detrimental to production goals, it may become desirable to weaken the group by making changes in its membership or by changing the formal relationships or work places of certain members. Since there are always underlying causes for informal group behavior, management before taking action to counteract any undesirable group behavior should make certain that its own practices have not contributed to the problem.

Résumé

The efficiency with which employees perform their work, the degree to which they work harmoniously with each other, and the satisfaction that they derive from their jobs can be no greater than the organization of a company permits. The organization thus provides the foundation for the management of personnel since it forms the basis for establishing the duties of the job and the nature of personnel's authority, responsibilities, and formal relationships. The most common structures into which the activities and personnel of a company are organized are the line and the line-and-staff types of structures. In the line type of organization, the functions that pertain to the management of personnel are performed exclusively by department supervisors. Through the development of a line-and-staff type of structure, it is possible to establish a personnel department to provide these supervisors with specialized assistance in the handling of personnel functions. While the functional authority that is assigned to the personnel department is intended to be merely advisory in nature, there is a tendency for this department in some companies to assume the responsibility for performing certain personnel functions and to dictate to supervisors how these functions should be performed. In order for line-and-staff departments in this type of structure to function as intended, the role of each department with respect to personnel management must be clearly established and understood by the members of the departments. If the necessary measures are taken to insure that it functions properly, the line-and-staff structure will lend itself to unlimited growth and will permit personnel functions under the leadership of the personnel department to be performed in a professional manner that is appropriate to the growing importance of this field.

The interrelationships between organization and human behavior have become the subject of greater emphasis and research. The size and shape of the structure, and the extent to which authority is centralized, can have a significant effect upon the individuals within the structure and upon their feelings of conflict, pressures, and frustration. The organization structure of the future, therefore, is likely to be more human-oriented and is likely to recognize the importance of creating the most desirable psychological climate within which people may work satisfactorily rather than being concerned primarily with the improvement of production technology.

DISCUSSION QUESTIONS AND PROBLEMS

1. How does modern organization theory differ from the traditional theory?

2. Would you agree with the conclusion reached by one study that top management has tended to assume a greater and more direct role in the administration of the personnel program as the importance of the personnel function has increased? Would it not be more logical for the personnel manager to be given a greater role under these conditions?

3. In many enterprises the functional authority of certain of the staff departments is continuing to increase. What are some of the possible reasons for this trend?

4. Why is it that many persons tend to resent having other individuals initiate action for them particularly if the individuals initiating it occupy a lower status?

5. Why do some individuals who have established themselves as the informal leaders of their groups fail to become effective formal leaders when assigned to supervisory positions?

6. Some companies have adopted the practice of assigning a member of the personnel department to each operating department in order to assist the supervisors in these departments with the performance of their personnel functions. What benefits and difficulties do you anticipate might result from this practice?

7. To what extent, if any, should the authority for recommending employees for promotions to supervisory levels be delegated to a management committee? If such a committee is established, to what extent should its recommendations be followed?

8. The engineering division of a large aircraft manufacturer maintained its own personnel department to handle the more than three thousand employees within the department. The company industrial relations director had been opposed to this department since its inception, but without success.

   a. How do you account for the fact that the engineering division was able to maintain its own personnel department in spite of the industrial relations director's opposition?

   b. What justification might be made for the existence of such a department within the engineering division and what problems might its presence create?

9. After spending several nights personally observing the work of two custodians who were suspected of stealing liquor from one of its stores, the personnel manager of a grocery chain was able to apprehend them in the act of committing another theft. What possible inferences might one draw from this event in terms of the company's personnel organization and management?

10. The president of a manufacturing concern employing about a hundred persons made the following statement: "We feel that a formal organization structure would impede our efficiency. In this company every executive and supervisor pitches in and gets the job done." Do you agree with this approach? Could it ever work successfully?

11. How may improvements in the organization of an enterprise contribute to the development of better human relations?

12. To what extent, if any, does the material in this chapter apply to the organization of student groups such as clubs, social fraternities, professional fraternities, and student associations? Suggest how the organization of formal groups to which you belong might be improved.

CASE 3-1

THE BRANCH MANAGER'S PROBLEM

The Home Owners Savings and Loan Association, with assets of over one hundred million dollars, was established in a growing metropolitan area. In addition to its main branch office downtown, the association also operated six other branch offices in the suburbs and in neighboring towns. The main branch, and each of the other branches, were organized as separate units under the supervision of a branch manager who reported to the executive vice president of the corporation. This latter officer with his staff was headquartered on the mezzanine floor of the main branch office. Each branch was organized into departments under the supervision of department managers who reported directly to the branch manager. These department managers, however, were also subject to certain supervision and control from the appropriate staff officers in the corporation office who exercised functional authority over them.

Relations between the branch offices and the corporate staff generally were satisfactory except at the main branch office. In this office the branch manager and his department heads often were bypassed by members of the corporate staff who had grown accustomed to seeking information and giving instruction directly from the personnel in the various departments of the main branch. The branch employees similarly were prone to seek the solutions to their problems by going upstairs to see someone at the corporate level. The immediate proximity of the corporate staff and their ability to make final decisions was a significant factor in encouraging employees of the main branch to consult directly with them. Thus, if the loan service officer in the main branch had a problem to solve, for example, he was likely to take it to the corporate vice president and loan officer for consultation rather than to his department head. Because of this practice both the manager and the department heads of the main branch tended to be bypassed frequently with the result that their authority and status were weakened. Employees within the branch, thus, lost some of their respect for their supervisors and for the manager of the branch. The branch manager was aware of the situation that existed but, since he had been in his position only a short time, he had been hesitant to challenge the practice because he did not want to risk antagonizing anyone at the corporate level until he felt more secure in his new position.

a. How should the manager of the main branch office attempt to correct the situation?

b. To what extent, if any, should his desire to avoid antagonizing corporate officers affect his decision to defer taking positive action?

c. What caused this problem to develop and how might it have been prevented?

d. How might an organizational chart contribute to the solution of this problem?

CASE 3-2

THE ASSISTANT FOREMAN

Pete Cole, the production superintendent for an automotive parts manufacturing company, received a visit one morning from Ellis Green, an assistant foreman. Green was disturbed about the way in which the new foreman of his department had been encroaching upon the authority of the assistant foremen. Whereas the new foreman's predecessor had given assistant foremen considerable freedom in scheduling work orders, in assigning specific jobs to their personnel, and in training the crew members within their sections, the new foreman assumed many of these duties himself. Specifically, Green complained that the new foreman had taken it upon himself to transfer personnel between sections claiming that the individuals who were involved needed a greater variety of work experience. In addition to having their crews broken up and their work schedules and job assignments interrupted, the assistant foremen, according to Green, were also being bypassed by the foreman who frequently gave work assignments and instructions to their personnel directly. Green complained also that he and the other assistant foremen had attempted, without success, to advise the foreman of the problems that he was creating for them. Green reinforced his complaint with a request that he be permitted to return to his former job as a production worker.

After listening patiently to Green's story, Cole asked him to defer his demotion request until the difficulty could be investigated. When Cole contacted the department foreman who was the subject of the complaint, he discovered that the foreman's version of the problem was somewhat different from that expressed by Green. The foreman complained that he felt his predecessor had relinquished virtually all of his authority to the assistant foremen who had become accustomed to operating their departments more or less as they pleased. The foreman went on to describe certain laxities which had developed within the department training scheduling that he was attempting to correct. He also enumerated instances of resistance that he had encountered from his assistant foremen. He cited Green in particular as being one of the assistant foremen who seemed to be most resentful of receiving any orders or suggestions regarding the operation of his section. Finally, the foreman stated his belief that the real problem stemmed from the fact that the assistant foremen had grown accustomed to exercising the authority of the foreman and that they resented having this authority withdrawn and reassumed by the foreman. Since Cole considered both individuals to be competent in their respective jobs, he surmised that at least a part of the difficulty stemmed from his own failure to give sufficient attention to lower levels of supervision within his department.

a. What steps do you feel Cole might take to correct this situation and to prevent the reoccurrence of similar ones in the future?

b. What possible reasons are there for the differences in the views expressed by the foreman and his assistant, Green?

c. What may be some of the underlying causes for the attitudes of the foreman and the assistant foremen? What may be some of the underlying causes for the difficulties that have arisen between them?

SUGGESTED READINGS

Albers, Henry H. *Principles of Organization and Management*, Second Edition. New York: John Wiley & Sons, Inc., 1961. Chapters 5–9, 11, and 12.

Bennis, Warren G. *Changing Organizations.* New York: McGraw-Hill Book Company, 1966.

Chruden, Herbert J., and Arthur W. Sherman, Jr. *Readings in Personnel Management*, Second Edition. Cincinnati: South-Western Publishing Company, Inc., 1966. Articles 3, 6, and 7.

Company Organization Charts, Studies in Personnel Policy, No. 139. New York: National Industrial Conference Board, 1954.

Dale, Ernest. *Management: Theory and Practice.* New York: McGraw-Hill Book Company, 1965. Chapters 16–21.

Davis, Ralph C. *The Fundamentals of Top Management.* New York: Harper & Brothers, 1951. Chapters 7–15.

Haire, Mason. *Modern Organization Theory.* New York: John Wiley & Sons, Inc., 1959.

Improving Staff and Line Relationships, Studies in Personnel Policy, No. 153. New York: National Industrial Conference Board, 1956.

Koontz, Harold, and Cyril O'Donnell. *Principles of Management*, Third Edition. New York: McGraw-Hill Book Company, 1964. Chapters 4, 11–19.

March, James G., and Herbert A. Simon. *Organizations.* New York: John Wiley & Sons, Inc., 1958. Chapters 1, 2, and 5.

Newman, William H., and James P. Logan. *Business Policies and Management*, Fifth Edition. Cincinnati: South-Western Publishing Company, Inc., 1965. Part III.

Sampson, Robert C. *The Staff Role in Management.* New York: Harper & Brothers, 1955.

Schell, Erwin Haskell. *The Technique of Executive Control*, Eighth Edition. New York: McGraw-Hill Book Company, 1957. Chapters 1, 4, 5, and 7.

4

The Organization of the Job

If it is to function effectively and to achieve its objectives, an enterprise must be organized so as to permit each employee to render the maximum contribution which he is capable of making. In order for him to be able to do so, however, the work that is to be accomplished by the enterprise must be divided into jobs that can be performed effectively and must provide a source of satisfaction to the persons who are assigned to them. The task of organizing and establishing the duties for each job within a company, therefore, is a most important function of personnel management that should receive careful attention and consideration.

In discussing the organization of the job, this chapter covers the following topics:

- The nature and function of the job.
- Work organization and the job.
- Describing the job.
- The job analysis program.

The Nature and Function of the Job

The *job*, it was revealed in the previous chapter, constitutes the smallest unit of the organization structure into which the activities of an enterprise are divided. The division of these activities should be accomplished in such a manner as to permit those that are a part of each job to be distinguished clearly. Thus, the job of key punch operator would entail certain duties and responsibilities that would be distinct from those of a secretary or a file clerk within the same office. The employee who is placed in this job then should be able to identify clearly what tasks or activities he is expected to perform as a part of his assigned duties and responsibilities.

Jobs that are similar in terms of the work performed and the qualifications that they require of employees may be grouped into job families known as *occupations*. These occupations may exist within a single industry or several industries.

If the work load of a particular job is sufficiently heavy, more than one employee may be required to perform it. Separate positions each involving the duties and responsibilities of this job would then have to be created to which additional employees would be assigned. A *position*, therefore, constitutes that portion of a job that is performed by an individual employee. The work load for a key punch operator, for example, may require the services of six employees each of whom will occupy a separate position involving similar duties and responsibilities. Before an employee can be hired, moreover, a position involving a particular job must exist for him. The number of the positions that have been budgeted within the organizational structure determines the number of individuals who can be employed since each of them must occupy a separate position within the structure.

Contribution to Organizational Operations

The job serves to define not only the activities of the organization that an employee is to perform but also the relationship of these activities to those being performed by other employees in the achievement of organizational objectives. The job provides the means for dividing and assigning the authority and responsibility that must be exercised by the incumbent job holders. It also establishes the foundation for selecting and training employees, for evaluating their performance, and for determining their rate of pay. The job and its requirements are important to the management of personnel since the manner in which activities are organized can have an important bearing upon the effectiveness with which the performance of these activities can be accomplished and controlled. The manner in which the activities within a job are organized can also be an important factor in the creation and solution of disciplinary problems and grievances.

The cause of job inefficiency at times can be due as much to the way in which the job is organized as it is to the caliber of the employee's performance. If the activities of a job are not organized properly, the confusion, interpersonal conflicts, and frustration that may result from this situation can cause the employee to become discontented and a problem to management.

Effect upon the Individual

The job, among other things, affects the employee's role within an organization. It represents the rung that he occupies on the organization ladder and from which he may hopefully move upward — or if less fortunate, slip downward. The location of the employee's job within the organization provides a measure of his relative worth in comparison with that of his co-workers and also provides a means by which he may gain self-esteem. Whiting Williams, an early and respected leader in the personnel field, had this observation to make after having spent an extended period living as a worker:

> . . . our hunger finds its chief and surest satisfaction in connection with our jobs, our work. I think I can claim rather varied contacts. To learn about people, I have associated with bums and with workers here and abroad, and I have sat with captains of industry in London, Paris, Berlin, Chicago, and New York. I give you my word, whether they were bums, board chairmen or in betweens, they were all just about equally less sure of themselves than they would *like* to be, all about equally as hungry to maintain "face," to have a word of approval.
>
> But here is the point. Whether they were at the bottom or the top of the ladder, every blessed one of them gave me as final, incontrovertible, proof of certificate: "This is my job; this is the kind of service I give my fellow men; this is the kind of equipment I make useful to my fellow citizens. On the basis of that I demand a certain amount of attention."[1]

Relationship to Status

Status refers to the rank that an individual occupies with respect to others in the social system. The nature of an individual's job and the relationship of the job to other jobs in the organization structure can have

---

[1]From *Connecticut Industry* (May, 1951), as reprinted with permission in Herbert J. Chruden and Arthur W. Sherman, Jr., *Readings in Personnel Management* (2nd ed.; Cincinnati: South-Western Publishing Company, Inc., 1966), pp. 147–158.

an important effect upon his status. The ability that the job demands of an individual, the duties, the working conditions and the pay that it entails, and the years of service accumulated by the employee represent still other factors that may help to determine his status. Tangible and visible expressions, which commonly are referred to as *status symbols*, can serve to call the attention of others to one's status. The location of an individual's desk or his work place, the tools and equipment that he uses, and the clothes that he wears may in some organizations symbolize status. At the executive level, office location and furnishings, reserved parking space, and the like are typical status symbols that may provide executives a source of ego satisfaction. While status symbols are important they can not be considered a substitute for pay to the extent that Figure 4-1 would imply.

Figure 4-1

"No raise, Durkin, but effective the fifteenth of next month you may start calling me by my first name."

Source: *The Saturday Evening Post.* Reprinted by special permission of Chon Day.

Since an employee's status can be affected by many different factors, it is quite possible for some of these factors to be inconsistent with others. This situation that is created is referred to as *status inconsistency*, and it may cause frustration and anxiety on the part of those who are the subject of the inconsistency. Employees, for example, are quick to resent the fact that someone in a job that is located on a lower level within the structure may be receiving higher pay or more privileges than they. Similarly, those individuals who have more status by virtue of their seniority, age, qualifications, or other factors may expect to receive preference with regard to work assignments and conditions of employment over other employees with less status. If these expected "privileges of rank" are ignored by supervisors when personnel decisions are made, it may generate resentment on the part of the individuals with status and cause them to become a problem. The employee's feelings of security and adjustment, thus, are likely to be more favorable if consistency exists with respect to the factors on which his status is determined. Inconsistency, on the other hand, can contribute to *status anxiety* in which the individual experiences a feeling of discomfort in not knowing how he ranks with respect to his colleagues.

Contribution of Job Organization to Teamwork

One of the main objectives in the organization of work is to bring about effective cooperation and teamwork among the various individuals and groups within an enterprise. This teamwork, in the opinion of Bakke, is achieved through what he calls the *bonds of organization* that he believes help "weld men together as partners of production."[2]

Teamwork is also dependent upon the ability of the members of the enterprise to adjust themselves to the demands of the organization and to achieve their personal objectives through the organization. Bakke calls the forces that serve to bring about adjustment between the individual and the organizational system in which he works the *fusion process*. This adjustment to the organization can contribute greatly to the individual's sense of psychological adjustment, which will be discussed in Chapter 16.

Work Organization and the Job

Traditionally the design and the content of the job have been determined by the requirements of the organizational structure and by the methods and processes that are established to perform the work. The primary objective of this approach to job design has been one of minimizing costs and maximizing output; or, in other words, one of achieving maximum efficiency. The traditional approach to job design, therefore, generally has concentrated upon limiting the number and variety of activities of a job and thus making these activities more repetitive. Attention

---

2E. Wight Bakke, *Bonds of Organization* (New York: Harper & Brothers, 1950), pp. 7–9.

also has been directed toward reducing the skill and training that an employee must have in order to perform the job effectively.[3]

Problems Relating to Job Design

The practice of reducing the variety of activities to be performed by a job is called *job dilution*. Such practices make the job easier to staff because less experience and training is required in order for the employee to perform it. The resulting job, thus, is well suited for mass production methods in which improvement in employee efficiency of even a slight amount can be multiplied into substantial savings because the activities that comprise a cycle of work are repeated over and over.

Unfortunately, the dilution of the job into more simplified and repetitive tasks can cause it to become more depersonalized and less satisfying for many people to perform. The mechanical pacing and repetitive nature of assembly line work, according to one study, has created a feeling of pressure — an anonymity among the employees working on the line. Many of them feel that they are performing as robots rather than human beings.[4]

Inasmuch as the dilution of the job reduces the skill and training that is required to perform it, an employee can be replaced more easily and, therefore, is afforded less security of employment. The absence of employment security that results can serve to reduce even further the satisfaction that his job may provide for him.

Improvement of Job Design

The reduction in the duties of a job in the shop or the office that, from an engineering standpoint, should contribute to increased productivity may fail to do so if it causes the resulting work to become more monotonous or boring for those who must perform it. Human as well as technical considerations, therefore, must be recognized in designing the job and in developing the methods and procedures for performing it. Thus, although it would appear that an employee should be able to become more productive if he had fewer duties to learn in a job, the reverse may be the case if this change reduced his interest in the job and the effort that he was able to exert. Instead of attempting to increase productivity by attempting to

[3]Louis E. Davis, "Job Design and Productivity: A New Approach," *Personnel*, Vol. 33 (1957), pp. 418–430.
[4]Arthur N. Turner, "Management and the Assembly Line," *Harvard Business Review*, Vol. 33, No. 5 (September–October, 1955), pp. 40–48.

simplify job duties, some companies, such as IBM, have attempted to add duties to certain jobs through a program of *job enlargement.* Through the process of job enlargement, the duties of several jobs are combined into one job. A machine operator, for example, in addition to handling his regular production runs might also be assigned the duties of setting up his runs, inspecting his completed work, servicing his machine, or performing other duties that were previously not a part of his job. While job enlargement programs have resulted in increased efficiency in some companies, the success of these programs to some extent may be attributed to the caliber and morale of the employees who participated, as well as to the caliber of management and the organizational climate within the company.

In addition to being stimulated through enlargement programs, job interest and satisfaction may be increased for some employees by rotating them among several jobs or by rearranging their work places to permit them to enjoy more group interaction. Managers also may be able to overcome the psychological limitation of work specialization by establishing subgoals, by giving employees a better understanding of their accomplishments and their contributions to the total production effort, and by using various financial and nonfinancial incentives. The advantages of job specialization, in comparison with those of job enlargement, can be as much a function of the individual as of the job. Work that is dissatisfying for one individual may prove to be quite satisfying to another. In dividing the work among jobs, therefore, recognition must be given to the type and caliber of the personnel who are to staff the jobs as well as to how the work might best be divided from a technical standpoint.

Human Engineering

The field of human engineering also is exerting a growing influence upon job design. While work in this field originated with the United States Air Force and has been advanced by aerospace agencies and companies, the potential contributions of human engineering are being recognized and utilized increasingly by other industries and government agencies. The emphasis in human engineering is upon adapting and developing machines, equipment, and jobs to match man's capabilities rather than upon getting man to adjust himself unduly in order to use the equipment. Human engineering thus requires the teamwork of psychologists, physiologists, engineers, and others in the solution of human performance problems. Its use in industry will place more emphasis upon designing the requirements of a job to fit the capacities of the individuals who are available to perform them.[5]

Attitudes Toward Work

In our culture work can be a source of self-respect and recognition as well as a source of income. Our society, for instance, provides many examples of individuals who have no financial need to work but who continue to do so because of the satisfaction that they obtain from it. The popularity of the "do-it-yourself" type of projects probably can be attributed partly to one's desire to demonstrate his skills and energies.

In spite of psychological and social pressures to work, however, there are still those individuals whose primary motivation for working is to earn a living. For these individuals, as Dubin points out, work is not a central life interest.[6] It merely provides a means of supporting interests and providing satisfactions that are obtained outside of the job. Efforts to make such individuals more interested in their work through job enlargement or changes in the design of the job may prove to be inadequate. Such efforts also may have to be supplemented by attempts to get these individuals to improve their attitudes toward their job and to identify themselves more closely with the organization as a whole or with the unit in which they may work. By giving employees more opportunities to participate in decisions and by keeping them better informed on developments that affect them and their work, management may be better able to help them improve their interest in and their sense of identification with their jobs. Making employees more aware of the importance of their particular job, the contribution that it renders to the organization, and how it relates to the total operation also can help to improve their interests and attitudes toward work in general. The use of financial and psychological incentives may provide still another means of gaining such improvement. A more detailed discussion of participation, communication, and financial incentive systems is included in Chapters 13 and 22.

Describing the Job

The duties that comprise each job should be determined as the result of formal planning which takes into account the contribution that the job

---

[5]Also see Ernest J. McCormick, *Human Factors Engineering* (New York: McGraw-Hill Book Company, 1964), pp. 580–586.

[6]Robert A. Dubin, "Industrial Research and the Discipline of Sociology," *Proceedings of the 11th Annual Meeting* (Madison, Wisconsin: The Industrial Relations Research Association, 1959), pp. 160–163.

is expected to render. This goal may not always be realized, however, since the duties of a job sometimes become those that the incumbent may assume, or be assigned from time to time on a hit-or-miss basis, rather than as the result of careful planning and organization. Although employees inevitably will help to make their jobs what they are, some degree of control must be established over them to insure that they are performing the duties that their jobs are intended to entail.

Controls can be provided by preparing a written statement of the duties and responsibilities of the job. A written statement of this type can serve to prevent a particular job from gradually being changed by the incumbent. It may also prevent differences of opinion from occurring between the incumbent and his supervisor over the nature of the duties that are to be performed by the former.

The written statement covering the duties and responsibilities of a job is commonly referred to as the *job description.* The personal qualifications that an individual must possess in order to carry out these duties and responsibilities are compiled into what is called the *job specification.* The job specification may be organized as a separate record or may be included as another part of the job description. The advantage of having a separate job specification is that the information contained in it is used for purposes other than those for which the information in the job description is used.

The Job Description

Since there is no standard form for their development, job descriptions will vary in content and organization from one company to another. The job description for a personnel clerk, shown in Figure 4-2, illustrates the organization, content, and writing style that may be followed. This description contains a rather typical organization pattern consisting of job identification, job summary, and job duties statements.

Job identification section. This section, by means of the job title and other identifying data, helps to distinguish a job from the others within the organization. The inclusion within the job title of such words as "senior," "junior," "trainee," "supervisor," "operator," or "clerk" can serve to indicate the duties and the skill level of the job.

Job summary section. This section, which is sometimes entitled "Statement of the Job," serves to provide a summary that should be sufficient to identify and differentiate the duties that are performed from those of other jobs.

Figure 4-2
SAMPLE JOB DESCRIPTION

JOB TITLE *Personnel Clerk*   DEPARTMENT *Personnel*

NUMBER OF EMPLOYEES IN   NUMBER OF EMPLOYEES ON JOB *3*

DEPARTMENT   *15*   DATE *February 10, 19--*

STATEMENT OF THE JOB

Under the supervision of the EMPLOYMENT MANAGER; interviews new workers in carrying out clerical routine of induction; performs miscellaneous clerical and stenographic work related to employment.

DUTIES OF THE JOB

1. Interviews new workers after they have been given induction information such as hours, working conditions, services, etc., to verify personnel information and prepare records; checks information on application, statement of availability, draft, citizenship, and the like; obtains necessary information for income tax withholding, and determines classification; prepares forms for hospitalization, group insurance, and bond deductions; assigns clock number, makes up time card and badge card.

2. Calls previous employer to get reference information while applicant is being interviewed; may check references by mail after employee is hired, and occasionally records information from Dun & Bradstreet or Retail Credit Association on personnel card.

3. Telephones employee's department or home after extended absence to determine when employee is expected to return, if at all; follows same procedure at end of leave of absence.

4. Handles stenographic work of EMPLOYMENT MANAGER.

5. Does miscellaneous clerical work; assigns clock numbers, and makes up time cards for employees transferred between departments; keeps record of equipment loaned to employees, such as micrometers, goggles, etc.; maintains current address file of employees in service; performs other clerical duties as assigned.

6. May substitute for RECEPTIONIST for short periods; give induction information to new employees in absence of PERSONNEL INDUCTION CLERK, escort new workers to departments; administer tests.

Job duties section. The major duties and responsibilities of the job are covered by brief statements that indicate: (1) what the worker does,

(2) how he does it, and (3) why he does it. The description of duties should also indicate the tools and equipment employed, the materials used, the procedures followed, and the degree of supervision received. An additional section of miscellaneous items may also be provided to indicate such things as the relationship of the job to other jobs with respect to transfer and promotion possibilities.

The Job Specification

The content and organization of a job specification, like that of the job description, will vary among companies. Generally, however, the items covered by a job specification may be divided into two groups: one group covering the skill requirements of a job and the other group covering its physical demands.

Skill requirements. The skill requirements include the mental and manual skills as well as personal traits and qualities that the job holder must possess to perform the job satisfactorily. Although a job specification may not contain each one of the following skill requirements, it generally will contain most of them.

Educational requirements. These requirements may include the minimum formal education, including special courses or technical training, considered necessary to perform the job.

Experience. The minimum amount and type of experience that is required in order for an employee to hold a job generally can be expressed in objective and quantitative terms such as years and months.

Specific knowledge requirements. Many jobs require the employee to possess specific knowledge that cannot be covered adequately by the education and experience specifications. These requirements might include a knowledge of certain materials, processes, equipment, systems, products, or other subject matter.

Personality requirements. These requirements often are the most difficult to describe because they are intangible and subjective in nature. Nevertheless, the ability of an individual to fit into a particular situation and to work harmoniously with others may have a much greater bearing than does his technical skill upon his success in performing a particular job. Information relating to these qualifications may cover such topics as social skills, judgment, initiative, cooperativeness, and creative ability.

Responsibility. Most specifications cover this qualification as a separate requirement because it is likely to include several types of responsibility. These types may include responsibility for the work of others, for equipment, for production processes, for company funds, for product quality, for safety, and for cost reduction.

Manual skill requirements. In the case of some jobs, manual skills can be covered in the items describing experience and training. For other jobs, however, manual skills may have to be defined in terms of the quantity, quality, or nature of the work to be performed, or in terms of the minimum scores that must be achieved on certain performance tests. Manual skills include clerical skills, such as typing, and shop skills, such as those that are required in order to make a pattern or a jig.

Physical demands. The physical demands of a job may include: (1) physical exertion, (2) working conditions, and (3) hazards that are encountered in performing the duties of the job. These demands are likely to be greater for shop jobs than for office jobs.

Physical exertion. Physical exertion covers such activities as walking, stooping, lifting, handling, or talking.[7] It includes not only the amount of physical effort required to perform a job but also the length of time during which such effort must be expended. A summary of the weights, pressures, or other quantitative measures of the exertion required can help to indicate the extent of the physical demands that are necessary.

Working conditions. This portion of the physical demands section pertains to the general physical environment or surroundings under which the job must be performed. It may indicate, for example, whether the lighting is adequate, whether the work is isolated, and whether the conditions are hot, cold, dusty, or cramped.

Hazards. The listing of unfavorable working conditions and hazards can help to call attention to them and encourage their elimination, and thereby contribute to employee health and safety. Certain jobs may remain hazardous in spite of all safety measures that can be taken. The specifying of hazards can help to insure that those persons who are placed in the hazardous jobs will have the mental and physical qualifications necessary to perform the work safely.

---

[7]U.S. Employment Service, Occupational Analysis and Industrial Services Division, *Training and Reference Manual for Job Analysis* (Washington, D.C.: United States Government Printing Office, June 1, 1944), p. 85.

Considerations Affecting Job Specifications

In developing the specifications for a job, every effort should be made to insure that the requirements set forth actually are necessary. It is quite possible, for example, that certain specifications such as those relating to age, experience, education, or physical qualification might be based more upon opinion or tradition than upon fact. A high school education might be specified, for example, when the knowledge that is required to perform the job does not exceed that which could be acquired before reaching the eighth grade. Similarly, an age limit for a job of 35 or 40 years might be entirely arbitrary in nature.

Avoidance of discrimination. Some of the requirements that are included in the specifications of certain jobs have been the subject of attack by those who feel that these requirements discriminate against members of their minority group. Leaders in one ethnic group, for example, have charged that certain minimum height requirements for policemen and firemen serve to discriminate against their members because these individuals on the average tend to be shorter in height.[8]

Requirements relating to race, religion, color, or birthplace, which once were not uncommon in job specifications, have to a large extent been eliminated by state and federal fair employment laws. Federal regulations such as those contained in the Civil Rights Act of 1964 also forbid items in the specification that discriminate against the employment of women. Some states forbid discrimination on the basis of age. In view of these trends to outlaw discrimination, therefore, it is reasonable to assume that specifications will have to be reviewed even more closely to prevent the inclusion of those requirements that are arbitrary or discriminatory in nature.

Influence of the space age. The "space age" has stimulated the creation of many new and highly technical jobs whose specifications are rather exotic and beyond the level of comprehension for most, except those persons who are involved directly with the job. An advertisement for *senior vibration analyst*, for example, is quoted as follows:

> Responsibilities call for airborne application of advanced techniques in shock, vibration, and reliability analysis, involving extrapolation of environment from individual components in the launch vehicle to still more advanced vehicles now in design stages.[9]

---

[8]*Sacramento Bee*, February 18, 1966.
[9]Russell Baker, "Ads For Help Wanted Puzzle Job Hunter," *New York Times News Service*, February 19, 1964.

Specifications of this type make the task of the personnel department that must utilize them a difficult one. The fact that few people are able to understand the specification, therefore, can limit its value. A complex specification, however, may serve to discourage certain applicants who might otherwise try to bluff their way into a nontechnical job by claiming to have the necessary experience and ability.

Style for Writing Job Descriptions and Specifications

Job descriptions and specifications should be written in a manner that permits all of the necessary information to be compiled accurately, clearly, and briefly. According to one authority:

1. The statements should be terse and direct, using the simplest possible wording.
2. All words and phrases which do not contribute to the description should be omitted.
3. Each sentence should start with a functional verb, present tense, with the implied subject being the worker holding the job.
4. Emphasis should be given to the skills involved and to the particular tools and equipment used.
5. Full capital letters should be used to spell out any job titles appearing in the description. The names of all departments, special equipment, and similar items should have the first letter in the word capitalized.
6. The term "occasionally" should be used to describe those duties performed "once in a while," and the term "may" should be used to describe those duties which are performed only by some of the workers.[10]

The job specification for a *personnel clerk*, shown in Figure 4-3, illustrates how the personal qualifications that are necessary to perform a job may be summarized. Since this is a specification for a white-collar job, it does not include items relating primarily to blue-collar work that were discussed in the preceding section.

Uses of Job Descriptions and Specifications

The value to be derived from job descriptions and specifications is determined to a large extent by the number of persons who make use of them and by the degree of use that they make of them. Even the job information that is prepared most carefully will be of little value if it remains stored in the personnel department files. The data pertaining to each job should be readily accessible to the job holder and to his supervisor. This

---

[10] J. L. Otis and R. H. Leukart, *Job Evaluation* (2nd ed.; Englewood Cliffs, New Jersey: Prentice-Hall, Inc., 1954), pp. 274–276.

Figure 4-3

SAMPLE JOB SPECIFICATION*

JOB TITLE: Personnel Clerk	CODE NO.:
DEPARTMENT: Personnel TOTAL POINTS:	CLASSIFICATION:

EDUCATION	Points

EDUCATION

High school graduate with typing and stenographic training.

EXPERIENCE AND TRAINING

Two to three weeks required to learn details of job. Three months required to perform job with minimum of supervision. Experience on job required to learn location of all departments, become acquainted with all FOREMEN, become skilled in the duties of other workers in the department for whom she substitutes occasionally.

RESOURCEFULNESS

Planning on a limited scale necessary in regulating and scheduling work in peak periods and in adapting routine to changed or new procedures. Some ingenuity involved in getting information from new workers, handling them effectively to give them a good first impression of the company, and explaining advantages of services provided for employees.

ABILITY TO DO ROUTINE WORK

There is considerable variety in this job. It is necessary that clerical work be accurate in order to avoid later mistakes in accounting for hours worked, in payroll information, and in payroll deductions.

MANUAL OR MOTOR (MACHINE) OPERATIONS

Must operate a typewriter to some extent, but typing speed is not an important element in the job; typing must be accurate, however.

CAPACITY FOR GETTING ALONG WITH OTHERS

Works in close sequence with three other employees in the department. Must avoid friction. Contacts with new employees, as well as with FOREMEN, very important.

CAPACITY FOR SELF-EXPRESSION

One of the most important aspects of the job; involved in explaining to and getting facts from new employees, former employees, FOREMEN, etc.

SUPERVISION

Supervision is almost always available; consults with superiors on any unusual situations. No supervision of others.

**RESPONSIBILITY FOR GOOD WILL
AND PUBLIC RELATIONS**

This job represents a key contact with new employees, affecting their initial impression of the company. The prime responsibility of this worker, however, is to present and explain clearly, thoroughly, and pleasantly the facts which the new employee is to learn at this point in the induction procedure. No highly developed techniques of salesmanship are required. Telephone contacts with employment departments of other companies are important.

WORKING CONDITIONS

Works in a large office with considerable traffic, frequent interruptions, and factory noise overhead.

	Total

*The column with the word "Points" at the head is used to assign point values to each of the factors that are arrived at through the process of job evaluation.

latter arrangement is of particular importance since employees are often hesitant to ask questions concerning their jobs for fear that such questions will be interpreted as a reflection of their ignorance.

Job descriptions can be utilized not only to inform and to remind employees about the details of their duties but also to provide them with a guide for improving performance and preparing for advancement. Job descriptions can serve as an important personnel tool for supervisors in helping them to orient and train employees, to reconcile employee griev-ances, and to support disciplinary action.

Job specifications probably are utilized the most in connection with the recruitment and selection of employees. Job specifications are par-ticularly essential in a large organization where applicants for a wide variety of jobs must be screened by employment specialists who may not be familiar with the jobs. In the determination of differences in wage rates through the process of job evaluation, the data that are contained in the job specifications also can serve an important use.

The Job Analysis Program

Information that is contained in job descriptions and specifications is gathered, analyzed, and recorded through the process known as *job analysis*. The data gathering process of job analysis thus must occur before the relative worth of jobs can be determined by means of *job evaluation*. The formal process of job analysis helps to reduce the influence of personal biases, opinions, or judgments on the part of those persons gathering or supplying the information by making it necessary for the information to be reduced to written form and supported by factual evidence.

Job analysis should not be confused with time and motion study which, while it also provides data relating to the job, is primarily an in-dustrial engineering rather than a personnel management function. Whereas job analysis helps to reveal in rather broad terms what an em-ployee does and the qualifications that he must possess, time and motion study is concerned with the details of the work activities that are per-formed. Time and motion study may involve the use of stop watches, photography, or predetermined time standards; and it is concerned with such factors as the nature of the motions performed, the time and dis-tances involved, and the sequence with which motions occur in performing the activities of a job. The results of job analysis are compiled in narrative and descriptive form. The results of time and motion study, on the other hand, are often quantitative and graphic in nature, for they are aimed at the improvement of work methods and the development of time standards.

Responsibility for Job Analysis

While the personnel department is the one that is primarily responsible for the job analysis program, it must receive the cooperation of the other departments if the program is to be successful. It is the supervisors and employees within each department who must supply most of the job data and who may even prepare the rough draft of the job descriptions and specifications.

If a personnel department is large enough to maintain a separate wage and salary division, the job analysis work is usually performed by members of this division. Those persons who specialize in compiling job data and in preparing and maintaining the job descriptions and specifications generally are given the title of *job analyst* or, in some cases, *personnel analyst.* Because this job requires a rather high degree of analytical ability and writing skill, it sometimes can serve as the initial job for college graduates who are seeking a career in the personnel field.

Compiling Job Information

The analyst may obtain job information by interviewing employees in each of the jobs and/or their supervisors, by having either of these groups complete questionnaires covering their jobs, by observing the jobs being performed, and by checking available production records. In many instances, all of these sources may be utilized.

Questionnaires have the advantage of permitting information pertaining to many different jobs to be obtained very rapidly. In order for the questionnaire method to be used successfully, employees who complete the questionnaires must have the ability to read and interpret the questions correctly and to supply the information requested in written and understandable form. The questionnaire method, therefore, is generally used more successfully with white-collar employees than with blue-collar groups. Even when employees are able to complete job analysis questionnaires or to prepare their descriptions by themselves, the analyst would often have saved time had he compiled the data himself because of the extent to which he must edit, correct, and supplement the information given by employees. For this reason, the interview method is generally used, at least to some extent, in gathering information for job descriptions and specifications.

If employees are requested to fill out questionnaires, the items must be clear and must solicit pertinent information without imposing an undue burden upon the employees. Figure 4-4, which lists the questions contained in a job analysis questionnaire used by Pitney-Bowes, Inc., illustrates the types of information that employees may be expected to supply through

Figure 4-4
JOB ANALYSIS QUESTIONNAIRE

Name_____   Date _____

Department _____   Department Head _____

Job_____   Length of time
                                         on this job _____

A. THE JOB

    (1) Describe exactly what the duties of your job are. Use extra sheets if necessary. Show average length of time (hours per week) required for each part of your job.

    (2) List various reports which you make out or assist in making out, designating whether daily, weekly, monthly, quarterly, or annually.

B. EDUCATION

    (1) Check below the basic general education which the job requires, *regardless of how it may have been acquired.*

High School	**Business College**	**College**
_____2 years	_____1 year	_____2 years
_____4 years	_____2 years	_____4 years

    (2) What additional education would be helpful, if any:

    _____

    (3) If college is required, state why _____

    _____

C. EXPERIENCE

    (1) Check below the length of time you think it will take a *new* employee with the educational background you have checked above to learn to do this job well.

        a. Less than 1 month_____   e. 1 to 2 years _____

        b. 1 to 3 months_____   f. 2 to 4 years _____

        c. 3 to 6 months_____   g. 4 to 6 years _____

        d. 6 to 12 months_____   h. 6 to 8 years _____

D. SUPERVISION RECEIVED

    (1) Are all questionable cases referred to supervisor?_____

    (2) Do you have to use own judgment in meeting new situations? _____ If so, give an example _____

    (3) Is your work checked?_____ If so, by whom? _____

(Figure 4-4 concluded on next page)

(Figure 4-4 continued from page 100)

E. ERRORS

    (1) What are the more probable types of errors you could commit, and their effect:

Types of Errors   **Effect**

F. CONTACTS WITH OTHERS

    (1) Do your duties bring you into contact with persons outside your own department?_____. If so,

With Whom	For What Purpose	How Made (Person, phone, or letter)

G. WORKING CONDITIONS

    (1) List below any disagreeable or hazardous conditions to which you are subjected in the course of your work, and how often subjected thereto.

Condition   **How Often**

H. SUPERVISION OF OTHERS

    (1) Do you supervise others?_____. If so, state below the number and extent.

Number   **Positions and Extent**

I. OFFICE EQUIPMENT

    (1) Do you operate office machines?_____

    (2) List of equipment.   Approximate number of hours per week actually operated.

ADDITIONAL COMMENTS   Use extra sheet if necessary.

---

this method. It will be noted that most of the questions on this form encourage brief answers. (In the actual questionnaire form, more space is provided for recording the answers to some of the questions.)

One of the more recent approaches to job analysis is that which is based upon the use of *critical incidents*. It involves recording factual incidents and events that have been observed to occur and which serve to distinguish effective from ineffective behavior on the job. The critical incident method, thus, can be particularly valuable when used to supplement the more conventional forms of job information since it focuses on the really important or critical behaviors associated with successful performance of the job that otherwise may be overlooked by supervisors and employees.[11]

The accuracy of job data. If job analysis is to accomplish its intended objectives, the data that are gained from it must be accurate. Persons who are responsible for gathering or editing the data need to guard continually against the omission of important facts, the inclusion of inaccurate statements, or the tendency of some personnel to exaggerate the difficulty or importance of their jobs in order to inflate their egos or their paychecks. When interviewing personnel or checking questionnaire responses, analysts must be alert for any statements which do not agree with other facts or impressions that the analyst has been receiving. It is the usual practice to have the descriptions for each job checked and approved by one or more of the employee's superiors. Unless the approval of these superiors is obtained, they may develop resentment and resistance toward the job analysis program.

As far as possible, the information pertaining to each job should indicate the specific results that are expected from an employee. Such information should enable the employee and his supervisor to have a mutual understanding of the performance that is expected in a job and thus be better able to evaluate and to discuss the performance results that the employee has achieved or is expected to achieve. Any special requirements that relate to an employee's success, particularly those relating to personality, should also be indicated. If, for example, a job requires a certain temperament in order to work for a particular superior or to get along in a particular work group, this fact may determine the success or failure of a job holder and should not be ignored even though it is of a delicate nature.

---

[11]John C. Flanagan and Robert K. Burns, "Employee Performance Record: A New Appraisal and Development Tool," *Harvard Business Review*, Vol. 35, No. 5 (September–October, 1957), pp. 95–102.

The Dictionary of Occupational Titles.   An important guide in the preparation of job descriptions is the *Dictionary of Occupational Titles*, which is commonly referred to as the D.O.T. It is compiled by the Bureau of Employment Security of the U.S. Employment Service. The third edition, published in 1965, contains definitions for 21,741 separate jobs which are known under 13,809 alternate titles, thereby making a total of 35,550 titles that are described in the *Dictionary*.[12] Volume 2 of the D.O.T. provides a classification system for grouping and identifying jobs. The type of descriptions contained in the *Dictionary* is illustrated by the description for a Production Lathe Operator job which follows:

> **LATHE OPERATOR, PRODUCTION** (mach. shop) **604.885. automatic-lathe operator; production-lathe operator.** Tends one or more previously set-up lathes, such as turret lathes, bar-machines, and chucking machines, to perform one or series of repetitive operations, such as turning, boring, threading, or facing, of metal workpieces according to specifications on production basis: Lifts workpiece manually or with hoist, and places and secures it in holding fixture or in automatic feed mechanism. Starts machine and turns handwheels to feed tools to workpiece, and engages automatic feed. Observes machining cycle. Verifies conformance of machined work to specifications, using fixed gages, calipers, and micrometers. Changes worn tools, using wrenches. May move controls to adjust rotation speeds, feed rates, and depth of cut. May assist LATHE SET-UP MAN. May work on non-metallic materials, such as plastics. May be required to have experience with particular materials or product, or with machine of particular size, type, or trade name.[13]

The D.O.T. descriptions have helped to bring about a greater degree of uniformity in the job titles and descriptions that are used by companies in different sections of the nation. This fact has facilitated the exchange of statistical information about jobs as well as the movement of workers from sections of the country that may be experiencing widespread unemployment to those sections where employment opportunities are greater. The D.O.T. numbers for jobs are also used in reporting personnel research, particularly as it applies to testing. The Validity Information Exchange (V.I.E.) of *Personnel Psychology*, for example, uses the job titles and code numbers of the D.O.T. in communicating information concerning tests for various jobs.[14]

---

[12]U.S. Department of Labor, Bureau of Employment Security. *Dictionary of Occupational Titles*, Vol. 1, Definitions of Titles (3rd ed.; Washington: U.S. Government Printing Office, 1965), p. XV.

[13]*Ibid.*, p. 413.

[14]While the V.I.E. was discontinued in 1966, it will continue to be valuable to users of psychological tests in business and industry.

Initiating the Job Analysis Program

A job analysis program that is well planned and organized should help to minimize any possible resistance from employees. This preparatory work can serve to clarify the purposes for gathering the job data as well as the procedures to be followed in collecting it. Before engaging in job analysis work, the groups of jobs to be included in the program, the order in which they are to be analyzed, the type of information that is to be obtained, and the method by which the information is to be gathered must first be determined. Analysts must be selected and trained and the necessary forms, instructions, and explanatory materials prepared. A full explanation of the scope, purposes, and benefits of the program to all personnel is, perhaps, the most important phase in the introduction of the program. The preparation of employees for the introduction of the program can do much to prevent the spread of false information about the program and can pave the way for the analyst's arrival in each department.

Gaining Acceptance of the Program

Developing acceptance for job analysis requires careful planning and effective communication. The purpose of the program, the benefits that will accrue to employees from it, and the methods that are to be used should be communicated to all individuals who are affected by it if their support is to be obtained. One of the first steps in planning a job analysis program is that of establishing and reducing to written form the objectives of the program and the policies and procedures governing its operation. The persons in charge of the program must have a clear understanding of what the program proposes to accomplish and how these accomplishments are to be realized in order to be able to explain the program to other members of the organization and to gain their support. Personnel throughout the enterprise should be made familiar with the purposes and benefits of job analysis through educational endeavors. Efforts along these lines may be aided by the use of printed materials, conferences, group meetings, and training classes. It is preferable to direct educational efforts to the supervisors first since the cooperation and support of supervisors in explaining the program to their operative personnel is so essential to the program's success.

Emphasizing program benefits to employees. The enlistment of employee cooperation and support should appeal to their self-interests by emphasizing the following personal benefits:

1. Job analysis can enable the employee to understand better the duties and responsibilities of his job and what is expected of him. Nothing can be more frustrating or demoralizing to an employee than not knowing the exact nature of his duties or his relationships with others.

2. Job analysis can provide important data that can be used to equalize the distribution of the work load among the employees. The data also can provide an objective basis for determining the rate of pay for each job and for evaluating employee performance. Employees want to receive fair and objective treatment and such treatment requires the existence of accurate job information that can be gained through job analysis.

3. The presence of accurate information concerning job requirements also can help to provide each employee with a guide for self-improvement, both with respect to his present and future jobs.

4. Finally, job analysis data can provide supervisors and employees with a more objective basis for defining and resolving certain of the grievances that may arise in connection with their job duties.

Introducing the program. The success of a program can be affected by the timing of its introduction. A program should not be initiated during a period of layoffs, economic uncertainty, or labor unrest since the employees are even more likely to view the program as a threat to their security. It is also important that a job analysis program be introduced within a department where the employees and supervisors are most likely to be cooperative and receptive toward it. Once the benefits of the program have been proved in one department, news of this fact will help to create an interest in job analysis in other departments.

Maintaining the Job Descriptions

Jobs, like the organizational structure that they comprise, are dynamic in nature. Changes in the size and nature of its organization or the introduction of new equipment, manufacturing processes, or products within a company, to mention but a few factors, can influence the duties and requirements of the jobs that are affected. Thus, job descriptions must be revised as changes within the jobs make these revisions necessary.

Many of the changes within the jobs are called to the attention of the personnel department as they occur through the requests of employees and supervisors to have the jobs reanalyzed and new descriptions prepared. The descriptions may have to be revised if significant changes are made in the duties or requirements of the job. Complaints over the classification or rate that is assigned to a particular job may also force a reanalysis of it and revision of the job description. In order to be certain that any changes in the jobs do not remain unrecognized, some companies make it a policy to review all job descriptions annually. This procedure can help to insure that job descriptions remain current and accurate.

Résumé

The caliber of an employee's performance and the feelings of satisfaction and recognition that he derives from his work will be influenced to a large extent by the demands that his job places upon him. His job, furthermore, can be a source of status to him and contribute to his sense of well-being both economically and psychologically. In organizing the work of the enterprise into jobs, it is important that jobs be designed so as to permit the employee who is assigned to it to perform efficiently and to achieve a feeling of satisfaction and security from his work. It is essential, in this regard, that the duties, responsibilities, and performance requirements of each job be established formally so that each employee and his superior will understand clearly what is expected of him in the way of performance. The requirements of each job should be determined objectively through the process of job analysis and compiled formally into job descriptions and specifications. The information contained in these descriptions and specifications can prove to be of considerable value in connection with the selection, evaluation, and training of employees and in resolving grievance and disciplinary problems. These statements need to be reviewed periodically for the purpose of insuring that the requirements demanded in a job are actually necessary and that they do not serve to discriminate unfairly against potential applicants from any particular group.

The responsibility for preparing and maintaining the job descriptions and specifications rests primarily with the personnel department. Since the information that is contained in these statements must be obtained from the personnel in departments where the jobs are located, individuals engaged in job analysis work must be sufficiently diplomatic and tactful to gain the cooperation of others. The cooperation of personnel can be gained more readily if they understand the purpose of job analysis and the possible benefits that they personally may derive from it.

DISCUSSION QUESTIONS AND PROBLEMS

1. What is it that makes a particular job satisfying to one individual but not to another? Why do some people prefer a particular type of work that others may dislike?

2. Suggest ways in which a repetitive type of job might be made more interesting.

3. List some of the status symbols that may be provided for people in jobs where you may work or have worked. Could these symbols be replaced by a 10 percent increase in pay?

4. As a project, prepare a description of the job at which you currently are working or have worked. Develop a specification listing the minimum qualifications that are necessary in order for one to perform this job. How do these requirements of the job compare with your qualifications?

5. Why is it that a college degree may be specified for a job when an individual actually could perform it without having had any college courses?

6. Why is it that the job specification rather than the job description is used primarily in connection with employee recruitment and selection?

7. Why would job descriptions and specifications tend to be more necessary in a line-and-staff type of organization with a central personnel department rather than in a straight-line type of organization?

8. Why are personnel more likely to support a job analysis program if they are permitted to participate in its development?

9. Some managers have opposed the preparation of formal job descriptions on the grounds that such descriptions encourage employees to do only the work that is required by their job descriptions. What is your reaction to this statement?

10. Several production supervisors have expressed strong opposition to a proposed job analysis program on the grounds that the gathering of job data would interrupt employees and supervisors in the performance of their work and thereby increase departmental operating costs. The supervisors also maintain that they and their employees have a better understanding than any job analyst regarding the duties of the jobs with which they have daily contact. If you were the personnel manager, how would you deal with this opposition to the development of a job analysis program?

11. In one company a new rule was issued requiring that the office employees punch in and out on a time clock. The rule had to be rescinded in the face of vigorous employee opposition. Only a minimum number of complaints had been received from production workers who had always used a time clock.
    a. How do you account for the opposition exhibited by the office employees?
    b. Should the use of a time clock also be eliminated for the plant employees?

CASE 4-1

THE DISGRUNTLED DELIVERYMAN

Bill Low was considered to be one of the Buffalo Distributing Company's most competent drivers. He was energetic, courteous, and usually completed his route in less time than the time standard established for it. The standards for each route had been developed carefully and had proved to be quite successful in controlling the performance of drivers.

The purchase of several new trucks one spring, however, forced an adjustment to be made in certain delivery routes and in the work standards for them. The new trucks were larger, faster, and the new body styles permitted more efficient delivery operations. Bill Low soon adjusted to the changes in his route and to the time schedule established for it. A short time later, though, the company found it necessary to use Bill's new truck on another route, and Bill received an older model as a temporary replacement. Although his new truck would be returned for short periods, some new emergency would occur to require its use elsewhere. Bill found himself being assigned to an older truck on practically a permanent basis. Soon his performance began to deteriorate, and his supervisor suspected that Bill often took extended coffee breaks and lunch periods. Frequently Bill required overtime to complete his route. His rate of absences for reported illness increased, and he made little effort to get along with his superiors or fellow drivers.

Bill's supervisor made a concerted effort to warn him about his poor record and to find out the cause for his deteriorating attitude. Bill was usually noncommittal when the subject was brought up; and when cautioned about his absences or his failure to complete his route as scheduled, he would improve sufficiently to meet minimum standards. Since Bill was doing enough "to get by" and since the union to which he belonged was quick to challenge disciplinary action by the company that was not clearly justified, his superior was reluctant to take any action against Bill even though it was obvious that he was performing far below his capacity. The situation continued until one of the senior drivers casually suggested to the supervisor that Bill's assignment to an older model truck might be one of the causes for the deterioration in his performance. Shortly thereafter Bill was permanently assigned another truck that had just arrived from the factory. Both his attitude and performance improved somewhat as a result of this gesture. From that time on his performance continued to be satisfactory, but he never again exhibited the superior performance that had once characterized his work as a deliveryman.

    a. How do you account for Bill Low's failure to return to his original performance level after getting a new truck permanently?

    b. Why didn't Bill tell his supervisor the reason for the deterioration of his attitude and performance?

    c. What lessons in personnel management might one draw from this case, particularly from the standpoint of job satisfaction?

SUGGESTED READINGS

Brennan, Charles W. *Wage Administration Plans, Practices, and Principles.* Homewood, Illinois: Richard D. Irwin, Inc., 1959. Chapter 7.

Langsner, Adolph, and Herbert G. Zollitsch. *Wage and Salary Administration.* Cincinnati: South-Western Publishing Company, Inc., 1961. Chapter 12.

Lanham, Elizabeth. *Administration of Wages and Salaries.* New York: Harper & Row, Publishers, 1963. Pp. 125–154.

Otis, Jay L., and Richard H. Leukart. *Job Evaluation,* Second Edition. Englewood Cliffs, New Jersey: Prentice-Hall, Inc., 1954. Chapters 7–9.

Patton, John A., C. L. Littlefield, and Stanley A. Self. *Job Evaluation: Text and Cases,* Third Edition. Homewood, Illinois: Richard D. Irwin, Inc., 1964. Chapters 4–5.

Personnel Recruitment

In order to maintain an effective work force, an enterprise must have accurate and continuing information as to the number and the qualifications of the persons needed to perform the various jobs within the organization. The qualifications that an employee is required to possess, it will be recalled, are determined by the duties and responsibilities of his job. The number of personnel needed to staff the various jobs in the organization is determined by the amount and type of work to be performed and by the efficiency with which this work is performed. It is determined also by technological changes and by changes in the organization structure that may occur and that may affect the number and types of jobs and positions to be staffed.

The staffing process of management, thus, is one of analyzing present and future manpower needs and of obtaining qualified personnel to meet these needs. Effective staffing requires that fluctuations in manpower requirements be reduced to a minimum so that it does not become necessary either to continue to employ persons whose services are no longer needed or to subject employees to a layoff. The staffing process also includes the developing and maintaining of adequate sources of manpower from which qualified applicants may be recruited and selected for employment. In order for qualified applicants to be recruited, positive action must be taken by the personnel department, not only to make these applicants aware of the employment opportunities that exist within the enterprise but also to induce them to apply and be considered for the openings that are or may become available.

The major topics pertaining to staffing that are covered in this chapter are:

- Anticipating personnel requirements.
- Locating qualified personnel.
- Policies relating to staffing.

Anticipating Personnel Requirements

Since considerable lead time may be required to recruit, select, and develop employees for many of the jobs within an enterprise, it is essential that job vacancies be anticipated as far as possible in advance. Similarly, the fact that positions are to be eliminated should become known sufficiently in advance to permit the employees affected to be retrained and reassigned, if possible, to other positions.

If the need to establish or eliminate positions can be identified in advance, it will be possible for the adjustments that are required within the enterprise to be made in order that an efficient and a more stable work force can be maintained. The anticipation of changes in manpower needs, particularly in terms of specific positions, requires effective manpower planning. Such planning, however, cannot be accomplished without effective sales, inventory, and production planning based upon objective data and research. It is, thus, the demand for its products or services and the competition that it experiences which will have a bearing upon the number and qualifications of persons that an enterprise must employ. These factors will affect its need for both white-collar and blue-collar personnel.

Sales Planning

The sale of its products or services constitutes the basic purpose for which a private enterprise exists. The sales function, therefore, affects the work load and the personnel requirements of all departments within the enterprise. Sales planning, if successful, will enable a company to anticipate the demand for its product or service and will help a company to achieve a more stable rate of production. Effective sales planning, furthermore, may help to influence the demand for the company's products by permitting these products to be designed on the basis of what research indicates the customer's wants are likely to be.

The pressure of unions for stabilized employment and the desire of management to reduce the high cost of employee turnover have caused many of them to devote more time to sales planning as a basis for stabilizing and maximizing sales. Efforts to stabilize sales are particularly essential for companies that are affected by seasonal fluctuations. Such efforts, therefore, may include planning for special promotional campaigns and price concessions to induce customers to buy during off-season periods or to purchase the product in smaller but recurring amounts; they may also include planning new products and services for which the demand is greater during the off season.

Changes in business activities resulting from fluctuations in the business cycle are more difficult to anticipate and to counteract than are those resulting from seasonal fluctuations. Through the use of forecasting techniques, a company may be able to discover cyclical trends affecting product sales and organizational growth and to project these trends into the future as a means of predicting its own business activity. Sales and personnel planning must also give consideration to government fiscal policies and regulations, to changes in the international situation, to technological breakthroughs, and to labor strikes.

Inventory Planning

A company's inventory of finished products can provide a flexible link between its sales and production programs. By increasing or decreasing the amount of inventory on hand, it is possible to stabilize production to a greater extent than otherwise would be permitted by the current sale of its products. While product size, perishability, and susceptibility to obsolescence or the limited financial resources or storage facilities of the company may not always permit production to be stabilized through the accumulation of inventory, effective inventory planning and record keeping can help a company to minimize overproduction and cutbacks in its work force.

Production Planning

The production rate of a company is generally determined by the customer orders that are on hand or are anticipated, with proper allowances being made for desired increases or decreases in inventory. Generally, overall production schedules are developed for a season or for some other suitable period of time and subsequently for monthly and weekly periods. While certain adjustments in long-term production plans are inevitable, their development is essential to good personnel planning. The procurement and development of qualified personnel for many jobs throughout the organization may require several months or even years of lead time which only long-term planning can provide.

Temporary fluctuations in the rate of production need not make necessary any changes in the size of the regular work force. Adjustments to temporary increases in the work load can be accomplished through the use of overtime, by subcontracting some of the work, by hiring temporary help, or by utilizing the services of companies that supply temporary manpower. Conversely, temporary decreases can be accommodated by shortening the workweek, encouraging the use of accumulated vacation time, or by assigning some employees to maintenance work or other projects that have been accumulated for just such "make-work" needs. Some companies, such as Procter & Gamble, which provide a program of guaranteed employment for their personnel insist upon having the freedom to shift personnel from one job to another as a means of meeting fluctuations in departmental work loads.

Personnel Planning in Public Enterprises

The need for effective personnel planning is by no means limited to private enterprises. Government agencies, educational institutions, hospitals, and other public enterprises also must operate efficiently within established budgets even though they are not profit-making in nature. Many of these public enterprises also experience long-term as well as short-term changes and fluctuations in the demand for their services. Changes and shifts in population, international tensions and conflicts, political pressures, and fluctuations in the business cycle may have an effect upon the services that a public agency or institution may be required to provide or upon the budget on which it must operate. These factors may also affect the number and types of positions that must be staffed for any particular period. Therefore, if possible, they must be anticipated as a part of the organization's personnel planning program.

Determining the Positions Required

The production schedule together with production standards provide the basis for determining the work load of each department and the manpower required to handle it. These manpower requirements, however, must be translated into specific job and position allocations for each department. In determining these allocations, adjustments must be made for the degree of competency that is possessed by the personnel who staff these positions. Adjustments also must be made for losses in productivity resulting from absenteeism, vacations, turnover, training assignments, and other factors affecting employee efficiency.

Authorizing Positions

The authority to staff the positions that are allocated to a department is provided by the department budget which authorizes the amount of wages that can be paid to each position. In evaluating their manpower needs, there is a natural tendency for managers and supervisors to feel that their departments are understaffed. Because of this tendency, they may seek more personnel for their departments than they require. One of the ways of discouraging this practice is through the use of accurate cost control procedures that reveal a manager's efficiency record. If managers are under pressure continually to improve these records by reducing their operating costs, the incentive will be for them to reduce rather than to increase the number of personnel within their departments.

In most companies the departmental operating budgets, which include payroll costs, serve to control the amount of money that can be expended for personnel within the department. The personnel budget may be augmented by means of allocation or manning tables that specify how the payroll is to be distributed in terms of the numbers, types, and remunerations of the positions allocated to a department. Through the use of these control records, managers are prevented from hiring personnel except for positions that have been authorized and for which vacancies exist. While these controls may prevent them from hiring unauthorized personnel, they do not prevent managers from trying to get an increase in their personnel budgets and allocations. It is, therefore, desirable for a company to establish those standards which permit manpower allocations to be made on an objective basis rather than on a subjective or political basis.

Locating Qualified Personnel

If the organization is to be staffed effectively, management must know where to obtain those persons who are most qualified to fill each position vacancy. Management must also have means for securing applications from personnel qualified for the vacancies. It can be just as important for a company to seek out the best sources of manpower as it is for it to seek out the best sources of raw materials, supplies, or equipment. In fact, effective procurement of both material and personnel requires that a company aggressively seek out the best sources of supply rather than merely utilizing those sources that may happen to be available.

In the case of personnel recruitment, the individuals who are the most qualified to fill a particular job vacancy are often the ones who are already employed and/or whose services are being sought by other employers. This fact is particularly true with respect to candidates for engineering, scientific, and similar jobs for which the supply of applicants may be extremely limited. Aggressive recruitment efforts, however, should be exerted even for those jobs for which there is an adequate supply of applicants since the objective of recruitment is to obtain that individual who is the best qualified person for a particular position rather than just any individual. This objective should hold equally true during recessionary periods when there is large-scale unemployment; for during these periods, the presence of competent employees can be vital to the survival of the organization.

As in the procurement of materials, the procurement of personnel requires the cultivation of many different sources of supply since jobs cannot all be staffed from the same source. A company would not be likely to obtain qualified engineers, for example, from the same sources from which it obtains clerical employees or shop personnel. Changes in business activity or other conditions also can affect drastically the number and quality of applicants that can be obtained from a particular source of supply. A company, for example, that had been able to obtain qualified applicants from among those seeking work at its employment office might find this source to be inadequate during a tighter labor market.

Internal Sources

In locating possible sources of supply, it is wise for a company not to overlook those sources that exist within its own organization. Internal sources of personnel are those that can be utilized through employee transfers, promotions, and recalls from layoffs. Most companies try to give first consideration to their own personnel in filling position vacancies before hiring persons from outside of the organization.

The development of computerized information retrieval systems has made it possible for data covering the qualifications of each employee to be stored on magnetic tape. All of the data formerly contained in the personnel folder can, in fact, be transferred to tape. These taped data permit a company to screen its entire force of personnel in a matter of minutes, or even seconds, when the need arises to locate those employees who may have a particular qualification or combination of qualifications for a specific opening. In a multiplant company this information can be drawn from the computer by means of teleprinters that are installed at each plant site and are connected by wire to the central computer. The data also can be used to prepare periodic personnel reports such as those covering manpower counts by department, job location, labor costs, absenteeism, or turnover. Most of the larger companies, such as the Ford Motor Company, Eastman Kodak Company, General Electric, and the various departments of the armed services, are compiling their personnel records on magnetic tape.[1]

In addition to permitting immediate access to any personnel data, the use of magnetic tape also permits the data to be stored in a fraction of the space that is required for conventional personnel records. The personnel files of Air Force Reservists, for example, which had formerly consumed the space of a large storage vault, were reduced to ten reels of magnetic tape.[2]

The use of internal sources, if it creates promotion opportunities or permits layoffs to be avoided, can benefit employee morale. A company also is likely to know its own employees better than it does applicants from the outside and may be able to capitalize on the training investment that it has in its employees if it makes maximum use of internal sources. Internal sources, however, are not always satisfactory because qualified individuals to fill certain vacancies may not be available within the company. It may be desirable, furthermore, to hire experienced personnel from other companies in order to acquire new technical information or new industrial "know-how." Outsiders often can bring new ideas and enthusiasm into a company and can help to revitalize it and prevent inbreeding. By giving too much preference to its own employees, a company may deprive itself of outside applicants who have superior qualifications. Furthermore, if employees must compete only with their co-workers and not with any outsiders in gaining advancement, the quality of the company performance may suffer from the lack of competition.

---

[1]"Describing Men to Machines," *Business Week*, June 4, 1966, pp. 113–114.

[2]D. M. Parnell, Jr., "The Air Force Automates Its 'Manpower Bank,'" *Management and Business Automation*, August. 1960.

External Sources

Some of the external sources that are used most commonly by companies are listed, although not necessarily in order of importance, as follows:

1. Advertising.
2. Educational institutions.
3. Employment agencies.
4. Employee referrals.
5. Unsolicited applications.
6. Professional organizations.
7. Labor unions.

Probably the external source that is relied upon the most is advertising. In one study of the methods used to recruit professional and technical personnel, 32 percent of the 148 companies (large and small) surveyed considered advertising to be the most productive source when cost and all other factors were taken into account. On-campus recruiting was considered to be the most productive by the next largest percentage of companies (23 percent), followed by field recruiting (16 percent), employment agencies (15 percent), and employee referrals (7 percent).[3] While it should be noted that the study was concerned with the recruitment of a very highly qualified group of applicants, the sources considered, with the probable exception of on-campus recruiting, would be applicable in the staffing of most jobs.

A survey of 35 large New York City firms conducted by the Commerce and Industry Association disclosed that the following methods, which are listed in order of their importance, were used to recruit operative employees over a five-year period:

1. Employee referrals.
2. Casual applicants.
3. Reemployment of former employees.
4. Company advertising.

The same companies in recruiting office employees ranked their principal sources of recruitment according to their value as follows:

1. Private agencies.
2. Employee referrals.

---

[3]*Solving the Shortage of Specialized Personnel*, Personnel Policies Forum, Survey No. 62 (Washington, D.C.: The Bureau of National Affairs, 1961).

3. Schools and colleges.
4. Company advertising.[4]

Advertising. Anyone who reads a newspaper is familiar with "Help Wanted" and "Situation Wanted" advertisements. For many employers advertisements may be the only source that is considered when seeking to staff position vacancies. Radio, television, posters, as well as magazines and newspapers, therefore, may be utilized as advertising media in attempting to reach interested applicants that might not otherwise be contacted. Advertising does have the advantage of permitting a large audience to be reached and of providing another possible source of applicants. If the advertisement is placed in a professional or trade publication that reaches a selected and desired group of readers, it is more likely to produce favorable results than if placed in a publication with mass circulation. Figure 5-1, taken from the *Wall Street Journal*, provides an example of advertisements that are directed toward business and professional readers.

The *Army Times*, *Air Force Times*, and *Navy Times* newspapers are examples of other media that can be used to reach a special group of applicants. This group includes members of the armed forces who are entering the labor market following the completion of their military obligation or their retirement from a military career. Individuals in this group have many varied types of training and experience which make them highly qualified for many civilian jobs.

The effectiveness of advertising as a recruitment tool is dependent, among other things, upon the nature of the appeal that it makes to the reader. While cleverness and exaggerated claims may sell household products, they are less likely to influence intelligent applicants in making job decisions that can affect their future careers, particularly if the job requires a reasonable degree of formal education. Similarly, the "blind type" ad or the ad that misrepresents or conceals the true nature of the job will attract only the more gullible applicants who, when the true facts about its duties are discovered, may become resentful or reject the job. The principal limitation of advertising, aside from the cost, is the unpredictable nature of its results. In some instances an advertisement may fail to attract any significant response, as apparently was the situation in Figure 5-2 on page 119. In other instances it may cause an employer to be overburdened with applicants. In spite of the fact that the qualifications desired for an opening are clearly specified in the advertisement, it may attract many marginal applicants who respond in hopes that there may be a remote possibility that they will be considered.

[4]Bureau of National Affairs, Inc., *Labor Policy and Practice*, Volume 4, 1966, pp. 201:103.

Figure 5-1

POSITIONS AVAILABLE POSITIONS AVAILABLE

DIRECTOR OF PERSONNEL

A major national manufacturing company with annual sales in excess of 900 million dollars and headquartered in N.Y.C. seeks a corporate personnel executive with an outstanding record of accomplishment.

Initially he will direct the development and installation of corporate programs for salary administration, management development and training. Present responsibilities will include administration of bentfit plans, medical and employment activities. Labor relations experience will be helpful.

This new position will report to the executive vice president. Vice presidential status is a definite possibility depending upon personal capacity.

Successful candidates should have a minimum of 10-15 years of diverse personnel relations experience with a large corporation.

Please reply in confidence detailing your experience, salary history and requirements to:

BOX J-242, THE WALL STREET JOURNAL,
30 BROAD ST., NEW YORK, N.Y. 10004

An Equal Opportunity Employer, Male and Female

PRESIDENT'S RIGHT-HAND MAN

Need ambitious, strong backboned MBA to work closely with president on new projects and existing operations. Requires working knowledge of finance and marketing techniques. Company is medium-sized dealing in a line of forest products. Located in Northern Calif. Position requires some travel, but you will have access to company's plane. Age: 30-40. Starting salary will be over $18,000, depending on experience. After first year, profit participation will be considered. Please send complete resumé to:

BOX 849 B, WALL ST. JOURNAL, S.F.

CONTROLLER

Challenging position with growing independent oil producing and land development company.

Must have broad oil production experience. CPA/MBA will have preference. Job location will be Apple Valley, California; a smog-free, high desert resort area. Salary $14,000 plus benefits. All replies in strict confidence. Send resumés to:

BOX 838 B, WALL ST. JOURNAL, S.F.

REGIONAL SALES MGR.

To manage Western Region for major manufacturer of magnetic recording tape. This position requires a man with sales management experience who has demonstrated the ability to direct and stimulate a professional sales force. You will be responsible for the sale of computer, instrumentation, video and sound recording tape to industry, government agencies, broadcasters and distributors.

Call Mr. R. E. Snare, Marketing Manager, at 931-1181 between 8 and 10 a.m. and 4 and 6:30 p.m., Thursday, July 7th, and Friday, July 8th, to arrange a local interview (or send resumé immediately).

REEVES SOUNDCRAFT
Division of Reeves Industries, Inc.
342 No. LaBrea Avenue Los Angeles 36, California
An equal opportunity employer

POSITIONS AVAILABLE POSITIONS AVAILABLE

CONTROL AND ADMINISTRATION

Controller needed by small rapidly expanding company in the plastics industry. Experience in systems work, cost accounting and budgetary controls required. We are seeking a man with a strong personality and drive, as well as the desire and ability to extend his scope of responsibility to other functions. Applicants should have a college degree and a minimum of 8 years' experience in industrial accounting. Earnings history should be included with detailed resumé. Compensation will be commensurate with capabilities and potential. Send resumé to:

PRESIDENT, BOX 741 R, WALL ST. JOURNAL, L.A.

SALES MANAGER

with experience in selling life care plan for elderly housing apartments. Project owned and operated by large religious order in the Midwest. Salary open.

Box CM 656,
The Wall Street Journal
711 W. Monroe St.
Chicago 60606, Ill.

ASSISTANT COMPTROLLER

Substantial East Bay company has once in a lifetime opportunity for an experienced accounting manager.

Applicant should have a degree in accounting and five years experience in a supervisory capacity. He should also be EDP oriented and have a background of Systems and Procedures work. To learn more about this key position please submit detailed resumé and salary history to:

Box 845 B, Wall St. Journal, S.F.

EXECUTIVE DIRECTOR
Redevelopment Agency

Applications for immediate employment invited. Salary open. Experience in this or comparable federal programs preferred, but not required. Submit resumé and salary expected.

REDEVELOPMENT AGENCY
City of Santa Monica
1685 Main St., Santa Monica, Calif.
Attention "Personnel".
An Equal Opportunity Employer

MANAGER—LAW OFFICE

Large growing law firm in So. California desires top executive to supervise personnel, accounting procedures, and non-legal business affairs. Salary open. Send resumé and salary requirement promptly to:

P.O. Box 1976
Santa Ana, California
Replies confidential

ADVERTISING MANAGER

for "group" advertising program in Oregon. Excellent opportunity for man with demonstrated ability. Grocery Management experienced desirable. Send resumé and salary requirements to

Box 814 B, Wall St. Journal, S.F.

Organic Chemist/Ph.D.

Research on organic synthesis of intermediates and finished pharmaceuticals. Experienced and publications. $12,000-18,000.
COLLEGE EMPLOYMENT AGENCY
811 W. 7th, L.A. 17 627-9075

POSITIONS WANTED—MALE

SALESMAN

Established 5-year old company wishes to hire salesman in the Los Angeles area with data processing, temporary help, or related experience. Excellent salary plus bonus. This position to lead to managership for the right party. Write fully in confidence to:
Box 739-R, Wall St. Journal, L.A.

SALES EXECUTIVE

Seeking Management position with aggressive, growing company. Leading salesman for large corporation past six years. For personal interview, write:

Box 847 B, Wall St. Journal, S.F.

CERTIFIED PUBLIC ACCOUNTANT

Experienced, to assume control of engagements, staff assignments and staff recruiting. This position includes partnership opportunity in a West Coast certified public accountant firm.

Call Mr. Dean (213) 383-1384
J. R. PIERCE ASSOCIATES AGENCY

Corp. Planning/Acquisitions

Wide experience merger analysis & negotiation. Seeks position expanding industrial company on business development acquisition staff. Wharton, Age 31.
Box 818 B, Wall St. Journal, S.F.

If you have capital for which you are seeking interesting possibilities tell THE MART readers.

Experienced nuclear electronic salesman. Top producer, management background. If you need a real salesman, let's get together. Must have a DRAW against comm. No sal. position considered.
Box 834 B, Wall St. Journal, S.F.

Source: *Wall Street Journal*, July 9, 1966. Reproduced with permission.

Educational institutions. The growing demand for personnel with scientific and technical training and with more extensive education has

Figure 5-2

"He has one big qualification for the job — he's the
only man who answered our ad!"

STRICTLY BUSINESS cartoon by Dale McFeatters, reproduced through the courtesy of Publishers Newspaper Syndicate.

prompted many companies to conduct vigorous high school, trade school, and college recruitment programs. Since these educational institutions eliminate many of the less interested or capable students, they also perform a certain screening function for employers. This fact, however, may tempt some companies to seek to fill positions with graduates who possess greater capacities than the positions will demand of these persons. When this practice is followed, it can be expected that many who are hired will soon lose interest and quit. Most schools and colleges operate a placement service which can provide the personal history records of those graduates who are seeking employment. These placement services can be of assistance to recruiters in helping them to locate and arrange interviews with qualified candidates and to disseminate company brochures, handbooks, and other literature about the company to interested persons.

The College Placement Council is undertaking a placement assistance program for employers and for college graduates and alumni to provide an information retrieval system that is operated nationally. This system which is known as the Graduate Résumé Accumulation and Distribution (GRAD) Program is designed to store on magnetic tape the personal placement files of graduates seeking employment. These files are made available to employers who are seeking applicants with the particular set of qualifications that are needed for a job opening. College graduates using the system have the advantage of being considered by an unlimited number of employers.

Employment agencies. It may be possible at times for employers to take advantage of the assistance of employment agencies in recruiting applicants. These agencies, which can serve as an extension of the employment department, differ considerably in terms of their policies, services, costs, and the type of applicants that can be obtained through them. Some agencies are publicly supported or are operated on a non-profit basis, while others operate as profit-making enterprises and charge a fee to the applicant and/or the employer. Employment agencies may supply applicants representing a variety of occupational areas, or they may provide applicants for only certain professional, technical, office, or domestic jobs. When seeking the assistance of an employment agency, therefore, it is advisable for a company to utilize those agencies that can provide the services and applicants that are needed at a cost which it can afford to pay. Three types of employment agencies that will be discussed in terms of their objectives and areas of service are the public employment agencies, the private employment agencies, and the management consulting firms.

Public employment agencies. Public employment offices are maintained in most of the larger communities throughout the nation, and part-time offices are located in many of the smaller ones. These offices are administered by the state in which they are located, but they are subject to certain general controls by the United States Employment Service (USES) since states receive financial support from federal tax rebates.

In order to be eligible to collect unemployment insurance benefits, an individual is required to register for work with his state employment service and to be willing to accept any suitable employment that is offered to him. This requirement serves to identify those persons who are unemployed and who may be referred to employers who are seeking employees. Since public employment agencies are administered by state governments, the type and quality of services that they provide tend to vary. In addition to supplying job applicants, the services of some state agencies may include assisting employers in performing employment testing, job analysis and evaluation, community wage surveys, and other personnel functions. By cooperating and exchanging job-market information, the state agencies have been able to help employers in those regions where there is a shortage or an oversupply of qualified employees.

In recent years the role of the USES has continued to expand much to the concern of the private agencies who feel that it is encroaching upon their area of service. Because of the need to provide more accurate and more current information about labor markets, unemployment conditions in different regions of the country, and the need to facilitate the shifting of unemployed individuals to areas of greater job opportunity, however, the role of the USES will undoubtedly continue to be an important one.

Private employment agencies. Because they charge fees, private agencies tend to provide more specialized employment services than public agencies and often cater to a particular class of clientele. Whether the employer or the applicant is charged the fee depends upon which of them is receiving the primary benefit. In addition to job referrals, services to the applicant may include vocational counseling and guidance or assistance in preparing personal résumés. Services to employers may include the advertising of vacancies so that the employer's identity is not revealed and the conducting of initial interviews. Having an employment agency advertise vacancies may be desirable if an employer wishes to consider persons outside of his own organization without the knowledge of his employees or if he wishes to avoid interviewing a large number of applicants who might respond to an advertisement.

Employment agencies that offer their services free or at a nominal charge may be sponsored by fraternal, religious, or civic organizations as a service to their members or to the community. Because of their small operating budgets, however, the services of the agencies in this group frequently are limited to acting as a clearinghouse for information concerning job openings and job applicants.

Management consulting firms. The growing need for persons with proven managerial ability and experience has encouraged the growth of consulting firms which specialize in the recruitment of management personnel. The fees for their services may cost an employer substantial sums to fill a single position. For this reason, consulting firms have an incentive to investigate and appraise very thoroughly those persons whom they recommend for executive positions. By means of personal inquiries, personal contacts, and selective advertising, firms that specialize in executive recruitment attempt to locate qualified executive prospects who are interested in changing their employment and improving their salaries. Qualified executives whose capabilities exceed the challenge or promotion opportunities of their present jobs are among the individuals that these firms seek to locate and refer to their clients. Some recruitment firms have developed personal data files covering several thousand executives in this category; through the use of computers, such files can be screened rapidly to locate possible candidates for a particular management opening.

Employee referrals. Employees may be used to help their company locate qualified applicants. High morale can make employees boosters of their company and can contribute indirectly to the recruitment of needed applicants. When applicants with skills that are needed are in short supply, the use of prizes and bonuses may help to stimulate employee recruitment efforts.

If an employee knows an applicant and thinks he would do a creditable job for the company and if the applicant is a person with whom the employee is willing to work and associate, the employee has a definite incentive to recommend the applicant. In recommending an applicant who is hired by the company, the employee, in a sense, places his own reputation at stake. This feeling of involvement can be advantageous in that the employee has a definite interest in helping to improve the individual's behavior and performance if it should prove to be unsatisfactory. On the other hand, even though employees may exercise caution in making recommendations, they can make mistakes or be influenced unduly by personal friendship. In utilizing employee recommendations as a means of filling vacancies, management must be alert to the potential danger of building up cliques composed of employees from the same school, church, lodge, or some other group. Furthermore, since it is natural for employees to refer as prospects persons who are like themselves, employers should exercise due care when considering those referrals made by their less satisfactory employees.

Unsolicited applications. Most companies receive varying numbers of inquiries about employment opportunities from individuals representing a variety of backgrounds and qualifications. These individuals may apply either by letter or in person. If they are knowledgeable about seeking employment, they may make use of a personal résumé similar to the one presented in Case 5-1 at the end of this chapter. A résumé, preferably only one page in length, provides the employer with a summary of the applicant's vital statistics, education, and work experiences. It can be used by the employer in screening the applicant's qualifications and can serve as a record to remind him of the applicant's interest in employment. The use of a résumé by an applicant permits him to write a letter of application that is brief and which serves largely to indicate his employment interests.

Although unsolicited sources may not yield a very high percentage of acceptable candidates, they should not be ignored. The fact that individuals take the initiative to apply for employment may indicate that they have a strong interest in the company and a definite desire to work for it. Because of this fact and the need to maintain good public relations, every person who applies for work should be treated with courtesy and consideration regardless of whether or not his application has been directly solicited.

Generally, the qualifications of unsolicited applicants will vary with the economic conditions, the company's reputation, the attractiveness of the employment opportunities, and the types of jobs to be filled. Unsolicited applications, therefore, can represent a fluctuating and unpredictable source of applicants, and often these applications are for job openings that do not exist. Nevertheless, unsolicited applications from persons who appear to be well qualified but who cannot be hired immediately should be kept on file, for these persons may provide a source of employees for future vacancies. It should be recognized, however, that such applicant files can become outdated very rapidly.

Professional organizations. Many professional organizations and societies operate a placement service for the benefit of members and employers. These societies may carry advertisements or lists of job openings and of applicants who are seeking positions in the journals that they publish.

The regional and national meetings of technical and professional societies have tended to attract increasing numbers of recruiters, sometimes to the consternation of the sponsoring organizations. This consternation has resulted from the fact that the lobbies and rooms where the recruiters have established their headquarters have often attracted a greater delegate interest than many of the conference sessions. Unfortunately, such conditions may discourage some companies from sending representatives to the meetings for fear that certain of their personnel may be recruited away by some other firm.

Labor unions. Labor unions are a principal source of applicants for certain types of jobs, particularly blue-collar jobs. In some industries the unions traditionally have been able to maintain control over most of the supply of a particular type of labor through their apprenticeship programs and through their labor agreements with employers.

Although a stipulation in the Taft-Hartley Act outlawed the closed-shop provisions in a labor agreement, which require that employers hire only union members, this portion of the act has not been enforced very vigorously. In the maritime, printing, and construction industries, for example, unions furnish a labor pool from which they can dispatch personnel to meet the short-term needs of employers. In doing this the unions provide a very useful economic service.

Underdeveloped Sources of Manpower

A number of special groups within our society include well-qualified individuals whose potential contributions have not been fully utilized. These groups consist of women, the physically handicapped, older persons, and culturally deprived persons. Because of prejudices toward applicants from these groups, many companies have deprived themselves of potential employees who have the talents and qualifications to render a worthwhile contribution. Society also has shared in the loss resulting from this waste of human resources.

Fortunately, there is a trend for more companies to utilize the services of individuals from those groups which previously were rejected for many jobs. This change of policy has resulted, in part, from the pressure of legislation governing employment practices and also partly from the growing realization by many employers that their reasons for rejecting these groups were neither valid nor based upon fact. As members of these groups have been given the opportunity to prove their qualifications, their performance records have helped to reduce prejudices and other barriers restricting employment for members of their groups. Starting with World War II, women had the opportunity to prove their capabilities not only in factory work but also in scientific, technical, and managerial positions. Efforts to encourage the hiring of the physically handicapped also have helped to prove that a handicap will not impede performance on many jobs and that with minor adjustments additional jobs can be performed successfully by the physically handicapped. When placed in jobs that they can perform, persons in this group accept the job as an opportunity to compensate for physical deficiencies and, as a result, often achieve better performance records than other employees.

The older person whose employment opportunities have been restricted has also been able to prove his value when given the opportunity.

Many individuals in the older age groups may actually be in better physical and mental condition than some of their juniors, and those who are not in this condition can still be utilized in many jobs.

Members of disadvantaged groups probably constitute the greatest problem because the prejudices that curb their employment opportunities are often more complex and deep-seated. Restrictions in the employment of members of these groups result not only from the prejudices of employers but also from the prejudices of the employees with whom the culturally deprived individuals may work, as well as from the reluctance of some unions to admit them to membership. While educational campaigns and legislation have helped to reduce employment discrimination, the performance records achieved by members of disadvantaged groups have probably been one of the most important factors contributing to the improvement of employment opportunities for them.

Policies Relating to Staffing

It is as much to the company's benefit to have qualified applicants seek employment with it as it is to the applicants' benefit to be considered by the company for employment. This fact, therefore, should be reflected in the company's staffing policies and procedures to insure that all applicants receive fair and considerate treatment. It may be desirable, also, for a company to establish special policies and procedures governing the staffing of those jobs for which there is a scarcity of manpower or which present special problems of recruitment and selection. Other policies that may have to be established are those that relate to the employment of moonlighters (those who already hold another job), to employment in overseas assignments, or to scientific and technical positions.

Public Relations and Recruitment

A company's recruitment and public relations programs are closely interrelated. The ability to attract qualified applicants is affected by a company's public image. The pride that employees feel toward their company and the favorable comments that they make about it in public contribute to its recruitment efforts. Thus, factors which have an impact on the recruitment function are operating continually even though a company may be unaware of such factors.

Many individuals may experience their only contact with a company in connection with their application for employment and may develop a lasting impression of the company from this contact. It is important, therefore, that representatives of the personnel department, as well as those from other departments who may have contacts with job applicants, make every effort to generate goodwill through these contacts. A company can do much to preserve goodwill by providing courteous treatment to all applicants and by advising those who are being considered for a position promptly and tactfully when the position has been filled. A company's reputation will also be aided if the employment conditions that an employee must endure are accurately and completely described, even though these conditions may be such as to discourage some applicants from accepting employment.

Large companies, when entering a small community, have at times created considerable ill will by disrupting the local labor market with their high wage rates and by drawing good employees away from local establishments. While the employees in any community should have the opportunity and freedom to improve their lot by changing employers, companies must use care and discretion in situations in which they might be accused of disrupting the local labor market.

The practice of hiring away employees from other companies, if it should become too common, could impair a company's image within the community. While the practice of taking customers away from another firm is considered to be entirely acceptable, the hiring of its employees sometimes is regarded as an act of "piracy." If viewed objectively, however, it is difficult to see why it should be wrong per se for a company to hire an employee away from another company if it can offer him a better employment opportunity. Furthermore, the fact that the employee is offered a better job sometimes may indicate that the former employer did not do all that he could for the employee. If the recruitment of an individual away from another company constitutes a violation of business ethics, therefore, it is more likely to be due to the purpose for which he is recruited or to the methods that are used to recruit him. Recruiting employees in order to gain access to a competitor's secrets or using a professional relationship with a client company to make contact with his employees would be examples of unethical (and possibly illegal) practices.

Recruiting Scientific and Technical Personnel

The limited number of applicants who possess scientific and technical training has made the recruitment of these applicants increasingly difficult. There is little likelihood that the situation will improve within the near future because the need for personnel with such qualifications probably will continue to increase. By recognizing that the ultimate solution to the problem is one of substantially increasing the available supply, a number of companies are attempting to utilize promotional materials, part-time employment, and plant visitations as a means of acquainting high school and college students with the opportunities available to them in the scientific and technical fields. Some companies also are attempting through films, exhibits, and other educational aids to develop a greater interest among students at the high school and even lower grade levels in scientific and technical careers. Company sponsored scholarships in these fields are becoming increasingly common.

Aside from the problems relating to the scarcity of the supply, the recruitment of scientific personnel also involves the problem of motivating these individuals to join a company since the things that they look for in a job may be different from those sought by other groups of applicants. According to one study, the following are some of the employment conditions that aid in attracting scientists and engineers:[5]

1. Freedom to publish and discuss work with other members of the scientific community.
2. Association with and stimulation from high-caliber colleagues.
3. A technically trained management — particularly for those managers who are in charge of laboratories.
4. Freedom to choose a research problem and to pursue it without too much management contact.
5. Reputation of the company as a leader in technical progress, especially in an applicant's particular field.
6. Adequate facilities, resources, and technical assistance for research.
7. Opportunities for advancement particularly for those individuals who wish to remain researchers rather than to become administrators.
8. Salary that is competitive with that paid by other companies but which cannot be considered as a substitute for other employment benefits.
9. Security, as evidenced by the company's record of retaining scientific personnel during bad as well as good economic conditions.
10. A good community in which to live — one offering good schools, libraries, and cultural activities.
11. Treatment as an individual and not as a part of a big machine.
12. Opportunity to continue formal education while working.

Besides directing attention to increasing the available supply of scientific and technical personnel and obtaining a proportionate share

[5]Douglas Williams, "Attracting Topflight Scientists and Engineers," *Personnel*, Vol. 34, No. 6 (May–June, 1958), pp. 79–81.

of them, companies frequently can do a more effective job of utilizing those that they already employ. There has been a definite trend in recent years for companies to assign many of the more routine duties of technical personnel to qualified assistants. This practice has permitted the technical personnel to confine themselves to duties commensurate with their education to the benefit of both the efficiency of the company and the morale of those affected.

Recruiting for Overseas Assignments

As their operations tend to become more international in character, companies are faced with the problem of selecting individuals to assume company jobs in foreign countries. The selection of persons for these jobs presents a definite problem since an individual who may be an excellent employee within the United States may prove to be highly unsatisfactory when placed in a job overseas. An individual chosen to work overseas, therefore, must be carefully screened in terms of his emotional stability and ability to adjust to the requirements of different cultures and living standards. Since the loss that can result from the choice of wrong persons for overseas assignments can be extremely high, it is important that special care be given to their selection. A personality evaluation and the careful analysis of work histories for evidences of emotional problems may be well worth the extra expense and effort that they involve.

If an employer is taking his family overseas, it might be well to also consider the personality of his wife in order to make certain that she will be able to adjust to the "cultural shock" of living in a foreign culture. Oxley defines this "shock" as "the state of confusion and tension that often arises when an American discovers many of his responses are not appropriate in a foreign culture."[6] Because they are aware of the significant contributions that a wife can make to her husband's career overseas, many companies are providing orientation and training programs to help prepare the wives for the foreign assignment.[7]

In general, persons and their families who adjust best to foreign jobs are more likely to be those who have a genuine interest in learning about the people, customs, traditions, history, and language of the country in which they are placed. For them a foreign assignment represents an educational opportunity rather than just a means of building a financial nest

---

[6]See G. M. Oxley, "The Personnel Manager for International Operations," *Personnel*, Vol. 38, No. 6 (November–December, 1961), pp. 52–58.

[7]"That Glittering Overseas Investment, The Executive's Lady," *Fortune*, June, 1966, pp. 132–139.

egg or of attempting to escape from those problems which they have not been able to solve at home.

Policies Toward Hiring "Moonlighters"

For a variety of reasons, such as the desire to use profitably the hours left over from a shorter workweek, many employees "moonlight"; that is, they hold down a second job. While some companies are hesitant to employ "moonlighters" and discourage their employees from holding a second job, others find "moonlighters" to be a valuable source of part-time employees. Retail and service organizations, in particular, use "moonlighters" to meet weekend and evening personnel requirements for temporary personnel. As efforts to achieve a shorter workweek are realized, there is every reason to believe that the number of persons seeking a second job will increase still further.

Policy Coordination

If a recruitment program is to be successful, it requires the coordinated effort of all departments within the organization. Pertinent information relating to sales, inventory, and production planning must be made available to the personnel department in order that it may be incorporated into the plans governing the personnel program. Conversely, anticipated shortages or surpluses of personnel that might make certain adjustments in production scheduling necessary should be communicated to the departments that might be affected as soon as it becomes known. If it is to be of value, therefore, data relating to the work force should be centralized and made readily available to other departments that might utilize it.

Résumé

If an organization is to operate efficiently, each position within the structure must be staffed by the person who is best qualified to perform it. Since lead time may be required in order to recruit and train personnel who will be qualified, it is necessary to anticipate personnel needs in advance of their occurrence. The satisfactory anticipation of manpower needs and of the factors affecting these needs will help to prevent a surplus or a shortage of personnel within a company from developing. It also will permit a more careful selection of new personnel and the location of new positions for those persons whose jobs are being eliminated by changes in organization or work load.

In order to obtain qualified personnel for each job, it is also necessary for a company to search actively for such personnel from a variety of sources both within and outside of the organization. The sources that may prove to be the most productive are likely to vary according to the type of job to be filled and the condition of the labor market. Regardless of which sources of applicants are utilized, consideration must be given to the effect that staffing policies will have upon the attitude of its employees and upon the attitude of the general public. Company reputation, employee morale, and recruitment all relate closely to and contribute to each other.

DISCUSSION QUESTIONS AND PROBLEMS

1. What are some of the possible reasons other than the starting salary that might affect your decision to accept one employment offer over another? Would these reasons outweigh a difference in starting salary of $150 per month?

2. An employment agency seeking to recruit salesmen for an insurance company advertised for applicants in the local newspaper. The position was described as a "management trainee" job with an insurance company. The advertisement did not list the name of either the employment agency or the insurance company but only the telephone number of the agency. What are the possible reasons for this practice? What would be your reaction upon reading the ad? Upon responding to it?

3. What are some of the possible strengths and limitations of a national placement file of job applicants such as that provided by the GRAD program?

4. Should the cost of the services provided by a private employment agency in filling a vacancy be borne by the applicant or the employer? Why?

5. The Green Engineering Company having recently been awarded a large government contract must enlarge substantially its engineering staff. The manager of the research department has suggested that the company provide a $100 bonus to employees for every candidate who is hired by the company as a result of their referral. Do you feel that this is a sound suggestion? Why or why not?

6. The manager of a company manufacturing novelty items maintains that production planning is impossible because of the difficulty of determining in advance which items will prove to be popular and the duration of their popularity. Do you feel that he is correct in his statement?

7. What are the dangers of attempting to hire applicants who are in short supply by either overselling them on the opportunities of the job or by hiring them at a starting wage that is too high?

CASE 5-1
PERSONAL RÉSUMÉ

JOHN M. WILLIAMS, JR.
135 Sutter Drive
Sacramento, California 95815   Telephone: 916-487-4644

    Marital Status: Single   Age: 28
        Height: 6'1''   Weight: 160 pounds

    Draft Status: 5A – Honorable Discharge, September, 1964, Staff Sergeant USAF

JOB OBJECTIVE

To begin work in the technical department of a company dealing with electronics with the purpose of qualifying eventually for full management responsibilities. No geographic limitations.

EDUCATION

    Sacramento State College   Class: February, 1967
                                          Degree: B. S.
                                          Major: Industrial Management
                                          Minor: Speech

HONORS

Dean's List, Beta Gamma Sigma National Honor Society in Business Administration, Blue Key National Honor Fraternity, Associated Students Service and Leadership Award, National Transportation Association Scholarship Award.

ACTIVITIES

Station Manager and Head Engineer of college radio station KERS – FM, member of the Society for the Advancement of Management, Vice – President of the Young Republicans.

EXPERIENCE

    United States Air Force, Electronics – Communications, 6/56 to 9/64.

        Duties and responsibilities: NCOIC Electronic Equipment Depot Overhaul and Fabrication Shop (supervised 8 men in the overhaul and building of weather and ionospheric research equipment), Shift Chief Long – Haul Transmitter Site (supervised 3 men in operation of 52 transmitters and 2 microwave systems), Team Chief Group Electronics Engineering Installation Agency (supervised 3 men on installing weather and communications equipment), Tech – Writer (wrote detailed maintenance procedures for electronic equipment manuals), Instructor in Electronic Fundamentals (continuous 3 – month classes of 10 men each).

        Special Qualifications: Federal Communications Commission First Class Radio – Telephone License. Top Secret Clearance for Defense Work.

        Summer and Part – Time Work: Manager, Campus Apartments; Disc Jockey for KXOA and KXRQ; Laboratory Assistant for Radio – TV Speech Department, Stage Technician.

PERSONAL BACKGROUND AND INTERESTS

Attended public elementary and high school in Crisfield, Maryland. Traveled while in Air Force through United States, Caribbean, Europe, Middle East, South Pacific, and Australia. Interested in water skiing, SCUBA diving, jazz, and building hi – fi equipment.

REFERENCES

References available upon request at Sacramento State College Placement Center, Sacramento, California 95819.

---

a. Comment on what you consider to be the strengths and weaknesses of this résumé in terms of organization and content.

b. If you were an employer, which of the data about Mr. Williams might impress you the most? the least?

c. Would you hire this man for a management trainee position?

CASE 5-2

RECRUITMENT PROBLEMS

The personnel manager of a large insurance company complained strongly to the dean of a state university business school located in the same city as the company's home office that his school was doing nothing to make its graduates aware of career opportunities in insurance. The personnel manager was particularly aggravated by the fact that during a recent recruitment visit to the school only four students appeared for interviews, and these students seemed to be mostly interested in gaining experience in interviewing recruiters.

    a. Do you feel that the personnel manager has a legitimate complaint?

    b. Is this university, as a tax supported institution, obligated to do anything more than it has been doing to assist the company in its recruitment efforts? Discuss.

CASE 5-3

THE ARTESIAN OIL COMPANY

For many years the Artesian Oil Company, located in the Southwest, had engaged in the production, refining, and distribution of petroleum products within a territory covering three states. Many of its oil producing and refining operations were located in semiarid regions that were well removed from any large city and which were not considered to be very desirable employment locations. Since some work experience in these operations was considered to be an essential part of the company's executive development program, college graduates who were selected for the program were required to spend a few years working and living at these locations. This factor caused a rather high rate of turnover among executive trainees. Other aspects of employment, however, were considerably better than average.

The company had a very comprehensive but rigid wage-and-salary system based upon job evaluation. The beginning salary and the fringe benefits for college graduates entering the program were above those offered by most companies. In addition to the base rate, the salary included possible extra allowances to be granted on the basis of the applicant's age, experience, marital status, and type of degree. For those college graduates who demonstrated satisfactory ability, advancement during their first few years with the company came very rapidly.

Through its annual nationwide college recruitment program, which it had initiated in 1938, the Artesian Oil Company had been able to select graduates who were considered to be outstanding. Because the company was one of the first to adopt such a recruitment program and had offered substantial employment inducements to those who were selected, it was able for several years to obtain the caliber of applicants that it wanted. Following World War II, however, other companies initiated similar college recruitment programs and offered employment inducements that compared favorably with those of the Artesian Company. As a result, the Artesian Company began to lose many of the outstanding graduates to other companies that offered special salary inducements or whose representatives arrived on campus first. In spite of this fact, the Artesian Company refused to lower its selection standards or to depart from its rather rigid policies covering starting salaries for college graduates. The company thus began to be faced with the problem of not being able to recruit a sufficient number of graduates of the caliber it wanted.

Since the company found its starting rates for graduates in line with those of other companies and also internally consistent with the other job classes in its rate structure, an increase in the starting rates did not seem feasible. While the company recognized that the prospect of being placed in one of its less desirable locations either as a trainee or ultimately as an executive was a factor that was contributing to its recruitment difficulties, the operations at these locations were vital to the company. Furthermore, work experience in the producing and refining operations at these locations was considered to be highly desirable, regardless of whether or not the trainees remained in the operating phase of the company. Those executives who were placed in this phase of the company, however, could anticipate spending a number of years at these less desirable locations.

Recognizing the growing recruitment and turnover difficulties that were confronting the company in its executive development program, the director of industrial relations asked his assistant to study the problem and to prepare a report recommending corrective action. This report was to be submitted to the executive committee for consideration at its next meeting. In studying the problem, the assistant recognized that it would be virtually impossible to gain an immediate increase in the starting salary for college graduates because this would create internal distortions within the company's wage-and-salary structure which, although highly formalized and rigid, was consistent from an internal standpoint. He also recognized that top management would be opposed to any appreciable lowering of its selection standards for executive trainees.

    a. In view of the limitations that have been set forth, what recommendation would you make if you were the assistant industrial relations director?

    b. If the company increased the starting salary for college recruits by 10 percent, what difficulties might it encounter within its formal wage-and-salary structure?

SUGGESTED READINGS

Building an Effective Workforce, Personnel Series, No. 165. New York: American Management Association, 1955.

Chruden, Herbert J. and Arthur W. Sherman, Jr. *Readings in Personnel Management*, Second Edition. Cincinnati: South-Western Publishing Company, Inc., 1966. Pp. 498–529.

Lipsett, Laurence, *et al. Personnel Selection and Recruitment.* Boston: Allyn and Bacon, Inc., 1964. Chapter 2.

Mandell, Milton M. *Recruiting and Selecting Office Employees*, Research Report, No. 27. New York: American Management Association, 1956.

——————. *The Selection Process.* New York: American Management Association, 1964. Chapters 8–9.

Moore, Franklin G. *Production Control,* Second Edition. New York: McGraw-Hill Book Company. Chapters 6, 15.

Stone, Harold C., and William D. Kendall. *Effective Personnel Selection Procedures.* Englewood Cliffs, New Jersey: Prentice-Hall, Inc., 1956. Chapters 1–4.

Voris, William. *Production Control: Text and Cases.* Homewood, Illinois: Richard D. Irwin, Inc., 1956. Chapters 2, 5.

ability - skill, knowledge
Aptitude -

Selection

6

Personnel selection is the process of determining whether candidates who have been recruited have the necessary qualifications for the specific job openings and of choosing those persons who best fit the job requirements or specifications. In the larger company there are likely to be several different jobs and/or positions vacant at a particular time, and there are many applicants who are interested in employment with the company so that the selection program should be designed to provide qualified personnel on a continuing basis for a wide variety of jobs. While the matching of talent and job specifications at best is often a compromise, it is essential to building an efficient work force.

Increasing numbers of employers are realizing the value of a sound selection program and are willing to spend more money for this important function. Applicants who have been selected carefully usually learn job tasks easier, become better producers, and are usually happier in their jobs than those who are selected on a casual basis. There is an additional incentive for management to improve its personnel selection policies and procedures if employees are represented by a union. If a poorly qualified applicant is hired and permitted to remain on the job, it becomes increasingly difficult for management to discharge him the longer that he remains on the job.

The achievement of a sound selection program is primarily the responsibility of the personnel department. However, it should work closely with the line and other staff departments to insure that the objectives and policies relating to selection are clearly understood and that all who participate in the selection process are oriented in and motivated to use scientific approaches to evaluating applicants.

In this chapter and in the following chapter on psychological testing, the selection function will be examined. This chapter will consider:

- Basic factors in selection.
- The selection process.
- Employment interviewing.
- The employment decision.

Basic Factors in Selection

In the preceding chapter the methods for determining manpower needs and developing sources of manpower were examined. It was observed that unless individuals with the greatest potentialities were encouraged to make application for employment the company would suffer by being forced to hire "bodies" rather than being able to make a choice from among several applicants. It is not always possible to be very selective, especially if there is a short labor supply; however, the importance of having a number of applicants whenever possible should not be overlooked. Unless there is a reasonable number of qualified applicants from which to choose, the advantages that are ordinarily derived from a well-planned and carefully managed selection program are lost.

Selection — A Cooperative Process

The important task of selecting the personnel for an organization requires the cooperative efforts of many of the individuals who are in the personnel department and of department managers and supervisors who have vacancies to be filled. The nature of the contributions that these individuals are able to make to the selection process will depend upon their knowledge and understanding of the jobs, their familiarity with the characteristics of successful and unsuccessful employees, and their ability to obtain pertinent information about job applicants and to assess such information accurately.

The decision to hire or to reject an applicant represents one of the most important decisions that is made in a company. Its effects may be as far-reaching as those decisions that are often assumed to be of much greater importance. Each new employee not only constitutes a production unit but his personality is felt in his work group, and sometimes throughout the entire organization. Thus, it is essential that the personnel department and managerial and supervisory personnel in all departments cooperate to make the selection process yield its maximum benefits to the organization.

Role of the personnel department. The personnel department typically initiates the development of policies and procedures to be used in the selection of personnel, especially for jobs below the executive level. Following approved policies, it establishes detailed procedures that will make it possible to obtain the necessary information required for making decisions about applicants who have been recruited. Some of the commonly used procedures such as interviewing, testing, checking of references, and physical examinations are handled by personnel who are directly supervised by the personnel manager. These members of the personnel staff are often experts with special talents that make them particularly skillful in assessing the potential success of job applicants. Their tentative decisions about applicants, however, must in the final stages withstand the scrutiny of the managers and supervisors in the various units of the organization served by the personnel department.

Role of managers and supervisors. Once the personnel department has screened the applicants and selected those candidates who are considered to be best qualified, the manager of the department in which there is a vacancy is then asked to interview the candidates and express his decision. At this stage of the selection process, there is room for freedom for the manager to choose the candidates who he feels will be best for the job. While his choice may be made primarily on the basis of his feelings about the candidate rather than on a rational basis, the fact that the candidate has the boss's emotional support can go a long way toward making him successful in the new job.

The personnel department, as the coordinating agency, is responsible for insuring that the selection objectives are met. Since there is usually a need to compromise between the type of persons who are desired to fill a vacancy and the qualifications of the applicants who are available, overall guidance is needed so that those involved in the decision-making process will keep the objectives of selection in focus.

Objectives and Policies

The primary objective of recruitment and selection is to choose those individuals who are best qualified for employment and to place them in jobs for which they are best suited. This objective should be achieved at a reasonable cost under conditions that will promote good public relations. While it is essential to have overall objectives such as these, it is also advisable to have more detailed policy statements covering recruitment, selection, and placement which can guide those engaged in selection in achieving these objectives and serve as a basis for evaluation of the selection program. A policy statement reduces considerably the number of times that the personnel department must call upon management for a decision on problem areas and also helps to insure that the selection function is consistent with other aspects of the personnel program.[1]

The policy statements of a company are likely to cover employment priorities for present or former employees, "pirating" of personnel from other companies, nepotism, and any other matters that are deemed to be important enough to be stated as company policy. Some of the more significant types of policy statements also may relate to fair and equal employment practices and the utilization of handicapped persons.

Fair and equal employment practices. Up until a few years ago companies were free to establish their own policies with regard to the hiring of persons from various ethnic groups. Those, however, that were engaged in programs supported by the federal government were among the first that were required to abide by the various executive orders forbidding discrimination on the basis of race, nationality, or creed. In addition, about a third of the states and a number of cities passed legislation against discrimination in hiring personnel. More recently, Congress passed the Civil Rights Act of 1964 which was designed to prevent discrimination in all important facets of an individual's personal, social, and economic life.

Title VII of the Civil Rights Act establishes a federal right to equal opportunity in employment and creates an Equal Employment Opportunity Commission to assist in implementing this right. Employers, labor unions, and employment agencies are required to treat all persons equally without regard to their race, color, religion, sex, or national origin. At the present time employers with 100 or more workers are required to adhere to the provisions of the act; but by July 2, 1968, those with 25 workers or more will be covered. Public employers, private clubs, educational institutions, and some other employers are exempt from these provisions.[2]

Most of the provisions of the Civil Rights Act, as they relate to discrimination because of race, color, religion, or national origin, did not

[1]*Recruiting and Selecting Employees,* Studies in Personnel Policy, No. 144 (New York: National Industrial Conference Board, 1954). pp. 8–9.

[2]Special Bulletin, *Civil Rights Digest* (Washington, D.C.: U.S. Commission on Civil Rights, August, 1964).

come as a surprise to most employers. The provision relating to discrimination because of sex, however, has resulted in some interesting cases. Women have applied for mechanics' jobs that were formerly designated under "Help Wanted — Male" columns in the classified sections, and men have applied for jobs as airline stewards within the continental United States — jobs typically held by women. Other jobs will undoubtedly present interesting and challenging situations under the new legislation.

Policies concerning handicapped persons. As a result of the success that has been experienced in the employment of handicapped persons, the slogan, "Hire the handicapped — It's good business," has become a standard employment policy for many organizations. This slogan does not suggest that handicapped persons can be placed in any job without giving careful consideration to their disabilities, but rather that it is good business to hire qualified persons who can work safely and productively. Members of the personnel staff should be trained in the assessment of individual variations in types and degrees of limitations and be aware of how these restrictions are related to different jobs in the organization. Handicapped persons may often qualify for certain jobs if those jobs were modified in some manner or if special equipment were provided. Under careful selection, training, and supervision, the handicapped person will not only be able to perform as efficiently as a nonhandicapped person but also is less likely to quit voluntarily.[3]

Assessment of Human Differences

The careful assessment of the individual applicant that is essential for effective selection and placement should not be restricted to handicapped persons but should be given to all applicants. Once the specifications for jobs have been clearly established as valid standards that should be met in hiring personnel and there are a reasonable number of suitable applicants from which to make a selection, the assessment of these applicants is the next important step in the selection process. Before discussing the selection methods that are commonly used in obtaining information, it is desirable to examine more closely the nature of differences among people and some of the important considerations in assessing these differences.

How individuals differ. The fact that people differ from one another in their physical appearance is readily recognized and used as a basis of

---

[3]Employee Relations Division, *Hiring Handicapped People* (New York: National Association of Manufacturers, 1957) and "Employment of the Handicapped — A Good Management Practice," *Personnel Management Bulletin No. 65-1* (Sacramento: California State Personnel Board, January 8, 1965).

identification. While Mr. Adams has physical features that are quite different from those of Mr. Baker, these characteristics are of little value in personnel selection, unless perhaps one is casting for a motion picture or television production. In fact, as will be explained later, too much attention to physical features may result in erroneous judgments concerning personal characteristics of job applicants. The differences among people that should be of primary concern to those engaged in the selection process are not readily observable, and the recognition of such differences depends upon the skillful application of the most objective methods available.

For purposes of examination, modern industrial psychology has categorized the important segments of human characteristics into (1) abilities and aptitudes and (2) personality, including character, interests, and attitudes. While the individual organism functions in a total or holistic manner, the segments listed above provide a useful basis for a more precise examination of the components that comprise the individual's behavior. Abilities (including both knowledge and skills) and aptitudes (the potential that an individual possesses) are of primary importance to the prospective employer. Above all, he is concerned with hiring individuals who will be able at the outset, or with some training, to perform job tasks at a satisfactory level of performance. The employer should also be concerned that the applicant possess personality characteristics that will enable him to be motivated to work productively and to get along with his fellow employees, his supervisor, and customers.

These two major segments of human characteristics, when translated into the fundamental requirements that concern the employer, may be expressed as *can do* and *will do* factors. An applicant not only must be able to do the job (or learn it in a reasonable period of time), but also must have the motivation necessary to put his abilities to use in the effective performance of the job. It should not be inferred, however, that motivation is an attribute that is independent of the job. Employers have a responsibility to create the job conditions that motivate their employees in the satisfaction of organizational and individual goals. Since not all individuals have the same pattern of needs and wants, special attention should be given to these factors. While it is often difficult to assess the needs of an individual applicant and to predict how he will fit into a work group under a particular supervisor, increasing attention is given to these intangibles that are as important to employee success as the possession of abilities or aptitudes.

The measurement of differences. One of the major problems in determining whether or not an applicant qualifies for a job is that of obtaining information about him that is sufficiently reliable and valid to be used as a basis for prediction. Early studies in determining the reliability or consistency between interviewers revealed considerable disparity between interviewers in their evaluation of an applicant. In one study, for example, an applicant, rated best by one interviewer, was rated by another interviewer in 57th place out of 57.[4]

Even interviewers who evaluate the same individual at a later time with no additional evidence available may perceive him differently. Likewise, a psychological test that has low reliability is just as worthless a measuring device as a scale that gives different readings when the same object is measured. In addition to the necessity for having reliable estimates of a person's suitability for a job, it is essential that the information obtained be valid. It most certainly should be valid in the sense that it represents a true statement about the individual. If the applicant claims that he has had five years' experience in a job with the Rodgers Electronics Company, the information should be verified to determine its validity. It is also essential that the information obtained in the selection process be valid from the standpoint of being predictive of success or failure on a particular job. While many interviewers believe that they know what *can do* and *will do* factors are needed for a particular job, such beliefs are often based on hunches and biases and have never been subjected to scientific scrutiny or even checked by the simple process of determining the degree of success on the job of those persons who were hired.

In the Space Age it should hardly be necessary to warn against unscientific methods in personnel selection, but occasionally one finds trained and experienced personnel managers who rely to some degree upon astrology, handwriting analysis (graphology), facial characteristics (physiognomy), and other pseudoscientific approaches to personality assessment. A study conducted by Waterworth revealed that even trained interviewers, who were aware of the fallacy of judging character and personality on the basis of facial features, fell into the trap of making such judgments under experimental conditions that provided a "Can't tell from the picture" as one type of response.[5] One might assume, therefore, that interviewers and others engaged in personnel selection may, either consciously or unconsciously, be using methods that should be examined more closely to determine how much harm they are doing to the applicant, to the company, and to society.

---

[4]H. L. Hollingworth, *Vocational Psychology and Character Analysis* (New York: D. Appleton & Co., 1929), pp. 115–119.
[5]William H. Waterworth, *Analysis of Physiognomic Stereotypes Held by Professional Interviewers* (Master's thesis, Sacramento State College, 1960).

The Selection Process

The selection process is initiated when the personnel department receives a formal requisition from another department for additional or replacement personnel. Ordinarily the requisition is prepared by a supervisor and approved by his department head. Upon receiving the requisition, the personnel department checks to determine if the position to be filled is one that is authorized by the personnel budget. If the vacancy is in an authorized position, action is then taken to fill the requisition. The first step is to check the files of applicants previously found to be qualified but not hired. These applicants are contacted to determine if they are still available for and interested in employment with the company. If qualified individuals are not available, it is then necessary to recruit candidates.

The need for the interviewers and others engaged in making the selection decisions to have a clear understanding of the job specifications cannot be overemphasized. It is desirable, therefore, that interviewers maintain a close liaison with supervisors of requisitioning departments and, if possible, that the interviewers obtain firsthand knowledge of the jobs with which they are concerned. In large companies each interviewer may fill only the jobs in a particular class which enables him to obtain a more detailed knowledge of job specifications than is possible when the interviewer handles several job classes.

The following steps are typical of a full-scale selection process:

1. Reception of applicants.
2. Preliminary interview.
3. Application forms.
4. Employment tests.
5. Interview.
6. Background investigations.
7. Preliminary selection in personnel department.
8. Final selection by supervisor.
9. Physical examination.
10. Placement on job.

The number of steps in the selection process and their sequence vary not only with the company but also with the type and level of job to be filled, the cost of administering the particular function at each step, and the effectiveness of a step in eliminating unqualified candidates. The selection of employees for some jobs may be accomplished successfully with only an interview and a physical examination, whereas several interviews, a battery of tests, and elaborate investigations are required for other jobs. Those procedures which provide the most definitive information concerning the probable success or failure of a job applicant usually come first in order that the applicant who fails to meet the basic requirements may be rejected as early as possible in the selection process. In the discussion that follows, the selection forms and procedures that are commonly used as a basis for obtaining information about an applicant will be examined in detail.

Reception of Applicants

Usually the receptionist in the employment department is prepared to provide information about the company and current job openings and to assist with the completion of application forms. In addition, he or she may arrange schedules for interviews, tests, and other steps in selection. A sincere, helpful, and tactful approach by the receptionist and a pleasant physical environment are not only desirable from a public relations point of view but can go a long way in creating the type of attitude in the applicant that will improve communication and cooperation during the selection process.

Interviews

The applicant may be interviewed by one person or by several, depending primarily upon the importance of the job. The interview serves many purposes and thus may be used at different stages in the selection process. The preliminary interview is often used to screen out those who are obviously unqualified, and it may be conducted on the basis of a preliminary questionnaire that the applicant has completed in the waiting room. Throughout the selection process the interview may be used to verify and clarify application blank data; to obtain further information concerning the applicant's abilities, motivation, and attitudes; to provide information to the applicant concerning job opportunities, company policies, etc.; to sell the applicant on the idea of working for the company; and to observe the candidate as he answers questions. Because of the important decisions that are made on the basis of interview data and since interviewing plays a predominate role in personnel selection, it will be examined more thoroughly later in this chapter.

Application Forms

Most companies require application forms to be completed because they provide a fairly quick and systematic approach to obtaining a variety of information about the applicant. Such information as educational background, work history, and character references can usually be re-corded more efficiently by the applicant, if he is able to read and write with any degree of facility. Even the best educated applicants rebel at times, however, because in many companies the application forms have grown with successive generations of personnel managers until they have reached unwieldy proportions. It is essential that forms be reviewed periodically for the purpose of eliminating any items no longer absolutely essential. Time and tempers may be saved by using a short application form (often a 5″ by 8″ card) which provides the basic information needed during the preliminary interview and serves as a permanent record of applicants. Those who pass the preliminary interview successfully may then be given a longer, more detailed form to complete.

In recent years many companies have found it desirable to revise their forms or have been required to do so. Emphasis on nondiscrimination in employment has resulted in changes in hiring procedures. Since laws require that persons be hired and promoted without regard to race, color, religion, national origin, age, or sex, it is illegal in most instances to ask a person to reveal information about himself that would be in one of the above categories. Similarly, the requirement of a photograph is likewise illegal.[6]

At the present time the application form is typically used as one more source of information about the candidate. With this information and that obtained from other sources, the interviewer or personnel technician gains an impression of the individual. While there may be some agreement on impressions, very often the impression is influenced by personal biases just as in the interview. In an effort to eliminate biases of this type, the more progressive personnel departments use an objective approach in evaluating application form data. This approach involves determining the relationship between items on the application form and success or failure.

One company employing approximately 1,500 chemists and engineers used this approach to personnel prediction when it found that the interview did nothing more than weed out obvious misfits. A systematic evaluation was made of background information provided on the original application blanks of chemists and engineers hired over the past five years. The infor-mation for high-performance employees was then compared to that for all others (including some who had been encouraged to leave). As a group, the high-performance men were found to differ significantly from the others on a number of application blank items, such as amount and type of

6Paul Bullock, *Combating Discrimination in Employment* (Los Angeles: Institute of In-dustrial Relations, University of California, 1961).

extracurricular activities in college, previous experience, and honor society memberships. Weights were then assigned to the various items based upon the magnitude of the differences between the high-performers and all others, and the original application forms of 239 employees were scored accordingly. It will be noted in Figure 6-1 that the high-performance employees in the group studied scored considerably higher than the others on the application blank. Similar results were obtained on another group, thus confirming the original findings.[7] A company which has collected such information can construct a template or scoring key for use in scoring the application blanks of new applicants. It should be recognized, however, that the specific weights assigned to the application form items must be kept confidential and new analyses of the weighting must be made periodically.

Figure 6-1

APPLICATION BLANK SCORES FOR 239 TECHNICAL MEN

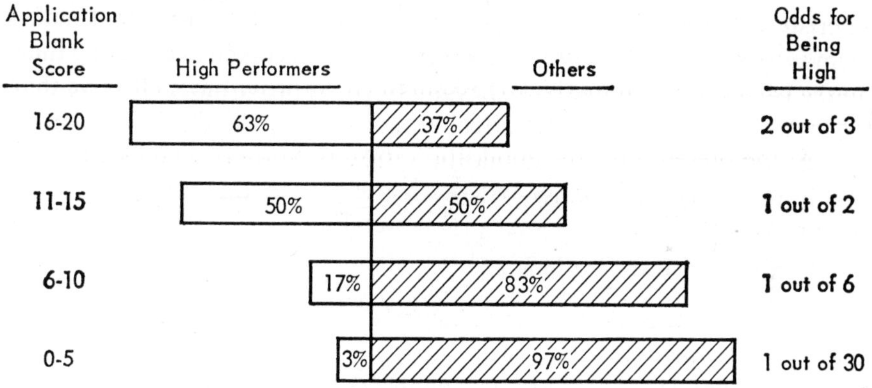

Application Blank Score	High Performers	Others	Odds for Being High
16-20	63%	37%	2 out of 3
11-15	50%	50%	1 out of 2
6-10	17%	83%	1 out of 6
0-5	3%	97%	1 out of 30

Source: J. R. Hinrichs, "Technical Selection: How to Improve Your Batting Average," *Personnel*, Vol. 37, No. 2 (March–April, 1960), p. 59. Reproduced with permission of the American Management Association.

Employment Tests

It has been noted that one of the essential aspects of selection involves the assessment of differences in abilities, aptitudes, and personality characteristics that exist among job applicants. While some of the differences may be readily observed, the ones that are most significantly related to job performance usually can be measured more accurately and reliably by tests

[7] J. R. Hinrichs, "Technical Selection: How to Improve Your Batting Average," *Personnel*, Vol. 37, No. 2 (March-April, 1960), pp. 56–60. The process of confirming the original findings is technically referred to as *cross validation*. For a further discussion of this process, see pages 185–186.

that have been carefully chosen. The assessment of what an individual *can do*, for example, can be done more effectively through tests of ability that are constructed or selected for the specific job than through an interview that is unstandardized and incomplete in its coverage of the skills or information required for satisfactory job performance and in which the interviewer's biases may cause him to overlook important and relevant information. The tests, however, must first be used under "try out" conditions and chosen on the basis of their ability to predict success in the job. Because of the importance of this try-out or validation procedure, it will be discussed in detail in the following chapter.

One of the problems in the use of tests in personnel selection is that management personnel often have extreme viewpoints concerning tests. There are some who overemphasize the importance of tests while others reject them completely. A more realistic approach recognizes the values to be derived from properly validated tests as they are used along with other data in assessing the abilities, aptitudes, interests, and personality characteristics of applicants. There is nothing about tests, per se, that makes them superior selection devices. However, if care is taken in choosing them on the basis of validation data, they are likely to prove more effective than the interview whose validity is often minimal. It should also be recognized that the interview may and should be validated to determine its effectiveness in the selection process.

Background Investigations

Since most job applicants are eager to obtain employment, it follows naturally that many of them will distort information pertaining to their abilities or experiences; and some will give completely false information in order to attain their objective. These tendencies require the employer to exercise every precaution in determining the value that he places on information furnished by applicants.

Validity of employment histories. The need for verifying the statements of job applicants is made quite evident by a careful study of 325 individuals whose statements about work history in a special interview were validated by obtaining employment records from their employers for at least five years preceding the interview. It was found that on only 3 of the 11 work history items studied did the proportion of valid information exceed 70 percent. On four items, 40 percent or more of the interview information was invalid. It was also found that information for the interviewee's present job was no more valid than for past (or earlier) jobs, thereby indicating that poor memory was not the only factor operating to cause a discrepancy.[8]

Traditional sources of verification. Former employers, teachers, credit bureaus, and individuals named as character references are usually contacted for verification of pertinent information such as length of time on the job, type of job, highest wage earned, and educational achievements. This can be done by writing for verification of information or by using a telephone check. The latter is not only quicker but usually brings the most candid type of reply and, therefore, is the most valuable.

Magee, of Helene Curtis Industries, recommends that the responsibility of checking references fall on the employment interviewer, not a clerk. After proper identification, some of the questions that would be asked in checking references over the telephone are:

> From your records, can you tell me when he started with your firm and when he left the company?
> What was his job classification with your company, and what were his job duties?
> How would you rate his job performance in terms of work volume and work quality?
> Did he receive any promotions or demotions while with you?
> As his supervisor, what did you find was the most effective way to motivate him?[9]

Newer methods of verification. In addition to the traditional methods of verifying an applicant's statements, some companies are now using the polygraph (lie detector). The device is attached to the applicant's hand and/or arm, depending on the type of equipment, and involuntary physiological responses are recorded as the individual answers questions about his former employment record, subversive activity, prior arrests, and other areas believed to be important.

While effective results have been obtained by this approach, the use of the polygraph raises many questions. Are the polygraph operators adequately trained for the work? Since they are probing and revealing a person's innermost secrets, can they be trusted to use the information wisely and honestly? Should they advise the police if they uncover information about a person that represents illegal behavior? These and other questions have been raised by many thoughtful individuals who are

---

[8]David J. Weiss, Rene V. Dawis, George W. England, and Lloyd H. Lofquist, *Validity of Work Histories Obtained by Interview.* Minnesota Studies in Vocational Rehabilitation: XII (Minneapolis: Industrial Relations Center, University of Minnesota, 1961).

[9]Richard H. Magee, "Reference Checking — Objectives and Techniques," *Personnel Journal,* Vol. 43, No. 10 (November, 1964), pp. 551–555.

concerned about the rights of individuals in a free society. It would appear that before attempting any use of the polygraph, a company should investigate the legal, ethical, and human relations aspects of its use in its particular setting.

The AFL-CIO has launched a wide-scale attack against the polygraph and other devices such as peepholes, see-through mirrors, hidden cameras, and microphones — all of which are viewed as infringements of the basic right of American citizens to personal privacy. It plans to press first for legislation that would outlaw the use of lie detector equipment in employment situations. Already, in five states such equipment may not be used: Alaska, California, Massachusetts, Oregon, and Rhode Island.[10]

Physical Examination

A preemployment physical examination is commonly required in a large percentage of manufacturing firms and in many companies having primarily office workers. One study of 426 manufacturing firms hiring from as few as 250 employees to 5,000 and over revealed that 85 percent of the companies required a preemployment physical examination.[11] This practice has the advantage of protecting the company against compensation claims for pre-existing disabilities, as well as determining if the applicant has the physical capacity to do the job. A pre-employment physical of the most cursory type should at least include tests of vision to determine if basic requirements are met. Similarly, auditory acuity can be tested quickly and inexpensively, thus providing the employer with information important to employee safety and welfare. By having audiometric data on employees, claims for loss of hearing as a result of job conditions can be adjudicated fairly.[12]

Employment Interviewing

It would be extremely difficult to find an employer in the United States who did not insist on having an interview with a job applicant before hiring him. Even for jobs in which standards are clearly established and documentary evidence can be submitted to show that the individual meets the

---

[10]"Unions Act in Threats to Privacy," *Business Week*, March 13, 1965, pp. 87–88.

[11]*Office Personnel Practices: Nonmanufacturing*, Studies in Personnel Policy, No. 197 (New York: National Industrial Conference Board, 1965) and *Personnel Practices in Factory and Office: Manufacturing*, Studies in Personnel Policy, No. 194 (New York: National Industrial Conference Board, 1964).

[12]Laurence Lipsett, Frank P. Rodgers, and Harold M. Kentner, *Personnel Selection and Recruitment* (Boston: Allyn and Bacon Inc., 1964), pp. 12–13.

required standards, the employer would probably feel that if the applicant had not had an interview he would not know all that he should about the applicant. Consequently, a considerable amount of time and expense on the part of both applicants and prospective employers is spent in going through this process.

While many employers interview job applicants just because it has always been done that way or because everyone else is doing it, most of them probably assume that the information obtained from the applicant and the observations made by the interviewer during the interview will provide a sounder basis for deciding whether or not to hire the individual. It is doubtful, however, if most employers have ever evaluated the interview as it is conducted in their companies to determine the extent to which it is accomplishing its intended purpose. Many of them, likewise, have given little or no consideration to the importance of selecting interviewers and in training them for their assignments.

Selection and Training of Interviewers

The employment interviewer has not only one of the most important jobs in the organization but also one of the most complex. He must be familiar with the specific requirements of the jobs for which he is selecting personnel, and he must be able to create a climate in which the applicant is encouraged to provide information and to express his feelings in an honest manner. Finally, he must possess the personality characteristics that enable him to synthesize all of the information and observations into conclusions that, when used with other selection information, contribute to the accuracy of selection. The interviewer's job is obviously not one to be assigned to those who have been failures in other types of work, to those who have basic personality problems, or to those with limited ability in conversation, perception, and limited experience in dealing with all sorts of people.[13]

A description of the detailed characteristics that an employment interviewer should possess is somewhat more difficult to construct, primarily because of the complex nature of an interview. An interview is conducted for many purposes; the individuals subjected to it possess a wide variety of backgrounds; and it is directed by individuals who may be equally quite successful even though different from one another in personality. Therefore, it may be expected that an individual who is effective as an employment interviewer in one company or in working with applicants for certain

---

[13]Milton M. Mandell, *The Selection Process* (New York: American Management Association, 1964), p. 187.

types of jobs may not be as effective in another company or in interviewing for a different group of jobs. However, there are some qualities that should characterize the individuals who are selected for the job of interviewing. The most fundamental quality should be humility because it motivates the interviewer to avoid hasty judgments, to improve his skill, to obtain the evaluations of others, and to rely on other selection devices. Other specific qualities that are desirable for interviewers are: ability to think objectively, critically, and systematically; experience in associating with people who have a variety of backgrounds; recent extensive experience with people similar in age and occupation to those being interviewed; association of experience with people in particular occupational groups; freedom from overtalkativeness, extreme opinions, and biases; maturity and poise.[14]

The need for extreme care in the selection of interviewers cannot be overemphasized. It should be recognized that interviewers are not born with all of the attitudes, knowledge, and skill that this complex job requires. Many companies, however, fail to provide any special training for their interviewers. In a study conducted by the AMA, it was found that only 22 percent have training programs for their interviewers.[15] While some of the interviewers may have had college courses in interviewing, mere textbook knowledge of interviewing seldom proves entirely satisfactory. Training programs for interviewers should include a review of the job descriptions and specifications that will be used by the interviewer, instruction in the theory and application of the various interviewing methods that are available, and experience in conducting interviews under supervision.

Those companies that have training programs have their interviewers study and analyze recorded practice interviews and check each other by interviewing the same person and comparing results. Such common interviewer faults as poor techniques, too much talking, and making "snap judgments" can readily be detected by this method. The recorded interview, which should be made with the applicant's permission, provides an especially valuable training and research tool because the content of the interview can be related to subsequent performance of the individual if he is employed. Months later the interviewer may "go back" and determine what was particularly significant in the interview in relation to the employee's present behavior. This research approach to interviewer training has proven to be one of the most effective ways in which to improve the validity of employment interviews.

---

[14]*Ibid.*, pp. 189–192.

[15]Milton M. Mandell, *The Employment Interview*, American Management Association Research Study 77 (New York: American Management Association, 1961), p. 71.

Interviewing Methods

Employment or selection interviews may be classified according to the methods or approaches that are used. In addition to the unplanned interview (which has no place in personnel selection) and the planned interview involving no special techniques, there are certain types of interviews with which the student should be familiar. These are used in varying degrees to meet the requirements of different personnel programs.

Patterned interview. The *patterned interview* is a well-planned and organized interview designed to overcome many of the faults and limitations of ordinary interviewing procedures. Through training in the use of special interview and evaluation forms, the interviewer's skill in obtaining information and in making judgments about applicants is improved considerably. According to McMurry, who developed the patterned interview, it has these important advantages over ordinary methods:

1. It makes possible a systematic and complete coverage of all necessary information for predicting the applicant's probable success on the job.
2. It guides the interviewer in getting the facts and discovering valuable information about the applicant.
3. It provides a set of principles for use in interpreting the facts obtained for the purpose of judging what the applicant *will do* alongside of what he *can do*.
4. It provides a means for minimizing the interviewer's personal biases and prejudices.[16]

McMurry has prepared different interview forms for applicants for office and factory positions, for sales positions, and for executive positions. A section from one of these interview forms is shown in Figure 6-2 on page 152.

Note that the form contains questions to be asked of the applicant together with questions beneath the line in small type (and in color on the original form) that are designed to help the interviewer to obtain complete information, to interpret its significance, and to become aware of inconsistencies. The interpretations are later recorded on a summary sheet that is completed on the basis of information obtained from the interview and from the application blank, tests, telephone checks, and other sources of information about the applicant. Companies that have used the patterned interview have generally found they have greater success in predicting the applicant's performance on the job than when other methods are used.

---

[16]Robert N. McMurry, *Tested Techniques of Personnel Selection* (Chicago: The Dartnell Corporation, 1955).

Figure 6-2
McMURRY PATTERNED INTERVIEW FORM (page 1 only)

S U M M A R Y

Rating: [1] [2] [3] [4]   Interviewer_____   Date_____

Comments (List both favorable and unfavorable points) In making final rating, be sure to consider not only the man's ability and experience but also his stability, industry, perseverance, ability to get along with others, loyalty, self-reliance, and leadership. Is he mature and realistic?

Is he well motivated for this work? Are his living standards, finances, his domestic situation, and the family influence favorable to this work?

Does he have sufficient health and physical reserve?

Position Considered for_____

Name_____   Telephone Number_____   Is it your phone?_____

Present Address_____ City_____ State_____
Will this location affect his attendance? Is this a desirable neighborhood? Does it appear consistent with income?

Date of your birth_____ Age_____ Have you served in the Armed Services of the United States? ☐ Yes, ☐ No

(If yes) What were the dates?_____19__to_____19__ If rejected or exempted, what were the reasons?_____
Discuss military service as a job in chronological order with other jobs. Will this affect his performance on our job?

Why are you applying for this position?_____
Are his underlying reasons practical? Does he have a definite goal?

Are you employed now? ☐ Yes, ☐ No; (If yes) how soon available?_____
What are relationships with present employer?

WORK HISTORY: LAST OR PRESENT POSITION   Dates from_____ 19___to_____ 19___
If out of work—how long?

Company_____ Division_____ Address_____
Does this check with application?

How did you get this job?_____
Did he show self-reliance in getting this job? Stability of interests? Perseverance?

Nature of work at start_____ Earnings at start_____
Did this work require energy and industry? Close attention? Cooperation?

How did the job change?_____ Earnings at leaving_____
Was progress made? Any indications of strong motivation?   Is this in line with what he can earn here?

What were your duties and responsibilities at time of leaving?_____
Did he accept them? Indications of industry? Self-reliance? Perseverance? Leadership?

Superior_____ Title_____ How was he to work with?_____
Was this close supervision?   Are there indications of loyalty? Hostility?

What did you especially like about the position?_____
Has he been happy and content in his work? Indications of loyalty, ability to get along with others?

What did you especially dislike?_____
Did he get along well with people? Is he inclined to be critical? Were his dislikes justified?

How much time have you lost from work?_____ Reasons_____
Is he regular in attendance on the job? Are there other interests?

Reasons for leaving_____ Why right then?_____
Are his reasons for leaving reasonable and consistent?   Do they check with records?

Part-time jobs during this employment_____
Does this indicate industry? Ambition? Lack of loyalty? Lack of interest in duties of position?

NEXT TO LAST POSITION   Dates from_____ 19___to_____ 19___
Any time between this and last job?

Company_____ Division_____ Address_____
Does this check with application?

How did you get this job?_____
Did he show self-reliance in getting this job? Stability of interests? Perseverance?

Nature of work at start_____ Earnings at start_____
Did this work require energy and industry? Close attention? Cooperation?

How did the job change?_____ Earnings at leaving_____
Was progress made? Any indications of strong motivation?   Is this in line with what he can earn here?

What were your duties and responsibilities at time of leaving?_____
Did he accept them? Indications of industry? Self-reliance? Perseverance? Leadership?

Superior_____ Title_____ How was he to work with?_____
Was this close supervision?   Are there indications of loyalty? Hostility?

Form No. EP-312   Copyright 1955, The Dartnell Corporation, Chicago 40, Ill., Printed in U. S. A.
Developed by McMurry, Hamstra & Company

Source: Published by the Dartnell Corporation, Chicago. Reproduced with permission.

The training required for this type of interviewing, as well as the standardized procedure, probably contributes to its reported success.

Nondirective interview. In the nondirective interview the applicant is given considerable leeway in expressing himself and in determining the course of the discussion. This is achieved by the interviewer asking broad, general questions, such as "Tell me more about your experiences in your last job," and by permitting the applicant to express himself fully with a minimum of interruption. Brief interviewer responses, as for example "What happened then?" or "What were the circumstances?", are used to keep the applicant talking about the subject. In general, the nondirective approach is characterized by such interviewer behavior as listening carefully, not arguing, using questions sparingly, not interrupting or changing the subject abruptly, phrasing responses briefly, and allowing pauses in the conversation. This latter technique is the most difficult for the beginning interviewer to master, perhaps because our everyday conversational folkways dictate that someone should be talking if two or more persons are gathered together.

The greater freedom afforded to the applicant in the nondirective interview provides an opportunity for him to discuss in depth any points that he would like to talk about. This may be particularly valuable in bringing to the interviewer's attention any information, attitudes, or feelings that are often concealed by more rapid questioning of the applicant. On the other hand, the interviewer should not come to a nondirective interview without some objectives to be achieved.

Other interview methods. While most employment interviews will be of the patterned or of the nondirective types, or modifications of them, there are some other more distinctive types of interviews with which the reader should be familiar. The *group interview* (also called a group oral-performance test) is a popular approach in the selection of executive trainees. When the group interview approach is used, a half dozen or so candidates assemble for a group discussion. Seated to the side or behind the group will be company executives who observe and evaluate the candidates as they engage in a round-table discussion with or without a leader. Revlon, Inc., reports that this method not only saves top executives' time but seems to result in better selection decisions.[17] While the group interview is generally used along with other selection techniques, it has been found to facilitate observations of such factors as initiative, aggressiveness,

---

[17]Jules Z. Willing, "The Round-Table Interview — A Method of Selecting Trainees," *Personnel*, Vol. 39, No. 21 (March-April, 1962), pp. 26-32.

poise, adaptability to new situations, tact, ability to get along with people, and similar qualities.[18]

One type of interview, commonly used by government agencies including the military services, involves having a panel of interviewers or observers who sit as a "board" and question and observe a single candidate in what is called a *board interview.* Another type that was developed during World War II as a technique for selecting military espionage personnel places the candidate under considerable pressure and hence is known as the *stress interview.* Its potentialities for business are limited.

Conducting the Interview

Many books and articles have been written about the interview and how to conduct it. Most of them contain advice that is useful and helpful, but only a small part of the advice is based on evidence obtained from studies made of actual employment interviews. Rather, the advice emerges from experimental studies carried out in other areas of psychology that are presumed to have some relationship to what transpires in the employment interview. However, there have been some recent approaches to the study of the interview that have proven fruitful and may lead to more profitable research in the future.[19] In the discussion that follows, some of the results from these studies will be combined with the more traditional advice that is given on how to conduct the interview.

Preparing for the interview. Even the most highly trained and experienced interviewer should prepare for this activity. The preparation typically includes an examination of the purpose of the interview and the outlining of areas and specific questions to be covered. A review of the application form, test scores, information from reference checks, and other pertinent data is essential. Preparation desirably extends to the interview climate to insure that the setting is private and as free from distractions as possible. Since the interviewer himself is an extremely important factor in the process, he should consider if he is free from extreme tension or pressures that would result in his being ineffective with a particular applicant.

Establishing and maintaining rapport. The first step in an interview is to establish friendly and cordial relationships with the interviewee. The

---

[18]Bernard M. Bass, "Selecting Personnel by Observation," *Personnel*, Vol. 26, No. 4 (January, 1950), pp. 269-272.

[19]An excellent bibliography of studies may be found in an article by Eugene C. Mayfield, "The Selection-Interview — A Re-evaluation of Published Research," *Personnel Psychology*, Vol. 17, No. 3 (Autumn, 1964), pp. 239–260. A decade of experimental research in interviewing is described in Edward C. Webster, *Decision Making in the Employment Interview* (Montreal: Industrial Relations Center, McGill University, 1964).

interviewer achieves this condition, referred to as *rapport*, by being pleasant in his greeting, by displaying sincere interest in the individual, and by listening carefully. Many interviewers achieve rapport by starting the interview with "small talk" about the day's baseball game or some other topic that may put the individual at ease. However, if the applicant is not interested in or knows little about baseball, the approach may increase the discomfort of the applicant who wishes to get down to business. It is usually better to talk about the applicant or the company since, presumably, there is a mutual interest in these topics.

It is the responsibility of the interviewer to maintain control of the interview situation in order that its objectives may be achieved in a reasonable length of time. The method used in questioning the applicant will depend largely upon the type of interview (patterned, nondirective, etc.); but regardless of which method is used, the applicant should have an opportunity to express himself fully and to bring out any points that will throw light on his qualifications. This requires the interviewer not only to ask meaningful questions but to listen carefully so that he understands what the applicant is saying as well as what the applicant is trying to say if he is having difficulty in expressing himself. The interviewer should not assume that he knows what the applicant means. Follow-up questions that begin with *why, what, when, where*, and *how* may be used appropriately to elicit more complete information. In phrasing such questions, however, one should have a pleasant tone of voice and not appear as a cross-examiner at a trial.

The interviewer must also be careful to phrase his questions so that whatever biases he has are not so apparent as to influence the applicant's responses. For example, the following different forms of a question concerning an applicant's college education would elicit different kinds of responses from an applicant:

1. Did you graduate from college?
2. Of course you graduated from college, didn't you?
3. When did you graduate from college?
4. So you went to college, did you?
5. How far were you able to go in school?
6. I suppose you're another one of those college graduates, eh?[20]

Similarly, if an applicant is asked a leading question like, "You don't mind shift work, do you?" he may answer "no" out of fear of being rejected. Later on, however, he may leave the job to avoid shift work, thus revealing that the interviewer failed to obtain an accurate assessment of his feelings.

---

[20]Roger M. Bellows and M. Frances Estep, *Employment Psychology: The Interview* (New York: Holt, Rinehart and Winston, Inc., 1954), p. 115.

Since the interviewer desires to obtain as much information as possible, he should avoid questions that can be answered with a simple "yes" or "no" since these answers often do not tell the whole story. At times the interviewer might wish that the story were shorter, but he should resist interrupting the applicant unless it is necessary. While it is the interviewer's responsibility to guide the conversation, he should not dominate it. A relaxed and warm manner in which the applicant feels free to talk is conducive to obtaining the information that is needed for making a decision.

Giving information. One of the distinctive features of the interview is the opportunity that it provides for giving information to the applicant. Some years ago Bingham pointed out that there are four duties of the employment interviewer that will never be delegated to a computer:

> (1) He must answer fully and frankly the applicant's questions about your business, the job, and the working conditions. Who has invented a regression equation which will do that? (2) He must convince the man he is interviewing that yours is a good firm to work for since it furnishes such and such opportunities for growth and advancement (if it does). In other words, he must be skillful in selling your firm to the applicant. (3) He must steer the applicant toward a job for which he is better suited, if there is one somewhere, lest he discover that job and shift to it only after you have spent a few hundred dollars in training him. (4) Finally, the interviewer should leave the prospect, in any case, with the feeling that he has made a personal friend.[21]

Making observations and inferences. In addition to providing an opportunity to obtain information from the applicant, the interview also provides a setting in which the applicant's personal characteristics such as his neatness, fluency of speech, correctness of grammar and pronunciation, mannerisms, poise, and other relevant and irrelevant characteristics may be observed.

In the typical interview, which is likely to be of short duration, judgments are made on the basis of a very small sample of an individual's behavior. Furthermore, since most applicants "dress up" for the occasion and usually go out of their way to make a good impression, the opinions that the untrained interviewer forms are likely to rest on shaky grounds. His opinion of the applicant may be influenced by his own biases and prejudices, which he is unlikely to recognize. One typical bias is the tendency to consider strangers who have interests, experiences, and backgrounds similar to his own as being more acceptable than those who differ from him. This type of bias is illustrated in exaggerated form in Figure 6-3.

---

[21]Walter Van Dyke Bingham, "Today and Yesterday," *Personnel Psychology*, Vol. 2, No. 2 (Summer, 1949), pp. 272–274.

Figure 6-3
AN EXAGGERATED FORM OF INTERVIEWER BIAS

"You're exactly the kind of man we need around here."

Source: *Dun's Review and Modern Industry*, March, 1957. Reproduced with permission.

Another problem in interviewing is the "halo error." This refers to the tendency to judge an individual favorably in many areas on the basis of one strong point. If the interviewer places a high value on personal neatness, he may judge the applicant who is neat to have many other favorable qualities that he may or may not possess, such as those pertaining to intelligence, honesty, and judgment. The "halo error" can also work in the opposite direction, in which case the above interviewer would probably assume that an unkempt individual is stupid and dishonest. Even among interviewers in modern business institutions, it is common to find those who rely on concepts such as "individuals who have shifty eyes are likely to be dishonest," "redheads are easily excitable," and "a high forehead indicates high intelligence." Similarly, many persons often reason incorrectly that the individual who dresses neatly is also likely to be neat in his work.

The fact that individuals happen to resemble each other can constitute a hazard for the interviewer. He may have had pleasant or unpleasant experiences with an individual who has long been forgotten. The fact that a job applicant with whom he is talking has facial characteristics similar to those of the person of long ago may result in his ascribing the same characteristics to this new person whom he hardly knows. Thus, while an interviewer may recognize physiognomy as being a pseudo-scientific approach to personality assessment, he fails to recognize that he has unwittingly fallen into the trap of using it himself.

Overemphasis on charm and "a good personality" can likewise blind the interviewer so that he fails to do a thorough job of obtaining all of the vital information that he needs. If he decides at the beginning that he likes the applicant, from that point on the interviewer is likely to select evidence that supports his original judgment and to ignore evidence that suggests the inaccuracy of the judgment. While awareness of the influence of selective perception is more important in selecting managers than in selecting nonmanagement personnel, its presence should not be ignored whether it occurs in the initial evaluation of personnel, later in performance appraisal, or in situations requiring disciplinary action.[22] Sometimes applicants are exceptionally shrewd and not only "turn on the charm," but also are skillful at placing the interviewer at ease.

On the basis of the information that the interviewer obtains and his observations, he makes inferences or interpretations about the individual's behavior. A useful form developed by Moyer of the New York Bell Telephone Company requires the interviewer to record his "findings" in one column and his "interpretations" of these findings in another column. This is particularly desirable since most interviewers, subject to human error, are likely to combine facts and interpretations together and assume that both are facts. For example, the interviewer might record the fact that the applicant "Sings in church choir." From this fact the interviewer might infer or conclude that the applicant's "Conduct is wholesome." While this may be a reasonably sound inference, it is still an inference and not a fact. One could also infer from the same fact that the applicant has a desire to make himself heard in the community or that he has a girl friend who sings in the choir.

Nervous behavior on the part of the applicant during the interview may be viewed by the interviewer as an indication of emotional maladjustment, and as the result of this impression, the interviewer may give the applicant a low rating. Actually, this is a very natural reaction and may be an indication of the applicant's intense desire to obtain employment with that particular company.

Since employment interviewing involves making inferences about an individual's probable success on the job, it is essential that the interviewer be required to examine the process by which he makes inferences. This can be accomplished through a training program for interviewers.

---

[22]Quinn G. McKay, "Red Flags Missed — Wrong Man Hired," *Business Horizons*, Vol. 6, No. 2 (Summer, 1963), pp. 47–52.

Recording results. Whether or not information is recorded during the progress of the interview will depend in part upon the nature of the interview. The patterned interview, for example, requires the recording of many details as the interview progresses while a nondirective interview may often be summarized best after it is concluded. It should be recognized by the interviewer, however, that rapport may be lost if the interviewer maintains closer contact with his papers than with the applicant. Furthermore, he should be alert to any signs that the applicant is threatened by having someone record certain facts about his life. In spite of the problems that may arise in these and similar instances, the interviewer should allow time at the end of the interview to record the facts and the impressions which were obtained. A company may develop its own record form or use one of the many forms that are commercially available.

Evaluating the interview. Professional interviewers in the personnel office as well as managers and supervisors in the hiring departments should be encouraged to evaluate their interviews. Many skilled interviewing practitioners are never satisfied with their proficiency and tape and criticize their interviews with the following points in mind:

1. Did I follow my pre-interview plan?
2. Did the interview ever degenerate into mere conversation?
3. What were my pre-interview objectives?
4. Were they accomplished? If not, why weren't they accomplished?
5. Was I prepared for this interview?
6. Was the applicant satisfied with the interview or did he leave confused, disgruntled, and upset?
7. Am I falling into any bad habits? (For example, failing to listen, missing danger signals, repeating questions which have been answered previously.)
8. Is my questioning technique awkward and stilted, or is it smooth with a transition from one series of questions to another?[23]

An effective interviewer will not stop with selection and placement on a job. He will keep a file on his turnover and periodically review his "batting average" with supervision and management.

The Employment Decision

While all of the steps in selection are important, the critical one is the decision to accept or reject the applicant for employment. It is at this point that the action of the personnel department will result in a gain or a

---

[23]Thomas L. Moffatt, "Where Interviews Fail," *Management of Personnel Quarterly*, Vol. 3, No. 3 (Fall, 1963), pp. 33–35.

loss for the company. By selecting an individual who later turns out to be a superior employee, it has realized a gain; by selecting a person who proves to be unsatisfactory or by rejecting a potentially productive person, it has added to the company's liabilities. The selection of an individual who proves to be unsatisfactory may result in further problems if his deficiencies are not discovered until after the probationary period has passed. With the shortening of the probationary period in many industries, it is essential that the decision made at the end of the selection process be based on sound evidence that is thoroughly and impartially examined.

Factors in Decision Making

In making decisions one of the major questions that arises is how much weight should be given to the facts about the applicants? For example, should test scores be given a priority over interviewer judgments? The desirable procedure is for each company to determine what information has high predictive value and to decide how this information can be obtained most effectively. It may be found that the verified work history and the judgments of the requisitioning department are the most valid indicators for some jobs, whereas for others test scores and evaluations made by former teachers are best. A desirable approach to the problem is the maintenance of flexible procedures that permit the use of the types of information which have proved to be the most valuable.

In weighing the facts it is well to keep in mind that, while it is important to reject those who do not meet minimal standards, the selection process should involve more than weeding out misfits. The applicant should be given an opportunity to show his strengths which, in some instances, may well compensate for any weaknesses that he may have. It has been suggested that every personnel department should question its approach in order to determine if it is hiring mediocre people free from any "weaknesses" or whether it focuses its attention on hiring people with strengths and potentialities.[24] Care should be exercised, however, in avoiding the establishment of unrealistic hiring standards which cause talented personnel to become dissatisfied and leave their jobs.[25]

Methods of Reaching a Decision

Unfortunately, in many employment situations little or no attempt is made to determine the value or validity of various types and sources of

[24]Glenn A. Bassett, "The Screening Process: Selection or Rejection?" *Personnel*, Vol. 39, No. 4 (July–August, 1962), pp. 31–37.
[25]Harold Mayfield, "Employee Selection — Don't Overshoot the Mark," *Supervisory Management*, Vol. 9, No. 7 (July, 1964), pp. 9–12.

information with the result that the employment decision often represents the combined intuitive judgments of persons who have examined various records and have interviewed the applicant. While one might assume that qualified personnel would be effective in making decisions of this type, in 20 studies only one had findings which support this notion. In 19 studies the predictions based on statistical approaches like those that are discussed below were more effective than those based on the personal judgment of experts.[26] Where interviews, application form items, and tests have been validated, these sources of information then provide the basis for a scientific method of selection. Three different methods that depend upon validated information will be described briefly.

The successive hurdles approach. The *successive hurdles approach* requires the applicant to clear in succession several hurdles such as those provided by the steps in the selection process. At each hurdle he is permitted to go on to the next hurdle or is rejected, depending upon whether or not he qualifies at that hurdle. The hurdles are arranged in the order of their importance in predicting the success or failure of an applicant in a particular job. For example, if a particular aptitude test were found to be the best single predictor of probable success on the job, it would be placed immediately following the initial interview. If the individual did not make a qualifying score on the test, he would be rejected at that point and would not proceed further in the selection process. Thus, under this method only those applicants who successfully meet the established requirements at all hurdles are hired.

Multiple correlation approach. The *multiple correlation approach*, like the successive hurdles approach, is based on analyses of the manner in which the test scores, interview ratings, application blank items, and other information are related to success on the job. The major difference, however, is that this method requires the applicant to go through the entire selection process in order that complete data may be obtained about him. These data, which are usually reduced to scores, are then combined. If the combined score is above the level needed to qualify, the applicant is hired; otherwise, he is rejected. Unlike the successive hurdles approach, this method is based on the assumption that strength in one ability may compensate for inadequacy in another important ability. Thus, if an applicant scores low on one test, he may still qualify by scoring high on one of the other selection devices.

---

[26]P. E. Meehl, *Clinical v. Statistical Prediction* (Minneapolis: University of Minnesota Press, 1954).

Discriminate analysis approach. *Discriminate analysis* is a statistical approach which predicts the probability of membership in alternative groups rather than placing individuals at a point along some continuum. It answers the question, "What group is this person most like?" With the increased use of high speed electronic computers, it is likely that the larger companies with large work forces will use this method of relating an applicant's talents to organizational needs.[27]

Regardless of which approach is used, there will be individuals who are rejected and must, therefore, be advised of it. While the general principle to be followed in rejections is to be as honest as possible with the applicant, it is necessary to maintain confidences and to minimize the possibility of creating more problems by the rejection. In addition, it must be made clear to the applicant that the rejection does not imply that he is generally inadequate but merely that there are others who are better suited for the particular job for which he applied.

Evaluating the Selection Program

The function of selecting employees is one of the most important aspects of the personnel program and, therefore, deserves more attention than is frequently given to it. Even though there are ways of improving the selection process, many businessmen believe that they "know people" and can select the potentially effective individuals through a brief interview. The suggestion that interviewing and other selection techniques could be improved may deflate some of the line members as well as members of the personnel staff, but positive steps should be taken to make necessary changes in the interests of better selection. Through analysis of information obtained from such sources as performance records, supervisory evaluations, and exit interviews, it is possible to realize the sources of errors in selection and to make corrections and improvements. Keeping the staff research oriented in the midst of filling personnel requisitions is not an easy task, but it is a necessary task if selection is to be successful and is to meet the objectives set for it.

Résumé

The process of selection involves obtaining as much information as possible about an applicant for the purpose of making a sound employment decision. While there is a practical limit to the amount of time and money

---

[27]Wendell L. French and Alvar O. Elbing, Jr., "Predictions for Personnel and Industrial Relations in 1985," *Personnel Journal*, Vol. 40, No. 6 (November, 1961), pp. 249–253.

that can be spent for this purpose, the collection of pertinent data covering many different facets of the individual can generally be profitable to the organization as well as to the individual. While the personnel department has a major role in the selection process, the success of the program also depends upon the efforts of the managers in the other departments who have an important role to play in the final evaluation of the applicants that have been initially screened. Since managers who are involved in the final decisions about employees may overlook the need and the opportunity to approach this task scientifically, the personnel staff should not only set a good example by its application of the most reliable and valid methods but should also endeavor to provide assistance and guidance to others who participate in the important process of selecting personnel.

In the cooperative process of selection, care must be taken to assess personnel on the basis of the qualities that are essential to the job. While it is usually easier to determine what a person can do, some judgment must be arrived at concerning what an individual will do if he is given the opportunity. It was noted that tests provide one of the most valid approaches to assessing ability and aptitude, whereas interviews and evidences from past experience may give insights that permit making some evaluation of what an individual will do. In the final process of arriving at a decision, however, all available information should be assembled and weighted in the light of its known validity in order that the selection process may contribute maximally to the total personnel program.

DISCUSSION QUESTIONS AND PROBLEMS

1. In selecting personnel for the following jobs, what procedures would give the best measures of what an applicant *can do*? Of what an applicant *will do*?
   a. Supervisor of an office force.
   b. Lathe operator.
   c. Research chemist in an oil company.
2. It was mentioned in this chapter that the Civil Rights Act of 1964 prohibited discrimination in employment because of sex.
   a. What are some of the problems that may arise from men working in jobs that were typically considered as women's jobs and women working in so-called jobs for men? Cite some specific examples.
   b. Do you view these problems as serious or insolvable?
3. As we observe situations in our everyday life, we are constantly making inferences or interpretations of the behavior of others. For example, if we observe that a fellow student is sleeping in class we may infer that he is bored, works the swing shift, etc. It is interesting to keep a diary for three or four hours in which observations and inferences are recorded in separate columns.

Make such a diary, and submit your list of observations to another person and ask him to report his inferences.

   a. How do his inferences compare with yours?
   b. How do you account for the similarities?
   c. How do you account for the differences?

4. In an advertisement for a personnel department interviewer, one company included the following statement: "Qualifications such as 'liking to work with people,' 'knowing people,' and 'good judge of people' are not wanted."

   a. Why were these restrictions included?
   b. What was the company probably looking for in its applicants for this position?

5. If an employee left a company after his first week on the job, what specific recruiting, selection, and placement activities would represent a personnel cost to the company? Make an estimate of the cost of each activity.

6. The Phoenix Mutual Life Insurance Company found in an analysis of personal data about its sales force that there were important differences between successful and unsuccessful sales personnel. The most successful salesmen had six-plus years of sales experience, were in the age bracket 33–38, and had three or more investments.

   a. What other types of personal data might be found to be related to success or failure in this type of job?
   b. What are some common assumptions made about personal data, such as that found on an application form, that may not be substantiated either in a specific company or in general?

CASE 6-1

THE BOSS'S FRIEND

This case involves the following individuals who held the positions indicated in a department of a government agency:

   Mr. Starbuck — Division Chief, who later became Department Chief
   Mr. Sparks   — Who replaced Mr. Starbuck as Division Chief
   Mr. Burns   — Section Chief
   Mr. Hughes   — Branch Chief
   Mr. Ronson   — An employee, later Branch Chief

At one time when Mr. Burns was away on temporary duty, his superior, Mr. Starbuck, hired Mr. Ronson and assigned him to Mr. Burns's section. Upon Burns's return to the office a week later, Starbuck advised Burns that he had done him a big favor by hiring such a capable man. He told Burns that he and Ronson had been friends for many years and that there wasn't a better man for the job. Burns checked Ronson's qualifications and was inclined to agree with Starbuck's action in hiring the man. Burns was advised that Ronson was hired at a salary only $300 less per year than Burns's salary.

About one month after Ronson was hired, Hughes retired and Ronson was assigned to his job. He was given this assignment primarily because of the implied direction from Starbuck. Ronson's new job required having knowledge of the office procedures, tact in dealing with office personnel, plus some individual judgment in case of work stoppage in the shops. Burns was aware that

Ronson did not have sufficient training to assume full responsibility as a supervisor; but since he was Starbuck's friend, he wanted to avoid any argument with Starbuck over the man.

About two weeks later Starbuck was promoted to Department Chief, and Sparks was promoted from another department to become division chief. Shortly after this transfer occurred, Burns reported to Sparks that Ronson was incompetent, a loafer, and was annoying women in the office. Sparks thereupon summoned Burns and Ronson to his office. He asked Burns for details and was informed by him that Ronson was not doing his job. Ronson admitted that perhaps there were certain procedures with which he was not thoroughly familiar, but he felt that with additional training he would be able to rectify the situation. Ronson also admitted that at times when things in the office were slack, he may have sat around and talked with people. He promised that he would discontinue this practice. In response to the charge about annoying women in the office, he expressed disagreement on the grounds that this accusation was not justified.

At Sparks's request, Burns arranged for additional training for Ronson. He also cautioned Ronson about loafing in the office and reminded him of his responsibility as a supervisor. Furthermore, he put Ronson on a 60-day trial period. Just before the trial period ended, Burns walked into Sparks's office and told him that Ronson must go. He stated that Ronson was not the man for the job and never would be. Sparks listened to Burns's comments and thereupon decided that, regardless of what Starbuck would say, Ronson would have to go. Sparks called Ronson into his office and told him that he would have to accept a nonsupervisory job or leave the organization.

The next day Starbuck summoned Sparks to his office and wanted to know what he was doing. As a result of his conversation with Starbuck, Sparks called Burns into his office. They reviewed this particular problem, and Burns reluctantly agreed with Sparks's decision that Ronson be put back on the job and be very closely observed. Sparks told Burns that proof would have to be presented before he could do anything.

About a week later the personnel division started a survey and reclassification of the office jobs. One of the jobs surveyed was Ronson's. The results of the job classification disclosed that Ronson was not fully qualified for his job but was qualified for another job. Ronson agreed to accept a cut in salary if he would be left in the office. Immediately, Sparks noticed a big change in Burns's attitude toward Ronson. All of the complaints and resentments disappeared. Ronson is still employed in the same office but in a different job.

a. Who made the first mistake? What could have been done to avoid the problem?
b. Do you feel that the lines of authority shown at the beginning of this case were followed at all stages in the development and solution of the problem?
c. Did the personnel division discharge its responsibilities satisfactorily?

CASE 6-2

THE MODERN DIOGENES

The executives of a large oil company with over 50 stations had good reason to believe that many of their employees were appropriating merchandise and trading stamps. Since a large part of the company profits came from the redemption of stamps and cash purchase of merchandise, the practice was as serious as if employees had considered free gasoline to be a fringe benefit. In an effort to reduce the loss of stamps and merchandise, the personnel manager decided to employ the services of an expert polygraph (lie detector) operator.

Thereafter, when applicants for service station jobs were considered for employment, they were interviewed by the lie detector operator. This process involved the use of standardized interview questions about past conduct and about any possible illegal activities. If the applicant lied while answering any of the questions, this fact was clearly registered on the polygraph dial. When an applicant was advised that he was apparently not telling the truth, the truth usually was revealed upon further questioning. In some instances crimes for which the individual had never even been a suspect were revealed.

In addition to using this procedure on applicants, company management decided that all employees who worked in the company's stations would be interviewed twice a year at random intervals. This procedure is now well established, and the management feels that it has the answer to the problem of dishonesty.

    a. Do you think it is wise and ethical to use this procedure on applicants? On employees? Why?

    b. What effects, if any, may such a practice have upon employee relations? Union relations?

    c. Do you have a better answer to the problem of dishonesty?

SUGGESTED READINGS

Bellows, Roger M., and M. Frances Estep. *Employment Psychology: The Interview.* New York: Holt, Rinehart and Winston, Inc., 1954.

Bingham W. V., B. V. Moore, and John W. Gustad. *How to Interview,* Fourth Edition. New York: Harper & Brothers, 1959.

Chruden, Herbert J., and Arthur W. Sherman, Jr. *Readings in Personnel Management,* Second Edition. Cincinnati: South-Western Publishing Company, Inc., 1966. Chapter 2.

Dunnette, Marvin. *Personnel Selection and Placement.* Belmont, California: Wadsworth Publishing Company, 1966.

Kahn, Robert L., and Charles F. Cannell. *The Dynamics of Interviewing: Theory, Technique, and Cases.* New York: John Wiley & Sons, Inc., 1957.

Lipsett, Laurence, Frank P. Rodgers, and Harold M. Kentner. *Personnel Selection and Recruitment.* Boston: Allyn and Bacon, Inc., 1964.

Lopez, Felix M., Jr. *Personnel Interviewing, Theory and Practice.* New York: McGraw-Hill Book Company, 1965.

McMurry, Robert N. *Tested Techniques of Personnel Selection.* Chicago: The Dartnell Corporation, 1955.

Mandell, Milton M. *The Selection Process: Choosing the Right Man for the Job.* New York: American Management Association, 1964.

Stone, C. Harold, and William E. Kendall. *Effective Personnel Selection Procedures.* Englewood Cliffs, New Jersey: Prentice-Hall, Inc., 1956.

Webster, Edward C. *Decision Making in the Employment Interview.* Montreal: McGill University, Industrial Relations Center, 1964.

Psychological Testing

In the preceding chapter the theory of personnel selection was discussed and some of the commonly used techniques for evaluating job applicants were examined. Because of the special role that psychological tests have in the assessment of an individual's qualifications and because of the need for managers and members of the personnel staff to understand the fundamentals of testing, this chapter will be devoted to this topic.

The primary purpose of tests in personnel management, as well as in other fields where tests are used, is not only to describe but to predict what an individual is likely to be able to do. The first question usually asked about a test score is, "What does it mean?" or, more specifically, "What does it mean in terms of an individual's likelihood for success in a particular endeavor?" The meaning to be derived from a particular score can be determined only after careful research has been done and the predictive value of the test is known. By having a reasonable degree of understanding of how predictive value is achieved, as well as other technical requirements of tests, members of the personnel staff will not only be able to use tests effectively but will be prepared to recognize and cope with the criticisms that managers, supervisors, employees, the unions, and others are likely to voice about tests.

Interviewers and personnel managers, as well as supervisors and executives, are required to make many judgments in the course of a day's activities. Tests provide one excellent source of objective information about individuals that may be used, along with other data, as a basis for personnel actions. In many instances, however, the tests are used improperly or without regard to their general or specific limitations. While it is not possible to give a thorough coverage of all of the important facets of psychological testing in one chapter, an attempt will be made to provide the reader with the fundamental concepts of testing as they relate to the management of personnel. The use of tests in schools, clinics, and various types of counseling activities present special problems that, for the most part, are beyond the scope of this book.

In the discussion that follows, therefore, the focus is on the scientific use of tests by management, primarily for the purpose of increasing efficiency and overall organizational effectiveness. It should be recognized, moreover, that these gains to the organization will in the long run ordinarily represent benefits to the individuals whose occupational destinies are affected by tests.

The topics to be considered are:

- Testing and the personnel program.
- Principles of psychological testing.
- Developing a testing program.

Testing and the Personnel Program

Since World War I, when about two million recruits were tested with the Army Alpha Test of mental ability, there has been an increased awareness and use of tests in personnel selection and placement. While tests have not always been used scientifically, as was particularly evident during the 1920's when many self-styled test experts operated on the American business scene, the personnel manager of today generally recognizes that, when used properly, tests can be of considerable value. Surveys reveal that personnel men are depending more and more on tests, especially in the larger companies,[1] and a review of the literature reveals a healthy interest in research in this area, much of which is conducted by persons affiliated with or serving as consultants to business, industrial, and governmental organizations.

---

[1]*Personnel Practices in Factory and Office: Manufacturing*, Studies in Personnel Policy, No. 194 (New York: National Industrial Conference Board, 1964) and *Office Personnel Practices: Nonmanufacturing*, Studies in Personnel Policy, No. 197 (New York: National Industrial Conference Board, 1965); "Jobs and Psychology: Personnel Tests Win Widening Business Use Though Critics Fume," *Wall Street Journal*, February 9, 1965.

Uses of Tests   *a test is a helper*

As a result of research in testing and the development of new approaches in measurement, the use of tests is no longer limited to that of
selection and placement. Tests are also being used by employers for such
purposes as determining who should be promoted, measuring progress
in training courses, and, to a limited extent, in counseling employees.

Employee selection and placement. In spite of their other uses, tests
are still used primarily for selecting and placing personnel. In using tests
for these purposes, it is of primary importance that the tests measure the
human characteristics that have been determined as essential for the job,
not only by the process of making job analyses and developing job specifications but also through the empirical determination of the relationship
between test scores and such criteria of success as productivity and/or
employee turnover. Because of the importance of establishing such a relationship through a process known as *validating* a test, a special section of
this chapter will be devoted to a discussion of this process. Unfortunately,
tests are frequently used as a basis for personnel decisions before they have
been validated fully, with the result that decisions are made on the basis of
test scores that bear little or no relationship to an applicant's later job
performance.

Promotion, A special type of placement action is that of advancing an
employee to a job which is higher in the organizational structure. Such
action requires that all available information about the employee be assembled and assessed. His personnel file should contain not only the information collected at the time he was hired but also subsequent information
such as performance evaluation reports, progress in training courses, and
scores from tests that he may have taken. Some companies have special
testing programs for those employees being considered for supervisory positions. One refinery of The Standard Oil Company of New Jersey found that
three tests were very useful in selecting supervisors, and other companies
have reported similar results.[2] The use of job-knowledge tests in promoting, as well as hiring, individuals in governmental agencies is fairly well
recognized. While very few companies use job-knowledge tests in evaluating persons for promotion, this approach should receive more attention
than it has because of the contributions that it can make through the assurance that individuals have the requisite knowledge for handling the demands of a higher-level job.

---

[2]Standard Oil Company (New Jersey), *Employee Relations Research in Standard Oil Company (New Jersey) and Affiliates,* Vol. 1, No. 1 (1956), pp. 107–110.

Managerial selection. Jobs above the first line supervisory level pose special problems in selection, primarily because of the broadening responsibilities that managers have for the long-range, overall objectives of the organization. In evaluating personnel for managerial jobs, attention must be given not only to the scope of information and understanding that an individual should possess for a specific managerial job but also for such factors as his ability to think critically and creatively, his temperament, facility in interpersonal relations, his ambition and drive, and other personality and motivational variables in executive success. Several companies, as well as research psychologists, are attempting to assemble tests that may be used as valid predictors of managerial success. While the tests currently used for the purpose have some value at least for research purposes, they have not been rigorously validated. The difficulty in defining managerial success, the limited number of persons in unique managerial positions, and difficulties in determining what traits make good predictors of managerial success are major deterrents to developing sound selection programs for managerial personnel. It should be recognized, however, that some of the tests that are currently available can be used effectively, along with other information, as a basis for judging a person's potentialities for a managerial job.[3]

Training. Tests may also be used to measure the effectiveness of training where abilities and skills are of such a nature that they lend themselves to typical testing procedures. For example, if the objective of a training program is to provide knowledge concerning union contracts, company policies, or similar factual information, objective examinations with multiple-choice and/or true-false items may be used to measure achievement in the program. The scores are useful as indicators of individual progress as well as of the total effectiveness of instruction. To obtain a true measure of the effectiveness of training, however, tests should be administered before and after training and the net gain computed against an untrained control group. Inventories may also be used to assess changes in attitudes or opinions in supervisory training programs. In the latter example, however, it should be recognized that an improvement in score does not necessarily insure a change in behavior in the supervisory situation.

Counseling. While tests are more commonly used for the purposes discussed above, recent surveys show that 36 out of 384 (9 percent)

---

[3]Robert M. Guion, *Personnel Testing* (New York: McGraw-Hill Book Company, 1965), Chapter 15.

manufacturing companies using tests indicated that they used them for employee counseling. Of banks and insurance companies surveyed, approximately 15 percent of them reported their use in counseling.[4] The specific purpose of the counseling was not reported, but it is likely that the tests were for career counseling of employees.

Contributions and Limitations

One of the major problems encountered in connection with tests for the various purposes discussed in the preceding section arises from their improper use by untrained persons. While it may be an overstatement, there is considerable support for the statement that there are no good or bad psychological tests — there are only good or bad test users.[5]

In companies where tests are used properly, both tangible and intangible benefits have been realized. Some of the tangible benefits obtained from the use of tests in the selection of personnel include reduced training costs, fewer accidents, and less turnover. Intangible benefits such as improved worker adjustment, increased job satisfaction, and better group morale have likewise been obtained through the attraction of better applicants and the "weeding out" of those whose lack of aptitude is readily detected by the tests.

The use of tests in selecting employees to be advanced to higher positions is not only desirable from the standpoint of placing the best talent in these positions but also has generally had a salutary effect on employees who realize that ability is given a higher priority than personal favoritism. While some tests may tend to favor certain persons and/or groups, the basis for favoritism may be detected, analyzed, and corrected much more easily than any type of personal favoritism, such as that which often occurs in an uncontrolled interview situation.

Although most of the limitations of tests can be overcome by using them effectively, there are some inherent characteristics that should be recognized so that tests may not be expected to contribute more than is possible. Three types of limitations of tests that should be recognized are:

1. Measurement techniques cannot be expected to make decisions for a person. They can only present evidence more clearly.
2. The best tests available cannot, at present, predict with great accuracy what a person will do in a complex learning or vocational situation.

---

[4]National Industrial Conference Board, *op. cit.*

[5]D. M. Goodacre, "Pitfalls in the Use of Psychological Tests," *Personnel*, Vol. 34, No. 5 (March-April, 1958), pp. 41–45.

3. Tests ordinarily cannot show why a person made a particular score but only that he did make the score. This is true of all measures of behavior.[6]

Since the publication of Whyte's *The Organization Man,*[7] there has been considerable discussion about the use of personality tests in industry. Some critics contend that requiring personnel to meet certain standards on these tests will result in the breeding of "organization" men, particularly at the supervisory and management levels. There is little evidence to support this claim, however, and the claim seems particularly illogical when one considers that there are not sufficient or adequate tests to measure all of the important aspects of personality even if a company wished to achieve conformity. Furthermore, most executives today realize that creative persons with differing interests and approaches are required to keep the large industrial organization competitive.[8]

A more valid criticism of personality tests arises from the manner in which these tests are sometimes used in personnel selection. While personnel records of any type should be seen only by those who must use them in their work, an individual's test papers and scores from personality tests should be seen by as few persons as possible, and they should be reminded of the need for handling the material in a strictly confidential manner. Those who will make judgments in part on the basis of personality test scores must realize that they are dealing with the type of test that is likely to be the least valid of any used in the test battery and that they should rely on the judgment of the test expert. Otherwise, many potentially valuable individuals may be rejected on the basis of a test score that was not viewed in the proper perspective. In view of these and other ethical problems, it has been suggested that a formal code of ethics, similar to that of psychologists, be developed for business executives who use personality tests.[9]

Attitudes Toward Tests

The determination of whether or not tests will be used in a company, and for what purposes if they are used, cannot be made solely on the basis

---

[6]Edward B. Greene, *Measurements of Human Behavior* (New York: The Odyssey Press, Inc., 1952), p. 16.

[7]William H. Whyte, Jr., *The Organization Man* (New York: Simon and Schuster, Inc., 1956).

[8]Andrew H. Souerwine, "More Value From Personnel Testing," *Harvard Business Review,* Vol. 39, No. 2 (March–April, 1961), pp. 123–130.

[9]Saul W. Gellerman, "The Ethics of Personality Testing," *Personnel,* Vol. 35, No. 3 (November-December, 1958), pp. 30–35.

of objective evidence concerning their value. The attitudes and opinions that executives, union leaders, and even applicants and employees hold toward tests will have important effects on the personnel manager's decision concerning the installation of a testing program. While his ability to "sell" a testing program will depend upon his own knowledge about tests and the degree of enthusiasm that he has for their use, the personnel manager will probably find that any action he takes will be based in part upon how others with whom he must work feel about tests. Although each situation involves people with differing attitudes, it is interesting to note some of the attitudes toward tests that may be found in certain groups.

Executives. A survey conducted by the Harvard Business School, of subscribers to the *Review*, reveals that while there is a strong minority of executives who are critical of tests, the majority of companies are using tests; and a large proportion of executives have been favorably impressed by them. It was found that the majority of those using tests were well aware of dangers connected with them and realized that tests could not be used in place of thoughtful judgment. Four out of five of the executives responding had taken one or more of the psychological tests themselves and as a group had a higher proportion of "most favorable" attitudes toward tests than those who had not taken tests.[10]

Union leaders. The attitudes of labor leaders toward tests are somewhat ambivalent. It is probable, however, that most union officials are not overly enthusiastic about tests because they introduce factors into the selection and/or promotion process that are not easily defined and that conflict with labor's emphasis on union membership, seniority, and other types of control. In commenting upon the use of psychological tests in industry from a trade union point of view, Gomberg states:

> The union, by its very nature, is forced to regard each of its members as an individual — particularly the man who is griping the loudest. Let us assume that some employee who feels that he ought to be entitled to try for a promotion is excluded by a psychological test. What will the attitude of the union be in this matter?
> Inasmuch as the tests themselves are so limited, the union will, in all likelihood, demand much more evidence than the test makes available that the man is not suitable for promotion. It is much more likely to insist upon seniority as a criterion of promotion. The union will demand much more evidence that the man with the highest seniority is not entitled to the promotion than is afforded by the simple test.[11]

---

[10]Lewis B. Ward, "Problems in Review: Putting Executives to the Test," *Harvard Business Review*, Vol. 38, No. 4 (July–August, 1960), pp. 6–15.

[11]William Gomberg, "The Use of Psychology in Industry: A Trade Union Point of View," *Management Science*, Vol. 3, No. 4 (July, 1957), p. 351.

Unions are also likely to insist that the validity of the tests themselves be proven in the selection or promotion system in which they are used. It is predicted that in the future companies that have not validated their tests for particular situations will come under increasingly heavy criticism and more and more cases pertaining to testing will go to arbitration.[12]

Applicants and employees. It is difficult to obtain meaningful expressions of opinion about tests from examinees. However, in a door-to-door interview study of over 600 persons, conducted by one of the authors, respondents were asked, "When applying for a job did the prospective employer give you any tests? If so, what was your reaction to being given these tests?" In this study there was a preponderance of favorable reactions to tests among those respondents who had been given tests; three respondents to one reported favorable reactions.

It should not be inferred from these findings, however, that applicants and employees may not be critical of tests for various reasons. Individuals who have had unpleasant experiences with tests in school and/or job testing are likely to react unfavorably toward tests. In fact there have been charges that employment tests may have been used, deliberately or inadvertently, as instruments of racial discrimination.[13] The now-famous Motorola case in which a Negro was awarded compensation in connection with failure to pass an employment aptitude test has served to open discussion on the whole topic of employment testing, especially where disadvantaged persons are concerned. Testing programs are subject to criticism not only because of failure to validate the tests but also because companies that routinely validate their tests shy away from any kind of research dealing with racial discrimination.[14]

The entire area of testing in relation to disadvantaged persons is extremely complex in that it encompasses such knotty problems as using the ratings of potentially prejudiced supervisors as criteria of job success, understanding cultural differences, defining the nature of intelligence and essential aptitudes, defining cultural deprivation, and considering the adoption of different standards for different groups of applicants.[15]

While all facets of the problem should receive the best efforts of all persons who can contribute to its resolution, Mayfield believes that:

---

[12]Wendell L. French and Alvar O. Elbing, Jr., "Predictions for Personnel and Industrial Relations in 1985," *Personnel Journal*, Vol. 40, No. 6 (November, 1961), pp. 249–253.

[13]"Hiring Tests Wait for the Score: Myart vs. Motorola," *Business Week*, February 13, 1965.

[14]Robert M. Guion, "Employment Tests and Discriminatory Hiring," *Industrial Relations*, Vol. 5, No. 2 (February, 1966), p. 28.

[15]The reader who is interested in the technical details of this issue should consult "The Industrial Psychologist: Selection and Equal Employment Opportunity (A Symposium)," *Personnel Psychology*, Vol. 19, No. 1 (Spring, 1966), pp. 1–39.

Tests, in short, reveal hard facts that need to be considered along with the many opinions that go into the employment decision. To junk this advantage for uncertain benefits would seem to be throwing out the baby with the bath water.

Of course, there should always be a place in the employment process for the exercise of judgment. Tests are just one phase of the process. In every good employment system, the person in charge is expected to override test results when other considerations are exceptionally favorable or compelling. But he should do so with open eyes, not blindly. He needs more facts, not fewer, in making such a decision.

Some well-meaning people are so intent on getting jobs for underprivileged people that they tend to overlook the other side of the coin. Placing a man on a job he cannot really handle is no favor to him or to the cause.

It's true that some apparently unqualified people perform beyond all expectations, but this phenomenon is not peculiar to underprivileged groups. To assume that a person will succeed merely because he is underprivileged is a sentimental fallacy. To follow a general practice of hiring people who by valid standards are unqualified is to abandon good sense.[16]

Mayfield concludes by suggesting that, rather than abolishing tests, employers take steps to insure that applicants with poor backgrounds are given a fair deal by (1) reexamining job requirements, (2) changing the hiring supervisor's middle-class attitudes about the disadvantaged person and his previous opportunities and experiences, and (3) intensifying recruiting efforts to include qualified disadvantaged persons.[17]

The criticisms of testing in recent years have by no means been confined to the issue of disadvantaged persons. Experts in the field of testing do not view tests as a panacea for all personnel problems, and probably the most critical remarks directed at efforts to test and evaluate people are those written by such experts. Others outside the field, including journalists, have come out with tirades against testing with the express intention of fomenting opposition to testing procedures. Such books as *The Brain Watchers*, *The Tyranny of Testing*, and *Testing, Testing, Testing*, are typical of the exposé type that presents biased views by persons who are not test experts. According to Flanagan, the best defense against their criticisms is to improve selection procedures through the systematic application of research and development methods.[18] These research and development

---

[16]Harold Mayfield, "Equal Employment Opportunity: Should Hiring Standards Be Relaxed?", *Personnel*, Vol. 41, No. 5 (September–October, 1964), pp. 8–17, as reprinted in Herbert J. Chruden and Arthur W. Sherman, Jr., *Readings in Personnel Management* (Second Edition; Cincinnati: South-Western Publishing Co., Inc., 1966), pp. 109–120.

[17]*Ibid.*

[18]John C. Flanagan, "What They Say About Testing—And What To Do About It," *Public Personnel Review*, Vol. 25, No. 3 (July, 1964), pp. 174–179.

methods will be discussed after a review of the principles of psychological testing.

Principles of Psychological Testing

The field of psychological testing is rooted in the curiosity and desire that man has to express events that occur in his environment in some numerical fashion. While we are all familiar with the use of rulers, altimeters, scales, and similar measuring devices, the measurement of human events or behaviors does not readily fall within the above categories. That is, as contrasted to measurement by ruler, the measurement of human behavior requires special devices which are based on radically different concepts of measurement. In using a ruler, for example, it is customary to start with the zero point and move toward the number of inches or feet encompassed by a given space. In the measurement of human abilities, personality traits, and other characteristics, the zero point does not mean "nothing" or the absence of a characteristic. This is readily apparent to the student who receives a zero on a test paper and who explains to the teacher that the score does not take into account what he has learned or accomplished. Measurement in psychological testing is, thus, of a different type.

Basic Characteristics

A _psychological test_ is an objective and standardized measure of a sample of behavior. Like other types of measurements mentioned previously, it involves the determination of "how much"; but, in this instance, reference is made to abilities, aptitudes, interests, or other characteristics about human behavior. While our language and our use of it in describing people tends to be of the either-or type, measurement of aptitudes and other characteristics reveals that individuals differ in degree rather than in kind. When large numbers of individuals are tested with a test that is of the appropriate difficulty level for the group being tested and when the individuals are selected at random, the distribution of scores will follow the normal probability curve as graphically illustrated in Figure 7-1.

If the numbers shown in Figure 7-1 are taken to represent scores on a particular test, it may be seen that few individuals attained extremely high or low scores; whereas most of them achieved scores in the middle range. If these numbers were test scores and an individual who took the test is told that his score is 20, this fact alone has little meaningfulness to him.

Figure 7-1

THE NORMAL PROBABILITY CURVE

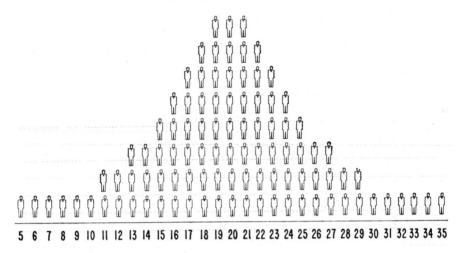

5 6 7 8 9 10 11 12 13 14 15 16 17 18 19 20 21 22 23 24 25 26 27 28 29 30 31 32 33 34 35

When large numbers of individuals are tested, the scores will distribute themselves in the pattern shown above if the test is of appropriate difficulty level for the group being tested and the individuals are selected at random rather than according to ability, experience, or other factors that would influence their test performance.

Drawing adapted from the Esso Scale for Performance Report. Reproduced with permission of Standard Oil Company of New Jersey.

On the other hand, if this individual has information, such as is shown in Figure 7-1, which enables him to determine the number of persons with the same score and those with scores above and below 20, he has a better understanding of how his score stands in relation to others. Thus, the significance or meaning of an individual's score is determined by the pattern of scores made by the larger group with which that person is compared.

In any one test an individual is required merely to respond to a limited number of items, or a sample. These items represent a carefully selected sample of problems that tap the total aspect of human behavior that the test is designed to measure. The proper sampling of behavior, whether it be verbal, manipulative, or some other type of behavior, is the responsibility of the test author. Where several tests are used, as in a battery, it is the responsibility of the test expert to select those tests that sample the many characteristics that are required for successful performance on the job.

The objective and standardized aspects of a test represent its most desirable features. Standardized procedures in administering, scoring, and interpreting results help to rule out subjectivity and, thus, permit comparisons to be made between individuals who may be tested in widely separated locations. In the large, multiplant company, as well as in governmental agencies including the military services, scores made by examinees throughout the world may be communicated and compared by means of a single digit.[19]

Types of Tests

Tests may be classified in different ways. Most tests are *group tests,* which allow for testing many individuals at one time. These are in contrast to *individual tests,* which require one examiner for each person being tested. Another classification is by the manner in which the individual responds to the test items. *Paper-and-pencil tests* require the subject to respond by writing or marking answers on a booklet or answer sheet, whereas *performance* or *instrumental tests* require him to manipulate objects or equipment. The Stromberg Dexterity Test shown in Figure 7-2 is an example of

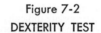

Figure 7-2

DEXTERITY TEST

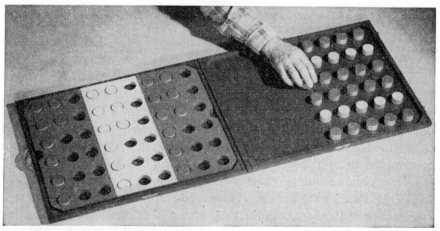

Reproduced with permission of The Psychological Corporation.

this latter type. In *oral tests* the examiner asks questions, and the subject responds orally to the question. Paper-and-pencil tests are the most commonly used since they can be administered easily to groups as well as

---

[19]The stanine scoring system, developed by the Aviation Psychology Program during World War II, uses a scale ranging from 1 to 9 with 5 as the median score. It provides for adequate differentiation between examinees and has the advantage of requiring only one column on the punch card commonly used in personnel record keeping or as input to a computer.

to individuals, and the expense of testing is considerably less than for the other types of tests.

In addition to these classifications, there is a more fundamental breakdown of tests according to the characteristics that are measured. Figure 7-3 provides one classification system which reflects the categories of tests as they are typically labeled by personnel workers. The figure also shows the degree of accuracy possible in measuring different human characteristics. Accuracy goes down as the characteristics become less tangible, and therefore harder to measure. Physical characteristics like weight and height, for instance, can be measured with the highest degree of accuracy and a personality trait like emotional stability, with the lowest.[20] It should be noted, however, that the statement with regard to accuracy refers to the tests as a group and should not be used in evaluating the accuracy of a particular test used in a testing program.

In a brief discussion of testing, it is only possible to list a few of the commercially available standardized tests that may be used in personnel functions. Figure 7-4 on page 181 is designed merely to familiarize the reader with some of those commonly used. The fact that a test is named should not be construed as an endorsement of the test for a specific purpose. Each test must be tried out in a specific situation to determine its value or validity.

Requirements of Tests

A large number of tests including those listed in Figure 7-4 have been standardized and are sold commercially to qualified users.[21] Others have been constructed for use by business and industrial firms, governmental agencies, military services, schools, and testing agencies and are not available for use because of their special nature or purpose. While test authors and publishers are responsible for the quality of product that they market,

---

[20]Herbert H. Meyer and Joseph M. Bertotti, "Tests: Their Use and Misuse in Selection," *Supervisory Management*, Vol. 2, No. 6 (May, 1957), pp. 20–27, as reprinted in Chruden and Sherman, *op. cit.*, pp. 101–108.

[21]Publishers of tests have rigid standards in order to insure that users will be qualified to administer, score, and interpret the test that they are using. The Psychological Corporation, for example, specifies three levels of tests in its catalog:

Level a — Those commonly used for employment purposes. Company purchase orders are filled promptly.

Level b — Available to firms having a staff member who has completed an advance-level course in testing in a university, or its equivalent in training under the direction of a qualified superior or consultant.

Level c — Available to firms only for use under the supervision of qualified psychologists, i.e. members of the American Psychological Association or persons with at least a Master's degree in psychology and appropriate training in the field of personnel testing. The qualified person may be either a staff member or a consultant.

Figure 7-3
ACCURACY OF VARIOUS TYPES OF TESTS

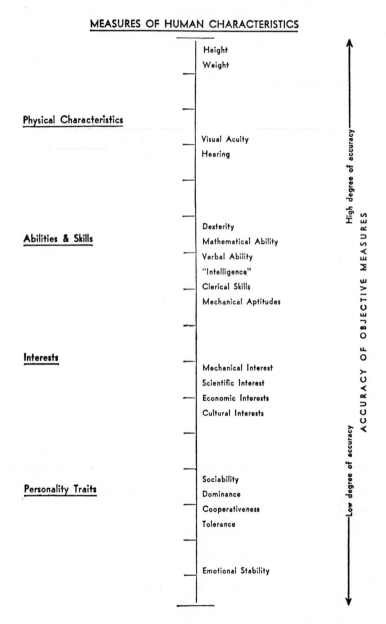

MEASURES OF HUMAN CHARACTERISTICS

Source: Herbert H. Meyer and Joseph M. Bertotti, "Tests: Their Use and Misuse in Selection," *Supervisory Management*, Vol. 2, No. 6 (May, 1957), pp. 20–27. Reproduced with permission.

Figure 7-4

SOME COMMERCIALLY AVAILABLE STANDARDIZED TESTS
COMMONLY USED IN PERSONNEL TESTING*

Name of Test	Examples of Jobs for Which Used
INTELLIGENCE	
Wonderlic Personnel Test	Clerical, factory, maintenance, and
Adaptability Test	sales jobs
Wesman Personnel Classification Test	
Concept Mastery Test	Managerial or executive job candidates
MULTI-APTITUDE BATTERIES	
General Aptitude Test Battery	United States Employment Service programs
Employee Aptitude Survey	All types of jobs from executive to unskilled
Flanagan Industrial Kit	Wide variety of jobs — battery includes 18 short tests covering 18 different job elements
DEXTERITY	
Stromberg Dexterity Test	Foundry moulders, punch press operators, assemblers
Purdue Pegboard	Radio tube mounters, production jobs
O'Connor Finger and Tweezer Dexterity Tests	Instrument assembly
CLERICAL SKILLS	
Minnesota Clerical Test	Office jobs
SRA Typing Skills	Typists
The Short Employment Tests	Office jobs
MECHANICAL ABILITY	
Test of Mechanical Comprehension	Variety of engineering and mechanical jobs
Revised Minnesota Paper Form Board Test	Mechanical shop work, drafting, design
PERSONALITY	
Gordon Personal Profile and Inventory	Office workers, computer programmers, others
Edwards Personal Preference Schedule	Salesmen, foremen
Guilford-Zimmerman Temperament Survey	Life insurance salesmen, office workers
INTEREST	
Strong Vocational Interest Blank	Administrative and sales jobs
Minnesota Vocational Interest Inventory	Various skilled jobs

*This list is merely to familiarize the reader with a few of the hundreds of available tests and some of the jobs for which they have been used. Since each test should be validated by the company using it, this list should not be construed as an endorsement of these tests for any specific purpose.

the fact that a test is published and commercially available does not mean that it can be used indiscriminately by a company. Publishers are ethically responsible to determine the qualifications of those in the company who will use the test as well as to make certain that the test itself meets the fundamental technical requirements for tests.

Reliability. One of the fundamental requirements of a test is *reliability;* that is, it must measure consistently whatever it measures. If a test is reliable, an individual's score remains approximately the same, or his standing in the group will show little change, the second time that he is tested. The use of an unreliable test is comparable to measuring a city lot with an elastic tape, which may give a different measurement each time. The reliability of a test is ordinarily discussed in the examiner's manual which accompanies the standardized test. While a test or other measuring device must be reliable in order to be of value, high reliability offers no assurance that the test is valid.

Validity. *Validity* refers to the degree to which a test predicts success in a particular activity. A test that is designed to predict success of applicants for the job of vacuum cleaner salesman would be considered highly valid if most persons scoring high on the test turned out to be top salesmen and if most of those who scored low turned out to be failures, as measured by their sales records, supervisors' ratings, and other possible criteria of success. Similarly, the validity of a test designed to measure potentiality for success in college would be measured by relating the scores on the test to grades earned or some other criterion of success.

While validity is ordinarily expressed by correlation coefficients, the nature of a valid and an invalid test is portrayed in Figure 7-5. It will

Figure 7-5
TESTS SCORES USED TO PREDICT CRITERION RATINGS

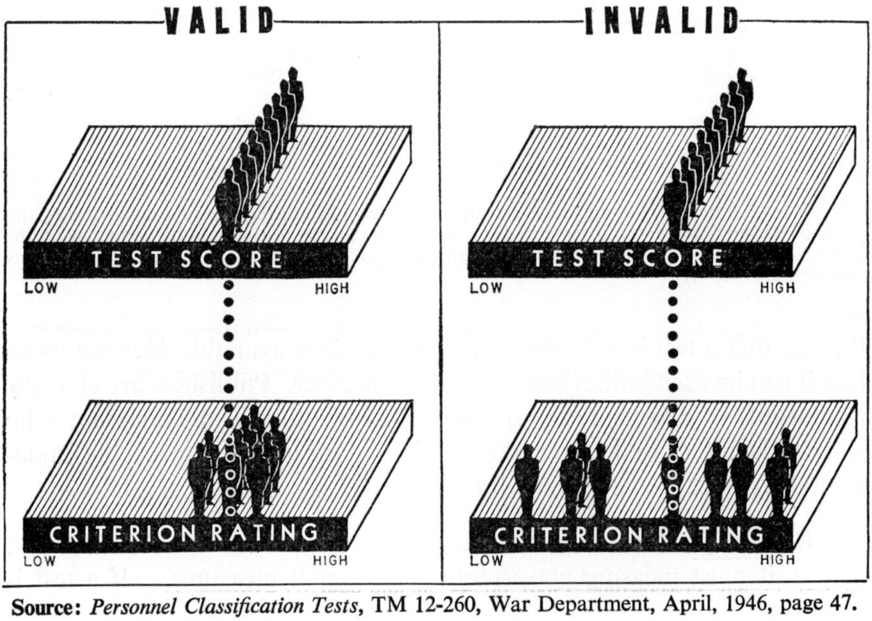

Source: *Personnel Classification Tests*, TM 12-260, War Department, April, 1946, page 47.

be noted that in the valid test men with the same test score achieve similar criterion scores (ratings in this case), whereas in the invalid test men with the same test score receive a variety of criterion scores or ratings.

✕ *Other requirements.* While reliability and validity represent the fundamental requirements for personnel tests, there are other requirements that apply especially to industrial situations where tests are used. These include:

1. *Cost.* There is little relation between the cost of tests and their quality, so that even a limited budget permits the use of well-constructed tests.
2. *Time.* Short tests are preferred, other things being equal. Too long a testing period bores the subject and makes him uncooperative.
3. *"Face" validity.* The cooperation of the subject is likely to be greater if the test appears to be related to the purpose for which the individual is being tested. However, "face" validity is not a substitute for empirical validity.
4. *Ease of administration and scoring.* Tests requiring the services of expert testers and scorers may not be feasible.[22]

Developing a Testing Program

Most companies of any size are confronted with the problem as to whether tests should be used in the personnel program. The problem cannot be easily solved by examining a few of the tests that have been listed, because any value to be derived from them is largely dependent upon the manner in which they are used. Like medicines on the pharmacist's shelves, they may be used to produce desirable results or may prove ineffective or even harmful if used without proper direction and control. Since there is no "package" of tests that will work for an organization without an analysis of its special needs, a testing program should not be undertaken without the assistance of a qualified person.[23] His special knowledge about tests is essential to getting the testing program started on a sound basis. In addition, his professional contacts enable him to obtain other expert opinion that adds to the value of his services. Once the testing program is established and operating smoothly, it may then be carried on by trained employees on the personnel staff with only occasional reference to the expert who set up the program. While the expert will be concerned with all of the major aspects of the program, his main focus will be on the experimental phase of the program where the critical issues are decided.

---

[22]Adapted from Lee J. Cronbach, *Essentials of Psychological Testing* (Second Edition; New York: Harper & Brothers, 1960), pp. 143–147.
[23]Harold E. Yuker and J. R. Block, "Common Sense About Psychological Tests," *Personnel*, Vol. 37, No. 3 (May-June, 1960), pp. 44–50, and Saul W. Gellerman, "A Hard Look at Testing," *Personnel*, Vol. 38, No. 3 (May-June, 1961), pp. 8–15.

The operational phase of the program will be more routine in nature although certainly just as important.

Experimental Phase

This phase of the testing program is where the important questions should be asked and satisfactory answers obtained before using tests in personnel management. Unless the pertinent questions are aired openly and definitive answers are obtained, testing is likely to be nothing more than a time-wasting formality. Answers to the following questions should be obtained before scores are used in making personnel decisions.

Are tests desirable? While a company endeavors to use all available techniques that will help its operations in any way, the fact that tests are used by other companies should not unduly influence it to adopt a testing program. Consideration should be given to such matters as the number of persons hired, the quality of personnel hired by existing methods, the size of the labor pool, the attitudes of labor as well as management toward tests, and any other related factors that are likely to enter the picture at the time that tests are considered.

Are criteria of job success defined? Since the purpose of tests is to predict success, it is essential that criteria of job success be clearly defined. This is the responsibility of management, and it might well be expected that managers would have clear definitions of what constitutes successful performance and what constitutes mediocre or poor performance. At this point in planning a testing program, however, it frequently occurs that management is not sure just what employees in a particular job are supposed to accomplish. Through discussion and investigation of job performance, usually it is possible to arrive at some definition of job success. Without it, there is nothing to predict, and it follows that tests cannot be used to predict something that does not exist. Some of the factors that may be used singly or combined as criteria of job success are production (quantity or quality), job tenure, accidents, commissions, and performance ratings. For each job for which tests are to be used, there should be definitely established standards based on criteria that are reliable (consistent), acceptable to line personnel, relevant to the job, and as objective as possible.

What tests should be used? The first step in attempting to answer this question is to turn to the job description and job specification. What, specifically, is required of persons in this job? Are they required to work rapidly with numbers, read drawings accurately, take shorthand, assemble electronic devices with precision? A study of what is required of the individual, including careful observation of several persons holding that job, will give clues as to the basic aptitudes and abilities that are essential for successful job performance. On the basis of his analysis, the expert will probably select several possible tests from commercially available standardized tests or, in some cases, he may construct tests.

Are the tests valid? Validity is not a characteristic of a test in general but, rather, refers to its value in predicting success of persons in a specific situation. The same test may be highly valid in selecting supervisory personnel for one company and may be practically worthless in another company. While there are other methods for determining the validity of a particular test or group of tests, a commonly used method is to try out the tests on present employees.[24] The focus in such a procedure is on "testing the test," and this fact must be communicated clearly to employees; otherwise, they may wonder what is going to happen to them. Enlisting their cooperation is, thus, an essential part of the tryout procedure. In addition, prior to the administration of tests, the quality of the performance of these experienced employees must be determined and expressed in terms of a criterion score, including supervisory ratings, production figures, or other management-determined criteria.

With several test scores and a criterion score available for each individual used in the tryout group, it is then possible to determine the relationship between test scores and the criterion score, as well as the relationship of tests to each other. Those tests which have little or no validity or that overlap too much with other tests are rejected. They are, in effect, the tests that are not sufficiently valid for the purpose. Those tests that are found to predict the criterion reasonably well are retained for use in testing job applicants and are combined into a test battery. A typical battery may include an intelligence test, one or two aptitude tests, a personality and/or interest test, and possibly some dexterity tests. Ordinarily the scores obtained on the tests are weighted according to the degree of their validity, and decisions are made on the basis of one of the approaches described on pages 161–162 in the preceding chapter. Prior to using the results operationally, however, it is desirable to repeat the

[24]This is commonly called the "present employee" method of validation. A better approach involves the method of predictive validity in which individuals are tested at the time of making application and criterion scores are obtained later. This latter approach, however, requires waiting for criterion data. In using these approaches supervisors must not be aware of the test scores of those persons whose performance they will evaluate. Otherwise they may judge performance with the individual's test scores in mind. When this occurs, it results in *criterion contamination*.

validation procedure with a group different from the one on which the tests were first validated.   This procedure, commonly referred to as *cross validation*, is especially important where the sample of cases of small and /or biographical data (application form) items are used as part of the selection data and handled like test data as described on pages 142–148 in Chapter 6.

> *Synthetic validity — a newer approach.*   A recent departure from the traditional validation design described above is known as *synthetic validity*. It involves inferring the validity of a battery of tests from predetermined validities of individual tests in the battery for specific components or elements of the total job.   An important difference between synthetic validity and the traditional validation approaches is the attempt to predict success on parts of the job instead of for the total job. The idea of synthetic validity was first used in small businesses; but trends toward job enlargement, technical employment, and service occupations and away from large numbers of workers performing identical functions make the need for synthetic validity greater.[25]   Before it can be perfected, however, job analyses will have to be refined and job elements detailed more accurately and uniformly. Some of the aptitude batteries developed for industrial use and listed in Figure 7-4 have been designed with job elements in mind. The aptitude tests developed by Flanagan represent pioneering efforts in this direction.

Operational Phase

Once the tests have gone through the experimental phase and a battery with a known validity has been assembled, it is then ready to be administered to job applicants. Because of the important use to be made of the scores, and because the operational use of the test must conform to the same rigid standards as the experimental phase, it should not be assumed that less diligence and caution are needed at this point in the program.

Administration.   Any factors that might influence the examinee's performance on the tests must be given careful consideration. The physical conditions of the test room, such as lighting, ventilation, and freedom from noise, should be carefully checked.   The examiner should insure that examinees are properly motivated, understand the instructions, and are doing their best. Those who are fearful of the testing procedure should be reassured. The examiner should also prepare himself by making certain that he understands the procedure for administration, has all of the

---

[25]Guion, *Personnel Testing, op. cit.*, pp. 169–174.

necessary materials available, and has arranged matters so that he will not be interrupted during the testing session.

Scoring. Most of the tests used in business and industry can be scored easily by means of a key or template, which is laid over the answer sheet and against which the answers are checked by trained clerks. In larger companies where many applicants and employees are tested, an IBM electric test scoring machine is valuable; or the services of electronic data processing companies may be used where there is a large volume of answer sheets and/or complex analyses to be made.

Interpretation of scores. The basic principle underlying all psychological testing is that individuals differ in degree with respect to their abilities, interests, personalities, aptitudes, and achievements. To the extent that these characteristics can be defined and measured, it is possible to compare individuals. The number of answers that agree with the scoring key is commonly referred to as the *raw score.* For example, if a test has 100 items and the individual answers 65 of these items correctly, his raw score is 65. But what does it mean? Without some basis for comparison, it is impossible to attach any meaning to the score, for it tells nothing about the individual's standing in relation to others who have taken the test. If the average (mean) score for a group of persons tested with this test is 60, however, it is then known that the individual scored slightly above average on the test. Ordinarily it is desirable to state scores in more specific terms in order that careful evaluations may be made.

When large numbers of individuals have been tested, the distribution of raw scores provides the basis for converting the raw scores into percentile equivalents as shown in Figure 7-6. It will be noted from this figure that a person scoring at the 50th percentile has exceeded the scores of half of those tested. Similarly, a person scoring at the 84th percentile on a given test has 84 percent of the individuals scoring below him.[26]

Establishing cut-offs. While the conversion of raw scores to percentile scores introduces a basis for comparing individuals who were tested, it does not indicate the point in the distribution above which a person should be carefully considered and below which he should probably be rejected. The score that an applicant must achieve before he is selected is referred to

---

[26]While percentile scores are easily computed and readily understood, they are somewhat limited in their application in testing for personnel selection purposes. Standard scores which are computed on the basis of the mean and the standard deviation of the distribution are normally used. An explanation of these scores may be found in most of the books on testing listed at the end of this chapter.

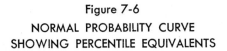

Figure 7-6

NORMAL PROBABILITY CURVE
SHOWING PERCENTILE EQUIVALENTS

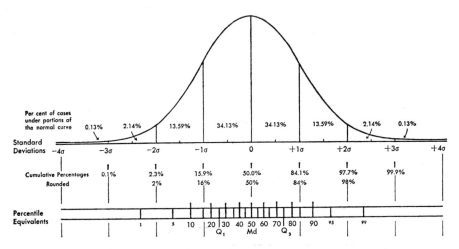

Source: Adapted from *Test Service Bulletin* No. 48, The Psychological Corporation, January, 1955, page 6. Reproduced with permission.

as the *cut-off* or *critical score.* This score is seldom constant since the number of applicants in relation to the number of job vacancies varies. Depending upon the labor supply, it may be necessary to lower or raise the critical score.

The effects of raising and lowering the critical score are illustrated in Figure 7-7. Each dot in the center of the figure represents the relationship between the test score and the criterion of success for one individual. In this instance the test has a fairly high validity as represented by the elliptical pattern of the dots. It will be noted that the individuals scoring high on the test are concentrated in the satisfactory category on job success, whereas the low scoring individuals are concentrated in the unsatisfactory category on job success. If the cut-off score is set as A, only the men represented by areas 1 and 2 will be accepted, and nearly all of these will be successful. If more men are needed, the critical score may be lowered to point B. Lowering the cut-off score in each case means that a larger number of potential failures will be accepted. Even when the cut-off score is lowered to C, the total number of satisfactory men selected (areas 1, 3, and 5) is considerably in excess of the total number selected who are unsatisfactory (areas 2, 4, and 6). This indicates that even when it is necessary to lower

Figure 7-7

A SCATTERPLOT SHOWING THE RELATIONSHIP BETWEEN TEST SCORES AND
THE CRITERION OF SUCCESS FOR A LARGE NUMBER OF INDIVIDUALS

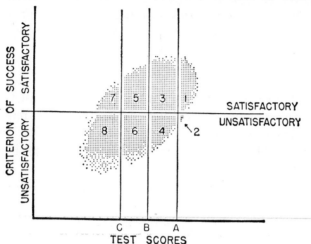

Source: *Personnel Classification Tests, op. cit.*, page 48.

the cut-off score to obtain the number of persons needed, the use of tests will result in the rejection of those applicants most likely to fail. In other words, *the test serves to maximize the selection of probable successes and to minimize the selection of probable failures.*

Using other norms. Up to this point the discussion has focused on the use of test scores and job performance of present employees as a basis for establishing the cut-off score for future job applicants. While this is the more desirable procedure, it is often necessary that another basis be used in interpreting test results because the company has not acquired enough data to warrant making generalizations. In such instances it is customary to use the norms provided by the test author. *Norms* are statistics that describe the test performance of specified groups assumed to be representative of a larger population. The manual for a typical standardized test provides norms based upon the prior administration of the test to a large number of persons in specified categories.

A survey by the Bureau of National Affairs of personnel executives of a large number of companies revealed that 42 percent of the companies used publisher's test norms, 38 percent said they used local (company) norms, and the remaining reported that they used both.[27] Where publisher's

[27]*Labor Policy & Practice — Personnel Management* (Washington, D.C.: Bureau of National Affairs, 1963), 201, 225.

test norms are used, the examinee's scores may be arranged on a *profile* that contains the names of the tests administered, the norms used as a basis of comparison, and the individual's raw score and converted scores on each test. Where company norms are utilized, the procedure for establishing cut-off scores discussed above, or some modification of it, will be used.

Evaluation of a Testing Program

✗ The testing program, as much as any other aspect of the personnel program, requires continuous evaluation. The personnel requirements of an organization and the sources of personnel from which selections are made are constantly changing. As a result, a test or test battery that is performing effectively at one time may not be as effective a few months later. A continuous check of the validity of the tests is essential if the testing program is going to serve its purpose.

In evaluating the success of a testing program, it is essential to think in terms of averages rather than specific cases. It is easy to point to the exceptional case and say, "There's a man who scored at the top on our test battery, but look at his poor job performance." It is just as true in testing as in other areas that exceptions occur, but they do not necessarily prove anything. The real value of a testing program lies in such benefits as the increase in average production, decrease in average absenteeism and turnover, decrease in average number of accidents, and other criteria that can be applied to a number of persons.

While it is sometimes difficult to show outstanding results from a testing program, even minor changes in such benefits can represent a sizable savings to the company. By maintaining adequate records on personnel who are hired, it is possible to calculate the savings resulting from testing and other personnel functions. Information concerning these savings should be reported to top management as well as to line personnel who are sometimes critical of the value of personnel services.

Résumé

While there are some businessmen who reject tests in their entirety, most of them recognize that tests can be valuable aids in personnel management if properly used. Before using tests operationally, it is essential that the necessary experimentation be carried out and that a definite relationship be established between test scores and criteria of job success. In order to establish this relationship, managers must first decide what constitutes acceptable performance on the job. These criteria may then be used in test validation, and they may be communicated to employees in order to give them a clear picture of what is expected of them.

The major contributions of tests lie in their objectivity. While tests have at times been judged as discriminatory against certain groups, they still represent the most objective method for assessing the important differences between individuals. This objectivity, along with the other standardized aspects of testing, is essential to effective personnel management.

DISCUSSION QUESTIONS AND PROBLEMS

1. It was mentioned in this chapter that disadvantaged persons often obtain low scores on employment tests.
   a. What is meant by a disadvantaged person?
   b. What causes many of them to obtain low scores on tests?
   c. Are there any characteristics of a paper-and-pencil test that may discriminate unfairly against a disadvantaged person?
   d. What can be done to overcome this problem immediately? in the future?
2. What do you see as some of the problems in selecting specific criteria (production, sales, errors, etc.) by which to evaluate job performance? Does this mean that little or no attention should be given to criteria in the management of personnel?
3. Recall some of the situations in which you were a member of a group being administered psychological tests. What do you recall about the administrators and their skill in giving the tests? What were your own feelings during the test period? How can you utilize these experiences if you are called upon to administer tests?
4. An applicant who is rejected because of his personality test scores wants to know why he did not get the job. Should he be told the real reason?
5. The vice-president of the company of which you are personnel manager calls you into his office and asks you to explain why a person who scored high on the test battery turned out to be a failure in the company after six months on the job. What would you tell him?
6. An industrial psychologist was offered an assignment to construct an attitude test that would serve to eliminate "union-minded" job applicants from serious consideration for employment.
   a. If you were the psychologist, would you accept the assignment?
   b. If you were the personnel manager of a company and the president suggested that such an assignment be offered to an industrial psychologist, what action would you take? Why?
   c. If such a test were used, might it be construed by the courts as violating federal legislation?
7. A battery of tests was administered to a group of employees who had been told that the tests were for experimental purposes only and that their scores would not be recorded on their personnel records. At a later date, after the tests had been proved to be valid, the personnel manager ordered that the

scores be entered on the employees' records. What is your opinion of the personnel manager's decision?

8. As a well-known and highly respected accountant, you are asked by the Civil Service Commission of your state to serve as a subject matter specialist in developing a test to be used in qualifying persons for accounting positions with state agencies. What contributions would you be able to make?

CASE 7-1

THE ANNUAL INVENTORY

The warehouse of a government agency that stocked several thousand different items had an annual problem of completing an inventory of the stock on hand. Regulations required that a physical count be made of each item because of the unusually high value of the goods. It was customary for the warehouse manager to obtain sufficient personnel on a loan basis from other departments in the agency for three or four days to complete the inventory. It was the practice of the lending departments to send personnel whose absence would least affect their respective operations. Therefore, the personnel who conducted the inventory were not of the highest caliber for the job, and the rate of errors was usually high.

As a result of an official visit of the chief inspector of the head office of the agency, permission was obtained to conduct the inventory on an overtime basis, thus eliminating any interference with the normal business operations. Because of the overtime wages, about three times as many employees as were actually required to complete the job made applications for this special assignment. One year's experience of hiring on a first-come-first-hired basis proved unsatisfactory. The personnel manager decided that only those who were particularly suited for this assignment should be selected and that this could be determined through the use of a test. He also believed that more time should be given to orienting and training the individuals who were selected.

An analysis of the inventory job revealed that the individuals performing this work should be proficient in performing simple arithmetic computations — addition, subtraction, multiplication — and in comparing stock numbers on the bins and cartons. Two tests were constructed: one included 25 arithmetic problems of the type performed on the inventory job; the other contained 100 problems with pairs of numbers and pairs of names to be matched. The matching problems were similar to those in standardized clerical aptitude tests. Each part of the test had a 6-minute time limit. Since the tests required only 40 minutes to administer (including directions) and about 50 persons could be tested at one time, it was considered an economical approach to the selection problem.

When the time for the next annual inventory arrived, an announcement was made about the availability of the inventory jobs and the fact that selection tests would be used. The usual number of individuals did not apply. Only about 100 — the number needed to do the job — made application. The tests were given, nevertheless, and everyone who applied was hired.

During the training session, the arithmetic items on the selection test were reviewed and practice problems in arithmetic were given to the trainees, and their solutions were checked for accuracy. The counting procedures to be followed, the method for recording numbers on the inventory cards, the safe use of ladders, and other related matters were also explained to the inventory crew.

At the close of the inventory, a spot check revealed that the percentage of errors was reduced considerably over previous years. A check of the number of items inventoried by each individual also revealed that those who scored in the upper 25 percent on the clerical aptitude test accomplished significantly more work during the inventory than those scoring in the lower 25 percent on the same test. It was decided that both tests were worthwhile and would be used again.

a. How do you account for the drop in the number of applicants the year the test was used for selecting inventory personnel?

b. Would practice on the arithmetic items be likely to improve the ability of the personnel in arithmetic? Why?

c. If practice had been given on the problems that involved the checking of pairs of names and numbers that were alike, would the personnel be expected to improve in this type of problem? Why?

d. Is the clerical aptitude test valid? Why?

e. Do both tests have "face" validity?

SUGGESTED READINGS

Albright, Lewis E., J. R. Glennon, and Wallace J. Smith. *The Use of Psychological Tests in Industry.* Cleveland: Howard Allen, Inc., 1963.

Anastasi, Anne. *Psychological Testing,* Second Edition. New York: The Macmillan Company, 1961.

Buros, O. K. *Sixth Mental Measurements Yearbook.* Highland Park, New Jersey: The Gryphon Press, 1965.

——————. *Tests in Print.* Highland Park, New Jersey: The Gryphon Press, 1961.

Chruden, Herbert J., and Arthur W. Sherman, Jr., *Readings in Personnel Management,* Second Edition. Cincinnati: South-Western Publishing Company, Inc., 1966. Chapter 2.

Cronbach, Lee J. *Essentials of Psychological Testing,* Second Edition. New York: Harper & Brothers, 1960.

Ghiselli, Edwin E. *The Validity of Occupational Aptitude Tests.* New York: John Wiley & Sons, Inc., 1966.

Guion, Robert M. *Personnel Testing.* New York: McGraw-Hill Book Company, 1965.

Harrell, Thomas W. *Industrial Psychology,* Revised Edition. New York: Holt, Rinehart and Winston, Inc., 1958. Chapters 5–6.

Lawshe, C. H., and Michael J. Balma. *Principles of Personnel Testing*, Second Edition. New York: McGraw-Hill Book Company, 1966.

Miller, Robert B. *Tests and the Selection Process*. Chicago: Science Research Associates, 1966.

Stone, C. Harold, and William E. Kendall. *Effective Personnel Selection Procedures*. Englewood Cliffs, New Jersey: Prentice-Hall, Inc., 1956. Chapters 9–13.

Tiffin, Joseph, and Ernest J. McCormick, *Industrial Psychology*, Fifth Edition. Englewood Cliffs, New Jersey: Prentice-Hall, Inc., 1965. Chapters 2, 5, 6, 7, and 8.

Wood, Dorothy Adkins. *Test Construction*. Columbus, Ohio: Charles E. Merrill Books, Inc., 1960.

f

8

Employee Development

The functions of recruiting and selecting employees represent only the initial stages in the building of an efficient and stable work force. It should be recognized that after being selected, employees require continuous development if their potential is to be utilized effectively. The development of employees, in fact, should be viewed as beginning with the orientation and continuing throughout their employment with the organization.

Employee development programs typically include a wide variety of activities that are concerned with informing employees of company policies and procedures, training them in job skills, motivating and evaluating performance, and providing counseling as it is needed. The primary purpose of these activities is to develop employees who will contribute more effectively to the goals of the organization and who will gain a greater sense of satisfaction and adjustment from their work. Development, therefore, is a process that ranges from training employees in job skills to assisting them in broader areas of personal and social adjustment in the interests of the individual as well as of the organization.

Because of the importance of employee development to the total personnel program, several of the chapters that follow will be devoted to an examination of the various functions that are established for that purpose. Among these other types of developmental activities are management development (Chapter 9), performance evaluation (Chapter 10), and supervisory development (Chapter 14). While the discussion of the principles of learning and the more general comments about training programs will be relevant to these other types of developmental activities, the emphasis in this chapter will be on the basic functions of providing information that employees require in order to perform their jobs effectively and on training them in job skills.

The major topics to be discussed in this chapter are:

- Orientation.
- Training programs.
- Psychology of learning.
- Evaluation of training effectiveness.

Orientation

The orientation of the new employee should give him an understanding of the importance of his job, the company's personnel policies and procedures as they concern him, as well as a broad picture of the role of the company in the business world and in the local community. While it is likely that he already has knowledge and opinions about the company and has some awareness of the importance of his job, it is essential that the new employee be furnished information that will enable him to find his place in the organization.

Although the type of information that he will need will vary with the job, it is customary to provide information about those matters that are of immediate concern to the new employee, such as working hours, pay, and parking facilities. The company, at this point, is also concerned that the new employee has a clear understanding of safety rules, security requirements in defense projects, and any other important matters of which he must be advised immediately so as to minimize the possibility of errors and subsequent embarrassment or tragedy. Later, attention may be devoted to informing the employee about those areas that are less urgent for him to understand and/or that require more time for presentation and comprehension.

Since a company must be dynamic in order to meet the ever-changing conditions affecting its operations, the organizational policies and procedures and the structure and content of jobs must change with it. Unless the employees are kept up to date on these changes, they may find themselves unaware of those aspects of the business of which the new employees are currently being advised. While the discussion that follows focuses primarily upon the needs of the new employee and how these may be met through an initial orientation program, the fact that all employees need to be kept oriented to conditions that are ever changing should not be overlooked. No employee likes to be advised about the new policies in his department by the man on the street who learned about them before he did.

A Cooperative Endeavor

The orientation program cannot be carried on effectively by either the personnel staff or the supervisors acting independently. For a well-integrated program that is carried out enthusiastically, cooperation between line and staff is essential. Ordinarily, there is no problem about the objectives of orientation which are: to provide the employee with facts about the company and his job, to build confidence in the employee, and to help him feel that he "belongs" in the company and in his work group. While the methods used to achieve these objectives may vary, it is essential that there be careful planning in order that new employees do not have experiences like that of the trainman in Figure 8-1.

Figure 8-1

"I'm new with the road. Where do I find track 14?"

Source: *Wall Street Journal:* May 17, 1962. Reproduced with permission.

The personnel department is ordinarily responsible for coordinating orientation activities in the company and for providing information concerning conditions of employment, pay and benefits, and other areas that are not directly under the supervisor's direction. It also is generally responsible for organizing and conducting orientation classes and for preparing handbooks, films, and similar materials. In many companies the employee may be scheduled for 30- or 60-day follow-up interviews with the personnel department as well as with his supervisor. This not only gives the personnel staff an opportunity to help in assisting the new employee with any problems but also enables them to obtain an appraisal of the effectiveness of the orientation program from the standpoint of the employee.

The supervisor has the most important role in the orientation program. The new employee is primarily concerned with his "boss" and will be likely to give closest attention to what he says and does. It is essential, therefore, that the supervisor allow sufficient time in order that he may discuss important aspects of the job on the employee's first day at work as well as establish a cordial relationship that will facilitate communication and learning. Prior to introducing the new person to the other members of the work group, it is also desirable for the supervisor to inform members of the group that a new employee is being added. Thus, if members of the work group have any questions about personnel changes, answers may be provided and any possible misunderstandings relating to their own job status or security may be resolved before the new employee arrives on the scene. Present employees may then be able to adjust more readily to the newcomer and in turn facilitate his adjustment to the job and the work group. Introduction of minority groups into a company or the merger of companies, for example, may make it desirable to discuss proposed changes with present employees and to make assignments of the new employees on a basis that will facilitate acceptance of the change by present employees.

Problems in Orientation

Those who plan orientation programs frequently expect the new employee to assimilate readily all types of detailed and assorted facts about the company, such as work rules, safety practices, executive biographies, and any other areas believed to be important. While the new employee should know these things eventually, it should be recognized that more learning may be effected if some things are covered over a period of time and in a series of meetings. To avoid overlooking items that are important to employees, many companies devise check lists for use by those responsible for conducting some phase of orientation. A check list developed by the General Electric Company (Figure 8-2) for use by supervisors insures that there will be no confusion as to whether or not a supervisor is expected to cover a particular item.

Figure 8-2

SUPERVISOR'S CHECK LIST

CHECK LIST FOR HELPING THE NEW EMPLOYEE GET STARTED

When Employee First Reports:

[ ] Welcome to Company and job.

[ ] Show locker or coat rack and wash room.

[ ] Acquaint employee with cafeteria and other lunch facilities.

[ ] Review security regulations including badge system.

[ ] Show work place.

[ ] Review rate, hours, use of time card.

[ ] Briefly describe group's work.

[ ] Introduce to fellow workers.

[ ] Start employee on job, remembering the four steps of instruction.

    1. Prepare the worker.
    2. Present the operation.
    3. Try out his performance.
    4. Follow up.

[ ] Briefly cover main safety rules and use of safety equipment.

[ ] Remind employee to come to you for information and assistance.

Later During First Day:

[ ] Review pay procedure.

[ ] Discuss parking, car-pools.

[ ] Explain dispensary facilities.

[ ] Review safety rules.

[ ] Briefly tell about work of department and how employee's job ties in.

[ ] Shortly before quitting time, check with employee on progress and any questions.

During First Two Weeks:

[ ] Review Benefit Plans*
    Insurance and M. B. A.
    Stock Bonus
    Pension
    Relief and Loan
    Suggestion System

[ ] Review items in "Your Guide to the River Works."

[ ] Check on safety habits.

[ ] Continue to follow up on progress and performance.

*Plans for which employee signed applications in Employment Office are underlined.

Source: General Electric booklet, "Orientating the New Employee." Reproduced with permission.

In developing and using check lists of this type, the personnel department should not fail to recognize the needs that special groups or individuals may have. A physically handicapped person, for example, may need additional information and/or facilities. Similarly, a new employee who is being sent to a foreign country will need to have information in addition to that given to those individuals working in the United States. In some instances it is not only a matter of providing special orientation for the new employee. Supervisors and established employees may also need to be oriented for certain situations. It is apparent, therefore, that the orientation program requires most effective use of communication techniques and media to insure the development of positive feelings as well as transmission of pertinent information.

Training Programs

The need to orient employees and to provide job information and training has been well recognized by managers and supervisors who are alert to the role that people play in the attainment of the organization's objectives. Through training activities old talents may be updated and new ones developed. Even if there has been no formal training program or training department, managerial personnel usually are aware of the important role of effective training even if they have not always acted accordingly. The impact of automation, however, has served to increase the importance of training. Three of automation's effects which have direct implications for industrial training are: (1) that some jobs will be enlarged, thereby requiring additional skills and knowledge; (2) that others will require a narrower range of skills; and (3) that many jobs will be replaced entirely by jobs newly created.[1] These changes in jobs resulting from automation will require a high degree of interaction and cooperation between line and staff personnel if employees are to be retained by the company and if they are to perform effectively.

In the larger company the personnel department may provide managers and supervisors with considerable assistance in conducting training activities, including the organization of formal training classes, the selection and training of instructors, the procurement of training equipment and other aids, and the establishment of liaison with educational institutions and government agencies. Frequently, in the larger company, these activities are handled by a separate training division within the personnel department. In the smaller company, however, most of the training tasks fall upon the managers and supervisors of the departments where employees work. In the latter situation, however, minimal assistance may be given by the personnel department, if one exists.

While they must never lose sight of the fact that they are performing a staff function, members of the training division may find it necessary to display considerable initiative in their attempts to strengthen the training program. They must, however, exercise tact in the attempt to accomplish their objectives, since training is a responsibility of each manager and supervisor in the organization. Managerial and supervisory personnel tend to be concerned primarily with meeting production standards, so they sometimes fail to recognize the need for and the benefits of training. It is, thus, the responsibility of the training staff to make certain that the needs

---

[1]William McGehee and Paul W. Thayer, *Training in Business and Industry* (New York: John Wiley & Sons, Inc., 1961), pp. 10–11.

for training are recognized and that the training function is given proper attention.

Determining Training Needs

The training division is responsible for making supervisors cognizant of the requirements for training and for working with them in planning and developing courses and other types of instruction. Certain evidence may reveal the need for training employees. If production records indicate, for example, that workers are not achieving production standards, additional training may be required. Similarly, an excessive number of rejects or a waste of material may be caused by inadequate training. An increase in the number of accidents is also an indication that employees need refresher training in the use of safety devices and in safe working procedures.

In order for training to be effective it must be accompanied by careful and continuous research. The determination of training needs, in fact, requires a careful and systematic investigation, something that about one company in ten does, according to one study.[2] As a result, many training efforts are ineffective and a waste of money. In order to overcome this failure to approach training needs more systematically, McGehee and Thayer suggest a threefold approach to thinking about the training requirements of an organization or a component of an organization. It consists of the following:

1. Organizational analysis — determining where within the organization training emphasis can and should be placed.
2. Operations analysis — determining what should be the content of training in terms of what an employee must do to perform a task, job, or assignment in an effective way.
3. Man analysis — determining what skills, knowledge, or attitudes an individual employee must develop if he is to perform the tasks which constitute his job in the organization.[3]

Organizational analysis places an emphasis upon the study of the entire organization, its objectives and resources, and how the resources are related to the organizational objectives. Indexes that may be used in organizational analysis include labor costs (direct and indirect), quality of goods or services, and employee morale. Operations analysis focuses on the task or job regardless of the employee performing that job. Indexes

---

[2]W. R. Mahler and W. H. Monroe, *How Industry Determines the Need for and Effectiveness of Training* (New York: The Psychological Corporation, 1952).

[3]McGehee and Thayer, *op. cit.,* p. 25.

that may be used here include data obtained from observing employees at work, much as is done in making a job analysis. Man analysis focuses on the individual in his present position and in possible future positions and may include units produced, cost of producing units, absenteeism, tardiness, and accidents.

While training represents a positive approach to the improvement of performance, it cannot provide the solution to all such problems. For example, if production is dropping because workers are disgruntled and resentful over working conditions, providing additional training for them will not be likely to increase production. It may, in fact, cause further resentment among employees because management may appear to them to be indifferent to the basis for their original feelings. The cause of each personnel problem, therefore, must be accurately determined and the most appropriate action taken.

In clarifying the objectives of training and in planning methods and procedures for attaining the desired outcomes, the training division should be careful when examining the programs of other companies. A "package program" taken over from another company may appear attractive in that its use does not seem to require any additional preparation. Such a program, however, is seldom adequate in its original form since it was designed to meet the needs of a different company. These needs may not be the same as those of the company that attempts to use the "package program." It should not be inferred, however, that a program prepared by a professional organization or by one company cannot be adapted to fit the needs of another company if the needs of both companies are similar.

Job Training and Retraining

One of the major types of training is commonly referred to as job training. The primary purpose of job training at the beginning of an individual's employment is to bring his knowledge and skills up to a satisfactory level. As the individual continues on the job, training may be used to provide him with additional information and to give him opportunities to acquire new skills. As a result of the training he may then be more effective in his present job and may qualify for jobs at a higher level.

The invention and installation of new equipment, much of which is highly automated, have resulted in many employees having skills that are no longer required by their employer or by any other potential employer. In order for these occupationally dislocated persons to remain on the payroll or to obtain employment elsewhere, it is necessary for them to learn new skills through some type of retraining. While many companies have their own programs for retraining employees whose jobs are changed by increased automation, the problem is of such a scope that federal and state legislation has been required to provide the funds needed to retrain occupationally dislocated persons.

ρ The Manpower Development and Training Act (MDTA) of 1962 authorized a national program of occupational training and basic manpower research and experimentation — all directed toward helping the American worker to develop his skills and potentials to the fullest and to find his place as a contributor to the economy. The major programs established under the provisions of the MDTA of 1962, as amended, are the Institutional Training Program and the On-the-Job Training Program.

In 1965, 145,000 trainees were enrolled in institutional training and 35,000 in on-the-job training. The majority of trainees enrolled in the institutional program received training in public and private vocational education or technical schools and more recently in Manpower Training Centers being established in the larger cities. Although classroom work is included, the emphasis is on shop work. In the on-the-job training program, an enrollee is actually hired and taught work skills while he is contributing to his employer's production. While the program focuses on providing the underemployed with the opportunity to upgrade their skills and to equip the unemployed with new skills required by a changing job market, the provisions of the act providing for training in basic education also helps workers to qualify for and benefit from occupational training.[4] Special efforts have been made in the programs to assist such disadvantaged groups as minority races, handicapped workers, public assistance recipients, and unemployment insurance claimants.

Other newer legislation related to the purposes and objectives of the MDTA that provides additional resources and avenues for manpower development activity is the Economic Opportunity Act of 1964. Federal programs under this act provide for training experiences to youth through the Job Corps and Neighborhood Youth Corps that serve over 500,000 youth with emphasis on basic schooling and reduction in the number of school dropouts.[5] Programs such as these indicate the present role of the federal government in manpower planning and the emphasis that is given to training activities.

---

[4] United States Department of Labor, Office of Manpower, Automation and Training, *Report of the Secretary of Labor on Manpower Research and Training Under the Manpower Development and Training Act of 1962* (Washington, D.C.: U.S. Government Printing Office, 1966).

[5] *Manpower Report of the President* (Washington, D.C.: U.S. Government Printing Office, 1966).

When Congress enacted the MDTA of 1962, it was authorizing a type of government program which had been in effect in most Western European countries throughout the postwar period and viewed as a permanent instrument of manpower policy. Such a program is thus considered to be as necessary in a period of full employment as in a period of unemployment.[6] The fact that the MDTA, EOA, and other programs contribute to industry's requirements for personnel does not absolve personnel departments from their responsibility for manpower planning. In fact, Cassell warns that the company that fails to emphasize the importance of manpower planning — including training and development of employees — may not in the future be able to compete effectively in the markets.[7]

While many companies have not yet organized formalized retraining programs, there are some who have done so and have some results to report. One study made at IBM was designed to determine the feasibility of retraining employees who were in excess of needs or whose skills had become technologically obsolete. One aspect of the study concerned itself with employee acceptance of the opportunity for retraining — an important factor in the learning situation. McNamara reports that employee acceptance of the opportunity seemed to be influenced by their interest in the work, their confidence in their ability to succeed, and the climate created by management. He also found that the number of employees that were not considered suitable for any type of retraining was very small provided the training time, when necessary, was increased with a resulting increase in cost per trained employee.[8] In this and similar training and retraining situations, management should recognize the value to be derived from an optimal level of motivation and sufficient time in which to learn new information and skills. It would appear that job training and retraining are taking on a new importance that will require the cooperative efforts of management, labor, and government as well as the best thinking and research of educators, psychologists, and specialists in other related areas.

Training Methods

Several different methods by which the objectives of the training program may be met are available. In the larger company all of the methods to be described will probably be used at one time or another.

---

[6]Margaret S. Gordon, *Retraining Programs — At Home and Abroad* (Berkeley, California: Institute of Industrial Relations, 1965).

[7]Frank H. Cassell, "Corporate Manpower Planning," *Stanford Graduate School of Business Bulletin* (Summer, 1965).

[8]Walter J. McNamara, "Retraining of Industrial Personnel," *Personnel Psychology*, Vol. 16, No. 3 (Autumn, 1963), pp. 233–247.

The use of a particular method, however, depends upon the objectives of the particular training course, the abilities and potentialities of the trainer and of the individuals to be trained, the probable number of trainees, the job level, and such factors as the time and expense involved. The training staff should assist line and staff personnel responsible for training in the selection of methods that have proven most effective in meeting the particular objectives of the training program. Too often a training method is chosen on the basis of tradition, habit, novelty, or other irrelevant factors rather than on its effectiveness in achieving the desired objectives.

On-the-job training. The most commonly used method in the training of employees is on-the-job training. It is conducted by the supervisor or by a senior employee who is responsible for instructing employees. It has the advantage of providing firsthand experience under normal working conditions. There is also a potential disadvantage in this method, however, if the supervisor emphasizes production rather than learning to perform the job in the safest and most efficient manner. Still, by allowing sufficient time for job training and by correcting the trainee's mistakes as they occur, the supervisor can also use this as an opportunity to build a good relationship with the employee.

Classroom training. Classroom training provides for handling the maximum number of trainees with a minimum number of instructors. It lends itself particularly to instruction in those areas where information and instructions can be imparted by lectures, demonstrations, films, and other types of audiovisual materials. If the size of the group is small, as is frequently the case in supervisory and executive development programs, instructional methods of a participative nature may also be used, such as role playing, sensitivity training, and discussion of cases.

𝒳 *Integrated on- and off-the-job training.* Classroom and job experiences are combined when the *integrated on- and off-the-job training* method is used. *Apprenticeship training* which is accomplished by assigning the novice to work under the supervision of a journeyman or master craftsman is one type of integrated training. The apprenticeship method is typically found in trades such as construction, printing, and metal crafts.

Another type of training which combines practical on-the-job experience with formal classes is *cooperative training.* The term "cooperative training" is used in connection with high school and college level programs which incorporate part-time work experiences. At the high school level such programs enroll students preparing for clerical, retailing, and manual jobs; students in college programs are preparing for technical and executive jobs. The company that participates in providing practical experience to students obtains a source of part-time workers and is also provided with an excellent opportunity to evaluate them for possible full-time employment upon their graduation.

Vestibule training is still another form of integrated training which is conducted by the company in an area separate from the production departments. Trainees are given instruction on the operation of equipment which is like the equipment they will use when assigned to operating departments. Advantages of vestibule training are that training activities can be conducted without interrupting the flow of work in operating departments, and the emphasis is definitely on instruction rather than production. Furthermore, under controlled training conditions it is possible to evaluate the progress of the trainee more accurately than where on-the-job training method is used. However, because of the expense involved in having duplicate equipment for training purposes, the equipment used for training sometimes is obsolete or worn out with the result that the trainee is required to make further adjustments when he is assigned to an operating department.

Supplementary training. Supplementary training provided by high schools, colleges, and universities has become increasingly popular. Many companies encourage participation in such training by reimbursing employees for tuition costs if the course is completed successfully. While not strictly a type of training, companies urge employees to join and participate in the activities of professional and technical organizations and often pay the costs of membership fees and the costs of attending meetings. By attending such meetings the employee is kept up to date in his particular field and, thus, can make a greater contribution to the company.

Simulators and other training devices. For some jobs it is either impractical or unwise to train the worker on the equipment that he will be required to use. An obvious example is found in the training of personnel to operate commercial or military aircraft and aircraft equipment. By using simulators in classroom situations, personnel may be given training and experience on airborne equipment under safe conditions. The design of simulators emphasizes realism in equipment and its operation so that the trainee learns how to perform the tasks in a setting as close to the real thing as is possible. Training devices are also used in teaching job skills and procedures of an industrial nature. An interesting training device known as Videosonics is being used to give employees step-by-step job procedures at their work benches. The device which looks like a portable TV set uses magnetic tape that is synchronized with 35 mm color slides. The slides together with the instructor's voice have been used successfully in describing and illustrating steps in the manufacture and assembly of electronic component parts.[9] Even after an employee has mastered an assembly operation, he can use this device to check on a particular phase of the work about which he may have some doubt or questions.

The steps involved in planning for and constructing a training device are similar to those which would be followed in preparing for any kind of training task. The recommended steps are as follows:

1. Prepare a task analysis of the job.
2. Select the tasks which are to be learned.
3. Decide on the level of skill expected of trainees.
4. Find out about the level of knowledge, abilities, and skills of probable trainees.
5. Find out about the level of knowledge, abilities, and skills of probable instructors.
6. Decide how the synthetic training will fit into on-the-job training.
7. Determine what controls, displays, and response-recording equipment will be necessary in the device for adequate training.
8. Integrate all information learned from steps 1–7 into a design recommendation.
9. Revise the design in terms of requirements of the trainer, trainee, and equipment.
10. Prepare instructions for use of the device in training.[10]

While most devices will accommodate only one trainee at a time, this is ordinarily not a serious factor since most equipment can be monitored by automatic response-recording devices, thereby reducing manpower costs of instruction. If many employees are to receive training in this manner, the costs of equipment may then be distributed over a large number of trainees.

Programmed instruction. Since the late 1950's companies have been making increasing use of programmed instruction in employee and executive development to the point that most training directors have some familiarity with this form of instruction.[11] While some of the programmed

[9]Theodore B. Dolmatch, Elizabeth Marting, and Robert E. Finley, *Revolution in Training* (New York: American Management Association, 1962). Videosonic is a registered trade name of the Hughes Aircraft Corporation.

[10]R. B. Miller, *Handbook of Training and Equipment Design* (Pittsburgh: The American Institute for Research, 1953), pp. 268–275.

[11]Ernest M. Schuttenberg, "Misconceptions About Programmed Learning," *Personnel*, Vol. 42, No. 3 (May–June, 1965), pp. 44–49.

materials use a book or manual format, teaching machines offer a more dramatic means of presenting programmed subject matter. A program represents an attempt to break down subject matter content into highly organized, logical sequences which demand continuous responding on the part of the trainee. After being presented a small segment of information, the trainee is required to answer a question either by writing an answer in a response frame or by pushing a button on a machine. Equipment calling for the latter type of response is illustrated in Figure 8-3. If the trainee's response is correct, he is advised of that fact and is presented with the next step (frame) in the material. If his response is incorrect, he is given further explanatory information and told to "try again."

Figure 8-3

A TEACHING MACHINE

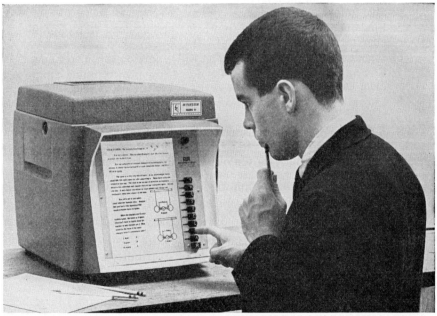

Source: The AutoTutor Mark II of U. S. Industries—Educational Science Division. Reproduced with permission of USI.

Programmed instruction has the advantage of recognizing individual differences in aptitude since each trainee learns at his own pace, and surveys have shown that trainees come away from this training experience with a higher disposition toward action and application. The major disadvantage is the cost in preparing special programs; but if sufficient numbers of personnel are to be trained, this cost can be readily absorbed.

Some typical users that have found it to be a valuable training method include the National City Bank of New York which trains new tellers on the intricacies of handling depositors and their money by this method. They also handle routine clerical training through programmed instruction. Humble Oil and Refining Company recently bought 2,500 programmed training devices to teach salesmen proper selling techniques, and DuPont has a library of almost 50 courses covering plant-level training programs.[12] Similarly, the Departments of the Army, Navy, and the Air Force have made increasing use of programmed instruction for training civilian personnel as well as men and women in uniform. In many instances programmed workbooks and textbooks are used in place of machines with somewhat lower costs and the advantage of portability.

While the first teaching machine was invented in 1922, the recent publicity given to this method may result in an uncritical attitude toward the device that some persons classify as a gadget. Certainly, the teaching machine is not a gadget if used properly, but those who propose to use it may fail to consider the objectives that they hope to achieve by its use because of the machine's novelty.[13] If used properly, learning can be accomplished by means of programmed instruction in a substantially shorter period of time than by conventional instruction, without loss in training or quality.[14]

Psychology of Learning

If the trainee has not learned, it is probably because some important principle of learning has been overlooked. Because the success or failure of a training program is frequently related to this simple fact, those who are concerned with developing instructional programs should recognize that attention must be given to the basic psychological principles of learning. The application of these principles, which are equally relevant to school classrooms and to company training programs, represents the major approach to making training effective.

Motivation

One of the fundamental conditions for learning is that the trainee be properly motivated. That is, for optimum learning the trainee must

---

[12]*Business Week*, July 4, 1965, pp. 67–69.

[13]One expert has written a provocative book about the need for clear statements of objectives of training programs — with or without teaching machines. See Robert F. Mager, *Preparing Objectives for Programmed Instruction* (San Francisco: Fearon Publishers, 1961).

[14]George D. Mayo and Alexander A. Longo, "Training Time and Programmed Instruction," *Journal of Applied Psychology*, Vol. 50, No. 1 (February, 1966), pp. 1–4.

recognize the need for acquiring new information or for having new skills, and he must maintain a desire to learn as training progresses. While people in industry are motivated by certain common needs, they differ from one another in the relative importance of these needs at any given time. The needs for recognition, for safety, and for self realization are among some of these needs that can be satisfied through training activities. Trainers should be alert to the individual's needs in the training situation and use them as a basis for motivating employees. Performance standards should be set so that an individual is not frustrated by the trainer who requires too much or too little. Learning is hindered by stress that may result from such frustration, or from anxiety, embarrassment, or confusion.

Knowledge of Results

As an employee's training progresses, motivation may be maintained and even increased by advising him of his progress throughout the training. His progress, as determined by tests and other records, may be plotted on a chart, commonly referred to as a learning curve. A learning curve for a group of employees is shown in Figure 8-4. Note that the curve expresses the relationship between time (in days and weeks) and units of production.

In many learning situations there are times when progress does not occur. Such periods of no return show up on the curve as a fairly straight horizontal line, which is called a *plateau*. A plateau may be the result of ineffective methods of work, or it may come because of reduced motivation. Proper guidance by the instructor may reveal the cause of a plateau and may enable the instructor to assist the trainee by such means as suggestions for new work procedures or aid in establishing new incentives.

While knowledge of results provides a strong incentive at all stages in learning, it is especially needed after the initial enthusiasm of the learning situation has diminished. It is important, therefore, that employees be advised of their progress during all of the phases of training and, preferably, throughout their careers with the company.

Closely related to knowledge of results is the principle of reinforcement. *Reinforcement* is anything which strengthens the response. It may be in the form of approval from the trainer or the feeling of accomplishment that follows the performance; or it may take the forms such as confirmation by a teaching machine that the trainee's response was correct. Regardless of the type of reinforcement, it is generally most effective if it occurs immediately after a task has been performed.

In training employees in how to perform their jobs more safely, it is important to reinforce safe actions. Conversely, however, studies have

Figure 8-4
LEARNING CURVES OF EMPLOYEES

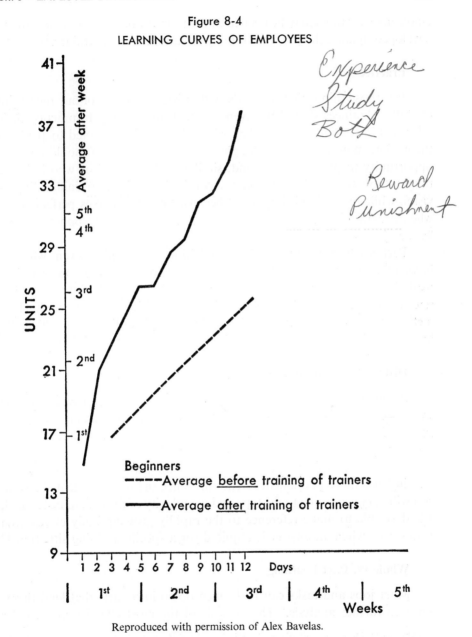

Reproduced with permission of Alex Bavelas.

shown that a wrong or unwanted response is more effectively eliminated simply by the absence of reinforcers than by presenting adverse or punishing consequences. The greatest danger in using punishment is that emotional reactions may be elicited in the learner and negative associations developed against the job, the training situation, and the trainer.[15]

Practice

It is those things that we do daily that become a part of our repertoire of skills. Trainees should be given frequent opportunity to practice their job tasks in the manner that they will ultimately be expected to perform them. The man who is being taught to operate a machine should have an opportunity to practice on it, and, similarly, the supervisor who is being taught "how to train" should have supervised practice in training. Supervision while practicing is important because "practice makes perfect" only when the trainee is performing correctly. The incorrect responses can be learned just as easily as the correct ones.

Participation facilitates the acquisition of learning even when it involves only oral material, as, for example, reciting what one has just read either to another person or to oneself. One method of study emphasizes reciting to oneself the main points covered in what was read. This method recognizes the fact that the reader's time is utilized more efficiently in reciting than in spending more time rereading the material.[16]

Distributed Learning

Another factor that determines the effectiveness of training is the amount of time given to practice in one session. Should trainees be given training in five 2-hour periods or in ten 1-hour periods? While there are operating problems to be considered in answering this question, it has been found in most cases that spacing out the training will result in more rapid learning and more permanent retention. Since the most efficient distribution will vary according to the type and complexity of the task to be learned, it is desirable to make reference to the rapidly growing body of research in this area when an answer is required for a specific training situation.[17]

Whole vs. Part Learning

Most jobs and tasks can be broken down into parts that lend themselves to further analysis. The analysis of the most effective manner for

---

[15]Marvin D. Dunnette and Wayne K. Kircher, *Psychology Applied to Industry* (New York: Appleton-Century-Crofts, 1965), pp. 67–68.

[16]The reader who desires to improve his reading and study skills will find the cited study method very effective. It is discussed in F. P. Robinson, *Effective Study* (New York: Harper & Brothers, 1961) and in his *Effective Reading* (New York: Harper & Brothers, 1962).

[17]*The Journal of Applied Psychology* is an excellent source of research studies of this type. Its articles are indexed in *Psychological Abstracts*.

completing each part then provides a basis for giving specific instruction. Typing, for example, is made up of several skills that are part of the total process. The typist starts by learning the proper use of each finger; eventually, with practice, the individual finger movements become integrated into a total pattern. Practice by moving individual fingers is an example of part learning. In determining whether part learning or whole learning is the most efficient approach, it is necessary to consider the nature of the task to be learned. If it can be broken down successfully for part learning, it probably should be broken down in order to facilitate learning; otherwise, it probably should be taught as a unit.

Individual Differences

In planning any type of training program, the intelligence, aptitudes, and interests of the trainees should receive special consideration. The extent of the differences among trainees should determine the type and amount of instruction required to attain the desired goal as well as the method by which materials should be presented. It is often desirable to group individuals according to their capacity to learn as determined by scores from intelligence and aptitude tests or to provide a different or extended type of instruction for those who need it.

Importance of Training Instructors

Research indicates that when instructors are given training the trainees will show much greater progress than when the instructors are not given such training. In one study approximately eight hours of special training by the discussion method were given to men who taught the operation of a stitching machine.[18] The effects of the training are shown in Figure 8-4, which was also used to illustrate the nature of learning curves. Note that the rate of learning a stitching operation was distinctly more rapid after the company trainers received the special instruction in teaching methods.

The Training Within Industry (TWI) Program of World War II emphasized the importance of training instructors in industry by means of the Job Instruction Training (JIT) Program. The basic ideas of the JIT Program were summarized on a reminder card which emphasized the following steps:

How to Get Ready to Instruct
1. Have a time table.
2. Break down the job.

---

[18]This study was conducted by Alex Bavelas.

3. Have everything ready.
4. Have the work place properly arranged.

How to Instruct
1. Prepare the worker.
2. Present the operation.
3. Try out performance.
4. Follow up.

This program, which was taught throughout the United States along with the other TWI courses in job methods, job relations, and program development training plans, undoubtedly provided the major stimulation for improved company training programs. Over 1,750,000 individuals received instruction under the TWI Program with the result that its effect has been felt in most companies.

Evaluation of Training Effectiveness

Training, like any other function of personnel management, should be evaluated to determine its effectiveness. The existence of a training staff and an array of courses and other training experiences for employees does not insure that learning is taking place. It is the responsibility of the training director to determine not only the needs for training but to have proof that the needs are being met through the program. Unfortunately, information concerning the achievement of goals and the most effective methods of reaching them are obtained in only a few instances, and then by research approaches that are often inadequate.

While an examination of various research approaches is beyond the scope of this book, there are certain basic principles that should be mentioned. In the first place, it is essential that experimental controls be employed in evaluation research. Not only should trainees be tested before and after receiving training, but the same tests or evaluations should be made of individuals in a control group which has not received the training and whose members are matched with the trainees on the basis of relevant variables such as intelligence, experience, and level of job.

Some of the criteria that are used in evaluating the effectiveness of training are: increased productivity, total sales, decreased costs and waste, and similar evidence of improved performance. If a course were designed to change the behavior of supervisors, the evaluation should be in terms of supervisory behavior, not knowledge. Measures used to evaluate training, such as production records, supervisory ratings, cost records, accidents, etc., should be sufficiently reliable or consistent to serve as dependable indicators. They should also be free from bias, if possible. Just because Roger Smith attended a particular training course does not insure that Roger actually benefited from the course in terms of the company objectives. His job performance, after training, should be observed and comparisons made with his performance before training on whatever measurable characteristics are considered pertinent. It is also unprofitable to ask Roger if he benefited from the training because the answer is usually in the affirmative and represents nothing more than a statement of appreciation for the opportunity given to him.

Training effectiveness may also be determined by studying learning curves prepared on the basis of individual and group performance (the latter being a combination of individual records). The visual display of the effects of training upon performance during the training sequence can be used to give the trainee an awareness of his progress, as mentioned earlier; it can also provide management with a picture of the extent to which its goals are being realized.

Résumé

Many companies recognize the values of personnel training; however, training is frequently relegated to a secondary position in the interests of meeting immediate production goals. The personnel department can help other departments in correcting such a situation by assisting in the orientation of new employees and by aiding in the efforts to achieve training objectives. While the personnel in each department should have an important part in the planning and carrying out of their programs, the training division should not wait until the other departments make their problems known. It should, like an educational institution, be looking ahead and anticipating the role that it can play in providing a service. The growing impact of automation and the importance of retraining require a high degree of cooperation between government and the training specialists in companies who must recognize the need for flexibility and adaptability and be prepared to handle all types of manpower requirements. In some instances the training division will be concerned with problems in teaching simple motor skills. At other times it will have the task of planning for the development of attitudes toward intricate social issues. Regardless of the area, training and development must be backed up by careful research. While new methods must always be considered and explored, the focus should be on the objectives to be attained through training. Whether or not the objectives are being met can best be determined by proper attention to evaluation.

DISCUSSION QUESTIONS AND PROBLEMS

1. A Wall Street Journal article of December 3, 1964, captioned "Aiding the Retarded — New Training Programs Help Many to Get Jobs," revealed that about 10,000 retarded persons (with IQs between 50 and 70) would get jobs that year in comparison to 5,900 in 1960.
   a. How do you account for the increases in job opportunities provided to these persons?
   b. What are some of the jobs that these persons should qualify for with some training?
   c. As a personnel manager what would be your opinions about hiring individuals in this category? What changes would be required in selection policies and procedures? What training methods would you use? Why?

2. A training manual was developed for training employees in the U.S. Employment Service and other agencies in how to use the Third Edition of the *Dictionary of Occupational Titles* (1965). The manual uses one of the programmed instruction techniques in which the blanks are filled in after reading a statement in the manual and often after consulting the D.O.T.
   a. What advantages is this method likely to have over a lecture on the same material? Over programmed instruction by a teaching machine?
   b. Why don't more employers use a similar approach in providing information to employees on how to perform their job tasks?
   c. How would you evaluate a training program in which programmed instructional methods were used?

3. At the General Motors Allison Division in Indianapolis, secretaries were given a turbine-engine course of 8 hours' duration. Attendance records were kept and certificates were awarded to each secretary attending all of the sessions.
   a. Of what value would such a course be to these individuals who would not be working on the engines themselves?
   b. Would this be a desirable procedure for other companies to follow? Are there any employees, other than secretaries, who might benefit from such an experience?

4. The production manager of a company blames the high rate of production waste on poor training. Would this necessarily be the cause? What factors other than training may be at fault?

5. At one company the new employee on his first day receives a 50-page employee handbook, a 70-page book of safety rules, and a half dozen pamphlets about different phases of the company's operations.
   a. What is your reaction to this practice?
   b. How would you handle the situation if you were in charge of orientation in this company?

6. Some companies use a sponsor or "buddy" system to aid employees in their initial on-the-job adjustment. Experienced employees are given the assignment in addition to their regular duties.

    a. What advantages are there in such an approach? What disadvantages?

    b. If you were given the assignment, what are the most important things you would feel you should do?

7. Obtain permission from your instructor to interview the training director of a company for the purpose of determining his opinion on such matters as:

    a. Line-staff responsibilities in training.

    b. Effectiveness of on-the-job training vs. other methods.

    c. Financial benefits of a training program.

    d. Effectiveness of supervisory training.

8. The task of instruction has been referred to as both a "science" and an "art."

    a. What are the scientific aspects of instruction?

    b. What aspects of teaching are more like an "art"?

CASE 8-1

THE GOVERNOR'S MAIL

Because of the importance of California's agricultural products to the state and to the nation, the California Department of Agriculture operates border stations in several locations where incoming automobiles are stopped for inspection. Uniformed personnel determine if an automobile is likely to have been through an area where plant pests might have been picked up by the vehicle or on produce carried by the occupants of the car. This is determined by questioning the driver and by visual inspection of the car.

In the course of thousands of inspections, a few travelers become disgruntled for one reason or another, and some even sit down later and write to the Governor or to the department in charge. As the correspondence began to exceed 100 letters in 1947, it was concluded that some form of corrective action was needed immediately.

The department investigated, and found that while most complaints were generally unfounded, there was a need for training the inspectors. A training program, therefore, was developed at each station that would include training in public relations with emphasis on how to approach persons entering the station, how to explain the purpose of the inspection, how to avoid complaints, and how to handle difficult cases. Training was also given in practical entomology, plant pathology, botany, quarantines, and inspection procedures.

The in-service training of border inspectors resulted in reducing the work load of the entomology and pathology laboratories in that over 75 percent of plant specimens taken at border stations are now identified by station personnel. Another benefit was the reduction in the number of complaints received by the Governor to only 36 in 1948 and to 26 in 1949. In addition to the reduction in the number of complaints, the inspections yielded better results as far as uncovering plant material in automobiles.

    a. How do you account for the apparent success of this training program?

    b. If you were asked to teach the public relations part of such a course, what instructional methods would you use? Why?

    c. Would the department be justified in firing border inspectors who were mentioned by name or badge number in letters of complaint? Should inspectors be interviewed about the complaints?

CASE 8-2

THE GOOD OLD DAYS

The following agreement was signed by a New England apprentice in 1640:
Know all men that I, Thomas Millard, with the Consent of Henry Wolcott of Windsor unto whose custody & care at whose charge I was brought over out of England into New England, doe bynd myself as an apprentice for eight yeeres to serve William Pynchon of Springfield, his heires & assigns in all manner of lawful employmt unto the full ext of eight yeeres beginninge the 29 day of Sept 1640 & the said William doth condition to find the said Thomas meat, drinke & clothing fitting such an apprentise & at the end of his tyme one new sute of apparell & forty shillings in mony: subscribed this 28 October 1640.*

a. How do the terms of an apprenticeship in 1640 compare with those of today?
b. Why has it been necessary to have federal and state legislation covering apprenticeship programs?

SUGGESTED READINGS

American Management Association. *Revolution in Training — Programmed Instruction in Industry*. New York: American Management Association, 1962.

Chruden, Herbert J., and Arthur W. Sherman, Jr. *Readings in Personnel Management*, Second Edition. Cincinnati: South-Western Publishing Company, Inc., 1966. Chapter 2.

DePhillips, Frank A., William M. Berliner, and James J. Cribbin. *Management of Training Programs*. Homewood, Illinois: Richard D. Irwin, Inc., 1960.

Gagne, R. M. (ed.). *Psychological Principles in Systems Development*. New York: Holt, Rinehart & Winston, Inc., 1962.

Gilmer, B. von Haller. *Industrial Psychology*, Second Edition. New York: McGraw-Hill Book Company, 1966. Chapter 7.

Glaser, Robert (ed.). *Training Research and Education*. Pittsburgh: University of Pittsburgh Press, 1962.

McGehee, William, and Paul W. Thayer. *Training in Business and Industry*. New York: John Wiley & Sons, Inc., 1961.

Proctor, John H., and William M. Thorton. *Training — A Handbook for Line Managers*. New York: American Management Association, 1961.

Servein, Oscar N. *Educational Activities of Business*. Washington: American Council on Education, 1961.

Taber, Julian I., Robert Glaser, and Halmuth H. Schaefer. *Learning and Programmed Instruction*. Reading, Massachusetts: Addison-Wesley Publishing Co., Inc., 1965.

Tiffin, Joseph, and Ernest J. McCormick, *Industrial Psychology*, Fifth Edition. Englewood Cliffs, New Jersey: Prentice-Hall, Inc., 1965. Chapter 10.

---

*From *Apprenticeship Past and Present:* U. S. Department of Labor, Bureau of Apprenticeship, 1952.

Management Development

Few if any functional areas of personnel management have been the subject of more interest and attention during the past decade than management development. This fact can be attributed not only to the growing need of companies for highly competent managers to handle the increasingly complex problems of modern business but also to a growing awareness among companies that the development of competency in management requires formal attention and effort. Because of its importance and the special problems relating to it, students should be aware of the role of management development in the personnel program and its relationship to other personnel functions. The principal topics discussed in this chapter on management development are:

- The nature of management development.

- The management development program.

- Methods for developing managers.

- Administering the development program.

The Nature of Management Development

The purpose of this function is to help develop management personnel in their existing positions and to provide a continuing supply of qualified individuals for management positions as they become vacant. Management development programs have grown rapidly during recent years. For example, Lawrence A. Appley, President of the American Management Association, estimates that at the beginning of this decade over 500,000 managers were enrolled in some type of formal management development program within their companies as compared with only 10,000 some 12 years earlier.[1]

A more recent survey of 167 companies conducted by the National Industrial Conference Board disclosed that the majority of these companies with more than 1,000 employees are engaged in management development activities. The survey further revealed that management development was also carried on in many of the smaller companies although it tended to be less formalized in nature.[2] There is every reason to assume that this growth of management development programs is continuing; and whatever the growing expenditures of money for such programs may be, these expenditures are infinitesimal in comparison with the costs, often hidden, that can result from incompetent and underdeveloped managers.

Changing Emphasis

Originally, management development, if it existed at all, was limited to the training of supervisors. The need for management development above this level became apparent during World War II when the war industries, because of rapid expansion and the loss of managers to the armed services, were faced with severe shortages of seasoned executive talent. The initial emphasis, therefore, was primarily upon the development of personnel for managerial positions where shortages of qualified personnel were most acute. Following World War II, most companies were confronted with the problem that their management ranks had grown older and that many management positions lacked qualified replacements. In addition, many of the individuals who were in management positions were incapable of coping with the many problems of organizational expansion, technological progress, and renewed competition that were arising during

---

[1]Lawrence A. Appley, "Management Training in Proper Perspective," *Management News* (April, 1960), p. 1.

[2]*Developing Managerial Competence: Changing Concepts — Emerging Practices*, Studies in Personnel Policy, No. 189 (New York: National Industrial Conference Board, 1964), p. 129.

the postwar era. In some companies, as a result of these situations, "crash programs" were organized to recruit and to accelerate the training and seasoning of promising junior managers for rapid advancement. Emphasis in these programs was placed upon providing courses and special work experiences in an effort to compress the years of practical experience normally required for management development. As the need for crash programs declined, however, management development programs became subject to more critical appraisal. Management development increasingly began to be recognized as something that was needed by all managers and not just by an elite group of management trainees. Instead of providing trainees with a prolonged period of special courses and work experiences and recognizing them as a separate group, furthermore, many companies began to assign their newly-hired management trainees to regular production jobs in which they were given their first opportunity to prove themselves.

Problems of Management Development

One of the major difficulties in the development of managers is the absence of a precise knowledge regarding the competencies which a manager should possess in order to be effective. Furthermore, even certain of the criteria that are used to evaluate successful managers may not be completely valid. Such criteria as sales, profits, returns on investments, or business growth, which are used frequently, can be influenced by conditions outside of the manager's control. Fluctuations in the business cycle, for example, can make a poor manager look good or a good one appear ineffective.

There have been many attempts made, on the basis of scientific research and practical experience, to define the qualities of a good manager. One researcher, for example, feels the following qualities typify the successful executives that he had studied:

1. Exhibit high frustration tolerance.
2. Encourage full participation.
3. Continually question themselves, i.e., try to analyze mistakes and to remain aware of their biases.
4. Admit that they are living in a competitive world and understand the "laws of competitive warfare."
5. Express hostility tactfully.
6. Accept victory with controlled emotions.
7. Are not shattered by defeat.
8. Understand the necessity for limits and "unfavorable decisions."

9. Identify selves with group.
10. Set goals realistically.[3]

Another list of qualities of a good executive compiled by one business leader includes the following: wisdom, integrity, courage, an interest in people, loyalty, imagination, and depth of interest.[4] Koontz and O'Donnell point out, however, that attempts to establish qualities that are common to all managers are complicated by the problem of terminology and by variations in the "mix" comprised of knowledge, experience, and personality that produce successful managers. They conclude that it is impossible to establish a specific set of qualities that a manager should possess.[5]

Research efforts and practical experience, thus, would seem to indicate that there are no universal qualities relating to managerial success and that the qualities which a manager should possess are affected by the situation in which he must operate. These conclusions appear to be particularly true with respect to managerial leadership. Thus, the selection and development of a manager must be accomplished in terms of particular situations which may tend to vary from one position to another. It must also be accomplished in terms of each individual's pattern of abilities and personality.

A major problem relating to the development of managers is that the success of the program is contingent upon the caliber of management that exists at the top. As they are developing for positions of greater responsibility, managers are likely to emulate many of the characteristics and practices of their superiors. The development of effective managers in an organization, thus, can be inhibited by ineffective top management. Furthermore, if an organization suffers from poor management, the need for devoting formal attention to the management development program may not be recognized; and the good management talent may be attracted elsewhere.

The Management Development Program

✗Even though it is difficult to define precisely the characteristics of an effective manager, it still is possible to improve the performance of managers if suitable conditions and a formal program are provided. The

[3]Chris Argyris, "Some Characteristics of Successful Executives," *Personnel Journal* (June, 1953). Also see Thomas W. Harrell, *Managers' Performance and Personality* (Cincinnati: South-Western Publishing Company, Inc., 1961), Chapter 2.
[4]William B. Gwen, Jr., "Must Managers Specialize? The Case for Executive Versatility," *Management Review* (November, 1956).
[5]Harold Koontz and Cyril O'Donnell, *Principles of Management* (Third Edition; New York: McGraw-Hill Book Company, 1964), pp. 401–402.

program should include analyzing the demands of each management position within an organization to determine what is demanded of the manager in terms of performance. On the basis of such analyses, the knowledge that the manager should possess in the position, the functions that he must perform, and the skills that he must exercise in order to perform his job can be determined. This required knowledge may include not only the details relating to the job, the company, and the environment in which it operates but also to that growing body of knowledge relating to the field of management that experience and research have helped to accumulate. It is also possible for competent managers to pass to their successors certain insights that they have acquired and to help their successors develop the attitudes and behavior that will contribute to successful performance.

The development of subordinates, however, may be hindered because formal attention is not given to their development. Unless formal attention is given to this function, even competent managers may become so preoccupied with their other duties that they may neglect this function. The existence of a formal program, therefore, should help to insure that the development needs of the organization, and of each individual, are recognized and that opportunities for development are provided.

In order to accomplish its objectives the management development program should provide for:

1. An analysis of the organization structure and objectives.
2. An analysis of manager requirements.
3. An inventory of management talent.
4. A determination of individual needs.
5. An appraisal of individual progress.
6. A means for program evaluation.

Analysis of the Organization Structure and Objectives

The duties of a manager and his role within the company are determined by the objectives of the company and by the organization that has been developed to permit their achievement. Whether the job of a manager is easy or difficult to perform and whether his efforts are effective or ineffective will be determined in part by the way in which his job has been organized. Rather than attempt to develop a manager to perform under extremely difficult job conditions, it is more logical to organize his job so that it can be performed with maximum effectiveness.

The first step in the establishment of a management development program should be a review of the company's objectives and its organization in order that subsequent development efforts may proceed in the right direction. The organization structure should be studied carefully for the purpose of correcting any unsatisfactory organizational conditions affecting its operation. These conditions might include unassigned or overlapping authority and responsibility, inappropriate division of duties, improper span of control, or the absence of clearly defined channels of authority. Thus, an important by-product of a management development program may be the improvement of a company's organization structure.

Analysis of Manager Requirements

An analysis of manager requirements should serve to identify the management jobs within the organization that must be staffed at present and/or in the future. Records containing information about each position, such as code number, title, department, physical location, name of incumbent, date for incumbent's replacement, and names of potential replacements, are usually desirable in order to identify the jobs in which and for which executives must be developed. These job records, which may also serve as a part of the inventory records of executive talent, may be represented by charts, tables, or record cards. The replacement schedule for management positions within the company in Figure 9-1, for example, identifies and indicates when each position is likely to become vacant and who the possible replacements for it may be.

Every management development program should include provisions for recruiting personnel with management potential from supervisory and lower levels. The practice of screening the lower levels of the organization for management talent may help not only to identify executive talent but also to encourage the future development of this talent. This practice enables individuals to be judged by their demonstrated abilities rather than, as sometimes happens, to be judged only by the formal education that has been acquired prior to entering the job market. While many personnel below the managerial level may have no desire to put forth the required effort to become managers, most of them will regard their company more favorably if they know that the opportunity for advancement does exist if they wish to take advantage of it.

Inventory of Management Talent

The management inventory records of a company help to provide information relating to the identity and the competency of the individual occupying each management position as well as the identities and competencies of possible replacements. These records may consist of

Figure 9-1

AN EXECUTIVE REPLACEMENT SCHEDULE

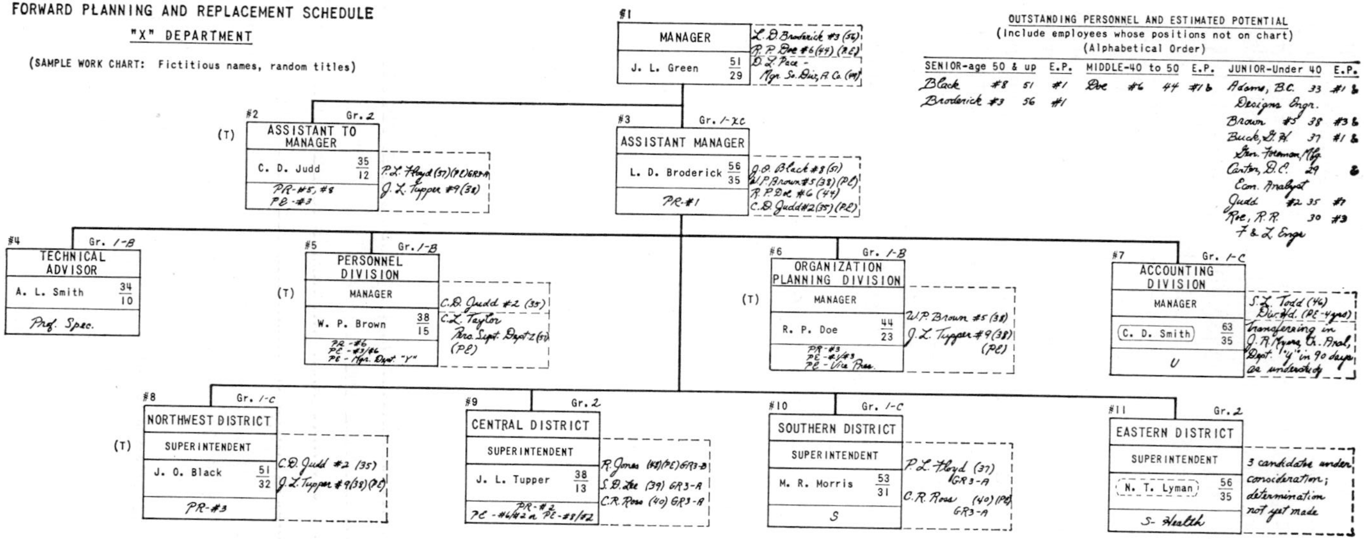

FORWARD PLANNING AND REPLACEMENT SCHEDULE

"X" DEPARTMENT

(SAMPLE WORK CHART: Fictitious names, random titles)

OUTSTANDING PERSONNEL AND ESTIMATED POTENTIAL
(Include employees whose positions not on chart)
(Alphabetical Order)

#1 MANAGER — J. L. Green — 51 / 29

#3 ASSISTANT MANAGER — L. D. Broderick — 56 / 35 — PE-#1

#2 ASSISTANT TO MANAGER (T) — C. D. Judd — 35 / 12 — Gr. 2

#4 TECHNICAL ADVISOR — A. L. Smith — 34 / 10 — Gr. 1-B — Prof. Spec.

#5 PERSONNEL DIVISION (T) — W. P. Brown — 38 / 15 — Gr. 1-B

#6 ORGANIZATION PLANNING DIVISION (T) — R. P. Doe — 44 / 23 — Gr. 1-B

#7 ACCOUNTING DIVISION — C. D. Smith — 63 / 35 — Gr. 1-C

#8 NORTHWEST DISTRICT (T) SUPERINTENDENT — J. O. Black — 51 / 32 — Gr. 1-C — PR-#3

#9 CENTRAL DISTRICT SUPERINTENDENT — J. L. Tupper — 38 / 13 — Gr. 2

#10 SOUTHERN DISTRICT SUPERINTENDENT — M. R. Morris — 53 / 31 — Gr. 1-C

#11 EASTERN DISTRICT SUPERINTENDENT — N. T. Lyman — 56 / 35 — Gr. 2

LEGEND

PR – Employee promotable and ready for position indicated.

PE – Employee promotable with further experience to position indicated.
For example: "PE-#1/#3 or #4" means promotable to Position #1 following experience in Position #3 or #4.

P? – Employee promotable but specific direction not yet known, e.g., new in job – or no higher job of his specialty in organization (such specialty may be noted for consideration elsewhere.)

S – Employee satisfactorily placed but will probably not progress beyond present position.

U – Employee on adjustment case (not properly placed or unsatisfactory performance.)

#3 Position Number (3).
Gr. Salary Group
(T) Good position for development and training.
54 Current year minus birth year.
34 Current year minus service year.
☐ Employee within 5 years of normal retirement.
☐ Employee probably replaceable within 5 years because of early retirement, health, etc.
☐ Replacement Candidates (See Note below)

IMPORTANT: TO ENSURE STRICTEST CONFIDENTIAL TREATMENT OF THE IDENTITY OF REPLACEMENT CANDIDATES AND APPRAISAL INFORMATION ON THIS CHART, NAMES OF SUCH CANDIDATES, OUTSTANDING PERSONNEL AND ALL APPRAISAL INFORMATION SHALL BE HAND-WRITTEN OR HAND-PRINTED IN THE RESPECTIVE BOXES BY THE INDIVIDUAL AUTHORIZED TO PREPARE THE REPLACEMENT SCHEDULE.

Appraisal Code (Summary of (GO-311, Sec. 15)

Reproduced with the permission of the Standard Oil Company of California.

replacement tables or charts of the type to which reference has already been made. It will be noted in Figure 9-1 that such information as the age, the years of service, and the potential of each manager can be gained quickly from a replacement chart. The replacement chart also serves to identify and provide similar information concerning possible replacements for each position and indicates when some positions may be vacated.

The personal history records of each manager and prospective manager can be reviewed for more detailed information about their qualifications. Their records may contain the various data gained at the time of employment as well as the record of their company work experience and their performance evaluations. Records of background investigations, psychological tests, and physical examinations are among those that may be included to make up the personal history records for each individual. It is from these personal history records that most of the information is obtained for replacement charts or other forms which summarize the status of a company's management force.

A company's inventory records of executive talent, which should be utilized in a confidential manner, can serve several purposes. First, the records can help to direct attention to the developmental needs of each individual in terms of his current job assignment and those into which he may be promoted. Second, the records can help management to anticipate vacancies resulting from expansion, retirements, or promotions sufficiently in advance to permit qualified replacements to be developed and, if necessary, recruited for these vacancies. Third, they can enable a company to be prepared to staff vacancies that may result unexpectedly from death or resignation. Finally, executive inventory records can contribute to better morale among management trainees and other personnel who are attempting to qualify themselves for eventual promotion into executive positions by helping to reassure them that management has been observing and keeping a record of their progress.

The evaluation of management performance, even if carefully conducted, will be of little value unless those who are evaluated are informed of their ratings and of their strengths and weaknesses. Discussions with superiors concerning these ratings are essential in order to help these individuals plan a course of action for overcoming their weaknesses. Performance rating interviews also can serve to reconcile any disagreements that the ratee may have regarding the ratings or comments that appear on his evaluation sheet. Interviews may also reveal misconceptions on the part of some persons regarding the opportunities and the requirements governing their promotions. When the individual's aspirations within the company, for example, are not consistent with his capacities or available opportunities, it is the superior's responsibility to help him to redirect his efforts toward achievable goals. The subject of performance evaluation and evaluation interviews will be discussed in detail in the next chapter.

Determination of Individual Needs

Because the requirements of each managerial job and the qualifications of each person are different, no two managers or management trainees will have identical development needs. A management development program in effect, therefore, serves to establish and to coordinate the personal development program of each individual in terms of the demands of his present job and his advancement potential. The individual's program for self-improvement should provide for those developmental experiences that will enable him to overcome such deficiencies as those relating to his knowledge, skills, or personality. Thus, for some individuals self-development may involve developing the ability to write reports, to give talks, or to lead conferences; for others, it may consist of learning how to supervise subordinates or how to gain the cooperation of others in the organization.

Figure 9-2 on page 228 illustrates how development needs are determined by one company and indicates the methods by which the development of managers is accomplished. Each of these methods of development, however, merely provides the opportunities by which the individual may improve himself. In the final analysis effective management development must consist primarily in guided self-development.

Appraisal of Individual Progress

The periodic appraisal or evaluation of each individual's progress is a very important part of an executive development program, and it should be a thorough and objective one. An objective appraisal can serve to measure the development progress of each individual and provide a basis for making those adjustments that appear advisable in the light of his progress. Performance appraisals also can permit each person to know how his superior feels about his performance and what weaknesses, if any, the superior considers should be corrected. As one management trainee expressed it, "They let you know where you stand in this company's program and if you are doing something wrong they tell you about it and try to help you." If objective standards of performance have been developed, the individual also should be able to judge his own accomplishments.

Figure 9-2

A COMPANY'S DEVELOPMENT PROGRAM

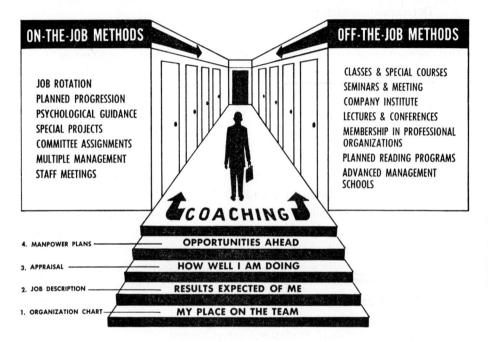

METHODS FOR DEVELOPING SYLVANIA MANAGERS

ON-THE-JOB METHODS

JOB ROTATION
PLANNED PROGRESSION
PSYCHOLOGICAL GUIDANCE
SPECIAL PROJECTS
COMMITTEE ASSIGNMENTS
MULTIPLE MANAGEMENT
STAFF MEETINGS

OFF-THE-JOB METHODS

CLASSES & SPECIAL COURSES
SEMINARS & MEETING
COMPANY INSTITUTE
LECTURES & CONFERENCES
MEMBERSHIP IN PROFESSIONAL
ORGANIZATIONS
PLANNED READING PROGRAMS
ADVANCED MANAGEMENT
SCHOOLS

COACHING

4. MANPOWER PLANS	OPPORTUNITIES AHEAD
3. APPRAISAL	HOW WELL I AM DOING
2. JOB DESCRIPTION	RESULTS EXPECTED OF ME
1. ORGANIZATION CHART	MY PLACE ON THE TEAM

Source: *Sylvania's Plan for Management Development*, prepared by Sylvania Electric Products, Inc. Reproduced with permission.

Considerable attention today is being given to the concept of *management by objectives.* This concept places emphasis upon the goals to be reached rather than upon the activities that are necessary to reach them. Accomplishments are the important thing rather than the performance of work for its own sake or the traits that the individual possesses.[6] These accomplishments are defined in terms of specific results that are expected on the job. The expected results might, for example, call for a manager to reduce his department's operating costs over a six-month period by 5 percent or for him to complete a particular project within a 30-day deadline. Once the expected results have been established, the appraisal of the manager's performance becomes largely a matter of comparing the results that

---

[6]National Industrial Conference Board, *Developing Managerial Competence: Changing Concepts — Emerging Practices, op. cit.,* p. 10.

were actually achieved against those that had been expected. The development of the manager, then, can be planned and directed toward achieving the expected results in the future.

The analysis of management requirements should serve to determine not only the number of managers that may be required but also the individual qualifications and competencies that are necessary to perform each job effectively. This latter information, which can be provided in the descriptions and specifications, should help to indicate the improvement that each manager must make in order to satisfy the requirements of his job.

Evaluation of the Program

It is desirable that a management development program be evaluated periodically to determine that it is meeting the development needs of the company and of its managers. This evaluation should include a reexamination of the program's objectives in order to determine if they are being pursued properly and if they should be modified to meet changing conditions that have affected the program. The solicitation of information through the use of questionnaires and by means of counseling sessions with participants can provide one source of information relating to changes in the program that may have become necessary. The effectiveness of the development program also should be reflected in the performance records of each department and of the company as a whole. An analysis of these records and of the performance rating of the managers thus can provide some basis for determining what improvements may be needed in the development program. Records relating to costs, output, production quality, and other achievements are typical of those which can indicate whether or not the development program is producing favorable results.

Unfortunately, the evaluation of a management development program must be based upon information that often is subjective in nature. Actually, there is no method for determining with complete accuracy the effectiveness of a development program. Neither is there any way of measuring precisely a program's contribution in terms of dollar savings or percentage increases in operating efficiency. The absence of such precise data, however, does not mean that attempts to evaluate a program are useless. Even subjective data can provide some basis for improving a program.

Methods for Developing Managers

A management development program generally should provide a variety of development activities and experiences for participants, because their development needs as determined by the requirements of their present and future positions and by their personal qualifications will vary widely. Developmental activities for the purposes of this discussion are grouped into two classes: those that occur on-the-job and those that occur off-the-job. This section covers some of the more common development activities and experiences in each of these two categories.

On-the-Job Activities

Management skills and abilities cannot be acquired merely by listening and observing or by reading about them in a book. They must be acquired through actual practice and experience in which a person has an opportunity to work under pressure and to learn by making mistakes and having them corrected. According to a study by the American Management Association, on-the-job experience is the method most commonly used by business firms to develop executive personnel.[7]

In order to have developmental value, work experience should be properly planned and guided. Otherwise, the experience may be no better than any regular job assignment. Some of the development activities that relate to on-the-job work experience are: coaching, understudy assignments, lateral promotions, special projects, committee assignments, staff meetings, and job rotation.

Coaching. An individual's daily job experiences are what provide the foundation for his development. If the individual is to profit fully from these experiences, however, he should receive assistance from those who have acquired greater wisdom and experience than he so that he may recognize and correct his mistakes. He may also require assistance in learning how to apply to his job such skill and knowledge that he may possess. The process of assisting individuals to perform their managerial duties and responsibilities more effectively is commonly referred to as coaching. Figure 9-3 illustrates how Sylvania Electric Products, Inc. believes that coaching can be conducted most effectively.

In contrast to the performance evaluation interviews that are conducted on a more formal and periodic basis, coaching tends to be of a more informal and continuous nature. The term "coaching" as it is used in connection with management development has much the same meaning as it has when used in connection with athletics. It involves observing a subordinate for the purpose of analyzing his performance and of assisting him

---

[7]*Management Education for Itself and Its Employees* (New York: American Management Association, 1954).

Figure 9-3

HOW CAN YOU IMPROVE DAY-TO-DAY COACHING?

— Set the right example
— Build on his strengths
— Delegate more
— Insist on completed assignments
— Let him "pinch hit"
— Seek his opinion
— Let him know how he's doing
— Broaden his viewpoint
— Use specific examples

Source: *Sylvania's Plan for Management Development.* Reproduced with the permission of the Sylvania Electric Products, Inc.

in improving it. Assistance may be provided in the form of a continuing flow of instructions, comments, criticisms, questions, and suggestions that the superior may offer to motivate the subordinate manager to develop himself further. Effective coaching also requires that a superior provide the correct example for subordinates to follow and that he establish high standards of performance for himself and his subordinates to observe. It also requires that the superior have and demonstrate confidence in his subordinates which in turn necessitates that he have adequate confidence in himself.

Understudy assignments. In some companies staff assistant jobs are created to provide development opportunities for those assigned as understudies to senior executives. The individual who is assigned to one of these jobs can relieve the superior of some of his work load while being permitted to learn as much as possible about the superior's job and his techniques for handling it. The understudy assignments can be used either for the trainee or for the experienced executive who is being groomed to take over the superior's job.

The benefits that an individual gains from his understudy assignment depend upon the time and interest that the superior devotes to him. If a superior permits his understudy to gain experience in handling important functions and gives him the help and suggestions that will enable him to develop, the understudy method of training can be very effective. If, however, the superior resents having to spend time with an understudy or feels that the understudy is a threat to his job security, the assignment may offer little development opportunity to the detriment of both the company and the individual.

Lateral promotions. Since it usually is not feasible to rotate experienced executives among different jobs for training purposes because of the salary costs that are entailed, it may be more desirable to broaden their skill, knowledge, and experience by means of a sequence of promotion steps through different departments. These promotions often are referred to as *lateral promotions.*

Positions in the industrial engineering or personnel departments are frequently among those in which executives may be given some experience particularly at the lower end of the promotion ladder. Work experience in these departments brings a candidate into contact with nearly every department within the organization and, thus, increases his knowledge concerning many different company functions. Lateral promotions, like rotational assignments, also provide an opportunity for individuals to receive guidance from a variety of managers and to observe many different management methods and techniques in action. A change in superiors can often be stimulating and bring to light certain abilities or deficiencies in the candidate that previously were overlooked.

Lateral promotions, however, have certain limitations. Some executives may be reluctant to have capable subordinates that they have developed assigned to other departments. The promotion of an individual into a new department, furthermore, may generate resentment among the personnel within the department who feel that one of them rather than an "outsider" should have received the promotion.

Projects and committee assignments. In most companies there are various projects for study that can be assigned to managers. These projects which can be assigned to them as individuals or as members of a committee can provide them with invaluable experience in analyzing and making recommendations on problems that concern company operations. Individuals who are given these assignments not only have the opportunity to broaden their experience and to demonstrate management skills and abilities but also to render an important contribution to the organization.

In some companies committees, which are referred to as "junior boards," are established to work on projects and to submit plans and recommendations for action to the board of directors. This practice, known as "multiple management," was introduced by the McCormick Company and derives its name from the fact that these junior boards exist in addition to the senior board. The function of the junior boards and the contributions that they may render, however, are similar to those of a committee.

Staff meetings. Participation in staff meetings offers another means of increasing knowledge and understanding, thus furthering the development of management personnel. These meetings not only enable participants to become more familiar with problems and events that are occurring outside of their immediate area but also expose them to the ideas and thinking of other managers. Staff meetings, furthermore, may give managers an opportunity to make presentations to the group and to have their ideas evaluated and improved on by others in the group. The developmental value to be gained from such meetings, however, will be contingent upon how well the meetings are planned, organized, and conducted. Like any other type of meeting, they can be extremely profitable or a waste of time, depending upon how they are conducted.

Job rotation. Job rotation is intended to provide a greater variety of work experience with which to broaden the knowledge and understanding that the individual requires in order to be able to manage more effectively. The rotation usually is among jobs on the same organizational level and for short periods of time. These jobs may be ones that have been established especially for training purposes, or they may be regular production jobs to which the trainee is assigned as a part of a "progressive experience program." Among the firms covered by an NICB survey, 76 percent indicated that they "use a preplanned sequence of relatively short-term training assignments" as part of their management development programs.[8] In some instances trainees may be placed in a "utility" or "flying" squad and assigned each day to those departments where extra personnel are needed.

The value of rotational training depends in large part upon the amount of supervision that the trainees receive and upon the seriousness with which these trainees pursue their job assignments. If the trainees are not coached effectively, or if they are given only routine "busy work" to perform, job rotation may do more harm than good as far as their development and morale are concerned. The movement from one job to another should be

---

[8]National Industrial Conference Board, *Developing Managerial Competence: Changing Concepts — Emerging Practices, op. cit.,* p. 62.

timed so that it occurs when the individual is ready to change jobs. Thus, the individual should be permitted to remain in a particular job long enough to profit from the experience but not so long that it ceases to provide a challenge.

In spite of its rather widespread use, job rotation can have certain limitations. One criticism of rotation is that it may discourage individuals from starting any long-range projects. Some critics feel that experience is not gained at a sufficiently high level to provide the ability that is needed to innovate and to make the bold decisions required of those in top management positions.[9]

Off-the-Job Activities

While on-the-job experience constitutes the basic phase of an executive's development, certain methods of development away from the job can be used to supplement work experiences. Off-the-job activities include those that can help to increase the individual's knowledge, broaden his perspective, influence his attitudes, or increase his sensitivity to the reactions of others. These activities may be provided on either an individual or a group basis and may be conducted during or after normal working hours. Such activities, which are not a part of the normal job duties, may involve either formal or informal learning situations.

The discussion of off-the-job training in the remainder of this section covers: company training courses, management games, role playing, sensitivity training, professional reading, and educational and professional organizations.

Company training courses. Many of the larger companies develop their own training courses for their management personnel. While these courses tend to be conducted through lecture or discussion sessions, some may be conducted on a home-study basis. Among the subjects most frequently covered by company training courses are those dealing with human relations, supervision, personnel administration, labor relations, general economics, general management, and communications. Many of these classes permit members to contribute from their own personal experiences as well as from their professional readings. Cases taken from a company's actual experiences or from published casebooks may be helpful in stimulating class discussion and the interchange of ideas. Case studies are particularly useful as a means for helping executives learn how to obtain

---

[9]George Strauss, "Organization Man for the Future," *California Management Review,* Vol. VI, No. 3 (Spring, 1964), pp. 5–15.

and interpret facts, to be conscious of the many variables upon which a management decision may be based and, in general, to improve their decision-making skills.

A variation of the case method is the *incident method*. In this method the participants are given only a brief statement of a problem or incident. Any details or facts that may be pertinent to the problem must be drawn from the discussion leader through questioning. Whether or not the group can gain sufficient information from the leader will depend upon its ability to determine what information is relevant and to elicit it from him.

The *in-basket training* technique is another method that can be used to stimulate a problem situation. In this technique the participants are given several documents, each describing some problem or situation the solution of which requires an immediate decision. This technique forces them not only to make decisions under the pressure of time but also to determine the priority with which each problem should be considered.

Management games. Case situations have been brought to life and made more interesting through the development of management games. Participants who play the game are faced with the task of making a continuing series of decisions affecting the enterprise. The simulated effects that each decision has upon each functional area within the enterprise can be determined by means of an electronic computer for which the game has been programmed. While management games do provide an exercise in decision making, they fall short of being able to duplicate the pressures and the realities of actual decision making on the job.

Role playing. Another management development training technique is *role playing*. It consists of assuming the attitudes and behavior of and acting out the roles of the individuals who are involved in a personnel problem, which usually are those of a supervisor and a subordinate. Role playing can help the participant to improve his ability to understand and to cope with the problems of other persons. It should also help him learn how to counsel others regarding their problems and how to gain the cooperation of associates. The participant may also come to recognize how, in his relations with others, his attitude and behavior may need to be improved. Thus, role playing can be an effective method for getting executives to recognize and to accept good human relations principles and for giving them an opportunity to develop skill in applying these principles.

Sensitivity training. One of the executive training methods that have grown rapidly in popularity is *sensitivity training*. This method, pioneered by the National Training Laboratories, is used with small groups — referred to as *"T"* (training) *groups* — whose members work together for a number of days. According to one study, the purpose of sensitivity training is:

> . . . to help men achieve a greater awareness of how human beings relate to one another. It accomplishes this by bringing to the surface, for conscious examination, the normally unquestioned assumptions about human relations.[10]

Sensitivity training, therefore, is intended to help managers learn more about their personalities and the reactions of others to them. It is believed that the insight thus acquired may provide them with a basis for modifying their behavior in such a way as to improve their effectiveness.

As the sessions progress the members' impressions and evaluations of one another tend to become quite frank and often rather critical. An example of some of the perceptions and reactions that may develop during sensitivity sessions is illustrated by the following excerpts taken from the diaries compiled by sensitivity training participants.[11]

EIGHTH MEETING: WHY DOESN'T BEN SAY ANYTHING?

Trainer: . . . Lew . . . asked Ben why he never saw fit to say anything in class.

Lew: Ben stated that he did not feel motivated. . . .

Hank: Some of these guys such as Lew and Al turn my stomach. They all jumped on Ben for not talking. They were reading all kinds of things into his nonparticipation in class. . . . I feel just like Ben; most of the time the discussions haven't been worth taking part in. . . . I would have laughed if some of these wise guys had hopped on me. . . . I wonder if they are just talking to appear to Irv as though they were working. Most of their remarks are just rehash of what someone else has already said. . . I don't think we should ever get so personal again, because before too long there are liable to be some pretty nasty remarks flying around.

NINTH MEETING: "TO HELL WITH IRV"

Duke: . . .My buddy, Ben, rated the highest. Immediately the pseudo-psychiatrists in the class jumped into the act and began studying him. It seems to me you can't even breathe without some idiot investigating why you do it. I am rapidly developing a temper restraint in this group lest I smash a few people in an emotional outburst.

Trainer: . . .After the experiment, which to many may well have been personally too threatening, the group floundered at length.

    [10]National Industrial Conference Board, *Developing Managerial Competence: Changing Concepts — Emerging Practices, op. cit.,* p. 91.
    [11]Robert Tannenbaum, I. R. Weschler, and Fred Massarik, *Leadership and Organization: A Behavioral Science Approach* (New York: McGraw-Hill Book Company, 1961), pp. 144–145.

Beverly: I'm afraid my reaction is despair bordering on disgust. . . . At this stage I question the value of letting the class flounder to the point of frustration, which I think we are reaching. . .

Frances: I wish the instructor would step in, clarify what has been going on, and give the group some leads as to why, how, and where we are being blocked. . . .

Trainer: At one point, while the discussion dealt with "feedback," Don asked me to define the meaning of the term. Before a reply was possible, Red burst out with the comment, "To hell with Irv" — followed first by a stunned silence, then by uproarious laughter. . .

Clinical
Observer: This meeting featured the "ritual slaying of the father." . . .

In spite of its popularity, there are those critics who question whether sensitivity training has much proven value in helping the manager perform his job more effectively. Furthermore, some of them feel that even though it may be beneficial for participants to discover how others in a group may perceive them, such experiences can penetrate the defense mechanisms of individuals who lack self-confidence. Odiorne suggests that the sensitivity training lab is:

> . . . a great psychological nudist camp in which he (the participant) bares his pale, sensitive soul to the hard-nosed autocratic ruffians in his T-Group and gets roundly clobbered. He goes away with his sense of inferiority indelibly reinforced.[12]

For this reason sensitivity training must be used with discretion and conducted only by persons who possess the training and experience necessary to conduct the course. Managers desiring to attend a training lab should be thoroughly briefed as to what to expect and, if they do not feel up to the pressure, they should be discouraged from attending. It is also advisable that an individual's training experiences be followed by positive assistance and counseling to help him apply any improvement that he may gain from the training situation to the practical problems of his job.

A management training method that bears some resemblance to sensitivity training is the *managerial grid* approach that has been developed by Blake and Mouton. This approach, which is discussed in Chapter 14, involves the use of problem-solving "laboratory seminars" to convince managers that they should give simultaneous attention to both production and people in developing a management style that is appropriate to the organizational setting.[13]

---

[12]As quoted by Spencer Klow, "Inside a T-Group," *Think Magazine*, published by I.B.M., 1965.

[13]Lyman W. Porter, "Personnel Management," *Annual Review of Psychology*, Vol. 17, 1966, p. 409. Also see R. R. Blake and J. S. Mouton, *The Managerial Grid* (Houston, Texas: Gulf-Publishing Company, 1964).

Professional reading. Many larger companies maintain extensive business and technical libraries for their personnel. Executives are encouraged to make maximum use of these facilities as a means of improving their knowledge and of keeping abreast of the latest management practices. Some companies also have inaugurated accelerated reading courses. These courses are designed to improve reading speed and comprehension and to increase executive efficiency in the handling of paper work. Reading improvement programs can be a device for improving executive capacity for self-development. Professional readers also have been employed to digest the information from the more significant articles appearing in professional and trade publications. This information is made available to management personnel by means of tape recordings or printed abstracts.

Educational and professional organizations. In conducting training courses, companies usually can secure assistance from educational institutions and professional organizations. Some companies encourage their managers to take advantage of such development opportunities by paying the tuition costs of those who participate or by having academic courses conducted on company premises for their personnel. Educational opportunities of this type frequently can prove to be more effective and more economical than those that a company might conduct for itself. Many colleges and universities now offer advanced and middle management programs to meet the growing demands of companies for management development assistance. These programs, which normally last from six to twelve weeks, place emphasis upon broadening the manager's perspective, sharpening his decision-making skills, and exchanging with other managers ideas and experiences in handling management problems.

Certain professional organizations, such as the American Management Association and the Society for Advancement of Management, have greatly expanded their executive development activities during recent years. Increasing numbers of regional conferences and seminars covering general and specialized fields of management are now being provided by these organizations. The American Management Association, for example, offers a continuing series of management seminars and conferences covering many areas of management to meet the constantly increasing demands of business and industry for such offerings.

Administering the Development Program

Because management development programs provide a variety of developmental activities involving managers in departments throughout the organization, some degree of coordination and control must be provided within the program. Although the personnel department must play a major role in the administration of the program, the active participation and support of top management and department heads also is required.

Management Participation

While the development needs of each manager participating in the development program are likely to be different, the opportunities for self-improvement and for promotion that are provided by the program should be fair and consistent. To insure this condition, the work experiences, training activities, and changes in position assignments must be well coordinated. Therefore, the authority and responsibility for conducting the program must be centralized and the responsibilities of each department manager and the personnel manager be well defined. In some firms the responsibility for directing and coordinating the development program may be assigned to a senior manager; in others, to the personnel department.

It is also advisable to have a management development committee composed of members of top management to provide assistance in the administration of the program. A committee can contribute strength to a development program because its members normally represent the major departments that provide the work experience and the advancement opportunities for participants in the program. Furthermore, a committee can help to guarantee that each individual receives proper consideration and attention and that company-wide support and cooperation are maintained for the program. It may review each participant's performance rating and approve any major changes in his position, including transfer, promotion, or dismissal. Periodic appraisals of training methods, program phases, company organization, job descriptions, future management needs, or any other factors related to the general program of developing managers may also come under committee advisement or control.

If the senior managers in a company can be encouraged to take an active part in the program, their subordinates, who have the direct responsibility for developing managers at the lower levels of management, will be more likely to take these responsibilities seriously. Top management can lend support to the program, either by conducting certain development course sessions or by taking some of the courses themselves. This active participation is one of the best methods for generating cooperation and enthusiasm for the program at lower levels throughout the organization. Managers at all levels are more likely to feel that "if the old man can learn something through the program, perhaps I can, too."

Responsibilities of the Personnel Department

The personnel department performs many functions in connection with management development, even though the responsibility for on-the-job experiences must rest with each department. The personnel department generally is assigned the responsibility of planning and scheduling training classes and of arranging other forms of off-the-job development. Class instructors or discussion leaders are likely to be provided or recruited by the personnel department. The department also normally handles the arrangements for executive personnel to enroll in courses, seminars, and development programs conducted by colleges or by professional organizations.

In the performance of many of its regular personnel functions, the personnel department often can contribute to the building of a good executive staff. In the selection of individuals for employment, the department can be alert for applicants who evidence executive potential. Applicants who are hired specifically as management trainees are usually screened first by the personnel department. The paper work and communication of information relating to the placement, transfer, promotion, or discharge of participants within the program are among the other activities performed by the personnel department. Furthermore, the personnel records of these individuals, including the employment histories and performance appraisals, are normally maintained in a central location by the personnel department, and information relating to management replacement needs may be gathered by it. Also, the department frequently is in a position to provide counsel and influence in connection with decisions involving the assignments and progress of the participants.

Requirements for Successful Management Development

Because management development programs are of relatively recent origin, it is to be expected that some programs may not have proven to be too effective. Some programs have suffered because of misplaced emphasis, some have relied too much on the use of gimmicks, and others have merely served as "window dressing."

One leading management consultant feels that management development has failed to achieve its intended objectives because of:

1. Programmitis — a blind faith in a set of procedures which purports to turn out well-machined, perfectly integrated management talent.

2. The failure to identify *from the beginning* what a manager must do in managing and to develop and train managers to do this work.

3. The assumption that managers can be trained to manage *away from the job*.[14]

If a program is to avoid the preceding as well as other criticisms, it must meet certain requirements. As in the case of other programs, management development programs must be tailored to the needs of a particular company and must have the active support and cooperation of top management. Each individual's development must be centered around his particular needs as well as around his work activities on the job. Any training that he receives off the job must relate to his particular development needs. Individual development must consist primarily of guided self-development in which the performance and growth of each manager or manager trainee is carefully observed and evaluated and in which continued improvement is stimulated by means of coaching from superiors and staff specialists. The climate within the organization and the incentives that are provided individuals should stimulate their continual development and yet not force them to be pushed too fast or beyond their capacities.

In the future more emphasis is likely to be placed upon training in a team setting. This approach is advocated by one author who suggests that:

> . . . management staff groups, project teams and special task groups should receive training as a group, working simultaneously with technical and communication problems. They should be learning to work more effectively not with strangers, but with each other.[15]

Résumé

While a formal management development program cannot supplant the initiative and responsibility that an individual should assume for his own development, it can provide a better opportunity for such development to be achieved more systematically. A formal program can provide a more reliable basis for determining the development needs of each individual and for permitting these needs to be satisfied. Individual development must be centered around the experience and assistance that a person receives in learning to perform the functions of his job more effectively. Personal development gained through work experience often can be supplemented or made more meaningful through participation in classroom or other formal learning activities that may be achieved outside of the job.

While many managers and manager trainees probably will find adequate opportunities to develop themselves, the presence of a formal

---

[14]Louis A. Allen, "Does Management Development Develop Managers?" *Personnel* (September–October, 1957), pp. 18–25.

[15]Malcolm Shaw, "Changing Concepts in Management Development," *Training Directors Journal*, Vol. 17, No. 9 (September, 1963), pp. 15–24.

program can help to prevent any gaps in their development from occurring. A formal program also can help to insure that persons with management potential are recognized and do not become forgotten in "blind alley" assignments. Thus, the trend among companies to establish formal development programs reflects the growing realization of the importance of these programs in developing the number of executives with the qualifications that are needed to meet current and estimated future needs for managers.

DISCUSSION QUESTIONS AND PROBLEMS

1. Why is it important that a manager be sensitive to the reactions of others toward his behavior? Is it not even more important for his subordinates to be sensitive to his reactions?

2. When the participants of university-conducted advanced management seminars are asked to complete evaluation questionnaires on the programs, the responses are often quite favorable. How much weight do you feel should be given to these responses?

3. What difficulties may be encountered if the responsibility and authority for management development are assigned to the personnel department rather than to the senior line executive?

4. Is the fact that many of the more efficient companies have formal management development programs one of the principal reasons for their competitive successes? Discuss.

5. Do you feel that an individual with a college degree should be chosen as a management trainee in preference to another individual who has approximately the same level of intelligence but four years of operative experience in the company and only a high school diploma? How is this question being resolved by those companies with which you are familiar?

6. A group of managers from different companies were discussing management development at a conference. One executive expressed the opinion that those executives who had the potential talent would find ways of developing themselves. Another one stated that his firm had several promising young men who were qualified for promotions but could not be advanced because all positions at the higher level were filled. He stated that his company would be wasting money in training persons either for positions that they had already outgrown or for positions that would not be open for several years to come. What is your reaction to the statements of each of these two men?

7. Some companies adhere to the theory that an effective manager should be able to manage any department of the organization. To what extent do you agree or disagree with this theory?

8. The statement frequently is made that experience is the best teacher. Would you accept this statement as always being valid? Does on the job experience necessarily provide development?

9. Distinguish between the incident and the in-basket methods of training.

10. How does the "results" approach to performance evaluation differ from other approaches?

CASE 9-1

THE FT. DAVIS DEPOT

Ft. Davis Depot was established at a small town in Arizona near the close of World War II for the purpose of repairing and storing Army vehicles. It was manned primarily by civilian personnel with a small number of military personnel assigned to the depot for administrative and training purposes. For the first few years, the civilian complement totaled about 700 persons. During the Korean War the number grew rapidly to about 3,500 and then stabilized at about 2,500.

The depot was organized into three principal operating divisions: storage, repair, and stock control; and five smaller divisions: civilian personnel, depot facilities, inspection, transportation, and controller. Except for the civilian personnel division, a military officer was in charge of each of the divisions. Most of the administration, however, was handled by civilian division heads, since the military officers were rarely retained in any one assignment for longer than a two-year period.

As operations began to stabilize following the Korean Armistice, the depot received a series of written and oral communications from Washington recommending that steps be taken to provide an executive development program for both military and civilian personnel. The directives pertaining to executive development were very favorably received by a number of the civilian division heads, who were under pressure to improve management practices and operating efficiency within their divisions. Many of these executives, however, were of the opinion that further development was needed by their subordinates rather than by themselves. The commanding officer of the depot was of the opinion that all executives could profit from a development program.

Since no specific program or training methods had been recommended by the Washington headquarters, the training director arranged to start the development program by having a college in a neighboring town offer a course in management with college credit. The tuition and book costs were paid by the depot, and half of the instruction was offered on government time.

Although enrollment in the course was voluntary, definite pressure was exerted upon executives in the upper and middle levels of the organization. As a result, most of the executives in these groups enrolled in the course, many of them because they did not want to appear to be disinterested in self-improvement. A number of these reluctant enrollees, however, soon found more urgent tasks to occupy themselves during the hours that the classes were scheduled. As soon as sufficient time had passed to make their withdrawal politically safe, most of these individuals, who constituted about 20 out of the 72 enrolled, dropped out of the course completely. Of those who remained, about 30 tried to put forth the effort required to gain something from the course, while the remainder continued to attend class sporadically because they wanted to have the fact on record in their personnel file that they had taken the course.

Only 15 of those who enrolled in the course had had any previous college work, and only three possessed college degrees. The lack of a college background created a feeling of insecurity among many of the executives in attendance, particularly among those in the higher level positions. Their insecurity was further increased by the fact that some of their subordinates, who were also in the course, were able to earn better grades on the examinations. This factor contributed in part to the greater dropout rate among executives from the higher levels.

At the conclusion of the first course, a second one was offered by the college. At this time, however, no pressure to enroll was exerted. The opportunity to take the course was extended to executives in the lower levels in order to replace members in the original group who did not again enroll. Of the 50 executives who enrolled in this course, only 5 dropped out before completing it. The interest and performance displayed during the second course for the most part was improved considerably.

As the second course drew to a close, the training director submitted a request to the depot commander for funds and permission to offer a third course in the area of human relations. The depot had just changed commands, however, and the new commanding officer raised several questions about the requested course and about the depot's executive development program in general. He questioned, for example, why those participating in the program varied so much from one course to another and why the same persons had not taken both courses. He also questioned why a master development program had not been organized and why other development opportunities besides college courses were not being stressed.

There was some doubt in the commander's mind as to whether the benefits derived from the courses were commensurate with the costs involved. He, therefore, requested his deputy commander to make a study of the depot's executive development efforts and recommend what future action the depot should take in providing such a program.

    a. If you were conducting the evaluation, what future action would you recommend that the depot take with regard to executive development? Should the series of college courses be continued?

    b. What are the main weaknesses in the executive development efforts of the depot? Do you feel that these efforts have been of any value thus far?

    c. Do you feel that the course offerings were of the proper type? Do you feel that any value may have been derived from them?

    d. Are there any factors that might tend to make an executive development program more difficult to operate in a government organization as compared with a private firm?

CASE 9-2

THE SALINE CHEMICAL CORPORATION

The Saline Chemical Corporation, with headquarters in the Midwest, was engaged primarily in the production and nationwide distribution of chemical products for industrial and retail markets. The company, like many others in its field, experienced very rapid growth both in its sales volume (number of products produced) and the size of its work force in the decade following World War II. At the time that the problem for discussion arose, the company employed about 30,000 persons, including those in its subsidiaries.

In the process of its expansion the company was continually on the lookout for opportunities to purchase mineral properties for future sources of raw materials as well as smaller companies that might enable it to diversify its line of products, to gain new channels of distribution, or to acquire nationally known brand names under which it could market certain of its existing products. Because of the rapid technological advances within the industry and the rapid expansion that had occurred within its work force, the company required a relatively large number of college trained personnel for both line and staff positions at the executive level. Although it had had difficulty during the postwar period in recruiting adequate personnel of the caliber desired, the company had been able to develop a technical staff composed of personnel who were extremely valuable to it.

One of the members of its financial research staff was J. Clayton Hall, who was about 38 years of age and an honor graduate with an M.B.A. degree from an Eastern university. He had acquired some ten years of experience with the company and was responsible for the analysis of financial data and the compiling of reports for top management that were used in making company investment decisions. His work was extremely important because it provided the basis for decisions involving the investment of millions of dollars. Hall was regarded by his superiors as an extremely hard working and conscientious individual who was outstanding in his type of work. His salary had been advanced rapidly and was above that being paid by other companies for similar types of work. His opportunities for advancement to positions of greater income and responsibility, although contingent upon additional years of service, were definitely assured.

In spite of his successful record and his value to the company, Hall did not feel that he enjoyed prestige within the company that was commensurate with either his ability or with that accorded to persons in supervisory positions who were much less competent and less valuable to the company. His contacts with certain of his college classmates who had risen to managerial positions of major importance caused him to be extremely sensitive of the fact that he did not have authority over anyone. Hall's failure to gain supervisory responsibility was due partly to the fact that he was more valuable to the company in the type of position in which he had been working and partly to the fact that he was totally lacking in human relations skills. Most company personnel who had any contact with him considered him to be an overbearing and extremely obnoxious individual.

Although Hall did not "rub" people the wrong way intentionally, he usually was so engrossed with the technical aspects of his work that he did not have time to give much consideration to the feelings of others. Although he had been reminded of his personality deficiencies during many previous performance rating interviews with superiors, he had never been able to improve these defects to any noticeable extent. Because of his outstanding performance in his technical field, however, Hall's personality deficiencies had not impeded his progress. Furthermore, the fact that he had relatively few contacts with other people caused his unsatisfactory traits to be overlooked.

After brooding for some time over his lack of positional status, Hall approached the head of his department with the demand that he be given a position involving supervisory responsibility or he was going to quit. His superiors were quite aware of the fact that he had received several recent offers from other companies and that he was in a position to enforce his demands. While the company did not regard any of its personnel as being indispensable, it recognized that even if it could employ another person with Hall's abilities, several years of experience would be required before the replacement could equal Hall's present contributions.

The possibility of giving Hall a position with a more prestige-lending title was considered but ruled out because it conflicted with rather rigid company policies and traditions, which caused executive titles to be reserved almost entirely for those positions of a managerial nature. The few senior staff positions that did carry executive rank and status were staffed by those persons who had at least 20 to 25 years of company service. Although Hall undoubtedly would eventually be able to achieve one of these senior positions that carried the prestige he craved, this prospect was at least 10 years away. There appeared to be only two alternatives in dealing with Hall's demands. One alternative was to disregard his personality and give him some supervisory responsibilities in which he could enjoy the title and prestige of a line executive position. Or, management could attempt to change his mind by pointing out his value to the company, the importance of his job, and the opportunities for status that would ultimately be available to him. There were strong indications, however, that Hall would not be satisfied with anything less than a supervisory position and that he would resign if he did not get one.

    a. What are some of the possible underlying reasons for Hall's demands?
    b. What action should his department head take?
    c. Why is it that jobs involving authority over people traditionally carry more prestige and salary than technical jobs which may require more education but no authority over people?
    d. Are the company's management development practices at fault?

SUGGESTED READINGS

Allen, Louis A. *The Management Profession.* New York: McGraw-Hill Book Company, 1964. Pp. 3–97.

Bellows, Roger. *Executive Skills.* Englewood Cliffs, New Jersey: Prentice-Hall, Inc., 1962.

Corsini, Raymond J., *et al. Role Playing in Business and Industry.* New York: The Free Press of Glencoe, 1961.

Dooher, M. J., and Elizabeth Marting (Editors). *Selection of Management Personnel,* Vols. 1 and 2. New York: American Management Association, 1957.

Executive Selection, Development, and Inventory, Personnel Series, No. 171. New York: American Management Association, 1957.

Greenlaw, Paul S., Lowell W. Herron, and Richard H. Rawdon. *Business Simulation in Industrial and University Education.* Englewood Cliffs, New Jersey: Prentice-Hall, Inc., 1962.

Harrell, Thomas W. *Managers' Performance and Personality.* Cincinnati: South-Western Publishing Company, Inc., 1961.

Houston, George D. *Manager Development, Principles and Perspectives.* Homewood, Illinois: Richard D. Irwin, Inc., 1961.

Jennings, Eugene Emerson. *The Executive — Autocrat, Bureaucrat, Democrat.* New York: Harper & Row, Publishers, 1962.

Kibbee, Joel M., *et al. Management Games; A New Technique for Executive Development.* New York: Reinhold Publishing Corporation, 1961.

Mahoney, Thomas A. *Building the Executive Team.* Englewood Cliffs, New Jersey: Prentice-Hall, Inc., 1961.

Maier, Norman F., *et al. Supervisory and Executive Development: A Manual for Role Playing.* New York: John Wiley & Sons, Inc., 1957.

Shartle, Carroll L. *Executive Performance and Leadership.* Englewood Cliffs, New Jersey: Prentice-Hall, Inc., 1956.

Tannenbaum, Robert, Irving R. Weschler, and Fred Massarik. *Leadership and Organization: A Behavioral Science Approach.* New York: McGraw-Hill Book Company, 1961.

Weschler, Irving R., and Edgar H. Schein. *Five Issues in Human Relations Training.* Washington, D.C.: National Education Association, National Training Laboratories, 1962.

Performance Evaluation

In the preceding chapters the policies and procedures for procuring and developing a competent and stable work force were examined. Throughout the various steps in the development of employees and managers the need for continuous evaluation was stressed. Because of the importance of its role in the development of personnel at all levels, the function of evaluation will now be considered in detail.

Performance evaluation occurs whether or not there is a formal evaluation program in an organization. Employers are constantly observing the manner in which employees are carrying out their job assignments and forming impressions as to their relative worth to the organization. Most of the larger and many smaller companies, however, have developed a formal program that is designed to facilitate and to standardize the evaluation of employees. Such programs exist under a variety of labels. The traditional term "merit rating" is associated with an evaluation plan whereby hourly employees are rated on scales that are assigned point values. The points are then used as part of the criteria for determining wages, promotions, and similar tangible benefits.

"Merit rating" is still used in referring to evaluations of employees in jobs that are typically paid on an hourly basis. However, with the extension of performance evaluation programs to personnel in white-collar and managerial jobs and with some deemphasis on assigning points to employee performance, such terms as "performance appraisal" and "performance evaluation" have become more popular. Other titles may also be found, but they all refer to essentially the same type of program.

The success or failure of performance evaluation is dependent upon the attitudes of supervisory personnel toward it and their skill in achieving the objectives of such a program. In order for superiors to indicate the performance strengths and weaknesses of their subordinates, they must give some attention to evaluating the individuals in terms of specific qualities of behavior and in communicating their findings in meaningful terms to the individuals concerned. As supervisors improve their evaluation skills, they are able to assist subordinates in the development of their personal job efficiency and are in a better position to make definite contributions to the human relations climate of the organization.

In discussing this topic, consideration will be given to:

- The process of evaluation.
- Methods used in evaluating personnel.
- Utilization of performance evaluation data.

The Process of Evaluation

The evaluation of one person by another is as old as man himself. Men have typically assessed the value of other men in a variety of situations and will probably continue to do so. Most assessments of this type, however, are made in a casual and unsystematic manner with little thought being given to the important elements involved in the evaluative process.

The success of a formal evaluation program is dependent upon managers and supervisors who understand the values to be derived from active participation in the program, who establish criteria of satisfactory job performance, and who develop skill in assessing individual differences in performance.

Purposes of Evaluation Programs

The fact that over two thirds of 426 manufacturing and 529 nonmanufacturing companies surveyed in one study were found to have individual performance evaluation programs indicates the general acceptance of such programs in industry. Further questioning of those companies that have formal evaluation programs reveals that data concerning employee performance serve a variety of purposes. The data in Figure 10-1 show: (1) the percentage of companies in the different industries that indicate the use of performance evaluations, (2) the specific reasons for such evaluations, (3) whether or not the supervisor discusses ratings with the employees, and (4) the basis for evaluation.

Figure 10-1

PERFORMANCE EVALUATION PRACTICES

(All figures shown are percentages)

	Office Personnel Practices: Nonmanufacturing (529 companies)	Personnel Practices in Factory and Office: Manufacturing (426 companies)		
Companies having individual performance evaluation program	67	67		
		Blue-and White-Collar Employees	White-Collar Employees	Blue-Collar Employees Only
Reason for rating job performance*				
Salary determination	89	69	90	76
Promotion	85	73	80	59
Help supervisor know employees	64	61	65	41
Let employee know his progress	66	61	74	24
Training and development	72	61	70	41
Transfers	71	59	58	41
Basis for follow-up interview	47	34	49	29
Discharge	54	46	38	6
Personnel Research	23	29	27	18
Layoff	25	27	25	24
Does supervisor discuss rating with employee?				
Yes	71	56	71	59
No	29	44	29	41
How employees are rated				
Mostly on job performance	55	55	68	58
About half job performance and half personality characteristics	45	45	32	42

*Some companies selected more than one reason.

Source: *Office Personnel Practices: Nonmanufacturing* (New York: National Industrial Conference Board, 1965); *Personnel Practices in Factory and Office: Manufacturing*, Personnel Policy No. 194 (New York: National Industrial Conference Board, 1964).   Reproduced with permission of the National Industrial Conference Board.

It is interesting to note that such a program is reported to serve many purposes — it may contribute in some degree to salary determination, promotion, helping the supervisor know employees, advising an employee of his progress, training and development, research, and such personnel actions as transfers, discharge, and layoff. In fact, personnel evaluation may be used to serve several purposes that may not be compatible with one another. For example, as a result of several empirical studies conducted by General Electric Company, it was concluded that where appraisal interviews are used to accomplish the two objectives of (1) providing a written justification for salary action and (2) motivating the employee to improve his work performance, the two purposes are in conflict. As a result, the interview essentially becomes a salary discussion in which the manager justifies the action taken, and the discussion has little influence on future job performance.[1] It would appear, therefore, that for best results the purposes must be clearly understood and their compatibility determined so that the maximum value may be obtained from a program whose influence generally pervades the entire organization.

Inasmuch as the evaluation program involves every person in an organization — either as an evaluator or as the one being evaluated, or in both capacities — it is important that, before attempting to use the program to serve the various purposes that have been described, it should be well established and operating effectively. While the personnel department is ordinarily charged with the responsibility for establishing and coordinating the program, it is advisable that members from all levels within the organization as well as those from the personnel department be represented on the planning committee. This representation insures that the viewpoints of members of these groups are known and may be considered in developing a program that will be acceptable and workable. The planning committee will probably be primarily concerned with establishing and clarifying the objectives of the program. These objectives, which are agreed upon by the representatives, should be communicated to all personnel in order that they will understand the purpose of the program and its importance to them as well as to the company.

Careful thought should also be given to the training of managers and supervisors who will be responsible for the success of the evaluation program. They must be assured of top management's interest in the program, and they must be given adequate time in which to perform the evaluations. While it may be assumed that they know something about evaluating their subordinates, a training program should include discussion of the important facets of evaluation that are considered in this chapter and their specific applications in that company.

---

[1]H. H. Meyer, E. Kay, and J. R. P. French, Jr., "Split Roles in Performance Appraisal," *Harvard Business Review*, Vol. 43, No. 1 (January–February, 1965), pp. 123–129.

Criteria of Satisfactory Job Performance

In any evaluation process it is important to consider the basis against which individuals are compared; namely, the job standards or criteria of satisfactory performance. While each person who is conducting an evaluation has some standard or guide against which he makes comparisons, these standards or criteria must be selected in advance on the basis of study and understanding of the requirements of the job.

In production work the output of an individual in terms of quantity and quality may be compared with the standards developed from time and motion studies. Similarly in sales and other types of jobs which provide reliable and valid numerical indicators of job success, it is indefensible to rely solely on subjective evaluations. In jobs where performance cannot be evaluated primarily in terms of output or in which such intangible qualities as persistence, initiative, speed in making decisions, and similar characteristics are considered essential, the personal observations and reports of supervisory personnel are traditionally used.

In recent years, however, as companies have become larger and their operations more complex and often international in scope, the need for communicating information about the performance of managerial and technical personnel has resulted in more realistic as well as more scientific reporting of their performance. Instead of emphasizing personality traits, attention is focused on what the individual accomplishes. In the case of executives, for example, criteria of success include such factors as profitability on the part of the company that he manages, inventory turnover record achieved, customer service, methods improvement, cost reduction, improving market position for a product, reducing lost-time accident rates, etc.[2] These types of data can be expressed quantitatively as illustrated in Figure 10-2. This figure illustrates one section of the appraisal form for plant managers used by the American Radiator and Standard Sanitary Corporation. The results expected and actual results achieved are compared. This approach illustrates the fact that the performance of persons holding nonproduction jobs can and should be assessed objectively. It also illustrates the need for establishing expectancies against which personnel can be evaluated. In some instances these expectancies or performance standards are established by the subordinate himself in consultation with his superior. Details of this approach are presented later in this chapter.

---

[2]C. Wilson Randle and Willys H. Monroe, "Better Ways to Measure Executive Performance," *Management Methods*, Vol. 19, No. 4 (January, 1961), pp. 64–66.

Figure 10-2

EXPECTANCIES AND ACCOMPLISHMENTS APPROACH
TO PERFORMANCE EVALUATION

PLANT MANAGER

RESULTS EXPECTED	ACTUAL RESULTS ACHIEVED
1. Production to meet monthly requirement schedules within plus or minus 9%.	1. Production averaged within plus or minus 7.8%.
2. Hold scrap loss to 5% and defective returns to 2%.	2. Scrap loss was 4.8%. Defective returns were 1.9%.
3. Install division-wide methods improvement program. Reduce overall direct labor cost 3.5%.	3. Direct labor cost up 2.6%. Only minor improvements made.
4. Get five times turnover of raw and in-process inventories.	4. Inventory turnover was 3.7 times.
5. Complete modernization program at plant within limits of authorized appropriation by January 1, 1960.	5. Work completed December 15, 1959, at $2,814 under appropriation.

Source: C. Wilson Randle and Willys H. Monroe, "Better Ways to Measure Executive Performance," *Management Methods*, Vol. 19, No. 4 (January, 1961), pp. 64–66. Reprinted by permission from *Business Management.* Copyright, 1961, Management Magazines, Inc.

Methods Used in Evaluating Personnel

Formal methods for evaluating personnel in industry grew out of procedures that were already in use in the Armed Forces. Some of these early methods were rather crude, as illustrated in Figure 10-3, but they undoubtedly served some purpose. Later on, during World War I a man-to-man rating scale, originally developed by Walter Dill Scott[3] for use in rating salesmen, was adapted to meet the needs of the Army. Since that time, business and government as well as the Armed Forces have given increasing attention to performance evaluation. In the days following World War I the focus in industry was on evaluating personnel in blue-collar and white-collar jobs who were lower in the organizational hierachy. In the period since World War II, however, increasing attention has been given to evaluating the performance of middle and top managers, as well as technical and professional employees. Somewhat less emphasis is being given to evaluating blue-collar workers and those white-collar workers who are unionized. Since seniority usually plays an important part in the determination of wages and the advancement of employees in companies that

---

[3]Dr. Scott was the senior author of one of the earliest textbooks on personnel management.

Figure 10-3
EXCERPTS FROM THE FIRST RECORDED EFFICIENCY REPORT IN THE FILES OF THE WAR DEPARTMENT

Lower Seneca Town
August 15, 1813

Sir:

I forward a list of the officers of the 27th Regt. of Infty. arranged agreeably to rank. Annexed thereto you will find all the observations I deem necessary to make.

Respectfully,
I am, Sir
Yo. Obt. Servt.
Lewis Cass
Brig. Gen.

* * * * * * * * * *

27th Infantry Regiment

Alex Denniston — Lieut. Col., Comdg.	— A good natured man.
Clardson Crolins — First Major	— A good man, but no officer.
Jesse D. Wadsworth — 2nd Major	— An excellent officer.
Captain Christiem Martel " Aaron T. Crane " Benj. Wood " Maxwell " Shotwell	— All good officers.
" Shotwell	— A man of whom all unite in speaking ill. A knave despised by all.
" Allen Reynolds	— An officer of capacity, but impudent and a man of most violent passions.
" Danl. Warren Porter	— Stranger but little known in the regiment.
First Lieut. Jas. Kerr " " Thos. Darling	— Merely good, nothing promising.
" " Robt. P. Ross	— Willing enough — has much to learn with small capacity.
" " Hall	— Not joined the regiment.
2nd Lieut. Nicholas G. Carner	— A good officer but drinks hard and disgraces himself and the service.
" " Stewart Elder	— An ignorant unoffending Irishman.
" " McConkey	— Raised from the ranks, ignorant, vulgar and incompetent.
" " Piercy " " Jacob J. Brown " " Thos. G. Spicer " " Oliver Vance	— Come from the ranks, but all behave well and promise to make excellent officers.
Ensign Behan	— The very dregs of the earth, unfit for anything under heaven. God only knows how the poor thing got an appointment.
" John Brown " Bryan	— Promoted from the ranks — men of no manner and no promise.
" Charles West	— From the ranks. A good young man who does well.

are unionized, ratings are not likely to play a major role in most of the important personnel actions even if a formal evaluation program does exist. However, an effective evaluation program can provide a formal record of the employee's performance and of past efforts to achieve improvement which can be used to substantiate disciplinary action taken by management.

The change in emphasis as noted above and the development of newer concepts of measurement have resulted in new approaches to evaluation.

However, since some of the older approaches are still used widely and provide a historical background for the newer methods, the traditional approaches will be examined first.

Traditional Methods of Evaluation

The older methods of evaluation usually attempted to qualify employee behavior on traits that were deemed to be important measures of an employee's worth to the organization. The emphasis was on attempts to measure these traits which were often stated vaguely. As a result they were usually viewed in different ways by managers, supervisors, and employees — if the latter were informed at all as to their ratings. As various inadequacies were noted in the traditional methods, experts attempted to recommend better procedures with some degree of success. For example, it was advocated that these forms should contain characteristics that are observable, that are universal to all of the jobs in which personnel are to be rated, and that are distinguishable from other behaviors.[4] They should also be designed in such a manner that the rater can render the most objective opinion or evaluation of the person being rated. Many forms still leave much to be desired. On the other hand, there are many of them still used in a well planned and efficiently functioning program where the inadequacies of the methods have been minimized.

Graphic rating scale method. The graphic rating scale method is the most commonly used type of rating scale. Each trait or characteristic to be rated is represented by a line or scale on which the rater indicates the degree to which he believes the individual possesses the trait or characteristic. An example of this type of scale is shown in Figure 10-4. If the characteristics are not too broad and the descriptions of behavior are meaningful to the rater, this type of scale is not only valuable for reporting purposes but may also be used effectively as a basis for discussion with the ratee.

One major hazard in using the graphic rating scale is that the rater, unless advised to the contrary, is likely to assume that each trait or characteristic has equal value. Similarly, those reviewing the form may make the same assumption and thereby be misled as to the real importance of the different traits listed on the form. For example, the employee who is rated average on seven traits (Figure 10-4) and high on attendance (VIII) and appearance (IX) would probably not be as valuable as one also rated

---

[4]Reign Bittner, "Developing an Employee Merit Rating Procedure," in M. Joseph Dooher and Vivienne Marquis (Editors), *Rating Employee and Supervisory Performance* (New York: American Management Association, 1950), p. 26.

Figure 10-4

A GRAPHIC RATING SCALE

PERFORMANCE REVIEW FOR SERVICEMEN

1. Rate the employee by placing an X in the space above the description which most nearly expresses your judgment on each quality.

2. Consider only one trait or quality at a time.

3. Consider the individual's entire work performance on each trait. Don't base your judgment on only one or two occurrences.

4. Use the space provided on the back page for comments and explanations.

5. Make your rating an accurate description of the one rated.

	1	2	3	4	5	6	7	8	9	10
I-QUALITY Consider the thoroughness of his work and ability to perform work of high grade consistently.	Work almost worthless.	Rather careless. Below standard	Just satisfactory.		Good quality.			Highest quality.		
II-DEPENDABILITY Consider reliability in execution of assigned tasks; dependability in following instructions; does he stick to his job and do good work without constant supervision?	Unreliable and irregular	Slightly neglectful.	Fairly dependable.		Trustworthy			Extremely dependable.		
III-CUSTOMER CONTACTS Consider tact and other qualities in dealing with customers; ability in maintaining favorable customer relations and company good will.	Displays little or no ability to handle customers.	Lacks qualities to do and say the right thing.	Average ability to get along with customers.		Makes favorable impressions with customers.			Builds excellent relations with customers.		
IV-QUANTITY Consider the volume of work accomplished under normal conditions and the promptness with which it is completed.	Very slow worker. Little output.	Barely meets requirements.	Average		Turns out good volume.			Rapid worker. Unusually big producer.		
V-MECHANICAL SKILL Has he consistently demonstrated the ability to cope with varied mechanical problems?	Requires continuous and repeated instructions.	Requires repeated instructions. Has some difficulty solving new problems.	Satisfactory on routine work; meets requirements on new problems.		Good ability in coping with mechanical problems			Exceptional ability in analyzing and solving mechanical problems.		
VI-COOPERATION Consider his attitude toward his work, company and his associates, and his willingness to work with and for others.	Dislikes to cooperate.	Has some difficulty getting along with others.	Acceptable		Willing worker. Cooperates readily.			Goes out of his way to cooperate.		
VII-PERSONALITY-DISPOSITION Consider behavior; effect of disposition on others.	Definitely unfavorable.	Behavior and attitudes disturb harmony occasionally.	Gets along well generally. Not good and not bad.		Gets along well with majority of associates.			Excellent behavior. Well liked by all associates.		
VIII-ATTENDANCE What attitude does he have toward attendance. Is he on the job?	Indifferent attendance.	Frequent absences.	Occasionally absent. Usually with good reason.		Very regular. Seldom absent			Excellent record.		
IX-APPEARANCE How is he in dress and personal appearance. Does he make a good impression?	Indifferent	Slightly indifferent.	Acceptable		Makes good impression.			Extremely impressive.		

Source: Pitney-Bowes Company. Reproduced with permission.

average on seven traits but high on quality (I) and quantity (IV). While some companies attempt to arrive at a rating score, such a score is practically meaningless if it represents nothing more than the simple addition of ratings on the separate traits.

Some rating scales are designed so that each rating may be substantiated by a comment, as shown in Figure 10-5. This not only requires the supervisor to "back up" his rating with facts, but it may help to overcome some of the errors that occur with this and similar types of scales. One rater, for example, may be quite lenient with the result that most of his subordinates are rated superior on many characteristics. Another rater may tend to give low ratings, while a third may have a middle-of-the-road approach to evaluation and group his ratings around the average.

In training raters it is now common practice to instruct the rater to distribute his ratings in accordance with a pattern that conforms to the normal frequency distribution (see Figure 7-1, page 177), thereby forcing him to assign low ratings to some employees and high ratings to others. This method has the advantage of requiring raters to observe differences; but it may force them to report differences which in fact do not exist, especially if the group is small and selected.

Other traditional methods. While the graphic rating scale is the most commonly used method, the student should be familiar with other approaches to evaluation. The *check list method* is one that involves having the rater check those statements on a list that he feels are characteristic of the employee's performance or behavior.

The *method of paired comparisons* involves comparing each individual with all of the others in the group. With ten individuals this involves 45 comparisons times the number of traits or characteristics to be considered —a sizable task for the rater.

The *ranking method* of evaluation requires each rater to arrange his men in rank order from the best to the poorest. This method has the advantage of being simple to understand and to use, and it is quite natural for the rater to rank his subordinates. One of the main disadvantages of this method is the unwarranted assumption that the differences between ranks are the same.

Newer Approaches to Evaluation

While the more traditional methods of evaluation are being used every day, there are newer approaches available that have become increasingly popular. As in other areas of personnel management, however, there is a

Figure 10-5

A GRAPHIC RATING SCALE WITH PROVISION FOR RATER COMMENTS

Appraise employee's performance in PRESENT ASSIGNMENT. Check (✓) most appropriate square. Appraisers are *urged to use freely the* "REMARKS" sections for significant comments descriptive of the individual.

1. KNOWLEDGE OF WORK:
Understanding of all phases of his work and related matters.

Needs instruction or guidance.	Has required knowledge of own and re- lated work.	Has exceptional knowledge of own and re- lated work. ☒

Remarks: *Is particularly good on gas engines.*

2. INITIATIVE:
Ability to originate or develop ideas and to get things started.

Lacks imagination. ☒	Meets necessary requirements.	Unusually resourceful.

Remarks: *Has good ideas when asked for an opinion, but otherwise will not offer them. Somewhat lacking in self-confidence.*

3. APPLICATION:
Attention, and application to his work.

Wastes time. Needs close supervision. ☒	Steady and willing worker.	Exceptionally industrious.

Remarks:

4. QUALITY OF WORK:
Thoroughness, neatness, and accuracy of work.

Needs improvement.	Regularly meets recognized standards.	Consistently maintains highest ☒ quality.

Remarks: *The work he turns out is always of the highest possible quality.*

5. VOLUME OF WORK:
Quantity of acceptable work.

Should be increased.	Regularly meets recognized ☒ standards.	Unusually high output.

Remarks: *Would be higher if he did not spend so much time checking and rechecking his work.*

Source: Part of an Appraisal and Development Form used by the Standard Oil Company of California. Reproduced with permission.

resistance to change. Nevertheless, many companies are trying new approaches, frequently in conjunction with the more traditional methods. Several of the new approaches that are being used are the results-centered, forced-choice, critical-incident, field-review, group-appraisal, and peer-rating methods.

Results-centered method. The results-centered method, which is consistent with Peter Drucker's concept of "management by objectives,"[5] is briefly described by the late Douglas McGregor as follows:

> The first step in this process is to arrive at a clear statement of the major features of the job. Rather than a formal job description, this is a document drawn up *by the subordinate* after studying the company-approved statement. It defines the broad areas of his responsibility as they actually work out in practice. The boss and employee discuss the draft jointly and modify it as may be necessary until both of them agree that it is adequate.
>
> Working from this statement of responsibilities, the subordinate then establishes his goals or "targets" for a period of, say, six months. These targets are *specific* actions which the man proposes to take, i.e. setting up regular staff meetings to improve communication, reorganizing the office, completing or undertaking a certain study. Thus, they are explicitly stated and accompanied by a detailed account of the actions he proposes to take to reach them. This document is, in turn, discussed with the superior and modified until both are satisfied with it.
>
> At the conclusion of the six-month period, the subordinate makes his *own* appraisal of what he has accomplished relative to the targets he had set earlier. He substantiates it with factual data wherever possible. The "interview" is an examination by superior and subordinate together of the subordinate's self-appraisal, and it culminates in a re-setting of targets for the next six months.
>
> Of course, the superior has veto power at each step of this process; in an organizational hierarchy anything else would be unacceptable. However, in practice he rarely needs to exercise it.[6]

This plan shifts the emphasis from appraisal to self-analysis and from focus on the past to the future, and the subordinate is helped in relating his career planning to the needs and realities of the organization through consultations with his superior. These consultations, if properly conducted, should strengthen the superior-subordinate relationship and might well lead to a type of relationship in which the supervisor concerns himself with what he can do to help the subordinate reach his "targets."

Kindall and Gatza believe that this type of approach: (1) tends to help people set targets that are both challenging and more realistic, (2) provides a method of detecting training needs, and (3) treats as a total process

---

[5]Peter Drucker, *The Practice of Management* (New York: Harper & Brothers, 1954).

[6]Douglas McGregor, "An Uneasy Look at Performance Appraisal," *Harvard Business Review*, Vol. 35, No. 3 (May–June, 1957), pp. 89–94.

a person's ability to see an organizational problem, to devise ways of attacking it, and to translate his ideas into action.[7]

The results-centered method, however, is not without its critics. Some of the major pitfalls in this method are:

1. It leads many managers to assume that there is now less need for them to counsel employees because the figures give each man a running check on how he has done (see Figure 10-2 on page 252).
2. The performance data used in the results-centered appraisals are designed to measure end results on a short-term rather than a long-term basis. Thus, a line supervisor may let his machines suffer to reduce maintenance costs.
3. The method does not eliminate the personal idiosyncracies that shape each manager's dealings with subordinates.
4. It may be questioned whether the understanding that is supposed to develop between supervisor and subordinate really comes about.

In addition to the above criticisms, there is the inability or unwillingness of supervisors to discuss personal characteristics of the subordinates with them which appears to be the fundamental problem with this and other performance evaluation methods. Professional assistance to managers and supervisors in evaluating personnel and in conducting interviews is recommended.[8]

Forced-choice method. Among the newest of the rating methods is the forced-choice method. While it is not used as extensively as some of the other methods, it was used widely following World War II for rating officers who were being considered for commissions in the Regular Army. More recently it has been used by consultants in preparing evaluation forms for large industrial firms.

The typical forced-choice rating scale requires the rater to indicate by a check mark those statements that best describe the individual being rated. Since several statements equally favorable or unfavorable appear, the person completing the forced-choice report form cannot be certain whether he is giving the employee a high or a low rating. An example of forced-choice scale is made of groups of four statements, known as *tetrads*.

1. Able to handle emergency assignments.
2. Hesitates to offer new ideas.
3. Definite in goals.
4. Gets confused under pressure.

[7]Alva F. Kindall and James Gatza, "Positive Program for Performance Appraisal," *Harvard Business Review*, Vol. 41, No. 6 (November–December, 1963), pp. 153–160.

[8]Charles J. Coleman, "Avoiding the Pitfalls in Results-Oriented Appraisals," *Personnel*, Vol. 42, No. 6 (November–December, 1965), pp. 24–33.

The rater is presented with a list of such tetrads and is instructed to indicate in each the one statement that is most descriptive and the one statement that is least descriptive of the individual being rated. In the above list of tetrads, statement "1" is on a par with statement "3" as far as rater preference is concerned. Similarly, statement "2" is on a par with statement "4" as far as the undesirable qualities are concerned, thus causing the rater to choose the statement because it is descriptive of the individual and not because it sounds a little better or worse than the other statement. Thus, the extent to which his bias may influence his ratings is minimized. Where the forced-choice method has been used, it has been found to correlate more highly with productivity than with subjective factors.

The forced-choice method is not without limitations, the primary one being the cost of establishing and maintaining its validity. The fact that it has been a source of frustration to many raters has sometimes caused it to be eliminated from evaluation programs. In addition, it cannot be used as effectively as some of the other methods in contributing to the commonly held objective of employing evaluation as a tool for developing employees by such means as the evaluation interview.

Critical-incident method. Another of the more recent approaches to evaluation is the critical-incident method, which involves identifying, classifying, and recording critical incidents in employee behavior.

> Briefly, an incident is "critical" when it illustrates that the employee has done, or failed to do, something that results in unusual success or unusual failure on some part of his job.
> Critical incidents are facts (not opinions or generalizations), but not all facts are critical. . . .
> Critical facts are the employee actions that really make performance outstandingly effective or ineffective.[9]

The use of this method involves spotting critical incidents of employee performance, classifying the incidents according to the headings given in the record sheet maintained on each employee, and recording them. Before every performance review, the detailed entries under the major headings are summarized. As illustrated in Figure 10-6, space is provided under each heading on the performance record form for recording the "blue" incidents (favorable) and the "red" incidents (unfavorable).

The Delco-Remy Division of General Motors Corporation, where this method was first developed, found that six minutes per day in recording critical incidents was the average time required for supervisors to keep the

---

[9]John C. Flanagan and Robert B. Miller, *The Performance Record Handbook for Supervisors* (Chicago: Science Research Associates, 1955), p. 6.

Figure 10-6

EXAMPLE OF RECORDED CRITICAL INCIDENTS

4. ALERTNESS TO PROBLEM SITUATIONS

a. Did not see problem; b. Overlooked cause of problem; c. Failed to see special situation.

A. Saw problem as soon as it arose; B. Recognized cause of problem; C. Recognized situation that might produce problems.

DATE	ITEM	WHAT HAPPENED	DATE	ITEM	WHAT HAPPENED
12/14	c	delay on special letter	11/2	C	furnace problem

RED

BLUE

A special delivery letter came in about the same time as the regular mail delivery. Instead of delivering the special letter at once, this employe put it in with the regular mail.

This fellow was working late one Friday. He discovered an electric furnace had been accidentally shut off. He phoned his supervisor at home. This prompt action prevented the furnace from freezing up over the week-end.

Source: John C. Flanagan and Robert B. Miller, *The Performance Record Handbook for Supervisors* (Chicago: Science Research Associates, 1955), p. 16. Reproduced with permission.

program going according to correct procedure.[10]   While recording incidents is only one part of the program, these figures do indicate that the "bookkeeping" task is not as time-consuming as it may appear to be.

This method, which emphasizes the importance of recording both strengths and weaknesses in specifically categorized areas, is potentially one of the most effective methods of achieving the results desired from the personnel evaluation program since it provides concrete information that can and should be discussed with the employee, preferably at the time the incident occurs.[11]   If, however, the supervisor merely records incidents and does not discuss them with the employee, or waits several months to do so, this method may be viewed by subordinates as the "little black book" approach to personnel evaluation.   As noted earlier, the critical-incident method also is one approach to job analysis.   Furthermore, it may also provide behavioral descriptions that become the items or scales on another type of rating form, such as the graphic rating scale that was discussed earlier.[12]

Field-review method.   This method as typically used provides the type of professional assistance in evaluation that managers and supervisors often need.   It derives its name from the fact that a representative of the personnel department goes into the "field," that is, he leaves his desk and

[10]W. H. Gilman and E. P. Comer, "Selecting a Method of Performance Evaluation for Hourly Employees," *Supervision* (November, 1957).

[11]Albert S. Glickman, "Is Performance Appraisal Practical?", *Personnel Administration,* Vol. 27, No. 5 (September–October, 1964), pp. 28–32.

[12]William D. Buel, "Items, Scales and Raters: Some Suggestions and Comments," *Personnel Administration,* Vol. 25, No. 5 (September–October, 1962), pp. 15–20.

goes to the workplace of the supervisor to obtain information about the work of individual employees. The personnel technician will ask the supervisor detailed questions about each employee's performance and then return to his office to prepare the evaluation reports. The reports are then sent to the supervisor who revises them, if necessary, and then signs them to indicate his approval.[13] This method not only provides professional assistance to managers and supervisors but makes for greater standardization in the evaluation process and helps in avoiding some of the problems that arise when each evaluator works independently.

Group-appraisal method. Like the field-review method, the group-appraisal method provides for personnel, other than the immediate supervisor, to participate in the evaluation of subordinates. A group of managerial persons who know the employee, including his immediate supervisor and his superior, join in conference with a coordinator whose primary role is to keep the evaluation objective. They discuss the evaluation that has been previously prepared by the supervisor after a discussion with the employee as to the job requirements. Following the conference, the supervisor has another conference with the employee in which they discuss such things as standards of performance, the employee's performance, and any development action required to improve performance. While the supervisor has the responsibility for evaluation under this method, the fact that he will discuss it with the group is likely to stimulate him to be more careful in performing his evaluation. The Bell Telephone System, which uses this method for managerial jobs, refers to it as the *coordinated group-discussion approach.*

Peer-rating method. While evaluation by one's co-workers has been used extensively in the military forces, industry has made little use of peer or "buddy ratings." Research indicates that employing this method need not result in popularity contests and that, if a peer group has sufficient interaction and is reasonably stable over a period of time, the ratings are reliable (consistent) and agree closely with ratings made by supervisors.[14] The advantage of peer ratings seems to be that peers may view behavior that cannot be seen by supervisors. In addition, where several individuals appear to be equally qualified to fill a leadership position, the organization might benefit from selecting the man who is seen by his peers as having the highest informal leadership status.

---

[13]Stephen Habbe, "Merit Rating-Plus," *Management Record*, Vol. 15, No. 9 (September, 1953), pp. 323–324.

[14]Gene S. Booker and Ronald W. Miller, "A Closer Look at Peer Ratings," *Personnel*, Vol. 43, No. 1 (January–February, 1966), pp. 42–47.

Analysis of Performance Evaluations

If care is exercised in planning the evaluation program, high-quality evaluations will usually result. Analyses of performance evaluations must be made, though, especially when evaluations are in the form of ratings; for only by means of careful analysis can the reliability and validity of the ratings be estimated. Although perfection cannot be achieved, every effort should be made to improve the reliability and validity of the evaluations. This improvement may be accomplished by a program of research which utilizes data available within the organization.

Study tendencies of raters. One approach to determining the validity of ratings is to study the tendencies that the various raters have in assigning their ratings to subordinates. Some will be quite lenient while others will be strict. As a result, the ratings assigned by the lenient supervisor cannot be compared with those made by the strict supervisor unless some allowance is made for the differences in their rating tendencies.

Note departmental and job differences. Where careful analyses are made of ratings within a company, it is not unusual to find that the ratings on employees in different departments or in different jobs vary sufficiently to warrant some adjustment.

A similar problem often arises in connection with different jobs in the same company. Usually those individuals in jobs that require little skill are rated lower than those persons in jobs requiring a high level of skill. Because of this tendency, it is desirable to compare the ratings of individuals holding the same job rather than to use the ratings from individuals on all jobs as a basis for comparisons.

Developing scoring systems. Many scoring plans provide for a weighting of the traits or characteristics used in the scale. Various weightings are assigned on the basis of the different jobs and their requirements. For example, in one job judgment may be an important factor; whereas, in another job there is no requirement for the exercise of judgment. Instead of using separate forms for the different jobs, it is possible to recognize the varying importance of a characteristic to the performance of different jobs by assigning different weights to it on the scoring key for the rating scale. This procedure also helps to avoid the fallacious concept among the raters that traits are additive or are of equal value.

Relating evaluation data to other information. Objective measures of job performance, such as production records, should be utilized wherever possible in evaluating personnel. Where ratings may be used as a basis for making decisions affecting personnel, it is advisable to study the relationship between ratings and other available data about individuals, such as accidents, disciplinary action, grievances, and absenteeism, that may prove helpful in determining the objectivity of the ratings.

Errors of Judgment

If it were possible to evaluate all employees in terms of the number of units produced, dollar-value of merchandise sold, or other objective criteria, the evaluation process would be relatively simple and accurate. However, since judgments are the basis of most evaluations, the evaluation process is thus subject to the same errors made in evaluating job applicants plus some additional errors.

Halo error. The most common error in evaluating others is the halo error, which is the tendency to rate an individual either high or low in many traits because the rater knows or believes the individual to be high or low in some specific trait which the rater likes or dislikes. This is a form of prejudice or bias which prevents the evaluator from perceiving the behavior of another person accurately. The halo spreads or generalizes to other areas. For example, the supervisor who values punctuality may tend to rate punctual persons high on characteristics other than punctuality. While punctuality may be an important job requirement, this characteristic should be viewed and evaluated separately and not confused with quantity and quality of production, initiative, cooperation, or other factors.

Overemphasis on recent behavior. While most evaluation reports are designed to cover a period of six or twelve months, it is quite natural for the supervisor to be influenced primarily by what the subordinate has been doing most recently. If his recent performance has been superior, it is likely that the subordinate will receive a superior rating, even though his performance up to a month or two ago may have been less satisfactory. Similarly, if his performance has been satisfactory until a month or two before evaluation and his behavior is now considered unsatisfactory, it is likely that he will receive an unsatisfactory rating. In order to guard against overemphasis upon recent behavior, some procedure should be established for maintaining continuous records of employee performance. The critical-incident approach provides a method for encouraging supervisors to be constantly alert to the importance of continuous rather than sporadic evaluation of their subordinates.

Personal bias. Supervisors, like employment interviewers, have their own likes and dislikes that often affect their opinions about a person. They will seldom admit that a subordinate's religion, ancestry, educational level, and similar characteristics have any part in influencing their opinions about an employee's performance. However, it is a rare individual who can overlook personal preferences and be entirely objective in viewing the job performance of a subordinate who does not conform to these preferences. For this reason provision is usually made for evaluations to be assessed by a reviewing authority. This action, however, is not entirely successful because the rater has usually, in the months preceding the evaluation, convinced the reviewing authority that the performance of the person being rated is as now described in the evaluation.

Utilization of Performance Evaluation Data

The careful attention that is given to the planning, rating, and analysis phases of the evaluation program will contribute substantially to the success of the program. For the most part, however, the success of the program is dependent upon the effective utilization of performance evaluation reports by supervisors, managers, and the personnel department.

Evaluation Interviews

When the performance rating report is used as a basis for counseling the employee, it is customary for the rater to first submit his ratings to his immediate superior for review. The review procedure provides the superior with an opportunity to evaluate the rating ability and tendencies of the supervisor and to indicate his agreement or disagreement with any of the ratings. If he believes that the supervisor has been unfair in assigning a rating to an employee or has overlooked some aspect of the employee's performance, he can make any necessary adjustment before further use is made of the performance reports. This review procedure is customarily followed in most companies even though interviews with employees may not be conducted. It should be recognized, however, that such interviews may serve many useful purposes and should not be ignored if maximum benefit is to be derived from the evaluation program.

Purposes of evaluation interviews. Only about 70 percent of the companies interview white-collar employees, and fewer interview blue-collar employees about their performance reports (see Figure 10-1). These interviews, however, have many advantages if they are handled correctly. The interview provides an ideal opportunity to explore with the employee his present performance and areas of possible improvement, and it provides an opportunity to identify and understand the employee's feelings and attitudes more thoroughly. If the supervisor has received training in conducting such interviews and is able to apply the instructions skillfully, the interview may improve communication between the supervisor and the employee and result in a feeling of great harmony and cooperation.

Some supervisors may be reluctant to discuss evaluations with employees because they feel incompetent as interviewers. They may excuse themselves by rationalizing that they might hurt the employee's feelings, or that most employees should consider "no news" from them to be "good news," or that they are too busy to take time out for interviews. Fear of the unpleasantness aroused by criticism is also an inhibiting factor. Few persons, including supervisors, like to be viewed unfavorably by others. Since most of the unwillingness to discuss ratings with employees probably stems from feelings of fear and inadequacy on the part of supervisors in handling the employee who is upset over his ratings, the best way to solve this problem is to help raters to improve their interviewing skills.

Conducting evaluation interviews. Since the primary purpose of the evaluation interview is to make plans for further development, it is important to have some guidelines in the making of plans. The General Electric Company stresses the following:

1. Make plans specific and concrete; where possible, show desirable timing.
2. Emphasize strengths on which the individual can build or which he can use more effectively rather than stress weaknesses to be overcome.
3. Avoid suggestions involving the changing of personal characteristics and traits; instead, describe behavior which has hurt the individual in certain situations and suggest alternate, more acceptable ways of acting.
4. Concentrate on the opportunities for growth which exist within the framework of the individual's present position, recognizing that advancement generally stems from outstanding contribution on assigned responsibilities.
5. Limit plans for growth to a few important items which are possible of accomplishment within a reasonable time period.
6. Focus the plans on an objective — for example, to increase effectiveness as a communications specialist or as a cost accountant — rather than on general improvement.[15]

[15]Marion S. Kellogg, "New Angles in Performance Appraisal," *American Management Association, Management Report No. 63* (New York: American Management Association, Inc., 1961).

While the above approach is certainly positive in nature, it does not suggest that all unpleasantness be avoided. Criticism should be expressed tactfully and in specific terms and should not be omitted for fear it will cause "hurt" feelings. Harold Mayfield states that most people can take more candor than they get and that it is a grave mistake to shy away from straightforwardness with *all* merely because a *few* might wither before it. Mayfield also states that most supervisors err on the side of reticence rather than frankness.[16] It should not be inferred, however, that the superior should do all of the talking. While he should certainly express his opinions and guide the interview, he should encourage the subordinate to express his opinions and feelings as fully as necessary in order to achieve effective communication.

The key to successful interviewing lies in a versatile and flexible approach with the procedure adjusted to the overall purposes of the evaluation and to the specific requirements of each person being evaluated. In some instances the supervisor may prefer to use the directive approach, in others the nondirective approach, and more often a combination of the two approaches for effective two-way communication.[17] Maier has studied in detail the cause and effect relations in three types of appraisal interviews listed in Figure 10-7 on page 268. He has found that the "tell and sell" approach is the most representative of the styles used in appraisal interviews. As contrasted to the "tell and listen" approach, it can lead to arguments with subsequent face-saving problems and has the tendency to make for conformity. Maier, therefore, recommends increased use of the "tell and listen" approach and the "problem-solving" approach. The latter is particularly recommended since the objective of evaluation normally should be to stimulate growth and development in the employee.[18]

Taking Appropriate Corrective Action

In many instances the rating interview with the employee will provide the basis for noting deficiencies in employee performance and for making plans for improvement. As a result, corrective action can be taken by those

---

[16]Harold Mayfield, "In Defense of Performance Appraisal," *Harvard Business Review*, Vol. 38, No. 2 (March–April, 1960), pp. 81–87.

[17]Raymond F. Valentine, "Appraisal Interviewing: Flexibility Is the Key," *Supervisory Management*, Vol. 10, No. 11 (November, 1965).

[18]Norman R. F. Maier, *The Appraisal Interview* (New York: John Wiley and Sons, Inc., 1958).

Figure 10-7

CAUSE AND EFFECT RELATIONS IN THREE TYPES
OF APPRAISAL INTERVIEWS

METHOD	TELL AND SELL	TELL AND LISTEN	PROBLEM-SOLVING
Role of Interviewer	Judge	Judge	Helper
OBJECTIVE	To communicate evaluation To persuade employee to improve	To communicate evaluation To release defensive feelings	To stimulate growth and development in employee
ASSUMPTIONS	Employee desires to correct weaknesses if he knows them Any person can improve if he so chooses A superior is qualified to evaluate a subordinate	People will change if defensive feelings are removed	Growth can occur without correcting faults Discussing job problems leads to improved performance
REACTIONS	Defensive behavior suppressed Attempts to cover hostility	Defensive behavior expressed Employee feels accepted	Problem solving behavior
SKILLS	Salesmanship Patience	Listening and reflecting feelings Summarizing	Listening and reflecting feelings Reflecting ideas Using exploratory questions Summarizing
ATTITUDE	People profit from criticism and appreciate help	One can respect the feelings of others if one understands them	Discussion develops new ideas and mutual interests
MOTIVATION	Use of positive or negative incentives or both (Extrinsic in that motivation is added to the job itself)	Resistance to change reduced Positive incentive (Extrinsic and some intrinsic motivation)	Increased freedom Increased responsibility (Intrinsic motivation in that interest is inherent in the task)
GAINS	Success most probable when employee respects interviewer	Develops favorable attitude toward superior which increases probability of success	Almost assured of improvement in some respect
RISKS	Loss of loyalty Inhibition of independent judgment Face-saving problems created	Need for change may not be developed	Employee may lack ideas Change may be other than what superior had in mind
VALUES	Perpetuates existing practices and values	Permits interviewer to change his views in the light of employee's responses Some upward communication	Both learn since experience and views are pooled Change is facilitated

Source: Reproduced by permission from N. R. F. Maier, *The Appraisal Interview* (New York: John Wiley & Sons, Inc., 1958).

who are in the best position to do something about it, namely, the employee and the supervisor. Unless an evaluation interview is conducted, deficiencies could continue until they become quite serious, and they can continue to the point where it is no longer possible to take corrective action. For this reason many companies provide for frequent evaluations and interviews for new employees. It must also be recognized that occasionally it is necessary for the supervisor to refer problem cases to his line superior or to the personnel department with a recommendation that certain types of action be taken.

Performance ratings are of little practical benefit if the results are merely filed away. In addition to taking action on problem cases that are referred to it, the personnel department should study, evaluate, and take action on the evaluation reports as they receive them. The reports should be examined for evidence that indicates the need for administrative action such as promotion, demotion, transfer, or counseling. If supervisory personnel fail to recognize the need for such action, the personnel department should bring it to their attention and recommend that appropriate action be considered for the employee in question.

Once the evaluation system has been found to be effective, it may be used to evaluate the various phases of the personnel program. It provides information that may reveal the need for improvements, especially in the selection, placement, and training policies and procedures. Performance evaluation reports have been found to be valuable as measures of employee success that may be used in validating the tests used in personnel selection. On the basis of information concerning the value (validity) of the tests, it is possible to make improvements in the testing program that will result in the selection of employees who are more likely to be successful. Performance evaluation reports may also provide information that reveals the need for corrections in the values used in determining the relative worth of the job under a job evaluation program. Finally, it is important to recognize that the success of the entire personnel program is dependent upon the knowledge of employee performance in relation to the goals established for them and for the organization of which they are a part. This knowledge can best be obtained from a carefully planned and administered personnel evaluation program.

Résumé

If a company is to utilize effectively the abilities and capacities of its personnel, it must continually evaluate their progress. Similarly, if employees are to direct their energies most effectively, they must recognize their strengths and weaknesses and be given assistance in making improvements. Throughout this chapter an attempt has been made to emphasize the importance of establishing objectives and developing objective means of evaluating progress toward goals. Objective evaluation may be achieved through careful selection of the methods to be used and through training of supervisors. As they receive training in evaluation methods and develop an awareness of the importance of objective and unbiased evaluations of their subordinates, they are likely to develop an appreciation of the importance of using the information as a basis for developing the competencies of their subordinates.

All too frequently insufficient time and attention are given to the evaluation interview. Unless supervisors are successful in conducting the interviews with employees, the evaluation program is of little value to the company or its employees because important information and knowledge is not communicated. It is essential, therefore, that a training program include instruction and practice in conducting performance evaluation interviews. Finally, as confidence in the evaluation program develops, evaluation can provide a basis for promotions, demotions, transfers, and similar personnel actions. This objective basis for making such decisions strengthens the personnel program.

DISCUSSION QUESTIONS AND PROBLEMS

1. The average rating of personnel in highly skilled jobs is found to be significantly higher than the average rating for those in jobs requiring less skill.
   a. How do you explain the differences?
   b. What significance does this fact have for training evaluators?
2. Some companies do not permit employees to see their performance ratings. What reasons might they have for following this practice and what disadvantages might accrue from it?
3. Consider a job in which you have worked or in which you have had an opportunity to observe others. Can you think of any critical incidents that appeared to distinguish superior from "run-of-the-mill" employees?
4. The group appraisal method described in the chapter is not used by many companies.
   a. What factors would operate against its use? Are these valid reasons?
   b. What advantages are there in this approach? Any disadvantages?
5. In a survey of merit-rating programs, Prentice-Hall, Inc., found that only 9.4 percent of the companies saw their program as providing a counseling and interviewing opportunity and only 4.7 percent believed that a principal advantage was to create better supervisory-employee relationships.
   a. How do you account for these findings?
   b. What significance do they have for students of personnel management?
6. Walter Dill Scott helped pioneer the use of personnel ratings in industry prior to World War I. The method used was the man-to-man comparison scale that required each rater to prepare a list of key individuals on a "master scale" ranging from satisfactory to superior. Persons to be rated were then compared with those persons whose names were listed on the master scale and assigned ratings in accordance with how they fitted into the master scale.
   a. Why would such a method be seldom used today?
   b. What are the merits of this method?
   c. What method of selecting personnel for promotion was probably used before the development of Scott's man-to-man scale?

7. Employees of government agencies are rated on a form that provides for three types of ratings: outstanding, satisfactory, and unsatisfactory. Most employees receive satisfactory ratings; very few receive outstanding or unsatisfactory ratings and then only when clearly justified in writing.

   a. What is your opinion on the restricting of raters to these three categories?

   b. What effect is this restriction likely to have on employee performance?

   c. How would you probably react to receiving a satisfactory rating over a period of years?

8. The executives of the Precision Die-Casting Company, a firm with over 1,000 employees who were represented by one union, decided to install a merit-rating plan as a basis for rewarding those employees who received outstanding ratings from their foremen. At the end of the first rating period so many grievances were filed that the company decided to abandon the rating plan.

   a. How do you account for the deluge of grievances?

   b. What should management have done before installing the plan?

   c. Is it hopeless for management to expect a merit-rating plan to work?

CASE 10-1

AN EVALUATION INTERVIEW

Frank Blackburn, supervisor of 12 women who performed clerical functions in the branch office of a nationwide advertising firm, was in the process of completing rating forms on his subordinates as required by the Madison Avenue office. Upon completion of the forms it was his intention to interview each employee concerning her performance during the six-month period covered by the ratings, as required in the office procedural manual.

One of his subordinates, Rosemary Adams, was completing a year's service with the company. She evidenced considerable interest in her job, was very proficient, and accomplished her assignment in a very satisfactory manner. However, in her relations with fellow workers and with clients' representatives she was quite lacking in tact and tended to ruffle their feelings. There had been a few complaints but nothing serious enough to warrant action at the time. Two of the items on the rating form, "relationships with others" and "promotability," reminded Blackburn of the complaints that he had received.

   a. If you were Blackburn, how would you discuss the problem of tact with Miss Adams? Would you use the tell-and-sell, the tell-and-listen, or problem-solving approach? Why? (Students may find it interesting to role-play the performance evaluation interview).

   b. Would it be better to avoid saying anything about the problem, wait for specific events to happen again, and then call it to her attention?

CASE 10-2

GIMBEL'S RATING PLAN*

Gimbel Brothers in New York City (a department store) uses the Field Review Method of employee appraisal. A representative of the personnel

---

*Adapted from article by Stephen Habbe, "Merit Rating — Plus," *Management Record,* Vol. 15, No. 9 (September, 1953), pp. 323–324, with permission.

department is equipped with a register of the persons who work in a given unit and with the name of their supervisor. He is also equipped with a definite list of questions, usually memorized in advance, which he will ask the supervisor about each employee. The questions are asked and answered orally. The personnel representative may make notes, or a secretary may be present for this purpose, but no paper work is done by the supervisor. After the interviews have been completed, the personnel representative returns to his office and dictates his notes. The reports are sent to the supervisor who revises them, if necessary, and then signs them to indicate his approval.

An overall rating is obtained for each individual employee in terms of outstanding, satisfactory, or unsatisfactory, and the supervisor is asked such questions as "Is additional training indicated?", "Is he promotable?", etc. Whatever the individual's rating, the personnel analyst probes for supporting evidence by asking such questions as "What facts can you cite to support this rating?"

An important "plus" phase of the Gimbel plan is the report which the analyst makes, department by department. Summaries of the ratings of employees are prepared for each department and comments about human relations conditions, training needs, situations requiring action, and other areas are included in the summary report prepared by the personnel analysts. In using this program, Gimbels has stressed two essential requirements: highly competent personnel analysts and strong line support, including the full backing of top management.

    a. What are the advantages of having personnel analysts interview the supervisors and prepare the individual evaluation forms?

    b. The Gimbel plan calls for an interview between supervisor and employee following the rating period. How would the earlier conference between the supervisor and the personnel analyst facilitate the interview between supervisor and employee?

    c. What effect would the analyst's request for justification of ratings have on the quality of overall ratings?

SUGGESTED READINGS

Fleishman, Edwin A. *Studies in Personnel and Industrial Psychology*, Second Edition. Homewood, Illinois: The Dorsey Press, Inc., 1967. Section 2.

Gellerman, Saul W. *Motivation and Productivity*. New York: American Management Association, 1963. Chapter 19.

Hepner, Harry W. *Perceptive Management and Supervision*. Englewood Cliffs, New Jersey: Prentice-Hall, Inc., 1961. Chapter 18.

Maier, Norman R. F. *The Appraisal Interview: Objectives, Methods, Skills*. New York: John Wiley & Sons, Inc., 1958.

Sartain, Aaron Q., and Alton W. Baker. *The Supervisor and His Job*. New York: McGraw-Hill Book Company, 1965. Chapter 21.

Tiffin, Joseph, and Ernest J. McCormick. *Industrial Psychology*, Fifth Edition. Englewood Cliffs, New Jersey: Prentice-Hall, Inc., 1965. Chapter 9.

Valentine, Raymond F. *Performance Objectives for Managers*. New York: American Management Association, 1966.

Whisler, Thomas L., and Shirley F. Harper. *Performance Appraisal; Research and Practice*. New York: Holt, Rinehart & Winston, Inc., 1962.

Administering Change

Modern society is characterized by changes that are occurring at an increasingly rapid rate and that are in a large part the result of scientific discoveries and technological developments. These conditions, therefore, demand that enterprises and the personnel within them be capable of adapting to changes, if they are to continue to function effectively. Managers, in particular, must be alert to the need for change and take appropriate action to effect it within their own departments as well as to influence change within their enterprise and within society as a whole.

Within an enterprise changes are taking place continually with respect to the structure, functions, and work load of the organization and with respect to the numbers and types of jobs that are to be staffed within the organization. Changes are occurring also in terms of the qualifications, capacities, attitudes, and behavior of the personnel who are available to staff these positions. Many of these changes may in turn necessitate changes in the placement of employees by means of transfers, promotions, demotions, or even layoffs. Regardless of their nature, however, placement changes should be accomplished so as to place the employee in the job for which he is best suited and most needed, thereby contributing to greater efficiency and morale within the organization. Changes in employee placement, therefore, should be governed by sound policies and procedures that permit these changes to be kept under control and to be compatible with company objectives and employee welfare.

In discussing the subject of changes and their effects upon placement, this chapter will be concerned with the following topics:

- The necessity for change.
- Changes in employee placement.
- Seniority considerations.
- Policies and procedures relating to placement changes.

The Necessity for Change

In order to survive in a competitive environment, any business enterprise must strive continually to improve its products or services and its methods of operation as well as to adjust continually to changes in this environment. Ultimately, any improvements and adjustments that are made will require certain changes and adjustments to be made by the employees within the enterprise. Employees may be required to change their workplace or their work group, or to change certain of their duties and responsibilities, or to perform some other job. They also may be subject to changes in the work load, in performance standards, and in the methods, procedures, and equipment used on the job. One of the major tasks of every manager, therefore, is that of creating conditions that will encourage personnel to accept and to adjust to these changes rather than resist them.

Cause for Resistance to Change

People may resist change because they fear that the proposed change may cause them to suffer the loss of employment or a reduction in their earnings or that they may be forced to work harder in order to maintain their existing rate of earnings. Employees also may fear that the change will impair their status or reduce the recognition or satisfaction that they have been receiving from their work. They may also perceive a suggested change as an expression of criticism of their performance or actions. Resistance may result in other instances from an unwillingness to relinquish firmly established habits or to engage in learning something new.

Social causes for resistance to change may be due to the reluctance of employees to break established social ties or to the fear that new social relationships will not be as rewarding as former ones. Individuals who have difficulty in meeting and becoming acquainted with others may be afraid that they will not be accepted by individuals with whom they may be placed as a result of the change. Employees who are a part of a closely knit group may object to change if they feel that the change is being imposed upon them, without their consultation, for the benefit of the company or others outside of their group.

Achieving Change

Basic to overcoming resistance to any type of change is the development of a climate that is favorable for change. A favorable climate is one that permits employees to feel that they are a part of the organization and are encouraged to suggest improvements. It is also one in which they feel assured that management will make certain that their personal interests are protected in the event of change. A previous history of fair and consistent treatment of employees provides one of the best ways of providing such assurance. A favorable climate also is one which offers employees an opportunity to participate in determining and carrying out the change and to voice freely their ideas and objections about it.

The introduction of any changes should, when possible, be preceded by careful planning that involves all phases of the change, the steps by which it is to be effected, and the objections and resistances that may be raised to the change, as well as methods that may be used to overcome them. Planning should also provide for introducing the change at a time that is not likely to coincide with events such as layoffs, production cutbacks, or labor disputes that are likely to disturb employees and to be aggravated further by the change. Plans for change also should establish the program for communicating the details of the change to the employees and for keeping them advised of the progress being made in carrying it out.

Perhaps most important, employees must be convinced that they will benefit from the change or at least not be adversely affected by it. If possible, changes should be introduced gradually in order to permit employees more time to adjust to the change. The use of financial incentive systems that permit those persons who are involved to share in any of the financial benefits that may stem from the change will also contribute to getting the change accepted.

Changes in Employee Placement

One of the principal forms of change to which employees are subjected in every organization is that which involves a change of job placement. A change of jobs may be made necessary in order to accommodate changes that are occurring in production loads or processes in the organization. Such changes also may be required to allow for changes that have occurred in qualifications, performance, or behavior of the employee. Job changes in other instances may be made in an effort to find a job which is better for the employee in terms of his capabilities or his ability to get along more effectively with others.

A change of jobs may constitute a transfer, a promotion, or a demotion depending upon whether the new job to which the employee is assigned involves more, less, or the same amount of responsibility, status, and pay. When the employee is removed from employment in any job, the action may constitute a layoff if he is eligible for recall, or a discharge if he is terminated permanently.

Transfers

A transfer involves the placement of an individual in another job for which the duties, responsibilities, status, and remuneration are approximately equal to those of the previous job. A transfer may require an employee to change his work group, work place, work shift, or organizational unit; and it may even necessitate his relocating in another geographic area. A transfer makes possible the placement of an employee in a job where there is greater need for his services; it often permits an employee to be placed on a job which he prefers and can perform more effectively; and a transfer sometimes enables an employee to join a work group in which he can work more cooperatively.

Transfers can also provide employees with training and development experiences. Employment in a variety of jobs and departments can help to prepare an individual for jobs at a higher level as well as increase his effectiveness at his present level. Transfers can serve to move employees from "blind alley" jobs to those where they will have better opportunities to achieve further training and advancement. Employees also may be transferred by management in an effort to rectify earlier mistakes in the selection and placement of these individuals or to avoid the necessity of taking discharge action. Transfers at times may be carried out in an attempt to find some job that an individual can perform more satisfactorily or to try an employee with another work group where his relations with others might be improved.

Control of transfers. Since some loss of efficiency is likely to occur while the employees who are transferred are learning and adjusting to their new jobs, some degree of control should be maintained over transfers. Accurate sales, production, and manpower planning and the exercise of greater caution in the selection and placement of personnel, furthermore, can reduce the need for transfers. The transfer of "problem employees" in particular must be carefully controlled since too often such action does not remove the cause of the problem but may merely pass the problem on to some other supervisor. In some instances, a problem which exists between a supervisor and an employee may be the result of a clash in personalities for which both have a measure of responsibility. Correcting such conditions involves proper counseling with employees and the training of supervisors to be more perceptive with respect to their own personality traits. Where the problem lies partly or entirely with the employee, effective training, a change of work within the department, or disciplinary action may provide the best solution. If improvement in an employee's behavior cannot be achieved by such means, it may be preferable to discharge rather than to transfer the individual from job to job. The postponement of discharge action through such transfers can make eventual discharge action more difficult.

Employees' transfer requests must also be kept under control to prevent some individuals from continually changing jobs in hopes of finding an occupational Utopia. An employee who is constantly seeking to change jobs may not need a change of environment as much as he needs psychological help. If too many transfer requests originate within a particular department, however, it could indicate that the fault lies with the supervisor or with the conditions within the department rather than with the employees.

Resistance to transfers. It is not uncommon for employees to resist being transferred to another job. Even if the new job is considered to be equally desirable, a transfer necessitates certain changes in well-established habits; for a new job requires adjusting to new social relationships, to a new supervisor, and to new procedures. While a new job may be a source of stimulation for some individuals, it can be a source of anxiety for others.

If a transfer forces an employee to move to another locality, strong resistance to the move may be encountered not only from the employee but also from his wife who may object to the tasks of packing, house hunting, taking the children out of school, making new friends, and the other unpleasantries that a move may create. Mr. Leonard Yaseen, a nationally known consultant in the selection of new plant locations, even goes so far as to state that dissatisfaction with a transfer usually can be traced to wives who, he feels, do not adjust to the environment of a new location as readily as men.[1]

---

[1] *Saturday Evening Post* (October 22, 1960), p. 148.

Supervisors also may object to losing their personnel to another department through transfers. This reaction may stem from an inclination to hoard manpower and from the desire to avoid losing individuals who have received a considerable amount of training. Resistance may be particularly strong if a supervisor feels that he is being required to supply those personnel that he has trained to departments in which the supervisors have failed to provide adequate training programs for developing the potential of their subordinates.

Some of the resistance to transfers can be reduced by communicating to personnel the reasons why the transfers are necessary and the bases upon which personnel are selected for transfer. Supervisors also may offer less resistance if they are given some voice in selecting the individuals who are to be transferred. When supervisors are given an opportunity to recommend employees for transfer, however, they must not be permitted to utilize this opportunity to eliminate the poorest producers from their departments. Similarly, transfer policies should prevent supervisors from raiding other departments of their more qualified personnel.

Promotions

A *promotion* involves a change of assignment from a job of a lower level to one of a higher level within the organization. The new job normally is one that provides an employee with an increase in pay and status, but demands more of him in terms of the skill or responsibility that he must exercise.

Purposes of promotions. Promotions permit a company to utilize more effectively any skills and abilities that individuals have been able to develop during the course of their training and employment. The opportunity to gain a promotion can serve as an incentive for individuals to improve further their capacities and their performance. Promotions can also serve as a reward and as evidence of appreciation for past achievements. If the promotion program is administered properly, it can serve to improve employee efficiency and morale and to attract new employees to the company.

Bases for promotion. The benefits to be derived from a promotion program are contingent upon having objective criteria available for selecting individuals for promotion. The use of such criteria permits promotion decisions to be made fairly and enables employees to understand the basis for them.

Merit and seniority normally provide the two principal criteria for determining promotions. While the term *merit* more correctly applies to an individual's record of performance, it also is commonly used in reference to his abilities. In its broadest sense, merit can be said to refer to both past performance and ability; for it is in this sense that merit is used as a criterion for determining that an individual is qualified to meet the requirements of a higher level job. Evidence of merit may be provided by performance ratings, personal history records, and test scores.

Seniority refers to the length of service that an employee has accumulated. While seniority lends itself to more objective measurement than merit, its determination can create various problems that will be discussed later in this chapter.

In giving recognition to merit and seniority, the problem generally is not one of deciding which of the two factors to consider; rather, the problem is to determine the degree of recognition which should be given to each of the factors. Rarely is either merit or seniority considered to the exclusion of the other, although employers generally prefer to give more weight to merit. Even when not restricted by a contract, however, a company may find itself giving considerable recognition to seniority because of the difficulty of effectively measuring relative merit and of effectively communicating to employees that the measurement is accurate and fair. If the differences in merit among employees are small or are difficult to measure, often managers will, consciously or unconsciously, award promotions to those candidates with the longer service.

By recognizing seniority, supervisors are able to avoid employee charges that promotions are determined on the basis of "favoritism" or "politics." If union contract provisions require that preference be given to seniority whenever the abilities of employees are equal, the burden rests with the supervisor to show that the chosen candidate has superior ability in the event that he does not have the most seniority. It is not surprising, therefore, that a supervisor is likely to recommend for promotion the eligible candidate with the most seniority rather than to take the chance of having his judgment challenged and reversed by the union.

In considering candidates for promotion, performance in their present job may not necessarily provide an accurate basis for predicting success in a job at a higher level. This fact is especially true if an employee is being promoted into a different type of job, such as occurs when an operative employee is promoted to a supervisory job. To the extent that the functions of the job for which a candidate is being considered are different, it is important that merit be judged in terms of meeting the requirements of the higher level job as well as in terms of meeting those of his present one. Since it is difficult to avoid being influenced by past performance records, an estimate of future potential is likely to be somewhat biased and is more difficult to substantiate.

Encouraging employees to accept promotions. In our society an individual is under considerable pressure to seek and accept promotions if only to convince others that he possesses the ambition and competence that is expected of him. In spite of the social and psychological pressures to the contrary, there are many individuals who will refuse to accept a promotion. The compression of the wage differentials between jobs on different levels has prevented promotions from providing pay increases that are commensurate with the added responsibilities of a promotion, thus causing them to be less attractive. The attractiveness of a promotion is also likely to be reduced if a large portion of an individual's wage increase is consumed by income taxes. The loss of certain authority and status that was once associated with supervisory jobs has also discouraged many qualified individuals from accepting a promotion. Reluctance to seek promotions may, in some instances, stem from feelings of insecurity and the fear of possible failure. This fear is likely to grow as an individual approaches retirement age and becomes concerned primarily with avoiding mistakes or failures that might jeopardize his retirement benefits.

In order to interest qualified individuals in promotions, management must make a promotion worthwhile in terms of the pay, status, and other benefits received. By giving candidates proper encouragement, coaching, training, and the opportunity to perform the duties of the job for which they are eligible to be promoted, management can do much to build confidence and enthusiasm for accepting the promotion. It may be well, however, for management not to be overly insistent that an individual seek and accept a promotion. As Levinson indicates:

> Most men know more about how they feel and their assets and limitations than those who seek to persuade them. Even if a man underestimates himself, he has to live with his judgment of himself, and how he feels about himself is more critical in his success or failure than what he is objectively.[2]

Furthermore, Levinson is of the opinion that a man should not accept a promotion that requires him to behave in ways which are different from the ways in which he customarily prefers to act.[3]

---

[2]Harry Levinson, "The Problems of Promotion," *Think Magazine,* published by IBM, January–February, 1965.
[3]*Ibid.*

Adjustment to promotion. A promotion can create a decided change in both an employee's work situation and his behavior. Not only must the individual adjust to the new relationships and the added responsibilities of a higher level job, but he must also learn how to use the additional authority that it provides him. Since many of his associates are likely to continue to react to him as they did formerly, he may be faced with the problem of trying to exert his new authority without being accused of having it "go to his head." He also may have to contend with the hostility and undercutting from certain individuals who may resent his being promoted. Furthermore, he may find himself being observed closely for evidence that will support the contention of these individuals that he did not possess the necessary qualifications for promotion. Thus, when an employee is promoted, he may find it as difficult to adjust to the changes in the reactions of others toward him as to adjust to the changes in the requirements of his job.

The unsuccessful candidates. The selection of an employee for promotion can result in disappointment for the other individuals who may have felt that they deserved favorable consideration. In particular, such reactions may be expected from individuals who have participated in training courses and programs with the hope that such training experiences would correct deficiencies which had previously blocked their advancement. The manner in which the situation is presented to the "also rans" can have a significant bearing upon their future performance and attitude toward the company. Management can help to minimize disappointments among unsuccessful candidates if it notifies them in a manner that preserves their self-respect and permits them to understand what improvements, if any, they will be required to make in order to be promoted at some future date. Furthermore, by pointing out clearly what the higher level job may demand of an individual, those who are less qualified or interested sometimes may be encouraged to eliminate themselves as candidates. The fact should be stressed that they were not rejected or considered to be inferior candidates but, rather, that the person chosen was considered to possess the qualifications that more closely matched the requirements of the job.

If management has been conducting its performance evaluations and evaluation interviews properly, candidates should know approximately where they stand with regard to possible promotions before vacancies occur. The reaction of a candidate to being bypassed for promotion is likely to be affected by any encouragement or discouragement that he has previously received concerning his performance and his promotion opportunities. If his work has been praised in the past, or at least not criticized, he may have had reason to assume that he was in line for advancement. It is, therefore, important that the supervisor in his relations with subordinates make them aware of their chances for promotion and what improvements they must make to qualify before any openings occur.

Demotions

A *demotion* consists of a change in assignment to a job on a lower organizational level and involving less skill, responsibility, status, and pay. Employees may be demoted because of a reduction in the number of positions of the type they are occupying or because their performance has not been satisfactory. Demotions also may be used as a disciplinary action to punish employees for their failure to correct their deficiencies or to comply with existing policies, rules, or standards.

Demotion problems. A demotion can create more personnel problems within a company than other assignment changes because of the psychological effects that such action may have upon the demoted employee or upon his fellow workers. It is difficult for most employees to accept and adjust to the loss of pay and status that usually results from a demotion. Even if an employee may be more effective and eventually happier in a job at a lower level, he may still experience difficulty in adjusting to what he considers to be a loss of face. It is important, therefore, that an employee who is demoted be given assistance in adjusting to his new job and be given any encouragement that may be warranted regarding his chances for returning to his former level. If a person can be convinced that he actually will be better suited to the lower level job or if he knows that he has an opportunity eventually to regain his former job, the adjustment problems arising from his demotion may be less significant.

Alternatives to demotion. Sometimes an alternative course of action may be preferable to a demotion. When the abilities and skills of a long-service employee decline below the requirements of his job, the problem may be solved by transferring some of the duties of his job to other jobs while allowing the title and pay of the job to remain the same. In other instances, the problem may be handled by "kicking the person upstairs" to a job with an impressive title and relatively little authority or responsibility. This latter course of action is usually taken when a company no longer is able to tolerate an employee's incompetence in a responsible job but may desire to keep him on the payroll until his retirement because of his years of faithful service or his large holdings of company stock.

If an employee's difficulties are due to a hostile attitude or to an emotional disorder, a demotion may serve only to aggravate the problem. If these difficulties cannot be overcome by means of counseling or similar corrective action, consideration of the individual for early retirement or discharge may be a better solution to the problem than demotion.

Layoffs

In Chapter 5 the advantages of stabilized employment to both the company and employees were discussed. In spite of its efforts to avoid the layoff of employees, a company may find it necessary to reduce the size of its work force as a result of a reduction in its work load, the elimination of certain jobs through reorganization, or the improvements made in production efficiency. While the reduction in the work force sometimes necessitates the permanent termination of the services of some employees, it can at times be accomplished by laying them off temporarily pending the resumption of business activity.

Nature of layoffs. The procedures by which layoffs may be accomplished and the nature of the reemployment of those affected by layoffs are usually covered in considerable detail by the labor agreement in those companies that are unionized. Adequate protection of job rights and equitable treatment of members whenever layoffs are necessary are among the benefits that individuals seek first from their union. Company policy as well as provisions in the labor agreement, therefore, should establish and define clearly the employment rights of each individual and the basis upon which layoff selections will be made and reemployment effected. The rights of employees during layoffs, the conditions concerning their eligibility for recall, and their obligations in accepting recall should also be clarified. It is common for labor agreements to preserve the reemployment rights of an individual receiving a layoff for periods of up to two years, providing that he does not refuse to return to work if recalled sooner.

Determination of the order of layoffs. The determination of the order of layoff for employees usually is based upon seniority and/or ability. Under some labor agreements seniority may be the primary consideration, as illustrated by the following provision:

> In all cases of layoffs or rehiring the principle of straight seniority by departments shall be observed and the length of service shall govern provided the employees shall have the skill, industry and ability to do the work they are required in a satisfactory manner.[4]

[4]Agreement between the Allen Manufacturing Co. and the United Auto Workers.

In other companies such factors as ability and fitness may take precedence over seniority in determining layoffs. For example, a labor agreement may provide that:

> ... in all cases of decreases in forces or recalls after layoff, the following factors as listed below shall be considered; however, only where both factors "a" and "b" are relatively equal shall continuous service be the determining factor:
> a. Ability to perform the work.
> b. Physical fitness.
> c. Continuous service.[5]

In the case of companies that are not unionized, definite policies and procedures should be established for conducting layoffs so as to insure that employees will receive fair and consistent treatment and be able to anticipate their vulnerability to layoff. Even when provisions governing layoff are contained in a labor agreement, it is still desirable to establish policies and procedures that can serve to supplement and clarify the terms of the agreement.

Compensation during layoff. There is a growing trend for companies to provide some form of compensation to employees who are laid off or terminated permanently. This trend began in 1955 when the United Auto Workers successfully negotiated a Supplemental Unemployment Benefit (SUB) plan with the automobile industry which established a pattern for other industries. The SUB plan permits an employee who receives a layoff to draw, in addition to his state unemployment compensation, weekly benefits from the company that are paid from a special fund created for this purpose. Many SUB plans in recent years have been liberalized to permit employees to receive benefits when the length of their workweek is reduced and to receive a lump sum payment if their employment is terminated permanently. The amount of these benefits is determined by his length of service and wage rate. Employer liability under the plan is limited to the amount of money that has been accumulated within the fund from employer contributions based on the man-hours of work performed in the company. In those states that forbid a worker from receiving SUB payments simultaneously with his state unemployment compensation payments, the benefits from each of the two sources may be drawn on alternate weeks; or the SUB payments may be accumulated and paid after all state unemployment compensation payments have been received.

State unemployment compensation. Employees who have been working in employment covered by the Social Security Act and who are laid off may

---

[5]Agreement between the U.S. Steel Corp. and the United Steel Workers, effective through July, 1968.

be eligible for unemployment compensation during their unemployment for a period up to 26 weeks. Eligible persons must submit application for unemployment compensation with their state employment agency, register for available work, and be willing to accept any suitable employment that may be offered to them. While the term "suitable" permits an individual to enjoy considerable discretion in accepting or rejecting job offers, he must, nevertheless, make weekly contact with the employment office in order to receive his weekly check.

The amount of the compensation that a worker is eligible to receive, which varies among states, is determined by his previous wage rate and previous period of employment. Funds for unemployment compensation are derived from a payroll tax based upon the wages paid to each employee, up to an established maximum. A separate account record is maintained for each employer; and when the required reserve has been accumulated within his account, the amount of his tax is reduced. Because of this sliding tax rate, the employer has an added incentive not to lay off his personnel since the unemployment compensation that these personnel will receive will deplete his reserve account and cause his payroll tax rate to increase again.

If the trend toward further liberalization of supplemental unemployment benefits and unemployment compensation continues, and there appears to be little evidence to indicate that it will not continue, a rather interesting paradox may develop with regard to employee attitudes toward layoffs. As the combined benefits from the two sources more nearly equal an employee's take home pay, a temporary layoff may be preferable to continued employment. One article reports that:

> Several UAW locals have asked that seniority rules be dropped when it comes to short-term layoffs. Older workers, they argue, should be given the choice between working full time at full pay or taking time off at 75% of base pay. The senior men, often in their late fifties or early sixties, would prefer time off, the younger workers say, for their children are grown up, their expenses are smaller and they are more likely to appreciate free time than the younger workers whose need for full pay is greater. . . .[6]

Funds that have been accumulated in their retirement, profit sharing, or company savings account also may provide some employees with an inducement to quit in order to be able to withdraw the money that is available. The situation portrayed in Figure 11-1 therefore may not be as unrealistic as it might seem to be.

---

[6]Thomas R. Brooks, "Bleaching the Blue Collar," *Dun's Review and Modern Industry*, Vol. 79, No. 1 (January, 1962), p. 61.

Figure 11-1

"I really hate to leave the firm, Mr. Brown, but I
can't afford to pass up the severance pay."

Source: *The Wall Street Journal*, January 31, 1962. Reproduced with permission.

Seniority Considerations

Seniority refers to the relative amount of service that an employee has
accumulated in a particular job category within a company and for which
he is entitled to receive certain rights and privileges. It has become well-
established in industry to give some degree of recognition to seniority even
among employees who are not unionized. Unions generally advocate
recognition of seniority because they feel that their members should be
entitled to certain job rights that are proportionate to the years that they
have invested in their jobs.

Whenever seniority provides a basis for determining or even influencing personnel decisions, the judgment and discretion of management is
reduced accordingly. Decisions based on seniority are relatively easy to

make since they require merely computing the amount of service that an individual has accumulated and, by referring to established policies and rules, determining entitlements to be derived from such seniority.

Advantages of Seniority

One of the principal advantages in giving recognition to seniority is that it helps to provide employees with a greater feeling of security since they know that their employment rights will be protected as long as they meet the minimum performance requirements for their jobs. Recognition of seniority also reflects an appreciation by the company for the years of service given by employees which can be an important factor in contributing to the development of employee morale. If a company is successful with its selection and training efforts and has eliminated at an early date those individuals who do not show promise, there is no reason why the growth and development of employees should not be consistent with their years of service. Seniority, moreover, lends itself to objective measurement; and when decisions are based upon seniority, disappointed employees have no justification to claim that favoritism or prejudice influenced the decision. Since seniority is a matter of record which can be understood readily by employees, they have more confidence in its use than they may have in other criteria. By way of contrast, it can be quite difficult to explain employee ability differences and to convince employees that the differences in ability have been accurately and fairly determined.

Disadvantages of Seniority

One of the major disadvantages of placing too much emphasis upon seniority is that the less competent employees receive the same amount of rewards and security as the more competent ones. Employees with outstanding abilities are faced with the alternative of seeking other employment where their abilities will be recognized more rapidly or of waiting out the time required for a promotion while their talents remain largely untapped and their ambitions may deteriorate. Individuals whose performance is of only minimal quality, on the other hand, are protected by seniority provisions from the competition of more competent employees who might otherwise move ahead of them. While it is important that employees enjoy a certain degree of job security, this security does not require that excessive recognition be given to seniority. The feeling of security that an individual acquires through the development of marketable skills or by achieving a level of performance that makes him invaluable to his employer may be preferable to that acquired by being sheltered through seniority provisions from the competition of other employees.

Seniority Provisions

In order to be able to compute the amount of an employee's seniority, it is first necessary to establish certain provisions governing the conditions under which it can be accumulated and applied. These provisions, which are usually covered in detail by the labor agreement, should clarify: (1) the organizational unit within which seniority rights may be accumulated and applied, (2) the conditions under which these rights may be accumulated and retained, (3) the rights and benefits that are to be determined by seniority, and (4) the groups that may be excluded from seniority provisions. The way in which these factors are decided can be vital to the company's operating efficiency and to the security of individuals and groups within the company, and, inevitably, the seniority provisions which are established will not prove to be satisfactory to everyone.

Seniority units. The organization unit within which seniority is to be accumulated may include the company as a whole, a plant, a department, an occupational group of jobs, or a single job. If a department is established as the seniority unit, for example, service in one department will not count toward the seniority accumulated in another department. Most companies prefer to limit the seniority unit to a workable size, such as a department or a group of jobs, in order to simplify administration. Unions, however, may tend to seek the size of unit that will provide the greatest protection for members of the faction that dominate the administration of the union.

Accumulation of seniority. Policies relating to seniority must establish the date that an individual will begin to accumulate seniority. This date might be the day that an individual is hired, that he reports for work, or that he completes his probationary period of service. Seniority policies must also clarify whether seniority shall be permitted to accumulate or even be retained when an employee is absent from his job. In regard to this policy, it appears to be fairly common for companies to permit employees to retain their seniority rights during periods of absence providing that the absences were justified and management was notified about them. Seniority rights also are usually retained during periods of strike or layoff, providing that the employee returns to work within a specified number of days following the end of the layoff or the strike. Most contracts, however, provide that seniority will be terminated whenever an employee quits, is discharged, or is absent for a period without giving proper notification or reason.

Seniority rights. Seniority has tended to be given greater weight in connection with decisions affecting layoffs than in connection with those involving promotions or transfers.

In a survey of labor agreements conducted by the Bureau of National Affairs, seniority was a major factor in determining the layoff or recall of production employees in 96 percent of the larger companies (over 1000 employees) and in 91 percent of the smaller companies that were studied. It was also the major factor in the layoff and recall of office employees in 32 percent of the companies studied.[7] Seniority, moreover, was referred to as *a* "factor" for determining promotions in 72 percent of the companies, *the* determining factor in 31 percent of the companies, and *the sole* factor in 2 percent of the companies where the employee was qualified.[8]

Exclusions from seniority. Most seniority systems exclude certain groups of employees from coverage. Personnel at the supervisory level and above are usually excluded from seniority provisions, and often some key nonsupervisory personnel that the company would want to retain in spite of layoffs are excluded. Shop stewards and other leaders within the union may also be specifically excluded from seniority provisions in order that the union organization will not be impaired by layoffs.

Policies and Procedures Relating to Placement Changes

Since changes in job placement can have a significant effect upon company efficiency and upon the morale and the lives of its employees, it is important that such changes give recognition to the needs of both the organization and the employees. Carefully prepared policies and procedures can help both to acquaint personnel with the circumstances under which changes in assignments are permitted and to prevent inequities and abuses from occurring as a result of such changes.

Authority for Making Placement Changes

In order for changes in job placement to be coordinated and controlled most effectively, they should be processed through the personnel department.

---

[7]Bureau of National Affairs, *Labor Policy and Practice*, Vol. 4 (Washington, D.C., 1961), pp. 207:401.

[8]*Ibid.*, pp. 207:102.

While department managers must have authority to make changes in employee job assignments if they are to be held responsible for the efficiency of their departments, they must make these changes in accordance with established policies and procedures. If they do not do so, it is within the functional authority of the personnel department to prevent the changes in placement from being executed. If some form of staff control were not provided, operating departments occasionally might make changes in job assignments that would ignore the rights of individual employees or the pertinent text of the labor agreement.

Since personnel in any one of several different departments may be eligible to fill a job vacancy or to receive a layoff, some centralized system of locating and screening eligible personnel is necessary. The personnel department, which usually is given the responsibility for maintaining personnel records, is the department that logically should be delegated the responsibility for administering this system.

Location of Eligible Employees

In larger organizations it is particularly desirable that a centralized record system be established that will permit the rapid location of personnel on the basis of specific qualification factors. The use of punch cards and electronic data processing systems, which are discussed in Chapter 5, can permit a company to locate qualified personnel to fill openings and can facilitate the accumulation of useful statistical data concerning its work force.

The location of employees for promotion or transfer also may be accomplished by means of a job-bidding system. Success with such a system is contingent upon a company being able to notify promptly all candidates who might be eligible about job vacancies and also to prevent employees from bidding indiscriminately. Some companies attempt to control indiscriminate bidding by restricting the bidding rights for a specified period of time for employees who have bid on jobs for which they are not qualified or who have refused to accept jobs on which they have bid.

Effecting Changes in Placement

The manner in which changes in job assignments are announced and made can have a very important effect upon an employee's attitude toward the change as well as his adjustment to it. Announcement by means of a personal interview generally is preferable to written notification since the former method reflects more human consideration and also permits the individual to ask questions and express his feelings and objections. If an individual is forced to learn about a change affecting his welfare by means of a written notice or, even worse, by way of the grapevine, he may conclude, and perhaps rightfully so, that management is not sufficiently interested in his welfare to notify him personally.

A company can improve an employee's attitude toward an assignment change, as well as his productivity, by helping the employee to "learn the ropes" of his new job and to be accepted into his new work group. If the change requires a move to a new location, management should make certain that there will be personnel at the new location available to help the employee get settled in the new surroundings. Compensation for moving costs, including the extra costs involved in house hunting, are becoming a more common practice in industry when the move is initiated by the company. A number of companies have also assumed the responsibility of selling the employee's home in order to protect him from losses that might be incurred by a forced sale.

In administering changes in job placement, it is to be expected that certain problems will be encountered both by individual employees and by the company. If handled on a systematic basis that is understood clearly by all employees and if information pertaining to changes is communicated effectively, however, such problems can be minimized. By giving individual consideration and attention to employees in helping them to solve their adjustment problems, management can do much to maintain their morale and efficiency during assignment changes.

Résumé

Every enterprise must be dynamic and undergo changes continually if it is to continue to exist and cope with the changes in various internal and external forces that may affect its operations. Changes that are required within an enterprise cannot be achieved unless the employees who are involved are willing to cooperate in making the change. Employee acceptance and adjustment to change can be achieved more readily if management exercises proper care in preparing, motivating, and assisting them in making the change.

One of the more important and frequent types of change that employees are required to make is that which involves their job assignment. When changes are necessary, the interests of both the employees and the company can best be protected through the development and enforcement of sound policies and procedures governing these assignment changes.

The condition and basis for making these changes should be thoroughly understood by all personnel, and sufficient control should be maintained by the personnel department to insure that changes in placement are made in a fair and consistent manner.

The program governing job changes should determine the recognition to be given to ability and seniority, and information pertaining to this subject should be communicated to employees. Since employee initiative and efficiency can be jeopardized if too much recognition is given to seniority, it is advisable for management to resist the inclusion of restrictive seniority; it should not be considered to the exclusion of ability. It is particularly important that management recognize that a change of jobs can provide a very critical experience for an employee even though the change may be accomplished merely by making minor entries in company personnel records. While an employee may only be a data card in a record system to a member of the personnel staff, he is a definite human personality as far as he and others around him are concerned.

DISCUSSION QUESTIONS AND PROBLEMS

1. Why do employees resist change? Under what circumstance may they seek to have change accomplished?
2. Would a manager who has recently taken over a department be in a better position than his predecessor (who had been the manager for a number of years) to install completely new operating procedures? Assume that the ages, experiences, and qualifications of the two managers are about equal.
3. To what extent, if any, should a company attempt to overcome the reluctance of apparently capable personnel to accept a promotion? How might such reluctance be overcome?
4. What explanation and justification can you give for the fact that seniority tends to be more of a determining factor in those decisions involving layoff than in those decisions involving promotion?
5. Could it possibly cost a company more to agree to strict seniority provisions in its union agreement than for it to give the union a ten-cent-per-hour wage increase? Discuss.
6. What problems are likely to develop as company supplemental unemployment benefits are increased? What effect may such a trend have, if any, upon management policies and practices?
7. Some unions have argued that since companies already provide guaranteed employment for management personnel it is only fair that operative personnel be accorded the same treatment. To what extent do you agree or disagree with this argument?
8. The personnel manager has received a request from an employee to be transferred to another department because the employee feels that his current supervisor is standing in the way of his advancement. The employee has requested that his supervisor not be advised of his interview for fear that

the supervisor might make future conditions unbearable. The personnel manager has heard a few other complaints about this supervisor, but none of them have been raised formally.

   a. What action should the personnel manager take?

   b. Should he disclose the request to the supervisor?

9. The management of a company with extensive operations in a number of foreign countries has become concerned over the fact that some of its personnel overseas appear to be "going native." Several employees have even refused to accept promotions that would take them back to the States. A few of them have married nationals in the countries where they have been working who might not be accepted socially by friends at home. The company is considering a policy which would limit the time that employees may live in a foreign country.

   a. How would you suggest that the company deal with this problem?

   b. Would you recommend that the length of service in a foreign country be limited?

CASE 11-1

A CASE OF HOMESICKNESS

The Franklin Electric Corporation, with headquarters in Chicago, manufactured and distributed electric motors throughout the United States and in many foreign countries. Early in February Mr. Timmons, the sales manager for the Eastern Division of the Company, received an office visit from Mr. Harold Enoch, a sales supervisor in one of the northern districts of the division.

Enoch was 32 years old, married, and had two children of preschool age. He had served four years in the Navy and had attended a state college in California following his discharge. He graduated four years later with a degree in business administration and had immediately joined the Franklin Corporation as a sales trainee. His first six months were spent in the company's program in Chicago and his next six months in the field under the supervision of a senior salesman. After a year of training, Enoch was assigned a territory in Oakland, California, where he worked for two years and made an outstanding record. Because of his record and executive potential, the company transferred him to the home office in Chicago so that he might acquire additional experience in its sales promotion division. After 26 months in Chicago, Enoch was sent to its Eastern Division where he was made a sales supervisor of one of the districts. Enoch had been in this position for about 5 months at the time of his visit with Timmons.

It was obvious to Timmons as Enoch entered his office that the young supervisor was quite disturbed about something. Timmons invited him to unburden his troubles. Enoch quickly accepted the invitation by stating that he would like to be transferred back to California. If necessary, he was willing to accept a demotion to a salesman's job in order to make the move. Timmons was surprised by Enoch's request to leave and by his apparent willingness to sacrifice his career with the company in order to get back to California. Upon questioning Enoch as to his motives, he learned that Mrs. Enoch had been very unhappy over being forced to live so far from her parents and friends in California. Her parents had not helped the situation by continually complaining about the location of their son-in-law's assignment and the fact they could not see their daughter and grandchildren more often.

In an effort to cheer his wife, Enoch sent her and the children home to California for a visit shortly after Christmas. When it was time for her to return, he received a letter stating that she couldn't face any more ice and snow and therefore was staying on with her parents. In discussing the problem further with Timmons, Enoch admitted that he too disliked the area and was homesick for California. At the moment, he felt his own and his family's happiness was paramount to his career with the company.

Timmons' first suggestion to Enoch was that he take some time off and visit his wife to see if he could persuade her to return and thus prevent the career sacrifice that would be involved for them both if he gave up his present job. Enoch stated that he had considered this possibility, but that he had given it up as being impractical.

Timmons admitted that he sympathized with Enoch's problem, but that there were no vacancies in the Western Division at the moment. He also reminded Enoch that the only way one could progress within the firm was to move where vacancies occurred and that failure to take advantage of the advancement opportunities provided by the company might possibly jeopardize his chance for further advancement.

Enoch replied that he liked the company and his work and that he realized some moving was necessary. He could not see, however, why employees from the East were transferred to the West Coast, while employees who had been raised on the West Coast were forced to move to the East Coast. Timmons replied that it was company policy to transfer employees to different sections of the country to provide them with training, to fill vacancies, to meet changing workload requirements. He also added that it was company policy, in the interests of fairness and efficiency, to transfer, promote, and move employees about within the company on the basis of their qualifications and eligibility for job vacancies, and not on the basis of their home town locations. After considerable discussion, Timmons suggested that the matter be postponed for a few days in order to give each of them a chance to think more about it and to investigate possible alternatives that might be considered in arriving at a solution. Enoch agreed to this suggestion.

In giving thought to the problem, Timmons found himself in sympathy with the emotional problems being faced by Enoch. The fact remained, however, that Enoch was not in line for another move for at least a year. Even if a salesman's job were open on the West Coast, it would probably mean a loss of rank, pay, and future promotion opportunities for Enoch. On the other hand, Timmons felt rather certain that Enoch would quit the company if he were not transferred to a job closer to his home. If this occurred, the company would lose a very promising young executive and a training investment of approximately $6,000. Timmons, feeling that the problem was beyond his power to handle, decided to call the home office and seek advice and assistance from the sales manager.

a. If you were the sales manager, what advice would you give Timmons?
b. Should Timmons have referred the problem to the sales manager, or the personnel manager, or should he have attempted to solve it himself?
c. Is the company at fault in permitting the problem to develop this far?
d. If a salesman's job were open in California, would it be advisable to let Enoch have it by taking a demotion? What new problems might this action create?
e. Do you feel that this case points up a need for a change by the company in any phases of its personnel program?

CASE 11-2

THE PLANT BULLY

The Supreme Oil Company maintains a nationwide system which is organized geographically into six marketing regions for distributing its products. Each of the regions is divided into sales districts containing one or more distribution plants from which the company's products are distributed to its service stations and commercial customers. Each marketing region is permitted a considerable degree of autonomy and most personnel below the management level normally spend their entire career with the company working within that region. Transfers to other regions generally are effected only for those employees who request such a move or for management personnel as a part of their career development. Within a region, particularly within the same district, personnel may expect to be transferred periodically as adjustments in the work force are made necessary by promotion, turnover, and work load changes within the various plants.

Once an employee has acquired a few years of service, company policy makes his discharge extremely difficult, with the result that it has not been uncommon for those employees who constitute a disciplinary problem to remain in a given location only for as long as it takes their supervisor to arrange to have them transferred to some other location. One employee in this category, Butch Graves, worked in the Riverdale distribution plant. Prior to his arrival, the plant had operated with efficiency and there was a minimum of discord among the personnel. Shortly after Graves was assigned to the plant, mistakes and delays in the processing of incoming and outgoing shipments began to occur. Although Graves had been involved in each shipment in which some problem had occurred, he usually had been able to absolve himself of any negligence by alibiing or by shifting the blame to someone else. In an attempt to escape the responsibility for a mistake involving one particular order, Graves went so far as to falsely accuse another employee of making the mistake. These false charges provoked the employee into a fight during which Graves beat him severely. As might be expected, Graves claimed emphatically that he had not been responsible for starting the fight and that he had merely acted in self-defense. Because there were no witnesses present to verify whether or not Graves had provoked the fight, the plant manager, Mr. Hammond, let the incident pass by giving Graves a strong reprimand for hurting the other employee.

Since he had begun to suspect that Graves was a troublemaker and the cause of many of the difficulties that suddenly had begun to be encountered within the plant, Hammond decided to investigate Graves' employment record by contacting managers at other plants where Graves had worked previously. It did not take long for him to discover that Graves had been involved in fights and various operating difficulties at each of those plants. For one reason or another, however, his previous supervisors had never been able to accumulate sufficient evidence to support formal disciplinary action against him, let alone discharge action. Consequently, as soon as the opportunity had presented itself, they had transferred Graves to another location. As a result of these transfers, Graves had been able to accumulate sufficient seniority to make his discharge extremely difficult.

Recognizing the handicap under which he was placed by company discharge policy, Hammond decided that some type of action was needed even if it might not conform to what would be considered acceptable personnel practice. When he learned, therefore, that Jim Riley, one of the new management trainees being assigned to his district, was a former college boxing champion, Hammond requested that the young man be assigned to his plant for training purposes. Since Riley neither looked the athletic type nor was prone to talk about himself, his boxing record remained unknown to the other employees at the Riverdale Plant except Hammond. Although he was very mild in temperament, it was not long before Graves began provoking him. Finally, Graves succeeded in goading Riley into a fight whereupon Riley beat Graves so severely that the latter was confined to his home for about 10 days. Unable to face the other employees following his severe defeat, Graves submitted his resignation.

    a. Do you feel that the approach used by Hammond was wise under the circumstances? What risks, if any, did this approach involve?

    b. What is your opinion of the company's policy concerning seniority and discharge?

    c. What bearing does this incident have upon company transfer policies?

    d. To what extent, if any, should greater cause be required to support discharge action against employees of more than 5 years of seniority? 10, 15, or 20 years of seniority?

    e. What types of personnel records or entries in the records might have proven to be valuable in this case?

SUGGESTED READINGS

Blum, Fred H. *Toward a Democratic Work Process: The Hormel-Packinghouse Workers' Experiment.* New York: Harper & Brothers, 1953.

Davis, Keith. *Human Relations at Work.* New York: McGraw-Hill Book Company, 1962. Chapter 17.

Nunn, H. L. *The Whole Man Goes to Work.* New York: Harper & Brothers, 1953.

Sartain, Aaron Q., and Alton Wesley Baker. *The Supervisor and His Job.* New York: McGraw-Hill Book Company, 1965. Chapter 14.

Severance Pay Patterns in Manufacturing, Studies in Personnel Policy, No. 174. New York: National Industrial Conference Board, 1959.

Wilson, Howard. *Changing Behavior and Preventing Resistance to Change.* Chicago: Administrative Research Associates, 1960.

12

Motivation

Whether or not a manager is successful depends in a large part upon how well his subordinates perform for him. His subordinates, therefore, must not only have the required knowledge and skills to perform their jobs but they must also be induced to release and direct their potential toward the accomplishment of goals that are significant to them and to the organization. Through an understanding of human motivation, a manager's competence in releasing potential and in achieving effective performance from others may be improved. Such understanding may also enable one to improve his own performance, although the unconscious nature of motivation makes it more difficult for an individual to influence his own behavior appreciably.

Motivation is concerned with the "why" of human behavior. Questions such as "Why does one man work diligently and another attempt to avoid work?" and "Why does one man find happiness in performing a job while another loathes it?" represent attempts to understand the motives for human behavior. The techniques used to motivate subordinates have changed with the passage of time in accordance with increased understanding of human motives and management's ability to apply this understanding to the supervision of personnel.

In a highly industrialized and urban society where people are interdependent upon each other for goods and services and where money has become increasingly important for normal existence, management, unions, and the employees themselves have placed considerable emphasis on money (or wages) as an incentive to produce more. This focus on money has tended to give a one-sided view of the employee and his needs. While the value of financial incentives cannot be minimized, the larger picture of human motivation must be examined if there is to be a fuller understanding of what men live and work for in our complex contemporary society. The focus in this chapter is, thus, on the broader aspects of human motivation including:

- Traditional and modern views of direction and control.
- Human needs: key to understanding behavior.
- Work and need satisfaction.
- Organizational climate and motivation.

Traditional and Modern Views of Direction and Control

The methods used to direct and control the activities of subordinates have undergone change just as the methods used by parents have been modified in controlling their children through the years. In the main these changes are the result of a more enlightened view of human personality that has grown out of research efforts of the behavioral scientists and has gradually filtered into the thinking of managers as well as the general public. While the extent to which businessmen have been influenced by modern concepts of human behavior will vary from one individual to another, an increasing number of managers recognize that the traditional views of direction and control are rapidly being replaced with modern theories that offer considerable promise for the fulfillment of individual and organizational goals. In *The Human Side of Enterprise*, McGregor contrasts the philosophy and the method for the traditional view of direction and control with a modern theory. An examination of these approaches reveals the striking differences between them.

The Traditional View

Theory X, as McGregor labels the traditional view, holds that:

1. The average human being has an inherent dislike of work and will avoid it if he can.

2. Because of this human characteristic of dislike of work, most people must be coerced, controlled, directed, and threatened with punishment to get them to put forth adequate effort toward the achievement of organizational objectives.

3. The average human being prefers to be directed, wishes to avoid responsibility, has relatively little ambition, and wants security above all.[1]

This view clearly dictates that motivation will be primarily through fear and that the manager or supervisor will be required to maintain close surveillance of his subordinates if the organizational objectives, and even the personal objectives of security, are to be obtained. In short, the manager must protect the employees from their own shortcomings and weaknesses and, if necessary, goad them into action, as suggested by the "big boss" in Figure 12-1. This view, while by no means without its supporters, is outdated in the light of modern concepts supported by research.

Figure 12-1

"My advice to you, Hawkins, is to take the pins out of the map and stick them into the salesmen."

Reprinted by permission of Chon Day.

---

[1]Douglas M. McGregor, *The Human Side of Enterprise* (New York: McGraw-Hill Book Company, 1960), pp. 33–35.

The Modern View

Theory Y, the modern view that McGregor labels "the integration of goals," holds that:

1. The expenditure of physical and mental effort in work is as natural as play or rest. Depending upon controllable conditions, work may be a source of satisfaction (and will be voluntarily performed) or a source of punishment (and will be avoided if possible).
2. External control and the threat of punishment are not the only means for bringing about effort toward organizational objectives. Man will exercise self-direction and self-control in the service of objectives to which he is committed.
3. Commitment to objectives is a function of the rewards associated with their achievement. The most significant of such rewards, e.g. the satisfaction of ego and self-actualization needs, can be direct products of effort directed toward organizational objectives.
4. The average human being learns, under proper conditions, not only to accept but to seek responsibility.
5. The capacity to exercise a relatively high degree of imagination, ingenuity, and creativity in the solution of organizational problems is widely, not narrowly, distributed in the population.
6. Under the conditions of modern industrial life, the intellectual potentialities of the average human being are only partially utilized.[2]

Theory Y, in contrast to Theory X, emphasizes managerial leadership through motivation by objectives and by permitting subordinates to experience personal satisfaction as they contribute to the achievement of objectives. This approach is consistent with modern theories of human motivation.

Human Needs: Key to Understanding Behavior

Human motivation is a complex process that is of interest to the psychologist, the manager, and the layman. In fact, one of the major concerns of human beings is their attempt to understand the basic reasons that lie behind the behavior that they observe in others. While the process of motivation is quite complex, one of the concepts that have been found useful in understanding it is that of human needs. As will be discussed later, individuals differ in their need patterns.

The Nature of Human Needs

All of the behavior that we observe around us is directed by a striving for the satisfaction of needs. Earlier theories of behavior tended to explain

---

[2]*Ibid.*, pp. 47–48.

all behavior on the basis of a single need (e.g., Freud's libidinal drive and Jung's need or drive to assert one's ego). Modern theorists typically list several needs ranging from three (physical needs, social needs, and egoistic needs) to fifteen in number. Since human needs cannot be seen but must be inferred from human behavior, it may be expected that there will be different theories about them and different systems for classifying them. In spite of the lack of uniformity in classifying human needs, a better understanding of human motivation may come from a study of what some of the behavioral scientists have proposed as a result of their objective and systematic analyses of human behavior in a wide variety of situations.

Classification of needs. One classification that is widely accepted comes from Maslow, a psychologist who has developed a theory of human motivation. He has organized or classified human needs into five categories: (1) the physiological needs, (2) the safety needs, (3) the belongingness and love needs, (4) the esteem needs, and (5) the need for self-actualization.

1. *The physiological needs.* Included in this group are the needs for food, water, air, rest, etc., that are required for maintaining the body in a state of equilibrium.
2. *The safety needs.* These include the need for safety and security, both in a physical and psychological sense. The need to be protected from external dangers to our bodies and our personalities are included in this group. Most employees, for example, desire to work at jobs that are free from physical and psychological hazards, and that provide tenure.
3. *The belongingness and love needs.* The need for attention and social activity are the major needs in this category. An individual desires affectionate relationships with people in general and desires to have a respected place in his group.
4. *The esteem needs.* These include the desire for self-respect, for strength, for achievement, for adequacy, for mastery and competence, for confidence in the face of the world, and for independence and freedom. Also included in this group is the desire for reputation or prestige or respect and esteem from other people.
5. *The need for self-actualization (realization).* This refers to a man's desire for self-fulfillment; namely, to the tendency for him to become actualized in what he is potentially. "What a man *can* be, he *must* be." This tendency might be phrased as the desire to become more and more what he is, to become everything that one is capable of becoming.[3]

The fact that human needs have been analyzed and categorized should not cause us to believe that we have a complete explanation of human

[3]Paraphrased and adapted from A. H. Maslow, *Motivation and Personality* (New York: Harper & Brothers, 1954), pp. 80–106.

behavior.   In analyzing the motivation of an individual, attention cannot be focused on any one of the needs to the exclusion of the others.   Behavior is multimotivated; therefore, several needs usually demand satisfaction concurrently.

Priority of needs.   According to Maslow's theory, human needs are arranged according to the priority shown in Figure 12-2.   In the first place, the physiological needs are the most fundamental; they require satisfaction before other needs.   Once the physiological needs are satisfied, the safety needs become predominant.   At this point an individual becomes concerned over his physical and psychological well-being.   Related to this concern is the employee's desire for security from injury as well as from adverse economic conditions and unpleasant or threatening behavior of other persons.

Figure 12-2

PRIORITY OF HUMAN NEEDS

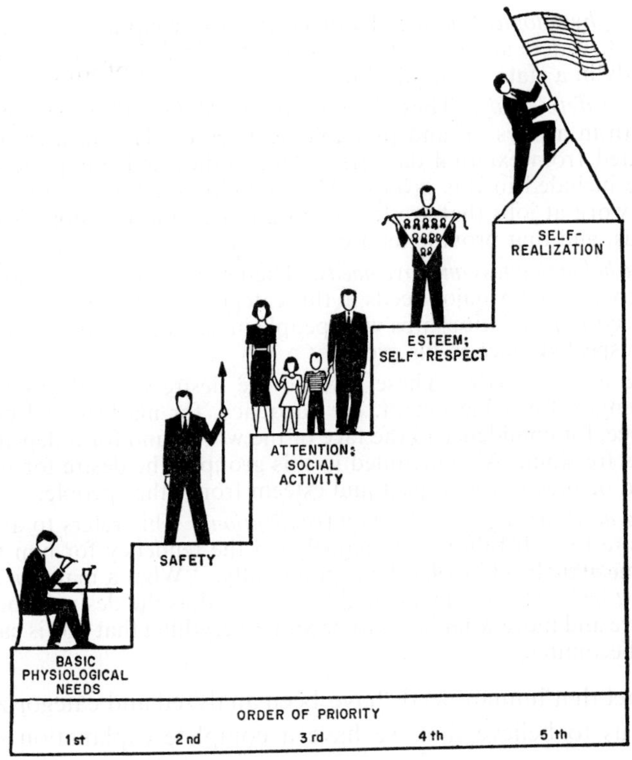

Source: Keith Davis, *Human Relations at Work* (New York: McGraw-Hill Book Company, 1962), p. 25.   Reproduced with permission.

If both the physiological and the safety needs are fairly well satisfied, the belongingness and love needs (the next step) will emerge as dominant in a person's need structure. His behavior will turn in the direction of seeking companionship with others and in striving for a place in his group. While much of the employee's need to feel that he belongs and is accepted by others may be satisfied through relationships with his family and his friends, this need should also be satisfied to some degree on the job. A large part of the individual's day is spent on the job in association with superiors and fellow employees. If relationships with them are friendly and congenial, this need will be satisfied to some degree. On the other hand, if dissension and disharmony prevail, one may expect the employees to look for satisfaction of this need elsewhere.

At the top of the ladder are the needs for esteem and self-realization. These needs include achievement, mastery, confidence, independence, recognition, and a realization of all that one is capable of becoming. As the lower needs are satisfied, these higher needs become dominant. Very few of us ever fully realize the fulfillment of these higher needs. In one study of the needs of middle-management and first-line supervisors, it was found that self-realization was the most critical need area of all in terms of both perceived deficiency in fulfillment and perceived unbalance to the individual. Furthermore, middle-management personnel did not perceive themselves as having the need for self-realization satisfied to any greater degree than the first-line supervisors who were studied.[4] It would appear, therefore, that top management should not fail to consider the needs of its middle-management personnel as well as those of first-line supervisors.

Differences in Needs of Employees

Management must recognize that the need pattern of each individual is different and not assume that a single approach can be used to motivate all employees toward the accomplishment of the organizational objectives. Because of the importance of these individual differences in need patterns, attention is now given to the ways in which individuals differ and the factors creating differences.

How individuals differ. According to Maslow, as needs at one level are satisfied needs at the next higher level come into predominance. Thus, a need does not have to be completely satisfied before the next need emerges. If, for example, the physiological and safety needs are 75 percent

---

[4]Lyman W. Porter, "A Study of Perceived Need Satisfactions in Bottom and Middle Management Jobs," *Journal of Applied Psychology*, Vol. 45, No. 1 (February, 1961), pp. 1–10.

satisfied in an individual and his love and self-esteem needs are 25 percent satisfied, his behavior will be primarily in the direction of satisfying the love and esteem needs with the physiological and safety needs taking a subordinate role. A millionaire executive, for example, may work as hard or harder than the individual who needs money for the bare necessities of life in order to satisfy his need for self-realization.

On the other side of the picture, we may find a person who is primarily concerned with earning sufficient money with which to buy the basic essentials of life. He may not expect to have the higher needs of belonging-ness, esteem, and self-realization satisfied to any degree through his job. The satisfaction of higher needs that he receives from his family, lodge, union, and participation in sports and hobbies compensates for the need satisfaction not attained through his job. In between these two extremes we are likely to find all shades of differences in what an individual aspires to attain from his job.

Factors creating differences. The differences in need patterns among a group of employees are as much to be expected as differences in interests, aptitudes, and attitudes among them. As a result of prior experiences, satisfactions, and frustrations in the life of the individual, some needs have become stronger than others. Childhood and youth experiences, previous employment experiences, and daily contacts with supervisors, fellow employees, and the family have played their part in developing unique motivational patterns within the individual employee.

Another factor influencing needs is that of class differences. Individuals from higher socioeconomic classes have different needs and aspirations than those from lower classes. The son of a bank president, for example, may feel that the job of machinist is not suitable for him, while the son of a bricklayer may feel that the machinist's job is a good choice. A person's socioeconomic class not only affects his occupational aspirations but also his attitudes toward work, authority, education and training, responsibility, and other factors that affect on-the-job performance.

While most of the preceding discussion focuses on Maslow's theory of human motivation, it should be recognized that there are other theories and classification systems. It is interesting, for example, to note the extended list of needs developed by H. A. Murray as part of his theory of personality,[5] and which were later used as a basis for a personality inventory known as the *Edwards Personal Preference Schedule*.[6] The *Edwards*

---

[5]Henry A. Murray, *Explorations in Personality* (New York: Oxford University Press, 1938).

[6]Allen E. Edwards, *Edwards Personal Preference Schedule* (New York: The Psychological Corporation, 1954).

Personal Preference Schedule contains 225 items that measure the relative strength of the respondent's manifest needs (those of which he is aware, in contrast to unconscious needs) in 15 areas, among them being needs for achievement, order, affiliation, dominance, and change.

It should be noted that this list represents a somewhat different organization of needs, as suggested by another eminent personality theorist. Hence, one should not assume that all of the questions about motivation are answered and that human needs have been isolated as precisely as the basic elements of the physical sciences. The Murray-Edwards listing of needs has stimulated considerable research, as has that of Maslow. There are other theories, too, that are not mutually exclusive. The reader, therefore, would be advised to recognize this fact and realize that it may require several hypotheses and many more years of research before precise understanding of human motivation is realized.[7]

Work and Need Satisfaction

While employees are continually attempting to satisfy their individual needs, management is primarily concerned with motivating employees to be more productive. There is somewhat of an inconsistency between these two strivings because an employee whose needs are satisfied is not a motivated employee. It is the striving that characterizes motivation, not the satiation of needs. On the other hand, it has been found that, unless certain needs are satisfied, employees will be unhappy in their jobs and avoid the unpleasantness that is associated with them. Hence, while management is concerned about motivating employees, it must also avoid creating dissatisfactions and frustrations in employees.

The motivating of employees to be more productive and to produce at a high level of quality often requires that a variety of incentives be used in varying proportions as best estimated by managerial personnel. Because of differences in need patterns and their ever-changing nature, the incentives that may be best for one group or an individual may not be effective for another at a particular time for reasons discussed previously. To illustrate the variety of incentives that are available, some of the commonly accepted positive incentives will be discussed; these will be followed by some of the negative incentives. Finally, a new theory of job motivation will be examined.

---

[7]T. C. Chamberlin, "The Method of Multiple Working Hypotheses," *Science*, Vol. 148 (1965), pp. 754–759.

Positive Incentives

The positive incentives that are used most widely in business and industry consist of (1) money, (2) security, (3) praise, (4) belongingness, (5) competition, (6) knowledge of results, and (7) participation. Money and security have often been overemphasized, and in many instances management has assumed that these are all that the worker expects from his job. Mayo has called this erroneous assumption the "rabble hypothesis."[8] Still, the nonfinancial incentives of praise, belongingness, competition, knowledge of results, and participation are not likely to replace the financial incentives of money and security, although they may be used to supplement them and to motivate behavior in the desired direction.

Money. In an industrial society money is the incentive used most frequently to stimulate the worker to greater production. When employees are asked to state what they would most like to receive from their jobs, however, pay is very seldom at the top of the list. This is in contrast to the demands of unions, which often emphasize increased pay for their members. While it would be foolish to assume that employees are not interested in a fair wage, some demands for wage increases may be the result of their inability to recognize or to verbalize other needs that are not being satisfied through their jobs. Furthermore, unions often ask for more money as a part of their bargaining strategy to gain more security and other benefits. Nevertheless, money is generally effective as an incentive. Wage incentive systems that relate wages directly to output are especially effective in stimulating production if standards are properly developed and the system is effectively administered. The support and the confidence of employees are important factors in determining the success of such systems. Profit-sharing, likewise, is effective as an incentive to greater production and has positive effects on employee attitudes.

Security. Most employees want to feel secure in their jobs. They want to feel that they will be protected against loss of job and earnings whether it be because of accident, illness, insufficient work to keep them busy, arbitrary firing, or other reasons. They are concerned over security in the years after retirement and do everything possible to protect it. The employee who is reasonably secure enjoys a type of freedom or independence that stimulates him to participate more wholeheartedly on the job and to work toward the achievement of the organization objectives.

---

[8] Elton Mayo, *The Social Problems of an Industrial Civilization* (Boston: Division of Research, Graduate School of Business Administration, Harvard University, 1945), Chapter 2.

He is in the position of being free to direct his energies primarily toward the goals of the company rather than toward the achievement of personal security.

Praise and recognition. It is important that employees be recognized and praised for a job well done. Praise, however, should be reserved for those instances where it is truly deserved and where it can be given with sincerity. If praise is used too frequently, it may become like an opiate in that it must be used in increasing amounts in order to be effective. If the praise is given sincerely, it should eventually be accompanied by more tangible forms of recognition, such as a pay increase or promotion; otherwise, its sincerity may be questioned. One writer questions the wisdom of praising employees. He feels that it is of limited value as a motivator and may actually serve as a barrier to communication since it may be an unconscious means of establishing the superiority of the praiser. As a result communication between the employee and his supervisor may suffer.[9]

Belongingness. In the years since the beginning of the human relations movement, increased emphasis has been given to making new employees feel that they are an important part of the group and that established members of the group are expected to contribute to integrating the newcomer. Since the need for belongingness and approval of the group is important to an employee's sense of well being, it may be assumed that frustration of this need is likely to contribute to job dissatisfaction and/or lower productivity.

Competition. Competition may be used as an incentive in stimulating certain types of desirable behavior. An employee may compete with himself, with other employees, or as a member of a group competing with other groups. In competing with oneself, such as when an employee tries to improve his own record, satisfaction may come to the individual, and no one loses face by not being the winner. Competition among individual employees or employee groups may be advantageous in stimulating increased safety, better housekeeping, and improved attendance as well as production.

Competition among employees for increased production may be stimulated by use of progress charts. It should be emphasized, however, that the charts should not be used as a basis for penalties or reproaches;

9Richard E. Farson, "Praise Reappraised," *Harvard Business Review*, Vol. 41, No. 5 (September/October, 1963), pp. 61–66.

but, rather, they should be used positively as a basis of encouragement and assistance.   One authority reports that where men found themselves competing against their own previous records, anything that tended to slow down production became as important to the workers as it was to the supervisor.[10]

Knowledge of results.   A knowledge of results serves as an incentive to better performance, and it also facilitates the learning of the job.   The following case shows how the desire for knowledge of results may operate on the job.

> A repair crew in the telephone industry objected to the procedure used in handling "repeats" (repair cases where a station is reported out of order two or more times in a month). The company procedure in such cases was to send a repairman who was not involved in the initial repair on such jobs. The crew argued that the company procedure gave them no way of knowing whether or not they had made the repair properly and they felt that they were entitled to know. They recommended, therefore, that the same man should be sent back on a repeat job with the foreman accompanying him. Under the latter procedure, which was adopted by management, repeats that consistently had constituted over 17 per cent of all service calls, immediately dropped to 4 per cent and remained at this or a lower figure.[11]

Participation.   Participation is recognized as one of the best incentives for stimulating employee production and for providing job satisfaction.   In addition to providing opportunities for the employee to participate in meetings and conferences, on committees, or through the suggestion box, greater attention can be given to participation in the making of decisions about the work itself and to the conditions under which it is accomplished within the work group.

Because of employee involvement and their personal stake in the success of the change, participation in decision making can help to minimize resistance to change.   It is normal for members of a work group to tend to resist change in their work procedures, as well as in other areas related to their employment, because habit patterns must be revised, and often the change is perceived as affecting the employee's security.   In addition, where changes are made, the social relationships among employees are often changed thereby affecting the satisfactions normally received from group association and interaction.   As a result, most employees, unless they have had some voice in the change, will respond to it

---

[10]Max B. Skousen, "Motivation Controls Help Employees Set New Records," *Supervisory Management*, Vol. 5, No. 5 (May, 1960), pp. 2–10.

[11]Norman R. F. Maier, *Psychology in Industry* (3rd ed.; New York: Houghton Mifflin Company, 1965), p. 461.

with some degree of resistance. Employees are likely to ask, "Is this change necessary?"[12]

In Figure 12-3 the motivating forces in a proposed change in work methods are shown. It will be noted that while more pay represents positive motivation for the new method, boredom, fear of management, and dislike of the time-study man are negative factors that may offset whatever positive motivational force is exerted by more pay. If employees can be made to recognize the need for the change or, still better, can participate in suggesting changes and in working out the details of the change, resistance will be minimized. Specific suggestions for providing for maximum employee participation in changing work methods, as well as in other matters, are examined in detail in Chapter 14.

Figure 12-3

INTERACTING FORCES IN A PROPOSED CHANGE

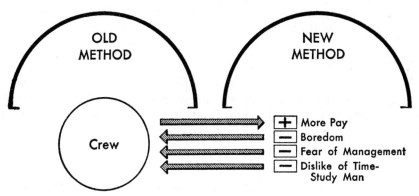

The forces (represented by *arrows*) are those set in motion when a foreman suggested a change in work methods. The direction of the forces (to right or left) is determined by the positive (*plus signs*) and negative (*minus signs*) motivational conditions aroused or removed, and they act upon the crew (*circle*) determining whether or not they will move from left to right. The left and right *arcs* at the top represent the "old" and "new" methods, respectively.

Source: Norman R. F. Maier, *Psychology in Industry* (3rd ed.; New York: Houghton Mifflin Company, 1965), p. 432. Reproduced with permission.

Negative Incentives

Negative incentives involve punishment or the threat of punishment to motivate employee behavior in the desired direction. The typical punishments in business are reprimand, monetary fines, layoff, demotion, and discharge. The reprimand is the method used most often to punish the worker for unsatisfactory performance or personal misbehavior.

---

[12]Nathaniel Stewart, "Change Requires Employee Support," *Nation's Business*, Vol. 47, No. 8 (August, 1959), pp. 33, 57–59.

Punishment or the threat of punishment is believed by many supervisors to be an effective device for securing obedience from employees, and it may occasionally have some value. More often, however, it introduces other factors that make it considerably less desirable than positive forms of motivation. For example, punishment is likely to frustrate the individual being punished with the result that he may become aggressive or perhaps childish in his behavior. These reactions usually make it more difficult for him to change his behavior in the desired direction. The threat of punishment may also cause the employee to become sufficiently fearful so that he is not able to respond in a positive manner to suggestions and instructions, and he is likely to develop unfavorable attitudes toward the job.

At this stage in our knowledge and understanding of human behavior, we cannot say that negative incentives should never be used. Some people respond effectively to fear especially if it is accompanied by a paternalism that overshadows the fear. Like any negative approach, however, one cannot accurately assess the damage that may occur to interpersonal relationships or to the individual personality.

Motivators Versus Hygiene Factors

Two of the major theories of personality — Maslow's and Murray's — that attach special importance to human needs were discussed earlier. These theories have been developed out of a study of people in a variety of situations that are predominately of a clinical or therapeutic nature. More recently, empirical studies of job motivation have been conducted by Herzberg, Mausner, and Snyderman, and other researchers that have presented some valuable insights into those job factors that may be considered motivating versus those that are of a hygienic or nonmotivating nature.[13] The basic study that has recently been replicated among Finnish supervisors and among several categories of personnel at Texas Instruments involved conducting interviews with 200 engineers and accountants in nine different companies in diversified locations about job factors that had important effects on their attitudes. The respondents were asked to think of a time when they felt exceptionally good or exceptionally bad about their job, either their present job or any other jobs they have had. Following the specific questions, to elicit these critical incidents, interviewers probed to get clarification on the nature of events and their personal reactions to these events.

---

[13]Frederick Herzberg, Bernard Mausner, and Barbara B. Snyderman, *The Motivation to Work* (Second Edition; New York: John Wiley and Sons, Inc., 1959); Frederick Herzberg, "The Motivation To Work Among Finnish Supervisors," *Personnel Psychology*, Vol. 18, No. 4 (Winter, 1965), pp. 393–402; M. Scott Myers, "Conditions for Manager Motivation," *Harvard Business Review*, Vol. 44, No. 1 (January/February, 1966), pp. 58–71.

Figure 12-4 portrays the original data on engineers and accountants. It will be noted that the largest percentage of the positive feelings at work were brought about by one or more of the *motivator* factors while a smaller percentage of the negative factors involved the motivators. Conversely, a larger percentage of the events describing dissatisfaction stem from *hygiene* factors or what more commonly may be thought of as a psychologically hygienic work environment (i.e., free from unhealthy working conditions).

In commenting upon motivator factors and hygiene factors, Herzberg, Mausner, and Snyderman conclude:

> Improvement in the factors of hygiene (company policy and administration, supervision, relations with supervisors, working conditions, etc.) will serve to remove the impediments to positive job attitudes. . . . When these factors deteriorate to a level below that which the employee considers acceptable, then job dissatisfaction ensues. However, the reverse does not hold true. When the job context can be characterized as optimal, we will not get dissatisfaction, but neither will we get much in the way of positive attitudes. . . .
>
> The factors that lead to positive job attitudes (the motivators) do so because they satisfy the individual's need for self-actualization in his work. . . . Man tends to actualize himself in every area of his life, and his job is one of his important areas. . . .
>
> It should be understood that both kinds of factors meet the needs of the employee; but it is primarily the "motivators" (achievement, recognition, the work itself, responsibility, advancement) that serve to bring about the kind of job satisfaction and . . . the kind of improvement in performance that industry is seeking from its work force.[14]

The Herzberg studies indicate that the needs at the top of Maslow's hierarchy — self-realization or self-actualization — are those that provide the greatest basis for motivating employees toward higher levels of job performance at least among the various occupational groups that they have studied. It is possible that these groups by their very nature are highly achievement-oriented and are not typical of all job groups.[15] The factors of hygiene cannot, of course, be ignored or slighted, but their satisfaction alone apparently will not result in the attainment of the desired goals. The basic question then becomes: what can management do to increase the presence of such motivator factors as achievement, recognition, the work itself, responsibility, and advancement?

Organizational Climate and Motivation

The development of an organizational climate that results in sustained motivation of employees toward the organizational goals is one of

---

14Herzberg, Mausner, and Snyderman, *op. cit.*, pp. 113–114.
15Robert B. Ewen, "Some Determinants of Job Satisfaction: A Study of the Generality of Herzberg's Theory," *Journal of Applied Psychology*, Vol. 48, No. 3 (June, 1964), pp. 161–163.

Figure 12-4

COMPARISON OF MOTIVATORS AND HYGIENE FACTORS

(Engineers and Accountants)

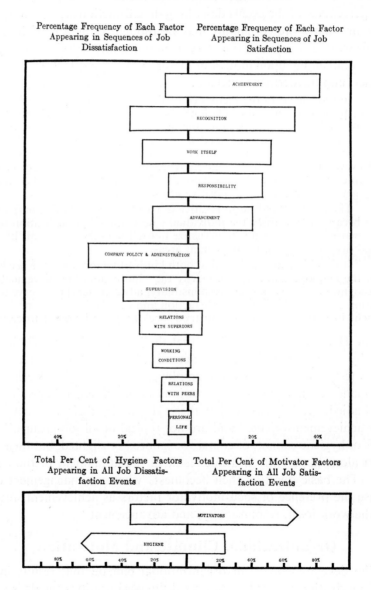

Percentage Frequency of Each Factor Appearing in Sequences of Job Dissatisfaction

Percentage Frequency of Each Factor Appearing in Sequences of Job Satisfaction

Total Per Cent of Hygiene Factors Appearing in All Job Dissatis-faction Events

Total Per Cent of Motivator Factors Appearing in All Job Satis-faction Events

Adapted from F. Herzberg, B. Mausner, and B. B. Snyderman, *The Motivation to Work* (Second Edition; New York: John Wiley & Sons, Inc., 1959). Reproduced with permission of John Wiley & Sons and *Personnel Psychology.*

the most important responsibilities of management. The late Douglas McGregor stated this responsibility most clearly when he advised that:

> The motivation, the potential for development, the capacity for assuming responsibility, the readiness to direct behavior toward organizational goals are all present in people. Management does not put them there. It is a responsibility of management to make it possible for people to recognize and develop these human characteristics for themselves.
>
> The essential task of management is to arrange organizational conditions and methods of operation so that people can achieve their own goals best by directing their own efforts toward organizational objectives. This is a process primarily of creating opportunities, releasing potential, removing obstacles, encouraging growth, providing guidance.[16]

It would appear, then, that management can create motivating conditions by adherence to many of the principles discussed earlier such as those relating to effective organizational structures, meaningful and realistic job assignments, and working conditions that provide an opportunity for individual achievement and recognition.

Organization and Management

The psychological and social climate of the company is largely determined by the individuals occupying the key positions in the organization. The attitudes and behavior of those at the top have a permeating effect on the motivational patterns of individuals at all levels in the organization. As a result, any attempts to improve employee performance must begin with a study of the nature of the organization itself and those who create and exercise major control over it. The factors in this connection that have a direct bearing on the motivation of subordinates include the efficiency of the organization and its operation, the delegation of authority, and the manner in which job activities are controlled.

Efficiency of organization and operation. A higher level of employee motivation is likely to be present where the duties and responsibilities of individuals are understood, where lines of authority are clearly indicated, and where the objectives are clearly defined. In developing the objectives for the work group, the manager is held responsible for the objectives of his component and for the integration of those objectives with the objectives of the company as a whole. He may, however, enlist participation by subordinates in setting work objectives but should reserve the final decision on

---

[16]Douglas M. McGregor, "The Human Side of Enterprise," *The Management Review*, Vol. 16, No. 11 (November, 1957), pp. 88–89.

the formal work objectives for himself. The fact that employees participate in the establishment of specific objectives will influence them to support their own ideas and will contribute toward their readiness to work productively. It will also stimulate them to assess progress toward the objectives more objectively.[17]

Delegation as a motivator. It was pointed out in Chapter 3 that superiors should delegate as much authority as possible to their subordinates. Where ample opportunity for decision making is provided within a job, interest and initiative are stimulated. Such interest and initiative grow out of the fulfillment of the needs for achievement, recognition, and responsibility. The self-realization that comes from being responsible, achieving the desired goals, and being recognized for a job well done is a type of need that is seldom, if ever, satisfied for a very long period. Like hunger for food, it recurs continually. As a result, it has continuing motivational value and, therefore, provides management with one of its strongest sources for stimulating employees to higher levels of achievement.

While special consideration is often given to creating a job environment that will appeal to the achievement needs of scientists and engineers, these needs should not be overlooked among personnel in other classes. It is true, however, that strong achievement motives are more likely to be found in certain groups or classes of society than in others. People in the so-called "middle-class" usually have more pronounced drives for achievement than either the "lower" or the "upper" classes.[18] Nevertheless, it should be recognized that the strength of the achievement motive in individuals in different groups is undoubtedly the result of cultural conditioning that may be changed as one has success experiences at school and at work. The Economic Opportunity Act of 1964, described in Chapter 8, offers some possibilities for providing significant success experiences to those who have been culturally deprived of these opportunities.[19]

Control but not overcontrol. Related to delegation is the matter of control. A conscious effort must be made to avoid overcontrol and

---

[17]David A. Emery, "Managerial Leadership Through Motivation by Objectives," *Personnel Psychology*, Vol. 12, No. 1 (Spring, 1959), pp. 65–79.

[18]The need for achievement may be viewed as an important facet of Maslow's need for self-actualization. The term is closely identified with the research of David C. McClelland. See his *The Achieving Society* (Princeton, New Jersey: D. Van Nostrand Co., Inc., 1961) and "Achievement Motivation Can Be Developed," *Harvard Business Review*, Vol. 43, No. 6 (November/December, 1965), pp. 6–16, 20–24.

[19]See Arthur Pearl and Frank Riessman, *New Careers for the Poor* (New York: The Free Press, 1965) for discussion of what can be done to create job opportunities — primarily in service occupations — for a large segment of the population of the United States who are on welfare or likely to be on welfare.

oversupervision of personnel. *Overcontrol* may be avoided by having accurate job descriptions, properly planned work schedules, and a system of internal checks. In one study involving office workers in several companies, it was found that lower productivity tends to be associated with close supervision; whereas, higher productivity tends to be associated with a more general type of supervision. The latter type of supervisor tends to specify the goals to be accomplished and gives subordinates some freedom in how the work is accomplished. On the other hand, those using close supervision methods are more likely to limit the employees' freedom to do the work in their own way and thus stifle growth and development.[20] This is only one example of how supervisory behavior affects employee motivation and performance. Other supervisory behaviors and their effects on employee motivation will be examined further in Chapters 14 and 15.

Job Content and Organization

Important factors in motivation are the content and organization of the job itself. Although a thorough exploration of this important topic would encompass many chapters, certain trends in this area that have some bearing on motivation should be noted. Among these are job enlargement and automation.

Job enlargement. Instead of limiting the employee to simple repetitive tasks, his job may be designed in such a way that he performs several related operations in a production cycle. He may also be teamed with other employees and made responsible for completing several operations. As noted in Chapter 4, this is the opposite of job specialization and is known as *job enlargement.*

Although job enlargement should help to reduce the monotony that is found in many jobs, there are differences in the manner in which individuals respond to monotonous tasks. What may be monotonous for one individual can be interesting and absorbing to another. Burtt cites the case of a woman who packed electric lamps, wrapping each lamp in tissue paper and putting it in a carton. She packed some 13,000 lamps a day and had been doing this for 12 years. When interviewed, she said that the work was interesting and pleasant. She went on to tell how she sometimes grasped the lamps differently for variety. She also let her imagination run as to where the lamps were going. She would spend the morning at Grand

---

[20]D. Katz, *et al., Productivity, Supervision, and Morale in an Office Situation:* Part I (Ann Arbor: University of Michigan Press, 1950), p. 17.

Central watching commuters, and then in the afternoon she might shift over to the dining room at the Waldorf.[21]

Since there are many different individual reactions to repetitive jobs, the first place to attack the problem is in the selection of workers. The intelligence of those who are selected for repetitive jobs should be commensurate with job demands. There is also some evidence to indicate that personality traits should be considered. Those who are extroverted are more likely to get bored than those who are introverted. Another approach is to make the job more interesting. Such methods as pointing out the significance of the employee's contribution, building a working environment that stimulates social interaction to a reasonable degree, rotating jobs, and providing rest pauses may also help to make the work more tolerable. Similarly, music has proved valuable in many companies for relieving monotony and improving the morale of those doing repetitive work.

Automation. Since the beginning of industrial mechanization, machinery and equipment have increasingly taken over functions that previously were accomplished by the worker. This has been the trend down to the present-day age of automation. In certain industries — especially the oil, paper, and chemical industries — many jobs have been reduced to dial watching. In other industries, such as the automotive industry, parts are machined by automatic equipment that incorporates a "feedback" device, which interprets and controls the machine. As a result of such devices, the operator's job may be reduced to that of a machine tender, but his responsibilities are often much greater because of the large array of equipment for which he is responsible.

In recent years the electronic computer has mechanized the office with the result that all types of office procedures, such as payroll computation, inventory, production control, sales forecasting, customer billing, writing insurance policies, and even personnel record keeping are handled by computers. The first business computers were delivered late in 1954 and at present there are about 15,000 installations. In 1963, U.S. industry spent over $2 billion for such equipment and by the 1970's the annual outlays are expected to be double or triple this amount.[22]

Increased automation of office jobs along with increases in automation of production jobs is certain to have some immediate as well as far-reaching effects on personnel. In an earlier chapter, the need for retraining

---

[21]Harold E. Burtt, *Applied Psychology* (2nd ed.; Englewood Cliffs, New Jersey: Prentice-Hall, Inc., 1957), pp. 440–441.

[22]G. Burck, "The Boundless Age of the Computer," *Fortune*, Vol. LXIX, No. 3, (March, 1964), pp. 101–110.

displaced employees was noted as one of the immediate problems of automation growing out of the rising level of skill and educational requirements accompanying automation.

Other problems center around the resistance of employees to changing work conditions as a result of automation. Attitudes toward the change appear to depend on the ability of the individual to deal effectively with the change and on the skill with which the organization manages the change. Office employees studied regarded the methods changes as temporarily disruptive but often welcomed the change. Similarly, automated factories are preferred as work places to less advanced plants. The sources of satisfaction with automation vary over the course of adjustment to automation.[23] This variance in sources of satisfaction is revealed in a study of an automated steel mill over a four-year period. Walker summarizes the finding of this study as follows:

> The majority of crew members, though not all, were able to move from semi-manual jobs to semi-automatic ones and derive personal satisfaction from the immediate job content of those positions. They did not derive this satisfaction at first but after a period of acclimatization and experience. The same job characteristics, all stemming from the automatic or semi-automatic operations of the mill which had at first been feared and hated, *were later the source of satisfaction.*[24]

In looking at the overall effects of automation on society, it seems likely that the trend toward further automation is likely to be accompanied by a shortening of the workweek for the individual worker. It is possible that this may introduce new problems of motivation. With the workweek reduced from 40 hours to 36 or 32 hours, there will be additional leisure time and increased attention to off-the-job interests. As a result, the job will be in greater competition with leisure-time activities which may prove to be more satisfying to the individual. It is important, therefore, that management be alert to the needs that individuals have and design organizational structures and plan jobs so that the talents and energies of human beings are utilized effectively. Consideration should be given to meeting social needs, recognizing the pay and status implications of automation, and recognizing the interests and the role of unions in protecting their members against the new technology.[25]

[23]William A. Faunce, Einar Hardin, and Eugene H. Jacobson, "Automation and the Employee," *The Annals* (Philadelphia: The American Academy of Political and Social Science, 1962), pp. 60–68.

[24]Charles R. Walker, *Toward the Automatic Factory* (New Haven: Yale University Press, 1957), p. 192.

[25]Frank T. Paine and Dennis R. Hykes, "Automation and Motivation: A Theory of Management," *Personnel Administration*, Vol. 29, No. 1 (January/February, 1966), pp. 26–32.

Social Organization

Every organization has a social system that in part follows the formal organizational lines but which also follows the informal patterns of interpersonal relationships. Although this patterning of social relationships in the company is quite complex, it cannot be overlooked. Important motivational aspects of the social organization are group approval, teamwork, and status.

Group approval. The Hawthorne Studies conducted at the Western Electric plant near Chicago, beginning in the 1920's and continuing for many years, revealed quite clearly that the attitudes of the work group constitute a powerful motivating influence. In the bank-wiring-room observations, several experienced workers were studied by an observer. The workers were engaged in wiring switchboards, a repetitive manual operation, under a wage-incentive system that did not function as management had intended. The workers decided among themselves that two units a day was to be their output. Those who exceeded this level were called "rate busters" whereas those who fell behind were known as "chiselers." Persons in both groups were controlled by sarcasm, ridicule, and "binging" (striking the upper arm with the fist) from the other members of the group.[26] This is an example of the fact that the control exercised by the group over its members cannot be ignored. It may well offset the motivational factors with the result that highly motivated individuals are prevented from producing through social control by the group.

Importance of status. Related closely to the need for recognition is the factor of status. As discussed earlier in Chapter 4, at all levels in the organization the personnel are seeking to maintain their status or to achieve a higher status in the formal and informal structure of the organization. The fact that people will work hard to achieve increased status should reveal to management the importance of insuring that opportunities are provided for advancement and that appropriate recognition is given for contributions to the organization.

Other Influences

The discussion up to this point has been mainly focused on the motivational influences that are available for management to use in the achievement of the company's goals and in the satisfaction of employee needs. It must be recognized, however, that all of the employee's needs will rarely

---

[26]Fritz L. Roethlisberger and W. J. Dickson, *Management and the Worker* (Cambridge: Harvard University Press, 1939), Chapter 18.

be met on the job. Other facets of life are required for satisfaction of man's complex pattern of needs, even for the individual who attains maximum satisfaction from the pursuit of his job. While management's emphasis must necessarily be focused on those aspects of motivation over which it has control, an understanding of the employee's behavior requires that some attention be given to other influences to which employees respond. These are many and varied because of the variety of backgrounds and experiences in the lives of the individuals. Certain influences, however, are generally applicable to personnel management and should be discussed. Among these are family influences, union influences, and economic conditions.

Family influences. The influence of the employee's family upon his attitudes toward his job and upon his job performance is difficult to measure. It is safe to assume, however, that the children and the wife in particular exert an influence upon an employee's behavior. The extent to which he responds to the incentives that management uses to motivate employees is somewhat dependent upon the manner in which his attitudes have been influenced by his wife who may have the opinion that her husband is underpaid. Her constant expression of that opinion may influence his job performance with the result that he turns out less (since he is presumably underpaid) or becomes dissatisfied and disagreeable on the job. He may even fail to recognize that he may be earning more than others in comparable jobs.

Family influences deserve the attention of management. Although attitudes and opinions are not easy to change, appropriate action should be taken to maintain or improve the outlook of the family toward the company and the employee's position. Communication should be maintained with the home. Therefore, employee publications should be designed with the family in mind. Social events, recognition banquets, and other affairs to which the families are invited can be helpful in developing favorable attitudes toward the company.

Union influences. Unions have developed and expanded in response to human needs. Workers not only have obtained higher wages and better working conditions, but also their needs for recognition and belonging have been satisfied to a considerable degree through their affiliations with unions. Since the union is able to play such an important part in satisfying employee needs, competition between management and the union in attempting to satisfy these needs may be expected.

Another item of concern in the area of motivation is the typical reaction of unions to management's attempts to stimulate workers to better performance. Since one of the primary goals of the union is to protect the worker from being displaced or having his pay reduced because of technological improvement, changes in work methods, production speedups, or attempts on the part of management to motivate workers to achieve greater production by any method may encounter resistance from the union. Some companies, however, have been successful in developing financial incentive systems with the cooperation of the unions. Because of their importance for employee motivation, such systems are discussed in detail in Chapter 22.

Economic conditions. The ability of management to make good on the financial incentives of pay and job security is largely dependent upon the economic conditions of the company and the nation. During the depression of the 1930's, for example, workers gave maximum performance for long hours at minimal pay. They were happy to have any kind of a job that would enable them to provide their families with the basic necessities of life. When economic conditions are reversed and there is a shortage of personnel to fill the jobs, some decline in the effectiveness of the financial incentive may be expected. Under these conditions the basic needs are satisfied, and employees expect to have the higher needs satisfied by their jobs. Even though they may be earning high wages, they would prefer to have a job that, in addition to paying high wages, meets their needs for self-actualization — to become everything that one is capable of becoming.

Résumé

Job performance is not only dependent upon the abilities and skills of the employees but also upon their motivation. Just because a man *can* do something is no assurance that he *will* do it. Thus, an understanding of the basic needs can be quite useful in motivating employee behavior toward the goals of management and labor. While it is essential for management to provide conditions that will avert job dissatisfaction, it must also give special attention to the motivator factors that provide for job satisfaction — such as content of the job, including task achievement, recognition for achievement, intrinsic interest in task, and advancement. Although financial incentives cannot be overlooked, they are too frequently overemphasized by management to the neglect of the nonfinancial incentives — often assumed to have little place in an enterprise built upon advanced technology. It should be recognized, however, that if the same ingenuity and perseverance that have been given to technological problems are given to problems of human motivation, the chances are greater that both management and labor will benefit.

DISCUSSION QUESTIONS AND PROBLEMS

1. Why do men work? Analyze this question in relation to what you have observed about your friends and acquaintances and what you have read in this chapter.

2. Why did you come to college? Analyze your own pattern of needs and then ask a fellow student to suggest needs that you may have overlooked.

3. It was mentioned in this chapter that one of the major concerns of human beings is their attempt to understand the motivation that lies behind the behavior of others. How do you account for this?

4. What have you observed about college students and their needs for achievement? How do you believe they would compare with noncollege individuals of the same age? What factors probably cause the difference?

5. Some individuals feel that attempts to motivate the employee are attempts to "manipulate" him. Is this true? What are the implications of this statement for the supervision of personnel?

6. It has been said that executives are often uninformed about the employee's needs for recognition. Do you believe this to be true? Why?

7. In an office employing 400 individuals engaged in writing insurance policies and keeping records on policies, it was announced that an electronic computer would be installed within the next few weeks and some personnel shifts would be required. Since details were not available at the time, it was stated that further information would be furnished later.

   a. How is this first announcement likely to be received by employees? What needs are likely to become predominant?

   b. What effect is the announcement likely to have on present job performance?

   c. Is this announcement likely to affect supervisor-employee relationships? How?

8. In recent years considerable emphasis has been given to creating job opportunities and training facilities for disadvantaged persons in our society.

   a. What are some of the problems in developing successful programs of this type?

   b. If you were a supervisor of individuals who had been placed in your unit for on-the-job training under such a program, what special attention would you give to the motivational factors discussed in this chapter?

9. In most jobs in government the financial incentives that may be found in many business and industrial jobs are not present.

   a. What effect is this likely to have on employee behavior?

   b. How can supervisors in government agencies motivate employees?

10. "Old-timers" are often heard to say: "People don't put forth the effort on their jobs like they used to."

    a. Do you believe this statement of old-timers is true? Why?

    b. Is the employee responsible for putting forth effort? Discuss.

CASE 12-1

THE OFFICE MOVE

A personnel research staff of a large government agency employed several technical writers and specialists in addition to the personnel needed to perform administrative and clerical functions. One of the technical writers, Priscilla Clemington, in her middle forties, had been with the organization for over a year. During that time she had made a distinguished record for herself as a result of her superior performance and her skill in working with specialists in the preparation of technical manuals. She was friendly, well poised, and in other ways revealed her keen interest in the work and in the people with whom she worked. Unlike many employees, she seldom talked about herself, and it was generally believed that she was enjoying life to the fullest. Only those who had interviewed her at the time she was considered for the job knew that she had just divorced her husband and that she was returning to work in order to earn a living.

One day while she was working away from the office, the manager decided that some physical rearrangements within the office were necessary for achieving greater efficiency. He called in his immediate subordinates, one of whom was Priscilla's chief, and discussed the need for making changes. All agreed that the changes were necessary, and the manager called the moving crews who reported promptly and rearranged the office according to plan. In the process of relocating furniture, Priscilla's desk and filing cabinet were moved about six feet from where they had been. Priscilla was, however, still next to the same people as before, and the lighting in the new location was superior to that in the old spot. It was anticipated that she should be pleased at the change and that she would feel that others were concerned about her interests.

About half an hour before closing time Priscilla returned from the place where she had been working for the day and quickly noticed that her desk had been moved and that things were not the way they were at the time she left the office that morning. She immediately burst into tears and left the office. Her supervisor tried to console her, but she would not listen to his reasons for the change. Priscilla then left for the day feeling very despondent.

    a. How do you explain Priscilla's attitude and reaction following her return to the office?

    b. What important lessons in human relations might one draw from this incident?

CASE 12-2

THE PAJAMA FACTORY*

Some years ago an experiment was conducted at the Harwood Manufacturing Company. The plant had about 500 women and 100 men engaged in manufacturing pajamas. The average age of the employees was 23 years, and the average education was 8 years of grammar school. Most of the employees were from the rural, mountainous areas surrounding the town and had no prior industrial experience. Because of its policies, the company had enjoyed good labor relations since the day that it commenced operations.

The experiment was designed to determine why employees often resist changes that are made in various aspects of their jobs. Management had determined that it was necessary to change work methods in order to reduce production costs and used this opportunity to study employee resistance to change.

One group of employees — the control group — went through the usual factory routine when their jobs were changed. The production department modified the job, and a new piece rate was set. A group meeting was then held in

---

*Adapted from an experiment by L. Coch and J. R. P. French, Jr., "Overcoming Resistance to Change," *Human Relations*, Vol. 1 (1948) pp. 512–532.

which the control group was told that the change was necessary because of competitive conditions and that a new piece rate had been set. The new piece rate was thoroughly explained by the time-study man, and questions were answered.

The experimental group was handled quite differently. In a group meeting that was held with all the employees to be affected by the change, the need for the change was presented as dramatically as possible by showing two identical garments produced in the factory; one was produced in 1946 and had sold for twice as much as the other one produced in 1947. The group was asked to identify the cheaper one and could not do it. The demonstration effectively showed the need for cost reduction. A general agreement was reached that a savings could be effected by removing the "frills" and "fancy" work from the garment without affecting the folders' opportunity to achieve a high efficiency rating. Management then presented a plan to set the new job and piece rate, as follows:

1. Make a check study of the job as it was being done.
2. Eliminate all unnecessary work.
3. Train several operators in the correct methods.
4. Set the piece rate by time studies on these specially trained operators.
5. Explain the new job and rate to all the operators.
6. Train all operators in the new method so they can reach a high rate of production within a short time.

The group approved this plan and chose the operators to be specially trained. A submeeting with the chosen operators was held immediately following the meeting with the entire group. They displayed a cooperative and interested attitude and immediately presented many good suggestions. This attitude carried over into the working out of the details of the new job. When the new job and piece rates were set, the "special" operators referred to "our job," "our rate," etc. The "special" operators served to train the other operators on the new job.

The results for the two groups that worked under the same supervisor were quite different. The control group improved little beyond their earlier performance. Resistance developed almost immediately after the change occurred. Marked expressions of aggression against management occurred, such as conflict with the methods engineer, expression of hostility against the supervisor, deliberate restriction of production, and lack of cooperation with the supervisor. There were 17 per cent "quits" in the first forty days. The experimental group, on the other hand, showed an unusually good relearning curve. At the end of 14 days, their group averaged 61 units per hour. During the 14 days, their attitude was cooperative and permissive. They worked well with the methods engineer, the training staff, and the supervisor. There were no "quits" in this group in the first 40 days.

a. What effect did employee participation in determining work methods have on their job performance?
b. Why did the employees in the control group act differently from those in the experimental group toward their superiors?
c. Is it good business practice to have employee participation in work methods and other matters related to the job? Why?

d. Have you ever observed resistance to change in yourself? What were the conditions that brought about the resistance?

e. What attitude should the supervisor have toward employees who are resisting change? What can he do to help reduce the resistance?

SUGGESTED READINGS

Bellows, Roger. *Creative Leadership.* Englewood Cliffs, New Jersey: Prentice-Hall, Inc., 1959. Chapters 4, 5, 6, 7.

Chruden, Herbert J., and Arthur W. Sherman, Jr. *Readings in Personnel Management,* Second Edition. Cincinnati: South-Western Publishing Company, Inc., 1966. Chapter 3.

Davis, Keith. *Human Relations at Work.* New York: McGraw-Hill Book Company, 1962.

Gellerman, Saul W. *Motivation and Productivity.* New York: American Management Association, 1963.

Haire, Mason. *Psychology in Management,* Second Edition. New York: McGraw-Hill Book Company, 1964.

Herzberg, F. *Work and the Nature of Man.* Cleveland: The World Publishing Company, 1966.

Herzberg, F., B. Mausner, and B. B. Snyderman. *The Motivation to Work,* Second Edition. New York: John Wiley & Sons, Inc., 1959.

Likert, Rensis. *New Patterns of Management.* New York: McGraw-Hill Book Company, 1961.

Lincoln, James F. *Incentive Management.* Cleveland: Lincoln Electric Company, 1956.

Maier, Norman R. F. *Psychology in Industry,* Third Edition. New York: Houghton Mifflin Company, 1965. Chapters 13–14.

Maslow, A. H. *Eupsychian Management.* Homewood, Illinois: Richard D. Irwin, Inc., 1965.

——————————. *Motivation and Personality.* New York: Harper & Brothers, 1954.

Sartain, Aaron Q., and Alton W. Baker. *The Supervisor and His Job.* New York: McGraw-Hill Book Company, 1965. Chapter 10.

Sutermeister, Robert A. *People and Productivity.* New York: McGraw-Hill Book Company, 1963.

Vroom, V. H. *Work and Motivation.* New York: John Wiley & Sons, Inc., 1964.

Williams, Whiting. *Mainsprings of Men.* New York: Charles Scribner's Sons 1925.

Communication

Effective communication at all levels within an enterprise is essential to the achievement of efficiency and morale among its personnel. It is of primary importance that every employee understand his job duties and the manner in which they are to be accomplished. Furthermore, it is important that he understand why he is doing something and how well he is doing it; otherwise, his motivation may decline with the result that grievances, accidents, waste, and other problems are likely to arise.

The successful operation of a business is dependent not only upon the contributions of its individual members but also upon the cooperation and teamwork that exists among them. Thus, the role of communication in the development and functioning of the group structure deserves careful attention by management. At all levels in the organization — among and between executives, managers, staff personnel, supervisors and foremen, and employees — the communication process is continuously in action conveying information, ideas, attitudes, and feelings among individuals and among groups of individuals. Communication is, therefore, often referred to as a network that binds all of the members of an organization together.

In the past management has frequently measured the effectiveness of its communication primarily in terms of how well it was telling its story. More recently, however, there has been an increasing recognition of the importance and values of obtaining feedback from employees. This view of communication, commonly called "two-way" communication, is the only approach to the development of mutual understanding between management and employees. Without understanding there is no communication.

The achievement of mutual understanding is the product of recognizing forces within the individual personality as well as those forces that are inherent in a functioning organization. Therefore, this discussion of communication focuses on the relationship between these two forces and includes these topics:

- The communication process.
- Communication and the organizational structure.
- Communication media.
- Barriers to communication.
- Developing and maintaining effective communication.

The Communication Process

The communication process is one of the primary tools of management. Without the transmission of information, ideas, attitudes, and feelings — both upward and downward — productivity and morale would soon suffer. It is essential, therefore, that management personnel at all levels understand the principles of effective communication and learn the skills that will enable them to communicate effectively. It should be recognized, however, that communication is the responsibility of every person in the organization. One's effectiveness as an employee, regardless of the job, is determined to some degree by his effectiveness in communicating with his supervisor, fellow employees, customers, and others.

Steps in Communication

An analysis of the communication process reveals that there are several steps, as shown in Figure 13-1. The first step is *ideation* by the sender. It represents the content of his message and is determined by his abilities and his objectives in the situation.

In the next step — *encoding* — the sender organizes his ideas into a series of symbols designed to communicate to his intended receivers. He selects suitable words or phrases that can be understood by the receiver, and he also selects the appropriate media to be used — for example, memorandum, conference, etc. The third step is *transmission* of the

Figure 13-1
THE COMMUNICATION PROCESS

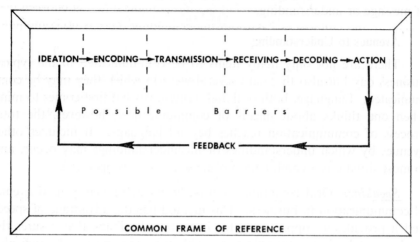

message as encoded through selected channels in the organizational structure. The fourth step is where the *receiver* enters the process. He tunes to receive the message. If it is oral, he must be a good listener. If the receiver does not function, however, the message is lost. The fifth step is *decoding*, as for example, changing words into ideas. At this step the decoding may not agree with the idea that the sender originally encoded because of the difference in perceptions between the receiver and the sender as to the meaning of words or semantics. Finally, the receiver *acts* or responds. He may file the information, ask for more information, or take other action.[1] There can be no assurance, however, that communication has taken place unless there is some type of *feedback* to the sender in the form of an acknowledgment that the message was received. It is desirable, therefore, that feedback be considered as an essential step in planning communications in business. Similarly, a common frame of reference which provides a common point of view for understanding improves the quality of communication.

On a typical working day the process described above occurs an infinitesimal number of times. The process is found in person-to-person communication, person-to-group communication, and group-to-group communication. A tally of all the attempts to communicate during a single working day would be almost incomprehensible in size, if humanly possible to make. Such a tally would include every order given by a superior

[1]Keith Davis, *Human Relations at Work* (New York: McGraw-Hill Book Company, 1962), pp. 349–351.

to a subordinate, all information passed back and forth between individuals whether written or spoken, as well as simple gestures conveying some type of message or understanding.

Avenues to Understanding

There are not only many items to be communicated in the typical business day but also there are several ways in which they may be communicated. Language, both oral and written, is what first comes to mind when one thinks about means of communication; however, the total process of communication reaches beyond language. It includes other avenues by which understandings or misunderstandings may occur, and in most situations a combination of these avenues is operating.

Speaking. Oral communication is the most frequently used avenue of communication in business. This method has the advantage of speed, and it provides an opportunity for immediate feedback that assures the sender that he is "communicating" with the other party. Speech also involves less work than written communication, but the fact that one should attempt to organize what he is going to say and give some thought to how he is going to say it should not be overlooked. The wise speaker will also convey to his listeners that he is willing to listen to them.

Listening. The most neglected avenue of communication is listening. Most of us feel that we are good listeners, but this usually means that we can remain passive and silent while the other fellow talks. Listening, however, is not a passive process; it requires action. One authority says:

> ... Figuratively or literally, too many of us "sit back and listen." This attitude may work well for music, but we need to "sit up and listen" when we're trying to take part in communication. A good listener's mind is alert; his face and posture usually reflect this fact. He may further show his interest by questions and comments which encourage the speaker to express his ideas fully. . . .[2]

It is only through this type of listening that *understanding*, the purpose of all communication, may be achieved. Unfortunately, however, most people are not good listeners. One test using a fairly simple spoken message lasting only a few minutes and containing only two major points proved difficult for businessmen who were tested. The average could summarize only a third of the content. It is suggested that among the reasons for this poor showing is that few people have been trained to listen. Even with the recent trend toward instruction in "the language arts" or in

---

[2]Lydia Strong, "Do You Know How to Listen?" in *Effective Communication on the Job* (New York: American Management Association, 1956), pp. 26–33.

"communication skills," listening has not received the attention that is devoted to reading, writing, and speaking. Several companies are attempting to improve listening by offering programmed instruction on listening. Over 20,000 persons in 50 companies have participated.[3]

Writing. Although there has been considerable emphasis on eliminating "red tape" and personalizing communication through the use of verbal communication, the written form is still essential. Those messages that are complex, that are quite important, that are of long-term significance, or that affect several persons are customarily written. Some common forms of written communication are letters and memoranda, newspapers, bulletin-board notices, signs, and posters. In written communication there is no personal contact; and unless the writer is available for discussion, his intentions may not be understood by the recipient. It is often necessary, therefore, that written communication be explained and clarified orally. For this reason management often requests that supervisors explain the contents of memoranda from top management to their subordinates in meaningful terms.

Nonverbal communication. Speaking, writing, and listening are recognized as the common ways in which communication takes place. More important than these ways, however, is action or inaction. Employees are primarily influenced not by what management says but by what it does. In fact, every behavior of a superior has some influence on the subordinates who observe it. The interpretation that is given to the behavior will vary according to the individual viewers. Nevertheless, there will be meaning attached to whatever action a superior takes, even if it be nothing more than a smile, closing his office door, or patting an employee on the back. Similarly, the superior assigns meaning to the nonverbal behavior of his subordinates. When he perceives them working diligently, daydreaming, or wasting time in talking with other employees, he is interpreting their behavior. In Figure 13-2 the boss has gone a step further and is interpreting the nonverbal communication that apparently has or is taking place between the members of the office staff. While there are many types of nonverbal communication that might be mentioned, the important thing at this point is for the reader to become aware of the role of nonverbal communication in the total communication process.[4]

---

[3]Walter S. Wikstrom, "Lessons in Listening," *The Conference Board Record*, Vol. 2, No. 4, (April, 1965).

[4]An interesting theoretical and pictorial presentation of this subject may be found in Jurgen Ruesch and Weldon Kees, *Nonverbal Communication* (Berkeley and Los Angeles: University of California Press, 1956).

Figure 13-2

ONE FORM OF COMMUNICATION

"They're not fooling me. They've got some kind of warning system."

—*Look Magazine*

Source: *Look Magazine.* Reproduced with the permission of the artist, Carl Thomas.

Communication and the Organizational Structure

Effective communication between friends is often difficult and at times impossible to achieve in spite of efforts to improve it. It may be expected, therefore, that where hierarchical relationships exist, as in an organization, and where interpersonal feelings are sometimes more negative than positive, the communication process will require even more attention and effort if it is to yield the level of understanding necessary for efficient operations. While it is generally agreed that there is need for an organizational structure, the development of the structure must necessarily be based on some consideration of the communication problems that may arise as a result of the pattern of interpersonal relationships established by the structure. In some instances it is possible to correct the problems; whereas, in other situations communication is blocked and travels by other means, such as through informal channels. In examining the communication process in relation to the organization structure, it is thus necessary to consider both formal and informal types of communication.

Formal Communication

Formal communication takes place between personnel according to established lines of authority or on the basis of established procedural relationships. A supervisor giving instructions to a subordinate is engaging in formal communication based on the lines of authority; whereas, the office secretary who discusses a correspondence problem with the mailing department is following procedural lines of communication.

Formal communication may flow in downward, upward, and horizontal directions.

Downward communication. This is communication that originates at any management level and is directed toward subordinate personnel. Basically, there are five types of communication down the line:

1. Specific task direction: *job instructions.*
2. Information designed to produce understanding of the task and its relation to other organizational tasks: *job rationale.*
3. Information about organizational *procedures and practices.*
4. *Feedback* to the subordinate about his performance.
5. Information of an ideological character to inculcate a sense of mission.[5]

Emphasis in the use of these different types of downward communication will vary from one organization to another and from one manager or supervisor to another. However, for effective employee performance, job satisfaction, and teamwork among the members of an organization, it is essential that there be effective communication from superiors to subordinates in all of the five types listed above.

Upward communication. Communication up the line is primarily concerned with the expression of a subordinate's ideas, attitudes, and feelings about himself, his job, his performance, and his problems; about others; about organizational policies and practices; and similar matters that he perceives as being acceptable material to communicate to management. The subordinate typically communicates directly with his superior either orally or in writing. The major exception is the submission of an idea or plan through the suggestion system. While management personnel may sincerely encourage upward communication or give "lip service" to it, there are barriers to its use which will be discussed later.

Horizontal communication. In addition to improving upward communication, management should also develop the type of conditions,

<hr>

[5]Daniel Katz and Robert L. Kahn, *The Social Psychology of Organizations* (New York: John Wiley and Sons, Inc., 1966), p. 239.

including the social climate, that facilitates *horizontal communication* —
communication among personnel at approximately the same levels in the
organization structure. Supervisors and the subordinates in different
departments, for example, should be encouraged and feel free to communicate with one another about common problems. Subordinates, however, should recognize the responsibility that they have for keeping their
supervisors advised of the general content of their communication with
personnel in other departments.

Informal Communication

Informal communication takes place between friends and acquaintances whose relationship to one another is independent of authority and
job functions. Rather, it has developed out of interpersonal relationships
in which the participants find harmony and satisfaction. While these contacts follow patterns that are independent of the formal organizational
structure, they nevertheless provide an important channel of communication, frequently referred to as the "grapevine" because it winds through
the organization without regard to the formal organization.

McMurry represents the informal organization in a company by a
circular or "beehive" chart which shows the chief executive in the center
and the other people at varying distances from him. In Figure 13-3 the
informal organizational chart of a particular company reveals that the
chief executive of the company really is the secretary-treasurer. (This is
because of the large stockholdings of his family.) The president, while
undoubtedly at the top on the chart of the formal organization, actually
takes orders from the secretary-treasurer. The vice-presidents, likewise,
are not in one ring next to the president but are at varying distances from
the center of the chart, representing different degrees of closeness to the
chief executive.

Such a chart made on the basis of the informal organization reveals
which communication routes are actually functioning. Notice that the
vice-president in charge of finance does not communicate directly with the
secretary-treasurer but goes through the vice-president in charge of sales.
The status of the personnel director in this informal organization is somewhat alarming. His role is apparently nothing more than that of a record
keeper since he is not in communication with anyone (as revealed by the
blank circle between him and the industrial relations director), and he is
quite remote from the key executives in the hub of the circle.

McMurry recommends that such a chart be prepared in every company in order that interpersonal relationships may be viewed realistically

Figure 13-3

CIRCULAR INFORMAL
ORGANIZATIONAL CHART

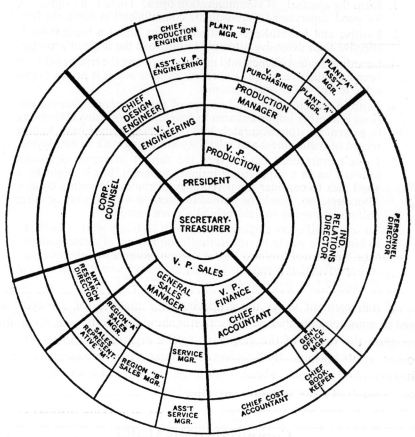

Source: Robert N. McMurry, *McMurry's Management Clinic* (New York: Simon and Schuster, Inc., 1960), p. 13. Reproduced with permission.

and adjustments made in the formal organization, where desirable, to facilitate communication and the achievement of the organizational objectives.[6]

Even outside the circle of executives and managers, news may travel quite rapidly over the "grapevine." In most instances it provides for a rapid transmission of information and misinformation and, therefore, presents a challenge to the planned communication of management. According to Hershey, however, there are some controls that can be used

---

[6]Robert N. McMurry, *McMurry's Management Clinic* (New York: Simon and Schuster, Inc., 1960), pp. 12–14.

to minimize the number and severity of rumors that are passed from one person to another over the grapevine. He recommends:

1. Keep the channels of communication open. There is no substitute for good supervisor-to-subordinate communication down the line.
2. Positive and truthful presentation of facts about a topic is more effective than defensive attempts to disprove the logic of a rumor.
3. Guarding against idleness and monotony among the troops has long been a military technique to prevent rumors and it is just as applicable to any other organization.
4. Faith in the credibility and source of management's communications is another important area to develop. A company attempting to present its story accurately and convincingly must have built a record of truthfulness and reliability in dealing with its employees.
5. I don't ever recall having seen the subject of rumor dynamics touched on in a supervisory training program, but it might be a good idea to consider the psychology of rumors in such a course. Managers, too, should be trained to question what anxiety or other attitude is coming to light behind a given rumor.
6. To sum up, if every employee knew with certainty all that mattered to him, there would be, theoretically, no rumors of consequence to "the business of business." But our communication processes are so imperfect that it pays to attempt to analyze rumors, understand them, and take positive steps to head them off.[7]

If management views the grapevine as a method for satisfying the need to communicate that neither can nor should be destroyed, it can then recognize the values of the grapevine to the organization in terms of its positive contributions. By listening to the grapevine, managers and supervisors can find out more about it and thus are better able to influence it in the direction of the organizational objectives.

Communication Media

It was noted earlier that communication takes place through different avenues but that the spoken and written word are the means most often depended upon for transmitting ideas, information, instructions, attitudes, and feelings in business. The different communication media involving language that are available to management may be classified under the headings of face-to-face communication and written communication.

Face-to-Face Communication

A large part of communication in business takes place on a face-to-face basis. This is probably because it is decidedly faster than most written

---

[7]Robert Hershey, "The Grapevine — Here to Stay But Not Beyond Control," *Personnel*, Vol. 43, No. 1 (January/February, 1966), pp. 62–66.

media if a limited number of persons are involved, and it provides for immediate feedback. Since understanding is the key to communication, the feedback gives the sender reasonable assurance that there is or is not a "meeting of minds."

Person-to-person communication. Most of the person-to-person communication within an organization occurs between individuals whose job procedures require it, as between the waiter and the cook and the cashier and the bookkeeper. Communication between supervisors and their subordinates represents the most critical area for the organization because of the supervisor's influence on the employee's behavior and morale. If the supervisor is an effective manager of personnel, he gives orders and instructions, he advises employees on matters that are of interest and concern to them, he advises and counsels with them on problem situations, and he communicates with them in many other ways. In order to communicate effectively with employees, it is important for the supervisor to understand the employees' viewpoint as well as that of management.

While this type of communication between supervisor and subordinate is highly personalized, it often leaves much to be desired. An employee may be given incomplete data needed for an assignment, top management policy may be misinterpreted, or the employee's attitude toward the supervisor may result in failure to understand what the supervisor is saying. Effective person-to-person communication is, therefore, dependent upon the accuracy and completeness of the information that the sender has, his ability to transmit it, and the receiver's ability and interest in understanding the intended meaning of the communication. Some of the shortcomings of the person-to-person method can be overcome by supplementing it with written communication.

Committees. Face-to-face communication among a number of persons is provided by committees. As was indicated in Chapter 3, the committee not only provides the advantage of group deliberation and judgment but also facilitates coordination and integration of the activities of a complex organization, especially at the higher echelons. By assembling representatives of different departments together with management personnel to discuss organizational problems, upward, downward, and horizontal communication may be facilitated. The success or failure of a committee meeting is largely dependent upon the composition of the committee, the skill of the chairman, and its assignment. While a committee may be composed of representatives from line and staff departments, it is essential that its members have some knowledge and understanding of the problems to be discussed. Otherwise, considerable time will be lost in briefing the uninformed, or they may try to "save face" by being overly critical of the proposals and comments of the others. The skillful chairman is usually able to deal effectively with such individuals and to provide for a balanced discussion among the committee members within reasonable time limits.

Brainstorming. In recent years the committee has been used quite widely for the purpose of obtaining new ideas. One approach is to conduct "brainstorming" sessions. The sessions are conducted on an informal basis, and the participants are instructed to "let themselves go" and state their ideas. No attempt is made to evaluate the ideas until the participants have exhausted all possibilities. As a result the participants are not quite as inhibited as they would ordinarily be in a meeting. American Greetings Corporation, a company that sold $77.9 million in greeting cards in 1965, uses this approach to obtain ideas for cards. According to their president, a group of employees gather together for a brainstorming session and "throw ideas at each other."

> "That's how our big Thanksgiving Hi Brow card was created," says Wilson. "We sat around and someone mentioned turkeys. Somebody else said that drumsticks were big with turkeys, weren't they? Somebody else said it was too bad a turkey had only two drumsticks. Finally, somebody said that if we crossed a turkey with a centipede there would be enough for everyone. I thought we had it but it got even better when someone else said it would be hard to catch. That made it — our best-selling card that year: 'For Thanksgiving We Crossed a Turkey With a Centipede and Now We Have Drumsticks for Everyone . . . If Only We Could Catch the Damn Thing!' "[8]

Other organizations use brainstorming not only for obtaining new and fresh ideas for new products but also new uses for old products and solutions to management problems. It should not be assumed, however, that a greater productivity of ideas will automatically result from brainstorming. Some recent studies indicate that individuals do not produce any more ideas in a group than they would produce alone. In fact, Dunnette recommends that brainstorming be done by individuals in private by dictating ideas and solutions into a recording device, thus avoiding inhibition of the best that may be available from individual problem-solving efforts.[9] Since further research is needed on brainstorming, it is suggested that it be used primarily in those situations where it can clearly be shown to be particularly useful and productive.

---

[8]_Forbes_, August 1, 1966, pp. 15–16.

[9]Marvin D. Dunnette, "Are Meetings Any Good for Solving Problems?" _Personnel Administration_, Vol. 27, No. 2 (March/April, 1964), pp. 12–16.

Conference. The committee and the conference are similar types of meetings with the exception that the committee implies a more or less stable membership and some regularity in meeting. The conference, on the other hand, usually is a one-time or infrequent meeting called for the purpose of obtaining and disseminating information and for exchanging ideas.

Surveys by the American Management Association, the National Industrial Conference Board, and the National Association of Manufacturers, as well as those made by many individuals and universities, show that the conference is firmly established as a desirable, if not indispensable, vehicle of management communication. Despite its drawbacks, which for the most part can be overcome through training programs, the business conference can accomplish multiple communication objectives of management: to keep people informed, to solve problems and make decisions, to consult and ascertain attitudes, and to provide a participation medium and climate.[10]

The face-to-face contact in conferences enables the participants to achieve a level of understanding that is not possible with the written word or with information or instructions passed through many intermediaries. As in a committee, the members are in a position to consider each other's ideas, to weigh the pros and cons of each suggestion, and to arrive at a decision in which each member has played a part.

Since the college student is likely to be a participant at a conference or a member of a committee upon obtaining employment, it may be helpful for him to have some ideas on how to be an effective participant. The following list of suggestions by Wiksell is recommended:

1. Understand the nature of the meeting. It is a cooperative effort.
2. Prepare for the meeting yourself, but do not let your preparation close your mind to new ideas.
3. Participate in the discussion frankly. Say what you think. Do not make a statement implying, "This is a fact," unless you are sure it is. Speak modestly by using such expressions as, "It seems to me," "In my opinion," or "As I understand it."
4. Listen thoughtfully. Show a deep interest in what others say in order to get their points of view.
5. Have an open mind. Be flexible. A collective change of viewpoint is one of the primary reasons for a conference.
6. Be courteous. The conference, like other communication situations, is no place for sarcasm, disparaging remarks, interruptions, arguments, or a monopoly of the talking time.

[10]Harold P. Zelko, "Dilemmas of the Conference Process," _Management of Personnel Quarterly_, Vol. 4, No. 3 (Fall, 1965), pp. 7–14.

7. Stick to the problem. Cooperate with the leader and the group by concentrating on the issue.
8. Be informal. The conference is no place for formality in material or manner, nor is it the place for speeches or parliamentary rules.[11]

Interviews. The interview is a special type of face-to-face communication. It is characterized by a higher degree of personal interest in the receiver when compared with other types of communication. The selection interview (Chapter 6), the performance evaluation interview (Chapter 10), and the personal adjustment interview (Chapter 16) are examples of different types of interviews. Many of the problems in communication discussed later in this chapter are as prevalent in the various types of interviews as they are in other media of communication.

Written Communication

While oral communication provides for feedback, it is too slow and is subject to too much distortion for top management to use when it desires to cover the broader and more complex aspects of the business. Because written communication generally carries greater weight and authority, special attention should be given to the style and quality of writing. It should be dignified without being pompous, consider the reader's needs, and possess such a high degree of clarity that it cannot be misinterpreted. While there is a wide variety of written media used in business, only a few will be considered here.

Job descriptions and procedural manuals. One of the most important media for communication with the employee is the job description. It enumerates in detail the duties that the employee is expected to perform, the equipment that he will use, and other important information necessary to his success on the job. Manuals in which operating procedures and rules and regulations are described are often made available to employees in order that a reasonable degree of uniformity, efficiency, and safety may be achieved.

Handbooks. Handbooks are often used to convey information of immediate concern to the employee. Employee services, sick leave provisions, insurance coverage, stock ownership plans, and other benefits are usually described in detail. An authoritative and condensed discussion of these topics is not only valuable to the employee but management may

---

[11]Wesley Wiksell, *Do They Understand You?* (New York: The Macmillan Company, 1960), pp. 167–168. Reproduced with permission.

also reach the employee's family through this medium, thereby increasing their understanding of and appreciation for the company.

The house organ. One of the most widely used media for downward communication within a company and for reaching the families of employees is the newspaper or magazine, commonly referred to as the *house organ.* News about employees and their families is still the backbone of the house organ, although there are indications that the reader desires more than this in his publication. Employees want news about those plans, policies, and operations that directly affect the security of their jobs, but they may resent having too many articles about the benefits of free enterprise forced upon them. Quite often employees look upon such articles as attempts by management to "brainwash" them. While management should not attempt to antagonize the employees through its publications, neither should it avoid the discussion of controversial issues. Among some authorities there is an increasing feeling that management should use employee publications to get its story across to employees, particularly in such matters as those involving union relations.

The Suggestion Program

The written media discussed above represent examples of downward communication; the suggestion program is an example of upward communication. The suggestion program is designed to encourage participation of the employee in the larger and more important aspects of the company's operations by rewarding him for suggestions that may be used to benefit the company. The suggestions may cover such areas as work methods and procedures, equipment design, safety devices, and other matters not related directly to production.

The suggestion program not only benefits the company but tends to focus the employee's attention and interest on his work and to make him aware that the company recognizes the importance of his daily tasks and is willing to reward him for improving the methods by which they are accomplished. A successful suggestion program is dependent upon management support. If, however, executives are as threatened by suggestions as the one pictured in Figure 13-4, the program is not likely to be very effective.

Supervisors should be instructed in procedures for assisting employees in preparing suggestions since they have considerable familiarity with the employee's job and the normal work procedures. Supervisors can assist in evaluating ideas and can be a source of encouragement. Inasmuch as

Figure 13-4

WALL STREET JOURNAL

A.S. HABBICK

"Fenton, are you coming up with all these marvelous suggestions just to make me look ridiculous?"

Source: *Wall Street Journal.* Reproduced with the permission of Cartoon Features Syndicate.

the status of the supervisor is enhanced if he is aware that a suggestion has been submitted, it is desirable that the supervisor be given a copy of the suggestion at the time it is placed in the suggestion box. Many suggestion systems specifically provide for this procedure in order to strengthen two-way communication between supervisor and subordinate. A suggestion system that fails to keep the supervisor informed may serve to antagonize him rather than contribute to the improvement of communication between him and his employees.

Some companies not only give a cash award to employees with the best suggestions but also reward the supervisor who encourages employees to submit suggestions, thus improving the supervisor's attitude toward the program. When supervisors are not rewarded, they may feel that the program is not important and that employees should not waste their time on such matters.

Barriers to Communication

While there are several avenues by which understanding may pass from one person to another as well as many media for promoting understanding, these avenues and media do not necessarily lead to the desired goal. The groupings of people into a complex organization impose additional conditions and factors affecting human relationships which may constitute potential barriers to communication. In order for communication to be effective, it is essential for the manager or supervisor to recognize these potential barriers and to plan communication so that these barriers may be overcome or at least minimized.

In a survey of over 750 company members, the National Industrial Conference Board asked, "What are the barriers to communication within a company?" The barriers cited fell into three major groups:

1. Barriers arising from the fact that individuals differ. These are barriers that a company inherits because they are common to society.
2. Barriers arising from the company's psychological climate which tend to stultify communication.
3. Barriers that are largely mechanical in the sense that they stem from lack of proper facilities or means of communication.[12]

Some of the major barriers in each of these groups are examined below for purposes of illustrating the problems that arise in attempts to communicate with others.

Differences in Individuals

One of the major problems in communicating with large numbers of individuals, as in a company, is the simple fact that no two individuals are alike. Individuals are born with different potentialities, they have had different experiences during their childhood and youth, and as adults they have had employers and supervisors who have exerted a variety of influences upon them.

Perceptions differ. One result of prior experiences is that each employee brings with him to the job his own unique way of looking at things, or in other words, his *frame of reference*. This frame of reference determines the manner in which he will interpret or perceive whatever he sees or hears. If the supervisor is viewed as a "father figure," the employee may accept or reject everything the supervisor says, depending upon the type of

---

[12]Barriers to Communication," *Management Record* (New York: National Industrial Conference Board, January, 1958).

relationship that he had with his father. Similarly, if the employee has been "let down" by previous supervisors, he is likely to view the new supervisor as someone not to be trusted.

Closely tied to perception and influencing it are the motivational and emotional states of the individual. The manner in which he interprets a situation will be largely influenced by his condition at the moment attempts are made to communicate with him. Haire points this out in a vivid example:

> During World War II, an aerial-gunnery student was taking a training flight over the Gulf of Mexico. The pilot, enjoying the ride and the scenery, pointed over the side of the plane, in a friendly spirit, to call the student's attention to a speedboat below. The gesture was clear to him, but the student referred it to his own acute terror of being in the air, and interpreting it to mean that his worst fears were realized, he parachuted over the side.[13]

Such misinterpretations frequently occur in the supervisor's attempts to communicate with employees where perceptions, motivations, and emotions of the sender and receiver are subject to continuous interactions. Gibb suggests, in fact, that one way to understand communication is to view it as a people process rather than as a language process. One way to improve communication is to reduce the defensive behavior that occurs when an individual is threatened. As a person becomes more and more defensive, because he feels threatened, he becomes less and less able to perceive accurately the motives, the values, and the emotions of the sender.

While we cannot always know the personal level of defensiveness of an individual, we can learn more about how the world looks to him or what motivational and emotional states he may be experiencing *by listening*. In addition, Carl Rogers suggests going one step further. Instead of following our natural tendency to judge, to evaluate, to approve (or disapprove) the statement of the other person as he expresses his views and opinions, we should listen *nonevaluatively*.[14] This means that we should try to understand the other person's frame of reference, his point of view; and once this is achieved, we have then overcome a major barrier to communication and mutual understanding is possible.

Semantics. Words, like gestures, can be interpreted in various ways thus creating a barrier to communication. Since there is not necessarily a connection between the symbol (the word) and what is being symbolized (the

---

[13]Mason Haire, *Psychology in Management* (Second Edition; New York: McGraw-Hill Book Company, 1964), p. 91.
[14]Carl R. Rogers and F. J. Roethlisberger, "Barriers and Gateways to Communication," *Harvard Business Review*, Vol. 30, No. 4 (July/August, 1952), pp. 46–52.

meaning), the communication may be received quite differently than was intended. The word "profit," for example, to the executive may represent a measure of success and a return deserved by a company; whereas, to the employee it may represent some of the funds that he should have received in the form of higher wages. In selecting words the communicator should consider his audience and its likely interpretation of the words he uses.

Status relationships. The position of the individual in the organizational structure will also influence the quality of communication that takes place. Persons of equal status, such as two supervisors, will probably find it easier to share information and feelings than a supervisor and a subordinate. In the latter instance, the differences in rank in the organizational hierarchy are likely to create barriers. The superior, because of his responsibilities to other subordinates as well as to higher management, is not "free" to disclose all that he knows about a particular subject to one of his subordinates. As a result, the quality of communication suffers.

A careful study of the communication efficiency of 100 representative business and industrial organizations reveals a tremendous loss of information as it passes from the board of directors downward through channels. As shown in Figure 13-5, by the time information flows downward through channels the plant manager had received only 40 percent of what had been transmitted to him, and the general foreman had received 30 percent. An average of 20 percent of the communication sent downward through the five levels of management finally gets to the worker level. Thus, in downward communication every effort must be made by executive and managerial personnel to reduce the amount of unnecessary *dilution* of information that takes place in order that subordinates may have as much information as possible for intelligent and enthusiastic job performance.

Subordinates when communicating with superiors, on the other hand, are even more likely to give only partial information and will frequently color events in such a manner as to conceal mistakes, failures, and other types of news that the boss may find unpleasant. This conscious manipulation of the "facts" to color events is called *filtering*. It is motivated primarily by the employee's desires to appear competent in the eyes of his boss because the boss controls and evaluates his performance. Because of its effects on the success of the organization, management should take positive steps to reduce filtering as much as possible. Some recommendations that have been offered include:

1. Tighter controls to ensure that upward communication contains a realistic estimate of the actual situation.

Figure 13-5

DILUTION OF INFORMATION IN DOWNWARD COMMUNICATION

Dilution of information occurs as a result of improper Communications flow . .

| 100% | 63% | 56% | 40% | 30% | 20% |
| BOARD | VICE PRESIDENT | GENERAL SUPERVISOR | PLANT MANAGER | GENERAL FOREMAN | WORKER |

Source: From a booklet published by Savage-Lewis, Inc., predecessor of The Erle Savage Company of Minneapolis. Reproduced with the permission of Erle B. Savage, Jr., President.

2. Building confidence by teamwork so subordinates see how their reports fit into the over-all picture of company operations.
3. Developing receptivity on the part of superiors to alleviate subordinates' fear of failure.
4. Improving the sensitivity of management to the problems, opinions, and feelings of subordinates so another method of expression is available to them besides the formal channel.[15]

Psychological Climate of the Organization

Organizations, like individuals, have "personalities." One organization may be permissive in that individuals have the freedom to express themselves and are encouraged to participate in many of the important activities. Another organization may be autocratic, that is, individuals are expected not to express their opinions and are otherwise discouraged from

[15]William G. Scott, *Organization Theory: A Behavioral Analysis for Management* (Homewood, Illinois: Richard D. Irwin, Inc., 1967), p. 305.

engaging in participative activities except in rare instances. In one company or department may be found individuals who are cheerful and friendly because the boss is relaxed; whereas, in another company or department individuals are disgruntled and uncooperative primarily because of a neurotic boss. Thus, the setting or climate in which individuals work influences their attitudes and behavior as well as the effectiveness of communication in the organization.

Personality of executives. Managers at the top of the organizational ladder can have considerable influence on a company's psychological climate. Their attitudes toward people, especially subordinates, the roles in the organization that they perceive for themselves, and their ability to be sensitive to the needs of others are major influences upon the total organization. The manager who is able to listen nonevaluatively to subordinates will later be able to make better decisions because he understood what the subordinates were trying to communicate to him. The impatient executive, on the other hand, who allows subordinates only five minutes to tell their story, may never get the facts that he needs for making intelligent decisions. The wise manager, therefore, plans his schedule so that he will have time for listening, and he attempts to create a relationship that will enable the subordinate to talk with him without feeling threatened by his presence and the realization that he is talking with the "brass." As noted earlier, threat is one of the major barriers to communication and, while not easy to allay, should be recognized by all persons in authority and minimized through the development of supportive climates.

Special groups and their effect. Within an organization there may be special groups or subgroups composed of individuals of various professions or occupations which have different value systems. Their differing values create barriers to communication that are frequently impossible to overcome. The accountants, for example, may not understand the attitudes that the research people have toward fiscal matters, just as the lawyers may not be able to understand the executive's attitudes toward government regulation of business. Differences in backgrounds and in the developing of "occupational personalities" may thus have profound effects on communication within the organization.

Mechanical Barriers

The barriers to communication that have been discussed represent those that are usually more difficult to overcome because they involve surmounting the idiosyncracies of human personalities or complex inter-relationships of people in groups. As a result, many companies do not attempt to overcome them and restrict their activities to removing the mechanical barriers to communication.

Lack of definite plans. In spite of the fact that the formal structure of the organization should be followed in communicating orders and information, it is fairly common for confusion to arise over the simple mechanics of who will do the communicating and when he will do it. If, for example, new work methods are to be introduced, should the announcement come from the president or the vice-president in charge of production? From there and on down the organizational structure, consideration should be given as to who will handle the various matters to be considered in relation to the change. Coordination between executives and managers is essential to having a presentation that will be complete and in proper focus in relation to the total operation of the organization.

Lack of clarity. Regardless of the educational or intellectual levels of the persons with whom one is attempting to communicate, understanding is less likely to occur if the material presented is not clear. Both the spoken and the written word may be misunderstood if the communicator uses words of many syllables or uses long, complex sentences. This type of speaking or writing has been labeled "gobbledygook" and should be eliminated through training and experience in plain talk and writing. The absurdity of gobbledygook is illustrated by a story about a plumber who was trying to communicate with a government agency in Washington.

> A New York plumber wrote the Bureau that he had found hydro-chloric acid fine for cleaning drains, and was it harmless? Washington replied: "The efficacy of hydrochloric acid is indisputable, but the chlorine residue is incompatible with metallic permanence."
> The plumber wrote back that he was mighty glad the Bureau agreed with him. The Bureau replied with a note of alarm: "We cannot assume responsibility for the production of toxic and noxious residues with hydrochloric acid, and suggest that you use an alternate procedure." The plumber was happy to learn that the Bureau still agreed with him.
> Whereupon Washington exploded: "Don't use hydrochloric acid; it eats hell out of the pipes!"[16]

Unfortunately, writing of this type is not confined to government agencies. Business firms have the same problem and should take positive

---

16From *Power of Words*, Copyright 1953, 1954 by Stuart Chase. Reprinted by permission of Harcourt, Brace & World, Inc.

steps to overcome deficiencies like these in communication. Many companies have improved communication by following the suggestions of Rudolf Flesch[17] who has developed techniques for making written material more readable.

Other mechanical barriers. The choice of media is often a barrier to communication. If persons who need to have information are not on the routing list or if they are not readily reached through one type of media, communication may suffer. The format for written communication may also be a barrier. Some persons, unless instructed, may assume that a mimeographed document is not as important as one that is individually typed; whereas, in many instances the reverse is true. Similarly, the misuse or overuse of a medium may cause people to ignore what comes over it, for they may come to have attitudes such as "it's not important" or "just more of the same." These and the other barriers mentioned need to be avoided if communication is to be effective.

Developing and Maintaining Effective Communication

Effective communication is dependent upon more than sound ideas and well-reasoned decisions that management desires to make known to employees. It is built upon continued attention to the many factors that are a part of the communication process and which make for understanding among those who are attempting to communicate with each other. In addition to those factors that have been discussed, consideration should be given to those matters that are less technical in nature but of equal and perhaps greater importance in developing and maintaining effective communication in the organization.

Sincerity

The sincerity or insincerity of management soon becomes apparent to employees. All too often management has plans for one type of action, but in communicating its plans to the employees, management attempts to hide the nature of the action or attempts to tell the employees what it believes they want to hear. It does not take many episodes of this type for employees to question the sincerity of management's intentions. If management has a record of fair and honest dealings with employees, its communication is more likely to be accepted.

---

[17]*The Art of Plain Talk* (1946), *The Art of Readable Writing* (1949), *How to Test Readability* (1951), and *How to Make Sense* (1954) (New York: Harper & Brothers).

Understanding Human Needs

Attention must be given to the persons who are to receive the information or instructions. What are their needs, interests, and attitudes? Since it is human nature to listen to someone who has something to say about those things in which we are interested, management's attention to employee's needs, interests, and attitudes can go a long way toward facilitating employee receptivity. For example, the manager is very likely to have an interested audience when he discusses prospects for continued employment with employees at a time when there are rumors of widespread unemployment in the industry. Similarly, the supervisor who calls a meeting of subordinates at a time when they are "griping" about working conditions will be appealing to the needs of employees to express themselves and will thus facilitate communication and morale.

The importance of the proper timing of a communication should not be overlooked. An announcement made at one time may be received enthusiastically by the employees. The same announcement made at another time may create havoc. For example, the premature announcement of the merger of two companies, both of which are considerably over-manned, is likely to create many problems. On the other hand, if the announcement is made after new contracts have been received or after arrangements have been worked out for placing excess personnel in other related jobs, it may be willingly received and accepted.

Evaluating the Effectiveness of Communication

Since communication is one of the most vital aspects of a company's operations, it is important that it be analyzed and evaluated. While there are no clear-cut criteria for judging the effectiveness of communication, certain indications can be used as guidelines. Freedom of expression among subordinates, which manifests itself in cordial relationships with their superiors, indicates a healthy condition.

One direct method that is commonly used to assess communication is the *employee attitude survey*, which is discussed in Chapter 16. The typical questionnaire includes items that ask the employee for his opinion of the effectiveness of communication within the company. A study of disciplinary problems, formal grievances, questions raised by employees, comments made during exit interviews, and the extent to which employees read company publications may also reveal something of the status of communication.

Effective communication yields benefits not only in terms of increased productivity but also in terms of improved employee attitudes, mutual confidence, respect, and understanding. The importance of these benefits to an organization is such as to require continuing attention from management as to the effectiveness of its modes of communication.

Résumé

The life of an organization is found in the people who occupy the positions and in the communication that they have with one another. If there is a free flow of information and attitudes from one person to another and from one level to another in the organizational hierarchy, the organization will most likely be strong and productive. If, on the other hand, communication is blocked at many points and information and attitudes fall on "deaf ears," the whole structure may be nothing more than a hollow shell pictured by names in boxes on an organizational chart. The chart has meaning only when the persons occupying the positions are able to interact successfully with one another in the accomplishment of the organizational objectives.

Many benefits will accrue to the company which has an enlightened understanding of the communication process and which makes a continuing effort to improve the effectiveness of its modes of communication. The efforts of all members of the organization to improve communication with those persons with whom they have a formal organizational relationship can be most effective in strengthening the organization. Thus, it is the responsibility of managers and supervisors to set the stage for all communication by nurturing the formal channels, reducing barriers, and developing a psychological climate in which the communication process may truly bind all of the members of the organization together.

DISCUSSION QUESTIONS AND PROBLEMS

1. In a Ph.D. dissertation (Yale, 1951), A. F. Wessen reported that in one large hospital 75 percent of the doctor's conversations were with other doctors, 60 percent of the nurses conversations were with other nurses, and 60 percent of the conversations of the workers of other groups tended to be with others in their own groups.
    a. How do you account for these findings? Do you believe they are typical only of hospital personnel?
    b. What significance do they have as far as the attainment of organizational objectives are concerned?
    c. What action could be taken to encourage greater interaction among personnel of different groups?
2. A few of the mechanical barriers to communication were mentioned in the chapter. Can you name some other possible barriers under these headings?

a. Written communication.
b. Oral communication.
c. Nonverbal communication.

3. Mr. Neil McElroy, Chairman of the Board of The Procter & Gamble Company, in a talk before a meeting of the National Industrial Conference Board said: "Starting with the foremen, we insist that each member of supervision be wholly responsible for that portion of the operation assigned to him. If questions are to be answered, he answers them. If company news is to be passed along, he tells it to his people. He is the Company management to the people under him."

   a. What is your opinion of this policy?
   b. What does it assume about the communication skills of foremen?
   c. What effect would it have on the formal organization of the company?

4. In our everyday language, especially when we talk about people, we use labels such as "businessman," "union leader," "good-looking secretary," "blue-collar worker," etc. What effect does this have on communication? Does the use of these labels facilitate or hinder communication? Explain.

5. Suggestion programs are reported to serve many effective purposes. However, some personnel managers feel that they often do not meet the objectives set for them. On the basis of what you have read in this chapter and any experiences that you may have had with suggestion programs, what do you believe are their inadequacies in meeting the objectives set for them?

6. Under what circumstances are rumors most likely to arise? What should management do to prevent them? After they are known?

7. Analyze the interactions among members of a committee or conference.
   a. What factors seem to make for good communication?
   b. Did you observe any behavior that appeared to be threatening to several members of the group? Describe the behavior and the indications of threat.
   c. How did the behavior of the leader of the group affect its members?

8. Ask a few teenagers to describe their interests, attitudes, and feelings about a topic of common knowledge. Then interview a group of middle-aged persons in the same manner with the same topic.
   a. Did you notice any differences in perceptions between the two groups?
   b. How do you account for these differences?
   c. What implications do your findings have for communication between these two groups?

9. Many companies make arrangements for their executives and managers to attend special courses devoted to improving reading speed and comprehension. How would this action benefit a company? What is there about the nature of modern management that necessitates such action?

10. How is the internal communication of a company related to its communication with customers and the community? Discuss.

CASE 13-1

SUSAN

It would soon be time for the annual award banquet held for employees of the Eastern Affiliated Insurance Company, and plans were being made for the gala event. Those employees with five years or more of service were scheduled to receive pins. Susan Hendershot, an employee with 35 years of service, was to be the guest of honor and was to sit at the head table with the president and other company officials. Public relations had sent out news releases, banquet programs were being printed, and the word was being spread throughout the community and the company that Susan with her 35 years of service was the pride of Eastern.

Three days before the award dinner the personnel manager and the executive vice-president were going over some problem areas in the company. They came to the conclusion that Susan had too many old-fashioned ideas that did not fit in with company policy and that the department of which she was manager was being operated in a manner that was not consistent with other departments. They decided to call Susan in that day and talk over these matters with her. The longer they talked with Susan, the more disagreeable she became until finally she stormed out of the room with the exclamation that she would see what could be done to improve her department operations but that she was not going to attend the award banquet.

    a. What are the implications of this situation in terms of good communication and management?

    b. How would you handle the problem?

CASE 13-2

FACTS AND INFERENCES*

Instructions

Read the following story and take for granted that everything it says is true. Read carefully because, in spots, the story is deliberately vague. Don't try to memorize it since you can look back at it at any stage.

Then read the numbered statements about the story and decide whether you consider each one true, false, or questionable. Circling the "T" means that you feel sure the statement is definitely true. Circling the "F" means you are sure it is definitely false. Circling the "?" means you cannot tell whether it is true or false. If you feel doubtful about any part of a statement, circle the question mark.

Take the statements in turn, and do not go back later to change any of your answers. Do not reread any of the statements after you have answered them. Such altering or rereading will distort the test.

The Story

John Phillips, the research director of a midwestern food products firm, ordered a crash program of development on a new process. He gave three of his executives authority to spend up to $50,000 each without consulting him. He sent one of his best men, Harris, to the firm's west coast plant with orders to work on the new process independently. Within one week Harris produced a highly promising approach to the problem.

Statements About the Story

1. Phillips sent one of his best men to the west coast plant........ T F ?
2. Phillips overestimated Harris's competence................... T F ?
3. Harris failed to produce anything new..................... T F ?

---

*From the "Uncritical Inference Test" by William V. Haney. Copyright 1961. Reproduced with permission of William V. Haney.

4. Harris lacked authority to spend money without consulting Phillips.. T F ?
5. Only three of Phillips' executives had authority to spend money without consulting him................................. T F ?
6. The research director sent one of his best men to the firm's west coast plant.. T F ?
7. Three men were given authority to spend up to $50,000 each without consulting Phillips................................ T F ?
8. Phillips had a high opinion of Harris...................... T F ?
9. Only four people are referred to in the story.............. T F ?
10. Phillips was research director of a food products firm........... T F ?
11. While Phillips gave authority to three of his best men to spend up to $50,000 each, the story does not make clear whether Harris was one of these men.. T F ?

Discussion Questions

   a. Why is it important to distinguish between facts and inferences?

   b. In what ways can the executive use his knowledge about facts and inferences in communications with subordinates?

SUGGESTED READINGS

Bellows, Roger M., Thomas Q. Gilson, and George S. Odiorne. *Executive Skills: Their Dynamics and Development.* Englewood Cliffs, New Jersey: Prentice-Hall, Inc., 1962. Chapters 5–9.

Bromage, Mary C. *Cases in Written Communication.* Ann Arbor: Bureau of Business Research, Graduate School of Business Administration, The University of Michigan, 1964.

Chruden, Herbert J., and Arthur W. Sherman, Jr. *Readings in Personnel Management,* Second Edition. Cincinnati: South-Western Publishing Company, Inc., 1966. Chapters 4–5.

Davis, Keith. *Human Relations at Work.* New York: McGraw-Hill Book Company, 1962.

Haire, Mason. *Psychology in Management,* Second Edition. New York: McGraw-Hill Book Company, 1964. Chapter 4.

Hay, Robert D. *Written Communications for Business Administrators.* New York: Holt, Rinehart & Winston, Inc., 1965.

Hayakawa, S. I. *Language in Thought and Action,* Second Edition. New York: Harcourt, Brace, and World, 1964.

Lee, Irving J., and Laura L. Lee. *Handling Barriers in Communication.* New York: McGraw-Hill Book Company, 1960.

Maier, Norman R. F. *Problem-Solving Discussions and Conferences.* New York: McGraw-Hill Book Company, 1963.

Newcomb, Robert, and Marg Sammons. *Employee Communications in Action.* New York: Harper & Brothers, 1961.

Redfield, Charles E. *Communication in Management.* Chicago: University of Chicago Press, 1953.

Zelko, Harold P., and Harold J. O'Brien. *Management-Employee Communication in Action.* Cleveland: Howard Allen, Inc., 1957.

Supervisory Leadership

In Part III the various personnel processes that contribute to the improvement of performance were examined. These processes are among the most important activities of managers and supervisors and for this reason were considered in detail. The total concept of supervision, however, is somewhat broader and should be analyzed not only in relation to these functions but also in the context of the organizational setting which prescribes the responsibility and authority of those in positions of leadership at various levels and which provides the conditions that help to determine employee performance, teamwork, adjustment, morale, and discipline.

The leaders of an organization — managers and supervisors alike — are a part of the total organizational setting and therefore are influenced by it. While it is generally expected that they will exercise a role different from that of their followers and display more initiative and concern for the achievement of the organizational goals, there has been increasing recognition of the need for *all* members of the organization to participate in the leadership function, even though formal authority has not been officially delegated to them. Thus, the present-day manager or supervisor is expected to solicit participation and at the same time retain the responsibility for the actions of his subordinates in this area. This trend toward greater participation by individuals and by the work group requires not only that managers be technically competent but also that they possess human relations skills and insights that enable them to share the leadership functions effectively. Because of the importance of the social context and group relationships in the supervision of personnel, a separate chapter — Chapter 15 — is devoted to this topic. The other aspects of the supervision of personnel which are discussed in this chapter are:

- Leadership in the organization.
- The supervisor's role in personnel management.
- Participative leadership.
- Improving supervisory leadership.

Leadership in the Organization

In Chapter 2 management was defined as the process of planning, organizing, staffing, directing, and controlling the activities and the personnel in order to accomplish the organizational objectives. This process by which managers contribute to the achievement of the organizational objectives through the efforts of oth rs depends upon a relationship in which there are leaders and followers. In an organization where authority is delegated from a superior to a subordinate within the chain of command and from that subordinate to his subordinate, some individuals serve both as a leader and as a follower. While both roles are essential to an organization's success, as implied in Figure 14-1, the focus in this chapter is on the leadership role.

The Nature of Leadership

In order for an individual in a leadership role to carry out his responsibilities, he must not only have authority but must also have the ability to exercise this authority over subordinates in such a manner as to obtain their cooperation. Authority and power in the formal organization are inherent in positions of a managerial or supervisory nature rather than in the persons who occupy these positions. This *positional authority*, as noted earlier in Chapter 3, should be broad enough to enable the manager or supervisor to carry out his job duties efficiently. Too frequently, however, the authority that is delegated to a position is so limited that the individual is unable to carry out his assignments in a manner consistent with his talents.

Many times, however, managers and supervisors possess positional authority on which they do not have to rely because of the respect and

Figure 14-1

"How do you know the fault is in my 'leading'? Maybe the fault is in your 'following'!"

Source: Reprinted with the permission of *The Saturday Evening Post* and Dana Fradon
© 1966, The Curtis Publishing Company.

cooperation that they command through their personal authority. As
early as 1916, Henri Fayol, a French industrialist and organization theorist,
said:

> Distinction must be made between a manager's official authority
> deriving from office and personal authority, compounded of intelli-
> gence, experience, moral worth, ability to lead, past services, etc. . . .
> In the make-up of a good head, personal authority is the indispensable
> complement of official authority.[1]

Today, we recognize that what Fayol referred to as personal authority
would relate primarily to the leader's personality characteristics. Such
characteristics as his ability to command the confidence and respect of his
subordinates, to maintain influence with his superiors, and to display

---

[1]Aaron Q. Sartain and Alton W. Baker, *The Supervisor and His Job* (New York: McGraw-
Hill Book Company, 1965), p. 47.

empathy toward subordinates determine how effectively he makes use of his positional authority.

An important factor in supervision is acceptance of leadership. If subordinates do not accept the decisions of their boss and carry out his orders enthusiastically, the quality of performance will suffer in some degree. The importance of subordinate acceptance of leadership is emphasized by those who subscribe to the _situational view_ of leadership.

The situational view is based on the assumption that traits are not what determines whether or not a person will be a leader; but, rather, the situation determines the outcome of his success as a leader. Thus, the situational view holds that an individual who is successful as a leader in one situation may not be successful in another situation regardless of the traits he possesses.[2]

The Hierarchy of Leadership

From the chairman of the board to the first-line supervisor in a typical organization, there will be many positions requiring skills that may be loosely referred to as leadership skills. As discussed in Chapter 9, many different lists of leadership skills and traits have been compiled in an effort to describe the ideal business leader. These skills, typically, are those that are not required of the salaried or hourly wage employees who occupy nonsupervisory positions. Such skills as making decisions, communicating orders and instructions, resolving conflicts between individuals and groups, and taking effective disciplinary action are typical of those that the superior must perform if he is to be an effective leader. Within the organizational hierarchy, however, various levels of formal leadership positions require different patterns of competencies that should be noted. These competencies will be considered briefly as they apply to top-management, middle-management, and first-line supervisory positions.

Top-management leadership. Those persons occupying positions in top management, that is, the chairman of the board, the president, and the vice-president, play a major role in establishing the psychological climate of the organization. Their attitudes toward other individuals, especially employees, will determine the type of loyalty and cooperation that they receive in carrying out the organization's objectives. Similarly, their approach to decision making will help to influence whether or not their

---

[2]For an interesting and authoritative review of studies pertaining to leadership, see Thomas W. Harrell, _Manager's Performance and Personality_ (Cincinnati: South-Western Publishing Company, 1961).

subordinates identify themselves with the company. If the top managers delegate very little, it may be expected that subordinates will soon demonstrate a similar reluctance to delegate or to exercise initiative. While top management must necessarily be concerned with many matters outside of the company that influence the company's operations, special attention should be given to developing a psychological climate that will permit employees to achieve a high degree of personal success while performing at maximum capacity for the company. An important factor in the development of an effective type of climate is the nature of the support and freedom of action that top management gives to its middle-management personnel who are most directly concerned with implementing the policies of top management and with getting things done through the efforts of others.

Middle-management leadership. Because of the important effects that middle-management personnel can have upon company efficiency, many companies are devoting more effort to creating conditions that will make middle-management jobs more attractive and thus enable the companies to retain personnel holding these jobs. While an individual in a top-management position should have a high degree of conceptual ability (ability to deal with ideas) that enables him to sense the total interrelationships of the different parts of the organization,[3] a person in a middle-management position must likewise possess a reasonably high degree of conceptual ability plus a reasonably high degree of skill in human relations. The middle manager must not only be effective in directing and controlling the efforts of his subordinates but must also be able to communicate essential information about his department, its activities and its people, to top management as well as to other department heads.

First-line supervision. Those persons holding positions as first-line supervisors are responsible for supervising directly the largest portion of a company's work force. It is through the employees who work under their direction that the detailed activities of the organization are performed. Within the limits prescribed by his superiors, it is the supervisor's responsibility to perform the basic processes of management within his own work group. It is his responsibility to insure that the work is accomplished on time and according to established standards and that a high degree of efficiency is maintained. These responsibilities require that he know the technical side of his job, that he be effective as an administrator, and that he be able to promote good human relations. His many contacts with

[3]Robert L. Katz, *Executive Skills: What Makes a Good Administrator?* (Dartmouth, New Hampshire: Amos Tuck School of Business, 1954).

employees in his work group and his effect upon the success and satisfaction (or the lack of it) that they derive from their employment results in many employees looking upon the supervisor as "the company." Because of the importance of first-line supervisors, the remainder of this chapter is focused on their role in an organization. Much of what is said about their activities in the handling of personnel also applies to individuals in higher management positions.

The Supervisor's Role in Personnel Management

The first-line supervisor may be a potent executive or a lead man stripped of his tools. He may supervise five men or 75.[4] The various aspects of the supervisor's job will range from one extreme to the other, depending upon the company, the department, and the organizational climate. By federal law the supervisor is considered to be a member of management and is defined as:

> ... any individual having authority, in the interest of the employer, to hire, transfer, suspend, lay off, recall, promote, discharge, assign, reward, or discipline other employees, or responsibility to direct them, or to adjust their grievances, or effectively to recommend such action, if in connection with the foregoing the exercise of such authority is not of a merely routine or clerical nature, but requires the use of independent judgment.[5]

Although supervisors are considered under law to be a part of management, the successful performance of their duties is dependent upon their identifying themselves closely enough with the employees whom they supervise in order that their leadership may be accepted by their subordinates. The fact that their attention and loyalty must be divided between subordinates and higher management frequently leads to problems that add to the supervisor's task of carrying out the many responsibilities that are normally part of his job. It is apparent to anyone who observes the supervisor at work that he is indeed a "Jack of all trades." While he also engages in such activities as planning, ordering materials and equipment, maintaining records, preparing reports, and many other activities relating directly to the technical phases of his job, the discussion that follows is focused on the supervisor's roles and responsibilities in the area of personnel management.

---

[4]John Perry, "New Patterns in Supervision," *Personnel*, Vol. 38, No. 5 (September-October, 1961), p. 30.
[5]National Labor-Management Relations Act (Taft-Hartley), 1947. Section 101, Subsection 2 (11).

Motivating and Controlling Employee Performance

Probably the most important functions performed by the supervisor are those of motivating and controlling employee performance. It is the supervisor's responsibility to establish goals and standards and to create conditions that will provide the incentives necessary to motivate employees toward the achievement of the departmental objectives. He must then determine the extent to which the goals are being achieved and whether or not prescribed quality standards are being maintained. He must also determine that employees are conforming to the policies, procedures, and regulations prescribed by management, by law, or by any professional or technical societies that may have a legitimate voice in the establishment of standards or determination of procedures.

Importance of human relations. It was once the common practice for management to view the supervisor primarily as a "driver" or a "bull of the woods." Little concern was given by management to the methods that he used to achieve results as long as he achieved them and carried out its directives. More recently, however, management has recognized that the supervisor must be more than a "driver." He must be able to promote good human relations with individual employees as well as with his work group, and, at the same time, he must insure that they meet production standards and requirements.

The promoting of effective human relations is frequently one of the more difficult aspects of supervision since effective human relationships depend upon attitudes as well as skills. Employees are quick to sense whether the supervisor's skills in human relations are based on sincerity or whether they are "management devices." Sartain and Baker are of the opinion that the average American is more suspicious of the boss than his father or grandfather was and that management tools for promoting good human relations on an insincere basis are likely to be recognized by subordinates. This suspicousness concerns two major issues. The first is that the supervisor is out for himself and will do anything to advance his own interests. Therefore, the employee learns to become a "yes" man or politician so as not to do anything that would be perceived by the boss as threatening to his own personal goal-seeking. The second basis of suspiciousness is a fear of manipulation. Managers who try to have good human relations may be thought of as attempting to mislead and deceive by pretending an interest that they do not feel. Sartain and Baker feel that many employees prefer the old time, hard-driving, supervisor since they always knew where they stood with him because he played with all of the cards on the table. The newer boss, according to them, is often thought of as clever and considerate — but also scheming, insincere, and manipulative. Sartain and Baker advise that every manager and supervisor needs to be on guard so as not to increase the amount of suspiciousness that already exists.[6] To tell managerial personnel that they should be sincere would probably result in only minor changes because most everyone feels that he is sincere in what he does.

Discussions of a manager's needs and aspirations and his technical and human relations skills can provide a starting point for improvement. As noted earlier, however, human personality must function within the total organizational climate, and the existing climate often creates formidable obstacles to the application of the best that has been taught in supervisory development programs. Nevertheless, as the important factors in supervision are identified, it is possible that the personal needs of employees and the goals of the organization may be brought into greater harmony. One of the major factors in supervision that have received increasing attention is the type of leadership.

Democratic vs. autocratic leadership. In recent years there has been considerable discussion about the types of leadership approaches and their relative effectiveness in motivating and controlling employee performance. While most supervisors vary somewhat in their leadership approaches from one situation to another, the democratic approach is typically emphasized in most supervisory training programs because it has been shown to result in more effective employee performance and better relations within the work group. While democratic leadership tends to focus on group relationships and the role of the group in decision making, the *democratic supervisor* is also characterized as one who emphasizes common goals, spends more time talking with employees, and uses a counseling approach in handling problems with employees. The *autocratic supervisor,* on the other hand, makes decisions himself, uses arbitrary methods in giving orders, and controls employee behavior through disciplinary action and legalistic approaches. Most of today's employees do not respond favorably to overdoses of this latter type of leadership because of prior training and experience at home and at school.[7]

---

[6]Sartain and Baker, *op. cit.*, pp. 184–185.

[7]In addition to the democratic and autocratic leaders, there is a third type known as the *laissez-faire leader* who permits each individual to do what he chooses and imposes very few limitations. This approach is seldom effective and not likely to be found in most organizations. Most of the discussion of leadership patterns, therefore, centers around the concepts of democracy and autocracy.

The criticism most frequently voiced about the democratic approach is that it is "soft" and is, therefore, an unrealistic supervisory approach in the business enterprise. Where this criticism has merit, it is common to find that a superior and/or his subordinates are not capable of performing effectively under the democratic process. With respect to the "soft" criticisms it should also be noted that, even where developed abilities in democratic processes exist, there will still be occasional employee infractions calling for disciplinary action and that there will be times when employees have grievances that require the supervisors' attention. (Both of these aspects of discipline are considered in detail in Chapter 17.)

Structure and consideration. Another approach to supervision is illustrated by the Ohio State leadership studies. One of the studies identified two major dimensions of supervisory behavior: consideration and structure. These two characteristics which were found to be independent of each other are described as follows:

> *Consideration* includes behavior indicating mutual trust, respect, and a certain warmth and rapport between the supervisor and his group. This does not mean that this dimension reflects a superficial "pat-on-the-back," "first name calling" kind of human relations behavior. This dimension appears to emphasize a deeper concern for group members' needs and includes such behavior as allowing subordinates more participation in decision making and encouraging more two-way communication.

> *Structure* includes behavior in which the supervisor organizes and defines group activities and his relation to the group. Thus, he defines the role he expects each member to assume, assigns tasks, plans ahead, establishes ways of getting things done, and pushes for production. This dimension seems to emphasize overt attempts to achieve organizational goals.[8]

Although the results varied somewhat with the situation, the most effective leaders have been found to be those who were above average in both consideration and structure. Those who are low on both dimensions or emphasize one to the neglect of the other are less effective. While the need differences between men and women are not as great as many believe, there is substantial evidence that women work best in an environment where the supervisor is high on the consideration scale. Women, for

---

[8]Edwin A. Fleishman and Edwin F. Harris, "Patterns of Leadership Behavior Related to Employee Grievances and Turnover," *Personnel Psychology*, Vol. 15, No. 1 (Spring, 1962), pp. 43–56.

example, may be more inclined than men to seek praise and attention from their supervisors and to want their supervisors to like them.[9]

Employee-centered supervision. It was once a common belief that the type of supervision which kept pressure on employees for production and which held rigidly to established procedures would yield the best results. It was assumed that, by giving close attention to production activities, results of high quantity and high quality would follow naturally. Contrary to this belief, however, experimental evidence shows quite clearly that the job- or production-centered supervisor is less effective in terms of production than the employee-centered supervisor who gives his attention to the people who do the work and who also has high performance goals and enthusiasm for achieving them. Figure 14-2 from Likert presents the findings from one study conducted by the Survey Research Center of the

Figure 14-2

EFFECT ON PRODUCTION OF JOB-CENTERED
AND EMPLOYEE-CENTERED SUPERVISORS

NUMBER OF FIRST-LINE SUPERVISORS WHO ARE:

	Job-centered	Employee-centered
High-producing sections	1	6
Low-producing sections	7	3

Source: Rensis Likert, *New Patterns of Management* (New York: McGraw-Hill Book Company, 1961), p. 7. Reproduced with permission.

University of Michigan. The findings shown in Figure 14-2 are typical of those obtained from several different studies in widely different kinds of work, such as clerical, sales, and manufacturing.

While the job- or production-oriented supervisor feels that he does not have time for employees until he has attained a satisfactory level of production, the employee-centered supervisor tends to have different attitudes which are revealed in such statements as:

I study the girls' work, find out who work together, and put them together. The main thing is to keep the girls happy. I talk with them and learn what their peculiarities are so that if a girl gets excited, I know whether it is important or not. Your girls have to feel that you are one of them, not the boss. Some girls get sort of cranky, and you can't just say, "Do it." It is much better to ask them to do the work in other ways; that's only human nature.

[9]Robert A. Sutermeister, *People and Productivity* (New York: McGraw-Hill Book Company, 1963).

It was found that the employees who worked for the employee-centered supervisor felt that he was personally interested in them, found him available for discussion, and saw him as a nonthreatening person. It was also found that the kind of supervision that results in the highest productivity also results in the highest morale. The employees of high morale groups mentioned more frequently than those of low morale groups that their supervisors engaged in such employee-centered functions as "recommends promotions and pay increases," "informs men on what is happening in the company," "keeps men posted on how well they are doing," and "hears complaints and grievances."[10]

Probably the most desirable attribute of the employee-centered supervisor is that he views his employees as worthwhile individuals who are deserving of his personal interest and attention. He is truly interested in them and recognizes that each one has his own unique pattern of personality characteristics. Furthermore, he is willing to tolerate personality differences and learns to adjust to these differences rather than to assume that anyone who differs with him should not be in his department. By focusing his attention on his subordinates and their needs and thereby building their morale, he is able to motivate them toward the goals that he outlines for them.

Developing Employee Efficiency

From the time that the new employee is assigned to his work group until he leaves, it is the supervisor's responsibility to provide the necessary training that will permit the employee to realize his potential to the fullest. The supervisor should also assist the employee in the solution of problems that may be directly or indirectly related to his employment with the company and that are likely to affect the employee's efficiency and/or adjustment.

An important part of developing an employee is the evaluation of his performance and the communication of this information to him in language that he can understand and with an attitude that will motivate him to better performance. Some of the methods used in employee development were discussed in Chapters 8 and 10. Other methods to develop employees and to insure efficient performance are considered below.

Time and motion study. Most companies, through the use of improved machinery, equipment, and production methods, hope to achieve a higher

---

[10]Rensis Likert, *Motivation: The Core of Management*, Personnel Series, No. 155 (New York: American Management Association, 1953), pp. 3–21.

level of production. Efforts to obtain maximum efficiency from the workers have also involved analyzing the motions required by the worker to complete a task or a series of tasks. These procedures are commonly referred to as time and motion study. While time and motion studies have had a long history and have yielded benefits to both management and employees, they have typically given rise to problems in human relations.

Trouble over time standards stems largely from an attitude of suspicion on the part of the workers and the unions which grows out of inadequate communications between management, employees, and the union. If it is suspected that the time studies are being used as a basis for speeding up production, eliminating jobs, and discharging workers or if the time study methods are not understood by employees, such studies will invariably lead to trouble.

Motion study may also create personnel problems. At the outset a change in methods is likely to create worker resistance, as any change may. The change may be perceived by the worker to mean that he has not been performing his job correctly and must now revise his working habits. Motion study may also cause workers to feel that the tasks are being standardized to the point that they will be required to use a certain pattern of motions, thus destroying opportunities for initiative and creativity. When the job can be made less arduous or incentive pay can be increased through the application of motion principles, these advantages should be pointed out to the workers.

The principles of the time and motion study have been adapted to office jobs where the need for maintaining a high level of employee efficiency is as important as in production jobs. In large government agencies, for example, where there are thousands of employees maintaining records, standards of performance are established. These standards provide the basis for manpower auditing to insure that acceptable levels of performance are achieved.

Supervisor resistance to time and motion studies. Not only do employees resist time and motion studies but many first-line supervisors may be psychologically threatened by them if they are not properly prepared for the introduction of changes suggested by the studies. The use of special staff personnel to conduct such studies within the working areas may be perceived by supervisors as affecting their status in the organization. Thus, like their subordinates, they too may resist such innovations and, as a result, may not be able to represent management's viewpoint enthusiastically. It is important, therefore, that higher levels of management provide opportunities for supervisors and employees to participate in the planning of method improvement programs and that management make provisions for training employees in the new methods in order that they will be able to achieve maximum competence and income as soon as possible. If employees suffer a loss in pay as a result of the new procedures, they are likely to resist the change. One way for management to minimize the possibilities of such difficulties is for it to work closely with the union before attempting to introduce any change in time standards or production methods and to make sure that employees will not suffer financially.

Effective personnel planning and control. It was noted earlier in Chapter 2 that effective planning contributes to employee efficiency as well as to a more desirable human relations climate in the organization. When the duties, responsibilities, and organizational relationships have been properly planned, organized, and communicated to them, employees are better able to direct their energies into productive and satisfying activities, and frustrations are minimized. As observed earlier, it is also desirable to plan for employees to have as much opportunity as possible for self-direction. However, this should not be construed as meaning that there are no controls on employee performance and behavior. A part of effective personnel planning is the establishment of sound work rules and other controls to govern the behavior of all employees in a reasonably uniform manner. Rules concerning working hours, coffee breaks, general safety rules, and other items that are essential to the maintenance of a good working environment should be established, communicated, and enforced. Similarly, in order to determine the extent to which subordinates are meeting their individual and/or group job standards, records should be kept of their performance that is compared against the standard. In a simple operation a supervisor can often control performance through overall observation. As operations become more complex, however, special strategic points may be used as a basis for assessing employee performance, thereby reducing the amount of time that a supervisor needs to give to this phase of his job.[11]

The Supervisor and the Union

The supervisor has an important role in the company's relationships with the union that represents the employees. His ability to foster good

---

[11]Harold Koontz and Cyril O'Donnell, *Principles of Management* (Third Edition; New York: McGraw-Hill Book Company, 1964), p. 544.

relations with the employee and the _union steward_[12] may have widespread effects on union-management cooperation. It is essential, therefore, that management do everything possible to prepare its supervisors in order that they may contribute effectively to good labor relations. Since the supervisor is responsible for enforcing the labor agreement, he must thoroughly understand it. Nothing can be more embarrassing to the supervisor than to find that the union steward in his working area knows more about the agreement than he does.

As a result of his experience in handling employee grievances, the supervisor is in an excellent position to determine what provisions of the agreement should be improved when a new agreement is negotiated. Management should encourage supervisors to submit suggestions for changes in order to have the benefit of their firsthand experiences and to insure that the agreement provisions are sound and realistic. Many companies have a representative group of supervisors sit on the company side at the bargaining table.

The Supervisor and the Personnel Department

Effective personnel management depends upon a high degree of cooperation between the supervisor and the personnel department. The supervisor is dependent upon the personnel department to recruit qualified personnel for his department, and he may also be able to utilize its assistance in the handling of such functions as training, employee rating and promotions, wage administration, and employee benefit and service programs. These services help the supervisor in performing his personnel activities and also relieve him of the necessity of performing those functions that can be handled more effectively on a company-wide basis through the personnel department. Similarly, the personnel department can assist supervisors by providing personal data on each employee which contain significant information and forms for maintaining information concerning production, attendance, and other items that stimulate the supervisor to think in terms of maximum efficiency and productivity.[13]

The personnel department, on the other hand, is dependent upon the supervisor for the effective accomplishment of its assigned functions. The supervisor who cooperates by providing information about employee performance, by fostering good human relations among the employees,

---

[12]The steward is an employee, often elected by his fellow-workers, who conducts union business in his department in addition to performing his regular job duties.

[13]Burt K. Scanlan, "Increasing Supervisory Effectiveness Through Personnel Management," *Personnel Administration*, Vol. 27, No. 5 (September–October, 1964), pp. 24–27.

and by making referrals to the personnel department of those who should be transferred to other jobs or considered for training or promotion contributes to the success of the company's personnel program.

While the personnel department should carry out its functions in a manner that will foster cooperation from other departments, it should not overlook its responsibilities to top management to determine that the established personnel policies are carried out. Personnel research studies and personnel audits are important sources of information which the personnel staff must use intelligently to form the basis for effective personnel control. However, the extent to which the personnel department can exercise control over the other departments will depend upon the concern of top management for the personnel functions. It is an axiom that management gives attention to the matters which it regards as important.[14]

Participative Leadership

In the discussion of employee motivation in Chapter 12, the incentive power of employee participation was mentioned. Because of its recognized value, increased emphasis has been given to leadership approaches that permit a high degree of participation by employees. Such participation is a characteristic of what is commonly referred to as democratic leadership. Where individual employees have mature relationships with one another and have feelings of responsibility toward the group and the larger organization, the democratic supervisor is likely to encourage the group to participate in the leadership role.

Group Participation in Decision Making

There are usually many activities within an organization in which employees may participate, including those of an educational and recreational nature, but the most important type of participation is that pertaining directly to an employee's job. The job is the area where the interests of management and those of the employees should come together. It is on the job that the actual production activities occur and where the employees expect to receive, and should receive, their major satisfactions. One of the primary sources of job satisfaction lies in the making of decisions relating to one's work, as evidenced by the large number of individuals who prefer to be their own "boss" and thus have their own business establishments. Much of the enthusiasm for his work that characterizes

---

[14]Charles C. Gibbons, "Control — A Neglected Dimension in Personnel Administration," *Personnel Administration*, Vol. 27, No. 3 (May–June, 1964), pp. 12–15.

the independent businessman can often be generated among employees by permitting employees to participate in the making of decisions concerning job problems. The extent to which employees participate in group decision making, however, often depends upon the supervisor's habits rather than upon his careful evaluation of the problem and the extent to which the group desires to have a voice in the decision. The supervisor who is effective in his relationships with the group recognizes the desires of the group and is flexible in his approach to carrying out his leadership responsibilities.

The continuum of leadership behavior. The supervisor, or manager, has a wide variety of leadership approaches available to him in determining the degree to which the work group may participate in the making of decisions. As shown in Figure 14-3, boss-centered leadership (the most autocratic type) is at one end of the continuum, and subordinate-centered leadership (the most democratic type) is at the other end.

Figure 14-3
CONTINUUM OF LEADERSHIP BEHAVIOR

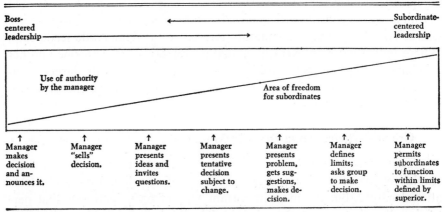

Source: R. Tannenbaum and W. H. Schmidt, "How to Choose a Leadership Pattern," *Harvard Business Review*, Vol. 36, No. 2 (March–April, 1958), p. 96. Reproduced with permission.

Each type of action is related to the degree of authority used by the boss and to the amount of freedom available to his subordinates in reaching decisions. At the one extreme the manager or supervisor maintains maximum control; whereas, at the other extreme he exercises minimal control. In between the two extremes are intermediate stages with varying degrees of "use of authority by the manager" and "area of freedom for subordinates." These two categories are equal or balanced on the continuum in Figure 14-3 when the leadership behavior is: "manager presents tentative decision subject to change."

Factors determining the choice of leadership approaches. Each situation or problem calling for a decision requires the supervisor to determine the approach to be used. The choice should be made on the basis of an evaluation of forces within himself, within his subordinates, and in the situation. *Forces within himself* include such matters as his confidence in his subordinates and his own inclinations as to how to handle the particular situation that calls for a decision. *Forces within his subordinates* include their interest in the problem, their understanding and identification with the goals of the organization, their knowledge, and their desire and expectancy to share in the decision making. *Forces in the situation* include such factors as the type of organization, the effectiveness of the group, the problem itself, and the pressure of time. The sensitivity of the supervisor to each of these forces at the time that a problem arises is the first step in effective leadership, but it is not enough.

> . . . The successful leader is one who is able to behave appropriately in the light of these perceptions. If direction is in order, he is able to direct; if considerable participative freedom is called for, he is able to provide such freedom.
> Thus, the successful manager of men can be primarily characterized neither as a strong leader nor as a permissive one. Rather, he is one who maintains a high batting average in accurately assessing the forces that determine what his most appropriate behavior at any given time should be and in actually being able to behave accordingly. Being both insightful and flexible, he is less likely to see the problems of leadership as a dilemma.[15]

It is thus the responsibility of the supervisor, as problems arise, to determine whether he should be permitting his employees more or less freedom in making the necessary decisions concerning these problems. There is, however, a need for the business organization operating in the democratic society to recognize the values of the democratic approach which characteristically provides for increased employee participation.

Developing Employee Participation

Most employees like to feel that they are contributing to the organization and that they are indispensable parts of the team. Most of them also like to believe that they are able to direct and control their work to a large degree. For these and other reasons supervisors have been encouraged,

---

[15]Robert Tannenbaum and Warren H. Schmidt, "How to Choose a Leadership Pattern," *Harvard Business Review*, Vol. 36, No. 2 (March-April, 1958), pp. 95–101.

mainly by human relations specialists, to move from the autocratic (boss-centered) type of leadership toward the democratic (subordinate-centered) type of leadership which provides for greater employee participation in decision making. It may be difficult at first, however, for supervisors who have never used the group-decision approach to find problems to which this approach may be applied. After a study of those problems that a supervisor may ordinarily solve by himself, however, several problems that could be decided by the group are evident. Changing work methods, scheduling coffee breaks and vacations, and handling excessive use of sick leave are a few of the problems that supervisors have successfully passed on to the work group for its decision. As a supervisor learns to trust his group and to recognize that it, too, can make good decisions, he is usually willing to let the group participate in decisions about more important matters. In any case, it should be realized that the supervisor may make decisions himself or submit to the group for decision only those matters or problems that fall within his jurisdiction or area of freedom. The diagram shown in Figure 14-4 illustrates that discussions would appropriately be limited to matters concerning the job (not religion, politics, or other matters) and that within a supervisor's job territory some activities have been taken from him or limited by union contracts, legislation, company policies and practices, etc. The remaining area — the area of freedom — falls within the authority of a given level of supervision, and problems in this area may be solved by group techniques.[16] It should be recognized, however, that group participation in a decision does not relieve the supervisor of his responsibility for the decision, even if he was of the opinion that it was a poor one.

The supervisor's role. The supervisor of a group of employees, according to Maier, has two roles when the group is involved in the decision-making process. In one role he is the *discussion leader* and has the job of conducting a good discussion about the problem under consideration. In the other role he is an *expert* who has certain information about the problem that should be made available to the group. The skills needed for the democratic type of discussion must be consistent with a permissive approach in which each member of the group is encouraged to present his opinions and feelings; however, no one should be permitted to dominate or to utilize the discussion for his own selfish purposes. Before attempting to use the group-decision approach, it is suggested that supervisors develop some competency in leading discussions, including the ability to:

---

[16]Norman R. F. Maier, *Psychology in Industry* (Third Edition; Boston: Houghton Mifflin Company, 1965), p. 174.

1. State a problem in such a way that the group does not become defensive, but instead approaches the issue in a constructive way.
2. Supply essential facts and clarify the areas of freedom without suggesting a solution.
3. Draw persons out so that all members will participate.
4. Wait out pauses.
5. Restate accurately the ideas and feelings expressed, and in a more abbreviated, more pointed, and more clear form than when initially expressed by a member.
6. Ask good questions so that problem-solving behavior is stimulated.
7. Summarize as the need arises.[17]

Figure 14-4

THE AREA OF FREEDOM FOR THE PRACTICE OF DEMOCRATIC LEADERSHIP*

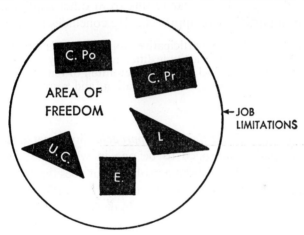

*The circle represents the limitations which the job situation imposes upon activity; *C. Po* and *C. Pr* represent the limitations imposed by company policies and company practices, respectively; *U. C.* and *L* represent activity areas removed by union contracts and legislation, respectively; and *E* represents problem areas solved by experts. The remaining area falls within the authority of a given level of supervision, and problems in this area may be solved by group techniques.

Source: N. R. F. Maier, "A Human Relations Program for Supervision," *Industrial and Labor Relations Review*, 1948, 1, pp. 443–464. Reproduced with permission of Dr. N. R. F. Maier.

Values of the participative approach. Maier's extensive experience and research conducted with various groups have revealed that the participative approach has several values. Agreement among participants has been high and has been a source of surprise to most supervisors. Employees are enthusiastic about the success of their decisions and cooperate in enforcing them. Furthermore, groups that participate in setting goals often place

---

[17] *Ibid.*, pp. 177–179.

higher demands upon themselves than the supervisors and methods engineers would make upon them.

Group decisions are usually of high quality; and because of their acceptance by the members of the group, the decisions are practically self-enforcing. Maier cites an interesting case to illustrate this fact. After a month's trial, a group of 30 women set a monthly tardiness figure of between 2.5 and 3 percent as a fair and reasonable objective. Over the following two-year period the figure never exceeded 3 percent as compared with the company average of 3.5 percent for that period. During the year prior to the time that the group decision method was utilized, the particular unit studied had a tardiness figure that exceeded 10 percent. Similar success has been experienced in establishing production goals.[18]

Maier and others cite similar results from other studies which show the benefits of a participative approach. He concludes that:

> Psychologically the participative approach adds up to sound motivation, clarification of attitude differences, security of group membership, constructive social pressure, prevention or removal of misunderstanding, good two-way communication, and respect for human dignity.[19]

Dangers of a pseudo-participative approach. Some persons have interpreted a participative approach to be one in which the supervisor has already reached his decision about a problem but goes through the motions of encouraging group participation in an effort to make the members of the group feel that they have had a voice in decision making. Attempts by the supervisor to convince members of a group that the decision is theirs, when he has actually decided the issue, are soon detected; and such attempts to manipulate the group are invariably resented by its members. If the supervisor feels strongly about a matter within his sphere of authority, he should not hesitate to use the boss-centered approach. His subordinates expect him to be autocratic at times in making decisions and would rather have it this way than to have the supervisor "make believe" that he is using a democratic approach. To avoid any confusion and to make his intentions clear, the supervisor should advise subordinates as to the degree of freedom that he is giving them (on the basis of the leadership continuum, Figure 14-3) when he brings a problem before the group. In this, as well as in other areas of personnel management, there is no room for hypocrisy.

---

[18]*Ibid.*, p. 184.
[19]*Ibid.*, p. 202.

Criticisms of the Participative Approach

It would not be fair to the reader to leave him with the impression that the participative or group-decision approach to management is accepted as being the "best way." There have been some experts in the field of management who feel that the realistic approach is to recognize that the typical organization has many characteristics that are incompatible with the participative approach. McMurry identifies these as follows:

1. Very few members of top management are by nature sympathetic to the "bottom-up" philosophy of management. They are more likely to be hard-driving, egocentric entrepreneurs. . . . Such men cannot ordinarily bring themselves to use any concept of management other than a purely authoritarian one.

2. Most commercial enterprises are very delicately balanced. One minor act. . . can have tremendous and often costly repercussions. . . . It is easy to see, therefore, why so many managers feel that little true decision-making may safely be delegated "down the line."

3. The democratic-participative philosophy of management is completely incompatible with the bureaucratic traditions of most corporations. Business enterprises. . . have a great attraction for those who have strong needs for security and status. Such people often make excellent subordinates. . . but they cannot administer, direct, or inspire others.

4. To a substantial number of employees, participative or "bottom-up" management is interpreted to mean that the employees have the right to veto management's decisions. Hence, while employees have few positive contributions to make, many are not at all reluctant to demand their "rights." Others interpret democratic supervision to mean lax handling by their superiors. They become resentful of any attempt to impose discipline.[20]

McMurry believes that the answer to more effective supervision lies in modifying the conventional autocratic-bureaucratic approaches by creating a benevolent autocracy which stresses the desirability of the humanistic, democratic philosophy of management but which also accepts people as they are and recognizes that most people prefer to be led. His theory is founded on the premises that there is a dearth of leaders in industry now and in the foreseeable future and that employees simply want a safe, secure job with someone to tell them what to do. These premises are likely to represent the thinking of many top management personnel.

A consideration of the participative approach should also note the argument of some that if subordinates have not been given sufficient opportunity to participate in decision making, it is not likely that they will understand what is meant by the process nor will they be likely to approach

20Robert N. McMurry, "The Case for Benevolent Autocracy," *Harvard Business Review*, Vol. 36, No. 1 (January–February, 1958), pp. 82–90.

it seriously or intelligently. It should also be noted that if supervisors have not been insightful and flexible in their leadership approaches and have used the participative approach as a way of handling every problem requiring a decision or have used it as a cover for autocratic motives, it may well be expected that such supervisors will seem ineffective to management and to their subordinates.

It seems desirable that greater attention should be given to making supervisors more insightful about the nature of the individual personality, the manner in which people interact in work-group situations, and the desirability of being flexible in the handling of problems requiring decisions. It does not necessarily follow that employee participation in decision making leads to lax discipline, failure to maintain satisfactory work standards, and employees "taking over" the organization anymore than a town hall meeting necessarily leads to anarchy. There are still the established lines of authority and responsibility to provide "limits" and to insure that the basic purposes for which the organization was created are not forgotten.

Need for Further Research

While a business organization must continue to function and managers and supervisors must decide what approach to use in accomplishing their assigned missions, it does not seem reasonable at this stage of our knowledge of supervision to conclude that the participative approach can be ignored. Research in leadership methods has hardly begun to explore the problem in terms of its scope and complexity. There is need for open-mindedness and a willingness to explore all dimensions of the problem of working with people not only as individuals but in the context of the group.

Improving Supervisory Leadership

As companies increasingly have come to recognize the importance of the supervisor's role within their organizations, they have devoted more attention to developing ways of improving supervisory leadership. Increasingly companies are also recognizing that special care must be taken to select those individuals who offer the most promise for success in supervisory positions and who can benefit from special training in supervisory attitudes and skills. Most companies of any size have established supervisory development programs similar to those designed for middle and top management (Chapter 9), and smaller companies encourage supervisors to obtain training that will enable them to be more enlightened leaders. While careful selection and special training are essential steps in improving supervisory leadership, the status that is accorded to the supervisors within an organization also is a vital factor in determining an individual's success in this capacity.

The Supervisor's Status

The role of the supervisor (or foreman) has undergone many changes. At one time he was not only knowledgeable about all activities under his purview but he was also able to maintain a practically unchallenged authority over those persons who were subordinate to him. With the growth of scientific management, the establishment of the personnel and other staff departments, and the growth of idealism with respect to human relations, however, the former role of the supervisor as an authority unto himself gradually eroded. One writer states that:

> In almost every area of his job he shares responsibility with functional specialists. "When" jobs are to be performed is often dictated in part by production planning specialists, the "how" is taken care of by methods specialists, to what standards the work is done is determined by quality control specialists, and in the personnel area many of the foreman's responsibilities are shared with employee relations specialists.[21]

The supervisor — a marginal man. The supervisor has been referred to as the "marginal man" — one who is on the periphery of the main stream of industrial events. He does not enjoy the high status the staff derives from technical specializations; he does not participate in the high status of line executives based on authority positions; and he does not have the security of production workers that arises from the collective strength of organized labor.[22] Lacking high status and job security and having to share authority with many other people in the functional areas of management, the supervisor may frequently wonder just what his role is supposed to be. According to Scott, the supervisor is paid mainly to be a "handler" of men — a human relations expert; but even in this area the foreman is "in the middle." He is accused of poor management if people are happy but the job does not get done; similarly, if an individual or two in his group is unhappy but the job does get done, he is still criticized.[23]

---

[21]Herbert H. Meyer, "A Comparison of Foreman and General Foreman Conceptions of the Foreman's Job Responsibility," *Personnel Psychology*, Vol. 12, No. 3 (Autumn, 1959), p. 451.
[22]William G. Scott, *Human Relations in Management* (Homewood, Illinois: Richard D. Irwin, Inc., 1962), p. 314.
[23]*Ibid.*, p. 317.

Importance of management's attitudes. If management ignores the fact that supervisors need status and incentives in order to be effective in their jobs, it should not expect much in return from them. The supervisor should be clearly recognized by management and the employees as being a part of the management team; and, furthermore, management should adopt policies and procedures that will contribute to the improvement of his status as a supervisor. Many persons who have observed that the supervisor's status has reached a low point have asked what can be done about it. The following suggestions are offered by Halsey:

1. A restoration of his standing as a person of some importance in the eyes of the people he supervises.
2. A clear definition of exactly what is his degree of authority in each phase of his work so that he will not be caused the embarrassment of having to back down from decisions he has made.
3. Adequate training in every phase of his work.
4. A feeling that he really is a part of management — a feeling which can be brought about only by his being actually consulted on important policy matters before final decisions are made.
5. An adequate differential between his pay and that of the highest paid worker under his supervision.
6. A feeling of security in his position, that he cannot be arbitrarily discharged or demoted without being given a reason and a chance for a hearing by top management.[24]

If these suggestions are heeded by management, it is likely that supervisors will be able to perform the important functions which are expected of them. Otherwise the chain of management from the top of the organization to the employees who must do the work will be broken at its most vital link with the result that production efficiency as well as human relationships will suffer.

Influence of the personnel department. In its relationships with the line, the personnel department must recognize that the supervisor has primary authority and responsibility for the operation of his department and must be careful not to encroach upon his authority in attempting to provide service and assistance. Otherwise the status of the supervisor may suffer; and if this occurs, cooperation between the supervisor and the personnel department is likely to become increasingly difficult to achieve. Effective personnel management depends upon cooperation between line and staff, and the personnel department should take the lead in developing this cooperation.

---

[24]George D. Halsey, *Selecting and Developing First-Line Supervisors* (New York: Harper & Brothers, 1955), Chapter 3.

Selection of Supervisors

The aim of any supervisory development program is to select the persons best qualified to meet the requirements of the supervisory positions. The achievement of this goal requires management to specify the requirements of the positions, to determine the qualifications of potential candidates, and to select the best qualified of the candidates on an objective basis. In determining the qualifications of potential candidates, several sources of information concerning present employees may be used.

Present supervisors. The role of the present supervisors in promoting the development program cannot be overestimated. Employees who show promise as candidates for supervisory positions may be identified and given supervisory responsibilities of a minor nature as opportunities arise. Since it is often undesirable to promote an employee to a supervisory position within the department where he has served as an operative employee, supervisors should be encouraged to identify talented personnel for possible assignment to another department.

Co-workers. The fellow employees of the individual who is being considered for upgrading to a supervisory position are often able to provide information concerning their estimates of the individual's capacity for leadership. In fact any individual who has already emerged as the informal leader of a work group is often an excellent candidate for a supervisory position since his personal authority and acceptance has already been demonstrated in the absence of any positional authority. Such recognition of his ability may deter his accepting an assignment with the union. Management should be careful, however, to determine that he is not a "false leader" who talks a good game or whom employees are letting "front" for them temporarily.

Personnel records. While supervisors can often be a valuable source of information about employees who have supervisory potentialities, the personnel department should screen the records of employees periodically to determine if there are any who have been overlooked. Performance evaluation reports, test scores, training records, and other data that may be found in an individual's personnel file may reveal candidates for supervisory jobs who have been overlooked.

College Graduates as Supervisors

Every year large numbers of recruiters from the personnel departments of many of the leading companies "make the rounds" of college campuses for the purpose of discovering new talent and encouraging students to consider career opportunities with them. Because they possess above-average intelligence, have broad educational backgrounds, and have received advanced training in one or more fields, college students are generally viewed as potential candidates for supervisory positions. Management recognizes that college students may not have supervisory experience, but their college education and specific training in supervisory practices will usually provide the necessary background for supervision if they are first given a minimum amount of work experience at the operative level.

It is likely that the success that the college graduate often experiences when placed in a supervisory position results not only from his knowledge and skills but from his ability to work effectively with higher levels of management personnel. Most of these management personnel are likely to be college graduates and very often accept the new supervisor as a member of the management group. This acceptance by higher authority is soon recognized by his subordinates and constitutes the *influence*[25] that the supervisor has with his group. Because of the support the supervisor receives from management, the group is willing to follow him and may even instruct him in areas where he may be lacking in knowledge in order to insure that the work is performed properly and that the group retains its strong position in the organization.

Training of Supervisors

The interest in supervisory training that was stimulated by the Training Within Industry Programs of World War II has continued to the present time. Much of this interest arises from the recognition by top and middle managers, as well as by supervisors, of the need for specialized training in this area. Some of the interest also grows out of the enthusiasm with which training directors, whose business it is to develop programs, "sell" them to other departments. Properly introduced and conducted, a supervisory training program can be effective in providing information and in developing skills that the candidates for supervisory positions, or even supervisors, do not possess at an adequate level for performing the many diversified tasks for which they are responsible.

While supervisory training programs may be designed to meet the special problems of a company and to cover any topics in which training is believed to be necessary, emphasis has been on the teaching of attitudes

---

[25]Donald C. Pelz, "Influence: A Key to Effective Leadership in the First-Line Supervisor," *Personnel*, Vol. 29, No. 3 (November, 1952), pp. 209–217.

and skills in human relations. The goals of human relations training programs are:

1. To gain a better understanding of one's self. To "know one's self" may range from resolving subconscious emotional conflicts to becoming aware of how others react to one's mannerisms.
2. To broaden and sharpen sensitivity to the feelings of others.
3. To develop respect for others and to accept individual differences. Reasonable as this may appear, human relations trainers find that an underlying cause of industrial conflict, often not consciously stated, is conflict between age groups, between male and female, between ethnic groups, or between those with varying physical appearance.
4. To establish the belief (rejected by authoritarians) that kindness is not a weakness.
5. To treat all human relations problems with a clinical approach — to be sympathetic and understanding as if seeking a cure for illness rather than to blame or make accusations as to motives.[26]

From these goals follows a further goal of human relations training: the overcoming of barriers to interpersonal communication in order to reduce conflict that arises from misunderstanding. Such methods as role playing, sensitivity training, and case discussion, described in Chapters 8 and 9, are commonly used to assist supervisors in overcoming these barriers and to develop more effective approaches to subordinates.

New materials for use in such training programs are being developed continually. One recent contribution is an analytical training approach which is closely related to the consideration and structure dimensions of leadership discussed earlier. In their book, *The Managerial Grid*, Blake and Mouton analyze managerial styles in detail, using the grid shown in Figure 14-5 as a basis for expressing the relationships between Concern for People (Consideration) and Concern for Production (Structure). The grid depicts five different patterns (the number 1 in each instance represents minimum concern, 9 stands for maximum concern), although 81 mixtures of these two concerns might be pictured.

As noted above, the grid provides the basis for training managers and supervisors. It puts the various methods of managing problems into a framework where the leader can identify, study, and change his own behavior.[27] One of the problems that frequently occur, however, is that the supervisor may find difficulty in applying on the job what he has been

---

[26]William H. Knowles, *Human Relations in Industry: Research and Concepts* (Berkeley, California: Institute of Industrial Relations, 1958), p. 94, and *California Management Review*, Vol. 1, No. 94.

[27]Robert R. Blake and Jane S. Mouton, *The Managerial Grid* (Houston: Gulf Publishing Company, 1964).

Figure 14-5

THE MANAGERIAL GRID

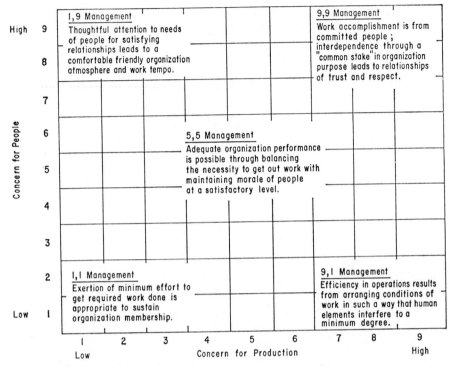

Source: Robert R. Blake and Jane S. Mouton, *The Managerial Grid* (Houston: Gulf Publishing Company, 1964), p. 10. Reproduced with permission.

taught in a supervisory training program. If the supervisor's superior is an autocratic leader, conflicts are likely to ensue, and the supervisor often learns to forget the training he has received in order to avoid further conflicts. Many supervisors would agree with Fleishman who, in summarizing the findings from a research study of the effectiveness of supervisory training in a large company, advises:

> The implication seems to be that certain aspects of the foreman's environment may have to be recognized if training is to be effective in modifying his behavior. It would appear, then, that more intensive training of supervisors above the level of foreman in the organization might be more effective in making the training effects more permanent among the foremen. If he could return to an environment where the boss behaved in a way consistent with what the foreman was taught in the training course, where these new modes of behavior were now the

shortest path to approval, we might expect a more permanent effect of such training.[28]

The values to be obtained from training supervisors in human relations attitudes and skills are thus dependent upon the psychological climate of the organization in which they will perform their supervisory duties. If the climate of the organization encourages supervisors to be sensitive to the feelings of others, to develop respect for others, to accept individual differences, and to treat personnel problems with a clinical approach, the quality of supervision in the organization is likely to be high even without special training. Under such conditions the training can be used to teach skills that supervisors will be motivated to learn because they recognize that what is being taught is consistent with the attitudes of management personnel at the higher echelons — the place where the nature and quality of leadership has its origin.

Résumé

The talents and enthusiasm of all of the members of an organization are of little value unless they are carefully directed toward the objectives that the organization is attempting to achieve. To provide the type of leadership that will result in this achievement is the responsibility of managers and supervisors at all levels. Because of his position in the organization, the first-line supervisor has one of the most important leadership roles. His responsibilities are many, but of primary importance is the part he plays in developing efficient employees and in motivating and controlling their performance. The manner in which he does this may vary from one individual to another, but the effective supervisor is one who is aware of the important factors in the leadership role and is flexible in his relationships with individuals and with the work group. The ability of the supervisor to provide for group participation in decision making was cited as one of the leadership skills that could be developed and would contribute to personal as well as organizational success. It was shown that the supervisor's effectiveness is dependent not only upon his own personal characteristics but upon the status he has in the organization primarily as a result of management's attitude toward the supervisor. The personnel department also has an important role in helping to preserve the supervisor's status, and personnel workers should recognize the value of the supervisor's contributions to the entire organization and especially to the personnel department.

---

[28]Edwin A. Fleishman, "Leadership Climate, Human Relations Training, and Supervisory Behavior," *Personnel Psychology*, Vol. 6, No. 2 (Summer, 1953), p. 221.

DISCUSSION QUESTIONS AND PROBLEMS

1. For some individuals the phrase "human relations" implies manipulating others. Is this interpretation correct? Why may they have this opinion?

2. One authority has described the foreman as the "master and victim of double talk."
   a. What does this statement mean to you?
   b. If you have been or are now employed, can you think of any examples that would illustrate this statement?

3. Why do most individuals respond without argument to a supervisor's orders? Is it desirable that they do so?

4. Assume that upon graduation from college you are employed by a company that promotes you to a supervisory position within a year or so. Shortly after your promotion an employee who has been with the company for several years is transferred to your work group. As you begin to explain his new job to him, he tells you that he has been around for quite a while and understands everything.
   a. What would you do?
   b. Why may the employee respond as he did?
   c. What are the broader implications in the situation for you as the supervisor?

5. In one large company all foremen are called "managers," and as far as practicable they have appropriate duties and authority. The manager-foreman of a section not only deals directly with his men in all technical matters of production but is also the prime authority in the hiring, promotion, or discharge of workers under his supervision.
   a. How does this company compare with other companies in the duties and authority it assigns to foremen?
   b. What advantages and disadvantages are there in the approach?
   c. What effect would this approach have on the personnel department?

6. One of the important skills in using the group-decision approach is the ability to state a problem to a group in such a manner that the members of the group will not feel threatened and become defensive. How would you state the problems in the following situations that concerned you as a supervisor?
   a. Employees have taken sick leaves far in excess of what they had taken at the same time a year ago.
   b. Some members of the group are not producing as much as they are able to produce, and other members of the group have to make up for their deficiencies in order to get the work accomplished.
   c. Employees are failing to heed safety rules and are taking dangerous short cuts in their work.

7. The article by Gibbons cited on pages 366–367 pointed out the personnel department's responsibility to top management in insuring that the personnel function in each department was being carried out at a high level of performance.
   a. What are some of the problems that the personnel department is likely to encounter if it is too demanding?
   b. What problems may arise if it is too lenient with other departments?

8. The manager of a retail store employing 25 persons used a laissez-faire type of leadership. On the other hand, supervisory personnel who were subordinate to him tended to be quite autocratic.

a. What effect would these different styles of leadership be likely to have on the employees?

b. How do you account for the supervisors' autocratic type of leadership?

c. How does laissez-faire leadership differ from democratic leadership?

9. An employee comes to the personnel department with the complaint that his supervisor is a "slave driver." What action should the personnel department take? Discuss.

10. Study the approaches used by different instructors under whom you have studied to motivate students, control their classroom behavior, and encourage or discourage discussion. How do these approaches relate to the descriptions of autocratic and democratic leaders found on pages 360–361?

11. The cartoon in Figure 14-1 shows a top executive with some of his immediate subordinates. His statement to them may be interpreted in different ways. How do you interpret it?

CASE 14-1

IS ANYBODY HOME?

In the Plans and Programs Department of a government agency, there were three branch chiefs who worked under the general direction of the department chief and his assistant. One branch chief, Bob Hanks, was a man in his middle fifties who supervised the work of six professionally trained men and women and about as many persons doing clerical work. While most of the individuals who worked under Bob's direction liked him, they soon learned that he was lacking in talents needed for the most effective direction of the work load assigned to that branch. The fact that he was hard of hearing did not help matters. It was also fairly common knowledge in the branch, and in the department, that Bob would doze off several times a day. The giggles that could be heard among his staff would provide the clue to the department chief, who sat behind a portable partition about twenty feet from Bob's desk, that Bob had "fogged out" again.

Upon hearing giggles one day, the department chief got up from his desk and moved as rapidly as possible toward Bob's desk. Just before reaching the desk Bob opened his eyes and with a startled look said, "Hello." Aggravated by this situation, the department chief sat down at Bob's desk and quietly told him that he would not tolerate any more of this sleeping on the job. Bob looked surprised and remarked that he had not been sleeping but was merely resting his eyes from the tedium of working with figures in a poor light. The department chief left Bob with the thought that he should set a better example.

a. Do you think the department chief handled the situation properly?

b. What effect is Bob's dozing likely to have on his employees?

c. What action should the department chief take if the situation continues?

CASE 14-2

TRAINING OFF THE TRACK

Mr. Chauncy Vanderhalt, Vice-President in Charge of Maintenance for the East-West Railroad System, was alarmed at the turnover rate among the men in the maintenance crews. He felt that the problem was primarily the result of the type of supervision that they received from the 30 division foremen and assistant foremen. There had been indications that these individuals were quite rigid in their attitudes toward subordinates and often treated them as if they were stupid and incompetent. Vanderhalt felt that this was a problem for the personnel department.

During a conference with Vanderhalt, the personnel manager, Mr. Smiley, and the training director, Mr. Roberts, recommended that the best approach to the problem would be to conduct a human relations institute for division foremen and assistant foremen. Plans were made for the institute to be conducted by five members of the faculty of a university that was centrally located in the system. The institute was scheduled for a two-week period in the following month.

On the eve of the day before instruction was to begin, the group of 30 participants assembled at one of the local hotels near the university for an informal get-together with the faculty. The highlight of the evening was a kickoff dinner at which the Vice-President in Charge of Maintenance and the university dean were the principal speakers.

The atmosphere was warm and cordial. A few of the members, however, relaxed too much and spent more time in getting acquainted with Jim Beam and John Barley Corn than they did with the faculty or their classmates. The Vice-President noted this and asked Roberts, the training director, who was in charge of the institute, to come to his hotel room after the kickoff dinner. Vanderhalt was quite disturbed over what he had seen and put the training director on the spot by asking him if this type of program was really going to be of any value. He wanted to see results! After all, the expenses for each man were $750 for the course, exclusive of his salary for the two-week period.

While the course proceeded fairly well, it was apparent after a few days that some of the participants were not giving it their full attention and effort. It was the first occasion in a long time that many had been away from their families and the rigors of the job, and many were inclined to stay out late at night. As a result, some of the men were not well prepared on their human relations cases and did not contribute much to the discussion. Others were finding it difficult to stay awake during the lectures. Roberts, who was sitting through the course, remembered the words of the Vice-President before he had departed and began to wonder if some incentive should be used. He believed that the men should be tested and graded on their work at the institute.

Roberts approached the faculty coordinator, Dr. Hammer, and made the proposal that tests be given to the men. Dr. Hammer agreed to discuss this matter with the faculty. The faculty, however, were quite firm in their belief that the men should not be tested and graded because they did not have equal backgrounds for the course, because grading would tend to make them feel insecure, and because a course in human relations is difficult to evaluate. Roberts was not satisfied with their response because he felt that he would need tangible evidence to present to top management to show that the course was worthwhile. He argued with Dr. Hammer that there should be some type of test that could be used for the purpose. Dr. Hammer and the faculty, however, maintained their original position, and no type of formal evaluation was made during the institute.

When the institute was over and Roberts returned to his office, he was asked by Smiley to prepare a report to Vanderhalt on the effectiveness of the institute in achieving the human relations objectives for which the institute was conducted.

    a. If you were Roberts, how would you evaluate the effectiveness of the course in your report to the Vice-President?

    b. Were the reasons given by the faculty for not evaluating the performance of the men justified? Why?

   c. Should management expect immediate results from such an institute?
      Why?
   d. Was improved human relations necessarily the answer to the high turn-
      over rate? If the turnover rate among the maintenance crew personnel
      remained the same, should the institute be considered a failure? Why?
   e. Would another type of course have been more suitable for the purpose?

CASE 14-3

SINGING SAM

Sam Miller was employed on the third (4 p.m. to 12 a.m.) watch as a Medical Technical Assistant at the Fernando Medical Facility which was operated by the State Department of Corrections. He had for some time been a source of difficulty to his immediate superior, Watch Sergeant O'Neil, who supervised the watch. It was Miller's responsibility to visit the inmates in his assigned sector according to an established schedule and to administer medications to the inmates that had been prescribed by the staff physician. While Sergeant O'Neil had no responsibility for the administration of medications performed by Miller, it was his responsibility to see that Miller followed the established medication schedule and that he observed all regulations and procedures pertaining to institutional security.

Miller's performance during the two years that he had been employed at the facility had been considered at best to be of only minimal quality. In fact, some doubts were raised when Miller completed his probationary period as to whether or not he should be retained. Sergeant O'Neil had helped to resolve the decision in Miller's favor because he felt that Miller might eventually become a good employee. Miller's difficulty from the start had been his defensive and resentful attitude toward his superiors whenever deficiencies in his performance were brought to his attention. Miller seemed particularly sensitive to the fact that he was a member of a religious minority group, and on more than one occasion had inferred that it was because of this fact that his performance had been the subject of criticism. He also complained that his religion was the reason why incidents of friction had occurred with certain of the cell watch officers with whom he came in contact while administering medications.

Among Sam Miller's favorable qualities was a fine voice and a musical talent that he put to work by organizing an inmate glee club. His work in behalf of the glee club was voluntary and under institutional regulations was supposed to be performed on his own time. Work with the glee club brought Sam some very favorable recognition that extended even outside of the institution; and as a result of it, Sam began to spend time with the club that he should have devoted to his regular assignment. This latter fact at times caused Sam to be late with his medication schedule. The maintenance of a definite medication schedule was quite important at the institution because psychotic patients were likely to become highly disturbed whenever there was a variation in the established routine. If a patient became disturbed, the officer in charge of a cell block often had to devote considerable time and effort in getting him to quiet down. The watch officers, therefore, had reason to resent Miller's failure to observe the schedule because of the extra work that was created for them. Several of the officers complained to Sergeant O'Neil about Sam's failure to observe his medication schedule which forced them to open the cell blocks that had been secured for the night. They reported that Sam had appeared indifferent to their complaints and that he appeared to feel that his glee club work gave him the right to be late. A few officers even hinted that this type of attitude and behavior was to be expected from members of Sam's religious group. Sergeant O'Neil cautioned the officers, whose statements reflected intolerance, about being prejudiced.

Since the evidence gathered by O'Neil clearly confirmed that Miller had been negligent in performing his duties, he arranged for an interview with Miller in the presence of Sergeant O'Neil's superior, Watch Lt. Ballard. After being reprimanded by O'Neil in front of Lt. Ballard for his negligence and cautioned that repetition of such incidents would result in formal disciplinary action being taken, Miller agreed to try to improve his performance. For a couple of weeks thereafter Miller appeared to be living up to his promises. One night, however, when O'Neil happened to be talking to the recreation director at the rear of the auditorium where Miller was rehearsing his glee club, he observed one of the inmates making the evening inmate count for Miller. Taking a count personally at prescribed intervals each day and reporting the presence of each inmate charged to his care was one of the most important duties of an institution employee. This procedure was designed to discourage inmates from leaving the facility before being officially released.

After witnessing his violation of roll call regulations, Sergeant O'Neil approached Miller who, realizing that the violation had been observed personally by his superior, appeared to be quite flustered. The ensuing conversation between the two individuals was as follows:

> O'Neil: Mr. Miller, are you aware that you have performed a serious error in allowing the inmate to make your count?
>
> Miller: I don't see anything wrong with it. I check when he is done; and, besides, I've been doing it for a long time, and I've never had a bad count yet.
>
> O'Neil: Are you aware of the correct departmental count procedure?
>
> Miller: Yes.
>
> O'Neil: Would you describe it to me so that I may be assured of your knowledge?
>
> Miller: Yes. (Gives complete description.)
>
> O'Neil: Then, Mr. Miller, I'm sure you realize that I have no other recourse but to bring formal charges against you for negligence and dereliction of duty?
>
> Miller: (Silence.)
>
> O'Neil: Would you step into the Watch Lieutenant's office? I'm going to inform him of the situation, and I would like you to be there so that you may have an opportunity to offer an explanation or rebuttal.

When Miller arrived at Ballard's office he appeared relaxed and, in a joking vein, attempted to minimize the seriousness of the incident. The discussion that took place in the Watch Lieutenant's office was as follows:

> O'Neil: I have just informed Lieutenant Ballard of the situation and of my intentions to take disciplinary action against you.
>
> Ballard: Mr. Miller, do you feel that you are being treated unjustly?
>
> Miller: No, I guess I knew I was wrong, but I just didn't see why it was so necessary for me to make the count when my helper could do it (produces tears and wringing of hands). I can't afford to have anything like this on my record; you know what it will

do to my chances of promotion? Look, Lieutenant, if you could see your way clear to give me a pass on this one, I promise you I'll never pull anything like it again.

Ballard: Sergeant O'Neil, do you think Mr. Miller has learned his lesson; do you think his past performance deserves giving him a pass?

O'Neil: No, I do not — for several reasons. First, Mr. Miller has not considered it important to follow procedures in the past. Secondly, he has been unreceptive to advice and counseling. Thirdly, this is gross negligence, and there is no excuse for Mr. Miller's action because he is well aware of the seriousness of his offense.

Ballard: Well, I think we can afford to let him off with a verbal reprimand this time, don't you?

O'Neil: Well — (sighs) I suppose so, but we're setting a precedent here, and I will be the first to remind you of it the next time I bring a watch officer to you under similar circumstances.

The interview was terminated by Lieutenant Ballard who administered a verbal reprimand to Sam Miller with a warning that any subsequent violations would result in written charges being filed against him.

On the following afternoon Sergeant O'Neil was called in for an interview by Mr. Ball, the Associate Superintendent, who was directly above the Watch Captain and the Watch Lieutenants in the chain of command. Mr. Ball informed O'Neil that Miller had expressed the intention of filing charges with the state civil service commission against him on the grounds that he had been prejudiced and discriminatory in his treatment of Miller. Sergeant O'Neil inquired if a formal written grievance had been submitted through Ball's office and was advised that it had not. After Sergeant O'Neil had stated his side of the problem, Mr. Ball advised him that he would talk with Miller and try to smooth things out. Ball then went on to criticize Sergeant O'Neil for not having made written documentation concerning his difficulties with Miller. At about this point in the interview, Sergeant O'Neil began to evidence anger over being made the defender in the case and suggested that Sam Miller be encouraged to file written charges. For one reason or another, however, formal charges were never filed by Miller who continued to do borderline work and to evidence a smug attitude toward O'Neil which indicated that he felt immune to the sergeant's authority.

  a. What effect, if any, do you estimate that this experience will have upon Sergeant O'Neil's future attitude and performance in his position?
  b. What important lessons of supervision and management might one draw from this case?
  c. How would you explain the attitude and behavior exhibited by Sam Miller?
  d. What role, if any, should the personnel department play in a case such as this one?

SUGGESTED READINGS

Argyris, Chris. *Personality and Organization.* New York: Harper & Brothers, 1957. Chapter 6.

Bellows, Roger. *Creative Leadership.* Englewood Cliffs, New Jersey: Prentice-Hall, Inc., 1959.

Chruden, Herbert J., and Arthur W. Sherman, Jr. *Readings in Personnel Management*, Second Edition. Cincinnati: South-Western Publishing Company, Inc., 1966. Chapter 4.

Davis, Keith. *Human Relations at Work*. New York: McGraw-Hill Book Company, 1962. Chapter 7.

Likert, Rensis. *New Patterns of Management*. New York: McGraw-Hill Book Company, 1961.

Maier, Norman R. F. *Principles of Human Relations*. New York: John Wiley & Sons, Inc., 1952.

Maier, Norman R. F., Allen R. Solem, and Ayesha A. Maier. *Supervisory and Executive Development, A Manual for Role Playing*. New York: John Wiley & Sons, Inc., 1957.

Pfiffner, John M., and Marshal Fels. *The Supervision of Personnel*, Third Edition. Englewood Cliffs, New Jersey: Prentice-Hall, Inc., 1964.

Richards, Max D., and William A. Nielander. *Readings in Management*, Second Edition. Cincinnati: South-Western Publishing Company, Inc., 1963. Section C.

Sartain, Aaron Q., and Alton W. Baker. *The Supervisor and His Job*. New York: McGraw-Hill Book Company, 1965.

Sutermeister, Robert A. *People and Productivity*. New York: McGraw-Hill Book Company, 1963.

Vroom, Victor H. *Some Personality Determinants of the Effects of Participation*. Englewood Cliffs, New Jersey: Prentice-Hall, Inc., 1960.

Walker, Charles R. *The Foreman on the Assembly Line*. Cambridge: Harvard University Press, 1956.

The Work Group

The successful supervisor is recognized as one who is effective not only in achieving results through individual members of his work group but is effective also in integrating the work group into a productive and harmonious team. While a group is composed of individuals, each of whom has his own unique pattern of abilities, aptitudes, and personality characteristics, it soon becomes apparent to those who observe and work with various groups that a group also has its own unique personality which distinguishes it from other groups. The distinguishing characteristics of a group are the result of such factors as the nature of the persons comprising the group, the nature of the interpersonal relationships within the group, the organizational climate, and the role of the group in the organization.

Within and between the work groups that have been formally organized according to the pattern of jobs and positions required for the accomplishment of the organizational mission are found subgroups that have emerged on an informal basis. Altogether these groups comprise what has already been referred to as the informal organization. In an examination of groups in an organization, attention should be given to both the groups that are formally organized by management and the informal groups. A study of the forces that are found in group behavior comprise the area of study commonly referred to as *group dynamics*.

The study of the forces inherent in a group represents one of the more advanced areas of research in the behavioral sciences that have been explored by psychologists and sociologists with increasing interest in the years since the classic studies at the Hawthorne Plant of the Western Electric Company were conducted by Elton Mayo and his associates.[1] It is recognized by most researchers that the study of the behavior of small groups, while extremely important, presents many problems in defining the factors or variables to be studied, in measuring them, and in controlling them in relation to other factors that are part of the total group process. Nevertheless, attempts to conduct research on small groups have yielded some valuable information that has provided managers and supervisors, as well as teachers and other personnel who work with small groups, with new concepts to guide them in their approach to problems that arise out of their attempts to direct a group toward defined goals. This chapter discusses groups and how they function and includes the following topics:

- Characteristics of work groups.
- Factors influencing behavior of work groups.
- Some problems of groups.

Characteristics of Work Groups

The primary emphasis of the discussions in preceding chapters has been upon the individual employee and management's relationships with the individual employee in efforts to utilize his talents most effectively. As has been pointed out, however, management must not only be concerned with its employees as individuals but must also recognize the importance of the influence of the various groups that emerge within the organization. At all levels in the organization, the informal groupings of employees exert a powerful influence on the behavior of their members. Similarly, formal groups such as committees, boards, and especially work groups affect the attitudes and feelings of their members. It should be recognized, therefore, that all types of groups — both formal and informal — have a vital role in the dynamic functioning of the organization. However, because of their importance and the large number of work groups in an organization, the emphasis in this chapter will be on work groups that are under the direction of first-line supervisors and the groups and forces that influence them. Studies of such groups have revealed the existence

---

[1]Elton Mayo, *The Human Problems of an Industrial Civilization* (Boston: Graduate School of Business Administration, Harvard University, 1946); F. J. Roethlisberger and W. J. Dickson, *Management and the Worker* (Cambridge: Harvard University Press, 1949). See also Henry A. Landsberger, *Hawthorne Revisited* (Ithaca, New York: Cornell University, 1958).

of certain characteristics which provide a basis for understanding group behavior. It should be observed, however, that these characteristics are not separate and independent of each other in the dynamic functioning of a group.

Leadership

The leadership role of the first-line supervisor was described in detail in the preceding chapter. It was noted that it is his responsibility to see that the work assignments of his unit are completed according to standards that are established and that a good human relations climate is developed among his employees. His ability to carry out these responsibilities depends in part upon his own leadership skills, upon the support that he receives from management, and upon the informal relationships among the members of his work group.

Formal leadership. The characteristics of effective supervision were discussed in the preceding chapter. In addition to those characteristics that were mentioned, the supervisor's role in the group is an important factor in his success as a leader. The University of Michigan studies reveal that the greater the supervisor's skill in using group methods of supervision, the greater the productivity and satisfaction of the work group is likely to be. In the high-producing work groups it was found that employees cooperate more and help one another in getting the work done on their own initiative. The willingness to help one another seems to come from a better team spirit and better interpersonal relationships that the supervisor has developed in the group. Likert describes the "group-centered" supervisor as follows:

> He endeavors to build and maintain in his group a keen sense of responsibility for achieving its own goals and meeting its obligations to the larger organization.
>
> The leader helps to provide the group with the stimulation arising from a restless dissatisfaction. He discourages complacency and passive acceptance of the present. He helps the members to become aware of new possibilities, more important values, and more significant goals.
>
> The leader is an important source of enthusiasm for the significance of the mission and goals of the group. He sees that the tasks of the group are important and significant and difficult enough to be challenging.
>
> As an overall guide to his leadership behavior, the leader understands and uses with sensitivity and skill the principle of supportive relationships.[2]

---

[2] Rensis Likert, *New Patterns of Management* (New York: McGraw-Hill Book Company, 1961), pp. 171–172.

Supportive relationships with a group are similar to those used with individual employees. Through the example that he provides, the supervisor may encourage the members of the group to be tolerant of the attitudes and behavior of the other members, thus creating an atmosphere in which all members are able to communicate with one another in a friendly and constructive manner. The supervisor who can develop a psychological climate that "brings out the best" in each individual and that encourages the individual to subordinate his selfish interests for the good of the group has achieved one of the most important objectives of supervision. Skill in achieving this objective is, in a large part, dependent upon the supervisor's sensitivity to the needs of individual members of the group and his ability to orient the group members toward building warm and effective relationships with one another. In a group in which individuals have mature relationships with one another and have feelings of responsibility toward the group and the larger organization, it is possible for the supervisor to permit the group to enjoy the benefits of participation in the leadership role, as described in the preceding chapter. His willingness to do this, however, is dependent in part upon the real or perceived authority that has been delegated to him. The effective supervisor is likely to be one who feels that he has adequate positional authority and is able to use it in making decisions. He feels secure and is confident that his decisions will be supported by his superior. This feeling of security reveals itself in the manner in which the supervisor approaches the various aspects of his job, especially in his relationships with subordinates. He can, for example, be more positive in his responses to employee questions than the supervisor pictured in Figure 15-1. The supervisor with a sense of security does not have to display his authority except in rare instances. He is able to treat his subordinates as equals and with respect, and they, in turn, respect him. While the supervisor possesses the authority to give any orders that are reasonable, he should be especially careful to avoid playing "favorites."

Informal leadership. Although the supervisor is recognized as the formal leader of the group by virtue of his positional authority, there may be one or more informal leaders in the group to whom the members of the group also give their allegiance. This allegiance to one or more fellow employees may result from the recognition by fellow employees of the unofficial leader's technical skill or knowledge, his seniority, the type of work he does, or more frequently his ability to communicate with others and to satisfy their personal needs. If the supervisor is able to recognize the informal leaders, he can often develop effective relationships with them

Figure 15-1

"My answer is maybe, and that's final."

Reproduced with permission of the *Saturday Review* and Brad Anderson.

that enable him to utilize the talents and energies of the group more effectively. If, however, the supervisor pays little attention to the informal leadership, he may encounter difficulties. The most effective way for management to handle informal leaders is to recognize their existence, to consider their influence, and to integrate the interests of the informal leaders and informal group with those of the formal organization. The informal leadership cannot, of course, be permitted to usurp the formal authority of the supervisor, but this problem is not likely to occur if there is successful leadership by the formal leaders.

Status

Being a formal or informal leader of a group distinguishes the individual from nonleaders and gives him status among the other members of the group. Status, as noted in Chapter 4, may also be associated with factors other than leadership, such as seniority, wages, having more modern equipment (such as an electric typewriter among those without electric machines), being a union steward for the group, possessing specialized skills, and other factors that distinguish one person from another or one job from another. Fortunately, there are many symbols of status so that each employee will be likely to possess a few of them and thus have his status needs satisfied to some degree. In his relationships with subordinates, the supervisor should recognize the sources and symbols of status and guard against any action that may jeopardize an employee's status.

Conformity

Much has been written about the "evils" of conformity in the modern business world. It should be recognized, however, that conformity does have values, providing it does not impede progress or destroy creativity. Because of the reinforcing effect of the first-line supervisor's attitudes and behavior on his subordinates, he can either stifle progress and innovation or he can facilitate it. The use of nonevaluative communication skills with individuals and groups as described in the two preceding chapters can help to provide a climate in which subordinates feel free to express their own ideas.

Keith Davis is of the opinion that the informal organization can create employee conformity of an even more serious type. While management expects employees to conform to the requirements of the work process in order that the operations may be completed successfully, it usually does not require *attitude conformity* on the part of its employees.[3] Forces at work within the informal group, however, may serve to keep the group uniform in its attitude toward the work, the supervision, and the other areas of importance. Such conformity may serve the interests of management — e.g., a group has a tradition of adhering carefully to company rules and exerts group pressure on an individual who has fallen into the habit of breaking certain rules. However, group requirements for attitude conformity may sometimes be contrary to management's interests — e.g., an employee is punished by the group for producing significantly more than the amount upon which the group has informally agreed. This latter type of situation is clearly illustrated by one of the workers in the pajama factory study (Case 12-2 on page 322) conducted by Coch and French. The curve in Figure 15-2 shows the influence of group pressures on the production of

---

[3]Keith Davis, *Human Relations at Work* (New York: McGraw-Hill Book Company, 1962), pp. 242–244.

that individual; as stated by Lippitt from the study by Coch and French at the Harwood Manufacturing company:

We see the day-by-day production curve of a girl belonging to a work group with a group production level of 50 units per hour represented by the dotted line. On the 11th and 12th days her production began to rise noticeably above the group standard and when she on the 13th day hit standard production of 60 (a psychologically very important deviation for the other members), she became a scapegoat of the group with a great deal of social aggression directed toward her. Under this pressure her production decreased toward the level of the other group members. After 20 days the work group had to be broken up and the members transferred to various other units. The scapegoated operator remained on the same job, alone. As can be seen, her production shot up from about 45 to 96 units per hour in a period of 4 days. Her production stabilized at a level of about 92 and stayed there for the remainder of the 20 days. Clearly the induced forces on behavior from a strong subgroup may be more powerful than those induced by a progressive friendly management, and by personal needs for economic reward.[4]

Figure 15-2
GROUP RESTRICTION OF PRODUCTION

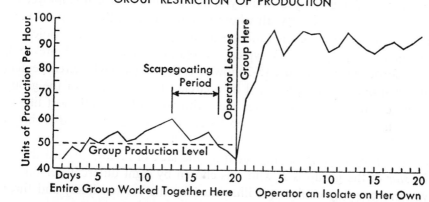

Source: Ronald Lippitt, "A Program of Experimentation on Group Functioning and Group Productivity," in Wayne Dennis, *Current Trends in Social Psychology* (Pittsburgh: University of Pittsburgh Press, 1951), pp. 25–27. From data obtained by Lester Coch and J. R. P. French, Jr., "Overcoming Resistance to Change," *Human Relations*, Vol. 1, No. 4 (1948), pp. 512–532. Reproduced with permission.

Evidence that the group influence often restricts the production of the individual members is available in many companies. However, we should not assume that the group influence is only restrictive. As noted in Chapter 14, the benefits of group participation in decision making are often quite pronounced.

[4]Ronald Lippitt, "A Program of Experimentation on Group Functioning and Group Productivity," in Wayne Dennis, *Current Trends in Social Psychology* (Pittsburgh: University of Pittsburgh Press, 1951), pp. 25–27.

Cliques

While the group may be able to demand conformity from its members, it does not follow that members of the group have the same feelings toward one another. Within a work group there will be smaller groups of individuals who commonly associate with one another and are frequently referred to as *cliques*. Such informal groupings of individuals are normal and need not interfere with the functions of the larger group if the supervisor is alert to their existence and does not permit a clique to divorce itself entirely from the larger group. The supervisor can usually notice cliques within the work group by observing who eat lunch together, who talks with whom during free periods, and by other evidences of exclusiveness and at times "snobbishness."

A more formal procedure in studying the makeup of the work group is through the use of *sociometry*, the measurement of relationships within the group.[5] The usual procedure is to have each member of the group rank his choice of individuals on the basis of answers to such questions as: "With which employee would you like to work? Which employee do you like the most?" or, "With whom would you most like to spend your time?" On the basis of the rankings a *sociogram*, showing the choices of individuals, is prepared. A typical sociogram is shown in Figure 15-3.

The sociogram in Figure 15-3 shows a work group of eighteen carpenters with each individual represented by a circle. Each member of the group was asked to nominate the three men with whom he would most like to work, and the total number of choices each individual obtained is shown in the circle. Individuals *A*, *Q*, and *R* are called *isolates* because they were not chosen by anyone (as indicated by the lack of arrows toward them). The *star* of the group is *K* who was chosen by eight different persons — five were one-way choices (as illustrated by the broken lines) and three were mutual choices (as illustrated by the solid lines).

While sociometry and sociograms have been used quite extensively in schools, their adoption by industry has been slow. Where they have been used, however, the results have been favorable. For example, Van Zelst found that a 5 percent saving in production costs was obtained by allowing carpenters and bricklayers to choose their teammates and by grouping the workers on the basis of the choices whenever possible, except that isolates were still assigned to groups. The value of the method is expressed by one of the workers as follows:

---

[5]The reader will find interesting variations of the sociometric technique discussed in *Sociometry*, a quarterly journal of the American Sociological Association.

Seems as though everything flows a lot smoother. It makes you feel a lot more comfortable working. I don't waste any time bickering about who's going to do what and how. We just seem to go ahead and do it. The work's a lot more interesting, too, when you've got your buddy working with you. You certainly like it a lot better anyway.[6]

Cohesiveness

Another characteristic of groups is their cohesiveness, or the extent of the loyalty of the employees toward their work group. Cohesiveness of work groups has been studied by two approaches. In one approach it is measured by the responses given by each employee to statements concerning his sentiments toward the group of which he is a member.[7] He is asked

Figure 15-3

A SOCIOGRAM

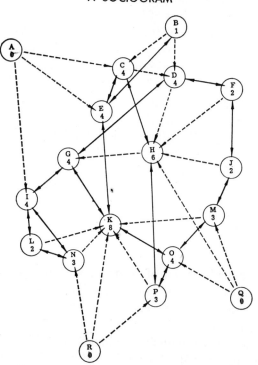

Source: Raymond H. Van Zelst, "An Interpersonal Relations Technique for Industry," *Personnel*, Vol. 29, No. 1 (July, 1952), p. 70. Reproduced with permission of the American Management Association.

[6]Raymond H. Van Zelst, "Sociometrically Selected Work Teams Increase Production," *Personnel Psychology*, Vol. 5, No. 3 (Autumn, 1952), pp. 175–185.
[7]Stanley Seashore, *Group Cohesiveness in the Industrial Work Group* (Ann Arbor, Michigan: Survey Research Center, 1954).

questions dealing with such matters as whether the workers in his group get along together, want to stay in the group, like to stick together, enjoy helping one another, and feel that they are a part of the group. In the other approach cohesion is judged in terms of concerted group activity. Cohesive groups are those in which the members act toward a common goal. Groups that are low in cohesion are characterized by an inability to achieve a degree of unification which makes group action possible.[8]

Analyses made by Seashore in one of the University of Michigan studies reveal the importance of group cohesiveness in understanding and influencing the activities of the work group. These analyses revealed that the degree of group cohesiveness is related to the influence which the goals of the group have on the performance of its members. If the goals of the group are to achieve high productivity and low waste, greater cohesiveness will enable them to attain these goals. Likewise, if the desire of the group is to reject the objectives of the organization and to restrict production, the greater cohesiveness will enable them to do this. Another important finding is that among work groups with high peer-group loyalty supervisors evidently tend to have the leadership ability to create relatively high performance goals.[9] Likert believes that on the basis of the research evidence the establishment of high performance goals and the achievement of them by the work group is largely fostered by leadership which uses group methods of supervision and which develops in the entire group a sense of responsibility for getting the total job done.[10]

Because of the importance of methods of supervision that emphasize group relationships, special attention is given to these methods following the discussion of the factors that influence work groups.

Role

In examining the behavior of groups, one should not lose sight of the fact that the group is comprised of individuals each of whom has a different role. A *role* may be considered to be a position that an individual occupies in a group. It is also defined as a behavior system which has been internalized and developed by a person for use in accomplishing objectives.[11] In a formalized role such as that of supervisor of a work group, the individual

---

[8]Leonard Sayles, *Behavior of Industrial Work Groups* (New York: John Wiley & Sons, Inc., 1958).

[9]Rensis Likert, *op, cit.,* p. 32.

[10]*Ibid.,* p. 34.

[11]John W. Thibaut and Harold H. Kelly, *The Social Psychology of Groups* (New York: John Wiley and Sons, Inc., 1959).

is expected to conform to behavior patterns that are defined by higher management and by the larger business society. Similarly, subordinates are expected to conform to behavior patterns that are typically associated with a subordinate's role. In either role — supervisory or employee — a reasonably wide range of behavior may be considered acceptable.

In an informal group members likewise fill different roles. One person may be the leader, another may be one who fosters good feelings among the members, another may be the critic, etc. As members of other groups, these individuals are likely to play different roles. For example, in discussions with the group at the office, Joe may play a listener role most of the time. At the ball game, however, he may be the one who typically lets the umpire know how he feels about his decisions. The fact that an individual plays different roles in different types of situations should be a clue to the supervisor of the complexity of human personality and the need for studying an individual in a wide variety of settings in order to understand his potentialities better and to communicate with him more effectively.

Katz and Kahn have given the role concept a central place in their theory of organizational behavior.[12] Certainly the concept of role is important in understanding the behavior of supervisors. How the supervisor perceives his role in the organization will largely determine his effectiveness in leading the work group. If his perception of his role is in conflict with that of his superiors or of his subordinates or if his role is ambiguous, he will not be able to achieve his full potential as a leader.

One common fault of supervisors is their failure to perceive the nature of their role as a manager. The supervisor is ordinarily expected to perform those tasks that are typically performed by managerial personnel and not to become engaged in the same type of work as the employees whom he supervises. While he may occasionally give a helping hand during an extremely busy period or if difficulties occur, his efforts should ordinarily go into doing those things that will prevent difficulties from occurring in the first place. The supervisor who constantly engages in production work alongside of the employees will not be acting in the best interests of the company, his employees, or himself, unless he is considered to be a *working supervisor*. However, a working supervisor, or lead man as he is often called, is not truly a supervisor in the sense in which the term is used in this chapter. He is an employee who is designated to perform very limited supervisory functions, usually of a minor nature, over certain aspects of production.

---

[12]Daniel Katz and Robert L. Kahn, *The Social Psychology of Organizations* (New York: John Wiley and Sons, Inc., 1966), p. 172.

Factors Influencing Behavior of Work Groups

The nature of the relationship between the work group and the larger groups of which it is a part is similar to the relationship between the individual and his work group. In both situations the smaller unit is functioning in a broader context. The smaller unit not only influences the larger unit but the larger unit, in turn, influences the behavior of the smaller unit. Work groups, like individuals, are subject to the influence of many factors that affect the functioning of the group and determine its cohesiveness as well as other characteristics.

Type of Work

The nature of the work performed by members of a group can appreciably affect its cohesiveness because of the environmental conditions created by the work. In the assembly line, for example:

> ... There is little in the way of a group to which he [the employee] can belong in a meaningful way. Perhaps the most important counterweight to anonymity and lack of belonging or purpose, if they exist in a factory, is the sense of belonging to a small work group. But the development of groups requires frequent and easy interaction (i.e. some form of verbal or nonverbal communication) between the members, and this is not found on the assembly line. For one thing, the noise in many sections of the plant interferes with interaction; so does the fact that most jobs, while simple, cannot be performed automatically, requiring constant attention as they do if the operator is to keep up with the line. Most jobs are performed singly, or with only occasional help from one "partner" performing similar work on the other side of the line.[13]

In other types of work where persons can communicate with one another freely, cohesiveness is more likely to develop and actually facilitates the accomplishment of the work. In contrast to the assembly line where each station must be manned, there are many work situations in which the absence of an employee does not require a replacement. Other members of the work group may absorb the tasks ordinarily performed by the absentee. Where cohesiveness is strong and the goals are well-defined, it is not unusual for production to remain at the same level in spite of absences. Interestingly enough, however, persons in groups with high peer-group loyalty are much less likely to be absent from work than persons in groups with low peer-group loyalty.[14]

---

[13]Arthur N. Turner, "Management and the Assembly Line," *Harvard Business Review*, Vol. 33, No. 5 (September–October, 1955), pp. 40–48.

[14]F. C. Mann and H. J. Baumgartel, *Absences and Employee Attitudes in an Electric Power Company* (Ann Arbor, Michigan: Institute for Social Research, 1953).

In many different types of organizations the employees are members of one group, but a large share of their working time is spent in interacting with members of other groups. An example is found in the restaurant industry where the nature of the work, and the interpersonal relationships required to accomplish it, have been studied in sufficient detail to provide some interesting and valuable insights into the types of problems that arise between groups. A study of the work flow has revealed that there are many opportunities for friction arising primarily out of who initiates orders and to whom. Whyte[15] reports that in one restaurant supplymen seeking to originate action (in getting food supplies) for cooks who were older, of greater seniority, more highly skilled, and much more highly paid caused friction between the two groups. Another problem area was found in the relationships between waitresses and countermen. In this industry, at least, men find it difficult to take verbal orders from women. It was found that when waitresses wrote out slips and placed them on top of a warming compartment that separated them from the countermen, less friction occurred. The written order in itself, however, was not enough to eliminate friction because opportunities for verbal interaction still existed. When conditions were changed so that the waitress and the counterman actually could not see each other, there was still less friction. Finally, the spindle — the round, metal wheel on which the waitress may fasten her order and from which the cook may take the orders — (see Figure 15-4) became the solution to the problem. It can be concluded from the study, therefore, that the layout of the work, the status of the different groups that are required to interact with each other, and the manner in which orders are initiated have been found to be important factors in determining the nature of relationships among people at work.

Influence of the Larger Group

Each member of the work group is also a member of other groups in society, such as the family, the church, a lodge, or other types of fraternal or social groups. In some instances there may be some degree of overlap, and in others no duplication between the composition of the work group and these groups exists. The influence of these groups not only affects the employee's behavior as a member of the work group but also affects his attitudes toward his job and other important areas of his life. It is important, therefore, that managerial personnel have some understanding of the

---

[15]William Foote Whyte, *Men at Work* (Homewood, Illinois: Richard D. Irwin, Inc., 1961), pp. 125–135.

Figure 15-4

THE SPINDLE

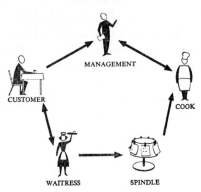

The introduction of the spindle breaks up the face-to-face relation between the waitress and the cook.

Source: Elias H. Porter, *Manpower Development* (New York: Harper & Row, Publishers, 1964), p. 5. Reproduced with permission.

other groups to which their personnel belong since these groups may influence the behavior of employees.

Occupational groups. Each member of a work group is also a member of an occupational group that is comprised of individuals performing jobs that are similar in nature. In many instances the employee is barely aware of his membership in this larger occupational group; whereas, in other instances membership in it may have fully as much significance for him as his membership in the work group. Professionally and technically trained persons, for example, are likely to feel that they not only work for the company or the supervisor but that they also are a part of a larger group that is dedicated to the attainment of a "cause." The scientist, for example, may be concerned not only with developing a method or technique that will benefit the company but will usually be concerned also about the broader implications of what he is doing. While he will be likely to seek recognition from the company, the scientist will have an even greater concern for recognition from fellow scientists in and outside of his work group.[16]

Persons working in professional-level occupations have long been aware of the importance of their relationships to other members of the profession and have ethical standards that govern their relations with one

[16]Barney G. Glaser, *Organizational Scientists: Their Professional Careers* (Indianapolis: The Bobbs-Merrill Co., Inc., 1964).

another. Members of groups in managerial, clerical, and skilled occupations have also gradually joined together in support of their common interests. National, regional, and local organizations, other than labor unions, attract the employee who has a specialty because they provide a meeting-ground for common interests and because the role of these organizations in influencing employers is well recognized.

In many of the trades, a "craft-consciousness" has developed that has resulted in a definition of what tasks a worker in a particular craft may legitimately perform and which tasks fall within the area of another craft. Craft-consciousness is particularly strong in construction and maintenance jobs where separate unions have been organized around such trades as carpentry, plumbing, electrical wiring, and bricklaying. Observation of individuals representing these trades at work in erecting a building soon reveals the fine lines that exist between one man's territory and that of another. This tendency of restricting one's activities to specified tasks is not limited to workers who are represented by a union but is a characteristic of most employees. Perhaps the desire to be recognized as capable of doing something that others cannot do underlies this behavior.

The union. While many managers feel that they never had any personnel problems before the existence of strong unions, this feeling probably arises out of forgetfulness or an inability to recognize that such problems did exist previously. Whenever people are grouped together for the purpose of achieving a goal, or even for fun, problems among them are likely to arise. The introduction of a union, with its emphasis on employee needs and wants and its affiliation with a larger, more powerful, national or international group, means that there will be outside influences on the work group as well as on management and the personnel department. As a result personnel management in the company will become more complex, and relations with employees and with the union will have to be carried out in accordance with the terms of the union agreement. Because of the importance of union-management relations, including the handling of grievances, Chapters 17, 18, and 19 are devoted to this topic.

The community. The presence of a company in a community affects the community economically, socially, and in other ways; and the community, in turn, exerts an influence upon the company. The influences of the local government and its leaders are apparent to the managers who must operate in accordance with local laws and regulations. Perhaps less obvious, but just as important, are the influences of the community that workers bring with them to the job. It is fairly well established, for example, that employees performing similar work will have common membership in a social class in the community. This common membership tends to influence their attitudes, values, and behavior in all areas of their lives including employment and may, at times, account for the likenesses among members of one group and the differences among members of different work groups. In many of the larger communities, members of an ethnic group are often found to live together within defined geographical areas; and because of their common background, they interact with each other more than with members of other groups. As members of these ethnic groups come together within an organization, they may gravitate toward certain jobs and thus provide a concentration of influence because of their similar attitudes and values.[17]

Management. The work group is also influenced by those management personnel who are superior to it in the organizational hierarchy. Each executive or manager contributes to the shaping of the larger environment within which the work group is required to operate. The fact that there are many work groups within the total organization and that they are under the direction of different executives and managers creates differences between groups within the organization. Some of the differences develop out of the manner in which policies are interpreted and rules and regulations are enforced. Other inconsistencies result from differences in attitudes toward people and approaches to supervision that have grown out of these attitudes toward people. As noted in the preceding chapter, the first-line supervisor who is inclined toward using democratic methods of leadership may experience considerable difficulty in doing so if his superior is extremely autocratic. On the other hand, if his superior uses democratic approaches in supervision, the supervisor will not only find it easy to use these approaches with his subordinates but will probably be encouraged to do so. While it is generally agreed that the democratic approach to leadership results in increased motivation of employees and improved teamwork, it should be recognized that the type of leadership approach that a superior should use at a particular time in handling a particular situation cannot be dictated by any theory of leadership. Rather, the type of leadership approach should be chosen on the basis of what the situation dictates, as perceived by the supervisor. It is a requisite of good

---

[17]The reader who desires to learn more about community influences on the company and its employees may refer to: *The Social Life of a Modern Community*, Yankee City Series, 5 volumes (New Haven: Yale University Press, 1941–1959), and *Democracy in Jonesville* (New York: Harper & Brothers, 1949).

supervision to perceive the situation accurately and to provide the type of leadership that will bring effective results from the group.

Some Problems of Groups

While an understanding of group dynamics will provide the basis for more effective supervision of work groups, there are problem areas that are likely to remain in spite of the best efforts of their leaders to eliminate them. However, special attention by supervisors and those in charge of supervisory training to these problem areas should at least reduce the severity of some of the problems that arise out of group functioning, and thus contribute toward a more desirable work environment.

Developing Effective Communication

The importance of communication in the functioning of an organization and ways of making communication more effective were considered in Chapter 13. It will be recalled that the supervisor plays a major role in organizational communications since management often depends upon him to interpret company policy to the employees in such a way that they will understand and accept it. The supervisor must also be able to communicate the feelings of his subordinates to management and to advise management of the progress and problems of his department. The supervisor who has the ability to give clear orders and directions that will be accepted and carried out, to conduct satisfactory interviews and discussions, and in other ways to communicate with subordinates in such a manner that improved attitudes and performance will result is a decided asset to the company.

The effectiveness of communication between superiors and subordinates may be assessed in different ways, ranging from the measurement of the outcomes of orders and directions to subjective impressions of the individuals concerned. One study by Hamann[18] reveals that superiors and subordinates have different perceptions of the degree to which the superior understands the problems of subordinates, as shown in Figure 15-5.

It will be observed in Figure 15-5 that at each level of supervision the subordinates feel that the superior understands their problems to a far lesser degree than the superior realizes. One explanation given by a research team is that subordinates fail to tell superiors about their problems, or superiors fail to listen, or subordinates are wrong in their estimates

18 J. R. Hamann, *General Management Series*, No. 182, Panel Discussion (New York: American Management Association, 1956), pp. 21–23.

Figure 15-5

OPINIONS AS TO THE DEGREE TO WHICH SUPERIORS UNDERSTAND SUBORDINATES' PROBLEMS

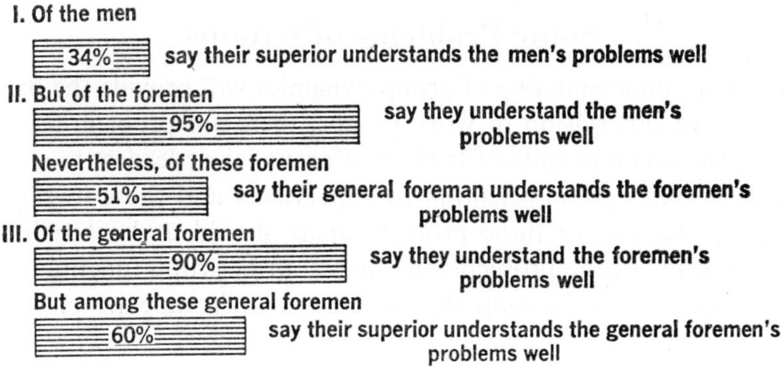

I. Of the men

34%   say their superior understands the men's problems well

II. But of the foremen

95%   say they understand the men's problems well

Nevertheless, of these foremen

51%   say their general foreman understands the foremen's problems well

III. Of the general foremen

90%   say they understand the foremen's problems well

But among these general foremen

60%   say their superior understands the general foremen's problems well

Source: Rensis Likert, *New Patterns of Management* (New York: McGraw-Hill Book Company, 1961), p. 52. Reproduced with permission.

of what the job obstacles are.[19] This failure on the part of superiors to understand subordinates as fully as they would like illustrates the need for communication of a type where nonevaluative listening characterizes the superior's behavior. The supervisor should develop skill in communicating with his subordinates as a group in order that he may mold its members into a harmonious and productive team. The use of the group decision conference described in the preceding chapter is one of the best approaches to the achievement of this objective.

Building Cooperation

The group approach introduces the possibility of either competitive or cooperative relationships. A cooperative or competitive relationship among the members of a group may be developed by the skill that the supervisor possesses in reinforcing one type of behavior over another. Through effective conference leadership, the supervisor can suppress behavior that may be self-serving to the individuals and encourage behavior that he views as being for the good of the group as a whole. Although much weight is given to the importance of cooperation, the impression should not be given that the best problem-solving groups are free of disagreement or conflict. The absence of disagreement suggests either lack of commitment or fear that causes the group members to suppress expressions of disagreement. However, whatever agreement or

[19]Likert, *New Patterns of Management*, p. 53.

disagreement exists should center about different methods for solving the group's problems and not for gaining advantage for one's self.[20]

It is natural for the supervisor to be interested primarily in his own group. However, every supervisor should be trained to recognize the importance of cooperation between groups in the organization. Schein suggests that the organization planner who wishes to avoid intergroup competition and conflict need not abandon the concept of division of labor but should follow these steps in creating and handling his different functional groups:

1. Relatively greater emphasis given to *total organizational effectiveness* and the role of departments in contributing to it; departments measured and rewarded on the basis of their *contribution* to the total effort rather than their individual effectiveness.

2. *High interaction* and *frequent communication* stimulated between groups to work on problems of intergroup coordination and help; organizational *rewards given partly on the basis of help* which groups give to each other.

3. Frequent *rotation of members* among groups or departments to stimulate high degree of mutual understanding and empathy for one another's problems.

4. *Avoidance of any win-lose situation;* groups never put into the position of competing for some organizational reward; emphasis always placed on pooling resources to maximize organizational effectiveness; rewards shared equally with all the groups or departments.[21]

Preserving Individuality

Many of the behavioral scientists as well as philosophers have indicated their concern over the effects of the formal organization, including the work group, on individual personality. Among the behavioral scientists who have devoted considerable attention to this topic is Chris Argyris. He believes, as noted in Chapter 3, that if the principles of formal organization are applied as they are defined,

> ... employees will tend to work in an environment where (1) they are provided minimal control over their workaday world, (2) they are expected to be passive, dependent, and subordinate, (3) they are expected to have a short-time perspective, (4) they are induced to perfect and value the frequent use of a few skin-surface shallow

---

[20]Timothy W. Costello and Sheldon S. Zalkind, *Psychology in Administration — A Research Orientation* (Englewood Cliffs, New Jersey: Prentice-Hall. Inc., 1963), pp. 430–432.

[21]Edgar H. Schein, *Organizational Psychology* (Englewood Cliffs, New Jersey: Prentice-Hall, Inc., 1965), p. 85.

abilities, and (5) they are expected to produce under conditions leading to psychological failure.[22]

On the basis of a logical analysis, he concludes that the formal organizational principles make demands of relatively healthy individuals that are incongruent with their needs. Frustration, conflict, failure, and short-time perspective are predicted as resultants of this basic incongruency.

Koontz, however, is of the opinion that Argyris has misunderstood and misapplied the principles of management and "has simply proved that wrong principles badly applied will lead to frustration." He urges that management theorists attempt to understand each other.[23]

More recently Argyris has written a sequel to his *Personality and Organization* (1957) entitled *Integrating the Individual and the Organization* (1964) in which he recognizes the importance of both the organization and the individual and the need for optimizing the effectiveness of both. He hypothesizes that

> . . . the incongruence between the individual and the organization can provide the basis for a continued challenge which, as it is fulfilled, will tend to help man to enhance his own growth and to develop organizations that will tend to be viable and effective. The incongruence between the individual and the organization can be the foundation for increasing the degree of effectiveness of both.[24]

In this recent book Argyris discusses the major personnel functions with the above hypothesis as the guiding principle in the discussion. It appears that this approach to the group is a sound one because, unless the groups are comprised of individuals whose needs are recognized and integrated into the functioning of the organization, the groups will be nothing more than aggregations of uninspired individuals who will contribute relatively little to the organization or to their own personal growth and psychological development.

Résumé

It has been emphasized that in order to be effective the supervisor must learn to integrate the individual members of his work group into a

---

[22]Chris Argyris, *Personality and Organization* (New York: Harper and Row, 1957), Chapter 3.

[23]Harold Koontz, "The Management Theory Jungle," *Journal of the Academy of Management*, Vol. 4, No. 3 (December, 1961), pp. 174–188. Also refer to Chapter 3 of this book, pp. 56–57.

[24]Chris Argyris, *Integrating the Individual and the Organization* (New York: John Wiley and Sons, Inc., 1964), p. 7.

productive and harmonious team. The ability to achieve a high degree of teamwork is dependent upon an understanding of leadership roles, pressures for conformity, cliques, and cohesiveness and how these factors influence groups. It is also important for the supervisor to understand how work groups are influenced by the job conditions, the union, the community, and the various levels of management.

The supervisor should be aware of these forces over which he has little or no control, and he should be concerned about the influence that his own behavior has on the work group. Through his efforts and those of other management personnel in developing effective communication, in building cooperation, and in preserving individuality, the needs of the individual and of the organization may be recognized and brought into greater harmony.

DISCUSSION QUESTIONS AND PROBLEMS

1. Some writers have been critical of large corporations because they view them as demanding conformity from employees. Do you agree with them? What specific evidence can you cite that would support your opinion?
2. Of what groups are you a member? How do you perceive your role in each of these groups? Insofar as you can determine, does your perception of your role differ from the perception that others have of your role?
3. In recent years there has been an increasing interest in group dynamics. At the same time the term "rank-and-file workers" has become less popular. What are the implications of these changes? How do you relate this change to your own preparation as a potential supervisor or manager?
4. In the discussion of the use of sociometry in industry, it was indicated that some favorable results had been obtained from using sociometric data in the assignment of individuals to a work group.
   a. What are some of the possible dangers in using such an approach?
   b. Is there any way that these dangers may be minimized?
5. Some managers feel that effective leadership is primarily dependent upon the quality of the relationships established between the leader and the individuals in the group and that too much emphasis is given to "group relationships."
   a. What is your opinion? What support can you cite for its validity?
   b. Can you think of any jobs where the supervisor must give close attention to group relationships as well as to individuals?
6. Study the work groups of a company in your community. Are there any common backgrounds among the members of the groups that would influence their attitudes toward their jobs, their supervisors, or management personnel? Of what significance is this type of information?
7. The next time that you go into a restaurant, sit where you can observe the interpersonal relationships between the counterman (or cook) and the waiters or waitresses. Make a note of what you see and hear and bring it to class. (In making your observations be as objective as possible, and look for pleasant exchanges as well as unpleasant ones).

CASE 15-1

THE EXTENDED LUNCH PERIOD

Mike Greer had been the swing shift foreman of the blueprint department in a large engineering company nearly three years. All of the employees on the shift were men whose age averaged about 20 years. After graduating from high school and completing two years in the military service Mike started as a folder in the department and progressed to his present supervisory position. Mike was well liked by his subordinates and production was high for the shift.

Mike permitted his people to have a maximum of freedom and as long as they did their work he was not strict in enforcing the time limits for the coffee and lunch breaks. His employees appreciated this consideration and tried to do their share of work to make up for it.

When Mike was promoted to a new position, he was replaced by Ron Wells who had a somewhat different philosophy of supervision. Ron was a recent college graduate with about six months of management experience. He believed in enforcing company rules, particularly those relating to the relief and lunch period schedules. Shortly after assuming his position Ron called a meeting and announced to the employees on his shift that in the future they would be expected to observe the time limits established for the relief and lunch periods. Although most of the personnel complied with his request, production in the department declined. A few of the employees who resented the new restrictions continued to take longer than the period permitted. When Wells discovered one of these employees returning from lunch about a half hour late, he warned the individual that he or anyone else would be sent home and not be paid for the remainder of the work period if they overstayed their lunch period in the future. The next evening the entire shift went out to dine together and were more than an hour late in returning to work. Faced with the alternative of backing down on his ultimatum or sending the entire shift home, Ron chose the latter course of action. The next day the division manager came to investigate the mass suspension and a short time later Ron was transferred to another department. Morale and productivity in the department continued to be poor, even after Ron's departure, until members of the shift were eliminated by transfers and terminations.

a. Did Ron err in:
   (1) Attempting to enforce the scheduled break periods?
   (2) Warning that those who were late in returning from their breaks would be suspended for the rest of the day?
b. What are the implications of the problems in terms of the role of the informal group?
c. If you had been the new supervisor, would you have continued to operate the department in the manner of your predecessor Mike Greer?

CASE 15-2

"LIMPING LARRY"

Larry Keene was a permanent U.S. Post Office clerk with six years of service. In addition to this regular job, Larry also served as the pastor of a small church. Although Keene's performance was generally poorer than that of others in his group, it was not considered to be sufficiently unsatisfactory to justify disciplinary action.

One year, during the Christmas season, Larry was assigned to work on the graveyard shift at the parcel post annex. About 2:00 a.m. on the first Sunday that he was assigned to this shift, Larry began to evidence a decided limp and to complain of pains in his left leg. After working about another hour he asked for and received permission from his supervisor, Paul Fern, to quit and go home. Since the volume of parcel post was heavy, his share of the work had to be assumed by other members on the shift. In addition, Keene left his work station, as he had on previous mornings, in a disorderly condition, with the result that his fellow workers also had to do his clean up work at the close of the shift. Because they believed that he was not assuming his share of the work load, therefore, other employees on the shift began to develop a resentment toward Keene. Some expressed their feelings openly to him but without stimulating any positive change on Keene's part. In fact, the quality and quantity of his work, if anything, tended to become even less satisfactory.

Furthermore, about 3:00 a.m. on the next Sunday morning his limp again developed, at which time he requested permission to go home. When the limping routine was repeated this second time, his supervisor was tempted to refuse his request. Since there was a slight possibility, however, that the complaint might be legitimate, and since there was no one available in the middle of the night whom he might consult with about Keene's condition, Fern let him go home with a warning to see a doctor the first thing Monday. On Monday when he reported for work Keene stated that his leg was much improved. Fern, however, informed him that he would have to get a report from a doctor as soon as he had an opportunity to see one, but forgot to follow up on the matter.

In the meantime, the other members of the group with whom he worked had become disgusted with Keene's behavior and had vowed to take the matter in their own hands if Keene did not change his ways. When the limping began on the third Sunday morning they were ready for action. At the suggestion of Ted White, to whom they looked for leadership, the other employees began to limp around complaining about their legs. Periodically, one of them would sit down complaining that he was unable to work and that he had to go home. Paul Fern, after observing the performance, promptly found urgent business to handle in another part of the building. About an hour later, Larry Keene's limping began to subside and he managed to complete the shift without requesting to go home. Although he never again complained about pains in his legs, Keene's performance as well as his relations with others in the group, did not show much improvement.

When the Christmas season was over and the temporary help was released, the graveyard shift was eliminated. Fern and his crew, including Larry, were returned to day work. Since Keene's performance and his relations with co-workers still presented a problem, Fern was determined to try and resolve it now that he had more time to devote to personnel matters.

a. What possible explanation is there for Keene's behavior?

b. What might be done with Keene to achieve improvement?

c. Was the supervisor correct in allowing the group to handle the limping problem?

d. Assume that you are Paul Fern, how would you attempt to discuss Keene's problem with him? Conduct the discussion by means of role playing.

SUGGESTED READINGS

Blake, Robert R., and Jane S. Mouton. *Group Dynamics — Key to Decision Making.* Houston, Texas: Gulf Publishing Company, 1961.

Chruden, Herbert J., and Arthur W. Sherman, Jr. *Readings in Personnel Management,* Second Edition. Cincinnati: South-Western Publishing Company, Inc., 1966. Chapter 5.

Davis, Keith. *Human Relations at Work.* New York: McGraw-Hill Book Company, 1962. Chapter 21.

Dubin, Robert. *Human Relations in Administration,* Second Edition. Englewood Cliffs, New Jersey: Prentice-Hall, Inc., 1961.

Dubin, Robert, George C. Homans, Floyd C. Mann, and Delbert C. Miller. *Leadership and Productivity.* San Francisco: Chandler Publishing Co., 1965.

Golembiewski, Robert T. *Behavior and Organization: O & M and the Small Group.* Chicago: Rand McNally & Co., 1962.

Gross, Edward. *Industry and Social Life.* Dubuque, Iowa: Wm. C. Brown Co., 1965.

Homans, George C. *Social Behavior: Its Elementary Forms.* New York: Harcourt, Brace & World, Inc., 1961.

Learned, Edmund P., and Audrey T. Sproat. *Organization Theory and Policy.* Homewood, Illinois: Richard D. Irwin, Inc., 1966.

Leavitt, Harold J. *Managerial Psychology.* Chicago: The University of Chicago Press, Phoenix Books, 1962.

Likert, Rensis. *New Patterns of Management.* New York: McGraw-Hill Book Company, 1961.

Maier, Norman R. F. *Principles of Human Relations.* New York: John Wiley & Sons, Inc., 1952.

Maier, Norman R. F., Allen R. Solem, and Ayesha A. Maier. *Supervisory and Executive Development, A Manual for Role Playing.* New York: John Wiley & Sons, Inc., 1957.

Olmsted, Michael S. *The Small Group.* New York: Random House, Inc., 1959.

Schein, Edgar H. *Organizational Psychology.* Englewood Cliffs, New Jersey: Prentice-Hall, Inc., 1965.

Whyte, William F. *Men at Work.* Homewood, Illinois: Richard D. Irwin, Inc., 1961.

Zelomek, A. Wilbert. *A Changing America at Work and Play.* New York: John Wiley & Sons., Inc., 1959.

Employee Adjustment and Morale

It is commonly recognized by the more enlightened managers that effective personnel relations require that emphasis be placed upon creating employment conditions that will contribute to the emotional adjustment and morale of employees as well as to their productivity. In the preceding chapters the contributions of selection, development, performance evaluation, motivation, communication, and supervision to employee adjustment and morale were considered. Since the individual employee functions as a total organism responding not only to the job environment but also to off-the-job conditions and to events in his own life history, it is important to understand the forces that affect him as a person. Through a better understanding of the individual — his needs, his feelings, his frustrations — it is possible for those in management positions to contribute to his emotional adjustment. Similarly, an awareness of the factors that contribute to individual satisfaction and group morale and a better understanding of how to assess satisfaction and morale are first steps in the creation of a work environment that contributes to employee emotional health.

Although some managers are inclined to feel that the personal adjustment of employees is not their responsibility, they should realize that good mental health is essential not only to the individual but also to the company and to society. Whether or not managers and supervisors are aware of the importance of employee adjustment and morale, the employees themselves and the unions that represent them are well aware of the fact that employment conditions which are detrimental to adjustment and morale need not be tolerated. They may recognize that there are other employers with interest in effective human relations who are able to create a pleasant and stimulating work environment. In this chapter the discussion goes beyond the techniques that may be used to create the desirable type of environment and emphasizes the individual and his intrapersonal life which often do not receive the attention and understanding that are required for effective personnel management. The discussion includes the following topics:

- Problems of employee adjustment.
- Symptoms of emotional problems.
- Facilitating employee adjustment.
- Building good morale.
- Morale surveys.

Problems of Employee Adjustment

The story is told of a psychiatrist who once had a sign on his desk which read, "If you have problems, tell me about them. If you don't, please tell me how you do it." Even though the story may be fictional, the significance of the statement on the sign cannot be disputed. It is common for all of us to have problems which grow out of our everyday activities and which affect our adjustment.

A Definition of Adjustment

Human beings are continuously engaged in adjusting to a variety of situations in an attempt to satisfy their needs and to maintain an emotional equilibrium that may be defined as a state of adjustment. They are not so much concerned with the satisfaction of the physiological and safety needs (Figure 12-2, page 302), as with the satisfaction of the needs for belongingness, esteem, and self-realization. It is the frustration of these latter needs that causes most of the problems of adjustment; and since the satisfaction of the needs for belongingness, esteem, and self-realization is largely dependent upon other persons, particularly those persons in positions of authority, it is important for supervisors to understand the nature of adjustment and maladjustment.

Surrogate – substitute parent

Although it is common to describe behavior in terms of opposites or extremes, adjustment, like intelligence, is not something that a person either has or does not have. It varies by degrees from one person to another. Adjustment also varies from one hour or day to the next. While most of us remain sufficiently adjusted to our social environments and to ourselves to function effectively on the job and away from the job, we often deviate from our normal pattern of adjustment as we are confronted with problem situations. Since adjustment is measured by degrees rather than kind, one may ask if it is possible to define "good adjustment" or "mental health."

One way of describing mental health is to describe mentally healthy people. The basic characteristics of people with good mental health, according to one authoritative source are: (1) they feel comfortable about themselves, (2) they feel right about other people, and (3) they are able to meet the demands of life. Some of the specific attitudes, feelings, and behaviors that are ordinarily considered are described in Figure 16-1. In studying these descriptive characteristics, it should be remembered that just one characteristic by itself cannot be taken as evidence of good mental

Figure 16-1
SOME OF THE CHARACTERISTICS OF PEOPLE WITH GOOD MENTAL HEALTH

1 *They feel comfortable about themselves.*

2 *They feel right about other people.*

3 *They are able to meet the demands of life.*

They are not bowled over by their own emotions—by their fears, anger, love, jealousy, guilt or worries.	They are able to give love and to consider the interests of others.	They do something about their problems as they arise.
They can take life's disappointments in their stride.	They have personal relationships that are satisfying and lasting.	They accept their responsibilities.
They have a tolerant, easy-going attitude towards themselves as well as others; they can laugh at themselves.	They expect to like and trust others, and take it for granted that others will like and trust them.	They shape their environment whenever possible; they adjust to it whenever necessary.
They neither under-estimate nor over-estimate their abilities.	They respect the many differences they find in people.	They plan ahead but do not fear the future.
They can accept their own shortcomings.	They do not push people around, nor do they allow themselves to be pushed around.	They welcome new experiences and new ideas.
They have self-respect.	They can feel they are part of a group.	They make use of their natural capacities.
They feel able to deal with most situations that come their way.	They feel a sense of responsibility to their neighbors and fellow men.	They set realistic goals for themselves.
They get satisfaction from the simple, every-day pleasures.		They are able to think for themselves and make their own decisions.
		They put their best effort into what they do, and get satisfaction out of doing it.

Source: *Mental Health Is 1-2-3.* Copyright 1951 by The National Association for Mental Health, 10 Columbus Circle, New York, New York. Reproduced with permission.

health, nor the lack of any one as evidence of mental illness. Instead the pattern of behavior should be judged against all three basic characteristics.

Throughout the course of a day even the best adjusted person is likely to have a few moments when he does not feel "quite right." He may be mildly depressed for a short period, he may experience a conflict over certain aspects of his work, or he may be frustrated because of temporary inability to solve an important problem. These and similar experiences are quite normal. Thus, good adjustment, as illustrated by Figure 16-1, does not imply freedom from all of life's problems but, rather, an emotionally mature orientation toward life that enables the individual to solve his problems constructively and to "weather life's storms" as he encounters them in his daily life. Even the best adjusted person is not free of problems, but he is usually able to handle his problems in such a way that his emotional equilibrium is restored quickly.

Problem Employees Are Employees with Problems

The person in a managerial or supervisory position soon learns that there are some individuals whose behavior at work reveals that they are having problems of adjustment that go beyond those that the average person experiences. Chronic absenteeism, accidents, turnover, grievances, alcoholism, and other types of problems including the many different forms of job dissatisfaction that are found in employment situations may be explained, at least in part, by emotional disturbance. Similarly, the worrier, the crank, the bully, the chronic complainer, and the other types of "problem employees" that frequently demand the supervisor's attention are people who are having difficulties in adjusting to the world about them. In most instances these individuals are also problems to themselves and feel uncomfortable about their own behavior. This fact indicates that the troublesome behavior of others has its roots in something deeper than a "desire to be a nuisance" or "sheer cussedness" which, unfortunately, are ways that supervisors often view maladjusted persons. A supervisor's knowledge of the psychological process of adjustment may then serve as a basis for understanding the problems that he may have with employees.

The Psychodynamics of Adjustment

It was noted earlier that human beings are engaged continuously in the process of satisfying needs and maintaining an emotional equilibrium. While there are minor fluctuations occurring all the time, one may periodically suffer a more severe disturbance that may last for a relatively short or long period of time. Basically, the disturbances center around one's needs and the effects that the environment has on the individual's ability to satisfy them. Two major types of processes involving one's needs and behavior related to their satisfaction will be examined briefly.

Frustration. In the discussion in Chapter 12, the various categories of human needs were examined with special attention to Maslow's five categories: physiological needs, security, belongingness, esteem, and self-actualization. In the study of any one of these needs, it is hypothesized that the need is accompanied by a drive or tension (imbalance) that results in a person's behavior being directed toward a goal that will satisfy the need and thus reduce the drive or tension. This sequence of events may be diagrammed as follows:

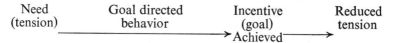

Need (tension)	Goal directed behavior	Incentive (goal)	Reduced tension
		Achieved	

One has only to examine his own daily life, however, to realize that need satisfaction does not always follow the above pattern. The path to the goal is often blocked as shown below.

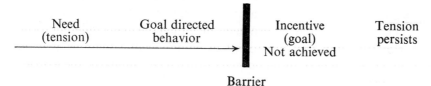

Need (tension)	Goal directed behavior	Incentive (goal) Not achieved	Tension persists

Barrier

As a result of failure to reach the goal, tension or imbalance will continue to persist until the barrier is surmounted or until a substitute goal is found that satisfies the need. The barriers to need satisfaction may be either external or internal. Some external barriers or obstacles to the satisfaction of needs are encountered by many employees in the form of discriminatory practices, hostile supervisors, monotonous jobs, unpleasant working conditions, economic insecurity, and similar situations. Some of the possible internal barriers that may frustrate the employee are poor habits and inadequate personality or aptitude for a particular job. A perceived inadequacy (imaginary barrier) is just as real to the person who sees himself this way as an actual barrier, substantiating the fact that in human affairs reality is a matter of personal interpretation.

Where the desire to reach a particular goal is strong and the barrier is another individual, it is quite common to find the frustrated individual engaging in some type of *aggressive* behavior toward the person creating the barrier which may range from gossiping about the frustrator to making an actual physical attack upon him. Although the manner in which frustrated individuals respond depends largely on their personality makeup, aggression is a common type of reaction to frustration.

Other reactions to frustration are *regression* (a return to childish actions), *fixation* (persisting in a type of behavior that is not adaptive), and *resignation* (giving up). While these are all symptoms of frustration, they tell us nothing about the cause of the frustration which can only be determined by a better understanding of the individual — his needs, his actual and perceived barriers, and his feelings. It is only through increased understanding on the part of superiors and fellow employees that the individual concerned may be helped in obtaining relief from the frustrating situation. It is clear that punishment only aggravates a state of frustration.

It should be recognized, however, that barriers may be temporary, that there are often ways around them, and that frequently one may be assisted in selecting satisfying alternative goals where barriers will not be encountered. For example, the individual who has a strong need to lead others and aspires to be a manager might have his needs satisfied if he were a first-line supervisor or an informal leader (a substitute goal).

Conflict. In frustrating situations we have seen that the person has no adequate response that will enable him to overcome the barrier. In a conflict situation, however, too many ways of responding may be available to him with the result that he is unable to decide which course of action to take. The employee who has an urge to ask his boss for a promotion and yet is afraid to do so is experiencing a conflict. The urge to ask because of the chances that he might be promoted and the fear of being told he is not qualified represent forces tugging at each other. The employee is in a sense being pulled in two directions — a characteristic of conflict situations.

Needless to say, frustration and conflict are present in our everyday lives and are usually dealt with successfully. However, where frustration and conflict persist and an individual's state of emotional adjustment is affected, some type of assistance is in order. In the discussion that follows, the symptoms that are indicative of major and minor disturbances in an individual will be described.

Symptoms of Emotional Problems

The manager or supervisor should be aware of some of the major symptoms of emotional problems in order that he can take appropriate action to provide assistance to the individual who may be in need of help. Some of the common symptoms of adjustment problems have already been mentioned. There are other more complex symptoms, however, that should be recognized as indicators that some type of help is needed. In some instances help may be given in the form of a brief talk with the individual; whereas, in other instances professional assistance may be required. The following discussion of symptoms progresses from those that are fairly common and are indicative of problems of a less serious nature to those that occur less frequently and reveal that the individual has serious problems.

Common Symptoms

All of us are subject to situations that produce frustration and conflict and we usually react in ways that are considered "normal." The behavior is viewed as normal because it is typical of that of a large segment of the population. This statistical concept of normality is not the only view of normality, but it is frequently used. For the purposes of this discussion, it is important to indicate the types and frequencies of behaviors that may be expected among large numbers of employees. Anxiety and defense mechanisms are the symptoms of emotional problems that will be seen most frequently.

Anxiety. Anxiety is a term commonly used to describe the response of the person who senses himself to be in danger. When anxiety exists, as contrasted to the existence of fear, the source of danger cannot be clearly identified, and usually the individual is not consciously aware of being in danger. Anxiety may account for various employee behaviors that are often misunderstood and misinterpreted. For example, resistance to change is fundamentally caused by the anxiety that arises from a proposed change in job, work method, or merely the relocation of a desk. Employees who resist changes, therefore, are not going out of their way to be "difficult" but, rather, are threatened or frightened at the prospects of a change. Unfortunately, anxiety affects managers and supervisors as well as employees. Their anxieties often lead to failure to delegate and to a distrust of those employees who exhibit any ambition.

Anxiety is accompanied by physical symptoms similar to those that one characteristically associates with fear, such as trembling, nausea, a pounding heart, and dryness in the throat. As a result of the physiological effect that anxiety has on the body, its persistence can lead to psychosomatic illnesses.

Studies show that almost 50 per cent of all people seeking medical attention today are suffering from ailments brought about or made worse by such emotional factors as prolonged worry, anxiety, or fear. Emotional tensions often play a prominent role in certain kinds of heart and circulatory disorders, especially high blood pressure; joint and muscular pains; skin disorders; and some allergies.[1]

Thus anxiety is not only unpleasant but may have serious physical effects on the body. In the interests of good physical and emotional health, managers and supervisors should do all that they can to reduce anxiety. It should not be inferred, however, that anxiety is always undesirable or indicative of maladjustment. A moderate degree of anxiety can serve as a drive to overcome shortcomings and is relatively harmless.

Defense mechanisms. Defense mechanisms are unconscious reactions that help to preserve one's self-concept from the psychological pain of embarrassment, defeat, or failure. Three major types of defense mechanisms are aggressive reactions, withdrawal reactions, and substitute reactions.

Aggressive reactions, as noted earlier, are common reactions to frustration. *Withdrawal reactions* include excessive daydreaming, engaging in childlike behavior, complaining that "things aren't like they used to be," or pushing unpleasant thoughts or feelings out of conscious awareness.

Most of the time aggressive and withdrawal reactions are not adequate for restoring equilibrium. *Substitute reactions,* involving a lowering of ambitions or the accepting of substitute goals, are more common, and they constitute a more satisfactory method of adjustment for the individual and for society. Common substitute reactions are compensation, rationalization, and projection. Most instances of *compensation* are those in which the person overreacts in the same general area in which he perceives himself to be inferior. For example, the individual who has little schooling and is concerned over it may use big words and complicated language in an effort to impress others. Another form of compensation is that in which the individual selects and attempts to achieve substitute goals to make up for his weaknesses. The borderline employee, for example, may become the star on the company baseball team.

Rationalization involves the giving of false reasons for one's behavior in order to preserve his own self-esteem and the approval of others. The employee who aspires to be a foreman but was passed over may say to himself and others, "It would hardly have been worth the small difference in pay." *Projection* is the act of blaming others for our own thoughts,

---

[1]*Emotions and Physical Health* (New York: Metropolitan Life Insurance Company, 1955).

feelings, or behavior. Some employees continually blame others because they sincerely believe that they themselves are not at fault. Of the substitute reactions, projection is the least desirable since it involves distorting an important part of the real world. In its most extreme form, projection is a central part of the psychosis known as *paranoia*. To some degree, however, everyone has paranoid tendencies.

Defense mechanisms are common modes of behavior that are used by all persons in an unconscious effort to maintain their own self-respect and the approval of others. Unless used to an extreme degree, defensive behavior is considered normal. Although an individual's defensive behavior should not be pointed out to him directly, it is a symptom of frustration and conflict and should be recognized as such by the supervisor who desires to understand his employees.

Neurotic Behavior

At least 5 percent of the population suffers from a mild form of emotional disorder that may be called a *neurosis*. It may take several forms, but seldom is it so severe that the person must be hospitalized. Usually the person is able to carry on the functions of everyday life but at a reduced level of efficiency.

> Characteristically, the neurotic is an anxious, unhappy individual, easily upset, lacking self-reliance and self-confidence, and prone to minor physical complaints such as fatigue, headaches, and indigestion. He often feels helpless, insecure, inferior, and inadequate. In brief, the neurotic is a maladjusted person whose inadequate behavior, due to excessive stress, renders him partially incapacitated to handle the life situations confronting him with normal efficiency.[2]

Besides their general feeling of inadequacy and their emotionally disturbed condition, neurotics may also have specific abnormal behavior patterns, such as an anxiety neurosis, a phobia, an extreme concern over health, or other behavior patterns. In general, the neurotic becomes a nuisance to himself and to others. He may have trouble getting along with other people in the shop or office and be generally disagreeable. More frequently, however, he is a nuisance to himself by constantly punishing himself. As a result, a psychosomatic ailment such as an ulcer, high blood pressure, or asthma may develop.

Since alcohol is especially effective in producing an escape from feelings of insecurity and inferiority, many individuals who have neurotic

---

[2]Floyd L. Ruch, *Psychology and Life* (4th ed.; Chicago: Scott, Foresman & Company, 1953), p. 166.

tendencies are likely to turn to this as a source of strength and relief from their frustrations and conflicts. Industry is faced with the problem of alcoholism that, according to announcements of the National Association for Mental Health, is estimated to cost industry a billion dollars a year. Only in recent years has industry taken an active part in facing up to this problem. Leaders in business today have come to recognize that they pay a price for the alcoholic, but even more important, they can help in motivating an alcoholic to seek help.

There are many good company programs for dealing with alcoholism. Some provide medical and psychiatric services while others use local alcoholism clinics and Alcoholics Anonymous. The success in handling alcoholics is dependent upon taking positive action promptly. Levinson advises that:

> When such a problem arises, the alcoholic should be told that despite his likely denials, he has a problem. He should be told further that he must deal with the problem, either through established channels or on his own. If he does not seek professional help and becomes intoxicated again, he will lose his job. If he does seek professional help, and if his drinking continues to interfere with his job, he will be placed on sick leave according to whatever provisions the company has for any severe or chronic illness. When his physician says that he has recovered from his symptoms and is able to work again, then he will be permitted to return to his job.
>
> When the company moves to support the ego of the alcoholic by confronting him with reality and limiting his alternatives, this often moves him to seek help. However, the company must take its firm position early in the course of the developing symptom or its leverage as a force to motivate the man will be lost. When a man has become so addicted to alcohol that his job means little to him, company policy loses its usefulness.
>
> The policy enunciated here is similar to that for any serious illness that threatened the man or the organization. In most companies, such illnesses as tuberculosis or heart disease would be handled the same way. Thus the policy enunciated is neither harsh nor unkind, but simply uses reality as a basis for judgment and action.[3]

The supervisor may play an important role in such a program. If the supervisor realizes that the problem drinker is going to be offered help and not fired, he will be anxious to help as much as possible. Many companies, including Consolidated Edison of New York, Du Pont, Standard Oil of New Jersey, Eastman Kodak, and Allis-Chalmers, have had considerable success with their respective programs. Allis-Chalmers, for example, estimates that their program saves over $80,000 yearly just in reduced

---

[3]Harry Levinson, *Emotional Health in the World of Work* (New York: Harper & Row, 1964), p. 143.

absenteeism. Their absentee rate has been reduced from 8 to 3 percent, and the firing rate for alcoholics has been cut from 95 to 8 percent.[4]

Psychotic Behavior

The more extreme forms of emotional maladjustment are known as *psychoses.* While there are many different classifications, certain characteristics are common among the psychotic. They are likely to have *hallucinations* (see, hear, or feel something in the absence of any stimuli) or *delusions* (strong, persistent beliefs that are contrary to fact). Other indicators of severe emotional illness include depression, marked change in mood or behavior from one's normal behavior, and extreme or inappropriate behavior. When a supervisor or associate of an employee observes such symptoms as these, he should ask himself, "What does this behavior mean?" While he should not view every little quirk as a major problem, neither should the supervisor observe these behaviors for a long period without taking action. The medical division of the personnel department, or other personnel designated in company personnel policy manuals, should be contacted for special instructions on how to proceed with the problem. They ordinarily will refer the employee to a psychiatrist, clinical psychologist, or mental hygiene clinic after consulting with the individual's family physician. In many instances the employee may be treated successfully as an outpatient, but in some cases it is desirable that he be hospitalized.

With improved methods of treatment, many individuals can be cured sufficiently to be released from the mental hospital and returned to work within a short period of time. This often poses a problem for the personnel manager who is faced with the problem of placing a new applicant or a former employee who has a history of emotional illness on a job. Personnel managers should recognize the responsibility that they have to society to give these individuals as careful consideration as they would to the individual who has a history of physical illness. On the other hand, personnel managers must also recognize their responsibilities to management in developing a sound and stable work force. While these individuals may pose a dilemma, there are often many jobs in which they may be placed. The advice and assistance of available medical personnel in evaluating their probable job success and adjustment should be sought if it is not offered. In many instances close liaison is established between the hospital and the employing company to insure that the job will facilitate the former

---

[4]"Industry and the Alcoholic," *Management Review*, Vol. 55, No. 3 (March, 1966), pp. 30–32.

patient's adjustment rather than hinder it. Forty of the Veterans Administration psychiatric hospitals, for example, have a special program whereby they place former patients in suitable jobs and maintain liaison with the individual's supervisor to insure that the hospital's therapeutic recommendations are carried out.[5] Such a program, in fact, provides the employer with individuals who have been fully tested, evaluated, and classified by psychiatrists. The company thus knows more about these people than it does about its other "more normal" employees who bring an assortment of unidentified problems with them to the job.

Facilitating Employee Adjustment

From the time that the employee is recruited until he is separated from the company, a large part of his life is influenced by the personnel policies and procedures of management, the supervisor for whom he works, and the relationships that he has with fellow employees. All of these influences, together with his past and present life experiences, determine his adjustment to his job as well as to other areas of his daily life. By establishing policies and procedures that facilitate employee adjustment, the company will not only contribute to the mental health of the employee but will also find itself in a favorable position from the standpoint of efficiency, absenteeism, turnover, and labor relations. Training supervisory personnel in human relations skills, including counseling methods, and in the making of referrals are further contributions that a company can make to employee adjustment.

Organizational Policies and Procedures

All of the personnel policies and procedures of a company affect the adjustment of employees in some manner. To be sure, the effects of a particular policy or procedure may range from very desirable to very undesirable, depending upon such factors as the personality makeup of an individual, his state of emotional adjustment at the time, and the importance of the policy or procedure to his life on the job. Attempts to generalize about the effects that any one policy or procedure will have on a particular individual would be risky. There are, however, certain major areas of personnel management that are generally viewed as having an important relationship to employee adjustment.

---

[5]Josef E. Teplow and Reuben J. Margolin, "The Former Mental Patient: An Untapped Labor Source," *Personnel*, Vol. 38, No. 1 (January–February, 1961), pp. 17–24.

Communication. The adjustment of employees depends in large part on their needs being fulfilled and upon their freedom from tension created by uncertainty. Where there is effective communication up and down the line between management and employees, the needs and concerns of employees may be made known to management with the result that appropriate action can be taken. Effective communication between management and employees, as described in Chapter 13, in which employees are kept advised about their employment status, future company plans, problems in production, and the many other aspects of their jobs, contributes to their adjustment.

Grievance handling. A system for filing grievances is a means of expressing complaints in a manner that is acceptable to management, the union, and the employees. The fact that a standard procedure exists contributes to the employee's mental health even if he never uses it. It is assurance to him that he can voice his complaints without fear of reprisal by management. It gives him a freedom that is based upon the principle that the individual in a democratic society has the right to be heard. If an employee files a grievance report, he knows that he will be heard even if it may be established later by a union-management committee that his complaint was unfounded or of little significance. The opportunity to express one's complaints in socially acceptable ways facilitates adjustment. Because of the importance of a grievance handling system in the nonunion as well as the union organization, this function of personnel management is considered in detail in Chapter 17.

Mental health programs. Many companies have wisely extended their health education programs to include a coverage of the principles and practices of good mental health. By means of films, lectures, and discussions, managers, supervisors, and employees can be provided with practical information that will help them in understanding their own problems as well as those of their co-workers. In recent years a wide variety of pamphlets has been prepared by various health agencies as well as by private companies, and many of them are found in reading racks established for employees. Such pamphlets are designed to indicate that common problems, such as those illustrated in Figure 16-2 from *The Worry-Go-Round*, should not be overlooked. Since major emotional problems can be precipitated by common occurrences such as those pictured, it is important that everyone concerned be aware of the fact that the everyday problems of everyday people at home and at work are deserving of attention. Correction of the situation that creates the problem appears to be the more fruitful approach. Prevention, as in the case of physical disease, is more economical than a cure. While it is hoped that managers would be motivated primarily by their interest in the employee's welfare, recent trends in workmen's compensation awards for emotional disturbance that is job related point to the need for prevention of emotional disturbances. A discussion of these trends may be found in Chapter 25.

Figure 16-2

THE WORRY-GO-ROUND

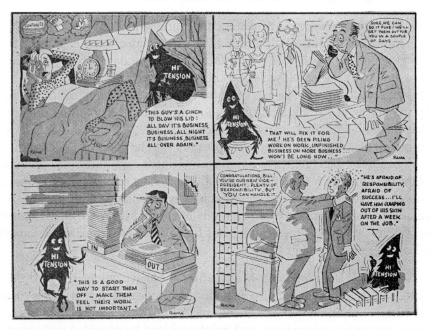

Source: *The Worry-Go-Round, How to Understand Your Everyday Tensions* (Hartford: The Connecticut Mutual Life Insurance Co., 1955). Reproduced with permission.

Many of the special publications for the businessman contain articles that are designed to promote interest in mental health and to provide practical suggestions on facilitating adjustment among executives and employees. One article, "How to Live with Job Pressure," includes advice by Dr. Robert H. Felix, Director of the National Institute of Mental Health, to those who are in business or are preparing for employment.

> Try to relate your job to a goal or purpose that is larger than your own narrow self-interest. In other words, don't let your pay check, or the next promotion, be your only motives for doing a good job.

Look for a challenge — even in the most routine and uninspiring sort of task.

It is natural and desirable to go as far as you can in your field. But don't overreach yourself. Every man has his limitations; know yours and stay within them.

Develop a pace to do your day's work, and, except in real emergencies, stick to it.

Don't waste today's energy stewing over yesterday's decisions.

Develop the kind of personal relations with your staff that will make it possible for you to blow your top occasionally without wrecking morale.

Don't take your business home with you every night.

Remember that you owe some time — and vitality — to your family.

Begin preparing now for retirement. Develop hobbies and outside interests.

Take at least one good vacation a year.

Don't build all of your relaxation around alcohol.

Don't badger your doctor for tranquilizing drugs.

Decide what philosophy of life can give ultimate meaning to your existence.[6]

These suggestions for withstanding job pressure should be followed as rigorously as one follows the principles of personal hygiene if one is to maintain an emotional equilibrium that will enable him to live a full and productive life.

Role of the personnel department. It is as true of the personnel department as it is of other departments that every action which it takes has some effect on the adjustment of one or more of the employees. There are, however, special areas in which the personnel department may contribute to employee adjustment, in addition to those mentioned above. In the recruiting and selection functions every effort should be made to detect those persons who are emotionally immature and are poor risks to withstand the normal job conditions. If an applicant is accepted, his assignment to a department should be based not only on his ability to meet the technical and skill requirements of the job but also on what is known about his personality characteristics and those of the supervisor to whom he will be assigned. Every possible effort should be made to match persons who will be compatible and cooperative. Although the nature of interpersonal relationships cannot be predicted with a high degree of success, attention given to this phase of placement can facilitate the adjustment of the supervisor and the employee to each other.

---

[6]Louis Cassels, "How to Live with Job Pressure," *Nation's Business*, Vol. 44, No. 9 (September, 1956), pp. 38–39.

The personnel department should establish training programs for managerial and supervisory personnel that include specific information about the problems of emotional adjustment, how to identify them through symptoms, and procedures for assisting employees with their problems. Such programs should include instruction in counseling techniques with opportunity to gain experience in using them through role playing.

Counseling by Supervisors

Many supervisors do not recognize the fact that some of their subordinates need to bring their problems to them and that they may be able to assist such subordinates with their problems. While many, if not most, supervisors would prefer not to be involved in such problems, it is apparent that both management and the employees expect them to serve as counselors, in addition to their other responsibilities. Since supervisors find it impossible to avoid some involvement in employees' problems, it is advisable that they become as skilled in counseling as possible. A good part of the skill is in knowing how far to go in the process and when and how to make a referral to professional persons. Helping employees who come for assistance with problems whose solutions are dependent upon more than mere information represents what is commonly referred to as counseling. Trying to "straighten out" problem employees who have the ability but for some reason are not able to use it effectively also calls for some type of counseling. While these two types of situations account for most of the counseling that supervisors will be called upon to do, it should be recognized that there are many types of situations in which the supervisor may be required to give some assistance even though professional counselors may be available.

Advantages and disadvantages. It should be recognized that there are advantages and disadvantages to the supervisor assuming the role of a counselor. The primary advantage is related to the fact that the supervisor has the opportunity to become well acquainted with his subordinates. He can learn the employee's pattern of judging, valuing, thinking, and feeling and, thus, can understand him better and even predict his behavior in many instances.

There are, however, many disadvantages to the supervisor assuming the role of a counselor. The daily interactions between the supervisor and his people may well lead to irritations and misunderstandings that will limit his effectiveness. His role as an authority figure may also make it difficult for him to be of assistance to an employee, especially if the employee has violated company rules or standards of good conduct. Similarly, the fact that the supervisor has status in the eyes of his subordinates may be a barrier to free and open communication about personal feelings. Finally, lack of training may well be a problem, although with training most supervisors can gain understandings about human problems and acquire skills for handling them.[7]

Counseling methods. In attempting to help an employee who has a problem, the supervisor may use a variety of counseling methods. All of them, however, depend upon active listening which, according to the message in Figure 16-3, is not easy for many persons. Sometimes the mere furnishing of information may prove to be the solution to what at first appeared to be a knotty problem. More frequently, however, the problem cannot be solved as easily as this because of frustrations or conflicts that

Figure 16-3

Source: *You Need Help, Charlie Brown* by Charles M. Schulz. © United Feature Syndicate, Inc., 1965. Reproduced with permission.

---

[7]Aaron Q. Sartain and Alton W. Baker, *The Supervisor and His Job* (New York: McGraw-Hill Book Company, 1965), pp. 286–292.

are accompanied by strong feelings such as fear, confusion, or hostility. In such cases the supervisor may be inclined to furnish advice to the employee and in most instances, but not necessarily all, advice-giving falls short of what is required in the situation. The maximum degree of assistance can often be realized by the use of the *nondirective approach* in which the employee being counseled is permitted to have maximum freedom in determining the course of the interview.

Nondirective counseling. The importance of nonevaluative listening as a communication skill was described in Chapter 13. Nonevaluative listening is also one of the primary techniques used in nondirective counseling. Fundamentally, the approach is to listen, with understanding and without criticism or appraisal, to the problem as it appears to the troubled person. He is encouraged through the counselor's attitude and reaction to what he says (or does not say) to express his feelings without fear of shame, embarrassment, or reprisal. As the interview progresses, the counselor should strive to reflect the feelings of the employee by restating them in his (the counselor's) own words. For example, if the employee has discussed several situations which indicate that he feels his supervisor has treated him unfairly, the counselor at the conclusion of this particular statement would probably say, "You feel that you have been treated unfairly." While questions are used at appropriate places in the interview, the interviewer should use general questions that stimulate the employee to pursue his examination of those areas which are troubling him. Questions that call for "Yes" or "No" answers on the part of the employee should be avoided.[8]

The following excerpts from an interview that a supervisor conducted with one of his employees illustrate the nondirective approach. In reading the interview excerpts particular attention should be given to: (1) the employee's release of pent-up feelings at the beginning of the interview, (2) the manner in which the supervisor reflects the employee's feelings and, (3) the insight into his problem that the employee gains as the interview progresses.

Supervisor: Joe, it's real good to see you again. I understand you have something on your mind.

Employee: Oh Boy! Have I got something on my mind! I'm burned up! There's a reason why I'm upset! I wouldn't be sitting here if I

---

[8]For a detailed discussion of nondirective techniques, see Carl R. Rogers, *Counseling and Psychotherapy* (Boston: Houghton Mifflin Company, 1942), and his *Client-Centered Therapy* (Boston: Houghton Mifflin Company, 1951). Specific applications of this method to business are discussed in Norman R. F. Maier, *Psychology in Industry* (3rd ed.; Boston: Houghton Mifflin Company, 1965), Chapter 20.

wasn't upset! Believe me I'm upset — burned up — mad — angry. It was a real bad trick you guys pulled last week.

Supervisor: You want to tell me about it?

Employee: Well, I don't think it will do much good. I've had this happen before. Put that other engineer in over my head and he failed to see that I've been here twenty-five years. The guy came right out of college, is single, and he gets it. I just wonder why it pays to work your head off. I really mean it.

Supervisor: This really hurts you?

Employee: Of course it hurts me — burns me up inside. I'm emotionally upset . . . I just don't know what you are up to — I can't get a feel for it — no help from you at all — none!

Supervisor: There's the feeling that somehow we're doing something here to you, or just kind of —

Employee: Sure, that's what I'm looking for, and do I get it. No! Not a bit! I don't say it's all your fault. It might be your boss's — like, you know, you're just taking what he says and bringing it back to me.

Supervisor: In other words, as you think it through, then it might not just be me that you're griping at, but you can see — it's the system.

Employee: Yeah, that's what it is! It's the system that's wrong. I've told you that before — you just didn't choose to see it.

Supervisor: I should have seen it then and I didn't.

The interview continues for a few minutes, and we look in again:

Employee: But you know something — I've got a feeling that the basic problem is — maybe rather than worrying about that guy, I should be learning some of these new trends myself.

Supervisor: So you've been holding on too long to this stuff here that hasn't any use.

Employee: Yeah, that's probably it.

Supervisor: Gee, I'm real glad you say this because I felt this way too and to have you really feel that this would be a good direction for you makes me feel real good about you.

Employee: Well, it's a thought I had and I don't say I developed it all by myself. My wife happened to mention it too and of course you know the reason I didn't do it before was that I felt I was just too damn old.

Supervisor: That's another one of the things that keeps cropping up here.

Employee: You can say this — you're a lot younger.

Supervisor: In other words, I can't really understand how you feel when you get to be your age. How old are you?

Employee: Forty-five.

Supervisor: You kind of feel like you're crossing over the bridge, huh? Critical time for you?

Employee: Right! This is a basic problem. But my wife convinced me that some guys go to college when they're forty-four. If they can do it, maybe I can do it.[9]

---

[9]Lawrence M. Brammer and Everett L. Shostrom, *Therapeutic Psychology* (Englewood Cliffs, New Jersey: Prentice-Hall, Inc., 1960), pp. 419–421. Reproduced with permission.

Values of nondirective counseling. The free expression that is encouraged in the nondirective approach tends to reduce tensions and frustrations. After the employee has had the opportunity to release his pent-up feelings through catharsis, he is in a better position to view the problem area more objectively and with a problem-solving attitude. The permissive atmosphere allows him to try to "work through" the entanglements of the problem and to see it in a clearer perspective. This approach has proved valuable many times in counseling "problem employees." At first such persons are likely to be on the defensive and to be critical of everything and everybody. Before the session is over, however, they often realize that their own behavior could be improved. The chances for improved behavior are found to be much greater under such circumstances than if the individual is threatened with punishment or admonished to "improve." Similarly, in other types of problem areas it has been found that if a decision is made by the client or interviewee he is more likely to carry through with the action than if a solution is given to him.

It should not be inferred, however, that counseling must be either directive or nondirective. Many counselors use a combination of techniques ranging all the way from the most directive to the most nondirective. As in the case of deciding which leadership approach to use (as discussed in Chapter 14), the effective counselor is one who is *flexible* in his use of counseling approaches. There are times during a discussion when an employee desires information and/or should be given it. This calls for the directive approach in which the information is given to him. When he expresses strong feelings about some problem, however, it may be that the exact nature of the problem is not recognized and that the employee probably would not appreciate nor benefit from advice. The nondirective approach has been found to be particularly effective in such instances in helping employees to clarify their problems and work toward solutions.

Use of Professional Counselors

Since he may not have the skill or time in which to handle the more complex personal problems that employees may bring to him, the supervisor should be able to recognize the need for making referrals to trained counselors in the personnel department or medical department. Such referrals should be made on the basis of the severity and complexity of the problem. Likewise, if the problem area is one over which the supervisor has little or no influence, as for example the employee's family relationships, supervisors are usually instructed to refer the employee to the medical or personnel department where specialists are available or may be contacted. Needless to say, the act of referring an employee for professional assistance requires considerable skill and tact. In their book, *Mental Health in Industry*, Dr. Alan A. McLean and Dr. Graham C. Taylor offer some helpful recommendations about how to make referrals:

> A word about how the foreman should refer an employee to a psychiatric consultant. Perhaps it is easier to say how it should *not* be done. Sometimes the foreman is tempted to tell a man that an appointment has been made with the psychiatrist and that he is to go to his office at such and such a time. The employee arrives feeling defensive, saying that he is not "nuts," and bearing resentment against both the psychiatrist and the foreman. Little good comes from such a referral. A foreman must speak to the employee about attitudes that he and the employee *both* recognize as inadequacies. Usually the matter for concern is a recent change in emotional reaction, in production, or in the employee's relationship to the work group. The foreman may refer to this change and suggest that perhaps the worker's health is impaired and that a talk with someone in the medical department is indicated. The goal is to motivate the employee to visit the medical department in the interests of his own health.
>
> If referral for help is made in terms of these changed reactions, it tends to be accepted with gratitude. When the employee has seemed depressed and unhappy, the foreman may suggest that he check with the medical department to see a doctor there particularly skilled in working with people who have problems that get them down in the dumps. If the employee seems to demonstrate an increasing tension and anxiety that intereferes with production, a frank discussion with such a person on the part of the foreman, pointing out that his nervous condition seems to be getting in the way of the job, is in order. More particularly, it is in order when the foreman can suggest steps to be taken to overcome the condition. These include the suggestion that the medical department has a consultant available whose speciality is helping people who are tense and nervous. Such a suggestion is rarely interpreted as an accusation that he is mentally ill.[10]

Several companies, including IBM, DuPont, American Cyanamid, and Metropolitan Life Insurance, employ full-time psychiatrists or clinical psychologists to assist employees with emotional disturbances. If a company is not able to support such qualified personnel on its own payroll, it should at least make referrals to clinical psychologists or psychiatrists through the medical staff working in cooperation with the individual's family physician. This is advisable because organic causes for an employee's illness should be considered first before psychotherapy is started. Furthermore, individuals with emotional problems requiring the assistance of professional persons should be referred to a specific individual whose qualifications are known, for there are many quacks ready to "serve" the

---

[10]Alan A. McLean and Graham C. Taylor, *Mental Health in Industry* (New York: McGraw-Hill Book Company, 1958), pp. 143–144.

unwary. Since both clinical psychologists and psychiatrists specialize in the treatment of emotional problems, professional competency should be the main consideration in engaging the services of a specialist in this area. This can be assessed most validly by those working in the field. The names of competent clinical psychologists and psychiatrists can best be obtained from the local mental health agency, the social welfare agency, the medical society, or a college or university department of psychology and/or psychiatry.

Building Good Morale

The emotional adjustment of the individual employee is not only essential from the standpoint of his feeling of well being and his job performance but also from the standpoint of the effect that his attitudes and feelings have on those who are working around him. His fellow workers are likely to respond to his reactions to frustration; and, as a result, their own feelings of frustration may be intensified. Because of this influence it is important for management to be alert to any situations that will affect the spirit and harmony of the group, which is frequently referred to as morale.

Each authority has a somewhat different definition of the word *morale*. Some prefer to restrict the use of the term to the group and describe a group with high morale as one in which such qualities as team spirit, enthusiasm, and achievement of progress toward a common goal are evident. Others extend the use of the term to include an individual employee's attitude toward his job, the degree of satisfaction that he obtains from it, and his personal adjustment. Individual employee attitudes and group morale are so interdependent that attempts to isolate them often prove quite difficult. In the following discussion, therefore, the word "morale" is used to cover all of the individual and group factors mentioned above.

Importance of Morale

The importance of morale to the successful operation of any endeavor has been clearly revealed in a variety of situations from the waging of war to the manufacturing of a product. The morale of his troops has long been a major concern of the military leader who recognizes its importance in the accomplishment of a mission. Merely providing the material and teaching the skills with which to fight are not sufficient. Such qualities as enthusiasm, personal satisfaction, and a willingness to work together — which may be considered as components of morale — are likewise essential for the continued success of any organization, whether its purpose be of a military or business nature.

Morale and productivity. The fact that groups with high group loyalty tend to be more productive should not be construed to mean that improvements in morale will automatically be reflected in higher productivity. It is possible to have groups with high loyalty that are not productive; and, conversely, groups with little or no loyalty may be quite productive. This does not mean that employee morale is of little significance. In fact, absenteeism and turnover — two major personnel problems — are often affected by it.

There is likely to be less absenteeism where morale is high. Employees who find their jobs interesting and challenging and the working conditions and relationships with supervisors and fellow workers pleasant will be less likely to stay away from the job than those who work under less favorable conditions. Turnover, like absenteeism, can often be related to low morale. Some of the reasons employees gave for quitting in exit interviews conducted in 48 companies were: dissatisfaction with pay, transportation, promotion opportunities, and working conditions; poor health; job insecurity; friction with co-workers; poor housing or excessive rents; personal unhappiness as affected by job experience; lack of ability of supervisor; broken promises by supervisor; lack of confidence in management; company disinterest in employee welfare; lack of freedom of communication with higher levels; poor recreational facilities; method of wage payment; and other problems.[11] These are among the typical factors that are covered in a morale survey.

Morale and public relations. The attitudes of employees toward the company quickly become common knowledge in the communities where employees work and live. As they associate with friends, neighbors, and businessmen, employees reveal their attitudes — both favorable and unfavorable. The criticism expressed by a few disgruntled employees to their friends can spread through a community and offset the best efforts of management to promote goodwill. As a result, customers who sense that morale is so low that labor disputes are likely to develop may hesitate to order the company's products for fear that the quality may be poor or that delivery will not be made on time. Low morale is also likely to affect the recruitment of new personnel. Desirable persons may not apply for jobs if they feel that they would also be unhappy if employed by the company.

---

[11]F. J. Smith and W. A. Kerr, "Turnover Factors as Assessed by the Exit Interview," *Journal of Applied Psychology*, Vol. 37, No. 5 (October, 1953), pp. 352–355.

Employee morale sooner or later will have its effects upon company relations with the union. When morale is good, the union often does not enjoy as strong a bargaining position as when morale is poor because employees are more likely to give their primary allegiance to the company. When employees are dissatisfied, it is easier for union leaders to gain the loyalty and support of the employees and to recruit new members. The type of experiences a company has with unions is thus determined to some extent by its own policies and procedures, which can have an important effect upon morale.

Factors in Morale

Morale is not something that can be dictated by management or built overnight. Employee morale is developed over a period of time as a result of sound personnel policies and procedures, good supervisory practices, and other influencing factors. The factors influencing morale should, therefore, receive careful attention by management, and continuous positive efforts should be made to build good morale. While every effort should be made to correct any undesirable conditions, the emphasis should be on positive action to develop the type of work environment that will contribute to good morale.

Satisfying employee needs and wants. The development of high morale depends upon taking action to satisfy as many of the employee's needs and wants as are consistent with the goals of management. Human needs and ways of satisfying them through the job were considered in Chapter 12. It was noted that much of an individual's motivation is unconscious; that is, he is not clearly aware of his own needs. *Wants*, on the other hand, are the conscious desires of individuals for those things or conditions that they feel will give them satisfaction. Although an individual's wants go beyond the area of employment, the nature of the employee's wants as far as his job is concerned is of particular interest to management in the development of good morale.

Within the past quarter century a number of surveys have been conducted to determine what satisfactions people seek from their jobs. The type of job a person has, the economic and social conditions at the time of the survey, the length of time on the job, and the personal factors such as age, intelligence, education, and personality all appear to have some effect on the survey results. In some surveys wages rank fairly high in the list of what people say they want in a job; in others it is of lesser importance. The same is true of security, working conditions, and other factors in job satisfaction. It appears that as wages approach the level that the employees desire or feel that employers can pay, other factors increase in importance. Because of the differences found among the various studies, therefore, it is not possible to make any conclusive statements about the priority of wants for employees.[12]

How supervisors view employee wants. One of the problems in determining the nature of employee wants is that management often relies on the judgments of supervisors rather than relying on the opinions of employees as gained from questionnaires. The findings from one study involving 24 plants revealed the necessity for obtaining impressions firsthand. In this study foremen were asked to rate the ten key factors which they considered to be the most important worker desires. Workers were asked to rate the same ten factors. A matching of the two lists is presented in Figure 16-4.

Figure 16-4
HOW FOREMEN AND WORKERS RATE
TEN JOB CONDITIONS

Job conditions	Worker rating	Foremen rating
Full appreciation of work done	1st	8th
Feeling "in" on things	2nd	10th
Sympathetic help on personal problems	3rd	9th
Job security	4th	2nd
Good wages	5th	1st
"Work that keeps you interested"	6th	5th
Promotion and growth in company	7th	3rd
Personal loyalty to workers	8th	6th
Good working conditions	9th	4th
Tactful disciplining	10th	7th

Source: William C. Menninger and Harry Levinson, *Human Understanding in Industry* (Chicago: Science Research Associates, 1956), p. 12. Based on data from *Foreman Facts* (New York: Labor Relations Institute, December 5, 1946.) Reproduced with permission of Science Research Associates and Labor Relations Institute.

The discrepancy between what the foreman rates as important to employees and what the employees themselves rate as important varies considerably. These differences between employee ratings and foremen ratings

---

[12]For a summary table of several studies, see Table 11–II in Thomas F. Harrell, *Industrial Psychology* (Revised edition; New York: Holt, Rinehart & Winston, Inc., 1958), p. 268.

reveal the importance of obtaining information about employee wants through more objective methods.

Studies of women's wants. Now that almost one third of the total labor force in the United States is made up of women it is realized that increasing attention should be given to any differences that may exist between the sexes. Probably the greatest difference lies in the area of attitudes and the manner in which they are expressed. Women seem to have greater facility than men in expressing themselves about such things as cleanliness of working conditions, pleasantness of social relationships on the job, and how their supervisors treat them. They tend to verbalize loyalty more than men but show less interest in pay, benefit programs, and opportunities for advancement.[13] While many of the employed women provide a supplemental income for the family and thus may have less interest in pay and advancement, even the career-oriented woman is primarily interested in working with a congenial group under an understanding and appreciative supervisor. A number of companies have found, for example, that the women who receive relatively little recognition at work are the ones most likely to be absent and that when women are upgraded or given more recognition as employees they are more regular in attendance.[14] The fact that such differences between men and women in attitudes toward various aspects of the job have been discovered should not lead one to the conclusion that these attitudes are inborn and unchanging. It is quite possible that, as more women are employed and as their role in business and industry continues to change, studies will likewise reflect some changes in attitudes as well.

Appraisal of Morale

Managers and supervisors as well as members of the personnel department should assess the state of morale among the employees on a continuous basis in order that any conditions that are disturbing morale may be corrected. Because of their frequent face-to-face contacts with the employees, supervisors appear to be in a good position to assess morale. However, evidence from experimental studies indicates that supervisors are not particularly effective in assessing the morale of subordinates as a group, where their estimates were compared with morale questionnaires

---

[13]B. B. Gardner and D. G. Moore, *Human Relations in Industry* (4th ed.; Homewood, Illinois: Richard D. Irwin, Inc., 1964), Chapter 18.

[14]Harry W. Hepner, *Perceptive Management and Supervision* (Englewood Cliffs, New Jersey: Prentice-Hall, Inc., 1961), p. 361.

completed by employees.[15] Nevertheless, managers and supervisors should be alert to changes in the quantity and quality of production, waste, accidents, turnover, absenteeism, and grievances as indicators of possible changes in morale.

The responsibility for employee morale rests primarily with the managers and supervisors in each department; however, the personnel department is responsible for assessing morale and advising top management as to how it may be improved. The suggestion plan provides a method for obtaining information concerning employee attitudes and recommendations for improving working conditions and other factors affecting morale. Interviews also provide an excellent source of information about employee morale and the factors that influence it. In its interviews with employees, the personnel department can obtain information about employee morale and can also improve morale through assistance to employees in the solution of problems either directly or indirectly related to their jobs. Finally, the personnel department has many records on file that can yield information concerning morale. A periodic review of these personnel records, particularly those relating to absences, turnover, formal grievances, transfers, and similar personnel actions, may point out the need for changes and improvements in personnel policies and procedures. Comparisons made between different departments may reveal that special action is needed in some places more than in others. While it is not the responsibility of the personnel department to make needed changes, it should make pertinent information and assistance available to managerial personnel in order that they may carry out their functions properly.

Morale Surveys

Management has found that one of the best ways it can appraise employee morale is through surveys. These surveys are usually conducted on a company or plant-wide basis and usually involve the administration of a questionnaire or inventory that has been especially designed for the purpose. Such questionnaires are intended to measure employee opinions concerning various aspects of the company and their jobs. On the basis of information obtained from questionnaire surveys, management may then take action to change those conditions that make for poor morale or attempt to change employee attitudes toward them. Before attempting any type of questionnaire study, however, management should ask itself if it

---

[15]Thomas H. Jerdee, "Supervisor Perception of Work Group Morale," *Journal of Applied Psychology*, Vol. 48, No. 4 (August, 1964), pp. 259–262.

sincerely desires to find out how its employees feel and if it is willing to accept the unfavorable comments that it may receive without becoming vindictive. If management is able to answer these questions in the affirmative, it may then proceed with the planning phase of the survey.

Planning the Survey

Careful planning of the survey is essential to its success. The objectives of the survey should be clearly determined by management and discussed with representatives of the various groups concerned, namely supervisors, employees, and the union. The suggestions from these various groups, as well as from counselors and other members of the personnel department, can not only be helpful but also will serve to enlist the cooperation of the personnel involved and help guarantee the success of the survey.

The confidence and cooperation of the employees are especially important. Management can increase the confidence of employees in management's intentions for conducting a survey by giving assurances that the responses will be made on an anonymous basis and that no punitive action of any kind will be taken. It is also essential that employees be advised that the results will be published and that action will be taken to correct unsatisfactory conditions wherever possible.

The personnel department, which should have the major role in planning the survey, may decide to utilize the services of outside consultants. These consultants frequently perform all of the functions connected with a survey from the development of a questionnaire to the preparation of the final report. Because of their experience in conducting surveys, these consultants usually have a better understanding of the detailed procedures to be followed. Although the expense of using their services may seem unnecessary, an improperly planned and carelessly administered survey may create more morale problems than it helps to solve.

Designing the Questionnaire

Once the objectives have been determined and preliminary plans have been made, the next step is one of designing the questionnaire. The construction of the morale questionnaire requires that careful consideration be given to the subjects to be covered and the types of questions that will furnish the desired information about those subjects.

Subjects covered. In a morale survey it is desirable to cover all phases of the job situation that in some way are believed to be related to morale. One commercially available questionnaire used by several large companies is the *SRA Employee Inventory* (Form A).[16] This questionnaire contains 78 statements that sample 14 areas related to morale that are listed in Figure 16-5 on page 442. It is only through a coverage of all major areas that possible trouble spots can be detected. While surveys in the past tended to be concerned primarily with "happiness and contentment" items, the approach today is to give considerable attention to job-related policies, procedures, and practices — issues directly related to getting the job done.[17]

Types of questions. The questionnaire method of appraising morale may include different types of questions or items. Agree-disagree items, multiple-choice questions, a check list of items, and open-ended questions to which the respondent comments in his own words are commonly used. The *SRA Employee Inventory*, mentioned above, contains items to which the employee responds that he "agrees," "disagrees," or is "undecided." A few typical items from this inventory are:

If I have a complaint to make, I feel free to talk to someone up-the-line.

My boss sees that employees are properly trained for the job.

Changes are made here with little regard for welfare of employees.

Poor working conditions keep me from doing my best in my work.[18]

It should be recognized, however, that for many items it is difficult for respondents to answer the questions with an "agree" or "disagree." The employee often finds that he needs to "shade" his answer away from an extreme position. The use of a scale with four or five positions may be desirable.[19]

Administering the Questionnaire

The conditions under which the morale questionnaire is administered are of vital importance to the success of the survey and to the morale of the participants. The planning of the survey should give special attention to this phase in order that employees will be fully oriented and will understand the purpose of the survey. Some thought should also be given to the "timing" of the survey. It might not be too meaningful, for example, to

---

[16]Prepared by the Employee Attitude Research Group of the Industrial Relations Center, University of Chicago, and published by Science Research Associates, Inc., 259 East Erie Street, Chicago, Illinois, 1951.

[17]A. J. Schaffer, "The Attitude Survey as a Management Tool," *Personnel Administration*, Vol. 26, No. 6 (November–December, 1963), pp. 36–39.

[18]*Ibid.*, reproduced with permission of Science Research Associates, Inc.

[19]Stephen Habbe, *Follow Up Attitude Survey Findings*, Personnel Policy Study No. 181 (New York: National Industrial Conference Board, 1961).

Figure 16-5. RESULTS FROM USE OF SRA EMPLOYEE INVENTORY

ATTITUDE YARDSTICK TO MEASURE MORALE IN YOUR PLANT=HOW ONE COMPANY'S EMPLOYEES FEEL

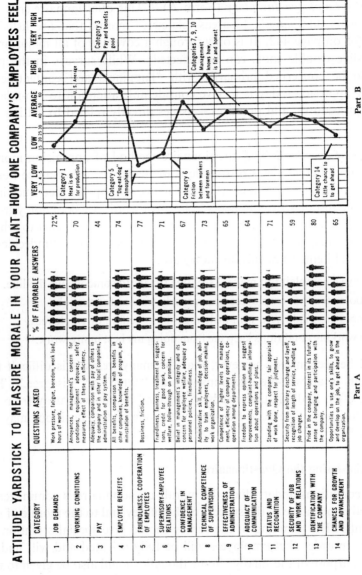

Part A

Attitudes of over 500,000 people in industry show how employees across the land feel about 14 major job-morale factors.

Source: David G. Moore and Robert K. Burns, "How Good Is Good Morale," *Factory Management and Maintenance*, Vol. 114, No. 2 (February, 1956), pp. 130–131. Reproduced with permission.

Part B

Profile chart takes national survey data as average. Against this norm, a metalworking plant plotted its employee's answers to a 14-category survey. They found over-all morale below average, pinpointed sore spots in some categories.

conduct a survey before or after a strike, a layoff, a wage reduction, or some similar event.

Several methods of administering questionnaires to employees are available. One method is to enclose a questionnaire with the paycheck, another is to mail the questionnaire to the employee's home, and another is to administer the questionnaire to employees in groups during working hours. Where it can be used properly, the group administration procedure is preferable to the other methods because it can give the worker a greater assurance of anonymity and insures that each employee will participate.

Utilizing the Results

It is highly important that management utilize the results of a survey as a basis for corrective action. Those employees who have gone to the trouble to complete the questionnaire will expect some type of action on the part of management and deserve to know what action is being taken by management or why action cannot be taken.

Interpreting survey results. Since the analysis and the interpretation of survey data require equally as much skill as is required in planning the survey, professional assistance can be used to good advantage if the data are to be analyzed and interpreted meaningfully.

A tabulation of results broken down by departments, male and female workers, hourly rated workers versus piece-rate workers, and other meaningful categories is the starting point in analyzing the data. The next step is to make comparisons with some standard. If data are available from previous surveys, comparisons can be made. Comparisons may also be made between departments of the company. Furthermore, where standardized questionnaires such as the *SRA Employee Inventory* are used, it is possible to compare the morale of personnel in one branch of a company with that of personnel in another branch. Because of the extensive use of this inventory, the opinions of employees in a company may also be compared against national figures. Data assembled from surveys of over 500,000 employees are represented in the cross-section of American workers whose attitudes are shown in Part A of Figure 16-5.

In Part B of Figure 16-5 results from a survey conducted in a metalworking plant are shown in profile form. Shown on the profile are interpretations of responses to some of the categories. In preparing the survey results for presentation to managers and supervisors, the findings should be interpreted in terms of possible specific causes of employee dissatisfaction. Such interpretations provide a basis for taking corrective action.

Companies that are operating on an international basis and employing personnel that are native to the various countries may wish to assess the attitudes and opinions of its workers. Interpretation of findings from a survey should take into consideration the effect that the particular culture will have on employee attitudes. In a study of employee attitudes in Japan and the United States, marked differences were found between native employees in the two countries, both of which are industrial. As an example, one item relating to employee identification with the company was answered as follows:

I think of my company as:	United States %	Japan %
1. The central concern in my life and of greater importance than my personal life.	1	9
2. A part of my life at least equal in importance to my personal life.	23	57
3. A place for me to work with management, during working hours, to accomplish mutual goals.	54	26
4. Strictly a place to work and entirely separate from my personal life.	23	6

There seems to be little doubt that Japanese participants are more willing to identify themselves positively with the company than are United States respondents. More than two thirds of the Japanese workers believed that their job lives were at least equally as important as their personal lives. The response pattern was almost reversed by United States participants.[20] It is also possible that companies operating on a national basis may find differences in employee opinions and attitudes that are affected by cultural differences of different geographical regions.

Some authorities believe that there are so many inadequacies in the employee opinion survey approach that it may prove of little value to the organization. Foegen believes that attitude surveys are suspect because (1) they are often too favorable, (2) there is possible bias on the part of those conducting them or interpreting them, and (3) only momentary opinions on specific issues are obtained.[21] The fact that the method is imperfect should not be discouraging, however, to those who recognize its limitations and use the findings with discretion.

Taking corrective action. The findings of the morale survey should be presented to department heads for their information and corrective action as well as to top management. It is not enough, however, to assume that advising a department head of deficiencies to be corrected is sufficient. It should be the responsibility of one individual or a committee to review progress continuously to insure that necessary action is being taken.

---

[20]Arthur M. Whitehill, Jr., "Cultural Values and Employee Attitudes: United States and Japan," *Journal of Applied Psychology*, Vol. 48, No. 1 (February, 1964), pp. 69–72.
[21]J. H. Foegen, "Why Attitudes Surveys Fail to Measure Attitudes," *Personnel*, Vol. 40, No. 2 (March/April, 1963), pp. 69–75.

Conferences with the managers and supervisors should be conducted in such a way as to facilitate corrective action and to minimize the possibility for "hard feelings." It should be recognized that the typical opinion survey bypasses the preferred channels of communication between employees and their supervisors and that this may result in some resentment by supervisors. Nevertheless, the opinion survey does provide a system for transmitting the type of opinions that employees have not felt free to discuss with their supervisors and/or the supervisors were unwilling or unable to pass on to higher management.

As corrective action is taken, employees should be advised through company publications, memoranda, and other media that such action is a result of the survey findings. This proof to the participants that their ideas and opinions are wanted and will be respected helps to guarantee the success of future surveys and facilitates other types of communication within the company, thus making a contribution to employee adjustment and morale.

Résumé

In this chapter the need for recognizing the symptoms of emotional maladjustment, for understanding its causes, and for helping disturbed employees to attain a more effective adjustment to their jobs has been emphasized. By viewing "problem employees" as employees with problems and helping them to overcome their difficulties, the supervisor is not only likely to help the individuals concerned but also to influence favorably the morale of the work group. In order that they may be able to assist others, it is recommended that persons in supervisory positions learn the techniques of counseling. Too frequently counseling is viewed as a technique to be used by specially trained persons; whereas, whether trained or not, each person in a supervisory capacity frequently assumes a counseling role. The supervisor, however, should be aware of the need for making referrals to professional persons when he encounters employees with problems that are beyond the scope of his competence.

While every supervisor should assess the morale of his group through feelings that are expressed to him by individuals, he should also be alert to other symptoms of poor morale such as absenteeism, turnover, grievances, and disciplinary problems that occur beyond the normally expected frequency. In addition to expecting supervisory personnel to be alert to such symptoms, the personnel department should conduct a continuous evaluation of the departments in order that it may be in touch with the total condition of morale in the organization. In order to be assured that it has its finger on the pulse of the organization, it is advisable for the personnel department to conduct periodic morale surveys in which each individual employee is given an opportunity to express his opinions anonymously with regard to those factors in the organization, the work group, and the job that are generally considered important. With such information about employee opinions, management may then correct those conditions that are detrimental to a high standard of personal adjustment and morale.

DISCUSSION QUESTIONS AND PROBLEMS

1. What should be the role of the personnel department in insuring that supervisors create a job environment in which employee adjustment is facilitated rather than hindered?

2. Some experts feel that mental health pamphlets, films, and similar educational materials do not contribute appreciably to an individual's adjustment. Do you agree? Why?

3. A personnel manager advises his staff that they must hire only normal applicants for jobs.
   a. Who is normal?
   b. What are some of the problems in determining normality?
   c. Should normality be given priority over skills and experience?

4. In view of the financial liability that the employer must now assume for the physical health and the welfare of his employees, what do you predict will be future trends in his responsibility for safeguarding the emotional health of employees?

5. Some executives are against conducting morale surveys because they feel that asking employees their opinions will create unnecessary problems and cause employees to become dissatisfied with what they have. What do you think of this viewpoint? As a personnel manager, how could you attempt to change it?

6. How would you plan a study to determine the relationship between morale and production in a company? What are some of the problems encountered in making a study of this type?

7. Some businessmen believe that the nondirective approach is not in keeping with sound management principles and that its use should be restricted to counselors and psychotherapists.
   a. Do you agree with their belief? Why or why not?
   b. What is the purpose of using the nondirective approach?
   c. In what way is the use of the nondirective approach consistent with the principles of effective communication as discussed in Chapter 13?

8. Duplicate the list of job conditions listed in Figure 16-4 on page 437, and ask a number of individuals to rate the job conditions according to their importance. How do the findings compare with those reported in Figure 16-4? How do you account for the differences and similarities?

CASE 16-1

THE SAFETY VALVE

Jack Rhoads had been employed by the Consolidated Telephone Company for 16 years. He was 38 years of age, married, and had two children of whom he was very fond — a girl, 7, and a boy, 5. Jack was usually rather quiet, minded his own business, and was well liked by his fellow employees. His health and attendance had always been good. During his period of employment, Jack had progressed through various job classifications and had acquired a lot of experience and knowledge about telephone installation work. He was a good worker, a competent craftsman, and several of his supervisors had received favorable comments from customers regarding Jack's neat work, courtesy, and cheerful assistance with their telephone problems.

For the past five years, Jack had been working as a PBX Installer and was assigned to an installation crew consisting of 7 PBX Installers and 3 Station Installers, who worked under the supervision of an Installation Foreman. For about two years, the foreman in charge of Jack's crew had been Sam Huse. Sam was a very capable and businesslike man who demanded and received high quality work from his crew, but he gave a strong impression of being cold in his dealings with them. He was completely impartial and honest in all of his relations, and his men liked him in spite of the high standards that he required them to maintain.

During a routine rotation of foremen, Huse was transferred to another branch and was replaced by Carl Robinson. Robinson was equally as experienced as Huse and, according to the "grapevine," was well liked by men who had worked for him. On the morning that Robinson took over the crew, Robinson and Huse sat down together to discuss the jobs on which the crew was working. When they were finished, the following conversation took place:

Huse: "Well, Carl, I guess that's about it. I think you'll like this district. There's always plenty to do and all the men are good workers. You don't have to worry about any of them not producing."

Robinson: "That's sure good to know."

Huse: "That Jack Rhoads, though . . . . I can't quite figure out what's gotten into him lately. About the last six months he's been acting like a bear. He's grouchy all the time, and he gripes about everything. Occasionally he gets real belligerent. He's even got the rest of the crew down on him now. They call him 'Jumpy Jack' behind his back. He used to be a real quiet, cheerful sort of fellow. Oh well, he still does a first class job. He'll probably get over whatever is biting him. You had better keep an eye on him, though."

Robinson: "Do you have any idea what the trouble might be?"

Huse: "No. He gripes about so many things it's hard to tell. Probably something personal . . . and I never get involved in things like that. Got enough headaches on the job without going into the employee's personal affairs. Well, I'd better get over to my new crew. I'll see you later."

During the next six weeks, Robinson's observations confirmed what Huse had told him about Jack Rhoads. He tried several times, without success, to get Jack to talk — to draw him out. One afternoon Robinson was at his desk in the storeroom when Jack stormed in to pick up some material that he needed for his next installation job. He slammed some boxes around, kicked an empty carton aside, and burst out with:

"This job is getting worse every day! Damn it all, somebody ought to straighten out those guys who make the assignments of lines. They're getting things fouled up more all the time. Seems like every assignment has something wrong with it. I could have had my last job finished before noon, except I had to spend a lot of unnecessary time calling in and getting their mess straightened out. It sure gripes me the way those guys goof things up!"

Robinson: "Yes, Jack, something like that can irritate you all right. It's a big help, though, that you've worked as a line assigner and know how to go about correcting such mistakes better than some of the men."

Rhoads: "Yeah, that does help, I guess, and I've got a couple of ideas that might help more. Oh well, it's not my funeral . . . . (Bitterly) Guess I'll get on over to the next job and see how much they've fouled that one up." (Starts out . . . hesitates . . . comes back to Robinson's desk.) "Sorry I blew my top, Carl. It's just that I get so darned griped. No reason to snort at you, though."

Robinson: "That's okay, Jack. Everybody's got to let off steam once in a while. Sit down for a minute and have a smoke. Your next job will wait for you that long."

Rhoads: "Seems like I'm always blowing up lately . . . guess the rest of the fellows feel I've been pretty ornery and unbearable most of the time . . . but I just can't seem to help it."

Robinson: "Something bothering you?"

Rhoads: "Oh, it's nothing you could help me with I'm afraid. But thanks for the offer." . . . . (Hesitantly) "I really get low sometimes. Everything seems to bother me and I snap at people without really meaning it."

Robinson: ?

(the interview continues but is not included here.)

a. Rhoads's behavior in front of the foreman (slamming boxes, kicking cartons, griping, etc.) might be construed by some supervisors as a sign of disrespect. Do you consider Rhoads's behavior disrespectful? Why?

b. Huse believed that the foreman should not get involved in the personal affairs of employees. How does Robinson's attitude toward problems of employees compare with Huse's attitude? According to the findings of the University of Michigan studies reported in Chapter 14, which individual — Robinson or Huse — is likely to have a more productive work group? Why?

c. What important clues as to the nature of Rhoads's problem are given in his statements?

d. If you were Robinson, how would you proceed in conducting the interview? What would be your response to Rhoads's last statement?

CASE 16-2

A MORALE SURVEY

The management of a Midwestern cannery employing 1,500 individuals engaged in preparing and canning baby foods for national marketing was concerned about the morale of its employees. There had been many indications in the past year that morale was lower than it had been in many years, in spite of steady employment and good wages. Management decided that it was time to make use of modern methods by which employee morale could be surveyed and hired a consultant to plan and conduct the survey.

For about two weeks, the consultant and the assistant personnel manager of the company met with representatives of management, the employees, and the union and discussed the objectives of the proposed survey, including the methods to be used in obtaining and in reporting the information to management and the employees. A definite date was set for conducting the survey, and all employees were given the details concerning the purposes of the survey and how it would be conducted.

On the day scheduled for the survey, employees were assembled in groups of 200 in the company auditorium. After a brief orientation by the assistant personnel manager, the consultant took over the meeting and administered the questionnaire. The questionnaire, prepared by a national firm and known to be among the best, contained about 100 items that the employees answered by checking "agree," "disagree," or "undecided" on separate answer sheets. Provision was also made for employees to write comments on the back of the answer sheet concerning any areas of their jobs that were particularly favorable or unfavorable. The only identification that employees entered on the questionnaire was their crew number.

After all employees had participated, the personnel department, with the aid of the consultant, tabulated and summarized the results. Reports, broken down by each major department in the plant and by crews, were prepared for submission to the department heads concerned and the plant manager. These reports included several scores, based on a standardized scoring system, that covered many areas under management's control. These scores represented the employees' attitudes concerning job demands, working conditions, communication, etc., for the crews and departments compared with other groups in the plant. The answers that employees had written to open-ended questions were studied and summarized to facilitate their use by those concerned.

The following is an extract from the company report that was sent to the manager of the Preparation Department. It concerns a crew of thirty female workers (Crew X-31) engaged in preparing meats and vegetables for canning. The crew is under the general supervision of the general foreman, who in turn has three foreladies who are responsible to him. Employees are paid on the basis of straight time, plus incentive bonuses.

EXTRACT OF REPORT

The statistical analysis of the morale questionnaires for this crew reveals that opinions toward the company as a whole, top management, and other areas measured are quite favorable. Employee opinions toward the following areas, however, are quite unfavorable:

Friendliness and cooperation of employees.

Supervisor and employee interpersonal relations.

Technical competence of supervision.

The comments that employees wrote on their answer sheets concerning the three areas viewed unfavorably were summarized as follows:

FRIENDLINESS AND COOPERATION OF FELLOW EMPLOYEES. There are apparently "Queen bees," i.e. older female employees who adopt a bossy and domineering manner regarding those with less seniority. These employees boss others around.

A common complaint among the employees is that the service boys cheat and that some employees are given better grade ingredients to process.

Those ordinarily engaged in the preparation of vegetables resent being transferred, when necessary, to the preparation of chicken on the basis that they cannot make a sufficient bonus. They suspect favoritism at such times.

SUPERVISOR AND EMPLOYEE INTERPERSONAL RELATIONS. The General Foreman many times bypasses the foreladies in contacts with employees.

There are frequent changes in work that come up without warning or explanation, allowing only time to give orders to change what is being done and to transfer employees over to other types of work where perhaps less bonus is to be made. The forelady, therefore, becomes more often than not the harbinger of bad news rather than the motivator.

Scheduling of rest periods is a problem.

TECHNICAL COMPETENCE OF SUPERVISION. Although there is possibly enough equipment available for the women to do their jobs, equipment does not seem to be in the right place at the right time. Food carts are one of the main shortages, and any change in work amplifies this.

Employees do their job the same way day after day, but the inspector can change his mind in interpreting procedure. He then writes a note about the employee, giving name and badge number to the plant superintendent. The employee sometimes gets a written reprimand and this causes friction. The employees feel that it should be brought to the employee's attention in some other way. There have been times when the employees tried to retaliate by damaging company property.

a. If you were the manager of the Preparation Department, what immediate action would you take on the basis of this report? What long range action would you take?

b. Are there any areas that seem to call for action being taken by other departments in the company?

c. Should the information contained in this report be released to other departments in the company?

d. Would the department manager be justified in recommending the replacement of the general foreman or the foreladies of Crew X-31 on the basis of the findings from this survey? Why?

e. Was this survey necessary? Could not management obtain the same type of information by just keeping its eyes and ears open? Discuss.

CASE 16-3

ALICE HALL
THE PROBLEM SUPERVISOR

At the time that the problem with her arose, Alice Hall had been employed by the National Phone Company for eight years as a clerk in the Accounting Department. She was thirty years old, married, but had no children. Alice was well liked by fellow employees and her work was above average. In recognition of her performance and seniority, Alice received a promotion to a supervisory position in the Estimate Section after six years of service with the company.

A few months following her promotion, Alice suffered a miscarriage, after which she requested and received a six-month leave of absence. At the end of this period she returned to work in her supervisory position. Alice had not been back long before her section had experienced a turnover of nearly 100 percent. She appeared to be unhappy in her position and to become easily upset over minor incidents. Whereas she previously had maintained a good attendance record, she began calling the office in the morning complaining that she felt ill and could not come to work. She also complained frequently about having headaches. Finally, one day she approached Mr. Webb, her boss, and requested a transfer to the Revenue Accounting Department, stating that the work there would be more enjoyable and involve less pressure. Mr. Webb contacted the Revenue Accounting Department and, upon finding that there was a position open, arranged to have her transferred.

After she had been in the new department for a couple of months, the manager there requested that she be returned to her former department because her performance had not proved to be satisfactory. Making another attempt to find a suitable position for her, Mr. Webb assigned her to the Distribution Section where she was in charge of only two other girls. Webb felt that the job would be sufficiently easy for her to handle. One day, however, when he asked her to expedite a job for him she broke into tears and stated, "I have more work than I can handle now." She then snapped, "I quit," turned and hurried out of the room. Her reaction caught Mr. Webb by surprise, since he was sure that Alice's work load was not excessive. A short time after her outburst, she returned to her desk and began working again. In view of her years of good performance, Mr. Webb was hesitant to push Alice on her threat to quit. Company policy, furthermore, was opposed to discharging an employee with her seniority except in extreme cases.

   a. What action would you recommend be taken?

   b. How does a manager cope with a pattern of behavior such as that exhibited by Alice? What possible explanation is there for her behavior?

   c. What are the extent of a company's obligations to an employee such as Mrs. Hall?

SUGGESTED READINGS

American Psychiatric Association. *The Mentally Ill Employee, His Treatment and Rehabilitation.* New York: Harper and Row, Hoeber Medical Division, 1965.

Argyris, Chris. *Integrating the Individual and the Organization.* New York: John Wiley and Sons, 1964.

Balinsky, Benjamin, and Ruth Burger. *The Executive Interview — A Bridge to People.* New York: Harper & Brothers, 1959.

Brammer, Lawrence M., and Everett L. Shostrom. *Therapeutic Psychology.* Englewood Cliffs, New Jersey: Prentice-Hall, Inc., 1960.

Chruden, Herbert J., and Arthur W. Sherman, Jr. *Readings in Personnel Management,* Second Edition. Cincinnati: South-Western Publishing Company, Inc., 1966. Chapter 4.

Harrell, Thomas W. *Industrial Psychology,* Revised Edition. New York: Holt, Rinehart and Winston, Inc., 1958. Chapter 12.

Kornhauser, Arthur. *Mental Health of the Industrial Worker.* New York: John Wiley and Sons, 1965.

Levinson, Harry. *Emotional Health in the World of Work.* New York: Harper and Row, 1964.

Luck, Thomas J. *Personnel Audit and Appraisal.* New York: McGraw-Hill Book Company, 1955.

McKinney, Frank. *Psychology of Personal Adjustment.* New York: John Wiley and Sons, 1960.

McLean, Alan A., and Graham C. Taylor. *Mental Health in Industry.* New York: McGraw-Hill Book Company, 1958.

Miner, John B. *The Management of Ineffective Performance.* New York: McGraw-Hill Book Company, 1963. Chapter 3.

Remmers, Herman H. *Introduction to Opinion Attitude and Measurement.* New York: Harper & Brothers, 1954.

Shaffer, Laurence F., and Edward J. Shoben, Jr. *The Psychology of Adjustment,* Second Edition. Boston: Houghton Mifflin Company, 1956.

Trice, Harrison M., and James A. Belasco. *Emotional Health and Employer Responsibility.* Ithaca, New York: New York State School of Industrial and Labor Relations, Cornell University, May, 1966.

Grievances and Disciplinary Action

In the preceding chapters the role of managers and supervisors in maximizing employee job satisfaction and adjustment was defined. While some managers overemphasize production efficiency to the neglect of humanistic values, the strictly production-centered manager is becoming less prevalent as he is replaced by his employee-centered counterpart on the management team. The latter type of leader who was described as being personally interested in his subordinates, available for discussion, and nonthreatening is the one who generally facilitates the achievement of satisfaction and adjustment.

In spite of the contributions of the employee-centered leader to employee satisfaction and adjustment as well as to production, there will be times, even under the best conditions, when employees are dissatisfied because of some specific action or lack of action on the part of the supervisor or higher managerial personnel in the company. It is now more clearly recognized that a system should be established in organizations to provide for the effective handling of complaints and grievances of employees that in earlier years, under different concepts of management, were considered impertinent and bordering on the illegal.

The management of large numbers of employees also requires that attention be given to the manner in which the attitudes and behavior of individuals affect the organization. Management, therefore, must concern itself with the quality of conduct or discipline of all its employees. It can best do this by establishing reasonable standards of conduct, by informing employees of these standards, and by enforcing them wisely. When such conditions have been developed and maintained by management, employees are more likely to have good morale and as a group will tend to enforce the standards by applying social pressure on those members of the group who get "out of line." Even in the organization where employees have a high degree of self-control, there are occasions when management must take some type of disciplinary action because rules have been broken. Effective policies and procedures for this action, as well as for the handling of employee grievances in both unionized and nonunionized companies, are essential to sound management and human justice. Such a judicial system provides for the just and equitable handling of problems that arise between labor and management. In a complex industrial society the rights of individuals, as well as of the company, must be recognized and protected by carefully designed procedures which operate to the mutual benefit of all parties and ultimately to all members of society. The discussion of the methods by which these rights may be protected includes these topics:

- Employee grievances.

- Formal grievance procedure.

- Disciplinary action.

Employee Grievances

In any employment situation there are likely to be instances when employees feel that they are not being treated fairly or that the conditions of employment are unsatisfactory to them. These dissatisfactions must be detected promptly and corrections made whenever possible. If the dissatisfactions of an employee go unheeded or if the conditions causing them are not corrected, the irritation is likely to grow and lead to unsatisfactory attitudes and reduced efficiency on the part of employees other than the individual concerned. Among other things, therefore, the effective supervisor is alert to signs of employee dissatisfaction and takes the steps necessary to uncover its causes.

Symptoms

It is fairly common procedure, especially in a democratic, permissive work environment, for employees to express any dissatisfactions concerning their jobs or working conditions directly to the supervisor. In expressing their complaints, it is irrelevant as to whether or not the supervisor can do anything to alleviate their dissatisfaction since the fact that he is a part of management makes him "fair game" for any problem that an employee may bring to him. The competent supervisor learns to listen to what employees have to tell him and to recognize that employee dissatisfactions may be revealed in ways other than through verbal complaints. Sometimes the employee cannot identify the exact cause of his dissatisfaction and, thus, is not able to talk about it. In other instances the employee may recognize the source of his ill-feeling but may be unable to find the words with which to express it to his supervisor. Thus, the supervisor must have skill in interviewing and counseling methods that will facilitate employee expression, and he must be able to recognize the common symptoms of dissatisfaction that may or may not be accompanied by verbal complaints.

While there is no one typical pattern of behavior, such signs as sullenness, moodiness, worrying, lack of cooperation, insubordination, decrease in the quantity and quality of work, and absence from the job often are indicative of dissatisfaction. It should be recognized, however, that these behavior patterns may also be symptoms of other problems that are unrelated to employment. For this reason it is important to uncover the true cause for the employee's change in attitude and/or behavior when handling complaints or grievances.

At this point in the discussion a distinction should be made between complaints and grievances. A *complaint* is any expression of discontent on the part of the employee; whereas, a *grievance*, according to union usage of the term, refers to improper treatment in terms of the labor agreement and typically involves such matters as discharge, wages, job classification, layoffs, promotions, transfers, and loss of seniority. As the term grievance is commonly used in personnel management, however, it refers to any employee dissatisfaction whether expressed or not.

Causes

Grievances, as expressed by the individual, often do not point to the heart of the problem. An employee may, for example, report that the physical conditions under which he works are unpleasant or unsafe. But a careful study of the situation by an impartial observer may reveal that the real reason for the complaint is that the employee does not like his supervisor because the supervisor is always "riding" him. In this instance the real grievance is over the nature of supervision and not the physical working conditions. Obviously, to correct the physical environment would not resolve this employee's grievance. Each grievance, therefore, must be carefully studied and analyzed to insure that the expressed grievance represents the heart of the problem. There are, however, some factors that are commonly found to contribute to employee grievances.

Management practices. Most companies have sound policies for the management of personnel, but the implementation of the policies often falls far short of what is supposed to be practiced. In addition there are many matters relating to personnel that are not adequately defined in the labor agreement with the result that any action that management may take is likely to result in grievances being filed. Grievances may also result from problems that could not have been foreseen at the time that the agreement was negotiated.

Poor communication between management and its employees is another cause of excessive grievances. If employees understood the reasons behind management's actions and had some voice in the making of decisions, they would often support management's actions rather than file grievances because of them. Management should also recognize that what may appear to it to be trivial and inconsequential may be important to employees. In one of the automobile assembly plants 32,000 workers walked out because the protective coverall furnished them at their request was referred to by the company as a "smock." An authoritative source commented: "I think this never would have happened if those garments weren't called 'smocks' at the start. The men feel they are being sissified. You might say this is the first semantical strike in the industry."[1]

Another source of grievances lies in supervisory practices. The supervisor's attitude and behavior toward individual workers and the union may provide a fertile source of grievances. The supervisor who plays favorites, fails to live up to promises, or is too demanding is likely to encounter many grievances from his workers. In addition to establishing good relationships with employees, it is the supervisor's responsibility to be familiar with the labor agreement and with company rules in order that he may protect the rights of the employees as well as those of the company.

---

[1]Reprinted from the June 9, 1951 issue of *Business Week* by special permission. Copyrighted 1951 by McGraw-Hill Book Company.

While these sources of grievances represent major areas of management and supervision and should not be overlooked, it is important that the personnel department (or employee relations department) carefully analyze all grievances in an attempt to arrive at their basic causes. Grievances should be viewed as manifestations of weaknesses in the management of personnel that can be minimized in the future by correcting the conditions out of which they grow. While a specific grievance must be handled carefully and thoroughly, it is an indicator of weaknesses in the total program that should serve as a warning of needed changes in personnel policies and/or procedures.

Union practices. The fact that a union can provide a voice for their grievances is a vital factor in motivating employees to join a union. Realizing that members expect action, union leaders sometimes are inclined to encourage the filing of grievances in order to demonstrate the advantages of union membership and to prove to the employees that the union is the organization primarily interested in their welfare. Where the union has not established itself securely as the bargaining agent for its members, it may conduct a campaign to "swamp" the company with grievances. Through such a "war of nerves" it may hope to marshal the support of its members and thereby place itself in a more secure bargaining position. Where union leadership itself is insecure, it may use these tactics to direct the attention of the members away from its own shortcomings. It sometimes happens that in the period immediately preceding contract negotiations the union may encourage employees to file more grievances than they ordinarily would. This often has the effect of strengthening the union's position with regard to some of the issues that the union leaders feel should be discussed and formally provided for in the new agreement. Regardless of the specific motives that the union may have in situations like those described above, it should be recognized that the grievance process can result in the gradual erosion of management prerogatives with the result that many of the major policies and procedures for operating a company are determined jointly by labor and management through the labor agreement.

Personality differences. In addition to management and union practices and their effects on grievances, the individual employee's personality has also been found to be related to job dissatisfaction. The employee who enjoys good physical and mental health is more likely to overlook minor annoyances and discrepancies while the less healthy individual may consider them to be of major importance and demand that corrective action be taken. Similarly, the employee who is beset with problems that are not directly related to his job may relieve tension that stems from other sources by filing a grievance. This may be viewed as a type of scapegoating, thus pointing out the need for ascertaining the true basis of the complaint or grievance.

Some employees are quite vocal and find fault with everything. They are sometimes referred to as "chronic grievers." One study of the personality characteristics of grievers and nongrievers revealed that the basic difference between the two groups was that grievers tended to be more "thin-skinned" and had their feelings hurt more easily. This finding suggests that some people may tolerate a certain condition without filing a grievance; whereas, others will protest.[2] While one cannot hope to remake such individuals, an awareness of the fact that there is this basic personality difference between grievers and nongrievers may prove helpful in working with these individuals.

Minimizing Grievances

Although there are always likely to be grievances wherever people are employed, competent managers can do much to prevent those situations that precipitate grievances. Whenever employee attitudes and feelings indicate that dissatisfactions may be developing, management should attempt to uncover the causes and take whatever corrective action may be feasible. In some instances the appropriate corrective action may require a change in work procedures or employment conditions. In other instances the appropriate corrective action may be achieved through proper communication; for example, proper communication may be achieved in an interview if a single employee is involved or by an announcement in which management states its position if grievances seem to be developing in a group of employees.

The degree of consideration shown to employees is an important factor in minimizing grievances. One study, for example, showed that the grievance rate was definitely associated with consideration. Consideration, it will be recalled, includes behavior indicating mutual trust, respect, and a warmth between the supervisor and his group, as well as encouragement of more two-way communication. Structure refers to the supervisor's overt attempts to achieve organizational goals (see page 361). An examination of Figure 17-1 shows that regardless of structure score, supervisors with

---

[2]Ross Stagner, *The Psychology of Industrial Conflict* (New York: John Wiley & Sons, Inc., 1956), pp. 394–395.

low consideration scores had high grievance rates. Similarly, those with high consideration scores had low grievance rates. The grievance rate of those with medium consideration scores is observed to vary with the amount of structure.[3] It would appear, therefore, that the attitudes and behavior of supervisors play an important role in the tendency of employees to file grievances.

Figure 17-1

COMBINATIONS OF CONSIDERATION AND STRUCTURE
RELATED TO GRIEVANCES

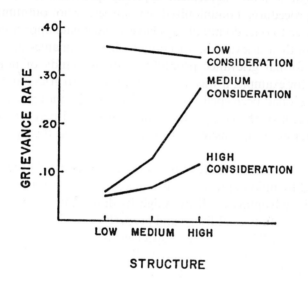

Source: E. A. Fleishman and E. F. Harris, "Patterns of Leadership Behavior Related to Employee Grievances and Turnover," *Personnel Psychology*, Vol. 15, No. 1 (Spring, 1962), pp. 45–53. Reproduced with permission.

Formal Grievance Procedure

The labor agreement typically outlines the grievance procedure by which employee dissatisfactions and disagreements between management and employees may be expressed. The *grievance procedure* is designed to facilitate the handling of complaints and disputes between the employee and the employer, as well as between the union and the employer, over the interpretation, administration, and enforcement of the labor agreement.

[3]E. A. Fleishman and E. F. Harris, "Patterns of Leadership Behavior Related to Employee Grievances and Turnover," *Personnel Psychology*, Vol. 15, No. 1 (Spring, 1962), pp. 45–53.

Since this agreement specifies in detail the conditions of employment, the grievance procedure provides a basis for handling many of the day-to-day problems that arise on the job concerning the interpretation of the agreement. While the grievance procedure is used primarily by employees and the union, it may also be used by management when it feels that it has received unfair treatment from an employee or the union. In practice, however, management customarily exercises its prerogatives and takes some type of disciplinary action against the employee who has acted contrary to established rules or standards of work.

Although a labor agreement typically provides for a formalized grievance procedure, nonunionized employees, who outnumber union members three to one, do not always have an adequate opportunity for the expression of their grievances, for nonunionized companies do not usually establish a formal grievance procedure. In one study of nonunionized companies, for example, it was found that the right to grieve and the means of exercising it had been spelled out in a formal grievance procedure in less than 25 percent of the companies. Employees in 75 percent of the companies, therefore, were unsure as to whether they had the right to voice a grievance.[4]

While many managers are of the opinion that a formal procedure, when not required by union agreement, is unnecessary or even undesirable, it is likely that its advantages will outweigh its disadvantages if the grievance procedure is carefully established and properly administered. In the unionized company the labor agreement specifies the steps to be taken in initiating grievances and the employees are well aware that the union will protect their rights and insure the effective and judicious handling of any grievances that are filed. In the nonunion company, however, management should establish a formal grievance procedure that meets the following requirements:

1. No fear of reprisal.
2. Employees understand system.
3. A problem solving atmosphere prevails.
4. The employee should not be at any disadvantage in handling grievances because of lack of skill in presenting his case.[5]

In order that the employees will know whether or not they have a legitimate grievance, it is desirable to restrict the use of the term "grievance" and procedures pertaining to grievances to misinterpretations or

---

[4]Walter V. Ronner, "Handling Grievances of Nonunionized Employees," *Personnel*, Vol. 39, No. 2 (March–April, 1962), pp. 56–62.
[5]Robert E. Sibson, "Handling Grievances Where There Is No Union," *Personnel Journal*, Vol. 35 (June, 1956), pp. 56–58.

misapplications of the company's personnel policies. It is important, therefore, that such policies be committed to writing and publicized.[6]

While this book focuses on personnel policies and procedures in business organizations, it should be noted that many nonbusiness organizations provide for the handling of grievances through formal systems. Scott describes in detail the appeal systems in the United Auto Workers Union, the Roman Catholic Church, the U.S. Army, and the federal government as examples of nonbusiness organizations that have formal grievance procedures.[7]

In spite of the fact that many more individuals are employed in nonunionized than in unionized companies, the number of nonunion companies with grievance procedures is small, and there is not the standardization in procedure that is typical of the unionized companies. Therefore, the discussion that follows focuses on procedures for grievance handling under the labor agreement. Many of the comments that are made, however, may be applied to the nonunionized company.

Steps in the Grievance Procedure

It has been noted that the steps through which a grievance is processed are usually enumerated in the labor agreement. The number of steps will depend largely upon the size of the company and the organization of the union. In the larger company a grievance may pass through four or more steps before being resolved; whereas, in the smaller company it may go through fewer steps. To facilitate the prompt and effective handling of grievances it is important that the number of steps be kept at a minimum.

In Figure 17-2, page 462, the steps and participants in the typical grievance procedure are indicated. Variations of this pattern depend upon the extent of the authority granted to union and personnel department representatives and the size and structure of the company and union.

Although grievances are usually presented by employees and/or the union steward, they may also be presented by union representatives at higher levels where a grievance involves several employees. While the general pattern for handling grievances is as shown in Figure 17-2, an examination of the grievance procedure as specified in a labor agreement will indicate the rigid standards as to time allotted at the different steps and the almost standard requirement for reducing complaints and replies

---

[6]Ronner, *op. cit.*, p. 60.

[7]William G. Scott, *The Management of Conflict — Appeal Systems in Organizations* (Homewood, Illinois: Richard D. Irwin, Inc., and The Dorsey Press, 1965).

Figure 17-2

STEPS AND PARTICIPANTS IN TYPICAL GRIEVANCE PROCEDURE

Step	Representing the Employee or Union	Representing the Employer
First (presentation)	Employee and/or union steward	Employee's foreman
Second	Chief steward	General foreman or department head
Third	Grievance committee	Personnel director or director of industrial relations
Fourth	Grievance committee and/or international representative or business agent of the international union	Plant manager
Fifth	Arbitration	

Source: Selwyn H. Toriff, *Collective Bargaining* (New York: McGraw-Hill Book Company, 1953), p. 292. Reproduced with permission.

to writing. The following paragraphs are extracted from an actual contract.

V — GRIEVANCE PROCEDURE — (a) The steps of the grievance procedure are a proper subject for local plant negotiation. The following general provisions shall be applicable to each local grievance procedure.

(1) All grievances must be reduced to writing and signed by a complainant before submission to the second step of the grievance procedure. The local grievance procedure shall provide for two steps and in no event more than three steps (exclusive of Impartial Umpire) after the grievance has been reduced to writing.

(2) The parties to this agreement recognize that grievances should be settled promptly and as close to their source as possible. Further, both parties will endeavor to present all the facts relating to the grievance at the first step of the grievance procedure in order that an equitable solution may be achieved. The Employer in each of the steps of the grievance procedure shall give written answer to the written grievance as soon after presentation as possible, but not later than three working days excluding Saturdays, Sundays and holidays unless extended by mutual consent. Should the Employer fail to give written

answer within the three-day limit, in the absence of agreement extending the period, at any step of the grievance procedure prior to the final step, the Union may submit the grievance to the next step without delay. It is recognized by the parties that it is desirable on occasion for department foremen to hold meetings with department union representatives for the purpose of discussing department matters of mutual interest. At least six (6) such meetings shall be held by each foreman annually. Designated Union representatives shall be paid at average hourly earnings for attending such meetings.

(3) A written decision at any step of the grievance procedure shall be considered as final unless the grievance is taken to the next step within fifteen (15) working days thereafter, excluding Saturdays, Sundays and holidays. No grievance, verbal or written, withdrawn or dropped by the union or granted by the employer, prior to the final step of the local grievance procedure, will have any precedent value. The sentence immediately above applies only to grievances resolved after the effective date of the 1961 company-wide agreement.

(4) The parties recognize that an employee who feels that he is aggrieved should submit such grievance claim to the grievance procedure without delay after the employee becomes aware of the occurrence of the incident giving rise to the grievance.

(5) When a supervisor discusses with an employee a matter likely to result in his discharge, or suspension, or when a derogatory notation is to be placed on his record, the employee will be reminded of his right to bring his Union representative into the discussion at that time and his Union representative will be informed of any action taken; then if an employee is to be suspended or discharged for any matter other than a violation of Article XII, he shall be brought into the office and informed of the action taken. If the employee files a written protest of the discharge or suspension within ten (10) working days, excluding Saturdays, Sundays and holidays, and such discharge or suspension is found to have been unjustified, the employee shall be reinstated to his former job and shall be compensated at his average hourly earnings for the time lost, less pay for any penalty time decided upon.

.   .   .   .

(b) Should negotiations between the Employer and the Local Union at the final step of the local grievance procedure fail to bring about an agreement between the parties with respect to any grievance which properly comes under the jurisdiction of the Umpire as hereinafter defined, either party may, within thirty (30) days, but no longer except by mutual agreement, after the final answer at the last step as outlined above, submit the issue to the Impartial Umpire. It is understood that a copy of the issue submitted will be furnished to the other party at the same time.

(1) On a date set by the Impartial Umpire, the parties shall at the time and place appointed by the Impartial Umpire, appear and present for his consideration a statement of the issues involved, either in writing or orally, as each party may desire.

(2) The Impartial Umpire shall render an award within seven (7) days following the hearing on every grievance which has been submitted to him.

(3) The decision of the Impartial Umpire shall be final and binding upon both parties and shall invoke immediate compliance by the parties.[8]

Initiating Employee Grievances

Customarily a grievance is first presented to the employee's immediate supervisor, either by himself or by the steward in his work area. If good relationships exist between the supervisor and the employee, it is quite likely that the employee will express his grievance orally to his supervisor. In many instances the supervisor will be able to resolve the grievance at that time or shortly thereafter. If, however, the employee is not satisfied with the supervisor's decision, he may appeal to higher authority. This is done by reporting his grievance on a special form similar to that shown in Figure 17-3 on page 465. These forms are usually prepared in multiple copies for distribution to company and union personnel concerned.

The use of an official grievance form requires the employee to assemble the facts and, in effect, to substantiate the basis for his grievance. This procedure tends to reduce the number of trivial complaints that are forwarded to higher echelons and minimizes the employee's opportunity for using this as a method for expressing hostile feelings that he may have that are unrelated to the reported grievance.

In writing up his grievance the employee usually obtains assistance from the steward who represents him. Because of his familiarity with the provisions of the union agreement and his experience in evaluating the validity of complaints, the steward's services can be especially valuable to the employee. If the steward is of the opinion that the complaint is valid, he can help the employee formulate the complaint in language that is appropriate for the official grievance form. On the other hand, if the steward feels that the employee does not have a valid grievance, he can discuss the employee's feelings with him to determine the cause. When there is a good relationship between management and the union, the steward can be particularly helpful in searching out the real sources of difficulties with the result that grievances which are filed are likely to come closer to representing the actual problems. A good steward can also assist the foreman by screening out chronic complainers or "grievers." It is in the

---

[8]Excerpts from Agreement between the Goodyear Tire and Rubber Company and Rubber Workers. Company-wide agreement covering hourly and piecework employees in 11 cities. In effect from April, 1965 to April, 1967.

Figure 17-3

GRIEVANCE STATEMENT

EMPLOYEE: Roland Smith_____ CLOCK NO: 65891_____ SHIFT: Swing___

JOB CLASSIFICATION: Bench Machinist___ PLANT: 2_____ DEPT.: 616___

DEPT. FOREMAN: R. M. Lancaster_____

STATEMENT OF GRIEVANCE: I received only a 7-cent wage increase on my eighth-month review. Everyone else in my department has received the top of the rate in the past. A man who hired in later than I did received the top of the rate. I am doing the same type, quality, and quantity of work as others in this classification who have received the top of the rate. When I hired in, the supervisor told me that I would receive the top of my rate on the eighth-month review. This was not the case. I feel that I have been discriminated against and should receive back pay to my eighth-month review for top rate of Bench Machinist.

EMPLOYEE: *Roland Smith*_____ DEPT. STEWARD: *Oscar Black*____
         Signature   Signature

RECEIVED BY: *R. M. Lancaster*_____ TIME: *9:30 a. m.* DATE: *1-16 —*
         Supervisor or Foreman

Prepare in quadruplicate for distribution

1. Original and one copy (Labor Relations)
2. Department   UNION FILE NO._____
3. Chief Steward
                                      LABOR RELATIONS NO. *1-59-32*

union's interest to restrict the filing of grievances to those that are basically sound because this places the union in a stronger position to gain satisfactory consideration on those grievances that are of major importance and for which there is an objective basis for demanding corrective action from management.

Resolving Grievances

Management and union representatives who have any part in the handling of a grievance must always keep in mind that a grievance is a very important matter to the employee who is aggrieved. In the interests of good personnel management, therefore, every effort should be made to insure that each grievance receives the careful consideration that it deserves. The facts must be determined, and all of the related aspects must be examined in a thorough and systematic manner with a view to arriving at a fair and impartial settlement of the case.

The first step. As is indicated in Figure 17-2, the first step in resolving a grievance is to present it to the aggrieved employee's first-line superior. Collective bargaining agreements often specify that a union representative be present when the employee meets with the supervisor. This is not only because the union often does not trust the supervisor but also because of the desire of union officials to show results to its membership.

The supervisor's skill in discussing the grievance with the employee and the steward and in taking prompt and appropriate action can reduce the number of grievances that must be handled at higher levels, can facilitate the restoration of goodwill, and can contribute to a considerable savings in time, energy, and expense. In 1965, 75 percent of the grievances filed under the agreement between General Motors and the United Auto Workers were settled at the first step (Figure 17-4). This achievement indicates ability and willingness on the part of both management and union in this instance to resolve grievances as quickly as possible.

Management should recognize the importance of the supervisor's role and train him in the handling of grievances. Training should include familiarization with the terms of the labor agreement, and it is desirable that counseling skills, discussed in the preceding chapter, be emphasized. Wherever a grievance can be resolved at the first step considerable time, cost, and bad feelings can be spared. By training supervisors in the skillful handling of grievances on an oral rather than a written basis, a true problem-solving approach may be facilitated. According to McKersie, who compared the old grievance system at International Harvester with the new one (in effect since 1959), the oral handling approach to grievances has these values:

1. Problems are settled where they arise and by the people concerned, and not at some higher level in the organization.
2. Grievances are considered while the facts are still fresh. Since details cannot be recorded, the parties have to grapple with the problem before the facts of the situation get away from them.
3. Employee complaints can be much more intelligently handled in oral discussion rather than in an exchange of written documents. Many foremen at International Harvester, as is the case with other

Figure 17-4
DISPOSITION OF WRITTEN GRIEVANCES

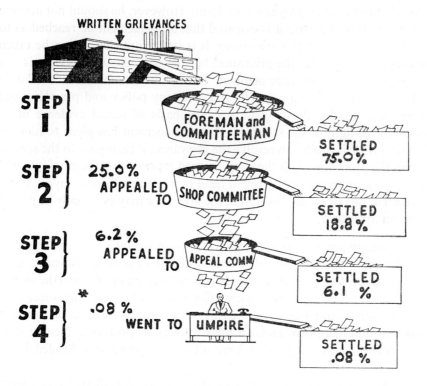

*An unsettled grievance will not necessarily be carried to the final step, hence the small unaccounted for difference at this point in the handling of written grievances.

Disposition of written grievances during 1965 under the General Motors-United Auto Workers National Agreement. Reproduced with permission of the Personnel Department, General Motors Corporation.

companies, find it difficult to understand the written word, especially complicated contractual language. It is much easier for the interested parties to get to the bottom of the situation with an oral investigation than it is with the submission of depositions.[9]

Another major feature of the International Harvester program is that the emphasis is on problem solving rather than defense of a stated position.

The training of supervisors should not only include instruction in counseling skills but should also provide role-playing experiences in handling grievances where the perceptual and motivational aspects of

[9]Robert B. McKersie, "Avoiding Written Grievances by Problem-Solving: An Outside View," *Personnel Psychology*, Vol. 17, No. 4 (Winter, 1964), pp. 367–379.

communication (see page 341) are displayed and examined.[10] The supervisor should be taught how to listen nonevaluatively so that he can obtain a clear picture of the employee's complaint. However, he should not hesitate to ask questions because it is essential that an agreement be reached as to the factual aspects of the grievance. It is important that action be taken immediately to resolve the grievance, but the competent supervisor is one who does not act in haste or in anger. Instead, he obtains the facts relating to it, checks the labor agreement and company policy and practices, and attempts to resolve the grievance on the basis of sound evidence interpreted in the light of the standards that management has given to him. If the supervisor is unable to resolve the grievance, it then goes to the second step in the procedure with the shop steward representing the employee and the general foreman or department head representing the employer. If not resolved at this or succeeding levels, the grievance may eventually be passed on to an arbitrator.

Necessity for mutual concessions. As representatives of management and the union sit down together in an attempt to settle a grievance, each side must maintain a flexible attitude and be prepared to discuss the matter in a give-and-take manner if their efforts are to be generally successful. A grievance should not be viewed as something to be won or lost but, rather, as an attempt to resolve a human relations problem. Neither side, furthermore, should expect to have all of the grievances decided in its favor.

When a grievance remains unresolved at the fourth step (see Figure 17-2), the following alternative courses of action are available. One of the parties may back down from the position that it has been holding, thereby resolving the difference. Or, if the agreement provides for arbitration by outside parties as the final step, the grievance can be submitted to arbitration. If, however, the agreement does not contain arbitration provisions and the deadlock cannot be broken, the aggrieved party will either have to drop the grievance or resort to a strike, a slowdown, or a lockout.

Grievance Arbitration

The final step in the typical grievance procedure is *arbitration*. It is a procedure that provides for an employer and a labor union to submit an issue of disagreement to an impartial person or group for a solution.

---

[10]For a fuller discussion of the role of motivation and perception in industrial disputes, see Ross Stagner and Hjalmar Rosen, *Psychology of Union-Management Relations* (Belmont, California: Wadsworth Publishing Co., Inc., 1965).

While only a relatively small number of written grievances reach this final step in the resolving of a grievance (Figure 17-4), arbitration is an integral part of the collective bargaining system in the United States. Most of the labor-management agreements have clauses that provide for arbitration as the terminal point for the handling of grievances. Such clauses also typically specify how arbitrators are to be selected, what issues may be subjected to arbitration, and the procedures to be followed. There are three types of grievance matters that may reach the arbitrator: (1) those involving conduct explicitly permitted or denied by the labor agreement, (2) those evoked by vague or ambiguous language or which uncover a conflict between several of the agreement's clauses, and (3) those with which the labor agreement fails to deal. In the first type the arbitrator is primarily a fact finder; in the second type he can exercise considerable judgment; and in the third type his authority is dependent upon the limits imposed by the parties in conflict.[11]

The arbitrator. The arbitrator[12] (or umpire, as he is sometimes called) may be one person or a tripartite board made up of representatives of management and labor plus an impartial chairman who is acceptable to both sides. He may be hired on a temporary (*ad hoc*) basis or on a fairly permanent basis for a specified period of time. The arbitrator is charged with the responsibility of arbitrating grievances that are submitted in a *submission agreement* or a stipulation to arbitrate. This document includes an agreement by the parties to arbitrate the dispute and a statement of the issue involved. Under typical arbitration procedures the parties agree in advance to accept the decision of the arbitrator, which makes him the final authority in the resolving of grievances.

Types of issues. Figure 17-5 lists the types of issues dealt with in arbitration cases ruled upon by arbitrators appointed by the U.S. Federal Mediation and Conciliation Service. The wide variety of problems indicates the broad scope of the arbitration process as well as the growing confidence labor and management place in the arbitration system. Chief among the types of issues that went through to arbitration were disciplinary problems, contract interpretation, and job classification and work assignment matters.

---

[11]A. W. Kornhauser, *et al.*, *Industrial Conflict*, "Arbitration," by Irving Bernstein (New York: McGraw-Hill Book Company, 1954), Chapter 23.

[12]Arbitrators are usually selected from lists of qualified persons with arbitration experience, including those whose names may be contained on the lists recommended by governmental agencies such as the Federal Mediation and Conciliation Service, state labor relations offices, or individuals who are members of the labor panel of the American Arbitration Association.

Figure 17-5

ARBITRATION ISSUES, FISCAL YEAR 1965

1. Partial writing of new contract 18
2. Total writing of new contract 6
3. Contract interpretation 660
4. Arbitrability, jurisdiction, or grievance 109
5. Auxiliary pay 36
6. Disciplinary 509
7. Guaranteed employment 26
8. Incentive rates — standards 44
9. Job classification and work assignment 345
10. Job evaluation and workloads 47
11. Management rights 290
12. Overtime and hours 199
13. Pay for time not worked 103
14. Health and welfare 23
15. Seniority in promotions 120
16. Seniority in demotion or layoff 134
17. Union security 20
18. Vacation and holidays 99
19. Working conditions 37
20. Miscellaneous 177

Source: *Federal Mediation and Conciliation Service, Eighteenth Annual Report* (Washington, D.C.: U.S. Government Printing Office, 1966), p. 64.

Precedent factors in arbitration. In carrying out his functions the arbitrator does not have a system of laws that must be followed. While there may be some legal implications in the matters that he is asked to consider, his primary function is to settle differences that have been stated in the submission agreement. With the increased use of arbitration as a method of settling grievances, however, there has developed, in effect, a form of legal background and precedent.

Though decisions are not considered as binding precedents, in the sense that court decisions are, they are fast becoming a major body of labor relations jurisprudence. For the parties to it, the award has the same binding and enforceable effect as a legal agreement; for other employees and unions, it is a valuable guide that shows what the problem was, what each side's contentions were, what the arbitrator decided, and why. The increasing use of arbitrators with professional stature and training has added considerably to the practical value of labor awards.[13]

[13]*Labor Course* (Englewood Cliffs, New Jersey: Prentice-Hall, Inc., 1962).

While the arbitration of past grievances does provide a background against which other cases may be viewed, it is important to recognize that each situation is different and that comparisons between arbitration cases are often difficult as well as dangerous. Furthermore, the primary objective of arbitration is to help to generate good labor conditions. Therefore, the manner in which previous cases were handled or resolved should not restrict the arbitrator in the effective handling of his cases.

Increased status of arbitration. The status of arbitration has been enhanced in recent years by Supreme Court rulings. In 1957 the Supreme Court decided in the Lincoln Mills case that agreements to arbitrate are enforceable under the Labor-Management Relations Act, when the agreement includes a no-strike provision. In another case, involving the Warrior and Gulf Navigation Company, the Supreme Court ruled that the presence of an absolute no-strike clause in the agreement subjects everything that management does to the agreement. As a result, the Supreme Court defines management rights as only those "over which the contract gives management complete control and unfettered discretion." For a company to prove that it has retained a management right, the Supreme Court insists that the exclusion of a specific management right from the grievance procedure be embodied either in the labor agreement or in a collateral agreement. In the absence of this, only "the most forceful evidence" will deter the operation of the grievance procedure in handling a grievance involving a claimed management right.[14]

The award. The arbitrator's decision is known as the *award.* In the statement of award, the arbitrator must cover every point of issue included in the submission agreement as well as an analysis of the issues which supports his decision. While the award must be stated positively, the statement of analysis of the issues which is part of the statement of award provides the arbitrator with an opportunity to include pertinent aspects of the issue that permit the "losing" side to save face. Since arbitrators derive their powers from the agreement between the disputing parties, they do not have the authority to make an award that affects the rights of anyone else. Generally, the arbitrator's award is enforced by the voluntary action of the parties concerned. It is, however, enforceable under common law and under state arbitration statutes.

While only a very small fraction of the grievances that are filed reach the final stage, arbitration is an important feature of the labor-management

---

[14]John J. McKew, "Supreme Court Looks at Arbitration," *Management Record,* Vol. 23, No. 4 (April, 1961), pp. 17–22.

agreement. Arbitration procedures insure that the rights of employees and management alike will be protected. In providing for equal justice to both sides, it serves to strengthen the free enterprise system that demands the cooperation of both management and labor.

Disciplinary Action

The discussion up to this point has focused on the grievance procedure, which is designed basically to protect the individual employee. As noted previously, management may also use the same procedure in cases where it desires to take action against the union or an employee who has violated company rules. The typical approach, however, in cases involving one or a few employees is for management to take disciplinary action against them.

Disciplinary action refers to the action taken by management to correct the attitudes and behavior of employees who have violated company rules, have failed to maintain required standards of performance, or have acted contrary to established policy. Such action may range from admonishments or reprimands to discharge from the company, depending upon the severity of the infraction and the number of times it has been repeated. While disciplinary action is taken by management, it should not be inferred that the union has no voice in the action. If the union believes that the action is unfair, it will counter management's action by filing a grievance in behalf of the employee concerned. In fact, grievances over discipline constitute one of the largest single groups of all arbitration cases;[15] and in half of these grievances, management's action is reversed or modified by the arbitrator. As increasing numbers of grievance cases go to arbitration and awards are made in favor of the employee and the union, management's authority to make rules and enforce them is correspondingly reduced. Even in nonunionized companies management's approach to disciplinary problems is influenced by the trend among unionized companies. The threat of unionization and tight labor markets in certain occupational fields actually limits management's ability to take disciplinary action. While management must maintain a strong but fair position in this area of personnel management, it can only do so by having policies and procedures that will withstand the various pressures to which they are subjected.

Effective Disciplinary Action

It is important to the welfare of the employees as well as to management that there be effective discipline or adherence to company rules,

[15]*Industrial Relations News* (August, 1960).

providing, of course, that the rules and regulations are just and reasonable. Most of the published rules are ordinarily of such a nature that they help to protect the safety and general welfare of the worker. Like civil laws, they are established to protect the group from the occasional misbehavior of some of its members. Merely having the rules, however, is not sufficient. Unlike civil laws, ignorance of company rules can be an excuse that the employee may use to vindicate his behavior. Therefore, rules must be explained to all personnel and enforced by management on an impartial basis if they are to yield the desired effect — namely, to emphasize to the employees the importance of abiding by the rules and regulations.

The supervisor's responsibility. It is the responsibility of the first-line supervisor to enforce the rules of the company. In most instances this is achieved without resorting to any type of disciplinary action. Occasionally, however, it is necessary for the supervisor to use his disciplinary powers. He should approach a disciplinary situation with a humanistic as well as a legalistic attitude. The causes underlying the employee's misbehavior are as important as the act itself, and any attempt to prevent further recurrence will require an understanding of the basic causes of the employee's behavior. It is often difficult for the supervisor to maintain an objective attitude toward infractions of employees; but if he can approach such problems with a problem-solving attitude, he is more likely to come up with a diagnosis that is nearer to the truth than if he used the approach of a trial lawyer.[16]

In attempting to uncover reasons for employee misbehavior, the supervisor should keep in mind the fact that the employee may not be aware that there is a rule covering such conduct or he may not know how it applies to a particular situation. While the employee may use this as an excuse, the supervisor should also consider whether or not he has given the employee careful and thorough indoctrination in company rules and regulations and whether the employee is competent to perform in accordance with the rules covering his job. The perceptive supervisor is able to assess the attitudes and behavior of his subordinates on a day-to-day basis and can mold an employee's behavior so that he will follow the rules because he wants to and not because someone was making him do it. This development of self-discipline in subordinates is certainly desirable; however, there

---

[16]For purposes of identifying personality characteristics with choice and actual implementation of various styles of discipline, Shell and Cummings have developed a scale for measuring attitudes toward discipline ranging from pure humanitarian to pure legalistic. See "Enforcing the Rules: How Do Managers Differ?" *Personnel*, Vol. 43, No. 2 (March–April, 1966), pp. 33–39.

will still be a need for an imposed discipline to reform the offender and deter others.[17]

Need for fair treatment. Definite policies and procedures for handling disciplinary matters are essential for insuring fair treatment of offenders. Each supervisor should be furnished with a written policy and a standardized procedure, including recommended penalties for specific infractions of the rules that may serve as a guide in determining what type of disciplinary action should be taken. While it is usually recommended that disciplinary action be handled on an impartial basis without regard for the specific circumstances involved, most individuals rebel against the imposition of inflexible rules. Rather than being forced into the rigid enforcement of rules and not being supported by management, supervisors will often "turn their heads" and fail to take any action on employee behavior that, according to the rule book, should be formally recognized and appropriately disciplined. In fact, this inaction on the part of supervisors, which has become commonplace, is referred to as the *indulgency pattern.*

One writer has suggested that rather than have inflexible rules that are not followed because of the additional problems created by their enforcement, it is more desirable to have a policy that allows for flexibility. Seybold suggests the following steps in planning such a policy:

1. Our objective must be to provide consistency of enforcement and predictability of company response. Consequently, rules and obligations must be clearly formulated and understood by all concerned.
2. Violations or deviations cannot be ignored, even if no penalties are forthcoming. The Company must make the offender aware of the fact that it knows of the offense.
3. Penalties (warnings, docking, disciplinary layoff, discharge) must be related to the offenses in such fashion that the violator can predict the probable area of his punishment. He need not be able to anticipate the precise degree of penalty to be meted out, but he must be able to judge *approximately* what the result will be.
4. Within this permissible area there is room for personalization, based upon such considerations as these:
    a. Were there extenuating circumstances?
    b. Was the violation such as to indicate contempt for authority, carelessness, absent-mindedness, loss of temper, etc.?
    c. How does this person respond to discipline?
    d. To what extent are there overtones of "test case" or "example" in the situation? Is the employee testing a rule? Is the company seeking an example? Are the motives in either situation pertinent?

---

[17]Aaron Q. Sartain and Alton W. Baker, *The Supervisor and His Job* (New York: McGraw-Hill Book Company, 1965), pp. 323–329.

    e. Is it feasible to share the decision (with respect to the degree of discipline to be imposed, within the permissible area) with others, especially union representatives?

    f. Can the company establish the basis for differentiating this situation from others? If so, is it feasible for the company to expect that these distinguishing characteristics can be understood and appreciated either by the union officials or by the rank and file?[18]

Seybold believes that if a personalized and liberal policy can be implemented without incurring ill will and creating jealousies or playing favorites, without sacrifice of production and efficiency, and without turning the personnel officer into a little paternalistic czar, then the art of industrial human relations will have been mastered.

Importance of facts and evidence. Before taking any disciplinary action, the supervisor should interview the employee with a view to obtaining his reasons for his behavior, his attitude, and any information that will enable the supervisor to understand the infraction. Even though the supervisor may be angry over what has happened, he should make every effort to approach the employee in an objective and understanding manner. It is particularly desirable that the supervisor avoid "taking personally" certain forms of employee behavior that may represent a reaction to frustration. The supervisor should react in terms of the situation rather than in terms of his own ego needs. It should not be inferred that disciplinary action should be avoided at all costs, but it should be based on understanding and good judgment rather than upon the supervisor's emotional reaction to the problem situation.

A record of offenses and disciplinary action taken is usually maintained in the employee's personnel file. This not only provides a complete work history of each employee but also serves as a basis for determining disciplinary action and evaluating the company's disciplinary policies and procedures. It is often found advisable to record the fact that the employee was reprimanded by a written notice. A copy of the notice is given to the employee and a copy sent to the personnel department for inclusion in the employee's file. With such records on file the company is in a better position to counteract any charges by the union that the employee was not warned and, therefore, should not receive disciplinary action.

Maintenance of proper records also provides management with valuable information about the worth of its rules and regulations. Those rules that are violated most frequently should receive particular attention.

---

[18]John W. Seybold, "How Personal Can a Personnel Policy Be?" *Personnel Journal*, Vol. 37, No. 8 (January, 1959), pp. 285–287.

The need for them may no longer exist or some alteration may need to be made that will facilitate their enforcement. If the rule has little or no value in protecting employee morale, safety, or company property, it probably should be revised or rescinded. Otherwise, employees are likely to feel that management is overrestricting their behavior and may retaliate by thinking up ways to harass the supervisory personnel, as illustrated in Figure 17-6. While the working conditions depicted in this cartoon are no longer typical of most factories, the principle illustrated is still applicable.

Figure 17-6

THE MAN WITH THE WHOA

Source: *Out Our Way* cartoons by J. R. Williams. Reproduced with permission of NEA Service, Inc.

Union reactions to discipline. The union is interested in the rules and regulations that form the basis for employee discipline because these matters concern the welfare of its members. If an employee is suspended or discharged for violating a regulation, the union is obliged to investigate and determine whether such action on the part of management was justified. The manner in which disciplinary cases are handled is usually an important factor in determining the attitude of union officers. Where objectivity and fairness prevail, the union is likely to be more reasonable in its reactions to disciplinary actions. Similarly, if the union is kept informed, there is less room for misunderstanding. It is usually helpful, therefore, to keep union representatives advised of infractions and any warnings that are issued to the employee.

In a thorough review of arbitrator's awards made over a twenty-year period, a labor-law expert has evolved a list of seven rules that will "stick." These are listed and pictured in Figure 17-7 on page 478. Even without an agreement, these rules are useful benchmarks in developing and maintaining discipline.

The development of the labor agreement and provision for arbitration of grievances have led to considerable centralization of the labor relations function in many companies. Because of the requirement that penalties be assessed under rules in harmony with the principles of the labor agreement and because there must be some consistency if a penalty is to stand the test of arbitration, disciplinary powers in many companies have been taken from the supervisor and placed in the hands of staff specialists or higher managers. Even where this has not been done, the supervisor relies upon the staff for advice in how to handle disciplinary cases. Otherwise, if a grievance results, the supervisor may find that his action is not supported by higher authority in the company.[19]

Employee Discharges

Discharge is the most drastic administrative action that can be taken. It is used against an employee who has committed a serious offense or has a record of repeated violations of company rules. It is also used to remove workers who cannot be utilized effectively in any job because of incompetence or inability to perform adequately. It was once a popular type of disciplinary action, but in recent years the trend has been for companies to resort to discharge action less frequently because of restrictions imposed upon them by the unions and by law. The shortage of trained personnel in many fields has also made discharge an unpopular way of handling problems with employees who have valuable talents but who may present behavior problems that occasionally disrupt the organization or infuriate the managers.

Authority for discharges. At one time it was customary to give the supervisor the power to discharge an employee whom he felt was not

---

[19]Dallas L. Jones, "The Supervisor and the Disciplinary Process in a Unionized Setting," *Personnel Administration*, Vol. 26, No. 1 (January–February, 1963), pp. 42–48.

Figure 17-7

7 Laws for
Making Plant Rules
That Will Stick

1. Make the rule reasonable

2. Stay out of private lives

3. Don't keep rules in your hat

4. Correct—don't punish

5. Make the punishment uniform

6. Don't double up punishment

7. Grant the benefit of the doubt

Source: An article by Paul A. King, "Tips to Successful Discipline," *Factory Management and Maintenance*, Vol. 116, No. 6 (June, 1958), p. 78. Reproduced with permission.

adequate for the job for any reason whatsoever, but this is no longer the accepted practice. Too many supervisors took advantage of the discharge authority as an opportunity to remove evidences of their own mistakes and inadequacies. While it is believed that the supervisor should have the authority to discharge or recommend that an employee be discharged from his department, it is generally agreed by management authorities that he should not be in a position to remove him from the company. It is possible that the employee could be effectively utilized in another job and under a different supervisor. In many instances the basic reason for the discharge action is a conflict of personalities that can only be resolved by placing the employee in a different department. Similarly, an employee's ineptness for one type of work may not interfere with his performing satisfactorily at another job. The personnel department must also avert any discharge action that may be in violation of the labor agreement or government regulations. Most companies thus provide for some type of review of recommended discharge cases to insure that fair and impartial consideration has been given.

When it is determined that discharge is warranted, every effort should be made by line and staff personnel to maintain pleasant relationships with the employee who is about to be discharged. When it can be done sincerely, he should be given as much help as possible in locating suitable employment. If the company employs counselors, they may be of further assistance at this time in helping the individual to realize his inadequacies and in helping him to become a more acceptable member of the business society.

Unfair practices. Since management is responsible for the effective operation of the business, it should be able to hire, discipline, discharge, promote, transfer, and take similar personnel actions subject only to the restrictions provided in the labor agreement. On the other hand, the union should have the opportunity to appeal any decision of management that it believes is discriminatory against the union or its members. The Labor-Management Relations (Taft-Hartley) Act, which is discussed in detail in Chapter 18, specifically recognizes the rights of employees and unions in this regard and provides for the redress of any action taken by management that constitutes an unfair labor practice. Therefore, in the interest of avoiding such charges and of developing effective human relations, management should have definite policies concerning discharges. The following policies are suggested by one authority:

1. Have as few disciplinary rules as possible, for the sake of simplicity; make them well known to the employees; and enforce them uniformly and strictly.
2. Have a well-defined or clearly understood seniority or other system to follow in the event of seasonal layoffs and business slumps, and adhere strictly to the system.
3. In taking back employees, following layoffs, follow seniority rules.
4. Give employees performing inefficient work sufficient and specific warning of their derelictions before invoking discharge.
5. Make absolutely certain that inefficient work, violation of rules, insubordination, and other offenses meriting discharge are actually the fault of the employee under suspicion.
6. Avoid giving favorable jobs and favorable treatment to nonunion employees over union employees, unless the employee's work actually deserves such treatment.
7. Do not discharge employees merely because they have incurred the displeasure of their union, unless it is for nonpayment of dues or initiation fees under a union shop contract.[20]

In addition to legislation concerning the rights of employees and unions, the fair employment practice legislation of the federal government and of several of the states and cities protects the employment rights of individuals. Such legislation, as noted in Chapter 6, is designed to prevent employers from discriminating against individuals because of their sex, race, color, creed, or national origin. Employers must not only be careful not to discriminate against individuals whom they are considering for employment but must also be cautious that employees are not discharged because someone in the company is prejudiced against them. By having sound policies for disciplinary action and effective procedures for implementing them, the rights of employees to fair treatment by the employer may be realized, and the company may benefit from the goodwill that usually follows.

Résumé

Throughout this chapter the importance of having established policies and procedures that will protect the rights of both management and labor has been emphasized. While harmony as well as productive results can usually be achieved and maintained through management's attention to motivation, communication, morale, and employee adjustment, occasionally it is necessary to use other processes. The dissatisfactions of employees may be openly and honestly expressed through the established grievance machinery. In this way, employee attitudes that have not heretofore been

---

[20]*Labor Course, op. cit.,* Paragraph 4304.

recognized and satisfactorily handled may be reconsidered by representatives of labor and management who are not directly involved in the grievance. Similarly, management dissatisfactions with employee performance and behavior may be resolved through disciplinary action. The grievance and disciplinary procedures thus serve as safety valves and help to preserve the type of relationship between management and labor required for harmony and productivity. While the existence of a grievance procedure may be limited to companies having a union contract, it can prove to be valuable to companies without such a contract. It provides an equitable and fair basis for handling employee dissatisfactions. Disciplinary actions should likewise be administered through a carefully planned program. Planned programs such as these are usually recognized by employees as attempts on the part of the employer to be "fair and square" — qualities that employees have come to expect.

DISCUSSION QUESTIONS AND PROBLEMS

1. One company gave a written warning to an employee for criticizing the integrity of the company in a loud and profane manner late one afternoon in a nearby tavern. The company justified its action on the grounds that the employee's conduct was detrimental to the company's reputation. The company further maintained that the employee had always been free to discuss his grievances with his foreman or to process them through the grievance procedure. What is your reaction to this incident?

2. The Oxford Paper Company has had fewer grievances since it established a standing committee composed of union and management representatives for the purpose of previewing company plans and discussing employee problems at each of its mills. Minutes of all meetings are reported in abbreviated form in plant newsletters.
   a. What is the probable reason for the decline in grievances?
   b. Should the personnel manager be on the committee? Why?

3. What are the implications and possible effects of an employee discussing a grievance with his steward before taking it up with his supervisor?

4. An employee of the Ajax Washing Machine Company had a sick sister and father. Because of this his job attendance was poor. In a six-month period he was able to work only 60 days. The company decided to discharge him.
   a. Was it fair in its action?
   b. Is it likely that the union will contest this action? Discuss.

5. Unions certified as exclusive bargaining representatives must handle grievances for employees who are not members of the union, according to a National Labor Relations Board ruling.
   a. What is the reason for this ruling?
   b. What is likely to happen if nonmembers were not represented?

6. Pfiffner and Fels (see suggested readings for this chapter) state: "It would seem that public and private management of labor relations are moving

toward each other in actual practice. Industry is taking on more and more of the legalistic job security aspect of civil service procedure, while government employees are becoming more widely unionized."

a. How do you account for these trends?

b. What implications do they have for students who are planning a career in business?

7. What action should management take if it finds that an unusually large number of grievances are filed by employees in a particular department?

8. The Eli Lilly Company's grievance procedure does not call for grievances to be put into writing until the third step. What effect is this likely to have on the number of grievances that ultimately go to arbitration? Why?

CASE 17-1

NO OVERTIME

The routemen of the Crispy Potato Chip Company receive a salary that is based upon a 40-hour week plus a commission. The company has never paid overtime since the routes were organized so that they could be completed within the allotted time. Furthermore, the men usually benefited from any additional time spent on the job through higher commissions. It was entirely up to the men if they wanted to work any time over the 40 hours.

The union officers discovered that several routemen showed up on their routes on days off and worked in excess of the 40 hours prescribed in the contract; and, as a result, the union demanded that thereafter the company pay overtime under such conditions. Management again advised the routemen that it would not pay overtime and that the routemen should be aware of this fact. Nevertheless, several of the routemen continued to work more than a 40-hour week, and the union demanded that they be paid for the extra time. Since the company still refused to do this, the union took the case to arbitration; and the arbitrator ruled that the company would have to pay for any overtime that had been worked.

At this point the company called a meeting with all of its routemen and the union representatives and advised everyone that from now on there was to be no overtime worked and no overtime paid. If there were any routemen who could not handle their routes in a 40-hour period, they were to speak up at that time so that necessary adjustments could be made. One man brought up the problem of his route at the edge of the city being longer than the others, so the company agreed to overtime on his particular route but not on any of the others. The union agreed to these arrangements.

a. Do you agree with the arbitrator's award? Why?

b. Is the union fair and realistic in making the type of demand that it did?

c. Should this case have been permitted to arise?

CASE 17-2

THE PRIVATE INVESTIGATORS*

After the theft of a few hundred pounds of copper tubing from a factory stockroom one weekend, management put a staff of investigators on the job. They arranged interviews on company time with all employees who might be

*American Arbitration Association Case No. L-15638-43. Reproduced with permission of the American Arbitration Association.

presumed to have information shedding light on the subject. The investigators had no authority to discipline anyone. All they could do was gather the facts and report to management.

Although none of the men questioned was accused of the crime, one employee demanded that a union representative be present during the interview. When this request was rejected, a grievance was filed to determine whether the contract, which provided for union representation in discussing grievances, applied to an interview by criminal investigators as well.

"Of course it applies," argued the union business agent. "The investigators' report might lead to action that would affect a man's job. Besides, we don't like the way some of these investigators have been carrying on."

The company answered: "The grievance procedure provides for union participation. If anyone is hurt by the investigation, that will be the time to complain and no one will bar the union. The investigators have the right to work in private. There is nothing in the contract to prevent it, and no one is deprived of his rights by this procedure."

Eventually, the case went to arbitration under the rules of the American Arbitration Association.

a. If you were the arbitrator, how would you rule in this case?

CASE 17-3

"BUCKSKIN BILL"

William "Bill" Miller was employed as a compressor operator by the Saturn Aero-Space Company at a U.S. Air Force missile installation in the western United States. The company performed service and maintenance work on missiles for the Air Force under governmental contract. Most of the employees of that company, like Bill, were members of an international union.

Bill had always performed his job satisfactorily and never been a problem to his supervisor until he won a whisker-growing contest. The contest had been sponsored by the local town as a part of its annual frontier days celebration. Although a number of employees had grown beards for the occasion, most of them shaved their beards off once the celebration was over. Bill Miller, however, stimulated by the contest results, continued to wear his beard and to let his hair grow even longer until he resembled a picture of Buffalo Bill. He adopted a complete Western outfit and looked as though he had just come off a Hollywood movie set. He bought a long bull whip with which he would practice during the lunch hour. He also began making personal appearances at local fairs and rodeos and even tried without success to obtain part-time roles in Western movies. He assumed the name of "Buckskin Bill" which he had painted on his car and horse trailer.

Needless to say, Bill attracted considerable attention at work but since he continued to do his job satisfactorily his supervisor decided not to make an issue over his appearance. When operating compressors, Bill took precautions to tie his hair up in a bandana so that it would not present a safety hazard.

Most of the employees with whom he worked liked Bill and gradually became accustomed to his appearance to the point of passing him off as a "character." Visitors to the base, however, were startled when they received their first glance of Bill who did not look like anything that they would expect to see at a space-age missile installation. Bill's department manager began to recognize that Bill's appearance was becoming a problem but still hesitated to take action. Finally, a general from Washington who was visiting the base was startled by the sight of Bill and stated bluntly that he did not want to see anybody who presented such an appearance working on the base.

Since Bill was scheduled to begin a two-week vacation, he was told that he would either have to come back without his long hair, beard, and Western attire or that he should plan not to return at all. His supervisor's parting words were, "I'm sorry, Bill, but if you are not cleaned up when you return I will have to fire you."

At the end of his vacation, Bill, who had refused to change his appearance did not return to work but instead filed a grievance with his union. In his grievance Bill charged that he was being discharged without "just cause" in violation of the labor agreement. His grievance went on to assert that his appearance had not constituted a safety or health hazard, that his work had always been good and that his record was free of any bad marks. Bill also maintained that there was nothing in company rules and regulations that forbade his style of appearance and dress and that the company's action infringed upon his freedom of choice of dress and style of personal grooming.

Since the company and the union were unable to agree upon a solution to the grievance, it went eventually to arbitration. By the time the case reached arbitration, however, Bill had received considerable publicity and support for his case, including two appearances on day-time television shows during which he presented his case to public viewers.

    a. What explanation can you give for Bill's behavior? Could this problem have been prevented from becoming an issue?

    b. To what extent does the employer have a right to dictate an employee's appearance and dress?

    c. Did the company in this case infringe upon Bill's legal rights?

    d. If you were the arbitrator, how would you rule in this case?

SUGGESTED READINGS

Chruden, Herbert J., and Arthur W. Sherman, Jr. *Readings in Personnel Management*, Second Edition. Cincinnati: South-Western Publishing Company, Inc., 1966. Chapter 11.

Davis, Keith. *Human Relations at Work*. New York: McGraw-Hill Book Company, 1962. Chapter 15.

Herron, John S., Jr. "Negotiating and Administering the Grievance Procedure," in Elizabeth Marting (Editor). *Understanding Collective Bargaining*. New York: American Management Association, 1958, 222–234.

Kuhn, James W. *Bargaining in Grievance Settlement*. New York: Columbia University Press, 1961.

Pfiffner, John M., and Marshal Fels. *The Supervision of Personnel*, Third Edition. Englewood Cliffs, New Jersey: Prentice-Hall, Inc., 1964. Chapter 7.

Scott, William G. *The Management of Conflict — Appeal Systems in Organizations*. Homewood, Illinois: Richard D. Irwin, Inc. and The Dorsey Press, 1965.

Stagner, Ross, and Hjalmer Rosen. *Psychology of Union-Management Relations*. Belmont, California: Wadsworth Publishing Co., Inc., 1965.

Stessin, Lawrence. *Employee Discipline*. Washington, D.C.: The Bureau of National Affairs, Inc., 1960.

Stone, Morris. *Labor Grievances and Decisions*. New York: Harper and Row, 1965.

18

The Union and Its Role in Personnel Management

The discussion of personnel management thus far has been concerned with the development of a personnel program in terms of company requirements and objectives. It has been stressed, however, that in unionized companies the type of personnel program which management may be able to develop and the ease with which the program can be administered are also contingent upon management's ability to gain union acceptance and cooperation with respect to the program.

Now that unions have become an established and accepted part of our industrial society with their collective bargaining rights protected by law, it is essential that management make every effort to work with those unions that may represent its employees. Management must also be prepared to maintain relations with any union that may represent its employees and do so in a manner that will conform to existing legal regulations and that will not needlessly antagonize the union officers with whom it may have to negotiate and administer a labor agreement.

In order to develop a working relationship with a union and in order to bargain effectively with its representatives, management should possess some knowledge about the objectives and problems of the union. While it may be difficult for some managers to avoid becoming resentful when union representatives challenge their actions and encroach upon what have previously been the prerogatives of management, these managers will be likely to cope with such problems more effectively if they have sufficient understanding of and empathy for the union's position. The purpose of this and the next chapter is to provide the reader with a better understanding of union objectives and practices as well as the laws relating to union-management relations and their implications for management.

The principal topics discussed in this chapter include:

- The functions of a union.
- The growth of organized labor.
- Union organization and leadership.
- Government legislation and its impact.
- Current problems and goals of unions.

The Functions of a Union

One of the primary functions of a union is to negotiate an agreement with the company covering conditions of employment for its members and to make certain that the company continually lives up to the terms of this agreement.[1] Another and equally important function of the union is that of protecting the interests of its members from unfair or arbitrary treatment by management and of assisting them in resolving any grievances that may arise in connection with their employment. In fulfilling these functions the union can have a decided impact upon the company's personnel program and upon its relations with employees. The union's presence can also bring about a change in the attitude and behavior of the employees toward the company by providing them with a sense of security, of importance, and of power in their relations with management that they previously did not possess as individuals.

Impact of the Union upon the Company

When a union is recognized and certified as the bargaining agent for its employees, a company is likely to have to use a portion of the time that it previously devoted to other personnel functions for negotiating the labor agreement and for discussing problems and grievances with union representatives relating to its administration. Additional and more accurate

---

[1]Although the terms contract and agreement tend to be used interchangeably, the term agreement is the more technically correct one since it lacks the requirement of specific performance — of compelling an employee to work against his will.

personnel and financial records may also have to be maintained in order to support the company's position during contract negotiations or grievance hearings. Greater care also will have to be given by the company in the development and enforcement of personnel policies and regulations so as to insure that employees throughout the organization are treated in a manner that is fair and consistent. Since a union is quick to detect and to challenge any inconsistencies in personnel actions or inequities in the treatment of personnel that may occur between departments, its presence is likely to make more centralized control over personnel policies and practices necessary.

The presence of the union may cause the company's relations with its employees to become more complex since many of the changes and decisions relating to wages, hours, working conditions, etc., that affect their welfare may first have to be discussed with and approved by union representatives. As a result of this condition, management's ability to resolve problems directly and quickly with the individuals who are involved may be lessened. First-line supervisors in particular may find their status and authority reduced and their relations with subordinates made more difficult because of the presence of a union steward who may challenge their decisions. Not only is the supervisor required to assume the added responsibility of enforcing the terms of the labor agreement but also he may find his efforts to maintain efficiency and discipline within his department challenged by the union. If supervisors have their disciplinary actions challenged by the union and reversed through the grievance procedure, the supervisors may be tempted to ignore rather than to face certain of the personnel problems that arise within their departments. Rather than take disciplinary action, for example, supervisors may be tempted to overlook certain violations committed by their subordinates. If management fails to help them in their relations with the union, the supervisors may feel that they are being sacrificed to the union by their superiors.[2]

The union quite often may seek the right to participate in company decisions which do not relate directly to the personnel program but which the union believes may indirectly affect the employment and welfare of its members. If the union is not granted the opportunity to participate or to be consulted with respect to these decisions, it may seek recourse by initiating a slowdown or a walkout or by challenging management's decisions through the grievance procedure. Specifically, the union may try to extend its right of participation in such management decisions as those relating to:

---

[2]See F. J. Roethlisberger, "The Foreman: Master and Victim of Double Talk," *Harvard Business Review*, Vol. 23, No. 3 (Spring, 1945), pp. 283–298.

the location of a new plant, the subcontracting of certain work, the introduction of new production equipment and methods, the scheduling of the work load, the establishment of production standards, and the determination of job content. While a company may want to exercise absolute authority over these or other decisions by claiming them as the exclusive prerogatives of management, it is likely to find that any such prerogatives are subject to challenge and erosion by the union.

Appeal of the Union to Its Members

There undoubtedly are employers who sincerely believe that a great many of their employees belong to a union only because they are compelled to do so by the union agreement or by group pressures. Available evidence, however, would seem to indicate that most union leaders today would have difficulty in compelling a majority of the employees in any company to remain in the union very long against their will. It also would appear that a large portion of those employees who belong to a union maintain their membership because they feel it is beneficial to them. Furthermore, many of those employees who are compelled to join a union initially in order to retain their jobs can come to accept the union after they have become involved with it.[3]

Satisfaction of Needs. According to Stagner and Rosen, a union comes into being when a large number of employees have or think that they have needs, such as those discussed earlier in the chapter on motivation, that are frustrated by the companies. The union thus provides a vehicle for the satisfaction of their needs even though these needs may vary considerably among employees.[4] Union membership also can provide certain employees with a means for releasing pent-up frustrations, for building self-confidence, or for putting dormant leadership capacities to work. It also may provide employees with new sources of interest, an outlet for their idle time, and a means of satisfying their desires for status, recognition, and group associations. Through their union employees often have an opportunity to become better acquainted and to fraternize with other persons who have similar desires, interests, problems, and gripes. Identification with the union can give the employee an added feeling of security and equality in his relations with his boss. As a member of a union he need have less hesitation in challenging those actions of his boss with which he disagrees

---

[3]Ross Stagner, *Psychology of Industrial Conflict* (New York: John Wiley & Sons, 1956), pp. 339–344.

[4]Ross Stagner and Hjalmar Rosen, *Psychology of Union-Management Relations* (Belmont, California: Wadsworth Publishing Company, Inc., 1965), p. 40.

or in expressing his sentiments freely about his job since he knows that the union is obligated to provide protection from possible retaliatory action by his boss.[5]

The economic advantages that a union can offer its members are among the most important and are usually the most frequently mentioned benefits of all. By bargaining collectively with an employer, employees have far greater strength than they would ever have as individuals, and they are able to demand more substantial economic improvements in their employment conditions.

Union services. Aside from representing and protecting the employment rights of its members, many unions are now providing, frequently with management cooperation, a broad range of personal benefits and services for employees and their families. It is becoming more common for unions to maintain vacation retreats and various recreation facilities for their members. Health clinics, legal aid, and urban housing ventures have also been sponsored by unions.[6] Other benefits include college scholarships for members' children, free eye glasses, prepaid dental plans, cut-rate drugs, psychiatric care, cha-cha lessons, and courses in oil painting. Unions also have sponsored community "watch dog groups" to insure that their members as well as other consumers are not cheated in the marketplace or are not subjected to exorbitant interest rates. A Los Angeles County Federation of Labor drive, for example, has helped to force the funeral industry in its area to make certain reforms. In Texas an AFL-CIO group has been contesting automobile insurance rates, and in Michigan and Ohio the United Auto Workers have been fighting to hold down increases in health insurance rates.[7] As a result of these and other efforts, unions are becoming more involved in civic activities and in promoting the welfare of the public as a whole, rather than just the welfare of the union members. Such efforts, aside from contributing to society, help unions to improve their public image.

The Growth of Organized Labor

Unions have existed in the United States since the Colonial Period although they have changed substantially in character and function since

---

[5]For an interesting article on the conflict between the personal needs of employees and their organizational environment see Chris Argyris, "Organizational Leadership and Participative Management," *The Journal of Business*, Vol. XXVII, No. 1 (January, 1955), pp. 283–298.

[6]*Wall Street Journal*, December 22, 1959.

[7]*Business Week*, September 18, 1965, pp. 150–160.

that period. Originally unions were local in scope and functioned largely as fraternal societies to provide mutual help and assistance for the members. The tendency of the union to refer to their members as brothers and sisters is a carry-over of this earlier concept of fraternalism.

Initial Employer Reactions to Unions

The early-day union seldom was able to exert much pressure upon employers. If the business panics and recessions did not curb their membership, the employer was able to do so by discharging the union members, by maintaining a blacklist with other employers of active unionists, by refusing to deal with union representatives, or by requiring new employees to sign a *yellow dog contract* in which they agreed not to join a union. If employers were unable to curtail union growth by these means, they could obtain court injunctions forbidding union organizing or strike activities, or they could charge unions with criminal action under the prevailing *conspiracy doctrine*. This doctrine held that union efforts to bring economic pressure to bear upon an employer were illegal acts of conspiracy.

Changing Attitudes Toward Unions

One of the first major victories of organized labor came with the reversal of the conspiracy doctrine in the *Commonwealth* v. *Hunt* Case of 1842. In reversing its earlier interpretations with respect to this doctrine, the judiciary undoubtedly gave recognition to the change that was occurring in public opinion toward unions. By this date public opinion was beginning to demand that improvements for the laboring man be made in the area of social welfare and in employment conditions. As compared with today's employment conditions, those at that time and even as late as the 1930's were often deplorable.

Much of the effort of unions during the 1800's was directed toward the promotion of social and political reforms, the achievement of universal suffrage, and the extension of free public education. A few unions became primarily ideological in nature and promoted such ideologies as socialism, Marxism, and syndicalism.[8] During this period unions also began to assume the role of minority pressure groups; they were intent upon generating favorable public opinion, upon rewarding political candidates and parties friendly to their cause, and upon withholding support from unfriendly political candidates and parties.

---

[8]Syndicalism was an economic movement aimed at the federation of workers in the various industries into autonomous associations for the purpose of enforcing economic demands through sympathetic strikes.

Development of National Affiliations

While the adversities experienced by unions caused their early growth to be slow, they still were able to achieve some progress. As early as the Colonial Period the local unions within some communities began to affiliate through local labor councils similar to those found in most communities today for the purpose of coordinating their activities and promoting the interests of labor within the region. By the middle 1800's certain local unions representing particular crafts had been able to unite and form what are now termed *national unions.* Following the Civil War a number of national unions affiliated to form the National Labor Union which, however, soon passed out of existence.

Knights of Labor. The first union federation to achieve significant size was the Knights of Labor, formed about 1869. This union welcomed individuals and local units into its ranks from all crafts and occupational areas. The Knights also actively engaged in several business cooperatives and in political activity. Although the union experienced a significant growth in size, its decline was hastened by the heterogeneous character of its membership, the lack of internal unity, the loss of several strikes, and the unfavorable public opinion which it encountered.

American Federation of Labor. The experiences of the Knights of Labor provided some important organizing lessons for its successor, the American Federation of Labor (AFL), which was formed in 1886 through the affiliation of some 25 craft unions. This federation under the able leadership of Samuel Gompers was able to profit from the mistakes of the Knights of Labor, and it became the first union to weather depressions and employer opposition. While the organization grew slowly at first and reached a membership of only 548,000 by 1900, it expanded rapidly to 1,676,000 members within the next four-year period.

The American Federation of Labor, as the term "federation" implies, was organized as a loosely-knit group of autonomous national unions which constituted the real power of the organization. The national unions within the federation originally were composed mainly of skilled craft workers; and although certain unskilled groups were also admitted, most of the craft unions were opposed to the admission of industrial workers into the AFL ranks. That more industrial workers were not admitted was the result of leadership inertia and the fear among certain craft groups that their status would be weakened by the admission of lesser skilled workers from the mass production industries. It was not until the Congress of

Industrial Organizations (CIO) began vigorously to organize industrial workers that the AFL as a whole became receptive to the admittance of industrial workers from the mass-production industries.

Congress of Industrial Organizations. The CIO was started when John L. Lewis, President of the United Mine Workers, together with the presidents of seven other unions formed a Committee for Industrial Organization within the AFL structure. The other unions in the Federation interpreted this action as constituting a threat to their security and in 1938 expelled the CIO group from the Federation. Shortly thereafter the expelled unions together with other unions held a convention and formed the Congress of Industrial Organizations.

Once established the CIO embarked upon a vigorous unionizing drive which was directed primarily toward industrial workers. The CIO unions therefore, are referred to as *industrial unions.* The CIO devoted particular emphasis to organizing new unions, to training personnel to handle the organizing drives, and to instituting educational and communication programs for the purpose of explaining the union's objectives and viewpoints to members, prospective members, and the general public. Although organizing, training, communication, and research activities were performed also by the AFL unions, these activities generally had not been emphasized to the degree that they were by the CIO.

In soliciting members the CIO has made a special effort to gain the support of minority groups by attempting to avoid racial and religious discrimination within its ranks. From the outset the CIO has placed considerable emphasis upon engaging itself in political activity at the local and national levels, a policy that Gompers and the AFL had opposed. This emphasis upon political activity eventually led to the establishment of the Political Action Committee (PAC) in 1943. Although the Taft-Hartley Act of 1947 placed certain curbs upon union campaigning for political candidates and upon the activities of the PAC, both the CIO and the AFL now participate in political affairs indirectly by giving their endorsement to candidates sympathetic to labor and by attempting to persuade their members to vote for these candidates.

Competition for members led to bitter jurisdictional conflicts between the AFL and the CIO union groups in their drives to organize different companies and occupational areas. The two groups, however, reunited in 1955 into a single AFL-CIO organization. A diagram showing the structure and composition of this new organization is contained in Figure 18-1.

Based upon data compiled by the Bureau of Labor Statistics, membership in this organization totals slightly over 15 million.[9]

Figure 18-1

STRUCTURE OF THE AFL-CIO

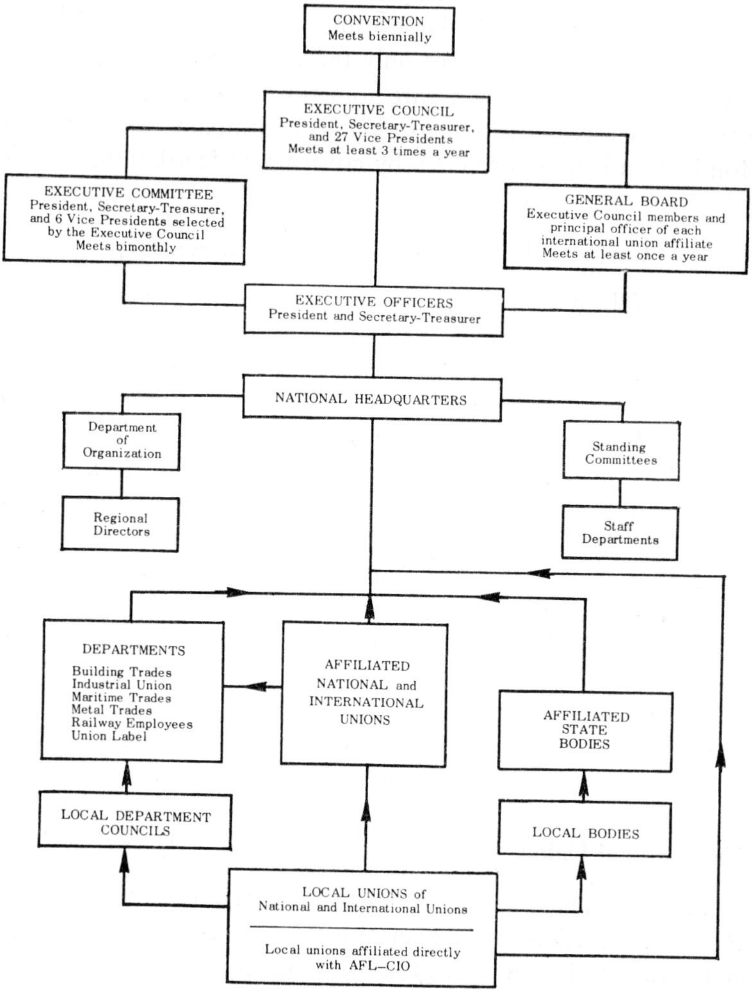

```
                        ┌──────────────────────┐
                        │     CONVENTION       │
                        │   Meets biennially   │
                        └──────────────────────┘
                                  │
                    ┌──────────────────────────────────┐
                    │      EXECUTIVE COUNCIL            │
                    │ President, Secretary-Treasurer,   │
                    │    and 27 Vice Presidents         │
                    │   Meets at least 3 times a year   │
                    └──────────────────────────────────┘
   ┌─────────────────────────┐                 ┌──────────────────────────┐
   │  EXECUTIVE COMMITTEE     │                 │     GENERAL BOARD         │
   │ President, Secretary-    │                 │ Executive Council members │
   │ Treasurer, and 6 Vice    │                 │   and principal officer   │
   │ Presidents selected by   │                 │      of each              │
   │  the Executive Council   │                 │ international union       │
   │   Meets bimonthly        │                 │ affiliate                 │
   │                          │                 │ Meets at least once a year│
   └─────────────────────────┘                 └──────────────────────────┘
                    ┌──────────────────────────────┐
                    │     EXECUTIVE OFFICERS        │
                    │ President and Secretary-       │
                    │        Treasurer               │
                    └──────────────────────────────┘
                                  │
                    ┌──────────────────────────────┐
                    │    NATIONAL HEADQUARTERS       │
                    └──────────────────────────────┘
   ┌──────────────┐                              ┌──────────────┐
   │ Department   │                              │  Standing    │
   │     of       │                              │ Committees   │
   │ Organization │                              └──────────────┘
   └──────────────┘
   ┌──────────────┐                              ┌──────────────┐
   │  Regional    │                              │   Staff      │
   │  Directors   │                              │ Departments  │
   └──────────────┘                              └──────────────┘

   ┌──────────────┐    ┌──────────────┐    ┌──────────────┐
   │ DEPARTMENTS  │    │  AFFILIATED  │    │  AFFILIATED  │
   │Building Trades│   │ NATIONAL and │    │    STATE     │
   │Industrial Un.│    │INTERNATIONAL │    │   BODIES     │
   │Maritime Trades│   │    UNIONS    │    └──────────────┘
   │Metal Trades  │    └──────────────┘
   │Railway Empl. │
   │Union Label   │
   └──────────────┘
   ┌──────────────┐                        ┌──────────────┐
   │LOCAL DEPARTMENT│                      │ LOCAL BODIES │
   │  COUNCILS     │                       └──────────────┘
   └──────────────┘
              ┌──────────────────────────────┐
              │     LOCAL UNIONS of           │
              │ National and International     │
              │         Unions                 │
              ├──────────────────────────────┤
              │ Local unions affiliated        │
              │ directly with AFL-CIO          │
              └──────────────────────────────┘
```

Source: *Directory of National and International Unions, 1964,* Bureau of Labor Statistics, Bulletin No. 1493, 1965, p. 147.

---

[9]U.S. Department of Labor, Bureau of Labor Statistics, *Directory of National and International Unions,* Bulletin No. 1493 (Washington, D.C.: U.S. Government Printing Office, 1964), p. 49.

Unaffiliated Unions

Although the majority of the national and international labor unions belong to the AFL-CIO, a number of unions, representing some 2.8 million members, are unaffiliated.[10] Among the more important of these unions are the United Mine Workers, the Railway Brotherhoods, and the Teamsters, the latter of which is the largest union in the United States. Those unaffiliated unions that represent only the employees within a particular company or part of a company are sometimes termed company unions. While this term was once used to refer to a company-dominated union, such domination is now forbidden by government legislation.

Union Organization and Leadership

In terms of the number of personnel who are employed by labor unions and the amount of funds that are handled by them, many of the larger unions today constitute sizable business operations. For example, according to the Bureau of Labor Statistics estimates, slightly over 13,000 full-time personnel are employed on the headquarters' staffs of the national unions.[11] These staffs, in addition to clerical personnel, also include attorneys, accountants, economists, statisticians, engineers, and other technical specialists. A union, like a business enterprise, therefore, must be effectively organized and administered if it is to function successfully. The basic organizational unit of a union is the local. Most locals are affiliated with a parent national organization which in turn is divided into regional areas or districts to service and to control certain of the activities of the locals. The functions of the national and the local union organizations, the relationship between them, and the problems that confront their leaders is the subject of discussion in the remainder of this section.

The National Union

The *national union* is the primary source of authority and control in any union organization whose operations extend beyond a local unit. The national's constitution provides the rules and conditions under which the local unions may be chartered and permitted to retain their membership in the national organization. While the degree of control that the parent organization maintains over its locals will vary, most national unions have regulations governing the collection of dues and initiation fees, the

---

[10] *Ibid.*
[11] *Ibid.*, p. 62.

administration of union funds, and the admission of members by the local. They also may require that certain standard provisions be included in labor contracts with employers. In return for the controls that it may exercise over the locals, the national union may provide them with professional and financial assistance during organizing drives and strikes as well as assistance in the negotiation and administration of labor contracts. The national unions also prepare various printed materials for use by the locals in their educational and public relations activities. A total of 189 publications, for example, are distributed by the national unions on a periodic basis.[12]

The negotiation of agreements that are purely local in scope usually are handled by the officers of the local. If assistance is needed in contract negotiations, however, national representatives may be called in by the local to provide moral and technical support or to help in overcoming a bargaining deadlock. When an agreement encompasses employers who maintain agreements covering more than one local, union representatives from the union's regional or national organization may conduct the negotiations.

Representatives from the national organization sometimes can assist an employer by exercising a stabilizing influence over the local bargaining committee and by preventing it from taking a drastic course of action. Because they are likely to have acquired greater experience and insight in labor relations, national representatives often can detect weaknesses in a local union's position and thus help its leaders to avoid bargaining difficulties.

Relations between the local and the employer, however, also can be impaired by the national organization if, for example, the national should insist that the local take strike action against its will to obtain the type of agreement that conforms to a national pattern. Again, if a local is forced by the national to spearhead new demands or to establish precedents that can be used as a pattern in dealing with other employers, a local may find itself involved in a strike over issues that are not particularly vital to its members and which may, in fact, be detrimental to the employees and the employer.

The Local Union

The *local union* is the organizational unit that maintains direct contact with the employers and with its members, and in many respects it is "the union" as far as both groups are concerned. The type of relationship that

---

[12]*Ibid.*, p. 63.

exists between the local union and the employer is influenced not only by the terms of the labor agreement but also by the abilities and personalities of the representatives on both sides who must negotiate and administer the agreement. Generally, when the provisions of an agreement are clear and both sides honestly try to cooperate in enforcing it, there is a greater likelihood that union-management relations will function smoothly.

Union-management relations also may be affected by the extent to which members concern themselves with union activities. Indifference and disinterest toward union affairs on the part of the more intelligent members unfortunately can enable an active minority of articulate but less competent members to assume control of the union. Sometimes the lack of participation in a union by the more intelligent members may be due to their fear that active participation will antagonize their boss and jeopardize their opportunity for company advancement. An employer's open contempt for a union, therefore, may be a factor in causing union leadership to go by default to persons who may find satisfaction in making trouble for the employer. Some students of industrial relations have advanced the argument that employers should encourage their more intelligent employees to take an active role in their union in order that the union will have able and responsible leadership.

Local Union Officers

The authority and duties of the local union officers as well as the rules governing their election, removal, and remuneration are usually set forth in the local union's charter and bylaws in accordance with the guidelines provided by the national constitution. In the locals of smaller size, the officers may hold full-time jobs and perform their duties of office without pay. In the larger unions a business representative may be employed to handle union activities on a full-time basis. This union officer, along with the stewards who are working in the companies represented by the union, is likely to be the person with whom these companies have the most frequent and direct contact. In many unions the business agent in the local is the major political power who actually runs the union. In such instances the president may occupy largely an honorary and minor role. In other unions, however, the president may be a full-time official who serves as the principal officer, while in still other unions the secretary-treasurer may be the most important officer. Regardless of which one of these representatives is the major power in a particular local, however, his attitude, competency, and behavior can be important factors in determining the degree of cooperation and harmony that can be achieved between the company and the union.

Business representative. Quite often the business representative is a member who has worked his way up within the local organization and who very likely has held other offices within it. He may exercise a considerable influence within a local union since he is in a position to gain the political support of the members by looking out for their employment interests and by being able to place friends in key assignments within the local. Besides making certain that employers abide by their labor agreements, the business agent usually exercises a key role in preparing for and in conducting the agreement negotiations. In addition to these activities he must be all things to all persons within the union. He frequently is forced into the role of counselor in helping the members with their personal problems. He also is expected to dispose satisfactorily of the members' grievances that cannot be settled by their stewards and also to help the employer correct members who are creating disciplinary problems.

The administering of the local organization is usually a significant part of the business representative's job. This task may include maintaining headquarters facilities, supervising an administrative staff, collecting dues, and recruiting new members. The handling of internal and external publicity for the local, coordinating social activities, and arranging for business and committee meetings also are generally a part of his administrative duties.

Shop steward. The shop steward represents the members with whom he works whenever they are unable to resolve their grievances with their foremen. He generally is elected by the members within the area that he represents. This area may be a certain unit within a plant, the entire plant of an employer, or the plants of several employers depending upon the number of members working in these plants. The general attitudes and actions of the steward can be important factors in determining the degree of cooperation that will exist between the union and the supervisor whose employees he represents.

Problems of the union officer. Some of the difficulties that employers experience with unions undoubtedly are due to their inability to understand the attitudes and problems of the union leaders. Employers may, for example, fail to recognize the political nature of the union officer's position which at times may force him to make demands that are neither wise nor reasonable. At times, for example, the union officer may be compelled to insist upon, or at least support, strike action over demands that he knows the company either cannot or will not concede to but which a majority of the members insist upon fighting for because they have become accustomed to receiving substantial gains with each new agreement.

At times the union officer may have to exhibit an aggressive attitude during sessions with employers in order to duly impress the union members who are present. Table pounding, exaggerated claims, and an outward appearance of belligerency may characterize his behavior while meeting with the employer in the presence of other union members. His private encounters with the employer, on the other hand, may be carried out on an entirely friendly and reasonable basis. Even though a union officer may feel quite cordial toward company executives and even socialize with them on occasion, he usually will find it wiser to maintain a safe social distance lest his members accuse him of maintaining a "sweetheart relationship" with management; that is, permitting his friendship with it to work to the detriment of the union.

David J. McDonald, for example, who was president of the United Steelworkers Union for a number of years, was unseated in 1965 by the union's secretary-treasurer, Mr. I. W. Abel. In spite of the gains that McDonald had been able to achieve for the union and his statesmanlike approach to labor relations, many of the rank-and-file members apparently felt that he had become too cooperative with management and had become a "tuxedo unionist." His successor campaigned as a "union man's" candidate who favored a more militant approach to union relations in contrast to the mutual cooperation (mutual trusteeship) approach that had been followed by McDonald.[13] While the outcome of the election was influenced by many different factors, the desire of the steelworkers to have a leader who was more militant and "more their kind of people" undoubtedly was a major contributing factor.

Aside from the politically insecure nature of the union officer's position, certain social and psychological factors may at times influence his relations with employers. Bitterness stemming from unfair treatment by employers during the time of his employment with them as well as the failure of many business executives to look upon him as a social or professional equal may cause a union officer to harbor resentments against employers. Thus, forcing employers to give concessions and to accede to demands can provide some union leaders with a means of "getting even" with employers as well as a means of strengthening the position of their unions.

Government Legislation and Its Impact

One of the most significant changes that have occurred within American society during the past three decades has been the substantial increase

---

[13] *Wall Street Journal*, January 5, 1965.

in the regulatory role of federal and state governments. The growth of government regulation has been particularly significant within the area of union-management relations. Until the 1930's, however, government did not involve itself to any extent in the area of labor relations, and very few state or federal laws dealing with this subject were in existence. Furthermore, prior to this time, the court decisions favored the employer who often was able to get injunctions against union activities; and prior to the *Commonwealth* v. *Hunt* decision, union efforts to achieve gains through the use of economic pressure were held to be a criminal act of conspiracy.

The Beginnings of Labor Legislation

The first federal legislation relating specifically to labor relations was the Arbitration Act of 1888 which was concerned with the arbitration of labor disputes involving the railroads. This act followed by one year the Act to Regulate Interstate Commerce which represented the beginning of government control of business activity. The Arbitration Act, while it represented a very modest beginning for labor legislation and sought only to encourage the voluntary arbitration of labor disputes, served to pave the way for the more extensive legislation that was to follow. The next legislation to be passed was the Erdman Act of 1898 that established an arbitration and conciliation commission to resolve grievances. It included provisions outlawing the use of "yellow dog contracts" by the railroads, a provision that was later held to be invalid by the Supreme Court. Other laws of minor consequence were subsequently passed dealing with the relations between the railroads and unions.

Antitrust Legislation

In an effort to curb the growing economic power and monopolistic practices of large business enterprises, Congress enacted the Sherman Antitrust Act in 1890. Although there have been differences of opinion as to whether or not Congress intended for this act to include the activities of labor unions, the Supreme Court in the famous Danbury Hatters case ruled that the provisions of the act were applicable to labor as well as to business. This case awarded $252,000 to the company for damages suffered as a result of the union's boycott of the company's product and served to curb drastically one of labor's most effective economic weapons, the boycott. It also threatened the financial solvency of unions by making them subject to civil damage suits.

When the Clayton Act was passed by Congress in 1914 to strengthen and to clarify the Sherman Act, it contained, in Sections 6 and 20, specific provisions exempting labor from antitrust prosecution. This feature of the act was widely heralded by labor unions as a victory for them. Later Supreme Court interpretation of the act, however, ruled that these sections did not give unions a blanket exemption from antitrust prosecution and that certain union activities, such as the boycott, if proved to be in restraint of trade could still be subject to criminal prosecution, damage suits, or court injunctions. It was not until the 1930's, therefore, that the federal government began to support rather than to restrict the activities of organized labor.

The Railway Labor Act of 1926

The first federal labor legislation of any real benefit to labor was the Railway Labor Act which was enacted to provide regulations on labor-management relations in the railroad industry. This act established the pattern for collective bargaining in the railroad industry that was later extended with the passage of the Wagner Act to cover companies outside the railroad industry.

While it did not prove successful in preventing strikes, the act did represent the beginning of official recognition and protection of employee bargaining rights for railway employees. The Railway Labor Act also established a National Mediation Board to mediate disputes and provided machinery for arbitrating those disputes that could not be settled through mediation. A 1934 amendment established a National Railroad Adjustment Board to provide arbitration services. Thus, the regulatory power of the federal government in the field of labor relations was exercised first over the transportation industries, where its constitutional authority was clearly established, and subsequently over other industries that were engaged in making or buying goods that crossed state lines. Government regulations, furthermore, were expanded from merely encouraging labor and management to settle their differences peacefully to protecting the bargaining rights of employees and to prescribing in detail what unions and employers were required to do in maintaining a bargaining relationship.

Control of Labor Injunctions

It was not until 1932 that labor was able to gain protection from the court injunction which had been an effective weapon of employers in curbing union strikes and boycotts. The passage of the Norris-LaGuardia (or Federal Anti-Injunction) Act of 1932 put such stringent restrictions upon the right of the federal courts to grant injunctions against union activities that their issuance for all practical purposes was prevented. The curtailment of injunctions was a significant victory for unions, for this legal device had previously enabled employers to force employees to return to their jobs under the threat of being held in contempt of court. If held in contempt, they could be sentenced without benefit of a jury trial. The act also outlawed the "yellow dog contract." In upholding the constitutionality of the act, the Supreme Court reversed its earlier decisions on the "yellow dog contract" and thus indicated that the more favorable public opinion toward labor had begun to influence the views of the Supreme Court.

Expansion of Federal Legislation

The Norris-LaGuardia Act marked the beginning of a series of favorable legislative enactments that gave government support to organized labor by recognizing their bargaining efforts and by curbing the efforts of employers to prevent the unionization of their employees. Because of such protective federal legislation as that provided by the Wagner Act of 1935, unions subsequently were able to expand rapidly from about 3 million to over 17 million in less than two decades and to use their growing economic strength to force employers to accept their demands. As their strength developed, unions no longer could be regarded as being champions of oppressed or exploited workers because their economic gains often enabled them to enjoy greater advantages than other groups of employees within society. This fact as well as various inconveniences experienced by the public as a result of crippling strikes gradually caused some of the public's earlier sympathy for organized labor to begin to wane. Public opinion began to press for the passage of legislation that would curb the growing economic strength of unions. Many legislators, furthermore, began to feel that some form of protection was needed by employers and individual employees against the possibility of unfair practices by unions or their leaders. In response to changing public opinion, therefore, the Taft-Hartley Act of 1947 and the Landrum-Griffin Act of 1959 were enacted.

The Taft-Hartley Act (Labor-Management Relations Act)

The basic federal statute governing union-management relations since 1947 has been the Taft-Hartley Act. This act was passed as an amendment to the earlier Wagner Act (National Labor Relations Act) of 1935. Since the relative strength of organized labor in comparison with that of employers was exceedingly weak at the time the Wagner Act was passed, it was designed primarily to encourage and to protect the efforts of employees to unionize. The Wagner Act established the National Labor Relations Board to determine bargaining units, to conduct union representation elections by secret ballot, and to prosecute certain anti-union activities (i.e., unfair labor practices) of employers that were declared illegal under the act. Since the act did not provide any restrictions covering their activities, unions were able to increase their membership and economic strength to the point that they were often able to enjoy a substantial advantage in their efforts to organize and bargain with employers.

In part, the intent of the Taft-Hartley Act was to equalize the bargaining relationship between unions and employers by subjecting union activities to certain controls similar to those that had been applied to employers some 12 years earlier. The act also provided certain amendments to the Wagner Act that were deemed necessary in light of the experience that had been gained from administering the Wagner Act and in light of the changes in conditions that had taken place since its passage.

Most of the basic provisions of the Wagner Act were preserved in the Taft-Hartley Act, including the following guarantee of employee bargaining rights under Section 7 of the Wagner Act:

> Employees shall have the right to self-organization, to form, join, or assist labor organizations, to bargain collectively through representatives of their own choosing, and to engage in concerted activities, for the purpose of collective bargaining or other mutual aid or protection. . . .

Unfair labor practices by employers. Activities of employers that violated the above-mentioned rights and that constituted unfair practices continued to be forbidden under the Taft-Hartley Act. These unfair practices included the following:

1. To interfere with, restrain, or coerce employees in the exercise of their rights guaranteed in Section 7.
2. To dominate or interfere with the formation or administration of any labor organization, or to contribute financial or other support to it.
3. To discriminate in regard to hiring or tenure of employment or any term or condition of employment so as to encourage or discourage membership in any labor organization.
4. To discharge or otherwise discriminate against an employee because he has filed charges or given testimony under this act.
5. To refuse to bargain collectively with the duly chosen representatives of his employees.

Unfair practices, it might be noted, are concerned only with those phases of employee relations which relate to their membership in a labor organization. The outlawing of such practices does not prevent employers from treating employees unfairly, as far as their conditions of employment are concerned, provided that such treatment does not relate to the union activities or membership of these employees.

Unfair labor practices by unions. In addition to those activities of employers that have been mentioned, the Taft-Hartley Act specified the following activities by unions as constituting unfair practices:

1. Restraint or coercion of employees in the exercise of their Wagner Act rights.
2. Restraint or coercion of an employer in his selection of the parties to bargain in his behalf.
3. Persuasion of an employer to discriminate against any of his employees.
4. Refusal to bargain collectively with an employer.
5. Participation in secondary boycotts and jurisdictional disputes.
6. Attempting to force recognition from an employer when another union is already the certified representative.
7. Charging excessive initiation fees.
8. "Featherbedding" practices requiring the payment of wages for services not performed.

Other provisions of the Taft-Hartley Act. One of the major effects of the Taft-Hartley Act was to relax the restrictions that the Wagner Act had placed upon an employer's freedom of speech. Under the Wagner Act a mere statement of opinion by an employer or his supervisors regarding the advisability of belonging to a union was in many instances ruled by the NLRB to constitute an interference with the bargaining right of employees and, therefore, an unfair labor practice. The Taft-Hartley Act helped to clarify the right of employers to free speech by giving them the opportunity to express their views regarding unions and unionizing efforts provided that no attempt was made to threaten or coerce or bribe employees concerning their membership in a union or their decision to join or not to join one.

Among other things the Taft-Hartley Act also required union officers to file anticommunist affidavits with the Secretary of Labor, a provision that has subsequently been repealed. In addition supervisors were denied legal protection in forming their own unions, the closed shop and the preferential hiring shop were forbidden, as was the practice of deducting union dues from the members' wages without having prior written consent. The act attempted, although without too much success, to reduce jurisdictional disputes and the mishandling of union welfare funds. The right of employers to sue a union for damages arising from the union's violation of the labor agreement or from unfair labor practices committed by it was clarified. The rights of individual members to submit their grievances directly to an employer without going through the union also was established.

The Taft-Hartley Act expanded the conditions under which court injunctions might be issued in labor disputes. It increased, for example, the opportunities for the NLRB to obtain court injunctions against certain illegal strikes and other unfair labor practices by the unions. The act also provided that the President of the United States, through the Attorney General, may seek an injunction against strikes or lockouts affecting the nation's health and welfare for a period of 80 days. If the dispute has not been settled after the injunction has been in effect for 60 days, the NLRB is required to take a secret vote among the employees involved in the dispute to determine if they are willing to accept the employer's "final offer." These injunction provisions of the act represent the basis for the "slave labor" charges that unions have leveled against it.

Enforcement of the Taft-Hartley Act. One of the major functions of the National Labor Relations Board is that of investigating and prosecuting unfair labor practices. These practices, however, are investigated by the Board only if a specific written complaint covering a violation is submitted to it. The Board's first action upon receiving the complaint is to have a preliminary investigation conducted by the nearest regional office. If the investigation substantiates the charge, the regional director generally tries first to get the violating party to cease the unfair practice voluntarily.

If a voluntary settlement cannot be achieved, a formal complaint is filed against the violator, and a public hearing is conducted by a trial examiner at which time the facts and testimony pertinent to the case are heard and recorded. The record of the hearing and the decision of the trial examiner, together with any statements of exception from the accused party, are forwarded to the NLRB. It is then up to the general counsel of the Board to decide whether or not the case should be submitted to the Board for review. If the Board upholds the decision of the trial examiner and if the violating party refuses to comply with its decision, the case must be submitted to the United States Circuit Court of Appeals which has the legal authority to order compliance with the Board's decision. Ultimately, a case can be carried through appeal channels to the Supreme Court.

Reactions to the Taft-Hartley Act. Like the reaction of employers to the Wagner Act, unions found it difficult to accept, to adjust to, and to comply with the provisions of the Taft-Hartley Act. Immediately following the act's passage, leaders of organized labor embarked upon a vigorous campaign to gain its repeal. However, because many of them were unwilling to accept anything less than the outright repeal of the act, their efforts were frustrated.

As time passed and there was an opportunity to observe the details of the act in operation, the need for certain changes in its provisions became more evident. Investigations into corrupt practices occurring within the field of union-management relations that were conducted by the McClellan Committee also helped to convince Congress that the existing statutes were inadequate to protect the rights of individual union members, to protect the equities of members in union welfare funds, or to prevent racketeering or unscrupulous practices from being committed by certain employers and union officers.

The Landrum-Griffin Act

The efforts of labor to amend certain provisions of the Taft-Hartley Act that were unfavorable to it and the efforts of others concerned with abuses that were occurring within organized labor resulted in the passage of the Landrum-Griffin Act. The act, which represented a compromise of several bills, has been difficult to interpret and enforce.

The Landrum-Griffin Act, which is known officially as the Labor-Management Reporting and Disclosure Act of 1959, is divided into seven sections or "titles." The first six titles concern the conduct of internal union affairs, and the seventh contains a series of amendments to the Taft-Hartley Act.

Bill of rights. One of the most important provisions of the act is the so-called "Bill of Rights of Union Members" which requires that every union member must be given the right to: (1) nominate candidates for union office, (2) vote in union elections or referendums, (3) attend union meetings, and (4) participate in union meetings and vote on union business. Members who are deprived of this right are permitted under the act to seek appropriate relief in a federal court which may include obtaining an appropriate injunction. Union members are also granted the right to examine union accounts and records in order to verify information contained in union reports and to bring suit against union officers to protect union funds.

Control of trusteeships. Another provision of the Act establishes certain ground rules governing the use of trusteeships by labor organizations in order to protect the rights of members within the trusteed locals.[14] A trusteeship may be required where the administration of a local union breaks down or where the officers refuse to comply with national regulations. Such action, however, can have the effect of depriving the local members of democratic self-government. The use of trusteeships in the past, furthermore, has at times been subject to abuses by national unions that have placed and kept certain of their locals in this category without just cause for a number of years. Members now can bring civil action against the national union to gain relief from trusteeships that have been installed in violation of the act.

Reporting and bonding provisions. Another important provision of the act concerns the reports that unions and employers are required to submit. This burden falls heaviest upon unions which are required to file an initial report with the Secretary of Labor and which, in addition, are required to file a financial report with him annually. Any conflict of interest by union officials, such as financial interest in the company being organized, must be reported as must any loans of union funds to union officers that are in excess of $250. Union officers are required to be bonded for an amount not less than 10 percent of the union funds that they are responsible for handling. In large unions the amount for which the national officers must be bonded may be substantial and involve large bonding fees.

Employers must report any expenditures that are made in attempting to persuade employees to exercise their bargaining rights. Labor consultants, similarly, must report agreements with employers involving efforts to persuade employees to exercise their bargaining rights or to supply information about union activities during a labor dispute.

Taft-Hartley amendments. Some of the amendments to the Taft-Hartley Act contained in the Landrum-Griffin Act provide for the tightening of the ban on secondary boycotts and prohibit "hot-cargo" agreements.[15] The Landrum-Griffin Act also prohibits picketing for the purpose of "shaking down" an employer, of forcing him to recognize a union, or of compelling his employees to join a union. Picketing conducted in connection with an organizing drive, furthermore, can be enjoined by the employer after 30 days if the union has not petitioned for a representation election. The restrictions on picketing, however, do not apply to a union

---

[14]A trusteeship is established when the national union takes the authority for administering a local union away from its officers and places it in the hands of a trustee appointed by the national organization.

[15]A *hot-cargo agreement* is one in which an employer agrees not to discipline employees for refusing to handle nonunion products or unfair products, which are termed "hot-cargo."

that has been certified and is attempting to force an employer to comply with legitimate demands that have been made upon him.

Unions were granted some minor concessions under the act in that the anticommunist affidavit requirements of the Taft-Hartley Act were repealed. Economic strikers, furthermore, were granted the right to vote in representation elections during the first year of their strike. Unions in the construction industry were permitted the right to sign prehire contracts with employers that require union membership as a condition of employment when the work force is recruited. This provision in effect legalizes a closed shop agreement.

Legislation and the Future

Since few employers, let alone labor leaders, would want to return to the pre-Wagner Act era, some form of government regulation of labor relations will continue to be necessary. Unfortunately, labor legislation, like other forms of legislation, rarely if ever has accomplished with complete satisfaction the intended purposes and has never been a satisfactory substitute for voluntary restraint and cooperation. Where unions and employees have developed a good working relationship, it generally has been because of intelligent action by both sides in recognizing the need and mutual advantages of cooperation rather than as the result of legal compulsion.

The fact that its employees seek membership in a union does not necessarily mean that a company has failed to develop an effective personnel program. The failure to develop such a program, however, can motivate employees to join or organize a union. Paternalistic and autocratic management practices, unfair and arbitrary treatment of employees, poor communication, inequities in the wage structure, or poor working conditions are but some of the factors that may serve to facilitate unionizing efforts.

Current Problems and Goals of Unions

Although organized labor experienced a decade of rapid growth following the passage of the Wagner Act in 1935, union membership, as Figure 18-2 illustrates, has leveled off and even declined during some of the years since early in the 1950's. There is considerable concern among labor leaders about this trend and about the need to develop new methods of revitalizing the labor movement and to reduce apathy among the members. The years ahead will undoubtedly produce renewed organizing efforts by many unions particularly with regard to organizing the growing segment of the labor force, namely, the white-collar employees. Drives also are likely to continue to be made for greater union participation in areas previously considered by management to be its sole prerogative (such as the establishment of work standards or the introduction of laborsaving equipment) in order to reduce the loss of jobs by members.

Figure 18-2

MEMBERSHIP OF NATIONAL AND
INTERNATIONAL UNIONS, 1930–1964

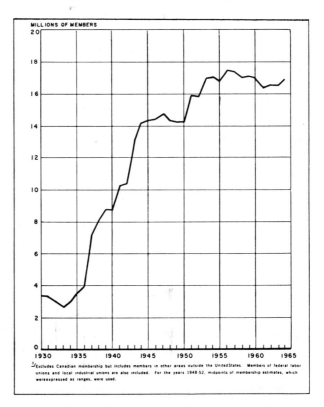

Source: *Directory of National and International Unions, op. cit.,* p. 51.

Problem of Membership Apathy

In some respects unions have become victims of their own successes in that they have reached the point of having satisfied most of the needs that their members expect them to satisfy. As a result of this condition, their leaders are being forced to help the members recognize new needs that the union can satisfy for them.[16]   Furthermore, according to one federal mediator, "The biggest problem that they (unions) have today is that they are running out of demands they can afford to make. Somehow, some way, they must maintain their protest function if they are to survive."[17] A veteran labor leader voiced the same view at an AFL-CIO national convention by stating that, "We can't get anywhere with unemployment slogans now. What we've (the AFL-CIO) got to find is some new slogan to stick on the bumpers of labor's shiny, new cars."[18]   A recessionary period, however, could quickly change the situation to which the leader refers.

The fact that most unions have done so well in achieving continuing gains for their members has had the effect of making many members rather apathetic toward the administration and progress of their union. These members include those whom Karsh calls the "crisis activists" and the "card carriers."[19] The crisis activists are those opportunistic members who rarely participate in union activities or attend union meetings but who can be counted on to turn up when there is some issue that affects them directly. They can also be expected to seek union support for any grievance that they may have with the company. The "card carrier" tends to be even more indifferent and uninformed about union affairs. Unfortunately for the union leader, these two groups often include a large portion of the membership, with the result that he may have to devote time that otherwise could be devoted to pursuing union goals in attempting to develop some degree of loyalty and support among them.

Employers also are competing more effectively for the loyalty of their personnel. The following statement by a union leader illustrates the union's problem of competing for the loyalty of employees:

> Many times, when I was servicing local unions, we would meet in a union hall and talk about the grievances that workers had brought in and what we were going to do about them. By the time I had arranged a meeting with management the next day, the problem had been corrected and the union didn't get credit for redressing the grievance. It's become a battle of loyalties. They want the worker to be loyal to them. This is our big problem: How can *we* get greater loyalty from the individual to the union? All the things we fought for the corporation is now giving to the workers. What we have to find are other

[16]Stagner and Rosen, *op. cit.*, p. 40.

[17]As quoted in Stagner and Rosen, *op. cit.*, p. 40.

[18]*Business Week*, December 18, 1965.

[19]Bernard Karsh, "Union Traditions and Membership Apathy," *Labor Law Journal*, Vol. 9, No. 9 (September, 1958), pp. 641–649.

things the worker wants which the employer is not willing to give him, and we have to develop our program around these things as reasons for belonging to the union.[20]

Organizing the White-Collar Groups

The growth problem confronting organized labor is perhaps best illustrated by the chart shown in Figure 18-3 and the graph in Figure 18-4. It may be noted from these two figures that, in terms of the percentage of

Figure 18-3

UNION MEMBERSHIP (EXCLUSIVE OF CANADA)
AS A PERCENTAGE OF TOTAL LABOR FORCE*

	Total Union Membership, Excluding Canada (millions)	Total Labor Force	
		Number (millions)	Percentage Union Members
1956	17.4	70.3	24.8
1957	17.3	70.7	24.6
1958	17.0	71.2	23.9
1959	17.1	71.9	23.8
1960	17.0	73.1	23.3
1961	16.3	74.1	22.0
1962	16.5	74.6	22.2
1963	16.5	75.7	21.8
1964	16.8	76.9	21.9

*Total labor force includes employed and unemployed workers, self-employed, members of the Armed Forces, etc. Employment in nonagricultural establishments excludes the Armed Forces, self-employed individuals as well as the unemployed, agricultural workers, proprietors, unpaid family workers, and domestic servants.

The ratio of union membership to employment in nonagricultural establishments is a rough measure of the organizing accomplishments of unions. Employment totals include a substantial number of people who are not eligible for union membership (e. g., executives and managers).

Source: *Directory of National and International Unions, op. cit.,* p. 51.

---

[20]Center for the Study of Democratic Institutions, "Labor Looks at Labor," 1963, pp. 16–17.

the total labor force that it represents, union membership has declined in most of the years since 1953. If organized labor is to reverse this regressive trend, it must make greater inroads in organizing those companies, geographic regions, and occupational groups that thus far have not been effectively unionized.

The white-collar workers as a group probably constitute the best unionizing opportunity, particularly in the manufacturing industries where the blue-collar workers are already unionized. In manufacturing industries organizing drives among the office workers will generally be supported by the plant workers whose refusal to cross a picket line established by the

Figure 18-4

UNION MEMBERSHIP AS A PERCENT OF TOTAL LABOR FORCE OF EMPLOYERS IN NONAGRICULTURAL ESTABLISHMENTS — 1930–1964

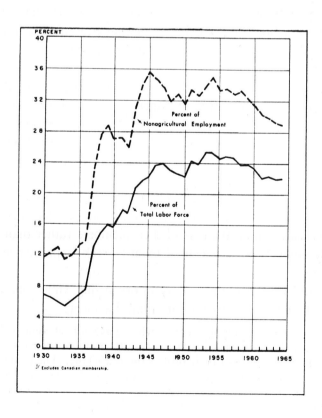

Source: *Directory of National and International Unions, op. cit.,* p. 51.

organizers is often sufficient to force company recognition of an office union. The fact that white-collar workers in many industries have fallen behind the unionized blue-collar groups in achieving new benefits has added to their discontent and has probably helped to reduce the white-collar workers' traditional dislike of unions. This fact is particularly true in the nonmanufacturing industries where office employees have not had passed on to them the benefits granted to the blue-collar workers in the plant. Automation in the office has also led to the elimination of many jobs and to more job insecurity within the office.

White-collar workers, however, do not constitute a homogeneous group, for they are employed in positions ranging from that of a file clerk to that of a professional engineer. Many of these white-collar groups, furthermore, prefer membership in the society or organization that represents their particular professional or technical field to membership in a union. Traditionally, white-collar workers, moreover, have tended to regard union membership as being somewhat degrading to their status; and they prefer to identify themselves with management whose ranks they may hope to join someday.

The reaction of professional employees is illustrated by the experiences of the Engineers and Scientists of America. This union, formed by the amalgamation of mine engineer unions in 1950 with 14,000 members, was able to expand to 25,000 members by 1956. As the result of internal conflicts and the defection and the dissolution of certain groups within the organization, however, membership in the union declined to 10,500 by 1960.[21] The difficulties encountered by this professional union are similar to those encountered by certain other white-collar groups where a loss of status and frustration on the part of their members rather than a dedication to the labor movement caused them to seek improvement through unionization.

The problem confronting unions in organizing white-collar groups is perhaps best summarized by the following statement:

> ... Professional employees as a whole have not yet come to understand fully the need for collective action to promote their own interests along with those of their profession as a whole. The trade union movement has not vigorously pursued the task of organizing this key group of employees or sought to profit from their successful experience. Nor has it established flexible enough approaches and adequate

---

21"Engineer Union Fights for Life," *Fortune*, May, 1960, p. 251.

facilities for experimenting with new forms that could attract this special group and respond to its peculiar needs.[22]

Adjustment to Automation

Another one of the more critical problems confronting many unions is that of protecting the jobs of their members against automation. The right to exercise control over changes affecting their members' jobs, including the installation of new equipment or methods, has in some instances become a more vital issue than increases in wages or fringe benefits. Automation, in addition to eliminating jobs, also has often reduced the ability of a union to strike in some companies where production can be sustained by a relatively small number of supervisory personnel who are pressed into service to operate the equipment.

While unions recognize that they cannot hope to hold back the tide of technological progress, they are attempting to force employers to cushion the unfavorable personnel effects of automation. In some industries unions have succeeded in negotiating agreements that require the company to establish funds for retraining workers displaced by automation and to provide separation benefits or early retirement benefits for those who cannot be retrained or placed in other jobs. The UAW and certain other unions also have been advocating that all employees, including the blue-collar workers, be placed on salaried status. Such status would permit employees to receive pay during those days when they were not able to work because of illness or lack of work.

One of the most revolutionary agreements of this type has been negotiated by the Westcoast Longshoremen; it provides that a portion of the savings derived by the installation of more efficient cargo handling devices be placed in a fund to provide earlier retirement benefits for members displaced by improved work methods. Another well-publicized agreement is the Kaiser Steel Union Sharing plan negotiated in 1963 between the United Steel Workers and the Kaiser Steel Corporation. This plan provides for the members to share with the company in the benefits of technological progress. Under this plan wages are tied in part to the cost savings achieved by the company. A plant-wide employment pool is also to be established to absorb as many workers as possible who are displaced

---

[22]Solomon Barkin, *The Decline of the Labor Movement* (Santa Barbara: Center for the Study of Democratic Institutions), p. 30.

by technological advancements. In view of the precedents being set in the steel and maritime industries, there is a greater likelihood that more joint efforts to solve and to cushion the problems of automation may be expected in the future.

Résumé

The growth in the size of labor unions has created problems of organization and management for unions to overcome that are similar to those encountered by a business enterprise. Today's union officers must, among other things, be effective managers and have the ability to anticipate changes that affect their organizations and to take appropriate action.

As with business organizations, unions today are continually being confronted with new problems which must be overcome if they are to survive. As unions have become larger, it has been more difficult for their officers to maintain contact with individual members, to stimulate the support of the membership, and to maintain in the membership a feeling of identification with the union and its goals. As the size and strength of unions have grown, they, like business enterprises, have also encountered increased governmental regulation. As contrasted to their former underdog role, unions are now considered by society to have reached a maturity requiring an exercise of responsibility such as is required of business enterprises. The growth of labor legislation, however, has shown that legislation to control labor or management or both cannot by itself develop good union-management relations. Good relations must be achieved by mutual cooperation between the union and management which is based on the recognition that each has a mission to achieve.

DISCUSSION QUESTIONS AND PROBLEMS

1. To what extent do you agree or disagree with the statement that "unions are running out of needs to satisfy"?

2. Are there any problems that may be encountered by unions as they expand the number of services that are offered to members such as free or low-cost eye glasses, drugs, dance lessons, etc.?

3. Why are unions becoming involved in such things as community welfare activities and consumer "watch dog groups"?

4. The Acme Poultry Company in an effort to reduce costs is developing plans for a mechanized processing line. When in full operation the new line will eliminate about 10 of the 25 employees in the processing plant. The employees learning of the company's plans have demanded that their union strike if necessary to prevent the company from installing the new line. The union president sympathizes with the problem confronting the members, but he also recognizes that the company will not be able to continue to compete with other companies unless its costs can be reduced. On the other hand, he realizes that the employees in the plant are sufficiently aroused by events to vote him out of office at the next election or to withdraw from the union and affiliate with a rival one unless he is able to protect their job rights.

   a. What action would you take if you were the business representative?
   b. Would you lead the union out on strike to prevent the installation of the equipment?

5. It has been stated by some authorities that management usually gets the type of union leadership that it deserves. To what extent do you agree and/or disagree with this statement?

6. Would it be wise and ethical for a company to hire an aggressive and skillful union leader who had succeeded in bargaining substantial concessions from them and place him on its bargaining staff? Assuming that the financial inducement were made sufficiently high to get this leader to accept employment, what difficulties might the company encounter?

7. What possible disadvantages may accrue to a labor union if it becomes active in politics?

8. Should unions as well as companies be subject to the provisions of antitrust laws? Discuss.

9. How do the purposes and objectives of the Landrum-Griffin Act differ from those of the Taft-Hartley Act?

10. Labor leaders at times have singled out such associations as the medical and bar associations as being the strongest unions in the nation. To what extent do you agree or disagree with this statement?

CASE 18-1

THE ANNIVERSARY WATCH

Jerry Rose, the business representative for Local No. 25 of the International Brotherhood of Plastics Workers, had relied heavily upon Mrs. Marconi, his secretary, to handle the operation of the local's office. Mrs. Marconi had served several previous business representatives during the nearly twenty years that she had been employed by the union. Although she sometimes tended to be a little domineering in her relations with union members, it was generally agreed that she had been of great service to the union.

In recognition of the fact that she was about to complete her twentieth year of service with Local 25, Mr. Rose decided to purchase an attractive wrist watch with an appropriate inscription engraved upon it for presentation to her as an anniversary gift. The cost of the gift totaled about $100.00 and was paid for from the local's discretionary fund. When Jerry Rose announced at the monthly union meeting that he had purchased the watch and that it was to be presented to Mrs. Marconi at a luncheon ceremony the next week, several of the members objected to the gift. They complained, in effect, that they felt it unfair to use the dues taken from their hard-earned wages to buy an expensive "luxury gift." One member complained that he did not feel that it was right for him to be contributing to such a gift for Mrs. Marconi when he had never been able to afford a decent watch for his own wife. After about an hour of heated discussion, the issue was put to a vote with the majority present supporting Rose's purchase of the gift. As might be expected, news reached Mrs. Marconi through the grapevine about the impending gift and about the controversy that it had created. While she never mentioned the fact, Rose could tell that she was aware of the objections raised about the gift by the way that she reacted to the watch when it was presented to her. The controversy over the watch also had dampened Mr. Rose's enthusiasm for the gesture, and he wondered if the gift did not now constitute a waste of the members' dues.

    a. How do you explain the attitude of the members who objected to the gift?

    b. Does this case indicate any possible problems that one might encounter in working for a union or for some type of fraternal organization? What motivates people to work for a union?

    c. If you did not have the hindsight provided by this case, would you have taken the same action as Mr. Rose?

    d. Do you feel that the practice of giving a present such as a $100.00 watch to mark a 20- or 25-year anniversary date constitutes a desirable practice?

CASE 18-2

THE NEW OWNER

The Custom Machine Shop, which employed about 50 persons in production work, had maintained a labor agreement with the Mechanics' Union for over 15 years. The agreement provided, among other things, for a two-week paid vacation after one year of full-time employment.

In January the company changed ownership, and shortly thereafter the new owner required that each employee fill out and sign a new application of employment on the grounds that they were now all new employees of a new company. When the vacation period arrived, the owner refused to honor the two-week provision in the labor agreement but agreed to concede one-week vacation on the basis of the six months that the personnel had been employed by him. The union immediately challenged the decision maintaining that the new owner was obligated to continue to honor the agreement negotiated by the previous owner until its expiration date. The new owner, however, held fast to his contention that the union's agreement ceased to exist once he assumed control of the company and that the union should have taken the initiative to negotiate a new agreement at that time.

a. Is the position taken by the new owner justified?

b. What developments do you anticipate will occur if the new owner maintains this position?

SUGGESTED READINGS

Black, James M., and George J. Piccolli. *Successful Labor Relations for Small Business.* New York: McGraw-Hill Book Company, 1953.

Chamberlain, Neil W. *Sourcebook on Labor.* New York: McGraw-Hill Book Company, 1958. Pp. 326–409.

Ching, Cyrus S. *Review and Reflection, A Half-Century of Labor Relations.* New York: Forbes, Inc., 1953.

Chruden, Herbert J., and Arthur W. Sherman, Jr. *Readings in Personnel Management,* Second Edition. Cincinnati: South-Western Publishing Company, Inc., 1966. Pp. 419–431.

Falcone, Nicholas S. *Labor Law.* New York: John Wiley & Sons, Inc., 1962.

Goldberg, Arthur J. *AFL-CIO Labor United.* New York: McGraw-Hill Book Company, 1956.

Labor Course, Current Edition. Englewood Cliffs, New Jersey: Prentice-Hall, Inc.

Labor Law Course, Current Edition. Chicago: Commerce Clearing House, Inc.

Labor Law Reporter, Fourth Edition. Chicago: Commerce Clearing House, Inc. Vols. 1, 2, 4, 4A, 5, and 6.

Labor Policy and Practice. Washington, D.C.: The Bureau of National Affairs, Inc. Vols. 1–5.

Marting, Elizabeth (ed.). *Understanding Collective Bargaining.* New York: American Management Association, 1958. Sections II and III, 61–146.

Mueller, Stephen J., and A. Howard Myers. *Labor Law and Legislation.* Cincinnati: South-Western Publishing Company, Inc., 1962.

Northrup, Herbert R., and Gordon F. Bloom. *Government and Labor.* Homewood, Illinois: Richard A. Irwin, Inc., 1963.

Peters, Edward. *Strategy and Tactics in Labor Negotiations.* New London, Connecticut: National Foreman's Institute. Chapters 1–4.

Peterson, Florence. *American Labor Unions.* New York: Harper & Brothers, 1952.

Progress in Labor-Management Relations, Personnel Series, No. 166. New York: American Management Association, 1956.

Reynolds, L. G. *Labor Economics and Labor Relations.* Englewood Cliffs, New Jersey: Prentice-Hall, Inc., 1959. Chapters 6–7.

Stagner, Ross, and Hjalmar Rosen. *Psychology of Union-Management Relations.* Belmont, California: Wadsworth Publishing Company, Inc., 1965.

Taft, Philip. *The A. F. of L. in the Time of Gompers.* New York: Harper & Brothers, 1957.

The Prentice-Hall Complete Labor Equipment. *Labor Relations,* Vol. 2 and *State Labor Laws,* Vol. 3. Englewood Cliffs, New Jersey: Prentice-Hall, Inc.

Unionization Among American Engineers, Studies in Personnel Policy, No. 155. New York: National Industrial Conference Board, 1956.

Young, Dallas M. *Understanding Labor Problems.* New York: McGraw-Hill Book Company, 1959.

Union - Management Relations

The type of relationship that exists between the company and the union is determined to a considerable extent by the terms of the labor agreement under which the two parties must operate. This relationship may be characterized by a condition of mutual cooperation and understanding between management and the union, or it may be fraught with discord and strife. Regardless of whether or not a harmonious relationship develops from the agreement, this document does serve to establish the rights of both the company and the union with respect to problems and decisions relating to employment conditions. It also affects interpersonal relations among company managers, supervisors, and union officials. Therefore, if the terms of the agreement and the respective roles of the union and management can be defined clearly, the likelihood that serious problems and conflicts will arise in connection with the operation of the agreement will be reduced.

The last chapter was concerned with the objectives and functions of a union and with government regulations affecting its operation. In this chapter the union-management relationships that result from the efforts of each party to achieve its objectives are discussed under the following topics:

- Developing a bargaining relationship.
- Union recognition and security.
- Negotiating the agreement.
- Characteristics of contemporary union-management relations.

Developing a Bargaining Relationship

When his employees become unionized, it is sometimes difficult for an employer to accept and adjust to the fact that he must bargain and consult with union representatives regarding conditions of employment for his employees. The union, in such instances, may encounter considerable resistance in attempting to establish its position as the bargaining representative for the company's employees. As a result the union may assume a militant role and try to attack the employer's reputation in an effort to strengthen its position and win over the loyalty of his employees. Considerable time may be required, therefore, before the hostility of either or both parties can be reduced sufficiently to permit a cooperative relationship to develop.

Unionizing Drives

Employee unionization drives may be the result of internal or external pressures. Internal pressures usually grow out of employee dissatisfactions that may develop when the needs of the employees are not being satisfied, when they feel that the company is not treating them fairly, or when they believe that they are not being provided with benefits equal to those offered by other companies. External pressures, on the other hand, result from the efforts of a union to convince the majority of a company's employees that it is to their benefit to become union members.

Since most national unions desire to expand their membership, they are not only ready to assist employees with their organizing efforts but also are eager to initiate an organizing drive if they feel that it will be successful. Most national unions today are continually on the alert for situations within companies which may provide them with an organizing opportunity. Sometimes a national union may even be pressured by a company whose employees it represents to organize the other companies in the industry that are in a more favorable competitive position as a result of paying less than the union wage scale.

Since an organizing drive is expensive to conduct, unions usually will not undertake one in a company until conditions appear to favor its success. The union, therefore, is likely to study a company first in terms of the readiness of its employees to organize and the vulnerability of the company to such union pressures as a boycott, a strike, or a picket line. If conditions for unionizing appear to be favorable, the union may then actively attempt to interest employees in becoming union members. After a nucleus of members has been recruited within the company, the union can increase the tempo of its campaign by holding meetings, by passing out union literature at the company entrances, and by personally contacting and encouraging the remaining employees to join the union. Employees who have become members can be particularly effective in encouraging and pressuring others to join. If feasible, organizing pickets may be placed at its entrances to put pressure on the company to recognize the union. After the union has gained recognition as the bargaining agent for its members, normally its next objective will be to work toward an agreement with the employer that will require all employees to become members.

Evolution of Union-Management Relations

An organizing campaign, like a political one, can become charged with emotion causing accusations and verbal insults to be exchanged freely and can cause bitterness and antagonism that may take years to eliminate. If the majority of a company's employees are to be organized, the union must be able to convince them that their employment conditions need to be improved and that the best hope for achieving improvements lies in their joining a union. In responding to the charges and accusations leveled against them by unions, companies must be very careful that they do not make replies or commit acts that can be turned against them or that may violate existing labor laws. While employers are now given greater freedom to express their views to employees concerning union activities and membership than was once permitted under the Wagner Act, it still is an unfair practice for them to attempt to discourage their employees from joining a union through the use of threats, coercion, or by offering bribes or rewards to keep the union out.

The transition from a condition of open hostility to one of mutual trust and cooperation often requires that union-management relationships evolve through several stages. The initial stage of hostility may last for a period of time until each party is convinced that the relationship will be a continuing one and that nothing is to be gained by attempting to weaken the position of the other party. Open conflict may gradually be replaced by a condition of "armed truce" in which both parties recognize the futility of conflict and make some effort to get along even if resentment and distrust still persist. Eventually the condition of "armed truce" may give way to one of mutual respect in which each party has some degree of empathy for the opinions and feelings of the other side. Labor relations can then assume a give-and-take pattern characterized by hard but intelligent bargaining rather than by divisive tactics, unrealistic demands, and emotionalism.

Union Recognition and Security

The achievement of recognition and security is essential to the welfare of any union. Until a union is recognized by the employer as a bargaining agent for his employees, it is not in a position to negotiate conditions of employment. Even after achieving such recognition, the union may still be confronted with the problem of securing its position within the company in order to avoid the loss of membership among employees within the bargaining area that it represents.

Gaining Recognition

The difficulty that a union encounters in attempting to gain recognition and to establish a formal bargaining relationship with an employer will, among other things, depend upon the amount of opposition that it encounters from rival unions. If no other union is seeking recognition and the employer is convinced that a sufficient number of his employees want it to represent them, he may simply agree to recognize the union and negotiate an agreement with it. If, however, the employer feels that a majority of his employees do not want to belong to a union or if more than one union is attempting to gain recognition, he may insist that an election be held to determine which union, if any, his employees prefer to have represent them.

Conducting union elections. Union elections are conducted by the National Labor Relations Board or by a state labor agency if the election is subject to the latter agency's jurisdiction. The petition to hold an election usually is initiated by the union although employers, under certain conditions, have the right to petition for one.

If the petition to hold a representation election is not contested by the union or employer or by a rival union, it can be conducted without holding a pre-election hearing. An election conducted under these conditions is known as a *consent election*. If conditions require that a pre-election hearing be held, the election is known as a *formal election*. All elections are conducted by secret ballot. Since the ballot permits employees the choice of "no union" in addition to the unions that are listed, it is possible that none of the choices will receive a majority of the votes if more than one union is listed on the ballot. In such instances, a *runoff election* must be conducted between the two choices receiving the largest number of votes. The union receiving a majority of the votes in the initial or the run-off election is certified by the NLRB as the bargaining agent for a period of at least a year, or for the duration of the labor agreement.

The bargaining unit. Before it can hold an election, the NLRB must first define the departments or the jobs within the company that are to be included within the bargaining unit to be represented by the union. The determination of the bargaining unit or units can be very important to certain occupational groups within a company. If a single bargaining unit is established for the company as a whole, for example, then white-collar and skilled groups of employees must be represented by the same union as the semiskilled production-line workers. If more than one bargaining unit is established, however, it may be possible for white-collar and skilled groups of employees to belong to unions that more closely represent their occupational interests or to refrain from belonging to any union. The existence of more than one bargaining unit within a company can compound the collective bargaining and union relations problems of the employer as well as reduce the strength of the union representing the majority. It may also help to stimulate interunion rivalry within the company and to precipitate jurisdictional disputes.

The bargaining history of a company and the wishes of the majority of its employees are among the major factors that are considered by the NLRB in determining the bargaining units. The Taft-Hartley Act, however, requires that under certain conditions separate bargaining units be established for professional and craft groups. This provision is designed to help insure that the special problems and interests of these smaller groups will not be submerged in a large industrial union.

Achieving Security

In order for a union to achieve maximum security, all of the employees working within the bargaining area that it represents should become members. Its security also requires that the union be capable of maintaining sufficient discipline among its members to compel them to observe union regulations and directives as well as the conditions of employment negotiated by it. A union, therefore, must have the ability to penalize its members for accepting employment conditions that are below the union scale, for performing a type of work that is forbidden by the union, for crossing union picket lines, or for engaging in any other acts that are contrary to union policy. If the union is able to achieve the degree of security that it desires, it will be in a stronger position to gain concessions from the company by exerting or threatening to exert economic pressure through strike action.

Forms of Security

The form of security that is granted to a union is determined by the types of "shop" that the union is permitted to maintain under the terms of the agreement and are listed in the order of the least important to the most important from the viewpoint of the union:

Open shop. An open shop exists where no union is recognized as the bargaining agent for the company's employees. Although there are no formal restrictions under this arrangement to prevent employees from joining one, the hostility toward unions on the part of management or certain groups of employees may effectively discourage union membership.

Bargaining for members only. This type of shop merely acknowledges the presence of a union and its right to bargain for those employees who are members.

Exclusive-bargaining shop. Although this type of shop does not compel employees to join the union or force an employer to give union members any preferential treatment, it does require an employer to bargain exclusively with the union over conditions of employment within that unit of the company that it represents.

Agency shop. Employees working in an agency shop need not become members of the union in order to maintain their jobs, but they are required to pay dues to it as if they were members. The argument for this type of shop is that it requires all employees to contribute to the support of the organization that has bargained in their behalf without forcing them against their wishes to affiliate with or to be subjected to its discipline. The agency shop originated in Canada and has been introduced in certain states as a means of circumventing a ban on the union shop.

Maintenance-of-membership shop. This type of shop, which originated as a compromise to the union shop, does not require all employees to join the union; but it does provide that employees who are union members after a given cutoff date must retain their membership in a union or suffer the loss of their jobs. Any employees who are hired after this date usually are required to join the union.

Union shop. In a union shop all employees in the bargaining unit represented by the union must become members within at least thirty days after being hired. Unions maintain that this type of shop is necessary in order to prevent certain employees from becoming "free riders" and capitalizing upon the gains that union members have received by supporting their union. Unions frequently claim also that they need this type of shop in order to maintain proper control and discipline over their members and that such control will benefit the employer.

Some employers feel that they can gain better cooperation from a union by having a union shop since it eliminates many difficulties that would otherwise exist if the union had to be concerned about maintaining its membership or if nonmembers were able to work beside and receive the same benefits as members. The presence of nonmembers in a shop, they believe, can lead to discord and even violence to the detriment of morale and efficiency. Other employers, however, are opposed to the union shop on the grounds that no person should be required to join a union against his will. Some employers, furthermore, believe that this type of shop gives too much power to a union. In spite of the controversy that may exist with respect to the union shop, however, this form of security is provided for in 53 percent of the labor agreements that were reviewed by the Bureau of National Affairs. The maintenance-of-membership shop and the agency shop, by way of contrast, were established in only 8 percent of the agreements.[1]

Closed shop. Under a closed shop arrangement an employer can hire only union members who are in good standing. Although banned under the Taft-Hartley Act, the closed shop does exist in disguised form in certain industries as the result of informal agreements.

Additional security. Most agreements that provide for the union maintenance-of-membership, or agency, shops also provide for a *dues checkoff.* Under this arrangement the employer agrees to deduct the dues of those members who have given him written authorization to do so and to forward these dues to the union treasurer. The checkoff benefits the union by reducing dues delinquencies. It also aids the employer by preventing a

---

[1] *Collective Bargaining-Negotiation and Contracts*, Vol. 2 (Washington, D.C.: Bureau of National Affairs, August, 1965), pp. 87:1.

situation from arising in which he might be forced to discharge a good employee for failure to pay his union dues.

Internal Unity and Union Security

The ability of a union to achieve recognition, security, and concessions from an employer is contingent, among other things, upon its internal unity and upon its bargaining strength. Conflict among factions within a union's ranks can weaken its strength. Union leaders, therefore, must be able to formulate objectives and policies that are acceptable to each of the special interest groups within the organization. In an industrial type of union, where the interests and backgrounds of the members are varied, this accomplishment may require considerable leadership ability.

In spite of a growing unity within the ranks of organized labor, rivalry between certain unions still exists, although probably not to the extent that is illustrated by the cartoon in Figure 19-1. Some rivalry has stemmed from personal competition among certain labor leaders who desire to become the dominant figures within their national organizations or within the labor movement. In other cases rivalry has resulted from the competition among unions over which one should have the right to perform a given type of work, particularly when technological changes have caused the work performed by members of one union to overlap into an area covered by another union or when new types of jobs not previously represented by any union are created. Union rivalry also has resulted from the drives of two or more unions to organize a particular industry or company or a certain group of workers.

Disputes between two or more unions over the right to represent a given group of workers or the right to have its members perform a certain type of work are called *jurisdictional disputes*. When disputes of this type cannot be resolved peacefully, they can be harmful to organized labor, to employers, to employees, and to the public. An employer and his employees, under such circumstances, can become the innocent victims of a picket line established by a union to which few, if any, employees belong. The unions themselves also may suffer from a loss of public support and goodwill since the public is rarely sympathetic with such disputes.

Jurisdictional disputes, fortunately, have decreased in recent years. Since the passage of the Taft-Hartley Act, the National Labor Relations Board has been required to give priority to holding elections in those plants where a jurisdictional dispute is hurting the employer, his employees, or the interests of the public. The merger of AFL and CIO organizations

Figure 19-1

WALL STREET JOURNAL

"I'd love to help you up, Mac, but
you know what a strong union we have."

Source: *Wall Street Journal*, April 23, 1958. Reproduced with permission.

also has permitted many of the jurisdictional problems that formerly arose among unions within these two groups to be resolved peacefully.

Negotiating the Agreement

At present there are over 150,000 labor agreements in effect within the United States, each of which represents a different bargaining relationship.[2] The terms of these agreements usually are the outgrowth of extensive negotiations between the representatives of the union and the company. During these negotiations each side, through the use of arguments, persuasions, and even threats, attempts to gain maximum concessions from the opposing side and to give up minimum concessions in return. While it is to the interest of each side to achieve its bargaining objectives by means of negotiation, the ability to do so also is contingent upon whether or not it is able and willing to resort to strike action in the event that negotiations are not productive.

---

[2]James J. Healy (ed.), *Creative Collective Bargaining* (Englewood Cliffs, New Jersey: Prentice-Hall, Inc., 1965).

Preparing for Negotiations

No matter how intelligent or skillful the negotiators on either side may be, it is advantageous for them to plan carefully their bargaining strategy and to assemble the data that will support the positions that they may take during negotiations. The file or loose leaf notebook into which these data are assembled sometimes is referred to as the *bargaining book*. The use of this book during negotiations can permit bargaining to be conducted on a more orderly, factual, and positive basis.[3]

Ideally, preparation for the negotiation of the agreement should start soon after the last agreement has been signed. Not only will this practice provide more time in which to collect, organize, and assimilate the needed factual material but it will also permit negotiators to review and to diagnose mistakes and weaknesses evidenced during the preceding negotiations while the experience is still current in their minds. Hopefully, these reviews can provide a basis for negotiating future agreements more effectively.

Sources of bargaining information. In preparing for negotiation, considerable information can be obtained from company records. Internal data relating to grievances, disciplinary action, transfers and promotions, layoffs, overtime, individual performance, and wage payments obtained from this source can be useful in formulating and supporting a company's bargaining position. The supervisors and executives who must live with and administer the agreement also can be a very important source of ideas and suggestions concerning changes that are needed in the agreement. Their contacts with union members and representatives provide them with a firsthand knowledge of many of the complaints that the union negotiators are likely to raise and the changes in the agreement that these negotiators may demand. Conditions outside of a company can also have an important effect upon bargaining demands and strategy. Statistical data concerning such factors as general economic conditions, cost of living trends, profit outlook for business, community wage patterns, fringe benefits and wage rates of other firms, and any other subjects that the union might introduce during the bargaining sessions should be compiled as a part of the bargaining book from the available sources of information.

Bargaining procedures and strategies. In preparing for negotiations, the company should first determine the course of action that it plans to follow. A planned course of action should take into account the proposals that the union is likely to submit, based upon the latter's agreements with

---

[3]*Preparing for Collective Bargaining*, Studies in Personnel Policy, No. 172 (New York: National Industrial Conference Board, 1959), p. 34.

other companies, and the demands that the union has achieved or is carrying forward from previous negotiations. The company should also attempt to estimate what new goals the union may be striving to achieve, as well as the concessions that it may be willing to make in order to realize these goals, and the extent to which it may be willing to compromise before resorting to strike action.

Certain elements of strategy are common to both the company and the union. Generally, the initial demands presented by each side are greater than those that it actually may hope to achieve so as to provide room for concessions. Each party, furthermore, usually will avoid giving up the maximum that it is capable of conceding in order to allow for further concessions, should this become necessary in order to break a bargaining deadlock.

Union strategy often involves the making of bridgehead demands — demands in some new area which the union hopes to achieve in some future agreement rather than in the current negotiations. Initial demands by unions for pensions, welfare benefits, and guaranteed employment that are quite modest in nature are examples of bridgehead demands that unions talk about and propose for several years before employers are willing to consider them, even on a modest scale. Once these demands are achieved, however, the union is in a good position to expand them further in subsequent negotiations.

Collective bargaining assistance. In order to negotiate more effectively, it may be advisable for management to utilize the services of professional negotiators. The use of these professionals has definite merit since they devote full time to union relations and thus are likely to have broader skills and experience than a company's own management personnel. Many companies utilize *bargaining associations* in order that their negotiations may be handled by professionals. These associations also can enable employers to present a united front against pressures exerted by the union; that is, association members can follow the principle that "a strike against one is a strike against all" and shut down their operations when the union strikes against one member company.

The Bargaining Process

The conditions under which negotiations take place, the experience and personalities of the participants on each side, and the strength of their relative positions are among the factors that tend to make each bargaining situation unique. Some labor agreements can be negotiated informally within a matter of a few hours particularly if an agreement's terms are based upon the pattern that has been established by the industry. Other agreements, however, may require months of negotiation before a final settlement can be reached.

After negotiators have had extensive experience in bargaining with each other, they often acquire the ability "to read their opponents' minds" and to anticipate their actions and reactions. Inexperienced negotiators working together for the first time, on the other hand, may misinterpret actions and statements of their opponents and may be able to react only to overt statements and pressures. Regardless of the variations in collective bargaining practices that may occur, however, there are certain rules and rituals that must be observed, and there are certain stages through which negotiations must progress if they are to produce results.

Opening the negotiations. The initial meeting of the bargaining teams is a particularly important one because it may establish the climate that will prevail during the ensuing negotiations. A cordial attitude with perhaps the injection of a little humor can contribute much to a relaxation of tensions and help the negotiations to begin smoothly. The first meeting usually is devoted to establishing the bargaining authority possessed by the representatives of each side and to determining the rules and procedures to be used during negotiations. If the parties have not submitted their proposals in advance, these may be exchanged and clarified at this time.

Analysis of proposals. The negotiation of an agreement often has certain of the characteristics of a poker game in which each side attempts to determine its opponent's position while keeping its own position concealed. Each side normally will try to avoid disclosing the relative importance that it attaches to each proposal in order that it will not be forced to pay a higher price than is necessary to achieve those proposals that are of the greatest importance. Thus, as in the case of the seller who will try to get a higher price for his product if he thinks the prospective buyer strongly desires it, the negotiator will try to get greater concessions in return for granting those that his opponent wants most.

The proposals that each side submits generally may be divided into those that it feels it must achieve, those that it would like to achieve but on which it will compromise, and those that it is submitting primarily for trading purposes. Proposals that are submitted for trading purposes, however, must be realistic in terms of the opponent's ability and willingness to concede them. Unrealistic proposals, such as union demand for membership on the company's board of directors, may serve only to antagonize the opponent and can precipitate a deadlock.[4]

The ritual of bargaining usually requires that each side go through the motions of resisting even those demands that it may be willing to concede. If either side, particularly the company, gives in too readily, it may cause the other side to believe that there is a good opportunity to gain still further concessions. Furthermore, if an employer concedes too readily to union demands, it may reduce the stature of the union leaders and cause their bargaining gains to appear less significant.

Resolving the proposals. The proposals submitted by either side, regardless of the degree of importance that is attached to them, must be disposed of if an agreement is to be consummated. These proposals may be withdrawn, or they may be accepted by the other side in their entirety or in some compromise form. In negotiations the proposals may be discussed in the order of their appearance in the agreement or in some other sequence. The sequence in which the proposals are to be discussed can in itself become a subject for collective bargaining since it can affect bargaining results for either or both sides. If the discussion of the more important proposals can be deferred until the last, these proposals may serve as leverage for gaining agreement on proposals of lesser importance which precede them. Since it is easier for the union to rally its members to strike over major issues, it is likely to try to place such major issues near the end of the bargaining agenda.

In order for each bargaining issue to be resolved satisfactorily, the point at which agreement is reached must be within limits that the union and the employer are willing to accept. Stagner and Rosen term the area within these two limits the *bargaining zone*. In some bargaining situations such as the one illustrated in Figure 19-2, the solution desired by one party may exceed the tolerance limit of the other party; thus, that solution is outside of the bargaining zone. If that party refuses to modify its demands sufficiently to bring them within the bargaining zone or if the opposing party refuses to extend its tolerance limit to accommodate the demands of the other party, a bargaining deadlock will result.[5]

Bargaining pressures and deadlocks. The knowledge that the opposing side is able and willing to use economic pressures to enforce its demands

---

[4]Edward Peters, "Only the Real Issues Count in Contract Bargaining," *Personnel Journal*, Vol. 32, No. 10 (March, 1954), pp. 367–373.

[5]Ross Stagner and Hjalmar Rosen, *Psychology of Union-Management Relations* (Belmont, California: Wadsworth Publishing Company, Inc., 1965), pp. 95–97.

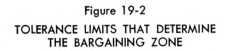

Figure 19-2

TOLERANCE LIMITS THAT DETERMINE
THE BARGAINING ZONE

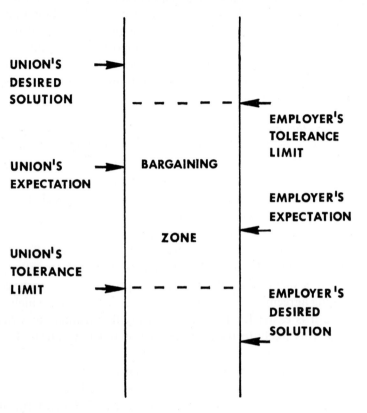

Source: Ross Stagner and Hjalmar Rosen, *Psychology of Union-Management Relations* (Belmont, California: Wadsworth Publishing Company, Inc., 1965), p. 96. Reproduced with permission.

may help to induce the other side to make greater effort to achieve a compromise. The union may exert economic pressures by striking, by picketing, or by boycotting the employer's products and encouraging others to do likewise. The mere threat to exert such pressures can also be effective. Employers who wish to exert economic pressure, on the other hand, may cease their operations and lay off their personnel, subcontract out their work, transfer work to another location, or threaten to do any of these things.

Strikes. A *strike* involves the refusal of a group of employees to perform their jobs. Since a strike can have a serious effect upon both the union and its members, the prospects for its success must be analyzed carefully before the strike is called. Among the factors which the union ought to consider before reaching a strike decision are the following:

1. The effect that calling a strike or, conversely, agreeing on a contract will have upon the union's policies, aims, and goals.
2. The long-term and short-term implication of settling without a strike.
3. The strength of the union and its ability to shut down the company's operations.
4. The degree to which striking members will be able to withstand the loss of pay checks.
5. The degree to which public opinion will be sympathetic — or at least, not antagonistic — to the purposes of the strike.
6. The role that federal, state, and local governments can be expected to take in the event of a strike.[6]

A strike can also create severe hardship for the company. In determining whether to concede to union demands or take a strike, the company must weigh carefully these considerations:

1. The extent to which a possible settlement is reconcilable with company policy.
2. What are the long- and short-term implications of settling without a strike?
3. The ability of the company to withstand possible loss of profits, customers, and suppliers.
4. The ability of the company to secure other employees and continue operations.
5. The effect of a strike on nonstriking employees.
6. The importance of the strike issues to union members.
7. The extent to which public opinion will support the company's position.
8. The extent to which the local union will receive financial and moral backing from its parent organization and other labor organizations.
9. The role that federal, state, and local governments can be expected to assume in the event of a work stoppage.[7]

Unions usually will seek strike authorization from their members to use as bargaining leverage in the hope of gaining concessions that will enable them to continue negotiating. A strike vote by the members, thus, does not mean that they actually want or expect to go out on strike; but, rather, it is intended as a vote of confidence to strengthen the position of their leaders at the bargaining table.

---

[6]*Preparing for Collective Bargaining-II*, Studies in Personnel Policies, No. 182 (New York: The National Industrial Conference Board, 1961), pp. 9–10.

[7]*Ibid.*, pp. 10–11.

Picketing. When a union goes on strike, it is general practice for the union to *picket* the employer by placing persons at the entrances to his premises to advertise the dispute and to discourage persons from entering or leaving these premises. Even when the strikers represent only a small proportion of the employees within the plant, they can often cause the shutdown of an entire plant if a sufficient number of the plant's employees refuse to cross their picket line. Also, a picket line can result in the refusal of employees from other companies to cross the picket line to deliver and pick up goods.

Picketing that is carried on by nonemployees is called *stranger picketing,* and it is sometimes used by unions in an effort to unionize an employer. Because peaceful picketing has traditionally been regarded as a form of free speech, the courts have been reluctant to curb it even when it has been used unfairly. If a strike fails to stop a company's operations, the picket line may become more than a passive weapon. Employees who attempt to cross the line may be subjected to verbal insults and even physical violence. *Mass picketing* in which large groups of pickets try to block the path of people attempting to enter a plant may then be used. However, the use of picket lines to exert physical pressure and to incite violence usually will succeed only in arousing unfavorable public opinion and legal restrictions.

Boycotting. Another economic weapon of unions is the *boycott.* This action can hurt an employer if conducted by a large enough segment of organized labor. For example, even though a manufacturer of work clothes is able to operate during a strike, he could suffer a substantial loss of sales because of the refusal of union members throughout the nation to buy the garments that he manufactures. Most unions levy heavy fines against members if they are discovered patronizing an employer who is the subject of a union boycott. The refusal of a union to allow its members to patronize a business enterprise where there is a labor dispute is a *primary boycott.* This type of boycott under most circumstances is legal. A union may go a step farther, however, and attempt to induce third parties, primarily suppliers and customers, to refrain from business dealings with the employer with whom it has a dispute. A boycott of this type is called a *secondary boycott* and generally is illegal under the Taft-Hartley Act.

Lockouts. A *lockout* occurs when an employer shuts down his plant in an effort to force the union to cease harassing activities or to accept certain conditions demanded by the employer. It is the employer's counterpart to a strike and is more likely to be used by employer associations to support members who have been subject to a strike. In recent years the lockout has perhaps been used most frequently by employer associations to support members who have been struck by a union. In such instances the lockout is invoked by the other members on the grounds that "a strike against one is a strike against all." Lockouts also may be used by employers to combat union slowdowns, damage to their property, or violence within their plant that may occur in connection with a labor dispute even though a strike may not be in progress. Employers have tended to use the lockout more as a defensive than as an offensive weapon. While threat of a lockout may be used to gain agreement from a union, employers are reluctant to resort to a lockout because of the loss of revenue during the shutdown and because of their fear that such action might generate unfavorable public opinion or result in legal action against them.

Overcoming bargaining deadlocks. If a strike or lockout occurs, it usually is not long before both parties begin to feel its effects. The company may suffer the loss of profits, customers, and public goodwill or may risk unfavorable government action. The union leaders may risk the possibility of losing members, of being voted out of office, or of having the employees vote the union out of the company. Unions also may experience the loss of public goodwill, may become involved in unfavorable legal action, or may suffer from subsequent legislation that is passed to regulate their activities. As the losses to each side increase, therefore, the participants usually become more anxious to achieve a settlement.

Conciliation and mediation. When the two parties are unable or unwilling to continue negotiations, an outside conciliator or a mediator can often be helpful. A *conciliator* provides a catalytic service by keeping the negotiations moving and thus helps the two parties arrive at their own solution. He does not attempt to suggest a compromise solution for them. A *mediator*, by contrast, exercises a more positive role in helping to resolve a deadlock by suggesting compromise solutions. In practice, however, the functions of conciliation and mediation often overlap. The conciliator may see fit to offer suggestions and thus perform the role of a mediator, or the mediator may attempt to let the two parties work out their own solutions and thus act merely as a conciliator. Since both the union and management usually are under pressure to achieve a settlement by the time he enters the picture, the conciliator (or the mediator) can help them to retreat from their deadlocked position without suffering a loss of face. Furthermore, the negotiating parties frequently will reveal to the conciliator a willingness to compromise at some point less than the one previously stated. By acting as an intermediary between the two parties, the conciliator can often detect and interpret the willingness of each to give ground and can thus gradually draw them closer together until an agreement point is reached.

Arbitration. In *arbitration* both sides agree to place the dispute in the hands of a third party and to abide by his decision. It is not used to resolve bargaining deadlocks nearly as much as it is used to resolve grievances arising from the administration of the agreement, for both parties are usually reluctant to have a third party determine the terms of their agreement. In most instances they would rather make concessions voluntarily or as the result of economic pressures than to be forced to accept whatever decision the arbitrator might see fit to render.

Government intervention. In some situations deadlocks may have to be resolved directly or indirectly as the result of government intervention, particularly if the work stoppage is a threat to the national security or to the public welfare. Government intervention may include plant seizure or the threat of seizure, the issuance of injunctions, or the cancellation of government contracts. The threat of punitive legislation or of public condemnation of either or both sides also can have a persuasive effect in achieving a settlement. Government pressure may be exerted through the appointment of a *fact-finding board* to investigate a bargaining deadlock. Although these boards do not have power to force the parties to reach a settlement, they do provide additional information that can serve to fix the responsibility for the deadlock. The influence of this information upon public opinion can place one or both parties under considerable pressure to reach an agreement.

The Content of the Labor Agreement

The development and ratification of a written agreement constitutes the final phase of the collective bargaining process. The wording of the agreement provisions can be extremely important, for the choice of words, phrases, or even punctuation marks may determine the outcome of disputes arising from the interpretation of the agreement. The written agreement provides a permanent record that can serve as a guide in administering those personnel functions covered by the agreement, and each agreement that is negotiated between a company and a union should prove more effective than the previous one. It is only as a result of experience gained from negotiating and enforcing several agreements that defects in an agreement and problems relating to its enforcement can be kept to a minimum.

The labor agreement typically is divided into from 20 to 30 articles or sections. Some of the principal subjects covered by these articles are discussed below.

General statement. An introductory general statement usually summarizes the scope and purpose of the contract and reaffirms the desire of both parties to exercise good faith in observing its provisions.

Union security. Articles covering union security typically deal with such things as type of recognition to be accorded to the union, dues check-off provisions, right of the union officials to enter or to have representatives within the plant, and similar subjects affecting union welfare. The union's right to be consulted or to participate in management decisions involving such matters as the subcontracting of work, the installation of newer equipment, or the changing of plant locations may also be included.

Functions or rights of management. While most unions are seeking to extend their areas of participation in personnel decisions, companies are striving equally hard to prevent such extensions. Companies frequently seek to define their rights or prerogatives to take independent action. For example, 65 percent of the labor agreements studied in one survey contained a statement of management rights.[8] The right to hire, fire, and discipline employees, to install new equipment, to establish work standards, or to subcontract work are among those subjects typically covered by statements dealing with management prerogatives.

Grievance procedures. Grievance handling is one of the first and most important subjects covered by the labor agreement as far as the union and its members are concerned. The steps in the grievance procedure, the provisions for arbitration, and, in some instances, the subjects that can be handled as grievances are among those described in this part of the agreement. An example of a grievance procedure was included in Chapter 17.

Seniority provisions. Articles covering seniority usually define the method of accumulating seniority and establish its effect upon transfers, promotions, and layoffs. The consideration to be given to seniority in the assignment of job duties, the granting of overtime, or other employment privileges may also be included.

Wages. Articles dealing with wages and hours usually specify the rates to be paid in the different job classifications as well as the policies that

---

[8]*Collective Bargaining: Negotiations and Contracts,* Vol. 2 (Washington, D.C.: Bureau of National Affairs, Sept. 25, 1964), p. 65:1.

govern the administration of the wage structure, the computation of wage payments, the method of making payments, and the premiums provided for overtime and holiday work.

Fringe benefits. Provisions for paid holidays, vacations, sick leave, supplemental unemployment pay, and various employee services also are typically included in a section of the agreement. The description of fringe benefits can be rather lengthy and, thus, is often included as a supplement to the main agreement.

Miscellaneous provisions. Miscellaneous articles can cover a variety of items such as safety, working conditions, union bulletin boards, military service, jury duty, leaves of absence, disciplinary procedures, and other subjects of a general nature.

Termination of agreement. The final article of the agreement normally defines the life of the contract and the procedures that must be followed in terminating or reopening it. There has been a trend for agreements to cover a period of more than a year's duration. A Bureau of National Affairs survey of a selected number of labor agreements, for example, disclosed that only 8 percent of them were of one-year duration, whereas 40 percent were of two-year duration and 47 percent were of three-year duration.[9]

Ratification of the Agreement

In some unions approval of the labor agreement by the national union is required while in others the ratification of the agreement by the general membership is sufficient. Company bylaws may require that the labor agreement be approved by the board of directors or even the stockholders before becoming final. In most cases the ratification of the agreement by both sides does not present a serious problem since those persons having the power of ratification usually are reluctant to undercut or cause a loss of face for the members of their negotiating committees.

Enforcement of the Agreement

A labor agreement, if it is to be of value, must be carefully administered and enforced. In order for the agreement to be enforced, the company and the union representatives who administer it, as well as the union members affected by it, should be thoroughly familiar with its provisions. Most unions do a fairly adequate job of educating their representatives and members as to the terms of the agreement. Many unions conduct

---

[9]*Ibid.*, p. 36:1.

classes for stewards and other union representatives in order to familiarize them with the provisions of the labor agreement and to prepare them for enforcing it.

Companies also are placing greater emphasis upon informing their managers and employees about the agreement. Communication and training efforts of the personnel department, in particular, have helped to put supervisors on at least an equal footing with the union representatives in their knowledge of the provisions of the agreement. Supervisors who have had training in the interpretation and administration of the agreement are less likely to violate its provisions and have their decisions reversed by higher management or by an arbitrator.

Characteristics of Contemporary Union-Management Relations

Since the passage of the Wagner Act, union-management relations in general have undergone substantial changes. Rationalism and give-and-take bargaining have tended to replace emotionalism and sheer economic pressures as the basis for achieving bargaining agreements. Increasingly employers are recognizing that the negotiation of a labor agreement is facilitated by the existence of a sound personnel management program. They also have learned the futility of attempting to destroy a union and of permitting themselves to always be on the defensive when negotiating with the union. Although some employers have been curtailed by their union in attempting to take advantage of technological advancements, an increasing number of them have been able to work out a system for introducing laborsaving devices that preserves the job rights of union members.

Increased Bargaining Initiative by Employers

Increasingly, since the enactment of the Taft-Hartley Act, there have been instances in which employers have attempted to take the initiative rather than assume the defensive in bargaining with unions. Under this more positive approach, a company usually determines what it feels it can afford to give the union in terms of current economic conditions and bargaining patterns. It then submits its offer to the union and, if possible, attempts to hold fast to this offer. Every effort is made to inform and sell individual employees on the merits of the offer; and after a given deadline, the increases and other benefits are granted to all employees except those covered by the agreement being negotiated. This procedure may place the union under considerable pressure to accept what has been offered to the other groups in the company since the union's members will lose what they otherwise could be receiving if a new agreement is not reached by the time the old one expires. As added pressure the company may indicate in advance its refusal to make any increases that are subsequently granted to the union members retroactive to the date that the general increases were granted.[10]

This new approach to collective bargaining quite naturally has not been enthusiastically received by labor unions. They regard it as an effort to avoid collective bargaining and to return to the tactics that were used before the passage of the Wagner Act. Any company attempting to use such an approach must be certain that it can maintain its bargaining position even if it precipitates a strike and that it can retain the individual loyalty of a major segment of its employees. Aside from the bargaining risks that are involved, this approach, depending upon how it is used, may risk the danger of being ruled as an unfair labor practice by the National Labor Relations Board. The Board, for example, has held that the General Electric Company's use of this type of bargaining with electrical workers constituted bargaining in bad faith.[11] The line of distinction between what constitutes good faith and bad faith in bargaining, therefore, is a fine one that the courts have yet to clarify fully. Regardless of where this line is drawn, however, many employers can be expected to take a more aggressive approach than had been the case in the past. In spite of these calculated risks, however, employers have in some instances been able, with considerable success, to exercise more initiative in bargaining with unions.

Possibilities for Union Cooperation

Possible areas of cooperation between employers and unions are often outlined in the labor agreement, such as provisions for the payroll deduction of union dues. Union participation in determining and administering time standards, in reducing waste, in promoting safety, or in handling various other operating problems also may be provided for in the agreement. Unions, in addition, may assist employers in solving certain of their personnel problems. Fines and reprimands and other forms of disciplinary action by the union can do much to discourage "quickie strikes," substandard performance, or violations of company rules by its members. Petty and unwarranted grievances can also be screened and resolved by union officers, and this serves to keep the grievance machinery available for the handling of the more serious cases.

---

[10]James Menzies Black, "Collective Bargaining: The Positive Approach Pays Off," *Dun's Review and Modern Industry*, Vol. 68, No. 1 (January, 1957), pp. 36–37, 52–65.
[11]*Wall Street Journal*, Dec. 17, 1964.

In the craft occupations union control over the training and performance standards at the apprentice, journeyman, and master levels can simplify the task of selecting and training employees. Unions in these and other occupational areas also may provide an important source from which to recruit new employees. Perhaps the ultimate in union cooperation, however, has occurred in those instances in which a distressed company has been helped through a difficult period by means of loans, voluntary wage reductions, or through the acceptance of deferred wage payments.[12]

Although the mutual benefits of cooperation are not always evident, numerous benefits exist which contribute to greater productivity. Higher productivity, in turn, can lead to organizational growth and higher profits for the company and more jobs, better working conditions, higher earnings, and increased job security for the union members.

Résumé

The right of employees to unionize, to bargain collectively with an employer over their conditions of employment, and to exert economic pressures to enforce these demands has become firmly accepted by American society. A growing body of law, furthermore, has been developed to protect these rights, to facilitate collective bargaining, to minimize conflicts, and to prevent abuse by either side in the maintenance of a bargaining relationship. While some employers may resent sharing with a union the authority to make various decisions relating to the operation of their companies, the existence of unions and their right to participate in these areas has become an established fact. It, therefore, is to the best interests of every employer who must deal with a union to develop the ability to bargain effectively and to maintain a satisfactory relationship with union leaders. Even those employers whose companies are not unionized cannot afford to ignore the subject of union relations or the laws pertaining to it since there is always the possibility that they may become the subject of a unionizing effort. It is important, furthermore, that a company attempt to maintain employment conditions comparable to those that exist within the industry as a whole as well as an effective personnel program. Such attempts will contribute to the maintenance of better relations with the union that represents its employees or that may at some future date gain the right to represent them.

Since it is the union-management conflicts that normally attract the public's attention, it is easy to ignore the fact that most relationships

---

[12]Ross Stagner, *The Psychology of Industrial Conflict* (New York: John Wiley & Sons, Inc., 1956), pp. 449–477.

between union and management are peaceful ones. Such relationships, however, do not "just happen" but, rather, have developed as the result of the skill and effort that have been exerted by representatives of both sides. While representatives with such abilities may be able to drive a hard bargain, they also are able to understand the position and problems of the opposing side and to avoid unrealistic demands and needless antagonism.

DISCUSSION QUESTIONS AND PROBLEMS

1. Can the fact that the labor agreement states that decisions, such as those relating to time standards or to discharge action, are the sole prerogative of management prevent the union from filing grievances relating to these subjects?
2. Why is a company more likely than the union to press for an agreement of more than a year's duration? Under what conditions will the union be more likely to agree to a longer term agreement?
3. In what ways does the political nature of the union leader's job influence his relations with management?
4. What is meant by the term "union security"? List the various types of security that a union may gain with an employer.
5. What is the purpose of picketing, and why have the courts been reluctant to curb its use?
6. Of what significance is the "bargaining zone" in the conduct of negotiations, and what determines the limits of this zone?
7. In view of the hardships that they create for the employer and union members, why is it that strikes occur as frequently as they do?
8. In the clause covering paid holidays, the company has proposed that the following statement be included in the agreement:

   > In order to be eligible to receive a holiday without deduction of pay, an employee must work the scheduled workday immediately preceding and immediately following the holiday.

   The union, however, has insisted that the wording be changed from "the" scheduled workday to "his" scheduled workday. What effect, if any, might this difference in wording have upon the administration of the agreement?
9. How does the more "positive approach" to collective bargaining differ from the approach that companies traditionally have taken? Why are some companies taking this positive approach?
10. At an election conducted among the 20 employees of the Exclusive Jewelry Store, all but two of them voted in favor of the Jewelry Workers Union, which was subsequently certified as their bargaining agent. In negotiating its first agreement, the union demanded that it be granted a union shop. The two employees voting against the union, however, informed the management that they would quit rather than join the union. Unfortunately for the store, the two individuals were skilled gem cutters who were the most valuable of its employees and would be difficult to replace if they could be replaced at all. What position should the company take with regard to the union shop demand?

CASE 19-1

THE STRIKERS' JOBS

The Modern Furniture Company had managed to maintain its production, although at a reduced level, during the two-month period that it had been the subject of a strike by the Woodworkers Union. Production had been maintained by hiring some new employees to replace those who had walked off the job and by using the services of a few employees who had returned to work after being on strike for a few days. Because the company was suffering a financial loss from the strike, it was anxious to reach a settlement with the union. As negotiations with the union continued, the company gradually was able to reach agreement with union representatives on all issues except those relating to the reemployment of the members who had been on strike. The union refused to accept anything less than the reemployment of all strikers on the grounds that its members might as well stay out on strike if some of them would not have a job to which they could return. The company, on the other hand, was equally firm in its refusal to discharge any personnel who had helped it to maintain production during the strike should such action be necessary in order to create jobs for all returning strikers. Because of the adamancy of both parties on this issue, there appeared to be little prospect for settling the strike in spite of the mounting losses being suffered by both sides.

a. What problems does each side face if it concedes on this issue? What problems does each side face if it refuses to make concessions?
b. How would you resolve this issue if you were called in as an arbitrator to settle it?

CASE 19-2

THE LOST WORK

Because of a series of labor difficulties encountered in the operation of its foundry, the Metal Products Company has decided to close down this phase of its operations and purchase its castings from another company. The union immediately filed an unfair labor practice charge against the company accusing it of attempting to coerce the union by threatening to close down the foundry. The union also stated that it would pull all of its members off the job and picket the company if it carried out its decision to subcontract its foundry work. The union has been guaranteed support by other unions within the plant who have promised not to cross the foundry workers' picket line in the event that they call a strike.

a. Do you feel that the subcontracting of the foundry work would constitute an unfair labor practice?
b. What implications may this dispute have from the standpoint of personnel management?

CASE 19-3

THE NEW STORE

The Appliance Repairmen's Local #480 had maintained a union shop labor agreement with the Factory Outlet Store for several years. The preamble of this agreement read, in part, as follows:

THIS AGREEMENT, made and entered into this 1st day of March, 196–, by and between THE FACTORY OUTLET STORE and the APPLIANCE REPAIR-MEN'S LOCAL #480 shall be . . .

While the labor agreement was still in effect, the company established a second store in a suburban shopping center of the same town and hired additional personnel to staff it. The union immediately demanded that the employees hired for the new store be required to join the union on the grounds that the new store was covered by the existing agreement. The company, however, refused to concede to the union's demands and maintained that its agreement covered only the store that existed and was mentioned in the agreement when it was negotiated.

    a. How should this disagreement over the interpretation of the agreement be resolved?

    b. What are the implications of this case in terms of employee bargaining rights at the new store and in terms of the union's security?

SUGGESTED READINGS

Chamberlain, Neil W. *Source Book on Labor*. New York: McGraw-Hill Book Company, 1964.

Chamberlain, Neil W., and James W. Kuhn. *Collective Bargaining*, Second Edition. New York: McGraw-Hill Book Company, 1965.

Davey, H. W. *Contemporary Collective Bargaining*. Englewood Cliffs, New Jersey: Prentice-Hall, Inc., 1959. Chapter 5.

Healy, James J. (ed.). *Creative Collective Bargaining*. Englewood Cliffs, New Jersey: Prentice-Hall, Inc., 1965.

Hutchinson, John G. *Management Under Strike Conditions*. New York: Holt, Rinehart and Winston, Inc., 1966.

Mabry, Bevars D. *Labor Relations and Collective Bargaining*. New York: The Ronald Press Company, 1966.

Marting, Elizabeth (ed.). *Understanding Collective Bargaining*. New York: American Management Association, 1958. Sections II and III, 61–146.

Peters, Edward. *Strategy and Tactics in Labor Negotiations*. New London, Connecticut: National Foreman's Institute. Chapters 1–4.

Preparing for Collective Bargaining-II, Studies in Personnel Policy, No. 182. New York: National Industrial Conference Board, 1961.

Walton, Richard E., and Robert B. McKersie. *A Behavioral Theory of Labor Negotiations*. New York: McGraw-Hill Book Company, 1965.

Warner, Kenneth O., and Mary L. Hennessy. *Public Management at the Bargaining Table*. Chicago: Public Personnel Association, 1967.

20

Job Evaluation

One of the basic objectives of a sound personnel program is to pay each employee wages that are commensurate with the demands of his job and are consistent with the wages paid to other employees performing similar jobs. In order to achieve this objective, a company must be able to determine with reasonable accuracy the relative worth of each job in terms of the demands that it makes of the employee who performs it. These demands and the personal qualifications that the employee must possess in order to perform his job, as disclosed in Chapter 4, are determined through the process of job analysis and are defined in the job specifications. On the basis of the information contained in these specifications, the relative worth of each job may be determined through the process of job evaluation. This process is discussed under the following topics:

- The job evaluation program.
- Job evaluation systems.
- The wage structure.

The Job Evaluation Program

While most companies attempt to determine an employee's pay upon the basis of what his job is worth, all too frequently this rate of pay ultimately is based upon personal judgment or upon the rate that the employee or his union is able to negotiate for the job. When pay rates are arrived at in this manner, it is not surprising that employees may wonder whether or not they are receiving their full entitlement. If employees are to receive the money to which they are entitled and if they are to be convinced of this fact, their rate of pay should be arrived at through some type of formal program of job evaluation.

Benefits of a Formal Program

A formal job evaluation program permits a company to determine more objectively and systematically the relative worth of each job within the company. While the job evaluation process is not scientific in nature nor entirely free from the influence of human judgments, it permits these judgments to be made systematically rather than on a hit-or-miss basis. The possibility of error, thus, is more likely to be reduced. Employees are also generally able to understand better how their wage rates have been determined and, as a result, may be more satisfied with these rates. Even though employee grievances may still arise in connection with their wages, the existence of a formal job evaluation program should, in the long run, reduce the number of grievances pertaining to remuneration.

Job evaluation can also provide a more objective basis for establishing the level of each job within the organizational hierarchy and the levels of authority and advancement that are provided by this hierarchy. This information, in turn, can facilitate the handling of employee training, promotions, transfers, and other personnel functions. In the process of analyzing and evaluating jobs, furthermore, the existence of safety hazards or of job duties that have been assigned improperly may be revealed and corrected to the benefit of both the company and employees.

Responsibility for Administering the Program

The primary responsibility for administering a job evaluation program normally is vested in the personnel department. If the company is of sufficient size, a wage and salary division may be established within the department to handle job evaluation as well as job analysis and classification. While the members of this division normally handle most of the details connected with job evaluation, including the clerical, statistical, and analytical work, the actual rating and classification of the jobs frequently is performed by a job evaluation committee.

A job evaluation committee generally is composed of representatives from the personnel department and the operative departments. The use of a committee permits the job ratings to be determined on the basis of group rather than individual judgments, thereby reducing bias. The inclusion of personnel from the different departments on the committee enables individuals who are personally familiar with most of the jobs that are to be evaluated and who have a direct interest in the results of the program to contribute to its operation. The presence of such individuals on a committee also will help to discourage any departments from attempting to exaggerate the importance of these jobs when they are being evaluated. Because job evaluation is a highly specialized and technical function, however, many companies have found it desirable to utilize the assistance of personnel consultants.

Job Evaluation Systems

It is possible to evaluate jobs formally by comparing them against one another or against a model or scale that has been constructed for this purpose. Either of these methods of comparison may be conducted on a nonquantitative basis, in which the jobs are evaluated as a whole, or on a quantitative basis, in which they are evaluated on the basis of each factor. These various methods thus provide a total of four different systems that can be used in evaluating jobs. As illustrated in Figure 20-1, these include the job ranking system, the job grade system, the point system, and the factor comparison system. Of these four systems, the point system is the one that is used most frequently, followed by the factor comparison system and the job grade system.[1]

Figure 20-1

COMPARISON OF JOB EVALUATION SYSTEMS

Basis for Comparison	Scope of Comparison	
	JOB AS A WHOLE (NONQUANTITATIVE)	JOB PARTS OR FACTORS (QUANTITATIVE)
Job vs. Job	(1) Job Ranking System	(4) Factor Comparison System
Job vs. Scale	(2) Job Grade System	(3) Point System

[1] Elizabeth Lanham, *Administration of Wages and Salaries* (New York: Harper & Row, Publishers, 1962), pp. 165, 189.

Job Ranking System

The simplest and oldest system of job evaluation is the *job ranking* or *order-of-merit* system by which jobs are arrayed on the basis of their relative worth. One technique that is used to rank jobs consists of having the raters arrange cards containing the specifications for each job in the order of importance of the jobs that the cards represent. Differences in the rankings made by the raters can then be reconciled into a single rating.

The basic weakness of the job ranking system is that it does not provide a very refined measure of each job's worth. Since the comparisons must be made on the basis of the jobs as a whole, it is quite easy for one or more of the factors of a job to bias the ranking that the evaluator gives to the job, particularly if the jobs are complex. Existing wage rates and job titles also may contribute to bias in the ranking. Furthermore, the rankings merely indicate the relative importance of the jobs but not the differences in importance that may exist between jobs.

Job Grade System

The *job grade* or *classification* system is more refined than the ranking system in that it permits the jobs to be classified and grouped according to a series of predetermined wage classes or grades. The federal civil service job classification system is probably the best known system of this type. The descriptions for each of the job classes constitute the scale against which the specifications for the various jobs are compared. The number of classes that are required for the system will depend upon the range of duties, responsibilities, skills, and other requirements that exist among the jobs to be evaluated by the system. Generally, it is necessary to provide separate systems for office, factory, sales, and supervisory jobs. The following classes, for example, might be established for jobs in the clerical and in the shop and service groups:

CLERICAL EMPLOYEES

CLASS

C-1   Routine clerical work such as typing; simple repetitive calculations; work under close supervision following definite rules.

C-2   Secretarial and advanced clerical work in which substantial judgment, discretion, and initiative are involved.

C-3   Supervision of three or more persons doing C-1 or C-2 work; substantial knowledge of some specialized field such as accounting; complicated calculations.

SHOP AND SERVICE EMPLOYEES

S-1   Repetitive work under immediate supervision and involving no unusual hazard or extra effort; requires no previous training.
         EXAMPLE: Watchman; Janitor.

S-2   Repetitive work under general supervision; repetitive work under immediate supervision, but involving unusual hazard or extra physical or mental application; no special training before employment, and very short training on the job.
         EXAMPLE: Guard; Routine inspection or assembly; Box maker.

S-3   Semiskilled work requiring exercise of judgment by employee in making decisions; specialized training or experience in operating tools required.
         EXAMPLE: Difficult assembly and inspection; Rough carpentry; Operation of machine tools to moderate tolerances.

S-4   Skilled work involving broad knowledge of a recognized trade; read and interpret difficult blueprints; responsibility for materials and equipment; set up and operation of a variety of machine tools to close tolerances.
         EXAMPLE: Machinist; Plumber; Carpenter; Steamfitter; Electrician; Supervision of S-2 or S-3 work.

S-5   Supervision of S-3 or S-4 work; precision work; highest degree of skill and experience; requires knowledge of two or more skilled trades.
         EXAMPLE: Tool and die maker; Instrument maker; Pattern maker; Lens grinder.[2]

The principal advantage of the job grade system, like that of the ranking system, lies in its simplicity. It is, therefore, suited to the needs of a small organization. A majority of the jobs that are evaluated under the job grade system will fall clearly into one of the established wage classes. The nature of some jobs, however, may cause them to overlap between two wage classes with the result that these jobs cannot be placed with complete accuracy in either class. This limitation, along with the fact that the system requires evaluating the whole job and therefore does not provide a very precise evaluation and the fact that classifications which are achieved can be biased by existing wage rates, probably explains why it is not used more extensively.

Point System

The point system developed initially by Western Electric has subsequently been used successfully by the United States Steel Corporation, General Electric Company, Metropolitan Life Insurance Company,

---

[2]Robert D. Gray, *Classification of Jobs in Small Companies*, Bulletin No. 5, Industrial Relations Section (Pasadena: California Institute of Technology, 1944), p. 21.

Montgomery Ward, and many other companies, both large and small.[3] This system permits jobs to be evaluated quantitatively on the basis of the factors or elements that comprise the demands of the job. The skills, efforts, responsibilities, and working conditions that a job usually entails are typical of the more common major factors that serve to make one job more or less important than another. The point system, like the job grade system, requires the use of a point manual or scale that contains a description of the factors and the degrees to which these factors may exist within the jobs. A manual also must indicate — usually by means of a table (see Figure 20-2)[4] — the number of points that are allocated to each factor and to each of the degrees into which these factors are divided. The specifications for each job then are evaluated by comparing them, factor by factor, against the description in the manual to determine the point value that the job is to receive. These point totals provide the bases for determining the relative worth of each job and for assigning it to the appropriate wage class.

Nature of the point manual. A variety of point manuals have been developed by companies, trade associations, and management consultants. Those manuals prepared by the National Metal Trades, the National Electrical Manufacturers, and the Administrative Management Society are among the ones most widely utilized. A company that seeks to use one of these or other manuals should make certain that it is suitable to its particular jobs and conditions of operation and, if necessary, should modify it to fit its needs. In many instances it may be preferable for the company to develop a manual of its own. If such a manual is developed, certain basic steps to be followed normally include:

1. Studying the jobs to be evaluated and determining the factors or characteristics to be used in measuring job worth.
2. Determining the degrees or levels needed to measure the presence of each factor in each of the various jobs.
3. Defining factors and degrees.
4. Assigning weight to the factors and the degrees of these factors in proportion to their relative importance within the particular firm.[5]

Construction of a point manual. The job factors and subfactors in the point manual should include those that are significant in measuring the

---

[3]John A. Patton, C. L. Littlefield, and Stanley Allen Self, *Job Evaluation* (Homewood, Illinois: Richard D. Irwin Co., 1964), p. 134.

[4]Figure 20-2 is taken from the point manual developed by the National Metal Trades Association and reproduced with their permission. The figure represents the table for assigning the point values for the various job factors covered by the manual and the degrees into which these factors have been divided.

[5]Patton, Littlefield, and Self, *op. cit.,* p. 136.

Figure 20-2

POINT VALUES FOR JOB FACTORS

Factors	1st Degree	2nd Degree	3rd Degree	4th Degree	5th Degree
SKILL					
1. Job Knowledge..........	14	28	42	56	70
2. Experience..............	22	44	66	88	110
3. Initiative and Ingenuity...	14	28	42	56	70
EFFORT					
4. Physical Demand........	10	20	30	40	50
5. Mental or Visual Demand.	5	10	15	20	25
RESPONSIBILITY					
6. Equipment or Process....	5	10	15	20	25
7. Material or Product......	5	10	15	20	25
8. Safety of Others........	5	10	15	20	25
9. Work of Others..........	5	10	15	20	25
JOB CONDITIONS					
10. Working Conditions......	10	20	30	40	50
11. Hazards................	5	10	15	20	25

Source: National Metal Trades Association.

worth of the jobs. The inclusion of those factors that are of a minor nature, that overlap, that are not clearly definable, that are not present in varying degrees among the jobs to be rated, or that tend to measure man or personal factors rather than job factors should be avoided.[6] The trend is for point systems to utilize fewer factors in support of the belief that a large number is unnecessary for effective job measurement. The number used ordinarily ranges from five to fifteen with the average being approximately ten.[7]

The job factors and subfactors that are illustrated in Figure 20-2 represent those covered by one particular point manual. Each of the factors listed in this manual has been divided into five degrees. The number of degrees into which the factors comprising a manual are to be divided, however, can be more or fewer than this number, depending upon

[6]*Ibid.*, p. 141.
[7]Lanham, *op. cit.*, pp. 177–178.

the relative weight assigned to each factor and upon the ease with which the individual degrees can be defined or distinguished. A factor such as experience (line 2, in Figure 20-2), which is assigned a proportionately large number of points and which may vary considerably for different jobs, could well be divided into as many as eight degrees. On the other hand, a factor such as working conditions (line 10, Figure 20-2) might well be divided into only three degrees if it were assigned a relatively small number of the total points or if it existed to approximately the same degree for all jobs.

After the job factors that are to be covered by the point manual have been divided into degrees, a statement must be prepared defining each of these degrees as well as each factor as a whole. The definitions should be concise and yet distinguish the factors and each of their degrees. Figure 20-3 represents a portion of a point manual used by the Allis-Chalmers Manufacturing Company to describe each of the degrees for the factors of experience and of initiative and ingenuity. These descriptions enable those persons conducting an evaluation to determine the degree that the factors exist in each job being evaluated.

Figure 20-3

SAMPLE MANUAL DESCRIPTIONS FOR JOB FACTORS AND FOR THEIR DEGREES

EXPERIENCE

This factor measures the length of time, *with the specified job knowledge,* that is required to obtain and develop the skills necessary to effectively perform the work. Where previous experience is required, time spent in related work or lesser classifications, either within the Company or other organizations, will be considered as contributing to the total experience required to effectively perform the work. Consideration must be given to continuous progress by the average individual, allowing sufficient practice time to encounter and satisfactorily resolve representative deviation in the work assignments that could normally be expected.

FIRST DEGREE:
Up to and including three months.

FOURTH DEGREE:
Over three years up to five years.

SECOND DEGREE:
Over three months up to one year.

FIFTH DEGREE:
Over five years.

THIRD DEGREE:
Over one year up to three years.

INITIATIVE AND INGENUITY

This factor measures the complexity of job duties in terms of the amount of initiative and ingenuity required for successful job performance. Consider the variation and involvement of the methods, procedures and practices; the degree of independent action and original thought required; the extent of supervision received; and the availability of standards, precedents, and shop practices.

FIRST DEGREE:

Instructions are received orally or written in nontechnical terms which can be understood and carried out with a minimum of initiative and judgment. Work is of such a nature that details left to the control of the employee are limited; operations are highly repetitive and minimum of responsibility for maintaining tolerances exists.

SECOND DEGREE:

Instructions may require explanation to the extent of using a single view or plan drawing. Procedures are normally detailed: the majority of work is similar in its overall requirement; however, minor variations exist in completing individual details which require the use of some judgment or initiative. Tolerances are easy to maintain, using scales, gauges, solid frame micrometers, templates, and related means of checking.

THIRD DEGREE:

Instructions may require explanation to the point of using multiple view or related part drawings. Work is of a varied nature within a well-defined field under standard practices and precedents. Operations can normally be accomplished by several methods or procedures requiring a selection to fit individual variations. Judgment or initiative are required within the limits of established standards. Tolerances are considered close and somewhat difficult to maintain.

FOURTH DEGREE:

Instructions available for job performance are few and of a general nature. Basic planning of successive steps together with consideration for related operations is necessary. Duties vary to the extent that assignments normally require drawing upon past parallel solutions for general guidance. Mental resourcefulness, initiative, and judgment are required to solve problems. Tolerances, sizes, clearances and balancing, testing, and related procedures are considered difficult to maintain.

FIFTH DEGREE:

Instructions, precedents, and standards for performance of the job are seldom available. Considerable planning and consideration of a variety of factors difficult to evaluate are necessary for successful completion of work. Duties involve the development of new procedures, processes, or methods with a minimum of technical guidance. Requires a high degree of imagination, ingenuity, and independent action.

Reproduced with the permission of the Allis-Chalmers Manufacturing Co.

The final step in developing a point manual is that of determining the number of points to be assigned to each factor and to each degree within these factors. Although 500 points quite often constitute the maximum point value for a manual, there is nothing to prevent the figure from being 400, 800, 1,000, or some other point total.

The system for distributing the point values among the degrees of a factor varies with different manuals. Some manuals increase the point values for each degree of a factor on an arithmetic basis — that is, by a constant amount, such as 5 or 14 points. This is the system of progression that is used in Figure 20-2. Other manuals increase the value of each degree by a constant percentage or by a geometric rate of progression, such as 2, 4, 8, 16, 32. Regardless of the system used, however, the distribution of point values must be accomplished in accordance with sound statistical considerations, preferably by job evaluation specialists.

Evaluating the jobs. Once a company has a point manual that is suitable for its needs, the final step becomes one of evaluating each job by means of the manual. The evaluation consists of comparing the job specifications, factor by factor, against the various factor degree descriptions contained in the manual. Each factor within the job being evaluated is then assigned the number of points that is appropriate on the basis of the degree descriptions contained in the manual. When the points for each factor (or subfactor) have been determined from the manual, the total point value for the job as a whole can be calculated. The relative worth of the job is then determined by the total points that have been assigned to it. The point values for the various jobs, in turn, can be converted into monetary wage rates by means of either a conversion table or a conversion (wage) curve. In order to simplify the establishment of wage rates, jobs may be grouped together into job classes at the point intervals that are desired. All jobs within the class or grade are then paid at the wage rate or rate range that has been established for their particular class. Although it is a less desirable practice, it is also possible for a separate wage rate to be established for each job that reflects the point value of the job.

Advantages and disadvantages of the point system.[8] The point system has several advantages, which probably account for its popularity. Some of these advantages are:

1. The system provides a basis by which errors in judgment can be minimized if the system is developed and followed carefully.

---

[8]See David W. Belcher, *Wage and Salary Administration* (Second Edition; Englewood Cliffs, New Jersey: Prentice-Hall, Inc., 1962) pp. 274–275; Lanham, *op. cit.*, p. 175.

2. The point values derived from evaluation can aid in the establishment of job classes and in job pricing.
3. The system provides for the use of a descriptive type of scale that many authorities consider to be more reliable and valid than other rating devices.
4. The degree definitions are relatively easy to use.
5. The system is less easy to manipulate than some of the other systems.

In spite of its advantages, however, the point system is subject to certain weaknesses:

1. It may be difficult to develop a point manual that will apply accurately to all jobs. No table of factors, degrees, and point values can be developed that will prove to be universally satisfactory or completely accurate. Some jobs, for example, may contain some requirements that are much more important than is represented by the maximum point value which can be allocated to them by the manual. A few jobs may even contain requirements that are not covered by a manual, for it is difficult to construct one which will properly fit all possible situations. (The personality requirements of a receptionist, the poise and appearance of a model, or the sensory power of a food taster could be cited as examples of job factors that might not receive an adequate point value because of the limits which the manual establishes for these factors.)
2. Regardless of the method that is used to allocate points among the various job factors and their degrees, this allocation cannot be accomplished easily without being somewhat arbitrary.
3. A high degree of skill is required in selecting and writing understandable definitions for the factors and degrees.
4. The system takes time to develop and install. Some authorities also question whether the use of such terms as degrees, point values, and weights does not make the system difficult for employees to understand.
5. There is also the danger that the numerical values provided in the manual and assigned ultimately to the jobs may cause the system to have a misleading appearance of objectivity.

Factor Comparison System[9]

The *factor comparison system* was originated by Eugene Benge about 1926. Like the point system, it permits the job evaluation process to be accomplished on a factor-by-factor basis. It differs from the point system, however, in that the specifications of the jobs to be evaluated are compared against the specifications of key jobs within the company, which serve as the job evaluation scale. Thus, instead of beginning with an established

[9]For further information about the factor comparison system, see Lanham, *op. cit.*, pp. 189–202; Belcher, *op. cit.*, pp. 252–271; Patton, Littlefield, and Self, *op. cit.*, pp. 113–131.

point scale, a factor comparison scale must be developed as a part of the job evaluation process. The factors of skill, mental effort, physical effort, responsibility, and working conditions are typical of those that may comprise the factor comparison scale. The steps that comprise the factor comparison system are:

1. Select the key jobs.
2. Rank the key jobs by each factor.
3. Apportion and rank wage rates of key jobs among the factors.
4. Compare factor ranking of jobs with wage apportionment rankings.
5. Construct factor comparison scale using key jobs.
6. Evaluate non-key jobs on the scale.

Select the key jobs. The key jobs of which the factor comparison scale is comprised should include jobs of varying difficulty for which complete and accurate descriptions and specifications have been developed. The wage rate for these jobs, furthermore, should be consistent both internally and externally and not be the subject of any grievance action. Usually 15 to 20 key jobs are a sufficient number for a factor comparison scale.

Rank the key jobs by each factor. This step is accomplished by ranking the key jobs on the basis of each factor. The factors most commonly used are skill, mental effort, physical effort, responsibility, and working conditions. Figure 20-5 on page 558 illustrates how a group of key jobs might be ranked (in the J. R. column) on the basis of each factor. (In order to simplify the discussion of the factor comparison system, fewer than the normal number of key jobs have been used in the figures illustrating the system.)

Apportion and rank the wage rates of key jobs among the factors. This step consists of determining what portion of the current wage rate each of the factors is considered to be worth. Thus, it will be noted in Figure 20-4 on page 557, for example, that the current hourly rate for a machinist is $3.48. The distribution of this amount among the various factors has resulted in the allocation of $1.36 to skill, $0.92 to mental effort, $0.32 to physical effort, $0.54 to responsibility, and $0.34 to working conditions.

When the wage rates for each of the key jobs have been apportioned among the factors, the jobs are then ranked on the basis of each factor according to the amount of money that has been apportioned to that factor. The columns in Figure 20-4 that are headed "monetary rank" indicate the ranking of the jobs for that particular factor. Thus, according to this figure the job of tool and die maker ranks first in terms of the money

Figure 20-4
WAGE RATE APPORTIONMENT TABLE

JOB	Present Rate	SKILL		MENTAL EFFORT		PHYSICAL EFFORT		RESPONSIBILITY		WORKING CONDITIONS	
		Rate	Monetary Ranking	Rate	Monetary Ranking	Rate	Monetary Ranking	Rate	Monetary Ranking	Rate	Monetary Ranking
Tool and Die Maker	3.68	1.48	1	.96	1	.36	3	.58	1	.30	5
Machinist	3.48	1.36	2	.92	2	.32	4	.54	4	.34	3
Millwright	3.23	1.14	3	.69	5	.52	2	.56	2	.32	4
Forklift Operator	2.74	.81	5	.73	4	.29	6	.55	3	.36	2
Assembler, Bench	2.67	.87	4	.86	3	.30	5	.36	5	.28	6
Janitor	2.10	.47	6	.34	6	.55	1	.34	6	.40	1

Figure 20-5
JOB RANKING AND MONETARY RANKING COMPARISON TABLE

JOB	SKILL		MENTAL EFFORT		PHYSICAL EFFORT		RESPONSIBILITY		WORKING CONDITIONS	
	Job Ranking	Monetary Ranking	Job Ranking	Monetary Ranking	Job Ranking	Monetary Ranking	Job Ranking	Monetary Ranking	Job Ranking	Monetary Ranking
Tool and Die Maker	1	1	1	1	3	3	1	1	5	5
Machinist	2	2	2	2	4	4	4	4	3	3
Millwright	3	3	(4)5	5	2	2	(3)2	2	4	4
Forklift Operator	5	5	(5)4	4	6	6	(2)3	3	2	2
Assembler, Bench	4	4	3	3	5	5	5	5	6	6
Janitor	6	6	6	6	1	1	6	6	1	1

allocated for skill, and the job of janitor ranks sixth. The job of janitor, on the other hand, ranks first among the key jobs in terms of the money that has been apportioned for physical effort and for working conditions.

Compare factor rankings of jobs with wage apportionment rankings. Figure 20-5 permits a comparison to be made, on the basis of each factor, between the way in which the jobs were ranked independently (shown in the J. R. columns) and the way in which the jobs were ranked according to the wage apportionments. If the job and money rankings made on the basis of each factor do not agree, efforts must be made to bring them into adjustment by reranking the jobs for those factors where there is disagreement or by reapportioning the allocation of wages for the jobs that are involved. If the differences between the job rankings and monetary rankings cannot be reconciled, the jobs that are involved should not be used as a part of the factor comparison table. Thus, it may be noted from Figure 20-5 that the original job and money rankings for the jobs of the *millwright* and the *forklift operator* (numbers in parentheses) did not agree in the case of mental effort and responsibility. The subsequent reranking of the jobs on the basis of these two factors, which is indicated by the numbers to the right of the ones in parentheses, permitted the rankings to be brought into agreement.

Construct the factor comparison scale using the key jobs. The next step in the factor comparison system is one of constructing a factor comparison scale of the type shown in Figure 20-6 on pages 560 and 561 and locating each key job on the scale according to the monetary value of each of its factors. The monetary value for each job factor is derived from the money rate column in Figure 20-4.

Evaluate non-key jobs on the factor comparison scale. The locations of the key jobs on the factor comparison scale and the specifications of these jobs provide the bench marks against which the other jobs are evaluated. As an example of how the scale is used, let us assume that the job of *drill press operator* is to be evaluated through the use of the factor comparison scale shown in Figure 20-6. By comparing the specification covering the skill requirement for a *drill press operator* with the skill requirements of the other jobs on the table, it was decided that the job demanded slightly more skill than a *forklift operator* but less than a *millwright*. The job therefore was placed at the $0.88 point on the scale. The same procedure was used in locating the job at the appropriate point on the scale for the remaining factors. As additional non-key jobs are added to the scale and are available

Figure 20-6
FACTOR COMPARISON SCALE

Hourly Money Rate	SKILL	MENTAL EFFORT	PHYSICAL EFFORT	RESPONSIBILITY	WORKING CONDITIONS
– 1.50					
– 1.48	Tool & Die Maker				
– 1.46					
– 1.44					
– 1.42					
– 1.40					
– 1.38					
– 1.36	Machinist				
– 1.34					
– 1.32					
– 1.30					
– 1.28					
– 1.26					
– 1.24					
– 1.22					
– 1.20					
– 1.18					
– 1.16					
– 1.14	Millwright				
– 1.12					
– 1.10					
– 1.08					
– 1.06					
– 1.04					
– 1.02					
– 1.00					
– .98					
– .96		Tool & Die Maker			
– .94					
– .92		Machinist			
– .90					
– .88	Drill Press Operator				

Figure 20-6
(continued)

Hourly Money Rate	SKILL	MENTAL EFFORT	PHYSICAL EFFORT	RESPONSIBILITY	WORKING CONDITIONS
—	Assembler				
— .86		Assembler			
—					
— .84		Drill Press Operator			
—					
— .82	Forklift Operator				
—					
— .80					
—					
— .78					
—					
— .76					
—					
— .74		Forklift Operator			
—					
— .72					
—					
— .70					
—		Millwright			
— .68					
—					
— .66					
—					
— .64					
—					
— .62					
—					
— .60					
—					
— .58				Tool & Die Maker	
—					
— .56				Millwright	
—			Janitor	Forklift Operator	
— .54				Machinist	
—					
— .52			Millwright		
—					
— .50					
—					
— .48					
—	Janitor				
— .46				Drill Press Operator	
—					
— .44					
—					
— .42					
—					
— .40					Janitor
— .38			Drill Press Operator		
—					
— .36			Tool & Die Maker	Assembler	Forklift Operator
—					
— .34		Janitor		Janitor	Machinist
—					
— .32			Machinist		Millwright
—					Drill Press Operator
— .30			Assembler		Tool & Die Maker
—			Forklift Operator		
— .28					Assembler
—					
— .26					

for comparison, it is possible that minor adjustments, upward or downward, may be made in the location of certain jobs on the scale. Further, as more non-key jobs are added to the scale, the jobs to be evaluated become easier to place on the scale because there are more jobs on the scale against which comparisons can be made.

The evaluated worth of the jobs added to the scale is computed by adding up the money values for each factor as determined by where the job has been placed on the scale for each factor. Thus, the evaluated worth of a *drill press operator* of $2.86 would be determined by totaling the monetary value for each factor as follows:

Skill	$ .88
Mental Effort	.84
Physical Effort	.38
Responsibility	.46
Working Conditions	.30
	$2.86

Advantages and disadvantages of the factor comparison system.[10] Some of the advantages claimed for the factor comparison system are:

1. It can be custom tailored to fit the particular jobs of a company.
2. It permits jobs to be compared against other jobs, including those of a similar nature, in determining their relative value.
3. It permits adequate weight to be allowed for factors that exist to an unusually high degree within a job because there is no maximum or minimum value to be assigned to any of the factors.
4. The evaluation of jobs by means of the scale can be conducted with relative ease.

Some of the disadvantages of the system are:

1. It may be difficult to locate a sufficient number of key jobs to comprise the scale.
2. Any inequities in the rates of the key jobs or errors in the specifications of these jobs will affect the system's accuracy.
3. The existence of monetary values in the system may tend to introduce certain bias on the part of those using it.
4. The system tends to be rather complicated and difficult for some employees to comprehend with the result that they do not have full confidence in its accuracy.

Variations of the system. In some systems percentages are substituted for monetary values in order to avoid the possibility of bias caused by making comparisons in monetary values. Points also may be used as a

---

[10]Also see, Belcher, *op. cit.*, pp. 269–270.

substitute for the monetary values. The profile method discussed below in connection with the evaluation of management positions represents still another variation of the factor comparison system.

Evaluation of Management Positions

Because they usually are more complicated and involve certain demands not found in jobs at the lower levels, some companies do not attempt to include management positions in their job evaluation programs. Those that do evaluate these positions, however, may extend their regular system of evaluation to include such positions, or they may develop a separate evaluation system for management positions. Any one of the four systems of job evaluation that have been discussed may be used to evaluate management positions, particularly if certain modifications are made.

Several systems have been developed especially for the evaluation of management positions. One of the better known of those which are gaining acceptance is the *profile method*.[11] The profile method combines certain features of the point, factor comparison, and ranking systems. The three basic factors or components that comprise the evaluation "profile" usually include knowledge (or know-how), mental activity (or problem solving), and accountability. The profile for each position is developed by determining the percentage value to be given to each of the three broad factors. Jobs are then ranked on the basis of each factor, and point values that go to make up the profile are then assigned to each job on the basis of the percentage-value level at which the job ranked.[12]

The Wage Structure

Once the evaluated worth of each job has been determined, it must be converted into the appropriate monetary value. In other words, the relative worth of each job in terms of its rank, class, points, or evaluated rate (depending upon which of the job evaluation systems is to be used) must be translated into an hourly, daily, weekly, or monthly wage rate. The wage rate that is established for a particular job, however, must take into account not only the relative worth of the job within the company but also the effect of such external factors as the available supply of labor, the company's ability to pay, the bargaining power of employee unions, wage

---

[11]See Edward N. Hay and Dale Purves, "The Profile Method of High Level Job Evaluation," *Personnel*, Vol. 28, No. 2 (September, 1951), pp. 162–170.

[12]For a more detailed description of the system, see Patton, Littlefield, and Self, *op. cit.*, pp. 183–185.

legislation, and the prevailing community wage rates. These external factors when considered together with the worth of the job provide the basis for determining the amount of wage that the job is to be paid and the differential that is to exist between that job and other jobs.

In order to simplify the determination and administration of wage rates, it is common practice to establish wage classes into which all jobs that fall within a certain range of difficulty may be grouped. The jobs within each class may be paid either at a single rate or at different rates within an established range that will permit differences in seniority and ability to be recognized. The wage classes and wage rates or rate ranges that are established serve as a basis for determining the rate that each person is to receive.

The Wage Curve

The relationship between the relative worth of the jobs and the rates that they are to be paid can be represented by means of a *wage curve* or *conversion line*. A wage curve can be plotted on a graph of the type illustrated by Figure 20-7. In this graph the base or horizontal axis indicates the relative worth of the different jobs in terms of points, class, or evaluated rate values, depending upon which job evaluation system is being used. The vertical axis of the graph, on the other hand, serves to indicate the wage rates for these jobs. A curve may be constructed graphically by preparing a scattergram consisting of a series of dots that represent the location of the jobs on the graph based upon their relative worth and current wage rates. A wage curve can be constructed by drawing a freehand line through the cluster of dots in such a manner as to leave approximately an equal number of dots above and below the curve, as illustrated by Figure 20-7. This wage curve will then establish what the relationship between the value of a job and its wage rate should be at any given point on the line.

While the curves that are developed by the freehand method are the simplest to construct, they are not as exact as those that are developed statistically. A statistical curve can be constructed by means of an algebraic formula on the basis of what is known as the *least squares method*. This method makes use of the same job data as those that would be used in constructing a freehand curve.[13]

Wage curves may be developed to indicate the relationship between the relative worth of the jobs within the company and the prevailing

---

[13]A description of the least squares method may be obtained from any basic business statistics textbook.

Figure 20-7
FREEHAND WAGE CURVE

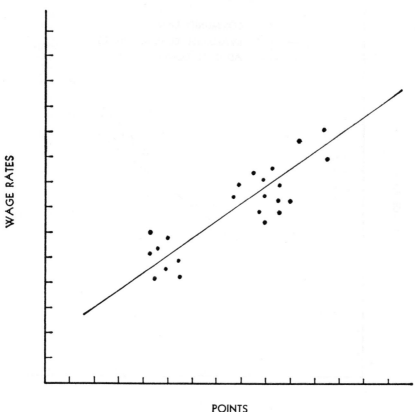

community rates, the existing company rates, or the proposed rates for these jobs. The initial wage curve, however, will normally show the relationship between the evaluated worth of the jobs within the company and the wage rates currently being paid these jobs. A second curve based upon the prevailing community rates may also be constructed on the same graph. These two curves can then serve as the basis for constructing the wage curve that the company proposes to use, which may have a greater or lesser degree of slope than the former ones. Figure 20-8 on page 566 illustrates the relationship of these curves. The rate differentials that a company desires to establish between jobs of varying difficulty, as well as the influence of collective bargaining agreements, wage legislation, and the other considerations mentioned earlier, may also help to determine the location and slope of any new wage curve that ultimately is adopted.

Figure 20-8

EVALUATED AND ADJUSTED COMPANY RATES AND COMMUNITY RATES

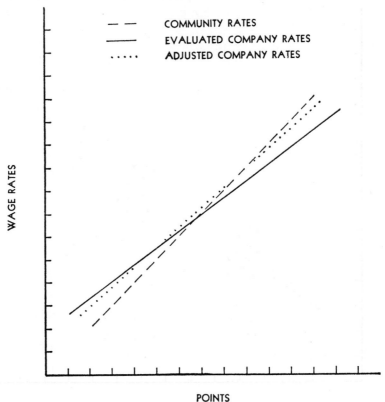

POINTS

Developing Wage Classes

It is usually simpler and more desirable from an administrative stand-point, as noted earlier, to group the jobs into wage classes or grades and to pay all jobs within a particular class the same rate or rate range. When the job classification system of job evaluation is used, the jobs are grouped into classes as a part of the evaluation process. In the case of the point and factor comparison systems, however, wage classes must be established at selected intervals of worth as determined by the point or evaluated rate value of these jobs. The graph in Figure 20-9 on page 567 illustrates a series of wage classes that have been established at 50-point intervals. The wage rate for the jobs within each class is indicated on the vertical axis of the graph.

Figure 20-9
SINGLE RATE STRUCTURE

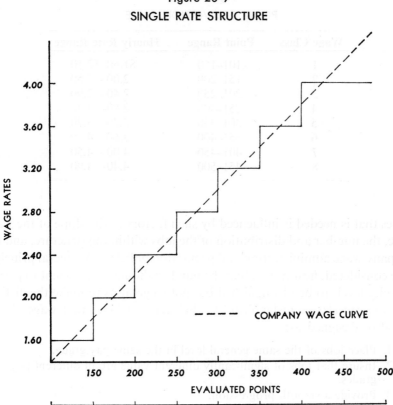

The relationship between the worth of each job and the rate that is paid to it also may be indicated by means of a conversion table. Figure 20-10 on page 568 provides an example of a conversion table that can be used to place each job into the appropriate wage grade on the basis of its evaluated point worth.

There is no fixed number of wage classes that should be established within a wage structure. Some structures may contain as few as four or five classes while other structures may contain several times this number, with the average being somewhere between 10 and 15.[14] The number of wage

[14]Lanham, op. cit., p. 228.

Figure 20-10

POINT CONVERSION TABLE

Wage Class	Point Range	Hourly Rate Range
1	101–150	$1.60–$2.10
2	151–200	2.00– 2.50
3	201–250	2.40– 2.90
4	251–300	2.80– 3.30
5	301–350	3.20– 3.70
6	351–400	3.60– 4.10
7	401–450	4.00– 4.50
8	451–500	4.40– 4.90

classes that is needed is influenced by such factors as the slope of the wage curve, the number and distribution of the jobs within the structure, and the company wage administration and promotion policies. A general principle to be considered, however, is that the number should be sufficient to permit difficulty levels to be distinguished but not so great as to make the distinction between classes insignificant.[15] Belcher concludes that wage classes should be designed to:

1. Place jobs of the same general level in the same pay grade.
2. Insure that jobs of significantly different value are in different pay grades.
3. Provide a smooth progression.
4. Insure that the grades fit the company and the labor market.[16]

Developing Wage Ranges

Once a system of wage classes has been determined, the next step is one of establishing the wage rate or the wage range to be paid to the jobs within each class. Figure 20-9 on page 567 illustrates a wage structure in which single rates are established for each class, and Figure 20-11 on page 569 represents a structure in which rate ranges are provided for each wage class. The rate ranges may be the same for all wage classes, or they may be proportionately greater for each succeeding wage class such as is the case in Figure 20-11. Usually, a wider range is more appropriate for those jobs in which the employee can maintain maximum control over the performance of his work and be eligible for merit increases. A wider range

[15]*Ibid.*
[16]Belcher, *op. cit.*, p. 316.

will be necessary if it is the policy of the company to grant wage increases that are larger or more frequent in nature. Regardless of the type of range that is developed, it is divided generally into a number of steps that permit those employees who qualify to receive wage increases within their class on the basis of seniority or merit, or a combination of these two factors. Most salary structures also normally provide for the ranges of adjoining wage classes to overlap somewhat. The reason for this overlap is to permit an employee with considerable experience to earn as much or more than an inexperienced or unproved person in a slightly more important job. Without some overlap no employee, regardless of how competent or experienced he might be, could ever be worth as much to the company, in terms of the wage he was being paid, as any man holding a job in a higher wage class. The amount that each class range may overlap with the preceding one tends to vary in accordance with the extent of the wage ranges, the slope of the wage curve, and the company's wage policies.

Figure 20-11

WAGE STRUCTURE WITH INCREASING RATE RANGES

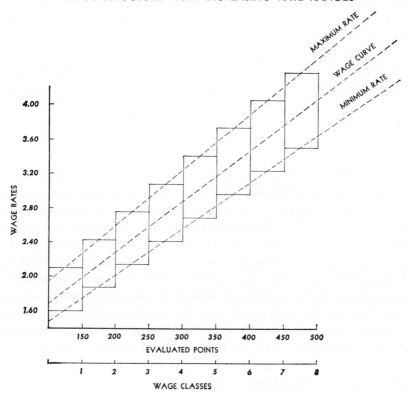

The Wage Survey

Before finalizing the wage structure it is advisable to compare the rates that are established for the various job classes with those that are being paid by other employers in the community for similar job classes. The data for this comparison can be obtained by means of a wage survey. These data are concerned not only with determining the minimum, maximum, and midpoints of the wage class ranges but also the indirect wages that are paid in the form of fringe benefits to employees working in the various classes of jobs. On the basis of the information gained from the surveys, it may be considered desirable to make certain modifications in the rate structure to permit the company to compete favorably for employees in the local labor market.

Classifying the Jobs

The final step in the job evaluation process is that of determining the proper wage class into which each job should be placed on the basis of its evaluated worth. This step in the job classification process may be accomplished by means of a conversion graph or a table of the types mentioned earlier. Job classification normally represents the phase of the evaluation at which complaints are most likely to be raised because it is at this stage that the job factors covered by the job specifications are translated into a pay rate. If an employee is dissatisfied with the classification of his job or with the rate that is established for his job, he is likely to demand that it be reevaluated or even reanalyzed and the specification for it rewritten so that the job will earn a higher wage rate.

It should be noted that job evaluation and classification normally are concerned with the job rather than the person performing the job. The fact that a particular employee may be exceeding the requirements of his job, therefore, can be acknowledged through merit increases within the class range or through a promotion to a job in the next higher wage class. It must be recognized, however, that to some extent the employee does influence the nature of his job. In view of this fact, some companies have attempted to evaluate both the job and the employee performing it and to establish the rate for each position on the basis of a combination of these two factors. It is quite likely that continued research and experience in the area of job evaluation may lead to the development of more effective means for recognizing the effect that an employee may have upon the worth of a job when making an evaluation of it.

Adjusting Rates to the New Structure

When a new wage structure is developed, the rates that are established for some jobs may prove to be above or below the wage rates that these jobs have been paid. If the job rates that are being paid are less than those provided for by the new structure, the situation can be corrected relatively easily by increasing such rates to the minimum level. In the case of those jobs that are being paid more than the new maximum rate established for their particular class, the solution may not be so simple. If the rates for these jobs are reduced immediately to conform with the new rate structure, it may create an unfavorable effect upon the morale of the employees who receive the wage cuts. Furthermore, such a reduction can create a feeling of insecurity and a desire to resist the program on the part of other employees who fear that they too may receive a wage cut as a result of the job evaluation program. Although some companies follow a policy of reducing as well as raising the rates previously paid to employees to make these rates conform to the new structure, the more common practice is to raise the rates of the underpaid jobs but not to reduce the rates of those employees who are being overpaid on the basis of the new rate structure. These overpayments of wages are thus permitted to continue until the employees receiving them have been terminated, retired, or promoted to a job in a higher wage class. New employees, however, who replace them are paid the new evaluated rates.

Reclassification of Jobs

Since jobs are dynamic in nature, their classifications are always subject to change. Changes in the skill, effort, responsibility, or working conditions of a job resulting from organizational, technological, or other changes are among the factors that can affect the job's nature, relative worth, and wage class. Furthermore, as increased experience is acquired by persons engaged in the job analysis, evaluation, and classification work, errors in the initial classification of some jobs are likely to become more apparent. There will always be some jobs, therefore, that are in the process of being reanalyzed and reevaluated either in response to employee grievances or in accordance with the review of all job classifications.

Résumé

The need for a company to have an objective and equitable system for determining wage rates cannot be overemphasized. To be fair and equitable, the job rates for each job should be consistent with both the relative demands and importance of these jobs and with the rates that other companies are paying for similar jobs. The systems and procedures for evaluating jobs and developing rate structures discussed in this chapter constitute the best means for determining wage rates. While none of these job evaluation systems can eliminate completely errors of human judgment that occur within the structure, they can permit these inequities to be reduced or to be detected and rectified more readily than otherwise would be possible without formal evaluation.

Although it usually is not feasible for smaller companies to attempt to develop an elaborate system of job evaluation, it is possible for them to develop some form of objective system for relating the wage rates for a job to the demands that it makes on the employee. Even if wages are determined by means of collective bargaining, job evaluation can provide objective wage data to use for bargaining purposes. Such data can provide the company with a basis for resisting those union demands which, if accepted, might create inequities in the wage structure. By preventing some jobs from being paid more or less than they should be paid, a formal job evaluation program should facilitate the control of labor costs and contribute to the improvement of employee morale and efficiency.

DISCUSSION QUESTIONS AND PROBLEMS

1. Why is job evaluation termed a systematic rather than a scientific approach to wage determination?

2. Why is it advisable for a company to eventually have its own personnel assume the responsibility for the job evaluation work even though consultants may be used to establish the program?

3. It has been argued that a formal wage structure works to a company's disadvantage by limiting the amount of money that it can pay in order to prevent a good worker in a particular job from being hired by another company. Do you agree with this statement? Discuss.

4. Since employees may differ considerably in terms of their job performance, would it not be more feasible to determine the wage rate for each employee on the basis of his relative worth? Comment on the advantages or disadvantages of this system.

5. What are some of the factors that may help to determine the number of wage classes that are established within a wage structure?

6. What does the job grade system have in common with the point system? Which of these two systems will produce the more accurate results? Why?

7. Although some companies have extended their job evaluation programs to include executive positions, most companies have been slow to do so. What are some of the possible underlying reasons for this fact?

8. As a result of an extensive modernization program the foundry operations of the Ferris Iron Works have been largely mechanized. Because of this program most of the heavy lifting and the hazards, as well as the smoke and heat associated with foundry work, have been eliminated. The number of employees in the department has been drastically reduced, and the work of those who remain is confined primarily to servicing and adjusting the equipment and taking corrective action when breakdowns occur. Do you feel that a restudy and reevaluation of these jobs would result in their being placed in higher or lower wage classes?

9. The union representing the employees of the Century Corporation has consistently opposed company efforts to determine wage rates on the basis of job evaluation on the grounds that wage rates can best be arrived at through collective bargaining. Do you agree with the union's position? What are the possible reasons for the union's position?

10. In general, the craft unions tend to prefer flat wage rates; whereas, the industrial unions often favor rate ranges. What are some of the possible reasons for this difference in union preference?

CASE 20-1

THE MISCLASSIFIED STENOGRAPHER

Velma Grey has been employed as a stenographer in the sales department of a furniture manufacturer for more than 20 years. Although the job specification for stenographers requires that they be able to demonstrate reasonable proficiency in typing and shorthand, Miss Grey's skills in both areas are very deficient. Because of this fact her job has been permitted to evolve, in the main, into one of handling filing and routine administrative assignments which would be more properly classified as the work of a clerk rather than as stenographer's work. As a result of a review of job descriptions and classifications by the personnel department and because of complaints from certain clerical personnel who resent the fact that Miss Grey is receiving more money than they, the office manager has concluded that some action must be taken to rectify the situation. While he realizes that Miss Grey is not performing the work of a stenographer and would be unlikely to meet the skill requirements for this job, he recognizes that to change the title, the wage classification, and the rate of Miss Grey's job to that of a clerk would be a severe blow to her and might reflect unfavorably upon the company in view of her years of service.

    a. What possible courses of action might the office manager consider in this situation, and which should he take?

    b. What implications does this case have for job evaluation?

CASE 20-2

PAID INITIATIVE?

Among the products manufactured by the Jupiter Electronics Company were electronic equipment testing consoles. During the production of an order for one particular model, it became necessary to make certain modifications in its electrical circuits. While it was the normal procedure for blueprints to be prepared first for the technicians to follow, the urgent need to meet a delivery deadline made it necessary to proceed with the console modifications without the benefit of the blueprints. The nature of the modifications desired was explained to the technicians by their supervisor who expressed confidence in their ability to utilize their talent and initiative in getting the job done. The ten technicians working on the project accepted the assignment as a challenge and were able to complete the order within the established deadline, thus saving the company from being forced to pay a penalty that otherwise would have resulted from a delay in the delivery.

About a week after the completion of the modifications project, however, the technicians who worked on the project filed a grievance through their union demanding that their jobs be reclassified to the next higher grade and that the reclassification be retroactive to the time that they began work on the project. In support of their grievance the technicians called attention to the fact that their job description called only for an ability to do work with the aid of blueprints. In being required to work without the aid of blueprints and to utilize their initiative in making the modifications, the technicians maintained that they were doing the work of junior engineers, the next higher grade.

    a. Should the company accede to the technicians' demands?

    b. What are the implications of this case from the standpoint of job descriptions? What are the implications with respect to employee training?

    c. How do you account for the fact that the employees filed a grievance when they had willingly accepted the additional responsibilities at the time the job was assigned?

SUGGESTED READINGS

Belcher, David W. *Wage and Salary Administration*, Second Edition. Englewood Cliffs, New Jersey: Prentice-Hall, Inc., 1962. Chapters 7–12.

Benge, Eugene J., Samuel L. H. Burk, and Edward N. Hay. *Manual of Job Evaluation*. New York: Harper & Brothers, 1941.

Brennan, Charles W. *Wage Administration*. Homewood, Illinois: Richard D. Irwin, Inc., 1959. Chapters 5–14.

Dooher, M. Joseph, and Vivienne Marquis. *The American Management Association Handbook of Wage and Salary Administration*. New York: American Management Association, 1950.

Evaluating Managerial Positions, Studies in Personnel Policy, No. 122. New York: National Industrial Conference Board, October, 1951.

Langsner, Adolph, and Herbert G. Zollitsch. *Wage and Salary Administration*. Cincinnati: South-Western Publishing Company, Inc., 1961. Chapters 6–13.

Lanham, E. *Job Evaluation*. New York: McGraw-Hill Book Company, 1955.

Otis, Jay L., and Richard H. Leukart. *Job Evaluation*, Second Edition. Englewood Cliffs, New Jersey: Prentice-Hall, Inc., 1954.

Patton, John A., C. L. Littlefield, and Stanley A. Self. *Job Evaluation, Text and Cases*, Third Edition. Homewood, Illinois: Richard D. Irwin, Inc., 1964.

"Pitfalls in Administering Job Evaluation," *Labor Policy and Practice*. Washington: The Bureau of National Affairs, Inc., February 24, 1955, 8.

21

Wage and Salary Administration

If a high level of efficiency and morale is to be achieved within a company, it is particularly important that employees receive a fair and equitable amount of pay. Although wages may not be the primary return that an employee seeks from his job, they are nevertheless of considerable importance to him, particularly as they compare with what other individuals are receiving in the company and in other companies. If employees develop the feeling that they are not being paid the amount of wages to which they are entitled, even though this feeling is not based upon factual evidence, their productivity and morale may suffer. It is important, therefore, that a company develop and maintain an objective wage structure that will provide a basis for determining as equitably as possible the amount of wages that each employee should receive as well as a basis for making him aware of this fact. This structure should provide the means by which the wages of each employee are related to the work that he performs and to the wages that are paid to other jobs within the company and within the community as determined through job evaluation and community wage surveys, which were discussed in the preceding chapter. It should also permit his wage to reflect the value of his performance and provide him with an inducement for improving this performance.

This chapter is devoted to the discussion of those factors that relate to the determination of wages and that must be considered in the development of a sound wage structure. The next three chapters discuss financial incentives, retirement, and other fringe benefits as a means of motivating and remunerating employee performance.

Among the topics relating to wage and salary administration discussed in this chapter are the following:

- Significance of wages.
- The wage program.
- Wage determination.
- Legislation affecting wages.
- The wage payment system.

Significance of Wages[1]

The amount of the wages that are paid to employees and the basis by which this amount is determined is of a matter of concern not only to employees but also to the employer and to society in general. Each of these groups is affected, although in a different way, by the company's wage policies and practices and the amount that the employee receives through direct wages and through indirect wages, commonly referred to as fringe benefits.

Significance to Employees

Wages are important to employees for a variety of reasons. First of all, wages can have an important bearing upon the comforts, services, and financial reserves that the employee can provide for himself and his family. The wages earned may also influence the employee's status in his community to the extent that status is measured by his material gains rather than by the caliber of his work, which may be known only by his immediate superior. Within the employee's company the wage received is also a source of status, for the wage the employee receives in comparison with other employees serves as a measure of his relative worth to the company. The possibility of earning a higher wage, moreover, may motivate the

---

[1]While the earnings that are paid on an hourly basis are referred to as *wages* and those earnings that are paid on a weekly basis are referred to as salaries, the distinction between the two forms of earnings is being reduced. Although employees on a salary traditionally have been guaranteed rather stable employment and income as well as paid holidays and vacations, wage earners also are rapidly being granted similar benefits. In the remainder of this chapter, therefore, in order to simplify the terminology that is used, the term wages will be used to include salaries.

employee to increase his worth to the company by improving his personal qualifications and his contributions to the company.

Significance to the Company

Wages are important to a company because they can provide a means of influencing employee productivity and loyalty. Wages also represent a significant part of production costs. For a selected number of industries, Figure 21-1 on page 578 shows the relationship of employee wages to the value of the product produced. This relationship is significant to a company because it indicates the extent to which wage increases will affect the cost, selling price, and competitive position of its products. According to Figure 21-1, wages in petroleum refining represent only about 6 percent of the cost of the product; whereas, in textile milling wages constitute 55 percent of the cost. The granting of a 5 percent wage increase to petroleum workers, therefore, would have much less effect upon the price of petroleum products than a similar wage increase for textile mill workers would have upon the price of textile mill products.

Increases in wage rates can be passed on to the customer in the form of higher prices, but this may result in a reduction of the sales volume and the profits of the company. If the cost of increased wages is not passed on to the customer, it must be offset either by greater efficiency or by a reduction in the profit margin. Those wage increases that severely reduce the company's profit margin can place the solvency of the company in jeopardy. If the margin is cut too far, the company may be forced to liquidate its assets as well as the jobs that it has been providing. It is, therefore, to the interests of every company to attempt to maintain a wage program that will provide it with a satisfactory profit and its employees with continuous employment and adequate wage payments.

Significance to Society

Wages can have an important effect upon the various social groups and institutions within the society. Higher wages, on the one hand, give employees more purchasing power which increases the prosperity of the community. To the extent that wage increases make higher prices necessary, on the other hand, they serve to reduce the standard of living for those persons whose incomes do not keep abreast of the rising prices. Higher prices, furthermore, may result in a reduction in the demand for the products or services that the employees produce and, thus, cause a reduction in the number of jobs within the community.

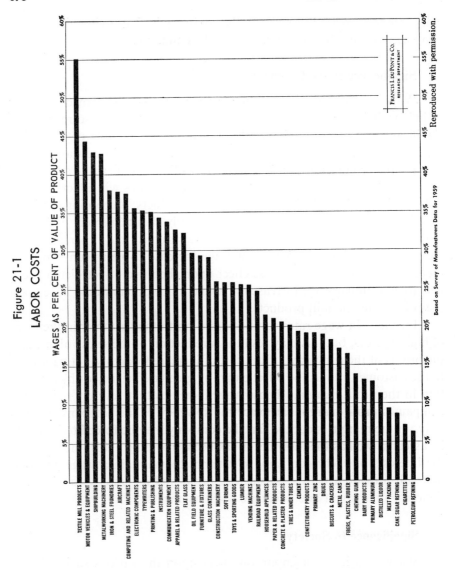

Figure 21-1
LABOR COSTS

The Wage Program

The wage program is an important part of the total personnel program because it affects the ability of a company to recruit and to retain capable employees and to motivate them to be cooperative and productive. The program, thus, contributes significantly to the achievement of an enterprise's objectives of producing a better product or service at a lower price.

The policies and procedures governing the administration of the wage program, for this reason, should be coordinated closely with the policies and procedures governing the performance of the other functions within the personnel program in the achievement of company objectives. The emphasis in wage administration, therefore, should be focused upon the objectives that are to be accomplished by the program rather than upon methods and techniques of dealing with wage problems.[2]

Relationship to Other Personnel Functions

Although an individual's decision to accept a job with one company rather than with another may be influenced by a number of factors, the differences in the wages that are paid by each of the companies is likely to be a significant if not the primary factor governing his decision. The wage that an employer is able to offer, therefore, will influence both the number and the quality of applicants who seek employment with him. The larger the number of qualified applicants that the employer is able to recruit, the more selective he can be in filling positions and the less the time that he will require to develop and train personnel to perform effectively. Provisions in the wage structure that allow increases to be granted can, if administered successfully, serve to motivate employees to improve their qualifications and their performance. The wage function, thus, is related closely to performance evaluation since the latter serves to determine whether or not an employee deserves a merit increase or whether he even deserves to be retained at his present rate of pay. A formal and systematic basis of wage determination also will serve to reduce grievances pertaining to pay as well as to resolve those grievances that do arise. If performance standards have been determined objectively, the company has a better basis for establishing the level of performance expected of an employee in return for his wages and can take disciplinary action when this level is not maintained. A sound and objective wage structure that provides employees with wages that are equal to or better than those paid by other employers also is likely to reduce possible difficulties between a company and its unionized employees; where the employees are not unionized, it may minimize the possibilities that the company may become the target of a unionizing drive.

---

[2]David W. Belcher, "Ominous Trends in Wage and Salary Administration," *Personnel*, Vol. 41, No. 5 (September–October, 1964), pp. 45.

Wage Policies and Procedures

In order to insure that decisions affecting wages are made in a consistent and equitable manner, formal policies and procedures must be developed to govern these decisions. If the wage structure contains a wage range for each wage grade, policies and procedures must be established to determine (1) the step within the range at which employees are to be placed when hired or promoted and (2) the basis upon which employees are to be advanced within the range or from one step to another. These policies and procedures also should provide the means for reviewing periodically the structure and the classification of jobs within the structure for the purpose of correcting errors or eliminating inequities. The procedures, furthermore, should establish the machinery that is necessary for processing employee grievances and complaints pertaining to wages.

Policies relating to merit. If the wage structure contains provisions for merit increases, wage policies should insure that the increases are actually earned on the basis of specific achievement. Merit increases also should be separated and distinguished from economic adjustments or financial rewards based on seniority. One of the goals of the wage administrator, it has been hypothesized, might be that of making employees dissatisfied with their rate of pay in order that they will work harder and avail themselves of the opportunity for merit increases.[3] This hypothesis conforms with some of the findings of Herzberg that were discussed in Chapter 12. Unfortunately, as Belcher points out, there is little evidence to indicate that a true merit philosophy actually is being followed in industry.[4]

Policies relating to wage rate increases. Since World War II there has been a trend for companies to grant across-the-board increases to all employees in order to satisfy union bargaining demands, to cover rising costs of living, or to keep wage rates in line with those of other companies; or because of a combination of these factors. Such increases have been either a flat amount, that is, a certain number of cents an hour for all jobs, or a percentage amount based upon the existing wage rate for each job. Flat increases have tended to be more commonplace and, as a result, jobs in the lower wage classes are receiving a larger percentage increase than those in the higher wage classes. This latter condition has had the effect of compressing the traditional rate differentials between the more highly

---

[3]*Ibid.*, p. 47.
[4]*Ibid.*, p. 44.

skilled and the less highly skilled jobs with the result that skilled wage earners no longer enjoy the same financial differential that they once did. If this trend continues long enough, it can severely curtail the incentive for employees to train themselves for jobs requiring greater skill. Percentage increases, therefore, have an advantage over flat increases in wage rates in that they permit wage differentials based upon the relative worth of the jobs within a company to be preserved whenever increases occur.

There are other practices in addition to the granting of flat increases that can bring about inequities within a rate structure. The rate structure can be distorted by such practices as hiring employees whose skills are in scarce supply at rates higher than the established rates or raising the rates of certain employees above the maximum limits established for their jobs. If a company can afford to do so, it is better for it to raise the entire rate structure rather than to distort the rate structure. If hiring conditions force a company to increase its starting wage for accounting trainees, for example, it should also grant proportionate increases to its senior accountants in order to preserve the added differential for their jobs. Similarly, if the union were to force the company to grant a 5 percent increase to its production workers, the company should also give the same increase to its office workers, supervisors, and other personnel not covered by the labor agreement in order to keep the wages of these personnel in line with those paid to the union members.

Responsibility for the Wage Program

In order that the wage program may be administered and its policies enforced consistently and uniformly within the different departments of an enterprise, some degree of centralized control must be maintained over it. The authority for exercising functional control over the program logically should be given to the personnel department and, more specifically, to the wage and salary division within the department, if one exists. Care should be taken to see that, in exercising control, the wage administrator does not function solely as a policeman whose primary job is to protect the company treasury. Instead, as Belcher suggests, the wage administrator should serve as an innovator and provide suggestions and leadership that will contribute to redesigning jobs, improved organization planning, and manpower budgeting.[5]

Many companies establish an advisory committee, such as the one discussed in the last chapter in connection with job evaluation, to assist

[5]*Ibid.*, p. 50.

with wage and salary administration. The value of such a committee is that it provides the departments who are represented on it with a voice in the program. Members of the committee, furthermore, may have greater firsthand knowledge of many of the jobs than the wage administrator and therefore be able to supply important technical information about job requirements and their wage rates.

In centralizing authority for wage administration, however, the role and authority of the supervisor should not be undermined. The supervisor should be permitted to exercise some discretion in obtaining increases for his people. It is the ability to "get something" for his personnel that can provide the supervisor with a certain degree of power that he can use in soliciting loyalty and performance from them.

Wage Determination

The subject of wage determination is a complex one because there are so many interrelated and variable factors that can exert an effect upon wage rates. Some of the factors which constitute what may be termed the "wage mix" include the prevailing rates, relative worth of the job, cost of living, and legislation. These factors, when acting independently of or in harmony with one another, can serve to force wages up or down depending on the effect that these factors exert upon wages. When acting as counter-vailing forces, however, such factors may serve to nullify one another and to stabilize wages.

Prevailing Rates

If an employer is to attract and keep competent personnel, he must pay them a wage that is comparable to that which other employers within the community are paying for similar jobs. Any comparison of prevailing wage rates, however, also takes into account any indirect wages that are paid to each job in addition to the basic wage. Moreover, the prevailing rate is affected among other things by the supply and demand for labor. If the relative supply of labor for certain jobs is scarce, companies may have to pay higher wage rates in order to recruit and retain qualified employees for these jobs; but higher rates may also help to attract workers from other areas and thus improve the local labor supply.

Some unions attempt to control or at least influence the labor market for certain types of skills. Where unions require new members to serve long periods of apprenticeship or where they have membership quotas, such requirements can be used to restrict the supply of certain types of labor skills and thus help to maintain a higher wage and employment level for union members. Even when there is a surplus of labor, the union through its ability to exert bargaining pressure upon employers may be able to maintain existing wage rates. Surpluses of labor such as may develop during a recession period, however, can lessen a union's power to maintain union wage scales and to prevent unemployed workers from accepting jobs at lower rates.

Relative Worth of the Job

From the standpoint of morale it is very important that the wages paid to each employee be properly related to the demands of his job and to the wages that are paid to employees in other jobs. Consistency of wage rates within a company is particularly important since the wages that an employee receives in relationship to what others receive often can be of greater significance to him than the actual amount of his wages. Wage inequities within a company's wage-rate structure can create equal if not greater problems, furthermore, than the inequities which may exist between its wage rates and those of other companies. A company, for this reason, should determine the relative importance of each job within its structure so that it may have an objective basis upon which to establish wage differentials between jobs that reflect the relative importance of these jobs.

Cost of Living

It is essential that a company pay wages that are sufficient to enable its employees to maintain an adequate standard of living. Otherwise, some employees may be forced either to seek employment elsewhere or to supplement their income by *moonlighting* — that is, by maintaining a second job. Inadequate wages may also tempt some employees to pilfer from the company, to embezzle company assets, or to contribute minimum effort to their jobs. Some firms, therefore, give consideration to employee cost-of-living requirements by providing special family allowances, particularly as a part of the starting wage for married applicants.

During inflationary periods general wages must be increased periodically if existing living standards of employees are to be maintained. Many union agreements therefore contain *escalator clauses* that provide for automatic cost-of-living adjustments. The escalator clause in the General Motors Agreement, for example, provides that a one-cent-per-hour change is to be made in the wage rate for each 0.4 change in the Bureau of Labor Statistics, Consumer Price (cost-of-living) Index (C.P.I.). An agreement between the Boeing Company and Machinists provided for a one-cent-per-hour change in the wage rate for every 0.3 change in the C.P.I.

Wage rates that are tied to a cost-of-living index, however, are not popular with the union during a period of declining prices. For this reason many unions may attempt periodically to have the cost-of-living increases which they have received incorporated into the basic wage rate for each job. For example, in 1964 the General Motors Agreement provided for 9 of the existing 14 cents cost-of-living allowance to be incorporated into the base rate. Other unions have considered it best not to have an escalator clause but, instead, demand general wage raises that are sufficient to cover or exceed any increases in the cost of living. Increases of this type are less likely to be lost when the cost of living declines.

Collective Bargaining

Collective bargaining in this country is widely utilized and accepted as a basis by which a unionized company's wage rates and fringe benefits are determined. The wage structure that is established as the result of collective bargaining by certain companies that provide leadership within an industry or geographic area may establish the pattern that other companies, whether unionized or not, have to follow. The continuing increases in the wage levels paid to employees and the expansion of employee fringe benefit programs is probably more the result of union bargaining pressure than any other single factor. The efforts of unions to organize companies, as well as the threat of organizing efforts, have served to bring about a greater uniformity of wage rates within industries and within and among geographical areas of the nation. In addition, unions have often been able to exert an influence upon the local labor market by controlling the supply of certain types of labor, and they have been active in helping to secure the passage of legislation governing minimum wage and overtime payments.

Company Ability to Pay

Ability to pay has frequently been used as a collective bargaining argument by the unions in attempting to prove that company profits are sufficient to support their wage demands. A company's ability to pay is influenced by such economic conditions as its competitive position within its industry and the prosperity that exists within the geographic region in which it is located. Ability to pay is also contingent upon the production of the employees within the company as determined by their willingness to work, by the existence of laborsaving equipment, and by the efficiency with which employees are managed.

Although companies sometimes use inability to pay as an argument for not meeting wage increases being granted by other companies, unions are reluctant to accept the argument particularly if they feel that this inability is due to inefficient management. It is not uncommon, therefore, for a union to take the position that its members should not be expected to subsidize either inefficient management or the continued existence of a submarginal enterprise.

Legislation Affecting Wages

Since the 1930's wage and salary administration, like the other areas of personnel management, has been the subject of many new laws enacted by the state and the federal governments. These laws have covered such subjects as minimum wage rates, overtime premiums, restrictions on child labor, methods of computing and disbursing wage payments, and the type of payroll records that must be maintained. During World War II and the Korean War, regulations were put into effect freezing existing wage rates and restricting the wage increases that could be granted to employees. Legislation, thus, can have an important effect upon a company's wage rates and upon its system for computing wage payments, and it probably permits ironical situations to develop, such as Figure 21-2 suggests.

The three principal federal laws affecting wages, in the order of number of employees covered, are the Fair Labor Standards Act, the Walsh-Healy Act, and the Davis-Bacon Act. These laws were enacted during the 1930's to prevent the payment of abnormally low wage rates and to encourage the spreading of work among a greater number of workers. The latter objective was accomplished by forcing companies to pay a premium rate for overtime work, that is, for all hours worked in excess of a prescribed number. This federal wage legislation with certain amendments has continued to exert an important influence upon wage policies and practices.

Fair Labor Standards Act

The Fair Labor Standards Act (FLSA), which is commonly referred to as the Wage and Hour Act, was passed in 1938 and subsequently has been amended several times. It covers those employees who are engaged in the production of goods for interstate and foreign commerce, including those whose work is closely related to or directly essential to such production. The act's coverage also includes employees of certain retail and service establishments whose sales volumes exceed a prescribed amount. In rendering decisions relating to the act, the courts also have tended to

Figure 21-2

"I'd like to pay you what you're worth Jackson. But the minimum wage law has teeth in it."

Source: *Wall Street Journal*, March 10, 1959. Reproduced with permission.

broaden their interpretation as to what business activities constitute interstate commerce and the types of businesses and jobs covered by the act.

The feature of the FLSA that perhaps creates the most confusion concerns the exemption of certain groups of employees from coverage by the act or from certain of its provisions. The act now provides for 40 separate exemptions covering individuals ranging from physicians to homeworkers making holly wreaths (apparently the use of some other material would subject the employer to government regulation) and from executives to newsboys. Some of these exemptions apply to only one provision of the act such as the one relating to child labor or to overtime but not to the other provisions. Other exemptions apply to certain groups of personnel within the company such as executives and administrators whose work is of the nature required to meet the necessary criterion.

Because of the complicated nature of the exemptions, it may be advisable for an employer to comply with all provisions of the act at least until he is certain which, if any, of his employees are exempted and the extent to which they are exempted. In addition to utilizing legal counsel, employers may find the major labor reference services, such as those published by the Bureau of National Affairs, Inc., by Prentice-Hall, Inc., and by the Commerce Clearing House to be helpful sources of information.

Provisions of the FLSA. The major provisions of the FLSA are concerned with minimum wage rates, overtime payments, and child labor.[6]

Wages. The minimum wage prescribed by the law has been raised several times from its original figure of 25 cents per hour to the rate of $1.60 per hour.[7] This minimum rate applies to the actual earning rate before any overtime premiums have been added, but it may include the reasonable cost of any facilities that are furnished, such as lodging.

Hours. An overtime rate of one and a half times the base rate must be paid for all hours worked in excess of 40 during a given week. The base wage rate from which the overtime rate is computed must include incentive payments or bonuses that are received during the period. For example, if a person who is employed at a stated rate of $2 an hour works a total of 45 hours and receives a bonus of $45, he is actually working at the rate of $3 an hour. His earnings for the week, which include 40 hours of regular time and 5 hours of overtime rate, therefore, would be computed on the basis of the actual rate of $3 per hour (which includes the bonus) as follows:

$$40 \times \$3 + (5 \times \$3 \times 1\frac{1}{2}) = \$120 + \$22.50 = \$142.50$$

If the bonuses are paid on a monthly or quarterly basis, all overtime payments during the period must be recalculated to include this additional incentive. If employees are given time off in return for overtime work, it must be granted at one and a half times the number of hours that were worked as overtime.

Although an employee may be paid a fixed weekly salary for working a varying number of hours each week, he is still entitled to receive overtime for all hours in excess of 40 that are worked in a given week. Thus, an employee who is paid $100 for working a varying number of hours per week would actually be earning $2 per hour during a week in which he worked 50 hours and $2.50 per hour during a week in which he worked

---

[6]Because the act is likely to be subject to future amendments, an employer should consult the appropriate publications of the labor services previously mentioned or the Wage and Hour Division of the United States Department of Labor in order to obtain the latest information regarding its provisions.

[7]The 1966 amendment provides for the minimum wage to be established at $1.40 per hour effective February 1, 1967, and at $1.60 per hour after February 1, 1968. This amendment also provides for the extension of the act to include about 8 million workers not previously covered. The minimum wage for most workers in this group will be increased through a series of four 15-cent increases to permit the $1.60 per hour minimum to be reached in 1971. A minimum wage for newly covered farm workers of $1.30 per hour will be reached in 1969.

40 hours. For the 50-hour week, however, the employee would be entitled to receive overtime for 10 hours computed on the basis of his hourly rate for the week of $2 per hour ($100/50 hrs.) This overtime premium, therefore, would bring his pay for the week to $110 instead of $100 as indicated by the following computation:

$$40 \times \$2 + (10 \times \$2 \times 1\frac{1}{2}) = \$80 + \$30 = \$110$$

The fact that an employee is paid on a piece-rate basis does not exempt his employer from paying a premium for overtime work. The employee still must be paid overtime based upon a rate that is computed by dividing the employee's earnings from piecework by the total number of hours of work required to earn this amount. Thus, if the employee produces 1,250 units of work at 10 cents per unit during a 50-hour period, he would be earning at the rate of $2.50 per hour:

$$\frac{1,250 \text{ units} \times 10\cancel{c}}{50 \text{ hours}} = \$2.50 \text{ per hour}$$

Since the 10 hours in excess of a 40-hour week constitute overtime, his total wages for the week would be computed as follows:

$$40 \times \$2.50 + (10 \times \$2.50 \times 1\frac{1}{2}) = \$100 + \$37.50 = \$137.50$$

In this example the overtime provisions of the FLSA would require that the employee be paid $137.50 for his week's work instead of the $125 that he would otherwise have received at the regular piece rate.

Determining number of hours worked. Under the FLSA, employee wage payments must include credit for the proper amount of the working time. This time may include periods when the employee is not engaged in actual production activities, such as when he is waiting for repairs, for work to arrive, or for loading and unloading operations to be accomplished. Employees must also be paid for the time consumed by rest periods, trips to the washroom, required travel during the workday, short meal periods, fire drills, compulsory physical examinations, or medical treatment of job injuries. In counting the number of hours worked by an employee, credit must also be given for any time that he is required to spend outside of normal working hours in order to hold his job or achieve advancement.

Working time under the FLSA, however, need not include the time spent on the company premises before and after the established starting and quitting times for a regular workday, including the time consumed by such activities as changing clothes, washing up, or walking between the working area and the plant entrance. The right to exclude these activities from wage payment calculations was established by the Portal-to-Portal

Act of 1947. This act was passed to relieve employers of back wage claims of sizable proportions filed by employees and by unions as a result of the Supreme Court ruling in the now famous Mt. Clemens Pottery case.[8] The act provides that the time for which employees must be paid is determined by the established work period rather than by the time at which they enter and leave the company premises. The principal exception to this provision is in such industries as mining and lumbering where portal-to-portal pay has always been the established practice or in those companies where it is authorized by the union agreement. Employers covered by the FLSA, however, must be careful that their employees do not remain in the plant for more than a "reasonable period" after the scheduled quitting time without punching "out" on their time cards in order not to be held liable for paying wages for this extra time. This is one reason, therefore, why close supervision must be maintained over company time records.

Child labor provisions. The FLSA forbids the employment of minors between 16 and 18 years of age in hazardous occupations, such as mining, logging, woodworking, meat packing, and certain types of manufacturing. Minors under 16 cannot be employed on any work destined for interstate commerce except when employed by a parent or guardian in nonhazardous occupations. Those minors who are over 14 years of age, however, can work in nonhazardous occupations under temporary permits issued by the Department of Labor.

Enforcement of the FLSA. The administration and enforcement of the FLSA is assigned to the Wage and Hour Division of the Department of Labor, which maintains regional and branch offices located throughout the nation for this purpose. The work of this division, which is headed by the Wage and Hour Administrator, includes the auditing of employer payroll records, investigation of complaints, supervision of back-wage payments to employees, issuance of injunctions against continuing violators, and the initiation of back-wage claim suits and criminal proceedings against employers when such action is warranted.

Walsh-Healy Act

The Walsh-Healy Act, which is officially called the Public Contracts Act, was passed in 1936 to prevent so-called "sweatshop goods" from being sold to the government. It covers workers employed on government contract work for supplies, equipment, and materials in excess of $10,000.

---

[8]*Anderson v. Mt. Clemens Pottery Company,* 6 WH Cases 83 — United States Supreme Court.

Employees of the contractor, however, who are not directly engaged in government contract work or who are engaged entirely in producing commercial orders are exempted from the act. This exemption includes such employees as those engaged in maintenance, clerical, administrative, plant protection, and similar types of work.

Minimum wage and overtime provisions. The Walsh-Healy Act requires contractors to pay those employees who are covered by the act at a wage that is equal to at least the prevailing wage rates established by the Secretary of Labor. It also requires these contractors to pay overtime at one and a half times the regular rate for all work performed in excess of 8 hours in one day or 40 hours in one week, depending upon whichever basis provides the worker with the larger premium. For example, if an employee worked 4 days of 12 hours each during a given week, he would be entitled under the Walsh-Healy Act to receive 4 hours of overtime on each of the 4 days or a total of 16 hours for the week. If this employee were employed at the rate of $2 per hour, his wages for the week would be computed as follows:

$$(32 \times \$2) + (16 \times \$2 \times 1\tfrac{1}{2}) = \$64 + \$48 = \$112$$

This amount constitutes twice the overtime that he would be eligible to receive if working under the 40-hour week provisions of the FLSA.

In computing overtime payments under the Walsh-Healy Act, as under the FLSA, the wage rate that is used must include any bonuses or incentive payments that may be a part of the employee's total earnings. The act, like the FLSA, also exempts certain industries and certain types of jobs from its overtime provisions.

Other provisions. In addition to its wage and overtime regulations, the Walsh-Healy Act contains restrictions covering the use of child and convict labor. The act also requires that the companies it covers maintain sanitary and nonhazardous working conditions, keep certain payroll records on those employees covered by the act, and preserve these records for a period of four years. Contractors who violate the act can have their contracts canceled and can be held liable for the payment of certain damages to the government, as well as back-wage claims to employees.

Problems of enforcement. In recent years the enforcement of the Walsh-Healy Act has been curtailed by court decisions involving suits initiated by industrial groups. These suits have limited the Secretary of Labor's ability to establish prevailing wage minimums by challenging the accuracy of certain prevailing wage minimums as well as the secrecy that is involved in the compilation of data upon which the minimums are based.

Enforcement of the act, as it is presently written, is therefore virtually impossible and, until it is revised, its impact upon wages is likely to be minimal.[9]

Davis-Bacon Act

The Davis-Bacon Act, which is also referred to as the Prevailing Wage Law, was passed in 1931 and is the oldest of the three federal wage laws. It provides that the minimum wage rates paid to persons employed on federal public works projects worth more than $2,000 must be at least equal to the prevailing rates being paid for similar jobs within the area as determined by the Secretary of Labor. These public works projects include subcontracts and work involving alterations and repairs as well as work on new construction.

The act does not contain overtime provisions since work on federal projects at the time of its passage was restricted by earlier laws to an 8-hour day, except during a national emergency. In 1940, the 8-hour day limitation was suspended and all hours worked in excess of this amount were required to be paid at one and a half times the regular rate.

The Wage Payment System

An effective wage payment system must provide the means for determining correctly not only an employee's wage rate but also the amount of work that he has performed at this rate and the amount of deductions that are to be withheld from his earnings. Accuracy is an essential requirement of any wage payment system since errors of even the smallest amount are unacceptable.

Determining the Amount of Work Performed

Wage payments to employees may be calculated either upon the basis of the amount of time that they have worked or on the basis of the amount of work that has been completed at the established rate. For the majority of workers in this country, wage payments are computed on the basis of some unit of time, such as hours or days. Under this system, which is commonly termed *daywork*, an employee is expected to meet certain minimum performance standards if he is to continue to receive the wage rate that has been established for his job. In order to provide employees with a greater financial incentive to increase their output, they may be

---

[9] *Wall Street Journal*, November 30, 1965.

paid according to the number of units that they produce under a system of *piecework*. Piece rates are determined by dividing the hourly wage rate for the job by the standard number of units that an employee is expected to produce in an hour. This standard represents the amount that an employee, working at a normal pace, should be able to produce and is determined by time and motion study or some other objective system of work measurement. There are also other incentive systems besides the piecework system that may be used in place of or in conjunction with daywork to reward employees for the extra effort that they exert. Some of these systems are discussed at greater length in the next chapter.

Advantages and Disadvantages of Daywork

Daywork is the system of remuneration most commonly used in industry because it is easy to understand and administer and because it enables both management and employees to compute wage payments readily. Time standards and records of individual output, although useful for purposes of control, are not essential for computing payments under this system. Daywork, furthermore, may be the only system that can be used when employees are learning a new job, when it is not practical to develop accurate time standards for them, or when there are frequent fluctuations in the rate of output which are not within the control of the employees. Daywork also is generally the more desirable system when emphasis is to be placed upon the quality as well as the quantity of production. Although some unions have accepted piecework or other financial incentive systems, daywork generally tends to be the system preferred by most labor unions and is the only system under which some will agree to work.

The principal weakness of daywork is that the wages an employee receives are not related directly to his work contribution during a particular pay period. An employee's wage payment may be just as large if he produces 90 units, for example, as it would be if he produced 100 units during the same period. The stimulation of performance beyond the minimum requirements, therefore, must be achieved through the use of forms of motivation other than direct financial incentives. The unit labor costs of production also are more difficult to predict under day-wage rates since the number of units that employees produce during an hour tends to vary, while the hourly wage remains constant, thus causing unit labor costs to fluctuate with the rate of output.

Handling Wage Payment Deductions

Normally, several deductions must be withheld from the wages that the employees have earned during the pay period in order to comply with existing legal and union agreement requirements. Deductions may be made for income tax, social security taxes, insurance premiums, union dues, savings plans, and other obligations that employees have acquired. Besides making additional calculations and records necessary, these deductions can constitute an additional source of complaints concerning the amount of the paycheck. In order to avoid such complaints, it is desirable to familiarize employees with the types and the amounts of the deductions that are withheld from their checks and to provide them with an itemized record of the exact amount that is withheld from each check. Furthermore, since some employees are likely to feel that their take-home pay is all that they receive, it might be well to keep the number of deductions to be taken from the pay check to a minimum. Normally, companies include the subject of paycheck deductions as a part of the orientation program, and some companies provide additional information of the type illustrated in Figure 21-3 in their employee handbooks. This information can help to make employees aware of the fact that the wages they have earned are considerably in excess of the amount of their "take home pay."

Résumé

Wage and salary administration constitutes one of the most important functions of the personnel program because it affects directly a company's ability to recruit and retain competent personnel and to motivate their performance. Wage administration affects and is related closely to the other functions performed by the personnel program and should contribute to the achievement of the program's objectives. The program, therefore, should place primary emphasis upon the objectives that are to be achieved rather than upon the wage administration methods and techniques.

In determining the amount of wages to be paid to each employee, such factors as ability to pay, bargaining pressures, condition of the labor market, prevailing community rates, and wage legislation may comprise the "mix" of factors that affect the amount to be paid each employee. In spite of the complexity of these factors affecting wages, many of which are beyond the power of the company to control, it is important that some system be established to determine in as objective and equitable a manner

Figure 21-3

METHOD OF EXPLAINING PAYCHECK DEDUCTIONS TO EMPLOYEES

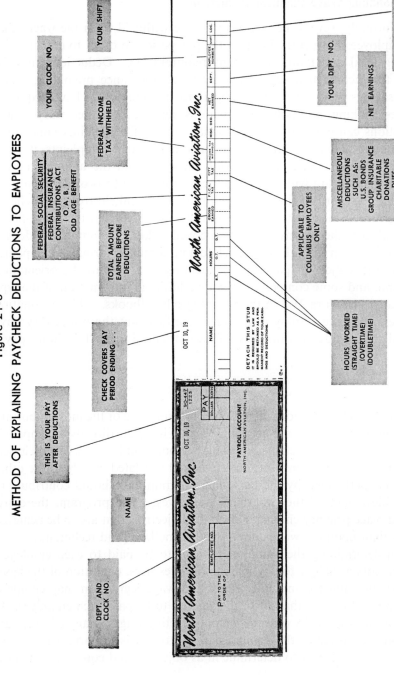

Source: North American Aviation, Inc. Reproduced with permission.

as possible the amount of money that each employee should receive for his services. If properly developed and administered, an objective wage structure and payment system will help to motivate the employee to render greater contributions to the organization rather than to merely do enough to keep from being fired. An effective wage program, furthermore, will not only help to insure that employees receive the wages to which they are entitled but will also make them aware of this fact through effective communication. An employee's efficiency and morale is affected not only by the amount of money that he receives in his paycheck but also by the amount that he receives in relationship to what his fellow workers receive for their work. It is only through the existence of an objective wage program which establishes formal wage policies and procedures and a sound system for administering it that a company can provide fair treatment and a basis for proper understanding relative to wage payments.

DISCUSSION QUESTIONS AND PROBLEMS

1. How does wage administration affect and relate to the performance of other personnel functions?

2. Why is it that students will make the necessary sacrifices to obtain a college degree which will qualify them to obtain certain jobs that may pay less money than many jobs for which only a high school diploma and a minimal amount of training are required?

3. Will a critical need for personnel to fill certain jobs or positions cause the rates for these jobs to be increased sufficiently to attract personnel to these jobs? Discuss.

4. During agreement negotiations unions have sometimes stated in reply to a company claim of inability to pay that the union should not be expected to subsidize inefficient management. To what extent do you feel that a union response of this type has or does not have merit?

5. Do you agree or disagree with the statement that employees should be made to feel dissatisfied with the wage that they are earning? Discuss.

6. One of the objections to granting wage increases on a percentage basis is that the lower paid employees who are having the most trouble "making ends meet" get the least increase while the highest paid get the largest increase. Is this objection a valid one?

7. Some people have criticized the child labor provisions of the FLSA on the grounds that it actually hurts rather than helps the nation's youth by denying them opportunities for employment. Do you agree or disagree with this criticism?

8. To what extent is it desirable and/or undesirable for the wage administrator to function as a "policeman" in controlling the expenditure of monies for wages?

9. Charles Bond was employed as an arc welder at the rate of $2.50 per hour. He also was paid an incentive production bonus based upon this weekly output. During the first week of August he worked a total of 50 hours and received a bonus of $25. The company computed his wages for the week, before deductions, to be $160. Bond complained that according to the provisions of the FLSA which covered his work, the computations were incorrect. Is Bond's charge valid? If so, how much more should he receive?

10. What are the principal differences between the Walsh-Healy Act and the Fair Labor Standards Act?

11. Ralph Garber is employed on a job which pays $3.50 per hour. His time card for one particular week is as follows:

Monday	12 hours
Tuesday	12 hours
Wednesday	4 hours
Thursday	9 hours
Friday	8 hours

Under which of the wage and hour laws would he receive the largest wage payment? How much larger would this amount be?

12. Clyde Burt was employed on piecework at the rate of 30¢ per unit. During one week he produced 600 units in a 60-hour period. How much should his wages for this week be before taxes, under the provisions of the FLSA?

CASE 21-1

SCIENTIFIC LABORATORIES, INC.

The Scientific Laboratories, Inc., recently had been encountering difficulty in recruiting qualified laboratory technicians at the starting salary that it had established for personnel in this classification. The existing salary range for technicians extended from a minimum of $475 to a maximum of $600 per month and was divided into five increments of $25 each. Employees in this classification were eligible to receive increment raises within this range up to the maximum each year on the basis of their seniority and merit. Although the company recognized that in the interest of maintaining a sound salary structure it should increase all steps within the technician range if it were to increase the starting salary, it also realized that such action would not be economically feasible because price competition within the industry had already virtually eliminated the company's profit margin.

As a solution to its problem the company decided to recruit any new employees who had previous experience at the second and third increments of the salary range. Shortly after the first experienced employee was hired at the starting salary of $525 per month, the personnel manager was confronted with a group of three technicians, all of whom had been hired within the last year, who were still earning only $475 per month. These employees demanded that they be immediately increased to $525 per month and that they be eligible also to receive their annual increment at the end of their first year. They enforced their demand with the statement that they planned to submit their resignations at the end of the month if the increase was not forthcoming by that time.

   a. What action should the personnel manager take with respect to their demands?

   b. How might a recruitment problem such as that facing Scientific Laboratories be handled?

CASE 21-2

THE DISPUTED HOLIDAY PAY

A company's labor agreement contained the following statement with respect to length of workweek and paid holidays:

> Forty hours shall constitute a week's work consisting of five consecutive eight-hour days, Monday to Friday inclusive, or Tuesday to Saturday inclusive.
>
> All regular employees shall be granted the following holidays without deduction of pay: New Year's Day, May 30th, 4th of July, Labor Day, Thanksgiving Day, and Christmas Day.

The preceding provisions appeared to be clear enough until May of the following year when the 30th of that month came on a Saturday. When the union realized that the terms of the agreement would permit some of its members to receive a paid holiday on the 30th but not others, it demanded that all members receive pay for the holiday. The company refused to concede to this demand on the grounds that it would be equally unfair to give the Monday through Friday crew a paid holiday for a day that they were not scheduled to work and thereby permit them to receive 6 days of pay for the week by working only 5 days. The Tuesday through Saturday crew, on the other hand, would be able to receive only 5 days pay for 4 days of work.

   a. How should the company resolve the problem confronting it?

   b. What dangers are inherent in its decision regarding this dispute?

SUGGESTED READINGS

Belcher, David W. *Wage and Salary Administration*, Second Edition. Englewood Cliffs, New Jersey: Prentice-Hall, Inc., 1962. Chapters 1–6, 12, 13.

Brennan, Charles W. *Wage Administration*. Homewood, Illinois: Richard D. Irwin, Inc., 1959. Chapters 1–4, 13–16.

Gilmour, Robert W. *Industrial Wage and Salary Control*. New York: John Wiley & Sons, Inc., 1956.

Langsner, Adolph, and Herbert G. Zollitsch. *Wage and Salary Administration.* Cincinnati: South-Western Publishing Company, Inc., 1961. Chapters 1–5.

Lanham, Elizabeth. *Administration of Wages and Salaries.* New York: Harper & Row, Publishers, 1963. Pp. 1–106.

Rothschild, K. W. *The Theory of Wages.* New York: The Macmillan Company, 1954.

Taylor, G. W., and F. C. Pierson (Editors). *New Concepts in Wage Determination.* New York: McGraw-Hill Book Company, 1957.

Tolles, N. Arnold. *Origins of Modern Wage Theories.* Englewood Cliffs, New Jersey: Prentice-Hall, Inc., 1964.

22

Financial Incentives

The previous chapter contained a discussion of how a wage structure may be developed to permit a company through merit raises and promotions to reward its employees for their contributions. Unfortunately, these rewards may not always be related directly or objectively enough to their contributions nor granted with sufficient frequency to induce employees to work and cooperate to their maximum ability. In an effort to gain greater motivational value from wage payments and permit these wage payments to be related more closely to organizational objectives, a variety of financial incentive plans have been developed and used by industry. These plans may range from those that include all employees to those that include only certain employees or groups of employees. The plans also may vary widely in terms of the methods and procedures by which the incentive payments are computed and disbursed and in terms of the extent to which employee involvement and participation in the plan are encouraged.

In this chapter the role of and types of incentive plans are discussed under the following headings:

- Role of financial incentives.
- Incentive plans for operative personnel.
- Incentive plans for sales personnel.
- Incentive plans for executives and professional employees.
- Company-wide incentive plans.

Role of Financial Incentives

Any incentive program, at best, can only be expected to contribute to the improvement of efficiency. It alone cannot overcome any basic weaknesses within the personnel program that may be contributing to low efficiency and morale. An incentive program, therefore, must be viewed not as a gimmick or a "cure-all" but rather as an integral function of the personnel program that must be coordinated closely with the other personnel functions.

Growth of Incentive Plans

The growth of financial incentive plans was stimulated by the scientific management movement which sought to bring about the improvement of efficiency in industry. The movement started from the contributions of Frederick W. Taylor and his followers who helped to make managers more aware of the need to develop improved methods and standards of performance by which employee output could be measured and rewarded. It was Taylor's conviction that employees could be induced to exert greater effort if they were provided with some financial incentive. Thus, he developed more accurate techniques for work measurement which made it possible for employees to be paid on the basis of the units of work that they produced.

Taylor developed a type of incentive plan called the *differential piece rate*. This system provided that employees would be paid at one piece rate if they produced less than the standard amount of output and at a higher piece rate if their output exceeded this standard. This plan thus stimulated employees to achieve or to exceed established standards of production. Taylor's incentive system was followed by a variety of financial incentive plans which bore the names of such leaders in management as Gantt, Emerson, Halsey, Rowan, and Bedeaux. While the plans varied somewhat in terms of the system that was used to calculate the incentive payments, they all represented an attempt to relate employee wages more closely to productivity. These attempts were directed not only toward the development of more accurate standards and measures of performance but also toward the development of more effective formulas for computing incentive payments.

Although the piece rate and other individual incentive plans can be quite effective in certain situations, they may prove unsatisfactory in others. As a result, other types of incentive plans have been devised which base incentive payments upon group contributions and cooperation. In recent years various systems, such as the Rucker and the Scanlon Plans, have been devised which reward employees for their cooperation as well as for their improvements in efficiency. Other plans such as profit sharing base these rewards upon company earnings. Profit-sharing plans usually include provisions for employees to participate in decisions affecting company operation, thereby affording them a further source of motivation.

Differences in Reaction to Financial Incentives

The motivational value to be derived from financial incentives will be affected in part by the need and the desire that the employees have to increase their income. Some employees and their families have a greater need to earn more money than others and, because of this fact, will make the effort and the sacrifices that are required for them to earn it. Other employees may place certain limits on the amount of time or energy that they are willing to contribute in order to obtain additional money. Employees in this latter group, therefore, would be less responsive to a financial incentive system than those of the former group.

Employees in a company also may differ in terms of their reaction to delays in the payment of the incentive. Generally, for employees in the lower socio-economic levels, the sooner the incentive is paid to them, the greater the motivational effect it will have upon them. For them the incentive comes from having the money to spend *soon*. Furthermore, those in the lower wage groups have more immediate need for the money, and its incentive value for them may be diminished if the payment is deferred for too long a period. Personnel such as managers and professional employees who earn at a higher level, by way of contrast, usually are better able to accept the deferment of their wages and can be motivated by the fact that incentive money is accruing to their account. By having the payment deferred, personnel in the higher wage classes also may be realizing certain income tax savings.

An individual employee's reaction to incentives also may be influenced by the attitudes and reaction of the group in which he works, which in turn may be dominated by the informal leaders within the group. If the group favors competition among members and stimulates their desire to earn higher wages, then financial incentives are more likely to prove successful. However, if the group informally establishes certain production limits or "bogeys" which members are under pressure to observe, a financial incentive system may do relatively little to stimulate increased production.

Group pressures to hold the rate of production within established limits may be prompted by the fear of its members that their incentive rates will be reduced or that they will work themselves out of a job if they produce at their maximum capacities. The fear on the part of the less efficient members that they will be placed in an unfavorable light by the superior producers can be another cause for pressures being exerted to control production rates. Individual and group pressures that may be exerted against such "pacesetters" by subjecting them to the "silent treatment," or to various forms of embarrassment and abuse, can be very effective in discouraging their desire to earn more incentive pay.

Requirements for Success with Financial Incentives

Unfortunately, the success and publicity that may be achieved by an incentive plan in a particular company sometimes has led to its adoption by other companies where it has not proven to be so successful. The reason for this fact is that the success of a financial incentive program, like any other program in personnel management, is not determined so much by the actual mechanics of the program as it is by the conditions under which it is operated and by the people who operate it. Often the effectiveness of a particular plan can be attributed to the personality and leadership of some particular individual — perhaps the owner or president of the company — in whom its personnel have considerable respect and trust. In companies where an individual of this caliber is not available or where morale or relations with the union are poor, however, even the best designed incentive program may be doomed to failure. One authority summarizes the requirements for a successful incentive plan with the following list of requisites:

1. Top management must understand the importance of integrity in standards for work performance.
2. A competent, experienced staff must install and maintain the system.
3. There must be an adequate budget to maintain and operate the system.
4. A good unit cost system (preferably standard cost or standard direct cost) must be available, and management must understand that lowest hourly wages seldom equal lowest unit costs.
5. Supervision must be thoroughly schooled in the workings of incentive wage plans.
6. Workers must be interested in high wages and high output.
7. The manufacturing engineering department must have competent methods men who are willing and able to work with supervisors and operators alike in developing the most economical methods of production.
8. The plant must have a good quality-control system that properly rewards high-quality output.

9. The production control department must be capable of providing the right tools, materials, and instructions to the right men at the right machines at the right time.

10. The most important ingredient in any effort involving people — especially where the effort involves wage rates and job security — is mutual respect, understanding, and trust.[1]

Problems Created by Incentives

A financial incentive system also can be a source of new problems. First of all, certain grievances and labor disputes may arise from the installation of and operation of the incentive system. When an incentive program is installed, employees may challenge those standards, measures, and performance records as well as company policies and practices that relate to efficiency.

Another managerial problem is created by the fact that a financial incentive program places management in the position of being obliged to provide and maintain facilities that will enable employees to earn maximum incentive payments. Any deficiencies that exist with regard to these facilities or to the management of them will be distorted and quickly become the subject of complaint.[2] If not corrected promptly, such deficiencies can have an adverse effect upon employee efficiency and morale.

A financial incentive program, moreover, is likely to create an additional cost of maintaining with accuracy those records that are necessary to administer the program. Financial incentives, furthermore, will require that management devote more attention to communication since the motivational value to be derived from incentives will be contingent upon the ability of employees to associate their contributions with the incentive payments that they receive. If a complicated financial incentive system is used, the task of educating and keeping employees informed about its operations can be substantial. In this regard one management consultant concludes that "top management too often wants to establish a pay plan in the terms it understands rather than the terms the worker understands."[3]

Incentive Plans for Operative Personnel

Financial incentive systems for operative personnel may provide that the incentive payment constitute their entire wage or that it be merely a

---

[1]"Tips on Effective Incentive Systems," *Steel* (August 10, 1964) as reprinted in *Management Review*, Vol. 53, No. 10 (October, 1964), pp. 69–70.

[2]Wilfred Brown, *Piecework Abandoned* (London: Heinemann, 1962), p. 10.

[3]*Management Review, op. cit.,* p. 70.

supplement to the regular wage that they receive for the time that they have worked. The amount of the incentive payment may be related directly to the number of units produced (as in the case of piecework), to established quotas (as in the case of bonuses), or be based upon improvements in company efficiency or profit records (as in the case of profit sharing and employee cooperation plans).

Piecework Systems

Under the straight piecework system wage payments are determined by multiplying the number of units produced by the piece rate for one unit, as expressed by the following formula:

$$
\begin{array}{ccccc}
\text{N} & \times & \text{U} & = & \text{W} \\
\text{(Number of Units)} & \times & \text{(Unit Rate)} & = & \text{(Wages)}
\end{array}
$$

The piecework system can provide maximum financial motivation for employees, particularly for those individuals who have a strong desire to increase their earnings, because the amount of wages that they receive is directly proportionate to their output. The wage payment for each individual is simple to compute, and the plan will permit a company to predict its labor costs with considerable accuracy since these costs are the same for each unit of output. The piecework system is more likely to be successful when units of output can be measured, when the quality of the product is less critical, when the job is fairly standardized, and when a constant flow of work can be maintained.[4] Employees normally are not paid for the time that they are idle unless the idleness is due to conditions for which the company is responsible, such as delays in work flow, defective materials, inoperative equipment, or power failures. In the case of delays for which the company is responsible, employees are paid a "down time" allowance for the idle period that is equal to what their average piece-rate earnings would otherwise have been for the period.

In spite of its incentive value, piecework is not nearly as prevalent in industry as is daywork. One reason for this fact is that production standards upon which piecework must be based can be difficult to develop for many types of jobs. In other instances the cost of determining and maintaining this standard may exceed the benefits to be gained from piecework. Jobs in which individual contributions are difficult to distinguish or measure, or in which the work is mechanized to the point that the individual exercises very little control over output, also may be unsuited to the use of

---

[4]David W. Belcher, *Wage and Salary Administration* (2nd ed.; Englewood Cliffs, New Jersey: Prentice-Hall, Inc.), 1962, pp. 384–385.

piecework, as may be those jobs in which employees are learning the work or in which high standards of quality are of paramount importance.

In his book describing the Glacier Project (conducted over a 15-year period at the Glacier Metal Co. Ltd. during which time piecework was being abandoned), Wilfred Brown concluded that the system tended to stimulate envy and greed. While he concedes that piecework stimulates a systematic study of work and the exposure of production problems as well as encourages inventiveness on the part of the operators working under it, he did not find that it causes people to work faster. He also concludes that piecework does not result in greater output or concentration on the work being performed but, rather, causes pressure to be exerted on the rate fix that results in the loosening of time standards.[5]

Deep-seated suspicion and resentment on the part of certain groups of employees and labor organizations toward piecework is another factor that has restricted its usage. There is still an underlying fear among some union leaders that management will use piecework to achieve a *speed up* (gaining more production from the workers for the same amount of money). There is also the fear that the system may induce employees to compete against each other and thereby cause a loss of jobs for those who are revealed to be less productive. Some leaders, furthermore, believe that the system will cause employees to work themselves out of a job or cause craft standards of workmanship to suffer.

In spite of opposition by some unions, piecework has had a history of success in the garment, leathergoods, and cigar-making industries where it has been used to the mutual benefit and satisfaction of management and the union. It should not be assumed, therefore, that union leaders as a group are opposed to the use of piecework. If the union has confidence in and a good working relationship with management and if it feels that its members stand to gain from the system, it will accept piecework.

Production Bonus Systems

Under a bonus system incentive payments, as indicated by Figure 22-1, are supplementary to the basic wage. This system has the advantage of providing employees with more pay for exerting greater effort while, at the same time, providing them the security of their regular wages. A bonus payment may be based upon the number of units that an individual or a group produces, as in the case of piecework. Thus, under a bonus system an employee who is paid at the rate of $2 an hour plus a bonus

---

[5]Wilfred Brown, *op. cit.*, pp. 8–28.

of 10 cents per unit would receive the following wages for producing 100 units during an 8-hour period.

$$(\text{Hours} \times \text{Time Rate}) \quad + \quad (\text{Number Units} \times \text{Unit Rate}) \quad = \quad \text{Wages}$$
$$8 \times \$2 \quad\quad\quad + \quad\quad\quad (100 \times 10¢) \quad\quad\quad = \quad \$26$$

Figure 22-1

WHAT is TIME BONUS?

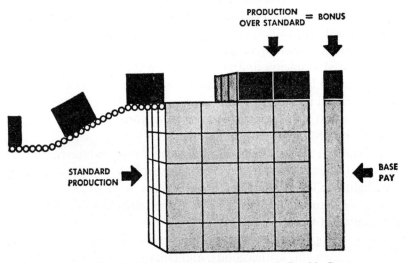

Source: Reproduced with permission of the Procter & Gamble Company.

Bonuses also may be based upon the amount of time that an employee is able to save in completing a task as compared with the standard time established for it. If, for example, one-half hour has been established as the standard time required to complete one unit of production and an employee is able to complete 20 units during an 8-hour day, he will accomplish the equivalent of 10 hours of work during an 8-hour period. In this type of situation, plans such as the *100 Percent Premium* plan permit the employee to receive the entire two-hour savings as a bonus. Under other plans, such as the *Halsey Plan*, the employee may receive only a portion of the two-hour savings as a bonus. The theory behind this latter practice is that the time which an employee saves is due in part to those persons who contribute indirectly to production.

Some wage incentive plans give consideration to factors other than output alone. One such plan is the *measured day plan*, a form of which permits employees to earn a bonus based upon the amount that their merit rating scores exceed a specified percent score. A person who receives a score of 70 percent or less, for example, might earn only his base rate; whereas, an employee receiving a score of 80 percent would earn 10 percent more than the base rate. The main weakness is that it may place the supervisor under considerable pressure to give higher ratings as well as to divert attention from the primary objective of a performance rating program, namely, to help employees improve their performance.

Group Incentive Plans

Piecework and production bonuses may be based either upon individual or group performance. Group incentives are the more desirable when the contributions of individual employees are either difficult to distinguish or are contingent upon group cooperation. If used under the proper conditions, such incentives can contribute to teamwork and to the maintenance of discipline within the group. As production has become more automated, as teamwork and coordination among workers has become more important, and as the contribution of those engaged indirectly in production work has increased, group incentive plans have become more popular. Most group incentive plans that have been developed in recent years, furthermore, base the incentive payments on such factors as improvement in company profits or efficiency or upon reductions in labor costs. These plans, in contrast with those based solely upon output, can motivate the employee for the total aspect of his contributions on the job.

Standards for Production Incentives

The success of incentive systems for production work is contingent upon the development of accurate work standards. These standards are essential not only in order to relate incentives to employee effort but also in order to maintain the confidence of employees in the system. If standards are set too "loose" (too low), the result may prove costly to management because employees are not required to put forth effort that is commensurate with the income they receive. Loose standards, moreover, are difficult to tighten without creating a loss of employee morale and cooperation. Standards that are set too "tight" (too high), on the other hand, may limit the employees' opportunities to earn incentive wages and provide them with very little inducement to work harder. Such standards also may become a source of grievances and ill will toward the company.

Use of the stop watch to compute time standards. One of the most common methods for determining time standards is by making actual time observations of the work being performed by means of a stop watch. The observed time that has been recorded then must be *leveled* to allow for the degree of skill and effort being exerted by the worker. For example, if the person being timed were judged to be working faster and more efficiently than is required to maintain an average work pace, the observed time for completing a work cycle would be increased by an appropriate amount of time. Conversely, if the person studied were judged to be working slower or less efficiently than he should be, the observed time for completing a work cycle would be reduced accordingly. The figure that is achieved after the observed time for a work cycle is leveled thus represents the amount of time that is required for an employee of average skill and effort to complete the cycle while working at a normal pace.

After the observed time has been leveled, further allowances must be made for work interruptions that may be required for employees to care for personal needs, to service equipment, or to wait for additional work to arrive. The time figure that is obtained after making these adjustments constitutes the standard time required to perform the task being observed.

The fact that time standards must include these adjustments and allowances which involve human judgment may cause employees to suspect and to challenge the accuracy of time standards. Actually, however, experienced time-study personnel are able to determine the amount of adjustment and allowance to be applied to the observed time with a high degree of accuracy. As a matter of fact, in some companies where wage incentive programs based upon time standards have become well established, the greatest number of complaints may be received from workers on straight daywork who want their jobs to be studied and included in the incentive program.

Computing the incentive wage rate. Although time standards establish the amount of time required to perform a given amount of work, they do not by themselves determine what the incentive rate should be. The incentive rates must be based upon hourly wage rates that would otherwise be paid for the type of work being performed under the incentive system. If, for example, the standard time for producing one unit of work in a job paying $3 per hour were computed to be 10 minutes, the piece rate would be 50 cents per unit. This piece rate is computed as follows:

$$\frac{60 \text{ (Minutes Per Hour)}}{10 \text{ (Standard Time Per Unit)}} = 6 \text{ Units Per Hour}$$

$$\frac{\$3 \text{ (Hourly Rate)}}{6 \text{ (Units Per Hour)}} = 50\cent \text{ Per Unit}$$

Other systems for determining time standards. Several methods of calculating time standards have been developed that do not require the use of a stop watch. One of these methods is *work sampling* which involves the application of statistical sampling principles to work measurement. Sample observations of jobs being studied are taken at random intervals for the purpose of estimating the percentage of time during the day that the employee is busy. Work-sampling techniques also provide for adjustments to be made for the skill and effort that the worker is observed to be exerting when each sample is taken.

Time standards may be developed from *standard element times* that have been computed for certain elements that are common to a number of different jobs. An element, for example, might consist of drilling a certain size hole, tightening a bolt, or setting up a production run. The standard time for a job is then computed by adding together the predetermined time standards for each of the various elements that are a part of it.

Incentive Plans for Sales Personnel

The enthusiasm and drive that must be exerted in most types of sales work require that salesmen be highly motivated which in part, at least, explains why financial incentives are utilized widely in sales work. Motivation is particularly important for outside salesmen who cannot be supervised closely and, as a result, must exercise a high degree of self-discipline. While the development of financial incentive plans for salesmen is of primary concern to the sales manager, it is the personnel department that has the responsibility for providing technical assistance in this area and for insuring that these incentive plans are consistent with the wage policies and practices of the company as a whole.

Most company incentive plans for compensating salesmen are, according to one survey, of the following types which are listed in order of their popularity: (1) combination plan, (2) straight commission plan, and (3) commission plan with a drawing account.[6] A more recent study by the National Industrial Conference Board revealed that 72 percent of the 405 manufacturing companies that were surveyed provided some form of extra compensation for their sales personnel. In 48 percent of these companies, the extra compensation was based upon the achievement of a quota or standard; in 32 percent, upon commissions; and in 10 percent, upon

---

[6]Harry R. Tosdal and Walter Carson, Jr., *Survey of Salesmen's Compensation* (New York: National Sales Executives, Inc., 1951).

company profits.[7] The fact that commission plans were second in popularity might well be indicative of a trend away from their usage.

Under the *combination plan* salesmen are paid, in addition to a fixed salary, a bonus that may be computed on the basis of such factors as their sales record, the increases in sales over a previous period, or the number of new accounts secured during a particular period. The salary of the salesman working under a *straight commission plan* is determined by multiplying his sales volume by the percent of the commission at which he is being paid. Since sales volumes will tend to vary from one month to another, the income of the salesman who is paid a straight commission will also tend to vary. When a *straight commission is augmented with a drawing account*, salesmen are advanced the difference between an established amount and that which they actually earn in commissions during a particular period. The amount of the difference must be repaid out of subsequent commissions earned in excess of the guarantee.

Incentive compensation plans for sales personnel, like those for operative personnel, often permit certain benefits to be realized at the expense of others. The straight commission plan, for example, may induce a salesman to exert maximum sales effort, but it may also cause him to concentrate on those accounts that produce the largest commissions and to neglect other phases of his job such as servicing small accounts, building goodwill, and cultivating new customers. Commission plans may also cause a salesman's income to fluctuate rather widely because of economic or other factors affecting sales that are beyond his control. Commission plans with a guaranteed drawing account help to stabilize a salesman's income; but when the account becomes too heavily overdrawn, he may become discouraged or may quit in the face of the mounting deficit. The combination salary and incentive bonus plan, on the other hand, provides certain advantages of both the straight salary and straight commission plans since it represents an attempt to supply to some degree the needs of employees for both a stable income and a performance incentive.

Incentive Plans for Executives and Professional Employees

Compensation plans for executives must be designed to stimulate an enthusiasm for their work, a loyalty toward their company, and a motivation which enables them to utilize their energies and abilities fully in contributing to company objectives. Among the specific objectives to be

---

[7]*Prevalence of Bonus Plans in Manufacturing*, Studies in Personnel Policy, No. 185 (New York: National Industrial Conference Board, 1962), pp. 53–54.

achieved through incentive plans for executives are the improvement of profits and return on investment, the reduction of costs, the achievement of greater individual and group effort and cooperation among company units, and the realization of satisfactory company growth.[8] Executive incentive plans, furthermore, must facilitate the recruitment of good executive talent and induce executive personnel to continue their professional growth and development. Above all, the plan should serve to encourage competent executives to remain with the company by providing them with opportunities to build an estate and to enjoy income tax advantages that they might otherwise experience as owners of a business. These principal goals of executive compensation have led to the development of a multitude of plans involving different methods of relating compensation to the contributions of executives. Many such plans contain provisions for deferring the payment of all or part of the incentive earnings until retirement and for the acquisition of stock in the company.

Problems of Determining Incentive Payments for Executives

The difficulty of devising accurate measurements of executive performance or of developing the criterion for determining the amount of incentive payments that an executive should receive constitute some of the major problems relating to the development of a good executive incentive system. While any achievements for which an executive is held directly responsible can serve as partial measure of his worth, such accomplishments are often the result of group effort or other factors that are beyond the control of one individual. Furthermore, the closer to the top of the organization that an executive climbs, the more he is likely to make his job what it is.[9] According to a survey by the National Industrial Conference Board, which was conducted among six major types of business, about 50 percent of the manufacturers and retail trade firms that were queried had an executive bonus plan. In contrast, only 25 percent of the fire and casualty insurance companies, 12 percent of the banks, 6 percent of the life insurance companies, and none of the utilities surveyed provided bonuses for their executives. The size of the bonus was also found to vary considerably between industries and to be the largest in retailing and in manufacturing.[10]

---

[8]Elizabeth Lanham, *Administration of Wages and Salaries* (New York: Harper & Row, Publishers, 1963), pp. 430–431.

[9]Arch Patton, *Men, Money and Motivation* (New York: McGraw-Hill Book Company, 1961), p. 57.

[10]*Top Executive Compensation*, Studies in Personnel Policy, No. 193 (New York: National Industrial Conference Board, 1964), pp. 1–77.

Cash payments have the advantage of helping executives to satisfy their immediate financial needs, which are often at a peak during the early stages of their careers. As an executive reaches the higher income tax brackets, however, the portion of a cash payment that is consumed by income taxes becomes greater. The tax-saving advantages of the deferred-payment plans, therefore, have contributed to their growth in popularity. Deferred incentive payments also can provide a painless way for executives to accumulate retirement benefits because the funds come from additional income that is less likely to be missed. One of the deferred-payment plans is that in which the incentive payment is made in the form of shares of stock rather than cash. Plans of this type not only permit a company to preserve its working capital but also help to reduce turnover among executives by enabling them to become part owners in the enterprise. Based upon these aims, some companies provide special benefits for their executives that are not available to other employees, such as life insurance, retirement annuities, club memberships, and stock purchase plans.

As with production and sales employees the problem of attempting to satisfy individual needs and preferences may be encountered in the development of incentive plans for executives. Some executives may prefer a plan that permits them to realize substantial tax savings or to accumulate a nest egg while others may want added income for immediate use. If possible, executive plans should permit individuals a choice in determining the form in which they are to receive their compensation so that it will serve their particular needs.

Incentives for Professional and Technical Personnel

During the past two decades the need for professional and technical personnel, particularly for scientists, engineers, and accountants, has increased substantially with the result that employers have been forced to compete vigorously for their services. This competition has not only led to improvements in the status, treatment, and compensation of these personnel but also has spurred the development of incentive bonuses for them.

While the money usually is not the most important return that a professional person seeks from his work, it nevertheless is a subject of concern to him as indicated by the fact that most of those persons contacted in a survey by Booz, Allen, and Hamilton expressed dissatisfaction with their existing system of remuneration. Furthermore, 56 percent of them indicated a desire for part of their remuneration to be of an incentive type.[11]

---

[11]James L. Wyatt, "Are Creative People 'Different'? Developing Incentives for Scientists and Engineers," *Management Review*, July, 1959.

In spite of the apparent interest of professional employees in financial incentives, such plans are still not prevalent in industry. A Conference Board survey of 405 manufacturing companies, for example, revealed that only 15 percent of them provided some form of extra-compensation plan to their professional-technical employees.[12]

The motivation of professional personnel through incentive pay should also permit ability to be recognized and rewarded by means of advancement opportunities. Unfortunately, in the past scientists and engineers usually were forced to assume an administrative assignment in order to advance beyond a certain point in the salary structure. Consequently, when these personnel were promoted, their professional talents ceased to be utilized fully with the result that the company perhaps lost a good scientist and gained a poor administrator. In an effort to avoid this type of situation, some companies have extended the salary range for personnel in scientific positions so that it equals or nearly equals the range for a department administrator. The extension of the range, therefore, provides a double-track wage system whereby the scientist who does not aspire to an administrative position can have an equal opportunity to gain salary advancement as a scientist.

There also has been a trend for some companies to make use of *maturity curves* as a basis for providing salary increases to professional personnel. These curves, such as the ones shown in Figure 22-2, provide for the annual rate of salary to be based upon experience and performance. Separate curves are established to reflect different levels of performance and to provide for annual increases. The curves representing the higher levels of performance tend to rise to a higher level and at a more rapid rate than the lower performance curves. The curves thus constitute both a salary structure as well as a means for recognizing differences in employee performance.

Company-Wide Incentive Plans

In recent years there has been a trend for companies to attempt to secure greater cooperation, efficiency, and loyalty from their personnel by providing them with an opportunity to participate in the profits derived from their efforts. Such participation has been accomplished indirectly through company-wide stock ownership, profit-sharing, and employee cooperation plans.

---

[12]N.I.C.B., Studies in Personnel Policy, No. 185, *op. cit.*, p. 81.

Figure 22-2

PROFESSIONAL MATURITY CURVES

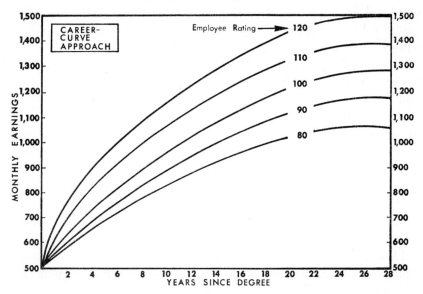

Source: Robert D. Sibson, *Wages and Salaries* (New York: American Management Association, 1960), p. 170. Reproduced with permission.

Stock Ownership Plans

While the depression of the 1930's resulted in a drastic reduction of employee stock ownership plans, the period following World War II brought about renewed interest in such plans and a substantial increase in their number. Stock ownership plans in general consist of two types: (1) those in which the employee purchases stock outright or receives it as a bonus and (2) those in which he is given an opportunity to buy a certain number of shares within a prescribed period and at a stated price.[13]

Stock purchase plans. If a company is publicly held, its employees, like the general public, are always free to acquire its stock through regular brokerage channels. Many employee stock ownership plans, however, permit them to acquire such stock at less than the quoted market price. Minnesota Mining and Manufacturing Company, Eastern Airlines, and Dow Chemical Company are among some of the companies that offer

[13]See *Stock Ownership Plans for Workers*, Studies in Personnel Policy, No. 132 (New York: National Industrial Conference Board, 1953).

their employees such a concession. Installment buying and payroll deduction provisions frequently are used to facilitate employee stock purchases. Stock purchase plans, however, may restrict the amount that an employee may buy to a percentage of his annual income or to a flat amount. Such plans may also require that stock be resold to the company whenever an employee decides to dispose of it. Companies also may protect their employees against sizable stock price declines by guaranteeing a specific repurchase price.

Some companies, such as Standard Oil of Indiana and the General Electric Company, give their employees company stock as a bonus for participating in a United States Savings Bond purchasing plan in order to encourage thrift and financial accumulations for retirement among these employees. Other companies pay incentive wages or profit shares to their employees in the form of company stock.

Stock option plans. A *stock option* is a right to purchase a specified amount of stock at a certain price within a stated period of time. The option price normally is less than the market price at the time that it is offered. The difference between the option price and the market price for the stock at any given time constitutes the value of the option. Although some company stock option plans permit all personnel to participate, most plans are for executive groups. Persons in this group are more likely to have the income and/or the capital necessary to exercise an option and to benefit from any income tax advantages that the option may provide.

A survey of 725 companies conducted in 1963 revealed the percentage of firms providing stock option plans for executives to be as follows: manufacturing companies (75 percent), retailing firms (60 percent), utility and insurance companies (33 percent), and banks (20 percent).[14] Since this survey was taken, however, the attractiveness of stock option plans has been reduced by legislation passed in 1964 which requires that the option price be 100 percent of the market value of the stock at the time that the option is offered, whereas previously it could be lower. Option prices, furthermore, cannot be reset if the market drops, and employees who purchase stock under an option plan must retain the stock for three years in order for any income realized from its sale to be treated as a capital gain.

Advantages and disadvantages of stock ownership plans. Stock ownership plans are intended to make employees more interested in the success of the company and more conscious of its problems and objectives as well

---

[14]N.I.C.B., Studies in Personnel Policy, No. 193, *op. cit.*, p. 6.

as those of the private enterprise system in general. These plans also help to provide a new source of capital and to spread the ownership of the company among employees. During inflationary periods investments in common stocks can also serve as a limited hedge for employees against inflation and can partially offset any decline in the purchasing power of the equity that they have in retirement funds, savings accounts, and insurance policies.

Stock ownership plans, of course, have their limitations in terms of their incentive value. Lack of funds with which to purchase stock may restrict the holdings of many employees to a token amount, and it is doubtful whether the possession of a small amount of company stock can by itself make employees feel any closer kinship with management. Furthermore, from an investment standpoint it is not considered the best practice for an individual to have both his job and his savings invested with the same company.

Another limitation on the value of stock ownership plans is that many employees are not in a position to risk possible loss in their equity through declining stock prices. For employees who cannot risk possible loss and who may have a limited understanding concerning corporation finances and stock market operations, suspicion and discontent can be created particularly during periods of declining stock prices. Memories of the 1929 crash and the suspicion of some union leaders that the loyalty of union members may waver if they become shareholders in the company also have been obstacles for company stock ownership plans.

Profit Sharing

Probably no incentive plan has been the subject of more widespread interest, attention, and misunderstanding than profit sharing. It has been estimated that between 32,000 and 34,000 plans were in existence by 1960 as compared with only 9,000 such plans in 1950 and only 105 plans in 1930.[15] A more recent survey by the Bureau of National Affairs disclosed that 20 percent of the companies included in their sample had a profit-sharing plan.[16]

According to the Council of Profit Sharing Industries, *profit sharing* is clearly defined as:

---

[15] *Wall Street Journal*, September 13, 1961.

[16] *Labor Policies and Practices* (Washington, D.C.: Bureau of National Affairs, Inc., 1966), p. 227:1.

> Any procedure under which an employer pays or makes available to all regular employees, in addition to good rates of regular pay, special current or deferred sums based upon the profits of the business.[17]

The payment of the funds that are distributed through a profit-sharing system may be distributed periodically as a cash bonus, or it may be deferred until retirement or some later period. The feature that distinguishes profit sharing from other incentive plans, however, is the source of the funds and not the fact that they serve to supplement the regular wage.

Purposes of profit-sharing plans. Profit-sharing plans are intended to provide employees with the opportunity to increase their earnings by contributing to the improvement of their company's profits. Their contributions may be directed toward improving product quality, reducing operating costs, improving work methods, and building company goodwill rather than just toward increasing their rate of production. Profit sharing can help to stimulate an employee to think and feel more like a partner in the business and thus to concern himself with the welfare of the organization as a whole. Its purpose, therefore, is to motivate the "whole man" rather than just specific aspects of his performance.

Among those companies that have experienced the greatest degree of success with profit sharing is the Lincoln Electric Company. This company reports that since installing profit sharing in 1934 it has been able to reduce the selling price of its motor-generator welders by 20 percent during a period in which labor rates for the industry have increased fivefold and the price of its raw materials has increased from three- to fourfold. In spite of these increasing costs of production the company paid out in 1959 an average of $10,467 per employee as compared with an average of $5,648 per employee in all manufacturing industries.[18]

Variations in profit-sharing plans. Profit-sharing plans differ as to the proportions of profits shared with each employee and as to the form of payment. The amount that is shared with employees may range from 5 to 50 percent of the net profit. Generally, however, most plans provide for the sharing of about 20 to 25 percent of the net profit. As is the case with executive compensation plans, profit distributions may be carried out in a variety of ways. The distribution may be made to all employees on an equal basis, or it may be based on their regular salary or on some formula that takes into account either or both of the factors of seniority and merit.

---

[17]Constitution and By-Laws of the Council of Profit Sharing Industries (1957), Article 2, Section I.
[18]The Plain Dealer (Cleveland, Ohio, December 10, 1961).

The payments may be disbursed in cash, they may be deferred, or they may be made on the basis of a system involving a combination of these two forms of payment.

Cash-payment plan. Under this plan payments are made at regular intervals. This practice offers the advantage of keeping employees more aware of the current earnings of the company and of their contributions to them and, therefore, tends to have more incentive value than a deferred plan. It also allows employees complete freedom of choice in disposing of their share of profit and permits them to have the opportunity to achieve an immediate improvement in their living standards.

Deferred-payment plan. The deferred type of plan provides for the employees' share of profits to be held in a trust fund for later distribution to them. The fund that is accumulated can be used to provide retirement income, disability payments, separation payments, or loans in the event of an emergency. Profits distributed in this manner can provide the company with a more flexible method of accumulating a retirement fund, or it can serve to supplement the benefits of a regular pension plan. Deferred profit-sharing plans, if they meet the requirements of the Bureau of Internal Revenue, can provide certain income tax advantages for the employees over the cash plans.[19] Furthermore, when the trust funds are invested wisely in high-grade corporate securities or in a mutual investment company, the dividends and the appreciation in the market value of the investment also may serve to increase substantially the amount of each employee's equity in the fund. A deferred type of profit sharing can have the added advantage of providing employees with an incentive to remain with the company.

Combination plan. This plan provides certain benefits of both the cash and the deferred plans. A combination plan generally provides that from one third to one half of an employee's total share of the profits be given to him as a cash payment while the remaining portion is retained in a trust fund. Such practice has the advantage of providing an employee with a direct incentive to increase his contribution to the company while permitting him to acquire savings that he might otherwise be unable to gain in any other manner.

---

[19]The Bureau of Internal Revenue permits a corporation to set aside from its profits an amount equal to 15 percent of its payroll. While the corporation may limit the coverage of its plan to a particular group — for example, to salaried employees — the plan cannot discriminate in favor of certain individuals within a group.

Considerations relating to profit sharing. Most authorities in the field are agreed that in order to have a successful profit-sharing program a company must first have a sound personnel program, good labor relations, and the trust and confidence of its employees. Profit sharing thus is a refinement of a good personnel program and a supplement to an adequate wage scale rather than a substitute for either one. As in the case of all incentive plans, it is the underlying philosophy of the management rather than the mechanics of the plan that may determine its success.

Some of the specific requisites of a good profit-sharing plan, based upon the experience of many companies, are:

1. There must be a compelling desire on the part of management to install the plan in order to enhance the team spirit of the organization. If there is a union, its cooperation is essential.

2. The plan should be generous enough to forestall any feeling on the part of the employees that the lion's share of the results of extra effort will go to management and the stockholders.

3. The employees must understand that there is no benevolence involved — that they are merely receiving their fair share of the profits they have helped create.

4. The emphasis should be placed on partnership, not on the amount of money involved. If financial return is emphasized, it will be more difficult to retain the employees' loyalty and interest in loss years.

5. The employees must be made to feel that it is their plan as well as management's and not something that is being done for them by management. The employees should be well represented on any committee set up to administer the plan.

6. Profit sharing is inconsistent with arbitrary management — it functions best in companies operating under a democratic system. This does *not* mean that management relinquishes its right and, in fact, its obligation, to manage but rather that management functions by leadership instead of arbitrary command.

7. Under no circumstances can profit sharing be used as an excuse for paying lower than prevailing wages.

8. Whatever its technical details, the plan must be adapted to the particular situation, and should be simple enough so that all can readily understand it.

9. The plan should be dynamic, both as to its technical details and as to its administration. Both management and employees — and in profit-sharing companies it is often difficult to find the demarcation line — should give constant thought to ways of improving it.

10. Management should recognize the fact that profit sharing is no panacea. No policy or plan in the industrial relations field can succeed unless it is well adapted and unless it evidences the faith of

management in the importance, dignity, and response of the human individual.[20]

In spite of the potential advantages of profit sharing it is also subject to certain weaknesses. As one author points out, the profits shared with employees may be the result of inventory speculation or many other factors that are beyond the influence of the employees. Conversely, company losses may occur during years when employee contributions have been at a maximum. When these bad years occur, employees may become less aggressive in their attempts to reduce costs. The fact that the payment of profit shares is rendered only once a year or deferred until retirement reduces the motivational benefits to be gained from these payments.[21]

Union reaction to profit sharing. Union attitudes toward profit sharing are so varied as to prevent generalizations. Some union leaders look upon profit sharing as a company device designed to weaken union power, to divert the loyalty of the members from the union, and to avoid giving employees any outright wage increases. Other unions are not opposed to profit sharing provided they are consulted in the adoption of the plan and provided that any share of profit received by employees is in addition to a good basic wage.

Certain unions, such as the United Auto Workers Union, have included profit sharing as one of their bargaining demands. The U.A.W. succeeded in negotiating such a plan with the American Motors Corporation in 1961. By the time that a new agreement was negotiated in 1964, considerable dissatisfaction with the plan had arisen among the United Auto Workers membership, and the future of the plan was in jeopardy. The fact that the benefits were based upon a formula that was difficult for the workers to understand and that did not provide cash payments contributed in part to the dissatisfaction. The plan that eventually was included in the 1964 agreement, therefore, was more simplified and provided for cash payments.[22]

Another plan which has received national attention is the Kaiser Steel Union Sharing Plan that became effective in 1963. It provides for a form of profit sharing that permits the workers to receive 32.5 percent of any savings from any cost reductions resulting from increased efficiency.[23] This plan, with certain revisions in the methods used to determine

[20]Sartall Prentice, Jr., "The Case for Profit Sharing," *Management Review*, Vol. XLI, No. 2 (February, 1952), pp. 85–86.

[21]Frances Torbert, "Making Incentives Work," *Harvard Business Review*, Vol. 37, No. 5 (September–October, 1959), pp. 81–92.

[22]Frederick Taylor, "Profit-Sharing Puzzle," *Wall Street Journal*, October 23, 1964.

[23]*The Kaiser Steel Union Sharing Plan*, Studies in Personnel Policy, No. 187 (New York: National Industrial Conference Board, 1963), pp. 3–30.

costs savings, was continued in the 1966 labor agreement. The revised plan, furthermore, removes some of the restrictions on the opportunity for certain workers to earn additional incentive income based on their performance.[24]

Just how strongly these unions actually want profit sharing is open to speculation. It is quite possible that the demands for a profit-sharing plan in some instances have been raised primarily for bargaining purposes, to be traded for other concessions from the company, since unions traditionally have sought to gain more for their members regardless of a company's profit outlook. The question of whether the union demands for profit sharing represent a desire to develop a new approach to management-union relations or just a strategic bargaining move, therefore, will require time in order to be answered.

Employee Cooperation Plans

In an effort to relate employee bonuses more closely to the effort and cooperation that they may put forth, during the years when company profits are poor as well as in years when they are good, some rather unique plans have been developed. Two such plans, which bear the names of their originators Joe Scanlon and Allen W. Rucker, are somewhat similar in that they place heavy emphasis upon employee cooperation and teamwork. The financial incentive features of these plans, while important, are not necessarily the primary factors that have contributed to their successful operation.

Scanlon Plan. According to one of Scanlon's associates effective employee participation, which includes the use of employee committees, is the most significant feature of this plan. The most important of these committees is the screening committee, composed of management and union officials and members. The committee's function is to review the production figures at the end of each month in order to determine the bonus or deficit that has been incurred. In addition the committee discusses problems relating to the administration of the plan and reviews suggestions relating to company efficiency that have been submitted to it by the various production committees.[25]

The financial incentives under the plan are normally distributed to all employees (a significant feature of the plan) on the basis of an established

---

[24]*Business Week*, March 19, 1966.

[25]Fred G. Lesieur, *The Scanlon Plans* (Massachusetts Institute of Technology: The Technology Press and New York: John Wiley & Sons, Inc., 1958), pp. 46–48.

formula. This formula is based upon increases in employee productivity as determined by improvements that are realized with respect to a "norm" that has been established for labor costs. The norm which is subject to review reflects the relationships of the payroll to the sales value of the company's products. The plan also provides for the establishment of a reserve, into which 25 percent of any earned bonus is paid, for the purpose of covering deficits encountered during the months when labor costs exceed the norm. After the portion for the reserve has been deducted, the remainder of the bonus is distributed with 25 percent going to the company and 75 percent to the employees. Any surplus that has been accumulated in the reserve at the end of a year is distributed to employees on the basis of the same formula.

Rucker Plan. This plan, which is also known as the Share of Production Plan (S.O.P.), normally covers hourly factory workers and executives. The financial incentive is based upon the historic relationship of the total earnings of hourly employees to the production values that they create. The bonus that is paid to employees, thus, is based upon any improvement in this relationship that they are able to realize. Thus, for every 1 percent increase in production value that is achieved, the workers covered by the plan receive an additional bonus of 1 percent of their total payroll costs. As in the case of the Scanlon Plan, maximum use is made of committees in administering the plan.[26]

Lessons to be gained. Perhaps the most important lesson to be gained from the Scanlon and Rucker plans is that any management that expects to gain the cooperation of its employees in improving efficiency must permit them to participate psychologically as well as financially in the company. Employees, if they are to contribute maximum effort, must be able to gain a feeling of involvement and identification with their company which has not been provided to them under the traditional manager-employee relationship. Consequently, it is important for companies to realize that while employee cooperation is essential to the successful administration of a financial incentive system the development of an incentive system will not by itself necessarily stimulate their cooperation.

---

[26]For an excellent evaluation of the Scanlon, Rucker, and other incentive plans see Frances Torbert, "Making Incentives Work," *Harvard Business Review*, Vol. 37, No. 5 (September–October, 1959), pp. 81–92, or as reprinted in Herbert J. Chruden and Arthur W. Sherman, Jr., *Readings in Personnel Management* (Second Edition; Cincinnati: South-Western Publishing Company, Inc., 1966), pp. 358–380.

Résumé

While money does not constitute the only return that employees seek from their job, it can provide them with an effective source of motivation, as well as an opportunity to earn more money. The mere opportunity to earn more money, however, will not assure that employees will exert themselves sufficiently to earn it since individual and/or group attitudes toward the incentive system will also affect their reactions toward the earning opportunities that it provides. These attitudes, furthermore, are in a large part a reflection of the informal leadership that exists within the group and the union as well as the confidence that the employees have in the company's personnel program and its willingness to look out for their interests. The conditions under which an incentive plan is to operate and in turn the attitude of employees toward the plan, therefore, can be just as important as the mechanics of the plan.

When conditions are favorable to its success and when the financial incentive plan has been tailored to fit the objectives and conditions of the company to the needs of its employees, a plan may operate most successfully. Such a plan can permit untapped capacity, which most all employees possess, to be released to the benefit of the company, society, and themselves.

DISCUSSION QUESTIONS AND PROBLEMS

1. What are some of the possible reasons that employees might have for not favoring financial incentives?
2. If the standard time for producing one unit of a product were 4 minutes, what should the piece rate per unit be if the established hourly rate for this particular type of work were $3 an hour?
3. Why is the attitude and philosophy of management so important to the success of a financial incentive plan?
4. What are some of the factors in an employee's background that might affect his response to a financial incentive plan?
5. Executives in government sometimes complain that they are handicapped in their efforts to improve employee efficiency because the government does not have an incentive wage system. To what extent do you feel that this complaint is justified? Discuss.
6. A company that paid its production employees entirely on a piece-rate system pointed with pride to the fact that it permitted its employees "to go into business for themselves." To what extent do you feel that this claim is true or untrue?
7. The supervisor of a production department was convinced that the standard for the incentive bonus plan within his department had become too loose.

Following an argument with an employee one day he took over the employee's job and during a half-hour period produced at a rate that was twice as great as that which the employee or others in his group had been averaging.

   a. Would the results of his action indicate that the standard should be tightened?

   b. What effect may the supervisor's action have upon future production within the department?

8. What are some of the problems that are encountered in attempting to develop financial systems for executive and professional personnel? Why are they more for these groups than for operative personnel?

9. What are some of the possible reasons why profit sharing has succeeded so well in some companies such as Lincoln Electric and yet failed to work successfully in other companies?

CASE 22-1

THE CHRISTMAS BONUS

During the previous eight years the Security Investment Company had given each of its employees a year-end bonus in an amount equal to from one- to two-weeks pay. Consequently, over the years the employees had become accustomed to using this bonus as a means of meeting their Christmas season expenses. Because of unusually poor earnings one year the company recognized that even if it did not pay a bonus to its employees it would be fortunate to avoid encountering a deficit. Since management recognized that a majority of its employees had worked hard during the year and were counting on receiving a bonus, it was reluctant to forego the payment of it even if it had to incur a deficit to pay it. Management also recognized that the company's bonus record was usually mentioned during employment interviews particularly when it hired clerical help whose salaries were not too high. As the first of December approached, management was faced with the problem of making a decision regarding the payment of the bonus.

   a. What decision do you feel that management should make concerning the bonus, and when and how should the information concerning it be communicated to the employees?

   b. What problems does this case indicate may arise in connection with the use of financial incentives?

   c. What future policy should the company establish concerning the bonus?

CASE 22-2

SUNRISE CROP DUSTERS, INC.

Sunrise Crop Dusters, Inc., was owned and managed by Emory Johnson. In addition to a service crew he employed four pilots. These pilots were paid a monthly salary plus a percentage of the gross profit as an incentive bonus. As Mr. Johnson was able to obtain additional accounts for his company, it became increasingly difficult for him to service customer demand with his existing staff. Mr. Johnson recognized that a fifth pilot would be required if he were to accept any more new accounts, but he also realized that he would need to obtain a substantial increase in business in order to cover the wages and bonuses that would be required to support the employment of this pilot. His pilots had expressed some objections to any expansion of their ranks that might serve to decrease their share of the company profits.

    a. Assuming that Emory Johnson is interested in continuing the expansion of his company, how might he cope with objections from his pilots?

    b. Should Johnson make any changes in his wage program? What changes, if any, would you recommend?

CASE 22-3

THE PROTEST WALKOUT

Two new employees, Max and Earl, were assigned to a work gang in the shipping department of the Garden Products Company at the task of loading boxcars. Both of them, working as a team, were paid an hourly rate plus an incentive bonus when they exceeded established loading standards. It was extremely difficult to earn a bonus, however, whenever they were forced to load irregular sized cartons because of the extra time required to arrange the cartons properly within the cars. After failing to earn any appreciable amount of incentive pay for several days, the two men complained one morning to the foreman that they were getting far more than their share of irregular sized cartons to load. When the foreman appeared unsympathetic toward their complaints, they told him that they were leaving their jobs at noon. In reply the foreman warned them that such action would result in their receiving a three-day suspension without pay. The two men, true to their threats, did not return to their jobs that afternoon. When they reported the next morning, they were told that they had been discharged, whereupon they immediately filed a grievance with their union business representative. The union, in support of their grievance, demanded of the company that the two men be reinstated at the end of a three-day suspension period since this was the penalty that they had been told they would receive if they walked off the job.

    a. If you were the personnel manager, what action would you recommend that the company take in response to the union's grievance demands? (Assume that the contract contains a provision for the arbitration of disputes.)

    b. What factors appear to have contributed to the development of this problem situation?

    c. Are there any changes in the incentive program that appear desirable in the light of this incident?

SUGGESTED READINGS

Belcher, David W. *Wage and Salary Administration,* Second Edition. Englewood Cliffs, New Jersey: Prentice-Hall, Inc., 1962. Chapters 14, 15, 19.

Brennan, Charles W. *Wage Administration.* Homewood, Illinois: Richard D. Irwin, Inc., 1959. Chapters 18–23.

Brown, Wilfred. *Piecework Abandoned.* London: Heinemann, 1962.

Jehring, J. J. *Profit Sharing for Small Business.* Evanston, Illinois: The Profit Sharing Research Foundation.

Knowlton, P. A. *Profit Sharing Patterns*. Evanston, Illinois: The Profit Sharing Research Foundation, 1954.

Langsner, Adolph, and Herbert G. Zollitsch. *Wage and Salary Administration*. Cincinnati: South-Western Publishing Company, Inc., 1961. Chapters 20–27.

Lesieur, Frederick G. (Editor). *The Scanlon Plan*. Massachusetts Institute of Technology: The Technology Press and New York: John Wiley & Sons, 1958.

Lincoln, James F. *Incentive Management*. Cleveland, Ohio: Lincoln Electric Company, 1956.

Patton, Arch. *Men, Money and Motivation*. New York: McGraw-Hill Book Company, 1961.

Prevalence of Bonus Plans in Manufacturing, Studies in Personnel Policy, No. 185. New York: National Industrial Conference Board, 1962.

Revised Profit Sharing Manual. Chicago: Council of Profit Sharing Industries, 1957.

Sibson, Robert E. *Wages and Salaries: A Handbook for Line Managers*. New York: American Management Association, 1960. Chapter V.

The Kaiser Steel Union Sharing Plan, Studies in Personnel Policy, No. 187. New York: National Industrial Conference Board, 1963.

The Prentice-Hall Complete Labor Equipment, Vol. 6. *Pension and Profit Sharing*. Englewood Cliffs, New Jersey: Prentice-Hall, Inc.

Top Executive Compensation, Studies in Personnel Policy, No. 193. New York: National Industrial Conference Board, Inc., 1964.

Whyte, William F. *Money and Motivation*. New York: Harper & Brothers, 1955.

Retirement

Employee retirement is one of the more recent personnel functions to be included in company personnel programs; provisions for retirement traditionally were viewed as being the private concern and responsibility of each employee. The cost of providing pension benefits for employees also has been a factor in deterring companies from becoming involved with a retirement program, particularly since these costs constitute long-term obligations that future company revenues may not be able to support. In recent years, however, companies have given serious consideration to installing retirement programs as a result of the changing attitudes of the public, the increasing concern of enlightened managers for the welfare of their employees, and the growing demand of employees and their unions for greater economic security during and following the normal working period of one's life.

The fact that some degree of financial assistance is now being provided to most of our retired population by the federal government through the social security program also has placed companies under some pressure to provide pensions to supplement social security benefits. As a result of the financial and other forms of assistance being provided to them, employees are becoming better able to cope with the problems that their retirement may create for them. Since many of these problems, however, must be solved by the individual employee, all that the company can do in many instances is to help its employees become better able to help themselves.

The discussion in this chapter covers the different types of assistance that are being provided employees to help them adjust to their retirement. The topics covered include:

- Company retirement programs.
- Pension plans.
- The Social Security program.

Company Retirement Programs

A formal company retirement program can help to facilitate the various adjustments that may be required within the company and on the part of the employees when they retire. Such a program also can help to permit an employee's retirement to be anticipated by the company and to be planned well in advance of its occurrence so that the problems of adjustment will be minimized. It also can help to insure that any pensions which are provided will contribute to the company's objectives and will be financially sound from the standpoint of protecting both the retirement benefits of the employees and the financial solvency of the company.

Facilitating the Adjustment of Retiring Employees

In spite of the favorable impression of retired life conveyed by pictures of a gray-haired couple enjoying a sunset, beaming over a brood of grandchildren, relaxing in hammocks, or pulling in fish from a river bank, retirement may prove to be anything but satisfying for a great many "senior citizens." Retirement often introduces a period of lonesomeness and boredom which many a retiree, such as the one pictured in Figure 23-1, would gladly trade back for the worries, pressures, companionships, and the "grind" of their former work activities. Retired personnel, therefore, must develop substitutes for those feelings of recognition, self-actualization, and belongingness that they formerly gained from their jobs; they must strive for new goals, sources of recognition, and social contacts. The help and assistance of a formal company retirement program often can do much to facilitate their social and psychological adjustments.

In an effort to assist their employees in adjusting more readily to retirement, many companies have inaugurated preretirement programs. In a survey of 974 companies conducted by the National Industrial Conference Board, for example, it was found that 65 percent of them provided some form of preretirement counseling for their employees.[1] One of the

---

[1]*Corporate Retirement Policy and Practices*, Studies in Personnel Policy, No. 190 (New York: National Industrial Conference Board, 1964), p. 69.

Figure 23-1

Source: *The Next Promotion* (Hartford, Conn.: The Connecticut Mutual Life Insurance Company). Reproduced with permission.

primary contributions of such programs is to make employees who are approaching retirement more aware of this fact, and in some instances to jolt them into thinking and doing something about it. Although some companies begin their counseling with employees as early as five years prior to their retirement, at least half of the companies in one survey do not provide it until a year or less prior to retirement time.[2] The shorter period, however, is not likely to allow individuals sufficient time to change their habit patterns. The percentage of companies that provided preretirement counseling on the following areas is indicated in parentheses:

1. Health problems of older people (72 percent).
2. Use of leisure time and recreation (68 percent).
3. Community resources for older people (50 percent).
4. Housing and living arrangements (48 percent).
5. Revenue-producing hobbies and activities (47 percent).
6. Family adjustment problems (42 percent).[3]

[2] *Ibid.*, p. 71.
[3] *Ibid.*, p. 72.

Adjustment to a reduction in income as a result of retirement is another critical step that an employee must take. Through preretirement counseling, therefore, employees should be encouraged to make downward adjustments in their spending habits and to eliminate their debts well in advance of retirement. Assistance in financial planning and budgeting, through meetings arranged by the personnel department, may help employees to avoid financial mistakes and the accompanying hardships.

A number of companies have prepared booklets, pamphlets, and other literature to use in their preretirement programs. Some companies also purchase subscriptions to senior-citizen magazines for employees nearing retirement. These magazines include *Aging*, published by the U.S. Department of Health, Education, and Welfare; *Harvest Years*, published by the Harvest Years Publishing Company; *Modern Maturity*, published by the American Association of Retired Persons; and *Retirement Planning News*, published by the Retirement Planning Council, Inc. According to a Conference Board survey, *Retirement Planning News* is the publication provided by the largest number of companies.[4]

The Esso Standard Oil Company is among those companies that have made a concerted effort to assist employees in making the adjustment to a retired life. For a number of years this company has been offering a series of discussion meetings covering various problems relating to retirement. Attendance has been on a voluntary basis, and the meetings are open to all persons nearing retirement age, regardless of their positions within the organization. The discussion meetings attempt to acquaint participants with the typical problems and characteristics of old age and to encourage them to develop a healthy and realistic view toward it. Suggestions on how to minimize the physical, financial, and social problems of retirement are also provided. In the course of the sessions, employees not only have the opportunity to share and receive ideas concerning retirement but also to lay the foundations for their own retirement plans. Other companies have developed somewhat similar voluntary discussion meetings. At Detroit Edison, for example, these meetings cover such subjects as psychological adjustment, mental and physical health, diet, finances, where to live, and use of leisure time.[5]

---

[4]*Ibid.*, p. 75. The interests of older persons are the special concern of the Office of Aging, Department of Health, Education, and Welfare, that issues many publications related to the problems of senior citizens.

[5]Irving Ladimer, "Preparation for Retirement: Boon or Boondoggle?" *Factory Management and Maintenance*, Vol. 3, No. 6 (June, 1953), pp. 88–91.

Organizational Planning for Retirement

The organizational adjustments that may be required because of retirements usually can be accomplished more easily and effectively if planned for well in advance. This planning should provide for the selection and training of replacements to fill the positions being vacated by retiring personnel as well as those vacancies being created as a result of the promotional chain reaction. Planning may also include transferring certain employees who are nearing retirement age to less demanding jobs or restructuring their jobs to permit these individuals to continue to perform them without impairing their health and/or the efficiency of the organization.

The gradual reduction of an employee's duties and work load may not only facilitate his replacement but may also help him to "ease into retirement" with a minimum of difficulty. There are several ways in which an employee's work load may be lightened and his active career with a company "phased out" gradually. One is to extend the length of his vacation period, and another is to reduce his workweek during the last few years of his employment. If a replacement is being groomed for the job, that person may gradually assume more of the responsibilities connected with the job. Regardless of what measures are used, however, a systematic plan for gradually reducing the work load of a retiring employee can help to make the transition an easier one for him and for the organization.

Maintaining Relations with Retired Employees

Most employees who have worked a number of years for a company are likely to have some feelings of belongingness and loyalty toward the organization. Continued contacts that the company may maintain with them after their retirement can serve to recognize and preserve these feelings as well as make these former employees realize that their past contributions have not been forgotten. Such evidences of consideration for retirees not only builds goodwill among those who are the recipients but it also demonstrates to its workers and to the public that the company is "an organization with a heart."

In order to maintain close contact with retired personnel, many companies keep their names on the mailing list for the company magazine, financial reports, and other literature, as well as invite them to company social activities and provide them with certain privileges and services that are furnished to regular employees. Some companies utilize their retired personnel in an advisory capacity or provide them with temporary work assignments during periods of peak work loads or vacation periods. Other companies encourage their employees to return for visits and may even sponsor special days in their honor. A number of companies also have given encouragement and assistance to the formation of a retired employees' club through which such employees can keep in touch with one another and can experience mutual help and assistance. A group of retired employees from one company has been instrumental in forming a club called SIR (Sons in Retirement) which meets once a month to hear speakers and/or visit local companies. This club, whose formal organization is minimal, has been growing rapidly in recent years.

Determining the Age for Retirement

One of the basic problems relating to retirement that must be resolved by a company is that of determining the age at which retirement is to occur. Some companies maintain a flexible retirement policy that permits an employee to keep working beyond the normal retirement age (generally 65) for as long as he continues to be reasonably efficient and physically able to work. The majority of companies, however, adhere to a policy of *compulsory* or of *automatic retirement* at an established age, at least for certain classes of employees.[6] *Compulsory retirement* is distinguished from *automatic retirement* in that it may include provisions by which the employee can continue to work on a year-to-year basis at the invitation of the company.

One of the arguments favoring a flexible retirement policy is that it recognizes the fact that the mental and physical condition of employees is not just a function of age and that some individuals, therefore, are capable of rendering valuable contributions to the company well beyond the normal retirement age. Thus, a flexible retirement policy prevents the company as well as society from being deprived of the contribution that individuals still may be able to render. A flexible retirement policy also permits employees who have not accumulated adequate pension benefits or who fear the adjustment problems of retirement to continue working.

Retirement flexibility also may be increased by permitting early retirement for employees who suffer a disability, a mental or physical decline, or who prefer to quit working before the normal retirement age. Early retirement also has been used as one of the means of coping with the introduction of laborsaving devices.

---

[6]*Ibid.*, p. 17.

Nearly all of the plans included in the N.I.C.B. study contained provisions for early retirement.[7] In most of the companies, however, eligibility to receive early retirement benefits is made contingent upon such factors as age, total years of service, and company consent. The ages 60 and 55 are prescribed by most companies as the minimum ages although a few plans set the age at 50 or even lower.[8] When employees retire early, their benefits usually are reduced by the actuarial equivalent of the number of years that they are retiring in advance. The United Auto Workers agreement with the major automobile manufacturers, for example, now includes provisions for retirement as early as the age of 55.[9]

If flexible retirement is to work successfully, a long-range form of preretirement program is particularly advisable to convince employees that they should begin preparation for retirement early enough. If the program prescribes the criteria upon which the retirement or the retention of personnel is to be decided, employees will have a better opportunity to judge for themselves whether or not they should retire. Furthermore, the evidence from one study would indicate that it is still possible to pressure people to retire who are not thought to be making a satisfactory contribution.[10]

A mandatory retirement policy, on the other hand, has the advantages of permitting a company to plan more effectively for employee retirements, to accomplish them on an orderly basis, and to avoid the unpleasant task of asking certain persons who are reluctant to retire to do so. While a mandatory retirement policy may cause some employees to retire before their physical condition requires them to do so, it also insures that those employees whose performance is declining will have to leave by a certain age. Furthermore, if employees know that retirement is compulsory at a particular age, they are more likely to prepare for it in advance. Compulsory retirement also serves to increase the advancement opportunities for younger employees who otherwise might be blocked by older employees, such as the old gentleman in Figure 23-2 whose retirement evidently is being strongly encouraged. It should be recognized, however, that when management adheres to a policy of mandatory retirement it is abrogating some of its discretionary power and perhaps is not maintaining the highest of personnel standards.

---

[7]*Ibid.*, p. 19.

[8]*Ibid.*, pp. 22–23.

[9]Harry E. Davis, "Changes in Negotiated Pension Plans, 1961–64," *Monthly Labor Review*, Vol. 88, No. 10 (October, 1965) pp. 1215–1218.

[10]Peter D. Couch and Carl F. Lundgren, "Making Voluntary Retirement Programs Work," *Personnel Journal*, Vol. 42, No. 3 (March, 1963), pp. 135–138.

Figure 23-2

"Of course, tomorrow's papers will report that after a long and
fruitful career, he decided to hand over the reins to a younger man."

Source: Courtesy of *True*, *The Man's Magazine*, and Donald Reilly. September, 1964, p. 73.

Pension Plans

Pension plans in this country have existed for less than a century. One of the first known pension plans was that initiated by the American Express Company in 1875. A few years later the Baltimore & Ohio Railroad also developed a pension plan for its employees, and it was followed by other railroads until the majority of the workers in this industry were covered by some form of plan. Personnel in the civil and the armed services of the federal government were also among the first groups to receive pension benefits. In industry most of the early pension plans included only the executive and other salaried employees. It was not until about 1935 that pension plans for wage earners became the subject of much attention.

It was the passage of the Social Security Act in 1935 that helped to stimulate employee and union interest in pensions. The meagerness of early social security benefits and the continuing increases in living costs caused employees to look to their employers for additional retirement income beyond that received through social security. The development of private pension plans during the 1930's, however, occurred at a relatively slow pace, and it was not until World War II that the growth of such plans received significant stimulation. Some 4,208 new plans qualifying for the tax-exemption provisions of the Bureau of Internal Revenue were inaugurated between 1942 and 1944. This number compared with only 843 new plans originating during the entire decade from 1930 to 1940.[11] The sudden interest of companies in pensions during World War II resulted from the fact that pensions, along with other fringe benefits, provided a means for attracting new employees at a time when there was a government freeze on wages. Furthermore, because of the "cost-plus" provisions of most war contracts and the high tax on excess profits, pensions in many instances cost companies very little to provide.

Prior to the 1948 NLRB decision in the Inland Steel Case, employers were not required to bargain with their unions on the subject of pensions.[12] Employers who did not want to establish pensions were able to forestall union demands for them on the grounds that decisions involving pensions were an exclusive prerogative of management. In the NLRB decision, which was later upheld by the Supreme Court, however, it was ruled that employers could not refuse to bargain over pensions; and as a result of this decision the way was cleared for union pension drives. Shortly thereafter a number of the major unions succeeded in negotiating pension benefits with some of the nation's largest companies, including those in the steel, automobile, and other manufacturing industries. The successes achieved by these unions helped to establish a precedent for unions in other industries to demand similar benefits from their employers.

Pension plans continue to grow as indicated by a study of union agreements made by the Bureau of National Affairs which revealed that over 70 percent of these agreements provided for pension benefits and that more than 84 percent were financed entirely by the company.[13]

Problems Related to Pensions

Pension benefits create many problems that are not encountered in other forms of remuneration since these benefits represent a long-term obligation that cannot be estimated in advance with complete accuracy. The age of a company's employees, the number of them who will remain with it until retirement age, the number of years that they can be expected

---

[11]Carroll W. Boyce, *How to Plan Pensions* (New York: McGraw-Hill Book Company, 1950), p. 4.

[12]*Inland Steel Company* v. *NLRB, NLRB* 77, 1 (1948).

[13]*Labor Policies and Practices* (Washington, D.C.: Bureau of National Affairs, Inc., 1966), pp. 227:1–4.

to live following retirement, and the amount of the benefits that they will receive, for example, are some of the factors which will influence the cost of the pension program. Employee turnover and inflation also may influence the cost of the pension program. Furthermore, the money necessary to provide pensions must come from future earnings that are subject to many uncertainties. If a trust fund is to be established from which the pensions are to be paid, an additional problem of investing and protecting the fund may be created.

In view of these and other problems concerning the administration of a pension program, it is not surprising that many companies, particularly those of moderate size and resources, have exhibited some degree of reluctance to provide pensions. The problems relating to pensions, however, are not insurmountable. Pension consultants can be of considerable help to a company in overcoming the many technical problems as well as protecting a company against the pitfalls that might otherwise be encountered in developing a pension program.

Methods of Calculating Retirement Benefits

The amount of pension benefits that a company desires to provide its employees and the basis upon which the benefits are to be determined are important considerations in the development of a benefit formula. A company, for example, must decide to what extent, if any, the payments are to be affected by such factors as years of service, amount of earnings attained by the employee, his retirement income requirements, or the amount of social security benefits that he may be entitled to receive. Also, a company must decide whether the size of the pension is to be a fixed amount or is to be contingent upon the contributions that have been paid into the fund on behalf of the employee. In general, there are four basic types of plans that can be used to compute retirement payments. These include (1) the flat benefit, (2) the percentage of income, (3) the percentage of income times service, and (4) the money-purchase pension types of plans. Within each of these basic plans there can be further variations.

Flat benefit plan. Under this plan each employee who retires receives a flat amount of perhaps $150, $200 or more a month regardless of his service or his earnings prior to retirement. A plan of this type tends to favor workers in the lower wage classes, but it may discourage the employment of older workers. The reason for this latter fact is that the company can gain a greater number of years of service from those employees who are selected at a young age before it is required to provide them with pension benefits. Sometimes flat benefit plans are tied in with the worker's social security benefits so that the company pays only the difference between the amount received from social security and the flat amount that is guaranteed by the company.

Percentage of income. Pensions under this plan of computation are based upon a percentage of the employee's earnings during a specified period of time. The earnings figure used might be the average earnings rate, the highest earnings rate during a given number of years, or the earnings rate received by the employee at the time of his retirement, depending upon the nature of the plan. According to a Department of Labor study of 16,000 pension plans, this type of benefit formula ranks second in terms of usage among private plans.[14]

Percentage of income times service. Benefits under this plan are based upon a percentage of an employee's monthly income (generally a figure of from one to two percent) multiplied by the number of years of service that he has completed. This type of formula is the one that is used most commonly among private plans.[15] It has the advantages of rewarding an individual's service and progress within the organization and of permitting a company to hire workers from the older age groups without experiencing higher pension costs.

Money-purchase plan. Under this plan the employer contributes a certain percentage of an employee's earnings into a retirement fund. When the employee retires, retirement benefits are purchased with the contributions and interest that have accumulated in his behalf. The size of his pension after retirement, therefore, is contingent upon the amount of funds in his retirement account and what these funds will buy in terms of pension benefits.

One of the simplest methods of providing pension benefits under this plan is through the purchase of insurance annuities, which provide the employee with a uniform monthly benefit for the remainder of his life. Arrangements can also be made with many mutual fund investment companies or with banks or trust companies to establish a pension trust fund from which the pension payments are distributed to each employee on the basis of his share in the fund and his period of life expectancy. Since the pension benefits under the money-purchase plan are determined by the

---

[14]Donald J. Staats, "Private Pension Plans: How Benefits Are Computed," *Management Review*, Vol. 54, No. 10 (October, 1965), pp. 33–36.
[15]*Ibid.*

amount of funds that have been accumulated for each employee, the company's financial obligations for providing such benefits are limited in nature.

Other Features of Pension Plans

Some plans permit an employee after a certain period of time to acquire a *vested right* or equity in the retirement fund that the company has accumulated in his behalf. This vested right may enable an employee to receive his equity in a lump-sum payment should he leave the company before retirement. In other instances the right may permit an employee who leaves the company to receive a pension at the established retirement age based upon the amount of entitlement that he has earned up to the time of his departure. There are plans also that permit employees to take their pension rights with them if they change employers. In certain industrial centers, such as Toledo, Ohio, employers have developed a group pension plan to permit employees to retain their pension rights should they transfer between employers in the group. Pension plans that are administered jointly with a union also permit the members to retain the pension rights while changing employers. Other features contained in some pension plans provide for disability payments for workers who are unable to work because of injuries and for lump-sum or pension benefits to surviving widows or dependents.

Financing the Plan

The success of any pension system is contingent upon sound financing — sound in terms of providing and protecting the funds necessary to meet pension obligations and in terms of the company's ability to support the costs. In addition, the system should meet all legal regulations pertaining to it and should provide maximum benefits and security for the employees as economically as possible.

The two principal methods of financing a pension plan are the *unfunded* or *pay-as-you-go* method and the *funded* method. The pay-as-you-go method is not used very much in comparison with the funded method.

Pay-as-you-go method. Under this method pension payments are made from current revenues. Since funds are not accumulated to meet the pension obligations, the money that might otherwise be set aside for this purpose may be reinvested in the company. Normally, a company should realize a higher return from funds that are invested in its own organization than from those invested in a trust fund or in insurance annuities with the result that the cost of the plan to the company is reduced. Unfortunately, the unfunded system often does not provide employees with complete assurance that they will receive pension benefits since these benefits are contingent upon the company's ability to survive and prosper. Economic reverses could force a company to reduce or even to default on its pension payments in order to avoid bankruptcy. The liquidation or the sale of the business, furthermore, could result in the loss of pensions for employees. These factors explain why this method of financing is seldom used.

Funded methods of financing. Under the funded method the money required to finance pensions is accumulated to cover part or all of a company's pension obligations before they mature. Pension funds may be derived from employee as well as employer contributions. The *noncontributory plan* in which funds are provided entirely by the employer, however, is the type preferred and most commonly negotiated by organized labor. This type of plan eliminates an economically unsound practice of taking back a portion of an employee's wages after the government has first removed its share of taxes. Employer contributions to the pension fund may be determined by an established formula, or they may be contingent upon company profits as a part of a profit-sharing plan. In some labor contracts, such as those negotiated by the United Mine Workers, employer contributions to the welfare and pension fund come from production royalties.

It is important that pension funds be invested where they will receive adequate protection and yet earn a satisfactory return. The earnings derived from a trust fund can be used either to increase the amount of money that is available for pension benefits or to reduce the amount of money that the company must contribute to the fund, or both. During inflationary periods a major investment problem is that of preserving the purchasing power of the pension funds as well as the dollar value of the funds. The loss in purchasing power of the pension benefits received by an employee can hurt him just as much as the loss of a comparable number of dollars from the fund. This fact sometimes is overlooked by companies through their failure to provide a hedge against inflation when investing funds for employee retirement.

The funds that are established to meet employee pension obligations may be managed by trustees appointed from within the company or by a bank or trust company that has been hired for this purpose. In other instances the funds may be used to purchase an insurance contract that will provide the retirement benefits. A plan that provides for trust funds is known as a *trusteed plan*; whereas, the plan that involves the purchase of an insurance contract is known as an *insured plan*.

Trusteed plans. In a trusteed plan the money that is necessary to fund a pension for each employee should be determined from actuarial computations and contributed annually to the fund, starting at the time the employee becomes covered by the pension plan. If pension benefits are to be computed on the basis of length of service, additional contributions may have to be made when a new plan is adopted to cover that service which has been performed prior to the creation of the plan. In such cases the funds to cover this obligation for past service may be built up over a 10-year, 20-year, or longer period of time after which there will be a full reserve fund available to cover pension obligations.

Insured plans. The insurance policy that is purchased to support retirement benefits under an insured plan may provide coverage on either an individual or a group basis. Frequently these policies also may provide for death and disability benefits in addition to the pension benefits. The policy premiums are computed so as to cover the costs of the benefits and the administrative expenses as well as a margin of profit for the insurance company. An additional loading charge may be included in the premium to provide a minimum margin of safety for the insurer. Policy premiums, depending on the contract, may be paid on an annual basis or in a lump sum on the date that each employee retires.

Comparison of insured and trusteed plans. Insured plans have the advantage of relieving the employer of the problems and the responsibilities of managing a pension fund as well as the possibility of criticism concerning its management. If the insurance contract is with a company that is financially sound, the employees are afforded a maximum guarantee that they will receive pensions of a stated amount. By knowing exactly what they may expect to receive at a given retirement age, employees will be likely to have more confidence in the plan; and, as a result, they will tend to have more confidence in the company's pension guarantees.

The disadvantage of an insured plan as opposed to a trusteed plan is that the amount of the pension annuity is fixed and thus may tend to lose its purchasing power during periods of inflation. For example, an annuity contract for a $75-a-month pension might have been quite adequate for an employee in 1935, but this amount would have had considerably less purchasing power and would have been less adequate for the employee who received the annuity pension some 20 years later. Aside from failing to provide protection against inflation, pension annuities may provide a smaller return on the money invested in them as compared with the money invested in many trust funds. For these reasons there has been a considerable trend in recent years for companies and unions to turn to trusteed plans and for more of the funds in these trusteed plans to be invested in high-grade common stocks as opposed to bonds.

The Social Security Program

While the number of persons covered by private pension plans has been growing rapidly, it is still considerably less than the number who are covered by the social security program of the federal government, which includes many of those persons who are also covered by private pensions. The discussion of retirement benefits, therefore, would be incomplete if some attention were not given to the Social Security Act.

The Social Security Act of 1935 represented a major step forward in the field of social welfare legislation. The act created a permanent federal program of social welfare that was designed to protect families against undue hardship when they were deprived of earnings due to the unemployment, retirement, disability, or death of the breadwinner. Since families of the lower income groups tend to suffer the most from such eventualities, the benefits paid to recipients in this group are proportionally larger with respect to their contributions than those paid to recipients in the higher income groups. One of the objectives of the act has been to develop gradually a program, supported by tax contributions from employees and employers covered by it, that will reduce the number of persons depending upon public assistance payments for their support. Most recently the Social Security Program has been expanded by Congress to provide health insurance for people over 65 under what is popularly known as "Medicare."[16]

Coverage of the Act

In order to receive benefits for himself and/or his family under the Social Security Act, an individual must have been engaged in some form of employment that is covered by it. Most employment by private enterprise, most types of self-employment including farming, active military service

---

[16]Since the Social Security Act has been, and probably will continue to be, the subject of amendments by Congress, students should refer to the current literature that may be obtained from their nearest Social Security Office concerning the latest provisions of the act.

after 1956,[17] and employment in certain nonprofit organizations and governmental agencies are subject to coverage under the act.

In spite of several amendments that have extended the coverage of the act, there are still some groups that are exempted from it. Some of these groups include the following:

1. Farm laborers earning less than $150 from any one employer during a calendar year.
2. Domestic servants receiving less than $50 cash in a given calendar quarter.
3. Casual employment (i.e., seasonal, incidental, or irregular in nature) for which less than $50 cash is received in one quarter.
4. Most types of family employment.
5. Ministers (unless he elects to be covered by filing a waiver).
6. Students employed by school, college, or one of its organizations while attending the institution.
7. Newsboys and news vendors.
8. Railroad workers (covered by their own system).
9. Student nurses and interns.
10. Employees of foreign governments.
11. Employees of nonprofit organizations (unless the employer and the employees request coverage).
12. Civil Service employees of the U.S. Government.
13. Employees of state and local governments (unless a majority of the eligible employees vote for coverage).
14. Employment outside of the United States, unless performed by a U.S. citizen for a U.S. citizen.[18]

Contributions Under the Act

The old-age, survivors, and disability program of the Social Security Program is supported by a payroll tax levied against both the employer and the employee. It is paid only on the first $6,600 of remuneration that an employee or self-employed person receives during a calendar year. The employer is required to send in the tax payments covering both his and the employee's shares. The employee's share of the tax is normally deducted from the wages he receives although an employer can pay the entire tax. A self-employed individual is required to pay his own tax at the time that he submits his income tax statement. The Social Security Program, as it

---

[17]Active military service completed between 1940 and 1956 inclusive was granted Social Security credit gratuitously based upon monthly earnings of $160 per month. If this credit is used for Social Security benefits, however, it cannot be counted toward any other federal service pension.

[18]For a more detailed account of exempted groups see the current editions of *Labor Course,* or *Tax Course* (Englewood Cliffs, New Jersey: Prentice-Hall Inc.).

now exists, provides for the tax supporting the program to be increased at periodic intervals until 1987. The tax rate for the employer and the employee, including the tax for Medicare, is scheduled to increase from 4.4 percent in 1967 to 4.9 percent in 1969 and ultimately to 5.65 percent by 1987. The corresponding tax for the self-employed person is scheduled to increase from 6.4 percent in 1967 to 7.1 percent in 1969 and to 7.8 percent by 1987. If the past trends are any predictor of the future, however, the tax rates may be increased still further before the present maximum is reached in 1987 in order to support the continuing liberalization of benefits that may be demanded by the public.

Retirement Benefits

In order to be eligible to receive retirement benefits, a person must have reached retirement age, must be retired, and be fully insured.[19] Whether or not an individual is fully insured is determined by the number of quarters in which he has received a prescribed amount of earnings. A calendar quarter is a three-month period beginning January 1, April 1, July 1, or October 1. For most kinds of employment a person must earn at least $50 in wages in order to obtain a quarter of coverage. Those persons who are self-employed must earn at least $400 a year, for which they receive four quarters of coverage. The exact number of quarters that a particular individual must obtain in order to be classed as fully insured will depend upon his date of birth or, if he dies or becomes disabled before reaching retirement age, upon the date of his death or disability. In no case can an individual become fully insured with less than six quarters of coverage and in no case will he need more than 40 quarters, regardless of his date of birth.

In order to be able to receive his monthly payment, an eligible person under the age of 72 must be retired — that is, he must satisfy the test of retirement. This test is that he not be earning more than $1,500 a year from wages or self-employment. Income from investments and certain types of royalties are not classified as earnings. Under the 1965 amendment an individual who earns more than $1,500 in one year will lose one dollar in benefits for every two dollars that he earns between $1,500 and $2,700 and one dollar in benefits for each dollar that he earns over $2,700. Regardless of how much an individual earns during a given year, however, no reduction will be made in his benefits during any month in which he earns $125 or less working for someone else, and if he is self-employed, during any

---

[19]Retirement age normally is 65. However, men and women may begin drawing retirement benefits at the age of 62 at a reduced amount and a widow of a fully insured worker may begin drawing reduced benefits as early as the age of 60 at a reduced amount.

month in which he does not render a substantial service to the business. (Normally this service is considered to be that which is less than 40 hours of work per month.) After the age of 72 there are no restrictions placed upon the amount that an individual can earn in order to be eligible for retirement benefits.

Since retirement benefits are computed on the basis of average earnings, a person's benefits are reduced by each year in which he does not work in covered employment. In determining this average, however, an individual is entitled to drop out the five years in which he had the least or no earnings. Thus, if an individual during a 20-year period in which he is eligible to be covered worked in covered employment for only 10 years, his average earnings would be computed on the basis of a 15-year period — that is, 20 years less the 5 years that can be dropped.

Retirement benefits under the act consist of a primary insurance amount that an individual is entitled to receive in his own behalf and auxiliary benefits that are paid to his eligible dependents. The *primary insurance amount* is based upon the individual's average monthly earnings and can be determined from a prepared benefit table. The largest amount that a retired person without dependents can receive is about $168, and the smallest amount is $44.

The *auxiliary benefits*, which are paid to eligible dependents of a retired worker, are based upon his primary insurance amount. Those dependents for whom auxiliary benefits may be claimed include the following:

1. Wife over 65 (or 62 at a reduced amount).
2. Wife caring for an unmarried child who is under 18 years of age or disabled.
3. Unmarried child who is under 18 or disabled.
4. Parent who is dependent upon covered individual for more than 50 percent of his support.
5. Unmarried children between the ages of 18 and 22 who are attending school.

The amount of benefits that an individual can draw for himself and his family is subject to a maximum limit equal to 80 percent of his average monthly earnings, or $368, whichever is the lesser. In no instance, however, can the total family benefits be less than $66 a month.

Disability Benefits

The Social Security program now provides benefit payments to workers who are too severely disabled to engage in gainful employment. In order to be eligible for such benefits, however, an individual's disability must have existed for at least 6 months and must be expected to continue for at least 12 months. Those eligible for disability benefits, furthermore, must have worked under Social Security for at least 5 out of the 10 years before becoming disabled. Disability benefits, which include auxiliary benefits for dependents, are computed on the same basis as retirement benefits and are converted to retirement benefits when the individual reaches the age of 65.

Survivors Benefits

Survivors benefits represent a form of life insurance that is paid to the family of a deceased person, providing it meets the requirements for eligibility. As in the case of life insurance the benefits that the survivors of a covered individual receive may be far in excess of their cost to this individual. Survivors of individuals who are currently insured as well as those who are fully insured at the time of death are eligible to receive certain benefits, provided the survivors meet other eligibility requirements. A *currently insured person* is one who has been covered during at least 6 out of the 13 quarters prior to his death. In the case of a currently insured person, the benefits are paid only to a widow or a dependent divorced wife with dependent children who are under 18 or are disabled, and these benefits cease when the youngest child reaches 18 or marries. The widow of a fully insured person is entitled to receive a monthly payment equal to 82½ percent of the primary insurance amount. An additional 75 percent is paid for each unmarried child of the deceased person who is under 18, who is under a disability that began before the child reached 18, or who is under 22 and a full-time student. The total family benefits for a widow and her dependent children, as in the case of those for a retired worker, may not exceed the lesser of 80 percent of the worker's average monthly earnings or $368.

The widow of a fully insured person whose survivor benefits have been terminated, if she meets certain conditions, can again start drawing Social Security benefits equal to 82⅓ percent of her husband's primary amount when she reaches the age of 62, or at a reduced amount at the age of 60. If they meet prescribed conditions, each of the dependent parents of a person who was fully insured at the time of his death may be able to qualify for a monthly benefit equal to 75 percent of the primary insurance amount earned by this deceased person upon reaching retirement age. If there is only one surviving parent, that parent may receive a benefit equal to 82½ percent of the primary insurance amount.

In event of the death of either a currently or fully insured person, the widow, widower, or, if none, the person paying the funeral expenses is entitled to receive a benefit equal to three times the primary insurance amount of the deceased. The amount, however, may not exceed $255 and must be applied for within two years after the death of the insured.[20]

Health Insurance or "Medicare"

Health insurance is the most recent addition to the Social Security Program. This insurance provides for *hospital insurance* and for *medical insurance* for persons over 65. Hospital insurance is financed by employer and employee contributions and covers most of the expenses of hospitalization for a period up to 90 days. It also covers a major portion of the cost for out-patient care, for post-hospital home care, or for nursing home care. The health insurance provisions of "Medicare" are provided to individuals who have been covered by the Social Security Program and, in addition, are available to those persons who have not been covered previously providing that they make application to the program. Starting in 1968, however, an individual must have at least six quarters of coverage to become eligible for hospital insurance, and the number of quarters required will increase progressively during each year thereafter. Medical insurance coverage requires the payment of a monthly fee of $3 by those who elect to be included. This coverage pays a major portion of the doctor's fees for medical services, including office calls, home visits, surgery, and various laboratory services.

Social Security Trends

Social Security is one government program that has the endorsement of both major political parties, and both parties have sought to gain additional support from their constituents by enacting amendments that have extended the act's coverage to additional people and increased the types and the amount of benefits covered by the program.

Unfortunately, the continued expansion of Social Security benefits also has necessitated further increases in the rate of tax required to support the program as well as increases in the maximum amount of income that is subject to the tax. The tax increases would have had to be even greater were it not for the fact that many persons continue working beyond retirement age and, therefore, do not become eligible for benefits. Also, many widows of deceased workers never draw survivors benefits because they continue to work or because they remarry.

---

[20]For further information on Social Security benefits, obtain a copy of "Your Social Security," Social Security Administration (OASI-35), latest edition.

It should be recognized, therefore, that the Social Security program is basically an insurance rather than a pension program. The tax that is collected to support the program is in effect a premium which the worker pays to cover a specific risk — namely, the loss of income for himself and / or his family due to unemployment, disability, retirement, or death. If the individual does not suffer a loss of income, he is in the same position with respect to collecting any return as the holder of a fire or accident insurance policy who does not suffer any losses.

Résumé

In recent years company personnel programs have given more recognition to the needs of employees relative to their retirement. Although primary attention has been directed toward meeting the financial needs of retiring employees, more attention also is being given to assisting these employees in coping with needs of a physical, psychological, and social nature. In spite of the trend for companies to broaden their retirement programs, however, pensions will continue to remain the most important part of these programs.

The administration of pension plans involves many problems not encountered in connection with other functions of personnel management because the obligations created by pensions are of a long-term nature and difficult to estimate with complete accuracy. As the size of the pensions and the life expectancy of those receiving them increase, the cost of a retirement program can place a severe drain upon the financial resources of a company and upon the amount of money that remains to support other functions of the personnel program. The retirement program, therefore, should render its appropriate contributions to the achievement of those objectives established for the personnel program as a whole. This criterion should be kept in mind when working out the technical details of a retirement program and when budgeting funds to support it; otherwise, it might be possible to utilize these funds to a better advantage in supporting other phases of the personnel program.

Since the lack of financial resources of most companies limits the pensions that they can afford to pay their employees to an amount that is considerably less than the wages previously received by the retired employees, such pensions are rarely sufficient to satisfy entirely their retirement needs. The retirement payments that are provided by the Social Security Act, therefore, serve as an important supplement to private pensions and as a vital source of income for those workers who do not receive any pension benefits from their former employers. Social Security retirement benefits are not now nor will they ever, in all probability, be sufficient by themselves to provide an adequate standard of living for retired individuals. It is important, therefore, that employees accumulate some financial reserves of their own to take care of their retirement needs. Some of the ways in which a company can assist its employees with this problem are covered in the discussion of financial services in the next chapter.

DISCUSSION QUESTIONS AND PROBLEMS

1. What are some of the adjustment problems that employees are likely to encounter upon their retirement? Can a company actually do much to help its employees resolve these problems?
2. What effect, if any, will retirement have upon the satisfaction of psychological needs listed in the chapter on motivation?
3. What factors may affect an individual's desire for retirement and his ability to adjust to it?
4. A primary desire of some people is to become financially independent at an early age in order that they may retire "before they are too old to enjoy retired life." Do you feel that this is a worthy or a realistic ambition?
5. How can a formal preretirement program contribute to the voluntary retirement of employees?
6. It has been argued by some that an employer who has compulsory retirement is actually being more arbitrary than he otherwise would be under a voluntary retirement policy. Do you agree with this view? Why or why not?
7. It has been stated by some that pensions merely constitute a reserve for human depreciation similar to that established for physical assets. Do you agree or disagree with this view?
8. Would it not be simpler and more desirable for a company to pay directly to each employee the money that it contributes toward his pension and let him accumulate his own retirement fund?
9. Distinguish between a currently insured worker and a fully insured worker in terms of requirements for coverage and benefits received.
10. Do you feel that it is fair or unfair for benefit payments under the Social Security Act to be reduced for those persons whose earnings exceed $1,500 a given year? Discuss.

CASE 23-1

PENSION PLAN PROBLEMS

The F. W. Matsu & Sons Nursery was founded by Fred Matsu with the help of his three sons in 1946. As the result of hard work on the part of the entire family and a favorable location in an expanding population area, the nursery proved to be a very successful business venture. By 1962 the number of persons employed by the nursery had grown to more than 100, and its gross sales had increased to well over a million dollars. Since Mr. Matsu by this time had reached retirement age, he decided to appoint his eldest son as the president of the organization and to assume the position of chairman of the board. While he continued to draw salary in his new position, he ceased to take an active part in the management of the business. Because he had worked hard all of his life, Mr. Matsu's retirement from this business forced him to undergo a significant personal readjustment. This experience caused him to become more aware of the personal problems that retirement would create for his employees particularly since they would not be in the same comfortable financial situation as he.

Because his nursery had enjoyed a good profit record and was forced to give a substantial portion of these profits to the government in the form of income taxes, Mr. Matsu reasoned that a pension plan could be established in the company without burdening it unduly from a financial standpoint. Mr. Matsu viewed a pension plan not only as a means of rewarding employees for their loyal service but also as a means of helping his sons to accumulate a financial nest egg for their retirement.

In order to gain information about the cost and the mechanics of a pension plan, Mr. Matsu called in his insurance broker for assistance. News of Mr. Matsu's interest in establishing a pension plan apparently reached persons outside of the company because it was not long before he was approached by various insurance brokers and mutual fund salesmen as well as by a representative from the bank where he had obtained his financing. Both the bank and the mutual fund representatives argued in favor of a trusteed type of pension plan as opposed to an insured plan on the grounds that the former type permitted the investment of pension funds in blue-chip stocks that could serve as a hedge against inflation. The bank representative, furthermore, stressed the fact that they had helped Mr. Matsu when he was in need of financial assistance; and, therefore, they felt it only fair for the bank to have this opportunity to administer the pension trust fund. After being subjected to a variety of types and sources of sales pressure, Mr. Matsu began to feel that it might be best if he gave up the idea of installing a pension plan.

    a. If you were in a position to advise Mr. Matsu, would you recommend that he should install a pension plan? How might he proceed?

    b. What problems does this case indicate which may be encountered by owners of small businesses in establishing a pension plan?

SUGGESTED READINGS

A Study of Industrial Retirement Plans, 1956 Edition. New York: Bankers Trust Company, 1956.

Buckley, Joseph C. *The Retirement Handbook: A Complete Planning Guide to Your Future.* New York: Harper & Bros., 1956.

Chruden, Herbert J., and Arthur W. Sherman, Jr. *Readings in Personnel Management,* Second Edition. Cincinnati: South-Western Publishing Company, Inc., 1966. Pp. 399–416.

Cochran, Howe P. *Scientific Employee Benefit Planning.* Boston: Little, Brown & Company, 1954.

Corporate Retirement Policy and Practice, Studies in Personnel Policy, No. 190. New York: National Industrial Conference Board, 1964.

Hall, Harold R. *Some Observations on Executive Retirement.* Cambridge: Harvard University, Graduate School of Business, Division of Business Research, 1953.

Hart, Gifford R. *Retirement: A New Outlook for the Individual.* New York: Harcourt, Brace & Co., 1957.

Kleemeir, Robert W. (ed.). *Aging and Leisure: A Research Perspective into the Meaningful Use of Time.* New York: Oxford University Press, Inc., 1961.

Mathiasen, Geneva. *Criteria for Retirement.* New York: G. P. Putnam's Sons, 1953.

——————————— (ed.). *Flexible Retirement.* New York: G. P. Putnam's Sons, 1957.

McGill, Dan M. *Fundamentals of Private Pensions.* Homewood, Illinois: Richard D. Irwin, Inc., 1955.

Pensions and Profit Sharing, Second Edition. Washington: The Bureau of National Affairs, Inc., 1956.

Problems of Retirement in Industry. Chicago: Chicago Heart Association, 1956.

U.S. Department of Health, Education, and Welfare. *Planning for the Later Years.* Washington, D.C.: U.S. Government Printing Office, 1965.

24

Fringe Benefits

Wages, it has been noted in earlier chapters, are not the only form of remuneration that an employee receives from his employer. As every employer well realizes, a significant portion of the total personnel costs are for items referred to as fringe benefits or "fringes." For the employee these benefits represent extra income, additional security, or more desirable working conditions that require no additional effort. Although the return from them may not be readily apparent to the employer, benefits often satisfy employee needs and wants that are not satisfied by wages and, thus, have considerable value in promoting employee morale. However, with the cost of fringe benefits continuing to increase from year to year, employers are becoming increasingly concerned over the extent of this cost. Fringe benefits, or supplementary nonwage payments, may range from 8 percent to over 70 percent of wages, depending upon the company and/or industry, with the average cost of fringe benefits now at one fourth the wages or payroll payments.[1] Even these figures do not include the costs of many of the services commonly furnished to employees which contribute to their welfare.

In view of the increasing costs of fringe benefits, which have been rising steadily since the 1920's, many employers are concerned not only about

---

[1]*Fringe Benefits, 1965* (Washington, D.C.: Chamber of Commerce of the United States of America), p. 6.

their cost but are questioning their value to the individuals and to the organization. Before unions achieved their present status, benefits were extended to employees largely as a result of management's desire to keep employees satisfied and to counteract the efforts of unions to organize their personnel. In recent years, however, most employee benefits have been initiated as a result of collective bargaining. In those companies that have not been unionized, many benefits have been installed in order to compete effectively for desirable employees. Similarly, benefits have been used to keep existing employees satisfied in their jobs and to forestall any organizing efforts of the unions. Fringe benefits, therefore, have become common supplements to wages but may or may not have the incentive value of wages. Because of their importance to employers, to employees, and to society, fringe benefits are considered in detail. The main topics discussed in this chapter are:

- Trends in fringe benefits.
- Building an effective benefits program.
- Types of fringe benefits provided to employees.

Trends in Fringe Benefits

The emphasis on fringe benefits, reflected by the amount of money spent to provide them, has been growing steadily over the past several decades to the present and is reflected in many different types of benefits. The number and variety of fringe items today is substantial. In fact one authority lists over 100 separate benefit items under five major categories: extra payments for time worked, payments for time not worked, payments for employee security, payments for employee services, and payments for nonproduction awards and bonuses.[2] Not all of the items are found in any one company, but each company has its own "fringe package" which often has grown in a piecemeal fashion over the years.

History of Fringe Benefits

While the major increase in fringe benefits has occurred since the middle 1940's, there were fringe benefits prior to that time. Many employers, as early as the 1920's, recognized the fact that their employees were entitled to have a desirable place in which to work as well as some degree of security in their employment and, thus, provided various types

---

[2]David W. Belcher, *Wage and Salary Administration* (Second Edition; Englewood Cliffs, New Jersey: Prentice-Hall, Inc., 1962), pp. 489–490.

of fringe benefits on a more or less informal basis. In many instances this action was undoubtedly motivated by a sincere belief by employers that employees were entitled to more of the benefits of capitalism than was represented by their wages. Other employers were motivated by a belief that employees, because of their lesser economic and educational status, lacked the ability to manage their own personal affairs and needed someone to "look after" them. This latter type of employer, frequently referred to as a paternalistic one, gave assurances to his subordinates that he would care for them in time of need or emergency and that they should feel secure in his domain. This paternalistic approach was not entirely unsuccessful, but with the growth of unions during the 1930's and 1940's and the increasing education and employment opportunities, employees soon recognized that their contributions to the employer and to society were worthy of reward and should not be left to the initiative of a benevolent employer. Union leaders, in their desire to obtain better working conditions for their members and to attract new members, pushed for additional fringe benefits at a time when employers were already attempting to use benefits to "keep employees in the fold" and dissuade them from the advances of the union. As a result employees were assured of receiving benefits either through the employer's initiative, the union's initiative, or both. Fringe benefits were at this stage in their history at the end of the 1930's.

Influence of World War II. One of the most important factors in the more recent development of employee benefits was the concern over inflation and the imposing of a ceiling on wages by the federal government during World War II. Under regulations that were established, employers could not increase wages and, therefore, did not have the customary bargaining power with which to attract new employees who were badly needed to replace those individuals who were called into the Armed Forces. The only way to overcome the restriction on wages was for a company to provide special inducements in the form of nonwage supplements, such as pension and welfare programs, paid vacations, sick leave, and health and life insurance. Although these benefits helped the employer to obtain needed personnel during the war, most employers found themselves obligated to continue the benefits after the war because employees and their unions were unwilling to give them up. The continued competition among companies for competent employees during the postwar period was also an important factor in their retention.

Post World War II Period. Following the removal of the wage freeze after World War II, union leaders concentrated their efforts on obtaining wage increases which they felt were long overdue. The inflationary results of World War II were apparent to everyone, and the unions were able to make an effective case for increasing wages in order that their members could maintain a satisfactory standard of living. As the costs of living began to level off about 1948, the unions' arguments for increased wages became less significant since the public began to look with disfavor upon continuing rounds of wage and accompanying price increases. It was generally accepted by the public, however, that employees should have better standards of health and welfare in their employment than they were receiving. Thus, fringe benefits became a bargaining issue that the unions could pursue realistically. Interpretations by the National Labor Relations Board and the Supreme Court to the effect that employers were obligated to bargain for pensions were also major factors that stimulated the spread of this type of fringe. In addition to these various influences that have been discussed, it should be recognized that the growth of fringe benefits has occurred at a period in the economic history of our country when profits have been high with the result that management has been under greater obligation to make available to employees benefits that would have been considered impossible "frills" during a time of economic recession or depression. During periods of high profits companies tend to be more reluctant to resist strike action by unions in support of their demands for greater fringe benefits. While profits have been high, the costs of fringe benefits have likewise risen.

Cost of Fringe Benefits

According to one Chamber of Commerce study (1965) with 1,181 reporting companies, payments for fringe benefits averaged 24.7% of the payroll. The percentage shown after each one of the five categories of benefits listed below represents a breakdown of the 24.7%.

1. Payments for time not worked, including paid vacations and bonuses in lieu of vacation, payments for holidays not worked, paid sick leave, and payments for State or National Guard duty, jury, witness and voting pay allowances, payments for time lost due to death in family or other personal reasons, etc. . . . . 7.7%.

2. Pension and other agreed-upon payments, including pension-plan premiums and payments not covered by insurance-type plan, life insurance premiums, death benefits, sickness, accident, and medical-care insurance premiums, hospitalization insurance, etc., separation or termination pay allowances, discounts on goods and services purchased from company by employees, free meals . . . (Employer's Share) . . . 7.7%.

3. Legally required benefits, including old-age and survivors insurance, unemployment compensation, workmen's compensation, railroad retirement tax, railroad unemployment insurance, state sickness benefits insurance, etc. . . . (Employer's Share) . . . 4.9%.
4. Paid rest periods, lunch periods, wash-up time, travel time, clothes-change time, get-ready time, etc. . . . 2.5%.
5. Profit-sharing payments, Christmas or other special bonuses, service awards, suggestion awards, etc., and special wage payments ordered by courts, payments to union stewards, tuition refunds, etc. . . . 1.9%.[3]

The average cost of these benefits was $1,502 a year per employee in the companies reporting in this study and $1,874 a year in 84 of the companies that have participated in similar studies over a period of years.

A comparison of the 1965 figures with the findings from earlier studies conducted in 1947 and biannually thereafter reveals some interesting changes. Over the 18-year period, the pension and other agreed-upon payments and payments for time not worked increased steadily largely as a result of collective bargaining. Translated into dollar costs, fringe benefits averaged $450 in 1947 to $1,004 in 1955 and to $1,874 in 1965, a rise of 316 percent in 18 years. Such increases in dollar costs, when translated into percent of payroll as shown in Figure 24-1, are from 16.1 percent to 28.1 percent.[4] This increase is sufficient to point out the importance of insuring that a fringe benefits program is making a maximal contribution to the total personnel program of a company.

Building an Effective Benefits Program

The fringe benefits provided by a company are not likely to be appreciated fully by the employees or to yield the maximum benefits to the employer unless considerable care has been given to the development of the program. Too often a fringe benefit is provided because "everyone else is doing it," because it is a whim of top management, or because of pressure from the union. The type of contribution that fringe benefits will make to the personnel program will depend upon the extent to which attention is given to certain basic principles that are discussed in this section.

Objectives

A fringe benefit program, like any other phase of the personnel program, should be carefully planned and objectives established for use as

[3]*Fringe Benefits*, 1965, *op. cit.*, p. 9.
[4]*Ibid.*, p. 27.

Figure 24-1

COMPARISON OF 1947–1965 FRINGE PAYMENTS FOR
84 IDENTICAL COMPANIES

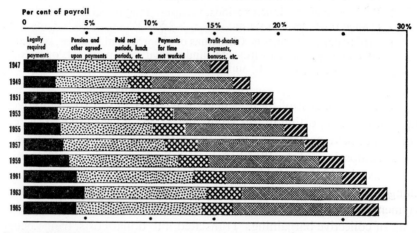

Source: *Fringe Benefits, 1965*, p. 28. Reproduced with permission of the Chamber of Commerce of the United States.

guidelines in the management of the program. All too often the fringe benefits or nonwage supplements paid for by many companies represent a "package" of miscellaneous benefits that were added at different times in the company's history as a result of different influences. Because of the different nature of the influences — some from within the company but probably more from outside — the package may bear little or no relation to what management feels is consistent with its overall objectives. It has been suggested that management give greater attention to determining the optimum combination of fringe benefits for its company that will maximize employee satisfaction and assure efficient production and thus serve as a standard against which to assess proposed additions and/or changes to the package. In determining the optimum fringe combination, Foegen suggests the following steps:

1. Assemble basic cost data of all of the fringe items.
2. Make a judgment as to how much money is available to cover the cost of all fringe benefits for a given future period.
3. Assign preference values to each fringe item, using some type of weighted numerical scale which takes into account the legal requirements, employee preference, and management preference.
4. Decide on the optimum combination of the various benefits. The person making the decision would carefully consider the various

fringe items possible, the relative preference shown for each by management and employees, the estimated cost of each, and the total amount of money available for the whole fringe package.[5]

It is suggested that such an approach to fringe benefits is not meant to be antiunion in any sense of the term, for if management takes "a logical, objective, planned, integrated attitude toward the fringe package, rather than the haphazard uncoordinated, passive one that has unfortunately been too often the case up till now, the long-run and even short-run welfare of both workers and company will be improved."[6] With a successful program, the company is in a better position to evaluate more carefully and intelligently union demands that often are made on the basis of collective bargaining trends rather than on the careful evaluation of a particular company's personnel program. Thus, by having a policy for its benefits program, the company is more likely to achieve goals that are in harmony with its overall personnel policies.

Many companies are adopting the principle of establishing objectives for its benefits program based on a social responsibility that in part, at least, is pragmatically motivated. In discussing employee benefits, Mr. William Vaughn, president of Eastman Kodak said:

> No one can prove it, but I venture to say that the intangible and incalculable rewards go a long way to offset the cost of the over-all benefit program. . . . The sense of job and income security means that an employee can concentrate attention on his job . . .
>
> Is it better to wage a tactical retreat, not conceding any new or improved benefit until the pressure for it becomes irresistible? Or is it better to exercise one's freedom of choice and planning, and treat responsibility more as an opportunity to be taken at the appropriate time, in the forward conduct of the business?[7]

Eastman Kodak's worldwide renown for enlightened relations with its people is sufficient answer, according to Wilson.

Employee Participation

One of the prime requisites of a successful benefits program is that it receive the support of employees. This support can best be achieved when employees are able to recognize management's willingness to be of assistance as a result of effective communication that encourages employees to express their desires. As noted above, before a new benefit is introduced,

---

[5]Joseph H. Foegen, "Product Mix for Fringe Benefits," *Harvard Business Review*, Vol. 39, No. 4 (July–August, 1961), pp. 64–68.

[6]*Ibid.*, p. 68.

[7]Joseph C. Wilson, "Social Responsibility of the Businessman," *Personnel*, Vol. 43, No. 1 (January–February, 1966), pp. 17–25.

the need for it should first be determined through some type of survey of the employees. Many companies establish committees composed of representatives of management and the employees that study needs and make recommendations concerning the benefits and services which are desired. The fact that employees are represented in making such recommendations not only helps to insure that management is moving in the direction that will satisfy employee wants but provides a basis for discussing some of the day-to-day personnel problems that are often associated with fringe benefits and of developing plans for minimizing their effects.

Two common fringe benefits, sick leave and the coffee break, are recognized as having considerable value to the employee's physical and mental health. However, most employers have experienced difficulty in controlling the misuse of these benefits and often find it necessary to appeal to the employees for cooperation and even to take disciplinary action against offenders. The major problem of sick leave is that employees feel that it is an entitlement, like a vacation with pay, which they have earned and therefore can use at their discretion. The fact that they are required to certify that they were ill when they were in fact able to come to work does not deter some employees from "using up" their sick leave. Controlling such misuse of sick leave is extremely difficult. However, frank discussion of the problem in shop committees and by supervisors in group and individual conferences with employees is often of some value.

The coffee break, like sick leave with pay, has become an "institution" in American enterprises, and employee rights in this matter are often jealously guarded. Such breaks in the work period tend to reduce psychological fatigue and probably help to increase efficiency in most cases. Problems, however, are encountered frequently in connection with the coffee break. Employees often overstay their allotted time and need to be reminded of their responsibilities. Others find the mid-morning break a convenient time for breakfast with the result that they may lack the required energy until after the break period. In spite of such difficulties, these and similar benefits will probably continue as accepted features of the personnel program, and supervisors will continue to find it necessary to remind employees of the rules governing the enjoyment of benefits. The use of the group decision approach, discussed in Chapter 14, has been used effectively in building group pressure for the enforcement of such rules, thus illustrating the values of employee participation in the solution of employee problems.

Control of Costs

One of the major problems confronting most companies is the increasing cost of providing fringe benefits. Since many of the fringe items represent a fixed rather than a variable cost, a company must decide whether or not it can meet the fixed costs under less desirable economic conditions. It is generally recognized that if a company is forced to discontinue a fringe benefit the negative effect may exceed any positive benefits that may have accrued from providing it.

In addition to the actual costs of fringe benefits are the costs of administering the program. For the larger company the overhead costs may be negligible. However, in the smaller company the personnel costs of managing the fringe benefits program may be sizable in proportion to the number of employees served. It has been suggested that this situation points up an apparent need for fringe benefit consultants who would establish and assist in administering such programs in small business firms.[8]

As a matter of sound administration as well as for collective bargaining purposes, it is important for a company to maintain complete records of its costs for fringe benefits. Such costs should be communicated to employees in order that they may understand that the paycheck tells only part of the wage story. One approach to employee education on fringe benefits is to speak of fringe expenditures in terms of additional employee "earnings" or "payments."

Another approach takes the form of statements such as, "This is what the company spends on each of you" or, "This is what it costs the company to provide these benefits." Sometimes this approach includes a statement similar to the following:

> The company, however, does not "give" its employees these things. No company can afford to give them, any more than it could afford to give away its products. Those who work for the company are entitled to them because they earn them. These job advantages, like the job itself, can be provided only by a sound business that is earning money. They are made possible by quality production, efficient operation, and hard selling — three things which can be achieved only through the combined efforts of all of us.[9]

Above all, in communicating with employees about fringe benefits, the information about complicated welfare and pension plans should be made crystal clear to the employees so that there will be no misunderstanding as

---

[8]John D. and Marjorie T. Stanley, "Fringe Benefit Policy: Orientation and Objectives," *Personnel Administration*, Vol. 25, No. 3 (May–June, 1962), pp. 19–28.

[9]*Computing the Cost of Fringe Benefits*, Studies in Personnel Policy, No. 128 (New York: National Industrial Conference Board, 1952), p. 5.

to what the plans will not provide as well as what they provide. Since employees are not usually skilled in technical or legalistic language, care must be taken to present the information in an understandable manner, using various media on a continuous basis.[10]

Problem Areas

It is generally assumed that fringe benefits contribute to higher morale among employees and thus are worth the cost. With the continuing pressure from the unions for additional fringe benefits, however, some companies have begun to question their value and scrutinize each fringe item with care. Employees have also questioned the value of some of the benefits, and they may actually prefer to have higher wages instead of the fringes. Under most conditions the individual employee is forced to take the whole fringe package whether or not it meets his individual needs.[11] He may prefer a wage increase to insurance, or he may prefer additional days of vacation with pay to having long lunch periods or supplemental unemployment benefits. In addition to restricting the individual's freedom of choice, there are also other problems that arise in connection with fringe benefit programs.

Continued demands for additional benefits. What may be considered a luxury at one time may be viewed later as a necessity. This has been true particularly of many employee benefits. Not too long ago vacations with pay were limited almost exclusively to executives and white-collar personnel. This situation no longer exists. Similarly, employer contributions to welfare funds to provide financial security for technologically displaced and for retired workers have become bargaining issues in recent years. Although it is difficult to predict what the future will hold as far as benefits and services are concerned, it may be assumed that employees, through their union representatives, will continue to ask for more fringe benefits. As soon as patterns are set in one industry and/or company, they tend to spread to other industries and/or companies with the result that a company often experiences considerable difficulty in maintaining its own planned program. With established policies, however, a company can resist some of the pressures for conformity that it encounters.

---

[10]Howard L. Peck, "Telling the Benefit Story," *Management of Personnel Quarterly*, Vol. 2, No. 1 (Spring, 1963).

[11]For an interesting article relating fringe benefits to psychological needs, see John Metzler, "Are Fringe Benefits An Answer?" *Personnel Administration*, Vol. 29, No. 4 (July–August, 1966), pp. 41–44.

New sources of grievances. As additional fringe benefits and services accrue to the employee as a result of bargaining, new potential problem areas are introduced. The cafeteria is a common target for complaints, some of which are perhaps justified. Health services are likewise criticized at times by employees who feel that they should receive better attention from the physicians and nurses. In fact, any of the benefits and services that are provided may become the subject of criticism and formal grievance action.

Charges of paternalism. In its desire to let employees know what the company is doing for their welfare, management may create the impression of being paternalistic. Benefits that are interpreted by employees as constituting gifts from a beneficient employer are seldom received enthusiastically by these employees. Most employees feel that they have earned these benefits and services and that they are rightfully entitled to them regardless of how the employer feels about the matter. This does not mean that employees do not appreciate benefits and services but, rather, that they prefer to feel that they have earned or are entitled to them. Mere existence of these programs, however, will not guarantee their effectiveness. "But when built upon a pattern of management attitudes and behavior which reflects a sincere appreciation of all the basic human needs of workers, these tangible benefits become convincing evidence that management recognizes workers as self-respecting individuals all of whom have the normal human desire to lead a happy, worthwhile, and productive existence."[12]

Some larger problems. While every employer is concerned with immediate problems, there are some far-reaching problems arising out of fringe benefits that sooner or later affect not only the employer but society as a whole. One of the most important and obvious problems is the effect that fringe benefits have on inflation. If the costs of fringe benefits can be paid from profits or from increased productivity, there would be no problem; but often the costs must be passed on to the consumer in the form of higher prices. The consumer, in turn, to meet the price must eventually demand a higher wage. With fringes becoming an increasingly greater percentage of payroll, they may be more important than wages. Since fringes tend to be paid across the board, the higher they become in relation to wages the more they will tend to negate the values of the objective standards of job evaluation. There is also the problem of increased benefits in

---

[12]Robert Saltonstall, "What Employees Want from Their Work," *Harvard Business Review*, Vol. 31, No. 6 (November–December, 1953), pp. 72–78.

such areas as unemployment compensation. With supplementary unemployment benefits some workers can now collect 65 percent of their previous take-home pay. As unemployment benefits increase, and it is predicted they will, and as they approximate normal wages, there is the possibility, as noted in Chapter 11, that people will prefer not to work especially in jobs or under conditions where it is difficult to obtain need satisfaction. Finally, as fringe benefits increase there is the tendency to freeze employees in their jobs since the benefits would be lost to them if they were to change employment. This tendency to freeze labor mobility may, in the long run, be detrimental to the economy.[13]

Neglect of other personnel functions. With increasing attention being given to fringes by the unions, there is always the possibility that executives and personnel managers will focus their attention on them and neglect other phases of the personnel program that may be more important. Similarly, overemphasis on fringe benefits may result in employees being more concerned about their security for the future than they are in "turning out a day's work." The many cartoons and jokes about the job applicant barely out of high school or college who wants a detailed description of a company's retirement program and other fringe benefits reflect the importance attached to job security and other fringes. Employers recognize the interest in fringes and induce applicants by emphasizing them in employment advertisements.

Types of Fringe Benefits Provided to Employees

Some of the benefits provided employees are discussed in other chapters. Unemployment compensation, for example, was considered in Chapter 11, retirement programs were examined in Chapter 23, and workmen's compensation for job-incurred illness or injury is discussed in Chapter 25. In addition to these benefits there are others that employers frequently provide to employees. Like any fringe benefit they represent a cost to the employer and an economic gain to the employees, since they would normally spend part of their wages in payment of these services if obtained from sources outside of the company.

---

[13]For a detailed discussion of the problems associated with fringe benefits, see J. H. Foegen, "Re-examining Fringe Benefits — 1. Fringe Detriments," *Personnel Administration*, Vol. 25, No. 3 (May–June, 1962), pp. 13–18.

Financial Services

Certain types of services made available by employers are concerned directly with the employee's personal finances. These services are designed to encourage thrift and to provide funds when needed at reasonable rates of interest. A common type of thrift plan is one whereby the employee can purchase stock in the company through a purchase plan such as that described in Chapter 22. Some companies also have plans whereby, instead of subscribing for a definite number of shares at a certain price to be paid for within a specified time, the employee builds up a fund through regular payroll deductions. The company either adds its own contribution to the employee's fund and buys the stock for him or gives him the stock as a bonus on his savings. The employee thus takes no risk of losing any money under this plan.[14] Much more common is the almost universally available thrift plan that is sponsored by the United States Treasury Department. Most employers cooperate in this plan by providing for payroll deductions for the purchase of United States Savings Bonds.

Credit unions. Credit unions have been established in many companies to serve the financial needs of the employees. The credit union encourages thrift by offering interest or dividends on deposits (usually in the form of $5 shares) at a higher rate of interest than that paid by most commercial banks. It also serves as a lending institution from which the employee may borrow money at a rate of interest usually not exceeding 1 percent a month on the unpaid balance of the loan. While employers often provide office space and a payroll deduction service, the credit union is an activity operated by employees under federal and state legislation and supervision. Its existence provides additional security to the employees of the company without management becoming involved in such detailed matters as approving or disapproving loans and enforcing payments on loans, which would not only be time-consuming but often embarrassing.

Company financial assistance. While the credit unions are lending institutions and in most instances are able to help an employee who needs financial assistance, there are occasional instances in which companies assist employees by granting loans at a low rate of interest or interest free. Some companies make loans to assist in the purchase of homes and provide other financial assistance that will contribute to employee welfare and morale. Those employees who wish to pursue an educational program

---

[14]*Employee Savings and Investment Plans,* Studies in Personnel Policy, No. 133 (New York: National Industrial Conference Board, 1957).

at a nearby school or college or by correspondence often can have all or part of the cost reimbursed by the employer. It is common, however, to require that the employee obtain approval to take the course and that he complete it successfully in order to be eligible for reimbursement of costs of tuition, books, etc.

With the national and international expansion of many companies and the requirement that personnel be moved from one location to another, much like that experienced by personnel in the Armed Forces, most of the larger companies have a planned program for paying the costs incurred in moving an employee, his family, and their household furnishings. Some companies will even pay the costs of transporting a horse or a goat if the employee happens to have one.

Insurance Programs

One of the oldest and most popular employee benefits is the group life insurance program. In 1961 approximately 90 percent of production and clerical employees in metropolitan areas were covered by group life insurance, and 81 percent of the average number of people employed in non-agricultural establishments were also covered. As a rule, the amount of life insurance coverage for an individual employee depends solely on his salary level; however, in manufacturing industries there are many plans which provide the same amount of insurance regardless of salary. The trend continues toward union-negotiated, company-financed plans; however, in some companies employees still pay the cost or it is shared by the employees and the employer. The most common types of group insurance for employees provide death benefits, and many include accidental death and dismemberment benefits.

Group medical, surgical, and dental plans and prepaid drug programs are also popular services provided by the employer through a master or group policy written by an insurance company, by an association such as the Blue Cross or Blue Shield, or through some type of organized group medical practice such as the Kaiser Foundation Health Plan. In 1962, for example, out of the 141.4 million Americans with health insurance policies, 110.7 million were covered by employee health benefit plans. About one third of all employee health benefit plans are negotiated plans. As a major buyer of health and welfare benefits, organized labor is in a position to exercise its purchasing power so as to effect important innovations in the financing and organization of medical care services. AFL-CIO leaders (and other labor officials) advocate further group-practice experimentation in the medical field, as contrasted with private practice, and more adequate prepaid protection.[15]

Professional Services

Many companies make the services of professional persons on its staff available to employees at no expense. Attorneys and accountants, employed in most of the larger companies, possess knowledge and skills that can be used to the advantage of employees. An attorney can contribute immeasurably to employee effectiveness by providing help in drawing up a will, giving advice on contracts, and assisting employees in locating qualified personnel to handle complicated legal cases. Similarly, the talents of an accountant can be made available, at least on a limited basis, to employees who need assistance in completing tax returns or who have minor problems in connection with the returns. The services of employee counselors, discussed in Chapter 16, and those of medical personnel, discussed in Chapter 25, likewise contribute to employee welfare and morale.

Recreational Services

The fact that many companies have a recreational program is some indication of the general desirability and need for it. The extent of the program, however, and the specific types of recreation should be determined largely by the expressed desires of the employees. Management should not plan an elaborate recreational program only to find that the recreational needs of employees are being met in other ways. Once the employees have indicated their interests in specific types of recreation, management should provide encouragement and assistance in working out the details. Wherever possible management should, however, let employees assume most of the responsibility for planning the program through committees and other forms of employee representation.

Athletic programs. Most companies offer some type of sports program in which personnel may participate on a voluntary basis. Bowling, handball, volleyball, golf, baseball, and tennis are quite common because a large number of employees may engage in these activities on an intramural basis. In addition to the intramural program, many companies have teams that represent them in athletic contests with other local companies and organizations. Employee participation in these contests has many desirable aspects. Management, however, should make every effort to insure

---

[15]John H. Simons, "The Union Approach to Health and Welfare," *Industrial Relations*, Vol. 4, No. 3 (May, 1965), pp. 61–76.

that an employee's worth to the company is not dependent upon his athletic prowess, a situation that is suggested in Figure 24-2.

Figure 24-2

"You're not being fired because of your work here . . . it's just that you haven't been holding up your end of the company bowling team!"

Source: *The Foreman's Letter*, January 27, 1958. Reproduced with permission of The National Foreman's Institute.

Social functions. While sports normally are provided only for employees, many social functions are for employees and their spouses or entire families. The company picnic is a typical institution among business firms that may be attended by personnel at all levels in the organization and their families. Dances, banquets, cocktail hours, stags, and other social events also provide an opportunity for everyone to get better acquainted and to strengthen interpersonal relationships. It is desirable that employees have a major part in the planning of such events if they are to be successful. Before planning such events, consideration should be given to some of the potential problems that may arise out of the behavior of some of the participants. Figure 24-3 illustrates one of the types of problems that may arise.

Other recreational activities. The importance of having a change of pace during the working day has been recognized by several companies that have provided a recreational program during the lunch hour. The Chrysler Corporation and North American Aviation are among those companies that have sports areas near to where the men normally eat their lunches. Some companies also provide movies as a noon-hour relaxer while others have hobby clubs which can make the lunch hour more interesting to many employees. It should be recognized, however, that employees may prefer a shorter lunch period in order to leave earlier at the end of the work shift. Management would, therefore, be wise to determine the desires of employees prior to establishing an elaborate lunch-hour program or any other type of recreational program.

Other Services

In addition to those services described above, other services have become popular with employees and serve to meet their needs. The services discussed in this section are merely typical of those provided and do not constitute an exhaustive list.

Purchasing assistance. Various methods may be used by the company to assist employees in purchasing merchandise more conveniently and at a savings. One type of enter-

Figure 24-3

"I didn't know you were such a close friend of the boss — calling him 'Old Baldy' all during the office party!"

Source: Publishers Newspaper Syndicate. Reproduced with permission.

prise is known as the "company store" or commissary and in its present form represents a real service to the employee, especially in remote areas where the community or a substantial part of it is owned by the company. In the past the company store often meant continuous indebtedness and overcharging of employees, but legislation, union pressure, and enlightened management have for the most part eliminated the undesirable aspects. Many companies also sell their own products at a discount to the employees, and in some instances certain items of other manufacturers are procured through the purchasing department for the employee at a discount if objections from local retailers are not too great.

Housing and transportation. A variety of housing services are offered to employees. At one extreme is the company town that for the most part is owned by the company and from which the employees rent apartments or homes. In other company towns most of the homes are owned by employees. An example of the latter is Midland, Michigan. The Dow

Chemical and Dow Corning companies have literally built the town (population 28,000), but 86 percent of the houses are owned by employees.[16] Since most companies have offices and plants located in established cities and towns, the most common type of housing assistance offered is advisory in nature and is usually restricted to maintaining listings of available housing or establishing connections with local real-estate agents and brokers who can be of assistance to the new employee. The same type of service is usually provided for employees who desire assistance in obtaining transportation to and from work. Share-the-ride listings are usually provided on bulletin boards in order that employees can make their own arrangements for car pools, which not only help the employees and their families but reduce the parking facilities that the company must provide.

Food service. Employee morale, health, production, and attendance are improved by a well-managed food service. A variety of facilities may be furnished, including a cafeteria, restaurant, snack bar, and food and beverage vending machines. The types of facilities provided will depend largely upon the location of the plant or office in relation to commercial restaurants, the size of the work force, and similar factors. Food service that is provided by the company or caterers saves time and eliminates the need for the employee leaving the company premises. Furthermore, the environmental conditions under which employees eat are usually made quite pleasant as well as sanitary.

The services described here are merely typical of those provided in most companies. There are many others that could be mentioned, some of which are peculiar to a particular company. Regardless of the company, employee benefits and services are most welcome and do the most effective job where they are established as a result of employee participation rather than presented as a "gift" from management.

Résumé

In recent years employees have learned to expect a variety of fringe benefits that are supplements to their regular wages. These benefits that now cost employers, and ultimately the consumers, billions of dollars a year represent a sizable portion of the wage costs in American industry. While benefits were originally initiated by management, they have more recently become bargaining demands of the unions. As a result, companies have

---

[16]*Time*, April 16, 1956, pp. 100–101.

often been forced to add benefits and services that may or may not yield an appreciable return to the company in terms of employee morale and efficiency.

Management should take positive steps to develop programs of fringe benefits, in cooperation with the unions, that will satisfy the needs of the majority of employees. Management should also attempt to hold the line against union demands for benefits that will not contribute to the company. Unless this is done, the benefit program will not achieve the desired objectives of improving the health, satisfaction, and security of employees and of providing management with an efficient and stable work force.

DISCUSSION QUESTIONS AND PROBLEMS

1. Many companies are concerned about the rising cost of fringe benefits and question their value to the company and to the employees.
   a. In your opinion what fringe benefits are of greatest value to employees? To the company? Why?
   b. What can management do to increase the value of fringe benefits to the company?
   c. How do fringe benefits in other companies affect a company's fringe benefit program?

2. What is meant by paternalism? Is it good or bad for management to be concerned about the welfare of its employees? Discuss.

3. The vice-president of a New York cosmetics firm said that he considered it a "terrible waste" to give factory employees Christmas bonuses.
   a. Do you agree with him? Why?
   b. Would you agree with him if his statement referred to management personnel? Why?

4. Sometimes at company picnics, and similar "short-sleeved" events, a few employees are likely to lose their inhibitions temporarily and express their opinions and feelings quite freely to management personnel.
   a. What advantages are there in such types of events? What disadvantages?
   b. Should executives fraternize with employees? What types of events are least likely to result in incidents that would be embarrassing to executives and employees?

5. Employees often fail to consider fringe benefits when wages are discussed and compared with those of persons doing similar work in a different company. What should a company do to make employees aware of the financial value of fringe benefits to them?

6. Fringe benefits were found to cost over $1,874 a year per employee in 84 United States companies surveyed by the Chamber of Commerce. What would you think of a plan that called for removing all fringes, except those

required by law, and giving the employees this amount in cash as part of wages? Discuss the advantages and disadvantages of such a plan.

7. Credit unions have had a remarkable growth in the United States. Find out as much as you can about their practices.
   a. How are deposits ordinarily made?
   b. How do their interest rates on deposits and on loans compare with banks and finance companies?
   c. What are their advantages to the employee? To the company?

8. Abuse of sick leave is so common that many companies question its value and resent its costs.
   a. What can management do to reduce its abuse under most sick leave plans?
   b. Would it be appropriate for a company to send a visiting nurse to the employee's home?
   c. Can you suggest a plan that would provide security for employees but would discourage them from using sick leave when they were not ill?

9. It has been found that work groups with the greatest employee participation in the company athletic program often have poor production records. How do you account for this? Does this mean that company athletic programs should be discontinued?

10. Employees in some instances may feel that management makes a profit on vending machines, cafeteria meals, and similar items that are sold on company premises. What action should management take to avoid such charges by employees?

CASE 24-1

THE SHORT FRIDAY

Friday, December 22nd, started like any other day at the Meyer's Meat Products Company. Since it was the last working day before Christmas, spirits were high among employees in the plant; and as the morning progressed these spirits soared still higher, with the aid of flasks that appeared from pockets and lunch boxes. After a while, individuals were forced to decide between whether they should try to maintain their capacity to work or the goodwill of those co-workers who insisted upon sharing their bottled cheer with all persons whom they contacted. In most instances, the urge to foster goodwill was stronger than the urge to continue working. The rapid developments within the plant caught the production supervisor somewhat off-guard; and as employees became more unruly, he grew more hesitant as to what action he should take for fear of what they might do to him. Finally, he decided to consult with Mr. Shultz, the general manager and one of the company owners, about the problem that was developing. As the two entered the plant area they were just in time to witness one of the workers being thrown, clothes and all, into the curing vat that was used in the processing of hams. The soggy appearance of the pair who were administering the dunking indicated that they had previously been accorded similar treatment.

The arrival of Mr. Shultz, with an enraged look on his face, helped to quiet conditions momentarily. Partly because he feared his rising blood pressure and partly because he feared that he, too, might get dunked in the pickling vat, Shultz managed to keep his temper under control. His only reaction was to order the workers to clean up their work places and leave the company premises immediately. While it had been customary to shut down the plant early on the last workday before Christmas, the 10:30 a.m. shutdown on the 22nd of December constituted a new record for the company.

   a. In order to avoid a repetition of the situation that developed at this plant, what preventive action should Mr. Shultz take in future years?

   b. Should disciplinary action be taken against those who brought liquor into the plant?

   c. What are the inherent dangers of permitting celebrations such as this to occur on company premises?

CASE 24-2

BEREAVEMENT LEAVE

It was the policy of the Acme Refining Company to give employees up to three days of compensation for the time that they were absent from work when a death occurred within their immediate family. Early one Thursday Ed Williams notified his supervisor that his grandfather had died in Centerville about 200 miles away and that he wanted to have the remainder of the week off in order to drive there and help with the necessary arrangements. The supervisor gave his approval, and Williams left immediately for Centerville. When the leave form covering the compensation for the two-day period of absence reached the personnel director for approval, however, he reduced the amount of allowable compensation for the absence to one day. He cited as reason for his decision the fact that one day constituted adequate time for Williams to reach Centerville and to attend a Saturday funeral. As additional support for his decision, the personnel director also pointed out that the term "immediate family" included only the parents and children of an employee and not grandparents, aunts, uncles, and other relatives of similar remoteness.

   a. What bearing does this problem have upon the enforcement of personnel policies and procedures and upon line-and-staff relationships?

   b. How much time off with pay, if any, should a company allow employees to take for attending funerals? What limits, if any, should it establish in granting time off?

SUGGESTED READINGS

Allen, Donna. *Fringe Benefits: Wages or Social Obligations?* Ithaca: New York State School of Industrial and Labor Relations, Cornell University, 1964.

Chruden, Herbert J., and Arthur W. Sherman, Jr. *Readings in Personnel Management*, Second Edition. Cincinnati: South-Western Publishing Company, Inc., 1966. Chapter 6.

Forde, Lois E. *Employee Savings and Investment Plans*, Studies in Personnel Policy, No. 133. New York: National Industrial Conference Board, 1957.

Fringe Benefits, 1965. Washington, D.C.: Chamber of Commerce of the United States, 1966.

Meyer, Mitchell, and Michael E. Edmonds. *Time Off with Pay*, Studies in Personnel Policy, No. 196. New York: National Industrial Conference Board, 1965.

Wistert, F. M. *Fringe Benefits*. New York: Reinhold Publishing Co., 1959.

25

Health and Safety*

In modern society an employer is expected to provide working conditions that are conducive to the physical welfare of his employees, and to a certain degree he is required to do so by law. It does not necessarily follow, however, that employee health and safety automatically result from the creation of desirable physical conditions at work. While physical environment is certainly an important factor, the maintenance of high standards of health and safety is even more dependent upon the attitudes and behavior of the personnel. In selecting personnel an attempt should be made to hire only those individuals who will be able to meet the health and safety requirements of the job. Once employees are hired, it is desirable to provide them with the necessary training in safe work procedures and to encourage them to adhere to the prescribed rules. Unless managers and supervisors view health and safety as important personnel functions, the most expensive and elaborate equipment that may be designed to protect employees will not prove to be very valuable.

While there are laws to protect the employee's physical welfare, most managers are motivated to provide desirable physical conditions at work by virtue of their sensitivity to human needs and rights. The more cost-oriented manager, furthermore, recognizes the importance of good work

*If it takes you one hour to read this chapter, during that time two persons will have been killed and 240 injured *at work* in the United States. (From *Accident Facts*, 1966 Edition, p. 12)

conditions since accidents and some illnesses represent avoidable and unnecessary costs of operation. When an employee is absent from his job, a replacement must ordinarily be furnished and paid for performing the absentee's work. Since the employee is compensated, at least partially, for his enforced absence, this represents an additional cost. Accidents that occur on the job also involve medical and hospital costs as well as disability benefits that must be paid directly or indirectly through insurance premiums. Accidents and illnesses that are attributable to the worker's employment may also have pronounced effects on employee morale and on the goodwill that the company enjoys in the community or in the business world. Any accident or illness which may indicate that management may be neglecting its duty toward its employees will affect the attitudes and the behavior of people in the community, customers and potential customers, union representatives, government officials, and others who in one way or another have some influence on the success of the company. Thus, there are many reasons why management should be motivated to create a working environment that will facilitate employee health and safety.

The discussion of these topics includes:

- Environmental factors in health and safety.
- Company health programs.
- Company safety programs.
- Workmen's compensation.

Environmental Factors in Health and Safety

Even though the maintenance of a healthful and safe work environment is primarily dependent upon the attitudes and behavior of supervisors and their subordinates, the importance of proper physical conditions in which employees work cannot be minimized. Health and safety hazards that may be found in the work environment may be controlled in part through intelligent behavior of employees. Often the control of such hazards, however, requires the installation of special protective devices, or other equipment, that management must provide for when planning the layout and design of the work area and its equipment. While certain types of jobs present special and unique conditions that may be hazardous to health and safety, this section considers some of the more common environmental factors influencing health and safety. It should be noted that efficiency and morale are also influenced in most instances by these environmental factors.

Lighting

Lighting has probably received more attention than other aspects of the work environment. It has long been realized that the quality of illumination affects employee efficiency, health, and morale, and is an important factor in the cause and prevention of accidents. While lighting is primarily the concern of industrial engineers, the personnel manager should be aware of the requirements of good lighting and its effect on employees. Distribution, intensity, and color are the three main characteristics of lighting that must be considered in planning for good illumination.

Atmospheric Conditions

The atmospheric properties of the work area may have an influence on the employee's behavior and thus affect the extent to which he is able to perform his work in a safe manner. Certain vapors, for example, create dizziness while others may cause drowsiness or visual disturbances. The atmospheric properties are also likely to affect the employee's health unless adequate safeguards are provided. Such atmospheric contaminants as vapors, gases, dusts, fumes, mists, smokes, and radiant energy (other than heat) require careful engineering control to protect employee health.

Noise

Noise has become a major industrial health problem in many companies. It is a problem primarily because its effect on hearing is not fully known and because there has been a sudden increase in the number of workmen's compensation claims for occupational loss of hearing. Because of individual differences in susceptibility to hearing damage, it is difficult to establish precise safe limits of noise. Beginning at 90 decibels,[1] however, the possibility of permanent auditory damage exists in highly susceptible individuals from long exposure. At 120 decibels the probability of permanent damage to the hearing of all individuals from long exposure is very high. Explosive noise is more damaging than continuous noise, and noise including the higher frequencies is more damaging than noise that is mostly composed of low frequencies. A good rule of thumb in maintaining auditory safety is that locations in which it is difficult for two persons to converse at close range should be studied with a sound level meter, a device that measures the intensity of sound.[2]

---

[1] A decibel is one tenth of a bel, the unit of loudness.

[2] George E. Shambaugh, Jr., "Noise Deafness," *Factory Management and Maintenance*, Vol. III, No. 12 (December, 1953), pp. 118–120. There are six articles in this issue devoted to industrial noise.

When a company is confronted with a noise problem, action should be taken to reduce or eliminate the noise through various soundproofing devices, including ear defenders (plugs) for the employees, and by establishing a hearing (audiometric) testing program. On the basis of hearing test results, the medical department can recommend individual or environmental corrective action where it is appropriate.

Other Factors

In addition to providing effective lighting, controlled atmosphere, and freedom from harmful noise, it is important that management give special consideration to the physical appearance and layout of the office and plant. The walls should be attractively painted, the windows should be clean, and the floors should be clean and free from grease or other substances that may cause an accident. Equipment, whether it be desks or machinery, should be in good repair and neatly arranged in such a manner as to provide an uncrowded and uncluttered appearance. Materials should be handled in conveyances that are safe and efficient, and waste should be removed promptly. Proper storage of materials and arrangement of tools at the work place, as well as proper work flow and scheduling, are also important. Attention to these and other phases of the work environment are not only conducive to better safety, but they are likely to affect employee morale.

Company Health Programs

The nature of the health program and the types of services provided to employees vary according to the size, location, and special needs of the company. It is generally agreed, however, that the company health program should be primarily concerned with education, diagnosis, and prevention. The therapeutic aspects of medicine are generally thought of as being the responsibility of the private practitioner rather than the industrial physician, although there are exceptions to this concept.

Recognizing and Controlling Health Hazards

One of the important ways in which the medical staff can contribute to good health and well-being among workers is by studying environmental conditions and individual health and sick leave records and by making recommendations for corrections. The effects of poor lighting, unfavorable atmospheric conditions, and other deficiencies often show up in their studies. Through close liaison between the medical staff and industrial engineers, deficiencies can be corrected before they create major medical problems among the personnel. In companies where employees work with chemicals, radioactive substances, and similar toxic materials, the medical staff can assist in determining the adequacy of protective devices and clothing; and through individual cases that come to its attention, it can assess the effectiveness of employee training for health and safety. Considerable improvements have been made in occupational health during the half-century since the founding of the Office of Industrial Hygiene and Sanitation of the U.S. Public Health Service. However, continuing attention must be given to recognizing and controlling health hazards.

> Although the health of the American worker is better than it has ever been, old and new health hazards related to his occupation still exist — and are often ignored because of misunderstanding, apathy, or overconfidence. Many companies have their own programs to prevent occupational disease and injury and treat them when they do occur. However, even in this age of great industrial operations, most American workers are employed in small plants — those with less than 500 workers. Few of these provide adequate health protection. A large part of the state's occupational health work is directed toward improving conditions in these plants and encouraging the development of preventative health programs.[3]

Personnel workers should also be alert to the need for recognizing and controlling health hazards and should maintain effective liaison with medical staff personnel and with industrial engineers. Their contacts with employees and access to personnel records together with their professional orientation in matters relating to physical and emotional health make them potentially valuable contributors to the health and safety programs. Since the personnel department is typically organized to include medical, safety, and training programs, as shown in Figure 3-4, the success of many of its programs that are related to more than one division in the personnel department depends upon adequate coordination among the personnel director and his assistant managers.

Providing Medical Advice and Assistance

The other divisions of the personnel department will find that the medical staff can furnish valuable assistance with such problems as worker fatigue, absenteeism, emotional disorders, and other problems. The medical staff is also in an excellent position to detect the quality of morale among employees on the basis of the complaints of illnesses that are

---

[3]U.S. Department of Health, Education, and Welfare, *50 Years of Occupational Health* (Washington, D. C.: U.S. Government Printing Office, 1964).

Figure 25-1
COMPANY SPONSORED MEDICAL EXAMINATIONS

Industry	Number of Companies	Percent Requiring Pre-Employment Examination	Percent Requiring* Periodic Examination During Employment	Percent Requiring* Examinations When Returning After Illness
Manufacturing Companies	426	85	30	Data not given
Insurance	129	70	16	29
Banks	158	50	9	11
Gas & Electric Utilities	92	95	10	43
Retail Trade	100	42	10	37
Wholesale Trade	50	30	4	8

* For one or more categories of personnel. These examinations are usually not required for all personnel.

Source: National Industrial Conference Board, *Personnel Practices in Factory and Office: Manufacturing, 1964; Office Personnel Practices: Nonmanufacturing, 1965.* Reproduced with permission.

expressed by absentees. A psychiatric study of many offices has revealed that the level of absences due to colds is directly related to the level of morale in an office. One psychiatrist said, "Where there's good supervision, there's low absence." It is simple for an employee to say, "I've got a cold." Any employee who wants to stay away from work can use this excuse whether he is sick or not.[4]

While a professional evaluation of the state of physical and mental health of employees is of primary concern to management, employees are probably more interested in the type of facilities for medical treatment that are available. In some companies only limited facilities, such as those needed to handle first-aid cases, are available. In others a company hospital with complete medical and surgical facilities is available for the employees.

Since prevention is one of the primary aims of the industrial medical department, provisions should be made for conducting periodic examinations that are reasonably thorough and for advising the employee of those

[4]"How To Cure Those Costly 'I've Got a Cold' Absences," *Management Methods*, Vol. 17, No. 5 (February, 1960), pp. 38–44.

conditions that require attention. Surveys by the National Industrial Conference Board, however, reveal that while preemployment medical examinations are used frequently, the periodic examination occurs less frequently. The data shown in Figure 25-1 indicate the need for greater attention to employee health. It is possible that some employees would view a periodical examination as an invasion of privacy, but the welfare of other employees and/or customers must also be considered. Teachers, for example, are required to have periodic tuberculin tests. On the other hand, an office employee is usually not subject to such periodic tests; however, he may very well be a "carrier," and his fellow workers may not know it until they contract the disease.

Executive Health Programs

In recent years there has been increased interest in the health of executives and the establishment of executive health programs. These developments are the result of an awareness that executives are in a hazardous position from the standpoint of health and that the company's investment in high-level talent is dependent upon safeguarding the health of executives.

Many companies believe that an executive health program should include more than a periodic physical examination. A successful program of executive health is dependent upon related factors, such as having (1) clearly defined areas of responsibility and authority within an organization, (2) written statements of policy, (3) regular communication channels, (4) executive development programs, (5) counseling and health education services for executives, (6) special vacation programs for executives, and (7) follow-up programs to encourage executives to get necessary remedial medical treatment.[5] Not only is the physically and emotionally healthy executive likely to be with the company longer but also the influence of his personality on subordinates is likely to promote their efficiency and adjustment rather than to affect them adversely, as the executive pictured in Figure 25-2 apparently does.

A prescription for executive emotional health is provided by one of the leading psychiatrists in the United States. The late William Menninger advises that the executive should be guided by these principles:

1. Have a periodic emotional check-up.
2. Take time to review his past and evaluate his present in the light of his goals — particularly in his family relationships.
3. Schedule vacations and hobby times.

[5]Doris M. Thompson, *Company Health Programs for Executives*, Studies in Personnel Policy, No. 147 (New York: National Industrial Conference Board, Inc., 1955).

Figure 25-2

"Ulcers, nonsense! My motto is: Give 'em, don't get 'em!"

Source: *Dun's Review and Modern Industry,* March, 1957. Reproduced with permission.

4. Improve his ability as a leader, on the job, at home, in the community.

5. Understand himself better — especially how he handles his hostile feelings.[6]

The wise executive is one who has learned to make effective use of the psychiatrist or clinical psychologist in resolving conflicts and reducing tensions that develop out of his complex pattern of activities and interpersonal relationships with others.

Training for Health

One of the main objectives of company health programs is to educate personnel in the principles and practices of good physical and mental health. The success of the program is dependent upon stimulating interest among employees. This may be done through the use of posters, films, and

---

[6]William C. Menninger, "A Prescription for Executive Mental Health," *Advanced Management*, Vol. 25, No. 9 (September, 1960), pp. 16–17. The entire issue is devoted to executive mental health.

pamphlets that have been prepared by various health agencies and by private companies, as well as by talks and interviews with employees. Some companies have special physical fitness programs for employees but more often special arrangements are made for executives.

It is being realized by more and more individuals that a moderate and regular exercise program can play a valuable role in the physical well-being of all persons, including executives. Too many busy executives, however, try to become weekend athletes with disastrous results. A program designed originally for the Royal Canadian Air Force has found acceptance in many countries, including the United States, where the U.S. Air Force has adopted it to improve the fitness level of officers and airmen. The RCAF plan for men (there is also one for women) is called the 5BX and takes 11 minutes a day to go through the five basic exercises. The exercise patterns are varied according to age levels, and a progressive pattern provides for moving upward to more difficult exercises as strength and endurance increase.[7] The role of diet, smoking, and consumption of alcoholic beverages in physical fitness should also be given careful attention. Perhaps the executive has the most to lose if loss of one's position and salary are valued highly. At any occupational level, however, physical fitness is an important factor in job efficiency, satisfaction, and emotional health. It would appear, therefore, that more companies should provide not only for periodic health examinations but also should have an active health training program. Such a training program should include appropriate training for supervisors.

Supervisors should be given some indoctrination in the symptoms of various physical and emotional disorders and should be encouraged to refer employees to the medical department for assistance. The method by which referral is made and the approach of the medical personnel are especially important in obtaining employee cooperation. Many individuals are reluctant to recognize that anything may be wrong with them and as a result may not cooperate with the supervisor in obtaining medical care unless they are handled skillfully.

Company Safety Programs

Considerable progress has been realized in making a job safer through the efforts of labor, management, government, the National Safety Council, the American Society of Safety Engineers, insurance companies, and

<hr>

[7]Richard E. Dutton, "The Executive and Physical Fitness," *Personnel Administration*, Vol. 29, No. 2 (March-April, 1966), pp. 13–18.

other groups. Nevertheless, there is still room for considerable improvement. In 1965 for example, 14,100 deaths and 2.1 million injuries resulted from accidents that occurred at work. The cost of these accidents is estimated to be over $6.4 billion including invisible and indirect costs.[8] Not reflected in these figures, however, is the human misery and suffering that accompanies any fatal or serious accident and usually affects not only those persons who are directly involved but also many other persons. In view of the gravity of the problem, management should do everything possible to reduce the number and severity of accidents.

Safety Education

Most companies have some type of safety education program that includes posters, warning signs, safety talks, and other media by which employees are given instructions in safe work methods and are urged to follow them. Some companies also conduct safety education courses that are aimed at reducing the number of accidents that occur off the job since these accidents can result in the temporary or permanent loss of employees just as much as those occurring at work. Safety education and other aspects of the safety program are usually coordinated by a safety director whose primary function is to enlist the interest and cooperation of all personnel. However, the safety director is largely dependent upon managerial and supervisory personnel for the success of the program.

On-the-job safety. Since most accidents are the result of unsafe acts, the supervisor should emphasize safety, beginning with the orientation of the new employee. He should not only talk safety but also, in demonstrating the proper procedures, should show his belief in safety by wearing the proper protective clothing or devices and by using safe methods. Whenever accidents do occur, the supervisor should discuss the findings with his men; and he should discipline employees who take chances, engage in horseplay, or in any way violate the established safe work procedures.

An important requisite of safety is a thorough understanding of what constitutes safe practices. Too frequently the assumption is made that the employees are knowledgeable about safety and other aspects of their jobs, which often is not the case. Revere Copper and Brass recognizes the importance of determining a prospective employee's safety knowledge through testing and thus learns what additional instruction he may need. Revere also tests those persons returning from lost time accidents with its *Safety Test*. In completing this test consisting of 54 items, the employee is

---

[8]*Accident Facts* (Chicago: National Safety Council, 1966), pp. 23, 24.

instructed to identify the practices that do not reflect the safe way in each item. Two items from the test are shown in Figure 25-3. (See if you can identify the unsafe acts and then check your responses against the key at the end of the chapter on page 700.) Item 5 is from Part I of the test on general safety and Item 33 is from Part II of the test containing items on piling, traffic, and carrying. After the test is scored the employee is encouraged to study the safety rules represented by the items that he missed by referring to a company publication on safety, *For Your Own Good, For the Good of Us All.*

Figure 25-3
ITEMS FROM THE REVERE SAFETY TEST

Source: Copyright Revere Copper and Brass, Incorporated. Reproduction rights granted, 1962.

One of the more common approaches to enlisting the support of management personnel and employees for safety, as well as that of the union, is through the establishment of committees in which these groups are represented. Membership of the committees is usually changed periodically in order that a large number of employees will have an opportunity to serve and through this participation may become ambassadors for safety. Several committees may be used to assist the safety director with the different phases of the program, such as inspection, accident investigation, publicity, and education. In addition to organizing the regular educational programs that are devoted to safety, safety directors often plan special safety compaigns. Such campaigns typically emphasize competition among departments or plants of a company with the department or plant having the best safety record receiving some type of award or trophy. In some companies cash bonuses are given to employees who have outstanding safety records. Contests have also been used to promote safety with some favorable results. Too often, however, employees forget about safety after the contest is over and the winner has been rewarded. The main objective in any safety program is to make safety an integral part of the job and to build safety into the working attitudes and habits of employees.[9]

Off-the-job safety. Seven out of ten accidental deaths and more than half of the injuries suffered by workers in 1965 occurred off the job. Production time lost due to off-the-job accidents totaled 60,000,000 man-days in 1965 compared with 40,000,000 man-days lost by workers injured on the job.[10] In view of these facts, many companies have been emphasizing off-the-job safety in their safety programs. One of the earlier programs of this type was developed by the California and Hawaiian Sugar Refining Corporation that has continually focused on highway and other off-the-job areas where good safety practices are as essential to employee morale and productivity as those that emphasize on-the-job safety. The success of this program is largely attributed to the participation of employees in its various phases.

Elimination of Hazards

Managerial and supervisory personnel should be continually alert to the presence of hazardous conditions and should take positive steps to eliminate them promptly. They should always be alert to the possible need for protective devices such as machinery guards, special switches for operating equipment, and warning signals. By calling upon the *human engineering specialist*, they may be able to have equipment redesigned so that their error-provocative features may be eliminated. While the most striking

---

[9]See James C. McHugh and Edward W. Sutton, "A Neglected Aid in Safety Management," *Personnel*, Vol. 43, No. 1 (January–February, 1966), pp. 48–53, for a discussion of the use of employee attitude surveys in improving the company safety program.

[10]*Accident Facts, op. cit.*, p. 33.

equipment changes that have been made on the basis of human engineering studies involve military aircraft dials and control levers, its basic principles may be applied to all jobs where equipment is involved. Human engineering specialists (or human factors engineers) are now employed in every branch of the military, in many independent research and consulting organizations, and in the aviation, automotive, electronics, communications, and home-appliance industries. Their work involves studying the man-machine relationships in all types of devices including space vehicles, highway signs, telephones, typewriters, machine tools, and kitchen stoves.[11] Their primary goal is to provide information leading to the redesigning of equipment that results in improved efficiency, safety, and reduction of fatigue.

Managers and supervisors should also recognize the need for instructing employees in safety regulations. Safety regulations and instructions are more likely to be followed if they are stated positively and some explanation or reason for the rule is given. The words "Keep Out" on an unlocked door are more likely to appeal to the employee's curiosity than to his sense of good discipline. A sign which reads "Danger — High Voltage" dispels the reader's curiosity and usually accomplishes the desired result. Similarly, positive instructions to use safety goggles and the reason for doing so have proved to be more effective.

While the traditional aproaches to the prevention of accidents are still to be found, there have been those who feel that safety posters, safety guards, and safety rules do not reach the crux of the problem — namely, the unconscious forces that are part of the individual employee's personality. It is recognized that most people who have accidents are usually normal but are often emotionally disturbed. By having an accident they attain the feeling of importance that they need through the attention and sympathy that they receive from others. One safety expert believes that warning signs, safety talks, and other traditional approaches to safety in fact provide a "trigger" to set off the unconscious desires in a person to have an accident when he is in an environment where there are some hazards.[12] It is recommended that while it is necessary to reduce hazards and to provide warnings to employees about dangers, it is equally important to train supervisors in leadership approaches that are consistent with

---

[11]Alphonse Chapanis, *Man-Machine Engineering* (Belmont, California: Wadsworth Publishing Co., Inc., 1965), p. 10. See also W. E. Woodson and Donald W. Conover, *Human Engineering Guide for Equipment Designers* (Second Edition; Berkeley: University of California Press., 1964).

[12]Evan Stallcup, "A Fresh Look at the Safety Program: I. When Enough Is Too Much," *Personnel*, Vol. 38, No. 6 (November–December, 1961), pp. 26–34.

those discussed in Chapters 10-17, inclusive. According to Stallcup, in order to reduce work injuries to a minimum, supervisors should:

1. Promptly and routinely correct any *definite* hazards and mechanical causes of accidents — without overly emphasizing the question of safety.
2. Be alert to changes in a worker's temperament, attitude, physical condition, or job satisfaction.
3. Be willing to listen without giving direction.
4. Build up the individual. Use praise generously; criticize rarely and constructively.
5. *Routinely* expect good performance and responsibility.
6. Never insult an employee's intelligence and trigger his resentment with "do's" and "don'ts" regarding safe procedure. All but the most complicated hazards he can see for himself.
7. Follow up on excessive minor injuries. These always indicate that a major injury is going to occur.
8. Never baby, give special privileges, or treat one employee differently than others. "Doing things" for those who react irresponsibly or in a maladjusted way always makes them worse.
9. Let everyone know what's going on in the company and in the department.[13]

The supervisor is considered the main element in the safety program. Training him to be effective in carrying out the above responsibilities is likely to be more productive than the more perfunctory approaches to accident prevention.

Accident Investigation

Every accident, including those that are considered minor, should be investigated by the supervisor and a representative of the safety organization in the company. Through such an investigation the causative factors may be detected and necessary corrections made before the accident is repeated. Correction may require that materials be rearranged, that safety guards or controls be installed, or more often that workers be given additional training in safety methods or that appropriate disciplinary action be taken. No employee should be permitted to "get away with something" where accidents are concerned. If the accident resulted from his taking chances or not following the prescribed procedure, the severity of his misdemeanor must be made clear to him if he is not already in the hospital.

---

[13]*Ibid.*, p. 33.

Accident records. An important part of the safety program is the maintenance of accident records and the dissemination of pertinent information to all managerial and supervisory personnel. This practice has the advantage of advising those concerned with accident prevention of the facts of each case and provides suggestions that they can use in their own departments. A daily accident record maintained at the plant health service calls attention to those workers who are having accidents as well as to machines or jobs that may be especially hazardous. This should not be construed to mean, however, that supervisors should wait for accidents to happen before attempting to do anything about them. Studying work accidents is less profitable than studying work conditions and near accidents.[14]

Accident proneness. A study of the accident records of individual employees usually reveals that there are some individuals who have many more accidents than others. The fact that a relatively large proportion of accidents are experienced by a relatively small proportion of individuals has led some experts to the belief that these few individuals are accident prone. *Accident proneness*, as the term is customarily used, refers to something in the biological and psychological makeup of these individuals that predisposes them to have "more than their share" of accidents. There is another group of experts, however, which says that the fact that a certain proportion of the workers have repeated accidents occurs purely by chance and is, in fact, a mathematical necessity. In studying the causes of accidents, it is important to recognize the possibility that those individuals with accident rates in excess of what would be expected on the basis of chance may be exposed to unusually hazardous situations more frequently than their fellow employees. Thus, their accidents are related more to their greater exposure to hazards than to their personal qualities. It is also possible that there is a relationship between so-called accident proneness and the tendency to report accidents versus concealing them.[15]

At the present time the most reasonable conclusion concerning accident proneness is that there is no clear case for or against either position. It seems desirable, therefore, that where there are individuals who apparently have more accidents than their colleagues every attempt be made to study all of the possible causative factors and to take whatever action is warranted rather than merely labeling an individual "accident prone" and immediately requisitioning a replacement for him. At the maximum,

---

[14]Leon Brody, "The Accident Phenomenon," *Personnel Administration*, Vol. 26, No. 6 (November–December, 1963), pp. 11–14.

[15]Gerald H. Whitlock, J. A. Barker, Frank E. Blackett, and Carl H. Stone, "The Relation of Accident Proneness and the Tendency to Report Injuries," *Personnel Psychology*, Vol. 16, No. 2 (Summer, 1963), pp. 163–169.

statistical analyses of accident data in which the chance factor was taken into consideration show that only about 15 percent of individual accidents can be accounted for by accident proneness. This leaves 85 percent of the accidents unaccounted for. To cover the 85 percent of the accidents that cannot be explained by the accident proneness theory, Kerr proposes two theories: the Goals-Freedom-Alertness Theory and the Adjustment-Stress Theory.

The *Goals-Freedom-Alertness Theory* states that accidents tend to occur in an unrewarding psychological work environment that is not conducive to a high level of alertness. The richer the climate in economic and psychological opportunities, the higher the level of alertness. The theory proposes that if the work climate provides the freedom to set reasonably attainable goals, the worker feels himself to be a significant participant, and this in turn leads to habits of alertness, problem raising, and problem solving. Studies on the effect of psychological climate on accident behavior lend considerable support to this theory.

The *Adjustment-Stress Theory* holds that unusual, negative, distracting stress upon the individual increases his liability to accidents. Negative stresses include diseases, toxic materials, temperature excesses, poor illumination, excessive noise level, and excessive physical work strain. Kerr states that it seems wise to emphasize that both of these theories of safety complement each other, as well as the existing proneness theory. He estimates on the basis of his own studies, and those of other researchers, that causes of industrial accidents are probably distributed as follows:

1. Accident proneness   1% to 15%
2. Goals-freedom-alertness   30% to 60%
3. Adjustment-stress   45% to 60%

He concludes that constructive thinking about the latter two theories should assist in escaping the defeatism of the overemphasized proneness theory and in better understanding and controlling of accidents.[16]

Accident rates. Two major national surveys of accidents are conducted regularly by the U.S. Public Health Service and the National Safety Council (NSC). They have different definitions of what constitutes an injury so that their survey figures vary somewhat. For brevity, only the NSC figures will be cited in this chapter. The NSC definitions of an accident and of disabling injury are:

---

[16]Willard Kerr, "Complementary Theories of Safety Psychology," *Journal of Social Psychology*, Vol. 45, No. 1 (February, 1957), pp. 3–9.

Accident is that occurrence in a sequence of events which usually produces unintended injury, death, or property damage.

A disabling injury is defined in the American Standards Association Standard Z16.1 as an injury which prevents a person from performing any of his usual activities for a full day beyond the day of the accident. The American Standard applies to work injuries, but the Council has adapted this definition to injuries in other categories.[17]

Other definitions that are important to understanding the charts that follow are:

Frequency rate is the number of disabling work injuries per 1,000,000 employee-hours exposure.

Severity rate is the total days charged for work injuries per 1,000,000 employee-hours exposure. Days charged include actual calendar days of disability resulting from temporary total injuries, and scheduled charges for deaths and permanent disabilities. These latter charges are based on 6,000 days for a death or permanent total disability, with proportionately fewer days for permanent partial disabilities of varying degrees of seriousness.[18]

It will be noted in Figure 25-4 on page 690 that during the past 25 years there has been a general decline in the frequency and severity rates, with the exception of the war period, 1941–1944, in all industries reporting to the National Safety Council. While such information is of general interest, the personnel department of a company would probably be more concerned with the frequency and severity rates of its particular industry. In Figure 25-5 on page 691 the injury frequency rates are presented on the left-hand side of the chart and the severity rates on the right-hand side. One need only look at the longest bars (at the bottom of the chart) to understand the concern and appeal of John L. Lewis for those workers he represented. While underground coal mining has the longest bars on both sides of the chart, it will be observed that a given industry will usually not have frequency and severity rates in the same relative position on the chart. The frequency rate (3.44) for the steel industry, for example, is below the average (6.53 — see arrow) for all industries, but its severity rate (744) is above the average (695) for all industries.

Workmen's Compensation

While the accident frequency and severity rates have steadily declined during the last quarter century, the individual worker who is unfortunate

---

[17]*Accident Facts, op. cit.,* p. 2, 97.
[18]*Ibid.,* p. 97.

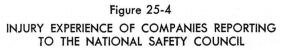

Figure 25-4

INJURY EXPERIENCE OF COMPANIES REPORTING
TO THE NATIONAL SAFETY COUNCIL

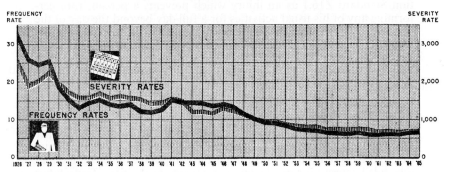

Source: *Accident Facts*, 1966 Edition, p. 28.   Reproduced with permission of the National
Safety Council.

enough to incur an illness or be the victim of an industrial accident is not
impressed by the statistics.   His temporary or permanent loss of earning
capacity, as well as the suffering and misery that usually accompany a
serious illness or accident, is a stark reality to him.   Should the worker
stand this loss even if he was primarily responsible for causing the accident
or for incurring the illness?   Society has answered this question quite
clearly.

Trends

The workmen's compensation laws that are now found in every state,
in the District of Columbia, and in Puerto Rico, and the federal workmen's
compensation represent a theory or approach to the employer's liability
in industrial illnesses and accidents that is radically different from that
which preceded it.   It is now recognized that the employer and society must
provide for the welfare of employees who become disabled as a result of
an industrial accident or disease.   This was not true of the provisions of
earlier laws.

Common law and employer liability laws.   At the beginning of the
Industrial Revolution the employee or "servant" had only one method for
securing damages from the employer (master).   This was by filing a civil suit
in the courts.   Under common law the master had certain specified obligations to the servant, such as providing a safe place to work and safe equipment; but if he performed them as a "reasonable man," he would not be

Figure 25-5

INJURY RATES BY INDUSTRY OF COMPANIES REPORTING
TO THE NATIONAL SAFETY COUNCIL

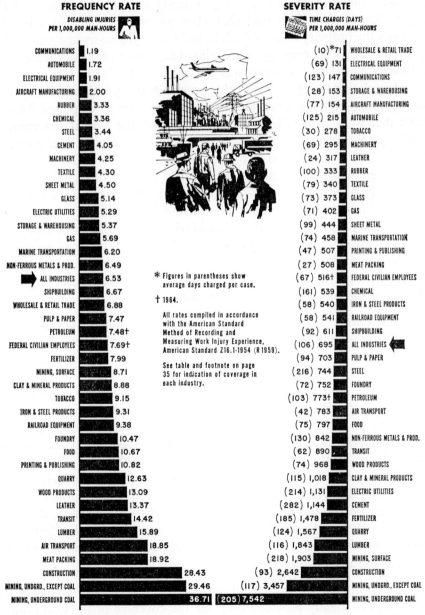

FREQUENCY RATE			SEVERITY RATE	
DISABLING INJURIES PER 1,000,000 MAN-HOURS			TIME CHARGES (DAYS) PER 1,000,000 MAN-HOURS	
COMMUNICATIONS	1.19		(10)*71	WHOLESALE & RETAIL TRADE
AUTOMOBILE	1.72		(69) 131	ELECTRICAL EQUIPMENT
ELECTRICAL EQUIPMENT	1.91		(123) 147	COMMUNICATIONS
AIRCRAFT MANUFACTURING	2.00		(28) 153	STORAGE & WAREHOUSING
RUBBER	3.33		(77) 154	AIRCRAFT MANUFACTURING
CHEMICAL	3.36		(125) 215	AUTOMOBILE
STEEL	3.44		(30) 278	TOBACCO
CEMENT	4.05		(69) 295	MACHINERY
MACHINERY	4.25		(24) 317	LEATHER
TEXTILE	4.30		(100) 333	RUBBER
SHEET METAL	4.50		(79) 340	TEXTILE
GLASS	5.14		(73) 373	GLASS
ELECTRIC UTILITIES	5.29		(71) 402	GAS
STORAGE & WAREHOUSING	5.37		(99) 444	SHEET METAL
GAS	5.69		(74) 458	MARINE TRANSPORTATION
MARINE TRANSPORTATION	6.20		(47) 507	PRINTING & PUBLISHING
NON-FERROUS METALS & PROD.	6.49		(27) 508	MEAT PACKING
ALL INDUSTRIES	6.53		(67) 516†	FEDERAL CIVILIAN EMPLOYEES
SHIPBUILDING	6.67		(161) 539	CHEMICAL
WHOLESALE & RETAIL TRADE	6.88		(58) 540	IRON & STEEL PRODUCTS
PULP & PAPER	7.47		(58) 541	RAILROAD EQUIPMENT
PETROLEUM	7.48†		(92) 611	SHIPBUILDING
FEDERAL CIVILIAN EMPLOYEES	7.69†		(106) 695	ALL INDUSTRIES
FERTILIZER	7.99		(94) 703	PULP & PAPER
MINING, SURFACE	8.71		(216) 744	STEEL
CLAY & MINERAL PRODUCTS	8.88		(72) 752	FOUNDRY
TOBACCO	9.15		(103) 773†	PETROLEUM
IRON & STEEL PRODUCTS	9.31		(42) 783	AIR TRANSPORT
RAILROAD EQUIPMENT	9.38		(75) 797	FOOD
FOUNDRY	10.47		(130) 842	NON-FERROUS METALS & PROD.
FOOD	10.67		(62) 890	TRANSIT
PRINTING & PUBLISHING	10.82		(74) 968	WOOD PRODUCTS
QUARRY	12.63		(115) 1,018	CLAY & MINERAL PRODUCTS
WOOD PRODUCTS	13.09		(214) 1,131	ELECTRIC UTILITIES
LEATHER	13.37		(282) 1,144	CEMENT
TRANSIT	14.42		(185) 1,478	FERTILIZER
LUMBER	15.89		(124) 1,567	QUARRY
AIR TRANSPORT	18.85		(116) 1,843	LUMBER
MEAT PACKING	18.92		(218) 1,903	MINING, SURFACE
CONSTRUCTION	28.43		(93) 2,642	CONSTRUCTION
MINING, UNDGRD., EXCEPT COAL	29.46		(117) 3,457	MINING, UNDGRD., EXCEPT COAL
MINING, UNDERGROUND COAL	36.71		(205) 7,542	MINING, UNDERGROUND COAL

* Figures in parentheses show
average days charged per case.

† 1964.

All rates compiled in accordance
with the American Standard
Method of Recording and
Measuring Work Injury Experience,
American Standard Z16.1-1954 (R 1959).

See table and footnote on page
35 for indication of coverage in
each industry.

Source: *Accident Facts*, 1966 Edition, p. 26.   Reproduced with permission of the National
Safety Council.

held liable. In addition, the employer had three common-law defenses that he would use, namely: (1) *the doctrine of contributory negligence*, which stated that the employer would not be liable if the injury of the employee was due wholly or in part to his own negligence, (2) *the doctrine of the assumption of risk* which held that when an employee accepts a job, he assumes the ordinary risks of the job, and (3) *the fellow-servant rule*, which provided that if the employee were injured as a result of the negligence of a fellow employee, the employer was not liable for his injury.[19]

Legislation that gave the working man a better position in the eyes of the law was gradually enacted. This took the form of employer liability laws that were enacted by both the states and the federal government. Although these laws generally represented an improvement over common law, the employee still had to file suit in a court of law and had to prove that the employer was negligent in his duty. This was often difficult to do and involved legal expense that was beyond the means of most employees. Furthermore, after paying legal fees, there was no assurance that the employee would win his case. If he should win his case, there was always the possibility that because of bankruptcy or other reasons the employee would not be compensated. These laws were also unsatisfactory from the employer's viewpoint since he was vulnerable to damage claims of large proportion if the employee should win a suit.

Workmen's compensation laws. The first workmen's compensation law to be passed in the United States was in Maryland in 1902, but it was declared unconstitutional. The first laws to be held constitutional were passed in 1911 by four states — California, New Jersey, Washington, and Wisconsin. Since that time every state has adopted some type of workmen's compensation act. Federal employees and others not working within the states are covered by separate legislation. Both state and federal workmen's compensation legislation is based on the theory that the costs of industrial accidents should be considered as one of the costs of production and should ultimately be passed on to the consumer. The individual employee should not be required to stand the expense of his treatment or loss of income nor should he be required to resort to complicated, delaying, and expensive legal procedures. The provisions of the newer legislation thus represent a radical change in the philosophy of employer responsibilities toward the employee.

Compensation for emotional problems. Workmen's compensation plans that originally provided only for the coverage of physical injuries have gradually been extended in many jurisdictions to cover emotional

[19]*Labor Course*, 1966 (Englewood Cliffs, New Jersey: Prentice-Hall, Inc., 1966).

impairments. For example, the person who suffers the loss of several fingers in a machine may develop a severe neurosis about working with any moving equipment. Even though he recovers from his physical injury, he may be emotionally incapable of performing the job for which he has experience. In this type of case, the courts have granted workmen's compensation — even where there is a lapse of as much as five years between the physical injury and the emotional upset. Similarly, those emotional illnesses that occur before they precipitate a physical injury have been found to be compensable. For example, it has been held by courts in several states that job-induced strain, stress, anxiety, or pressure that leads to a heart attack is compensable.

More recently, mental illness that can definitely be linked to job conditions has been found to be compensable in cases that were tried in Kansas, California, Texas, Louisiana, Massachusetts, West Virginia, Colorado, New York, and Michigan. In one case, a train dispatcher was awarded compensation for a nervous breakdown which developed under the pressure of routing trains and having people shout at him over loudspeakers. In another case, an assembly-line employee was awarded partial temporary disability compensation for a traumatic neurosis attributed to the emotional pressures resulting from his supervisor's criticism coupled with his inability to perform the job correctly. Trice and Belasco emphasize the need for companies to prevent and/or correct situations that lead to the precipitation of emotional disturbances. They recommend studying the personality readiness or vulnerability of the individual to emotional illness and the nature of the social climate in the work place.[20]

Provisions

Since each state has its own workmen's compensation laws, the provisions are not uniform. There are, however, many common provisions that should be noted along with some of the differences. For example, none of the compensation laws cover all types of employment. Agricultural and domestic workers are usually exempt. Employers hiring fewer than a specified number of employees are also exempt in 28 of the states. The most common exemption is for employers having less than 3 employees. In eight states, however, the numerical exemption ranges from 6 to 15 employees. Under some of the laws having numerical exemptions, the exemption does not apply under certain conditions or to certain specified occupations. For instance, in New Mexico the exemption does not

---

[20]Harrison M. Trice and James A. Belasco, *Emotional Health and Employer Responsibility* (Ithaca: New York State School of Industrial and Labor Relations, Bulletin 57, May, 1966).

apply if the injury occurs when the employee is working 10 feet or more above the ground; in Kansas it does not apply to employment in mines or building construction.[21]

Workmen's compensation laws may be classified as *compulsory* or *elective*. Under a compulsory law, every employer subject to it is required to comply with its provisions for the compensation of work injuries. These acts are compulsory for the employee also. An elective law is one in which the employer has the option of either accepting or rejecting the act, but in case he rejects it, he loses the customary common law defenses — assumed risk of the employment, negligence of a fellow servant, and contributory negligence. Although most employers elect to be covered by the act, some do not. In the latter case the employees may be unable to obtain compensation unless they sue for damages. The elective laws also permit the employee to reject coverage, but in practice this is rarely done.

Thirty[22] of the workmen's compensation laws are compulsory and twenty-four[23] are elective for most of the private employments covered. Under most types of elective laws, acceptance of the act by employers or employees is presumed unless specific notice of rejection is filed. Nineteen[24] laws make this presumption, but in the other elective laws the employer must accept the law in writing or show notice of acceptance.[25]

Workmen's compensation laws typically provide that the injured employee will be paid a disability benefit that is usually based on a percentage of his wages. Each state also specifies the length of the period of payment and usually indicates a maximum amount that may be paid. The weekly payment in many states does not exceed $35. In addition to the disability benefits, provision is made for payment of medical and hospitalization expenses to some degree, and in all states death benefits are paid to survivors of the employee. Unlike the former employee liability laws, it is not necessary for an injured employee to file suit in a court in order to benefit under workmen's compensation laws. Commissions are established

---

[21]U.S. Department of Labor, *State Workmen's Compensation Laws*, Bulletin 161 (Washington, D.C.: U.S. Government Printing Office, 1964), p. 13.

[22]Alaska, Arizona, Arkansas, California, Connecticut, Delaware, District of Columbia, Hawaii, Idaho, Illinois, Maryland, Massachusetts, Michigan, Minnesota, Mississippi, Nevada, New Hampshire, New York, North Dakota, Ohio, Oklahoma, Puerto Rico, Rhode Island, Utah, Virginia, Washington, Wisconsin, Wyoming, Longshoremen's and Harbor Workers' Act and the Federal Employees' Compensation Act.

[23]Alabama, Colorado, Florida, Georgia, Indiana, Iowa, Kansas, Kentucky, Louisiana, Maine, Missouri, Montana, Nebraska, New Jersey, New Mexico, North Carolina, Oregon, Pennsylvania, South Carolina, South Dakota, Tennessee, Texas, Vermont, and West Virginia.

[24]Alabama, Colorado, Florida, Georgia, Indiana, Iowa, Kansas, Louisiana, Missouri, Nebraska, New Jersey, New Mexico, North Carolina, Oregon, Pennsylvania, South Carolina, South Dakota, Tennessee, and Vermont.

[25]*Ibid.*, p. 3.

to adjudicate claims at little or no expense to the claimant. In general, the commissions have been increasingly liberal in the awards made to injured employees.

Financing Workmen's Compensation

The workmen's compensation benefits prescribed by law in the various states generally are financed by the employers. A few states require the employees to make small contributions, but these funds meet only a small part of the expense involved in paying the benefits. While payment of the benefits is an operational expense for the company, the customer ultimately pays the cost of benefits. Since the company must be able to meet the prices of its competitors, however, it is encouraged to do everything possible to prevent accidents from occuring, thereby reducing the cost of operation.

Two methods of providing for workmen's compensation risks are commonly used. One method is for the state to operate an insurance system that employers may join or in some states are required to join. Another method is for the states to permit employers to insure with private companies, and in some states employers may be certified by the commission handling workmen's compensation to handle their own risks without any type of insurance.

Under most state and private insurance plans the employer and the employee gain by maintaining good safety records. Employers are rated according to accident experience, and their casualty insurance costs are figured on this basis. The accident frequency rate and severity rate are used as the basis of such costs. Until an employer has had time to accumulate experience data and is given an "experience rating" (or "merit rating," as it is sometimes called),[26] the casualty premiums are based on the experience of the industry as a whole (*manual rating*) or on the basis of an examination of the safeguards used in the individual plant (*schedule rating*). Using the experience rating or merit rating for determining the insurance rate for an employer is the fairest method since it is based on actual experience in that particular company.

Under many compensation plans employees are encouraged to follow safe practices. In some states an employee's benefits under the law are reduced by a specified percentage if he is found to have willfully failed to use safety devices provided by the employer, willfully failed to obey safety

---

[26]Not to be confused with employee performance rating or merit rating discussed in Chapter 10.

rules, or if the injury resulted from intoxication of the employee. A method that provides the worker with reasonable compensation for injury but at the same time penalizes him for being willfully negligent in the observance of safety practices should help to promote safe practices. Since the employer also loses in the event of an accident, his continuing attention to fostering safety likewise pays dividends to him.

Résumé

It is recognized today that employee health is dependent not only upon the physical environment but on the social and psychological environment as well. While careful attention should be given to the physical environment and its effects on employee health, the personalities of managerial personnel should also be assessed to determine how they affect the emotional adjustment of subordinates. Since many illnesses are caused or aggravated by emotional conditions, the physical health of the employees is likewise affected. Therefore, in its efforts to provide a working environment that is as healthful and safe as it can be, it is important that the human factor receive the full attention of management.

Since the early 1930's the accident severity and frequency rates in American industry have gradually declined, and most employees are now safer at work than they are at home. This decline is largely the result of the combined efforts of many groups. It is likely that further improvements in the area of accident prevention will depend largely on the attitudes and behavior of individual employees. Because their attitudes and behavior will be largely determined by the effectiveness of the supervision that employees receive, it is essential that supervisors be trained in leadership skills that will promote safety among their subordinates. While the emphasis should be on supervisory training for safety, management must still give continuous attention to the physical environment and the effects that it has on safety and health.

DISCUSSION QUESTIONS AND PROBLEMS

1. The National Safety Council reports that its member companies generally have lower injury rates than nonmember companies.
   a. How do you account for this fact?
   b. What are the implications for personnel management?
2. It was noted in this chapter that many occupational health hazards no longer exist but that industry would have to remain vigilant to the possibility of new ones.

   a. What are some of the occupational health hazards that were once common but are seldom found today? What factors contributed to their elimination?

   b. What are some possible present and future hazards that did not exist in the past?

   c. What role would periodic medical examinations contribute to their detection and elimination?

3. Many companies are sponsoring off-the-job safety education programs.

   a. Why would industry be interested in such programs?

   b. Some individuals would say that this type of program is none of industry's business. Would you agree? Why?

   c. Do you feel that this type of program does any good?

4. An employee working in an engine test unit at an Air Force maintenance depot complains to his supervisor that his hearing is "going bad."

   a. What should the supervisor do?

   b. What are some of the implications of this problem for management?

5. It was stated in this chapter that the wise executive is one who has learned to make effective use of a psychiatrist or clinical psychologist.

   a. How do you react to this statement?

   b. What values would be derived from the executive consulting with such a professional person?

   c. What are some of the barriers that keep people from consulting a psychiatrist or clinical psychologist?

6. There are differing points of view about the amount of strain and stress to which an executive is subjected. One view is that the executive's job in itself is more stressful than a job lower on the organizational scale. An opposite view is that the executive's job is no more stressful for him than another job is for the person holding it.

   a. Which view do you favor? Why?

   b. What can an individual do if he feels that he is under stress?

7. Most states have specific schedules which indicate the amount of money a disabled employee will receive for the various types of disabilities, including permanent disabilities. The State of California has a different system in which the compensation for permanent impairments is based on a judgment as to the likely loss of earning power in view of the injured worker's age and occupation, as well as the nature of the injury.

   a. Which do you feel is the better approach? Why?

   b. Do you feel that the more flexible approach is likely to affect employee attitudes toward accidents?

8. In recent years there has been a campaign urging employers to hire the handicapped person.

   a. Find information about the accident rates for handicapped workers. How do their rates compare with the nonhandicapped?

   b. What precautions should the personnel department take in hiring a handicapped person?

   c. Who is a handicapped person?

9. A recent trend in workmen's compensation awards indicate that an employee who suffers an emotional illness because of his job may be awarded disability payments.

a. What effect is this trend likely to have on company employment procedures?

b. How can companies identify the person who is vulnerable to emotional illness?

c. What are the implications of this trend for management development and supervisory training programs?

10. Disabling back injuries on the job are estimated to total nearly a half million a year. Age is not found to be an important factor but rather the hour of the day is important with most back injury accidents occurring in the first few hours of work.

a. Of what value is information such as this?

b. How can this and similar types of information be utilized in a safety training program?

c. How should one proceed to lift a heavy box from the floor when no lifting equipment is available?

CASE 25-1

THE GOODCRUST BAKING COMPANY

In order to compete with other bakeries the Goodcrust Baking Company was automating various departments as rapidly as feasible. Each job had become easier but required faster working movements and more inspections. One employee, Harry Handem, who was about 40 years of age and had completed 15 years of service with the company, was having a difficult time in working at the faster speed. His inability to work faster may have been related to a war injury which required brain surgery and the wearing of a plate in the top of his head.

Harry's job was that of wrapping machine operator. It involved taking the loaves off the end of the wrapping machine, putting them on a tray, and putting the tray on a rack. He also had to watch the wrapping machine and check to make sure that setups were proper, that there was plenty of paper, that the loaves went through properly, that jams were released, etc. Harry was barely able to keep up with the increased operating speed and was unable to do any of the checking work which meant that he had an unusually large number of crippled loaves. The two crew members with whom he worked — both close relatives of his — said that they had had to "carry him" for a long time on the job and would not do it any longer.

The personnel department considered transferring Harry to a type of job that he would perform satisfactorily; but the only place where he would fit in would be in the sanitation department, and there were no vacancies there. In view of these circumstances the personnel manager decided, in spite of union opposition, to discharge the man.

a. In view of Harry's brain injury, should the company have hired him?

b. Is the company legally or morally responsible for retaining Harry?

c. What are the implications of this case in the hiring of employees whose jobs are likely to be automated?

CASE 25-2

TOO MUCH VANILLA

"Salty" Deaux, the special diet cook for a local hospital, reported to the personnel office that he had experienced an accident about a week earlier. According to his story he had slipped on some grease while carrying a large kettle of potatoes across the kitchen to the stove and had injured his left shoulder. He said that no one was present at the time because it was early in the morning following his return from his regular two-day break.

The personnel manager did not believe that Salty's injury to his shoulder was job incurred. In his opinion it was more likely that Salty had been drinking, had fallen down and hurt himself, and was now trying to get the hospital's insurance carrier to pay the bill. He told Salty, however, that he would look into the matter. Two weeks later Salty was caught drinking on the job, and because of the serious nature of the violation, he was discharged.

- a. To what extent should a personnel manager or a supervisor believe what employees tell him? Why?
- b. Was the hospital justified in questioning Salty's claim? In discharging Salty when he was discovered drinking?
- c. Would the fact that Salty was caught drinking constitute sufficient reason for denying his earlier injury claim?

CASE 25-3

ANOTHER STATISTIC

Harold Spence, safety director of the Metropolitan Printing Company, received word that John Newcomb had lost the tips of two of his fingers in an accident on one of the high-speed printing presses. No one observed the accident, but his foreman stated that it was clearly a case of carelessness on Newcomb's part. Newcomb had been working as a pressman on the high-speed presses for only a few weeks. Prior to that time he worked on some of the slower presses. During the two years that Newcomb has been in this department, he had had three other accidents. Two of the accidents involved the dropping of forms that were ready for the presses which caused only minor injuries to his feet, and one involved a fall down a flight of stairs in the plant. The fall incapacitated him for work for a week.

- a. Would you describe Newcomb as being accident prone? Why?
- b. Of what value is the foreman's opinion in this matter?
- c. What types of information should Spence obtain about the accident?

SUGGESTED READINGS

Brody, L. *Human Factor Research in Occupational Accident Prevention.* New York: American Society of Safety Engineers and New York University, 1962.

Burtt, Harold E. *Applied Psychology*, Second Edition. Englewood Cliffs, New Jersey: Prentice-Hall, Inc., 1957. Chapters 14, 15.

DeReamer, R. *Modern Safety Practices.* New York: John Wiley & Sons, Inc., 1961.

Ghiselli, E. E., and C. W. Brown. *Personnel and Industrial Psychology,* Second Edition. New York: McGraw-Hill Book Company, 1955. Chapters 10, 12.

Haddon, William J., Edward A. Suchman, and David Klein. *Accident Research: Approaches and Methods.* New York: Harper & Row, Publishers, 1964.

Heinrich, H. W. *Industrial Accident Prevention,* Fourth Edition. New York: McGraw-Hill Book Company, 1959.

Mee, John F. *Personnel Handbook.* New York: The Ronald Press Company, Inc., 1951. Chapters 9, 12.

Simonds, Rollin H., and John V. Grimaldi. *Safety Management,* Revised Edition. Homewood, Illinois: Richard D. Irwin, Inc., 1963.

Trice, Harrison M., and James A. Belasco. *Emotional Health and Employer Responsibility.* Ithaca: New York State School of Industrial and Labor Relations, Cornell University, May, 1966.

University of Michigan, Institute for Social Research. *Employee Health Services.* Washington, D.C.: Government Printing Office, 1957.

ANSWERS TO REVERE SAFETY TEST

Figure 25-3, Page 683

In items 5 and 33 the first two pictures of each item represent unsafe practices. The last picture in each item represents a safe approach.

26

Appraisal and Research

The importance of establishing a sound personnel program and the policies and procedures that implement this program effectively has been emphasized throughout the preceding chapters. It should be recognized, however, that the mere fact that a program is established is no assurance that it will be carried out. As in the case of other management programs, the personnel program should be appraised to determine if it is achieving its established objectives. While the appraisal or audit of a company's financial status is ordinarily conducted by a separate auditing department or by outside auditors, many personnel appraisals or audits are conducted by the personnel department itself. Some appraisals, however, are conducted by other departments in the company or by outside consulting firms, particularly if there is reason to question the program's effectiveness.

While an audit can reveal the effectiveness of a personnel program, it does not reveal the new practices and developments that might be incorporated in the program. In order to have a broader perspective of what the trends are in the field, personnel managers should familiarize themselves with the practices of other companies and with the findings from research studies conducted by other companies, research organizations, and individual scholars. Wherever it is feasible, personnel managers should also make provisions for qualified members of their own staffs to engage in research that will be of value to the company as well as to the profession.

Each company should, therefore, take a look at how well it is performing its personnel functions and should make use of the findings from research. This chapter is devoted to an examination of these important phases of the personnel program:

- Appraisal of the personnel program.
- Personnel research.

Appraisal of the Personnel Program

It is a universal practice to conduct a periodic audit or appraisal of the financial condition of a business in order that any deficiencies may be noted and necessary action taken to correct them. Such an appraisal may uncover not only the presence of deficiencies but may also reveal strengths which were not recognized. One might assume that an important function like personnel management would receive the same careful evaluation as the fiscal aspects of an organization in order that strengths and weaknesses could be known and used as a basis for intelligent action. Various studies indicate rather clearly, however, that a comprehensive appraisal of the personnel program is conducted in only a small percentage of companies. Many companies do, however, conduct appraisals of certain phases of their personnel activities, and many of them belong to associations that compile data regularly from member companies on such aspects of personnel management as wages and fringe benefits.

Personnel Appraisal Practices

The most widely used method of personnel appraisal is the analysis and evaluation of statistical reports that are received by top management on a regular basis. A study of 132 companies ranging in size from 300 to 199,200 employees reveals that in more than three fourths of the companies reports are received on total number of employees, on separations, and on accidents; in one half to three fourths of the companies, reports are received on group insurance, pension plans, compensation, employee hours worked, workmen's compensation, tuition-aid plans, and medical care. Top managements of less than two fifths of the companies receive regular reports on training; about a third are informed regularly on number of grievances. Indexes used by the largest number of companies are those on accidents, turnover, and absenteeism.[1] In addition to statistical

---

[1]Geneva Seybold, *Personnel Audits and Reports to Top Management*, Personnel Policy Study No. 191 (New York: National Industrial Conference Board, 1964).

reports, personnel functions may be audited by means of attitude surveys (discussed in Chapter 16), performance appraisal summaries (Chapter 10), interviews and group conferences between management and employees (Chapters 14 and 15), and formal grievance procedures (Chapter 17). These nonstatistical approaches are often more valuable in correcting problem areas in that they may reveal the causes of problems rather than merely indicating their existence. However, statistical data that reach top management can serve to stimulate corrective action.

The cost of manpower in the successful operation of a business should impress top management with the need for ascertaining the extent to which its personnel policies and objectives are carried out by managerial and supervisory personnel and by the personnel department. Too frequently, however, top management permits the personnel department to conduct a self-audit which is contrary to the usual procedures followed in appraising management functions.[2] Even if the personnel department conducts a careful and impartial appraisal of its own activities, it is desirable that the personnel department try to involve top management in the planning and conducting of appraisals. Top management will not only lend prestige to the personnel function but can facilitate the work of the personnel department in obtaining information needed for the appraisal and in authorizing whatever corrective action should be taken as a result of the appraisal.

Obtaining and Analyzing Information

The first step in conducting an appraisal of the personnel management function is to determine the personnel functions about which more information is desired. While it is usually preferable to make a comprehensive study, this is not always possible because of the time and/or expense involved. Thus, at the outset, the appraisal should be tailored to fit the needs of the company at the time of the appraisal.

After the major functions and principal subfunctions have been identified, the next step is to assess each activity in the light of the following questions:

1. What is the philosophy underlying the function?
2. What principles of management are being followed in carrying it out?
3. What policies have been established for this function?
4. What procedures have been established? Are they in line with the philosophy, principles, and policies?

---

[2]William D. Torrence, "Some Personnel Auditing Practices in Business and Industry," *Personnel Journal*, Vol. 41, No. 8 (September, 1962), pp. 391–394.

5. Are the procedures, policies, management principles, and philosophy of each function consistent with those of other, related functions?[3]

Once the first two steps are completed, the next step is to determine the sources of information. Since appraisal is a form of research, it is important that the findings be based on as objective, reliable, and valid data as can be obtained. Various existing records in the organization may provide the necessary information concerning some of the activities. Interviews and surveys may also be used. In most instances, however, the information on the records is valuable only when analyzed according to a rationale that takes into account the relationships between the specific behavior that is recorded (e.g., absenteeism, accidents) and its significance. Figure 26-1 on pages 706 and 707 shows the wealth of information available from company records and some suggested methods for analyzing it.

It will be noted in Figure 26-1 that one of the suggested methods of analysis is for a company to compare its findings with those of other companies. Through professional groups and employer councils and associations it may be possible to establish a clearing house for information concerning personnel policies, programs, and procedures. The data that are assembled may thus serve as bases of comparisons among companies. This plan is especially recommended for the smaller business that may not have a large personnel department.[4]

Absenteeism and Turnover

Most of the records listed in Figure 26-1 were considered in the preceding chapters. The first two records on the list, however, have been discussed only incidentally. Because absenteeism and turnover are symptomatic of the quality of the organizational climate, further attention is now given to these topics.

Absenteeism. The extent to which employees are absent from their work may serve to indicate the effectiveness of the personnel program of a company. A certain amount of absenteeism is due to unavoidable causes. There will always be some who must remain away from work because of sickness, accident, serious family problems, and for other legitimate reasons. Considerable evidence, however, indicates that there are many other absences which could be avoided. It is advisable, therefore, for a company to determine the seriousness of its absenteeism problem by maintaining

---

[3]Robert D. Gray, "Evaluating the Personnel Department," *Personnel*, Vol. 42, No. 2 (March-April, 1965), pp. 43–52.

[4]Harvey F. Marriner, "Rx for the Personnel Man with Too Many Hats," *Personnel*, Vol. 38, No. 2 (March–April, 1961), pp. 67–70.

individual and department attendance records and by computing absenteeism rates. While there is no universally accepted definition of absence nor a standard formula for computing absence rates, the method most frequently used is the one used by the Bureau of Employment Security of the U.S. Department of Labor. The general formula suggested by the Bureau is:

$$\frac{\text{number of man-days lost through job absence during period}}{(\text{average number of employees}) \times (\text{number of workdays})} \times 100 = \text{rate}$$

If a company employs 500 workers and during one month with 25 scheduled working days 300 man-days are lost through job absence, the absentee rate among the employees for that month would be determined as follows:

$$\frac{300}{500 \times 25} \times 100 = 2.4\% \text{ absenteeism rate}$$

While comparisons between companies are difficult, some general picture of the absenteeism problem may be obtained. Absenteeism rates for the first six months of one year reported by members of the Bureau of National Affairs Personnel Policy Forum showed the following relationships:

1. Absenteeism rates representing percentage of the total scheduled work-time lost ranged from a low of 1.30 to a high of 6.70; the median rate was 2.70.
2. Absenteeism rates generally were highest in January, February, and March, lowest in May and June.
3. Absenteeism rates were higher for female than for male employees in almost all companies.
4. Absenteeism rates were higher for plant than for office employees in most companies.[5]

An intensive study made with a large public-utility company revealed that absence rates were closely associated with employee attitudes toward management, their immediate superior, and fellow workers. With white-collar workers in this company it was found that absenteeism was related to the following:

1. Lack of freedom to talk job problems with supervisors.
2. Lack of feeling of group solidarity.
3. Dissatisfaction with chances for promotion.
4. Dissatisfaction with pay.
5. Lack of recognition for good work done.
6. Dissatisfaction with middle management (the supervisor's boss).

Absenteeism among blue-collar workers followed a similar pattern.[6]

[5]*Labor Policy & Practice-Personnel Management* (Washington, D.C.: The Bureau of National Affairs, Inc.), pp. 241:305–6.
[6]"What Makes People Absent," *Modern Industry* (June 15, 1953), pp. 47–50,

Figure 26-1

USING COMPANY RECORDS TO CHECK PERSONNEL PRACTICES

RECORD	SOME METHODS OF ANALYSIS
Employee turnover record	Analyze record for causes of employee's termination of service. Correlate data with sources of applicants, tests used in selection and placement, sex of employees, length of service, departments, and occupations. Check to see if turnover should be reduced. Also ascertain methods for cutting turnover. Compare with other firms.
Absenteeism record....	Check for possible causes of absenteeism. Correlate with age, occupation, and length of service of employees to see if any pattern is disclosed. Other items such as religion and community events may also be analyzed.
Accident frequency and severity	Compare departmental records for indications of problems in certain departments. See if time of day or length of day affects accident rates. Also compare with other firms. Show savings in reduced number of accidents.
Scrap-loss record......	Discover whether scrap loss is reduced by better training or different types of training. Compare with past scrap records. See if use of tests in placement of employees reduces this figure. Compare records to see if employee-rating plans help reduce scrap costs.
Employee requests for transfers	Correlate with training received, sex, length of service, placement methods, type of work, and supervision received.
Grievance records.....	Analyze subject, handling, cause, costs, and employee characteristics to effect reduction in number of grievances. Show savings in time lost in handling grievances. Check frequency of grievances to locate trouble spots and to make necessary changes in company policies or union agreement.
Personnel inventories...	Compare the number of employees required to handle certain functions with the number used for the same functions in other concerns. Check ages of personnel to see if young replacements are available for key jobs. See if employees are being trained for advancement. Also prepare for possible draft calls for employees.

Time standards and output records	Compare with other companies and with past records to judge effects of methods in improvements and training.
Job specifications......	Compare minimum personnel specifications before and after job analysis to see if savings have been effected in hiring employees with lower personal and job-skill requirements. See if better placement and less training time are required since the system was installed.
Costs of recruitment of employees	Study sources from which employees were drawn and correlate with success on the job to see if some sources should be dropped or other sources added.
Test scores before and after training	Check to see if there is an improvement in employee's knowledge as a result of training. Correlate with success on the job in order to check validity of tests and value of training.
Personal employee records	Determine by sampling if records are up to date and if they are used in making transfers and promotions.
Costs of training methods	Compare unit costs with other firms and costs before and after changes. Balance costs against savings from increased output, lower overhead, reduced accidents and turnover, etc.
Employee use of services such as publications, cafeteria, recreation centers	Determine whether percentage of employees using services is increasing or decreasing. Decide whether the service should be continued or changed. Check possible interrelationships of grievances and services, output and services.
Arbitration awards.....	Classify the subject, contract clause, and employees involved to determine needed changes in personnel policies or practices.
Payroll data...........	Compare with other companies in the vicinity and in the industry to see if wages are in line. Check effects of wage incentives on output, quality, and inspection costs.
Health records........	Analyze causes of illness to check defects in working conditions. Compare with general population and other firms. Compare with morale scales to see if health has affected morale or morale has injured health.
Suggestion records.....	Study to determine what percentage of employees are handing in suggestions, what type of suggestions. Check to see if more employees should participate. Estimate savings achieved.

Source: Thomas J. Luck, *Personnel Audit and Appraisal* (New York: McGraw-Hill Book Company, 1955), pp. 31–32. Reproduced with permission.

It would appear that one of the first things that management should do to reduce the absentee rate is to study the nature and quality of supervision that employees receive. Many of the more desirable supervisory practices discussed in Chapter 14 should be observed. It is quite likely, however, that special attention will still have to be given to those individuals who have the highest absenteeism rates and the cause of absence determined in each individual case. The use of counseling methods, followed by disciplinary action whenever the employee persists in being absent without legitimate and verifiable reasons, is one approach to the problem. A more positive approach, however, is the award of extra days off with pay for good attendance which some companies offer to their employees in an effort to reduce costly absenteeism.

Turnover. Turnover refers to the amount of movement of employees in and out of an organization, ordinarily expressed in terms of the turnover rate. The turnover rate for a department or a company can be an important indicator of the efficiency with which the various personnel functions are performed by managerial and supervisory personnel as well as by the personnel department. The turnover rate may be computed in terms of either accessions or separations, but the separation rate with reference to quits (employees who initiate the termination) is the one most used.

The quit rate is the number of quits during the month divided by the total number of employees on the payroll in the pay period ending nearest the 15th of the month. (Rates for layoffs, discharges, etc., may be computed in the same manner.) For example, if a company employed 500 employees (N) as of the pay period nearest the 15th of the month and there were 25 quits (S) during the month, the quit rate would be:

$$\frac{S}{N} \times 100 = T$$

$$\frac{25}{500} \times 100 = 5\%$$

Another method is one in which the rate is based upon unavoidable separations. If S equals the total separations in the selected period and US the unavoidable separations, the formula becomes:

$$\frac{(S - US)}{N} \times 100 = T$$

Unavoidable separations include termination of temporary employment, promotions, transfers, separations due to illness, death, or marriage.[7]

---

[7]*Labor Policy and Practice-Personnel Management, op. cit.,* pp. 241: 402–403.

This latter method yields what is probably the most significant measure of a personnel program's effectiveness since it can serve to direct attention to that portion of employee turnover that can be reduced. It also represents that portion of turnover that management has the most opportunity to control through its personnel program by means of better selection, training, supervisory leadership, improved working conditions, better wages, and opportunities for advancement. It cannot be used, however, when comparing a company's turnover rate with the figures reported in the *Monthly Labor Review.*

The turnover rate is not the only factor to be considered, however. The quality of personnel who leave a company is important since turnover among competent and desirable employees is a serious matter as compared with turnover among incompetent and undesirable employees. In an effort to determine why employees become dissatisfied and quit, many companies conduct exit interviews. A skillful interviewer can often obtain the type of information that will be helpful to the company in correcting conditions that are undesirable.

Another way in which to obtain information concerning the reasons why employees leave a company is to mail a questionnaire to them after a short interval has lapsed since the date of their termination. The questionnaire shown in Figure 26-2 illustrates the type of questions that may be asked of former employees. Because it is received after the initial anger (if any) has subsided and because the former employee already has the security of another job, a more honest evaluation is likely to be reflected on the questionnaire. The fact that this method is conducted anonymously rather than in a face-to-face confrontation with a member of the personnel staff is also likely to result in favor of a candid response.[8]

A study of turnover, as well as other factors that may be symptomatic of the condition of the organization, should not rely solely on employee opinions. The personnel department should conduct research studies that yield other types of information. Such studies are often reported in journals and provide information as to methodology that may be useful in planning similar studies. In one study of a central petroleum products credit card issuing and billing office employing 700 persons, biographical information from the employee's application forms was related to turnover. Through this procedure it was possible to determine personal characteristics of the employees associated with turnover. Such factors as age, proximity to work, and military service were found to be related in one

---

[8]Julius Yourman, "Following Up on Terminations," *Personnel*, Vol. 42, No. 4 (July–August, 1965), pp. 51–55.

Figure 26-2

A TYPICAL POST-EXIT QUESTIONNAIRE

CONFIDENTIAL COMPANY X QUESTIONNAIRE

DO NOT SIGN. Answer by a checkmark where choice of answer blank is offered. If you need more room for your comments, write "Over" and continue on the back of this sheet.

1. When you were first employed at Company X, were the duties and responsibilities of your job clearly explained to you? YES_____ NO_____ UNCERTAIN_____ COMMENTS _____

2. Were the conditions of work, salary, and other benefits, hours of work, etc. clearly explained to you? YES_____ NO_____ UNCERTAIN_____ COMMENTS_____

3. Did you know who was your immediate supervisor—the one person to whom you reported and from whom you were to receive instructions? YES_____ NO_____ UNCERTAIN_____ COMMENTS _____

4. When you needed information to do your job, were you able to get it easily, usually? YES_____ NO_____ UNCERTAIN_____ COMMENTS _____

5. When you had a suggestion about doing your work, could you discuss it easily with your supervisor? ALMOST ALWAYS_____ USUALLY_____ SOMETIMES_____ RARELY_____PRACTICALLY NEVER_____ COMMENTS_____

6. Frankly, what was the *real* (most important) reason for your leaving the company? _____

7. Could anything have been done to prevent your leaving? PROBABLY NO_____ PROBABLY YES_____ UNCERTAIN_____ COMMENTS _____

8. Have you secured another job? YES_____ NO_____ If "Yes," how does it compare with your last job with us? COMMENTS _____

9. Add here any other comments you wish to make about your work at Company X, your feelings as an employee, or suggestions for making Company X a better place to work. _____

_____. *THANK YOU FOR YOUR COOPERATION. PLEASE RETURN QUESTIONNAIRE IN ENCLOSED ENVELOPE. DO NOT SIGN YOUR NAME.*

Source: Julius Yourman, "Following Up on Terminations," *Personnel*, Vol. 42, No. 4 (July–August, 1965), pp. 51–55. Reproduced with permission.

way or another, thus providing information with which to explore further the characteristics to look for in job applicants in order to maximize length of employment. Since the factors will vary from one job to another and from one company to another, the specific information obtained in this study is not pertinent to the discussion.[9]

Taking Corrective Action

The value to be derived from information obtained from appraisals lies in the use made of it to correct deficiencies in the personnel program. Analysis of the information may reveal that changes in procedures for carrying out some of the personnel functions need to be revised. It is even possible that whole programs should undergo a thorough revision if they are to meet the objectives that have been established for them. Finally, the policies themselves for the various functions should be examined to determine their adequacy as part of the overall personnel policy. Changes in policies and in operating procedures that may be indicated by appraisal findings are often resisted by managerial and supervisory personnel. Nevertheless, if the personnel appraisal is to be of any value to the company,

[9]Gerald L. Shott, Lewis E. Albright, and J. R. Glennon, "Predicting Turnover in An Automated Office Situation," *Personnel Psychology*, Vol. 16, No. 3 (Autumn, 1963), pp. 213–219.

positive action must be taken by management to correct deficiencies as they are discovered from an analysis of objective information.

Personnel Research

Although every company should have an appraisal system that will provide it with accurate and current information concerning the adequacy of its personnel program, it should also attempt to improve its program through the use of personnel research data. There is a wealth of information that can be used in planning and improving a personnel program. Through research findings a business can benefit from the experiences that other companies have had in handling personnel matters. It may also benefit from the research of scholars in various subject-matter fields. In recent years an increased awareness that scientific methodology can be applied to human problems has stimulated research in the behavioral sciences. As a result many studies have been conducted and the findings made available through books and scientific journals.

Behavioral science research is being conducted at various colleges and universities, and considerable information on human behavior is coming from governmental agencies as well as private institutions and from companies that employ psychologists, sociologists, cultural anthropologists, and workers in related fields as members of their staffs. Along with the growth of personnel research, there has been a persistent interest on the part of management, the unions, and the employees themselves for dependable information that will make them better able to understand, predict, and control the behavior of others. Although research will probably never be able to provide solutions to all of the personnel problems of business and industry, the fact that more and more problems are being turned over to experts who use the scientific approach in the study of human problems is an encouraging development.

Importance of Research

Understanding of human behavior, it was noted in the first chapter, has lagged considerably behind man's understanding of his physical environment for various reasons. One reason is that man is a complex organism whose behavior is usually much more difficult to analyze than material or physical items. A second and probably more important reason is that all persons are inclined to feel that, as a result of their experiences, they have learned about human nature and that they understand its complexities as well as the next person. The same individuals, however, would probably be reluctant to admit that they possessed the same degree of understanding about the physical world.

While experiences that one has with people are undoubtedly quite valuable, they may not always result in improved ability to handle personnel problems effectively. Personnel research provides a way of taking an objective look at problems and of developing policies and procedures that are based on facts obtained through scientific study rather than on opinions that result from personal experiences. It is a common practice for the personnel manager to train his subordinates in the use of certain techniques that he has found useful, and subordinates, in turn, teach others these rule-of-thumb approaches. The honest personnel manager, however, must admit that he just does not have the answer to many of the problems that arise. Although he is required to cope with these problems and in many instances must take quick action, he often does so with a hopeful attitude that all will work out for the best. He does not have the controls that the laboratory scientist has in his work. He has many more variables to consider than the laboratory scientist, and he is not able to confine his subjects to the laboratory or a test tube but must deal with them in a social environment that usually defies rigid scientific controls. Furthermore, since he is a fellow human being subject to the influence of the environment that he is attempting to control in some degree, he often finds it difficult to make wise use of the knowledge and skills that he possesses.

While the inadequacy of present knowledge and skills in personnel management and related areas concerned with human behavior is partially the result of these complexities, this is no excuse for relying solely on common sense and experience. Although all of the answers do not exist to questions such as why men work, how raters can be trained to be more objective, or how work groups can be made more productive, the lack of complete answers should not be a deterrent to efforts to work toward sound answers to such questions. Fortunately, these questions become the stimulus for personnel research that in the future will provide partial answers at least. Only by keeping in touch with current research in the field and by applying sound research methods to problem areas can the personnel worker make an effective contribution to his organization.

Research Methods

In the "Space Age" the word "research" has become very common, and most educated persons have a fairly accurate understanding of what is meant by the term. The student of personnel management should, however, have a knowledge of the steps that must be followed in conducting sound personnel research. With such knowledge the student may not only be able to plan research studies of his own but he will have a frame of reference from which to read the reported research of others. The student should be able to read a report with understanding, to evaluate it critically, and to apply the information to current problems that he encounters at work. A knowledge of the types of studies, the steps in the experimental method, and some of the tools used in personnel research are essential to understanding its significance.

Types of studies. Various approaches may be used to obtain information, to analyze it, and to arrive at a conclusion that has some value in predicting and controlling the behavior of people at work. The type of approach that may be used depends on such factors as the nature of the problem, the available data, and what is likely to be accepted by those persons who are being studied. While the experimental approach (to be discussed later) represents the most refined type of study, there are others that are often found to be useful in personnel research. *Surveys*, in which facts are obtained on a topic or problem from a variety of sources, are often used in research on wages, fringe benefits, and labor relations. *Historical studies* are sometimes used to trace the development of problems with a view to understanding them better and in isolating possible causative factors. *Case studies*, like those found at the end of each chapter of this book, may be developed for the purpose of exploring all of the details of a particular problem that is believed to be representative of other similar problems. All of these types of studies have their place. It should be recognized, however, that they lack the precision of the experimental method which is commonly referred to as the scientific method.

The scientific method. While it is sometimes difficult to consider personnel research as being scientific, it should be remembered that what makes a study scientific is not the subject matter but the manner in which one deals with it. A brief examination of the following steps in the scientific method should reveal its applicability to the study of human behavior:

1. Define and delimit the problem. Do not attempt to work on too large an area at one time.
2. Find out through reference to books and journals what others have done on this and related problems.
3. State your problem in the form of a hypothesis or assumption. For example, the hypothesis "workers who are supervised too closely produce less than those workers who receive more general supervision" or "older employees use more sick leave than younger employees" may be tested.

4. Decide on such details as which workers will be used as subjects, how many subjects are needed, the types of control groups, the statistical techniques to be used, etc.
5. Collect the necessary data. This may involve administering questionnaires or tests, conducting interviews, studying available records (personnel, production, etc.).
6. Interpret the data. At this point the hypothesis is either accepted or rejected.
7. Cross-check or verify your findings, if possible, by using another method of gathering data or another group of subjects (if all available subjects were not used in the original study).
8. Publish the findings and distribute. If the report is being prepared for top management, it should be reduced to the essentials and should include positive recommendations that management may either accept or reject on the basis of the findings plus other factors that must usually be considered.

The approach of the scientist is characterized by certain attitudes that affect the results of his efforts. In the first place, the scientist is interested in making systematic rather than aimless observations. He sets up hypotheses (questions) to be tested and he makes observations that will provide him with answers to these questions. His search for the answers is conducted on an impersonal basis. He does not try to prove that the ideas or opinions that he already holds represent facts. Since the observation of human behavior is subject to the pitfalls of bias and prejudice, he may find it advisable to obtain the observations of many individuals rather than to rely merely on his own impressions. Finally, as a check on his objectivity, the scientist reports his experimental procedures and the results in such a manner that it is possible for other scientists to repeat the experiment for purposes of verification.

Errors in conducting research. Although most scientists or researchers are dedicated to following the principles and procedures of science, there is considerable opportunity for error. Those errors that occur most frequently and are most serious are failure to define and delimit the problem, making faulty generalizations, and failure to verify findings.

Unfortunately some experimenters attempt to obtain information without first clearly determining the nature of the problem they are attempting to solve. Obviously if one does not have a clear perception of what the problem is, it is doubtful that he will solve it no matter how much data are collected. In recent years scientists have emphasized the need for asking better questions, that is, asking questions in such a way that it is possible to obtain meaningful answers. This usually involves stating the problem in specific terms rather than in broad, general terms that are too inclusive.

Since a hypothesis should be stated in specific terms and the experimental design set up to evoke the answer to the problem or question, the findings should not be construed as having a wide applicability. For example, if the hypothesis "women employees in the *X* Company over 40 years of age have fewer accidents at work than do women employees under 40 years of age" is tested, certain restrictions must be observed in generalizing from the data. It would be improper, for example, to make any generalizations from the obtained data concerning male employees or accidents away from work. Also, since the study was made in the *X* Company, the findings apply only to that company and not to other companies that were not included in the study.

Finally, the need for verification of research findings should be reemphasized. This is the only way in which the researcher can determine the worth of his original findings. If the results from two studies do not agree, it would be a very questionable procedure to use the findings as a basis for any important personnel or administrative action until the cause for the difference was determined. Unfortunately, even among prominent experimenters, verification has often been a neglected phase of research. Before conducting research of any type, therefore, one should become familiar with studies that are reported in journals and should learn to evaluate them. The checklist for evaluating scientific articles in Figure 26-3 may prove useful for this purpose.

Use of statistics in research. In all types of studies it is usually desirable to quantify the data being collected. This facilitates analysis and summarization of the data and permits generalizations to be made through the use of statistics. Because of the increasing need for the personnel worker to understand and to know how to use statistics, it is recommended that the student learn all that he possibly can about statistics. The old idea that "intuition is enough" has given way to a more scientific approach, which includes the use of statistical concepts.[10]

The personnel worker should not only be familiar with the statistics typically used in business but should at least examine a book in psychological statistics since most personnel research that is reported in the various professional journals employs psychological statistics. It would also be desirable for the personnel worker to familiarize himself with the rapid advancements that are being made in the applications of electronic data processing (EDP) equipment to personnel research. While

---

[10]Stephen Habbe, "Statistics and the Personnel Director's Job," *Management Record,* Vol. 21, No. 6 (June, 1959), pp. 198–201.

Figure 26-3

A BRIEF CHECKLIST FOR EVALUATING SCIENTIFIC ARTICLES

1. The analysis of the purpose of the article:
   - is the purpose clearly stated?
   - will the purpose be supported or refuted by the kind of data collected?
   - is sufficient account taken of previous studies in this particular field?

2. The analysis of the design of the sampling procedure of the experiment involved:
   - is the design of the experiment so formulated that it will give an adequate answer to the purpose of the experiment?
   - how are the subjects selected: from the total population, a restricted population, or other?
   - is the number of subjects adequate to take care of the purpose of the experiment satisfactorily?
   - are there proper and adequate controls (e. g., have controls been properly equated with experimental group)?

3. Analysis of the procedure of the scientific article:
   - are the procedures so described that any other experimenter could duplicate the experiment to check the findings?
   - are the data systematically collected and presented?

4. Analysis of the results:
   - are results correctly and clearly presented?
   - are the units of measurement sound?
   - are graphs properly drawn?
   - are tables properly constructed?
   - are statistical procedures essentially sound?
   - are the proper tests of significance made?
   - do the verbal statements agree with the quantitative and tabular data?

5. Analysis of conclusions:
   - are the conclusions warranted by the data presented?
   - are significant trends recognized?
   - are the limitations of the experiment recognized?

Source: Harry W. Hepner, *Psychology, Applied to Life and Work* (Fourth Edition; Englewood Cliffs, New Jersey: Prentice-Hall, Inc., 1966), p. 603. Reproduced with permission.

punch card systems of various types have always been useful in personnel research, the electronic computers have opened a vast new area of opportunity for research that requires that many variables be manipulated. The availability of computers and other electronic equipment not only facilitates the accomplishment of research studies but also will inevitably stimulate more research in areas where heretofore only feeble attempts could be made to study the many complexities of human behavior in the work situation.

Use of PERT and CPM in personnel operations. As new techniques of work control are developed, managers should consider the possibilities of adapting them for personnel projects. For example, some companies have used PERT (Program Evaluation and Review Technique) to integrate planning, evaluate program status, and identify potential trouble spots. The Sandia Corporation has applied the method to its college recruitment. Prerecruitment activity was broken down into 23 specific tasks that had to be accomplished during the summer months prior to actual campus recruitment, such as analyzing results of prior recruiting efforts, analyzing work load, selecting salary projections, and establishing salary guides. The data were fed to a computer which came out with deadlines that had to be met to keep on schedule. A large chemical company has used the critical path method (CPM) in transferring key personnel and in moving personnel and offices of a product division to its headquarters location.[11]

Research Efforts

Throughout this book reference has been made to the many research studies that have provided partial answers to some of the problems that have faced personnel managers over the years. There are still many unanswered problems that need to be solved through research. Fortunately, there is heightened interest in personnel research, but the basic problem is that research in areas related to personnel management has not kept pace with that in the physical sciences and technology. The rapid changes in technology have created new problems in the management of personnel with the result that an increasing number of new problems will come along before the old problems are solved. The urgent need for greater research effort in areas related to personnel management is well expressed by Peter Drucker who said:

> During the period ahead, in any event, the greatest need for innovation seems more likely to lie in the social than in the technological

---

[11]Geneva Seybold, *Personnel Audits and Reports to Top Management, op. cit.,* p. 113.

area . . . the need is for effective innovation in the management of workers and in the organization of work; despite the progress in this area, it may well be the most backward sphere, and the one with the greatest potential for increased productivity.[12]

While there has been a lag in personnel research, there are many factors that tend to favor more research, and it is possible that the outlook may not be as unfavorable as Drucker forecasts. Increased interest in science and a shortage of scientific personnel have stimulated research in the area of selection. Similarly, a shortage of executives has prompted studies in how to select and train executives for modern complex organizations. The growth in size of many companies and an emphasis on human relations has stimulated interest in studying job satisfaction, morale, supervision, communication, and social interaction within groups. Increased automation has likewise focused on the need for research.[13]

Research in the several areas of study or the disciplines upon which personnel management relies for many of its methods and research in personnel management itself is being conducted by a variety of organizations. A comprehensive study by Goode reveals that personnel research is divided among organizations as shown in Figure 26-4. The financing of the costs of carrying on personnel research studies is as follows: federal government, 67 percent; foundations, 16 percent; business and industry, 13 percent; and state government, 4 percent.[14] The role of the federal government in making research possible is apparent. The main advantage of this support, aside from the fact that research is recognized as important, is that the findings from most of the studies are made available to all organizations regardless of whether they are governmental, business, or industrial in nature.

The approach to research taken by most of the organizations shown in Figure 26-4 is toward the solving of problems that are viewed as critical. In contrast to former methods in which an experimenter often worked on a problem alone because it had a special appeal to him, the trend today is in the direction of using teams to work on research problems. It is not uncommon for these individuals to represent several areas of study or disciplines. Hence, the term "interdisciplinary research" is becoming more popular and will probably characterize a large part of future research.

The findings from research studies, however, are of little value unless they are used in improving personnel policies and the manner in which the

---

[12]Peter F. Drucker, *America's Next 20 Years* (New York: Harper & Brothers, 1957), p. 16.
[13]Cecil E. Goode, *Personnel Research Frontiers* (Chicago: Public Personnel Association, 1958), pp. 14–15.
[14]*Ibid.*, p. 18.

Figure 26-4
WHERE PERSONNEL RESEARCH IS PERFORMED

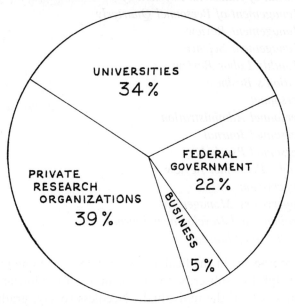

UNIVERSITIES
34%

FEDERAL
GOVERNMENT
22%

PRIVATE
RESEARCH
ORGANIZATIONS
39%

BUSINESS

5%

Source: Adapted from chart and data in Cecil E. Goode, *Personnel Research Frontiers* (Chicago: Public Personnel Association, 1958), p. 21. Reproduced with permission.

various personnel functions are performed. Personnel workers must, therefore, keep themselves informed of the findings from the research conducted by others. In order for the personnel worker to keep abreast of the times, it is helpful to read professional publications. Some of the journals that often contain pertinent articles are:

Advanced Management Journal
Business Horizons
Business Topics
Business Week
California Management Review
Conference Board Record
Dun's Review and Modern Industry
Harvard Business Review
Human Organization
Industrial and Labor Relations Review
Industrial Psychology
Journal of the Academy of Management
Journal of Applied Psychology

Journal of Business
Journal of Industrial Psychology
Management of Personnel Quarterly
Management Review
Management Science
Monthly Labor Review
Nation's Business
Personnel
Personnel Administration
Personnel Journal
Personnel Psychology
Public Personnel Review
Supervision
Supervisory Management
Training and Development Journal
Wall Street Journal

As one progresses in the field and his interests become more specific, it is usually helpful to subscribe to one or more of the journals that meet the particular needs of the individual. Needless to say, graduation from college does not mean the end of learning. Actually, commencement marks the beginning of a career that will require continuous study if success is to be realized in a world that is changing at a more rapid pace than ever before in its history.

Résumé

The need for appraising the work of the personnel department has been considered in this chapter along with the need for making use of available information obtained from research studies. While those who are engaged in the management of a particular function usually believe that they are doing the best they can "under the circumstances," they should try to recognize that improvements can always be made if facts rather than opinions are used in guiding their decisions.

Several sources of factual information with which to conduct an appraisal of the personnel program are available. The more progressive companies use such information not only to correct bad situations but also to plan for future operations. Thus an efficient and sound personnel program is made even better as a result of using appraisal techniques. These companies are also likely to be alert to the value to be derived from research findings, and they usually use them wherever they are applicable.

While the term "research" is academic to some people, for the practical man it represents an effort to do things better. It represents also a problem-solving attitude. Personnel workers who adopt this attitude will probably be among those who are viewed by management and their colleagues as being "out in front" in the field.

DISCUSSION QUESTIONS AND PROBLEMS

1. Even though manpower represents one of the major costs of a business, many companies do not audit their personnel activities with the same degree of thoroughness as they do their fiscal activities. In fact, many companies appear to be "penny wise and pound foolish."
   a. How do you account for the fact that management gives little attention to personnel auditing?
   b. Should personnel managers attempt to do anything about it ? Why?
2. Some companies employ specially trained consultants to conduct audits of their personnel programs.
   a. What are the advantages and disadvantages of using consultants for this purpose?
   b. Consultants often compare the audit findings from a company with other companies with which they are familiar. Of what value are such comparisons?
3. It was stated in this chapter that a study of turnover as well as other factors that may be symptomatic of the condition of the organization should not rely solely on employee opinions.
   a. What other sources of information are available?
   b. What can they contribute to an understanding of causal factors that may not be revealed by employee opinions?
4. How is absenteeism related to the various personnel functions that have been discussed in the various chapters of this book? How far should a manager go in attempting to control it?
5. One of the first steps in conducting personnel research is the formulation of specific hypotheses. Formulate five hypotheses for studies that could be conducted by a personnel department. Have other members of the class criticize your hypotheses using the information contained in the section "Errors in conducting research" on pages 714–715 as a guide.
6. One company research administrator recently said that personnel managers have all types of research data laying around them and have often been the last to recognize its possibilities for use.
   a. What types of data do personnel managers have available to them?
   b. In what ways could they make use of it?
   c. Why do they fail to recognize its possibilities for use?
7. There is often a considerable lag in the application of behavioral research findings to personnel management problems.
   a. What is the reason for the lag?
   b. How can it be reduced?
   c. What effect does this lag have on the value of the research findings to practical problems?

8. Examine recent copies of the journals listed on pages 719–720. Write a brief résumé of the types of articles that are found in these journals. Which journals appear to be of most value to you at this stage in your career? Have you considered subscribing to one or more of them to enhance your professional growth in this area of management?

CASE 26-1

AN APPRAISAL PROGRAM*

The Industrial Relations Department of the Crucible Steel Company of America maintains a continuous appraisal program that is conducted by members of its own staff. Its purposes are (1) to see whether specific programs are hitting their targets and (2) to give top management a continuous overall view of results and trends. The seven major sections of the Industrial Relations Department whose functions are evaluated include: administration, safety and suggestions, training and employment, public relations, company newspaper, labor relations, and salary administration.

Crucible's "Industrial Relations Index" includes almost every aspect of the department's activities. It is a seven-page report prepared in such a way that comparison between different plants of the company is facilitated. Space is provided for inclusion of cumulative year-to-date averages as well as averages for the previous year, thus permitting comparisons to be made from one period to another as well as between the various plants for a particular month. The Index is distributed monthly to all company officers, department and section heads, plant managers and their assistants, and all supervisors in the industrial relations department of Crucible Steel.

In the chart below, some data for three of the plants are presented:

	Plant A	Plant B	Plant C
EMPLOYEES, WAGES AND HOURS			
Number of wage employees	2,646	2,230	1,144
Total employees	3,165	2,522	1,377
Total man-hours (1,000)	561	309	235
Average weekly wage	$ 93.31	$ 79.57	$ 89.84
Average hourly wage including overtime	$ 2.16	$ 2.18	$ 2.17
Premium overtime cost per hour	$ 0.11	$ 0.00	$ 0.11
Premium overtime cost	$51,998	$ 1,055	$20,935
EMPLOYMENT			
*Applicants	24.3	73.0	97.3
*Accessions	7.6	15.9	17.4
Separations	15.2	21.0	10.9
% Turnover rate per month	1.5%	2.1%	1.1%

*Adapted from Seward H. French, Jr., "Measuring Progress Toward Industrial Relations Objectives, *Personnel*, Vol. 30 (March, 1954), pp. 338–347, with the permission of the American Management Association.

LABOR RELATIONS

*Grievances pending first of month...	16.4........	7.5........	2.9
*Grievances filed during month......	1.6........	.4........	0
*Total grievances settled during month..........................	2.5........	3.6........	.7
*Grievances pending end of month......................	15.5........	4.3........	2.2
Work stoppages — man-hours lost...........................	0........	0........	0

SAFETY

Frequency rate.....................	8.01........	2.82........	3.88
Severity rate......................	6.46........	.06........	.11
Compensation cost per 1,000 man-hours.....................	$ 94.23........	$ 0.68........	$ 14.46

SUPERVISORY TRAINING

Average hours in training............	0........	0........	0

SUGGESTIONS

*Received........................	9.5........	7.5........	.7
*Adopted.........................	3.8........	2.0........	0
*Declined.........................	6.3........	4.8........	0
Tangible savings...................	0........	$15,957........	0

a. What interesting relationships do you observe between the figures for the various personnel activities of the three plants for the month indicated?

b. If Crucible's reports showed that a plant had a high turnover rate, plus a high accident rate, many grievances and a few suggestions, what is likely to be the cause?

c. If the hours spent in supervisory training remained at a high peak over a 5-year period, production remained high, and the number of grievances dropped significantly, what hypotheses would be suggested? How could these hypotheses be tested?

d. What advantage is there in having reports monthly by plant with cumulative totals distributed to all company officers, department and section heads, plant managers and their assistants? How does this type of report compare with various fiscal reports?

CASE 26-2

EVALUATION OF SUPERVISORY TRAINING

The committee on supervisory training, established as an advisory body to the training director of a government agency, recommended to Mr. Nickerson, the training director, that supervisors be given a course in the psychology of supervision. They suggested that he employ a professor from one of the local universities who had training and experience in this field, to which Mr. Nickerson agreed. Dr. Rogers was recommended by the university and assented to consider the assignment which was to include a series of ten weekly sessions of two hours each during regular working days. Dr. Rogers met with the committee and presented his ideas as to what should be included in such a course. The committee felt that his ideas were practical, and arrangements were made for the course to begin within a few weeks.

---

*Per 1,000 employees.

Prior to the opening meeting of the course, the committee met and further discussion of the course ensued. It was agreed that the course should be evaluated like all of their courses had been. Since this was the first time a psychology course had been offered, there was some confusion as to what outcomes should be expected. It was decided, after some discussion, that a test should be administered to each supervisor who would attend. The test would be one that the committee had developed for appraising supervisory attitudes and behavior. Each individual would answer these questions so as to indicate his attitudes and behaviors as he perceived them. Each person scheduled to attend the course completed the test to which he was asked to sign his name in order that comparisons could be made with the retest that would be made at the end of the ten-week period.

The course itself included lectures, films, and role-playing exercises covering those aspects of supervision in which psychology played a major part. The major topics were motivation, attitudes, emotions; interviewing and counseling techniques were stressed. While factual material was presented and discussed, the participants were subjected to a considerable amount of "soul searching."

In the week following the final meeting, the committee on supervisory training met again and made arrangements to have the test administered for the second time to the participants. The pre- and post-instructional self-evaluations were then compared. While a few of the participants made higher scores on the post-test, indicating more favorable supervisory attitudes and/or practices, many of the participants' scores did not change significantly; and a few individuals even obtained lower scores on the post-test than on the pre-test. The committee was concerned that the findings were not more favorable, and some of its members felt that the program had been a "waste of time" in spite of the many favorable comments received from the participants. The committee even asked Dr. Rogers to discuss the findings with them and at that time advised him of the type of evaluation that had been conducted.

a. How do you account for the fact that some individuals obtained lower scores on the post-test?
b. Should Dr. Rogers have known about the evaluation before the results were submitted to him? Why?
c. Can you suggest a better type of evaluation for such a course?
d. What are some of the problems of evaluating training courses? What problems might accompany the evaluation of other functions of personnel management?

CASE 26-3

THE TAXPAYERS' PRODIGY

The taxpayers of Wells County felt that they were fortunate to have had Abner Slocum as their county treasurer for over 25 years. Economy always had been Slocum's primary objective during his tenure in this appointive office. His greatest feelings of accomplishment occurred during those years when he was able to return at least 10 percent of his department's operating budget to the general fund. In recognition of these achievements, which were realized more years than not, Slocum received a letter of commendation and a certificate from the county commissioners. The certificate was framed and placed on a wall of his office, which had become well covered by such certificates and by similar commendations during his tenure in office.

In order to achieve economies, Slocum kept a tight rein over all expenditures, and he found the approval of any expenditures for new equipment extremely distasteful. Some of the equipment in his office had become "collectors items." More than one typewriter remained in operating condition only because its user had provided for its maintenance with his own money.

Payroll costs also were kept under close surveillance by Slocum who seemed to be ever-present in the office and quick to investigate any apparent instances of idleness. Male employees were permitted to go to the vending machines for refreshments but were expected to return immediately and consume these refreshments while working at their desks. Women employees were permitted to have a ten-minute rest period every four hours, but only because such periods were required by state law. Whenever possible, Slocum utilized temporary employees who could be laid off whenever the office work load declined or before they became eligible for a salary increase.

Although the clerical staff in the office was supposed to work under the supervision of Elmer Smithers, chief clerk, this individual was bypassed frequently by Slocum who gave assignments directly to employees. At times Slocum would countermand the instructions or assignments that Smithers had given the employees without notifying the latter about the change. While Smithers occasionally had heated discussions with Slocum about such practices, improvements seldom materialized, and Smithers had become resigned to putting up with conditions until Slocum retired.

As might be expected, the employees in Slocum's department were not as enthusiastic toward his methods of operation as were the county's taxpayers. Turnover in the department was extremely high; and except for employees who had accumulated appreciable retirement benefits, the only others who remained were those who were unable to get another job because of their advanced age or general incompetency. Members of the county personnel department, knowing the situation in the treasurer's office, were hesitant to refer those applicants with ability to Mr. Slocum; and, as a result, he received largely those applicants who could not be placed in other departments.

Both morale and efficiency within the department were poor, and errors in record keeping were not uncommon. Citizens having contact with the office were often treated in a curt or even discourteous manner. The county commissioners who were responsible for Slocum's appointment to office began to become more aware of the unsatisfactory conditions that existed within the office. Two of the commissioners who had been friends of Slocum for many years attempted without success to convince him that improvements were needed in the management of his office staff. The commissioners as a group, however, were hesitant to terminate Slocum as treasurer because of his popularity with taxpayer groups and with many of the "old timers" in the community. While his position of treasurer was an appointive one, Slocum did have tenure rights under the county's civil service code that would have prevented his being discharged completely from county service. In addition to job tenure Slocum had also accumulated, during his service with the county, rights to a comfortable pension which he would be eligible to receive in approximately four years at the age of 65. The amount of his pension would be based upon a percentage of the salary received during the five years preceding retirement multiplied by the number of years of service. It was this latter factor, in particular, that made the commissioners hesitant to force the resignation of Slocum from the position that he had occupied for so long. The commissioners also did not have a suitable replacement for the office in mind if they were to decide to remove Slocum from it.

There was a division of opinion on the board regarding Smithers' aptitude for the office. Some members felt that he had never been given a chance by Slocum to demonstrate his ability. Others felt that Smithers was reluctant to assume responsibility.

The chairman of the board of commissioners was the individual in whose hands the responsibility rested directly for initiating any corrective action. Having known Slocum since high school days, the decision for him was a difficult one.

a. What action would you take if you were chairman of the board of commissioners?
b. What factors complicate the reaching of a decision in this case? Would the problem be any different if it occurred in a private company?
c. Would there be an advantage in having an outside consultant appraise this situation? Why?
d. To what extent should economy be the objective of a manager in a government agency?

SUGGESTED READINGS

Conant, James B. *Modern Science and Modern Man.* New York: Columbia University Press, 1952.

——————. *Science and Common Sense.* New Haven: Yale University Press, 1951.

Goode, Cecil E. *Personnel Research Frontiers.* Chicago: Public Personnel Association, 1958.

Hertz, David B. *The Theory and Practice of Industrial Research.* New York: McGraw-Hill Book Company, 1950.

Komarovsky, M. (Editor). *Common Frontiers of the Social Sciences.* Glencoe, Illinois: The Free Press, 1957.

Litterer, Joseph A. *The Analysis of Organizations.* New York: John Wiley & Sons, Inc., 1965.

Luck, Thomas J. *Personnel Audit and Appraisal.* New York: McGraw-Hill Book Company, 1955.

Mee, John. *Personnel Handbook.* New York: The Ronald Press Company, Inc., 1951, Section 20.

Seashore, Stanley E., and David G. Bowers. *Changing the Structure and Functioning of an Organization,* Report of a Field Experiment. Ann Arbor: University of Michigan, Survey Research Center, 1963.

Seybold, Geneva. *Personnel Audits and Reports to Top Management,* Studies in Personnel Policy, No. 191. New York: National Industrial Conference Board, 1964.

Shuchman, Abe. *Scientific Decision Making in Business.* New York: Holt, Rinehart, & Winston, Inc., 1963.

Strother, George B. (Editor). *Social Science Approaches to Business Behavior.* Homewood, Illinois: The Dorsey Press, Inc. and Richard D. Irwin, Inc., 1962.

Whyte, William F., and E. Hamilton. *Action Research for Management.* Homewood, Illinois: Richard D. Irwin, Inc., 1965.

Personnel Management in the Future

Throughout this book an attempt has been made to present a philosophy of personnel management and to consider various objectives, policies, and procedures that are consistent with that philosophy. It is recognized that the philosophy presented may in some respects have appeared to be idealistic when compared with the current practices of certain companies. This fact, however, does not necessarily invalidate the philosophy that was expressed, but, rather, it may indicate that such practices of these companies may have become outmoded or may not have been implemented effectively. Personnel management as practiced is often a process of meeting immediate operational needs (the "putting out of fires") rather than a total, integrated approach to the use of human talents. In times past a relatively loose, informal approach to the utilization of personnel was often adequate. In the period since World War II, however, there has been an increasing challenge for management to reassess its philosophy of personnel management and its practices for carrying out this philosophy. The next decade will present new and exciting challenges that will require the attention of executives, managers, and personnel researchers. Legislators, judges, and government officials, as well as educators, union officials, and the many professional and technical persons whose areas of responsibility and interest involve various aspects of personnel relations will likewise be involved in the task of helping to meet the demands of a rapidly changing society.

In the half century that personnel management has developed into an important functional area of business management, there have been many economic, technological, and social changes that have influenced the role that human beings will have at work. Concurrent with these changes have been changes in the composition of the labor force, in legislation, and in the concepts concerning the utilization of manpower. The field of personnel management has been and will continue to represent the dynamic interaction of many forces that require careful study and analysis followed by appropriate action at each point in its day-to-day emergence.

In the preceding chapters the policies, objectives, and procedures for carrying out the functions of personnel management have been considered in detail. As the discussion of this area of management is brought to a close, it is appropriate to look to the future and to speculate about what is likely to occur that will influence the nature of personnel management. Such speculation is, of course, largely dependent upon the trends that have been observed and are predicted to continue. After an analysis of these trends and their accompanying problems and possible solutions, the outlook for personnel management as a career will be discussed. Hence the major topics of this chapter are:

- Trends, problems, and solutions.
- Personnel management as a career.

Trends, Problems, and Solutions

Significant changes in the field of personnel management are occurring rapidly as a result of the dynamic interaction of all of the forces that dictate its role in a business enterprise. It is exceedingly difficult, therefore, to "stop the clock" at a given moment and obtain a true picture of the field. It is even more difficult to be assured that all of the influencing economic, political, social, and psychological forces were considered in such a picture. Any attempts to look into the future and predict what is likely to happen as far as the total picture of personnel management is concerned must, therefore, be viewed quite tentatively. Nevertheless, it is essential that continued attention be given to the forces that impinge from all sides. Within an organization these forces should be studied by executives, managers, and supervisors in order that they may be in a position to act intelligently with regard to the company and its employees. It is also desirable for employees to be aware of trends affecting their employment in order that they may make wise decisions concerning their own individual destinies and may participate intelligently in the activities of various groups.

In the organizational hierarchy, the personnel manager, as any other manager, must make use of all available data and try to predict what the future of his field will be like in order that he may not only be prepared for the future but may contribute to shaping its future. It is apparent that there are many factors over which he has no direct control, but there are some factors which he can control in varying degrees and which require action on his part if personnel management is to continue to serve the organization and society. As Thomas G. Spates so ably states it:

> In rendering his service to the organization, the officer for, or director of, personnel administration will depend primarily and consistently, but not exclusively, upon patience, perseverance, and persuasion.[1]

These essential qualities of a personnel manager must be supported not only by knowledge of the present but by an awareness of the changes that are taking place in the field, some of which will be considered.

Manpower Trends

One of the areas of major concern to the personnel manager is the availability of manpower for staffing his organization. While there are specific qualities that he considers when recruiting and selecting personnel, the nature of the manpower resources that are available has considerable influence on the degree of success that he experiences in filling job vacancies. The composition of the labor force and its distribution also affect such personnel functions as supervision, fringe benefits, wage and salary administration, and union relations. In fact there is probably no function of personnel management that is not influenced in some manner by manpower trends. It is desirable, therefore, to understand some of the changes that are taking place and their implications for personnel management.[2]

---

[1]Thomas G. Spates, *Human Values Where People Work* (New York: Harper & Brothers), 1960, p. 214.

[2]Unless otherwise indicated the data on manpower trends are from the *Occupational Outlook Handbook*, 1966–67 Edition, Bulletin 1450, U.S. Department of Labor. The projections are based on four fundamental assumptions:

(1) That high levels of economic activity and employment will be maintained over the long run, even though there may be temporary recessions;

(2) That there will be no major war, but at the same time, the defense programs will continue at about the current level;

(3) That scientific and technological advances will continue;

(4) That the institution and fundamental economic structure of the United States will not change significantly.

It is anticipated that the population of the United States will increase from 195 million to a projected 226 million people in the period from 1965–1975. During this same period it is estimated that the number of men and women age 14 and over, who are working or looking for work, will grow from 78 million to 94 million — a growth of almost 20 percent. The growth in the labor force, however, is really a story of young people, as shown in Figure 27-1.

Figure 27-1

CHANGES IN THE LABOR FORCE 1965–1975

Labor force group	Number of persons (in millions)		Percent change, 1965–75
	Esti-mated, 1965	Projected, 1975	
Age 14 and over, both sexes	78. 4	93. 6	19. 4
In the formal education age range, 14–24:			
Men	10. 5	13. 9	32. 0
Women	6. 3	8. 6	36. 3
In the career commitment age range, 25–34:			
Men	10. 7	15. 0	40. 4
Women	4. 2	6. 1	45. 0
In the career peak age range, 35–54:			
Men	21. 7	21. 5	−. 8
Women	11. 5	12. 6	9. 7
In the advanced career age range, 55 and over:			
Men	9. 0	9. 9	10. 3
Women	4. 6	6. 0	32. 4

Note: Because of rounding; sums of individual items may not equal totals. Percentages computed from unrounded figures.

Source: U.S. Department of Labor, *Occupational Outlook Handbook*, 1966–1967 Edition, Bulletin 1450, p. 18.

Young men and women between the ages of 25 and 34 will increase in number at a rate double that for the labor force as a whole. The people who will be in the 25 to 34 age group in 1975 are today in the 14 to 24 age bracket — an age group whose primary concern now would ordinarily be with education and training. The federal labor experts advise that the demand for better educated and trained workers appears to extend to all categories of jobs, and they advise youth to complete as much schooling as possible. Unemployment falls heaviest on workers with the least education with the result that young workers having completed less than eight years of school are expected to have 7 times the unemployment rate of college graduates. Similarly, workers in the least skilled group — laborers — are seven times as likely to be unemployed as professional workers.

The need for education is likely to be even greater in the future as a result of technological developments that may require a person to face several job changes during his working career, hence the wise concern of the young man pictured in Figure 27-2. No longer can a person expect his education and training at the time of graduation or his initial occupation to last for a lifetime. To remain employable, he may be forced to change jobs and his occupation several times during his working life. One, therefore, must have an educational background broad enough to provide a foundation for further training and education that may be necessary.

Figure 27-2

"Mostly, I want to make sure I get into a job
they're not apt to invent a machine for."

Source: *Wall Street Journal*, June 12, 1959. Reproduced with permission.

Since unemployment is higher among those with the least education, it is essential that guidance and counseling services be expanded and improved in schools and that all forms of training on the job, including apprenticeship for the skilled trades, be increased.

At the other end of the age scale, the projections are also for a larger percentage of individuals 55 years of age and over in the labor force, thus requiring that management give special attention to the health, adjustment, and safety problems of employees in this group. Government and industry working cooperatively will find it necessary and desirable to provide training and retraining of older persons to help keep them up to date on technological changes.

Another important change in the composition of the labor force is in the number of women workers. The estimated number of working women in 1965 was 26.6 million, which comprises over one third of the total work force. The projections are for an increasing number of women to be employed.

Another significant trend, namely toward increased moonlighting, has already been observed in Chapter 5. As more individuals hold two jobs, there will likely be a change in employee interest in benefit plans. Some individuals, for example, are overinsured by being covered on two jobs or by having a wife covered on her own job and through her husband's job.[3]

While there will be a change in the size and the composition of the available labor supply, there will also be changes in the developments of major industries and the kinds of jobs for which industry will need workers. Figure 27-3 shows how the major industries are expected to grow in the next ten years. The three major areas with more-than-average projected employment growth are government, service, and contract construction industries. Government — mostly state and local — will be a major source of new jobs in the coming decade. The federal government has fewer than 2½ million civilian workers, and its employment needs are expected to change little during this period. Among the service industries for which considerable growth is predicted are medical and health services and business services — advertising, accounting, auditing, and data processing.

Manpower requirements in educational services (public and private) are expected to grow especially fast as more young people attend schools at all levels. Manpower requirements in education are also expected to be affected sharply by expanded government programs that provide vocational and adult education and training and education for youth, the poverty-stricken, and the unemployed.

The change in industry growth rates is reflected in the changing composition of the nation's work force. As noted in Figure 1-2 on page 8, employment in white-collar jobs has exceeded that in blue-collar jobs and this trend is likely to continue as a result of increased mechanization and streamlining of jobs. The major occupational groups that are affected in this trend are shown in Figure 27-4 on page 734.

---

[3]California Institute of Technology, Industrial Relations Section. *Annual Report 1959–1960*, (September, 1960).

Figure 27-3

**WHILE TOTAL EMPLOYMENT WILL GO UP BY
ONE-FOURTH BY 1975 . . . .**

Industry Growth Rates Will Vary Widely

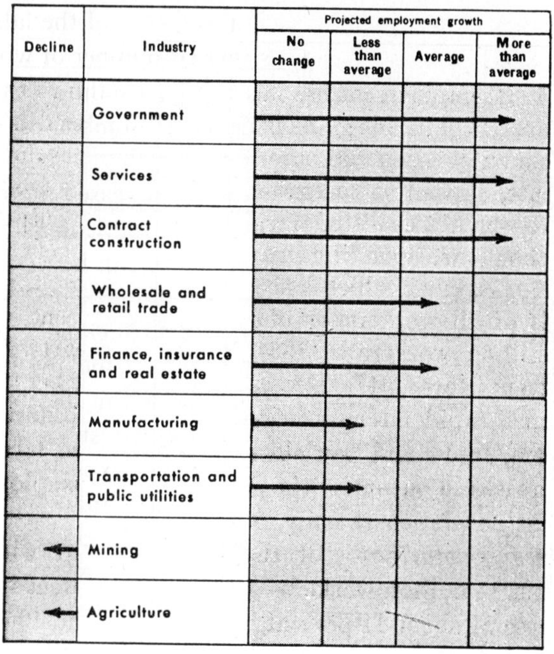

Decline	Industry	Projected employment growth			
		No change	Less than average	Average	More than average
	Government				→
	Services				→
	Contract construction				→
	Wholesale and retail trade			→	
	Finance, insurance and real estate			→	
	Manufacturing		→		
	Transportation and public utilities		→		
←	Mining				
←	Agriculture				

Source: U.S. Department of Labor, *Occupational Outlook Handbook*, 1966–1967 Edition, Bulletin 1450, p. 13.

All of these changes in the composition of the labor force and the demands of industry for personnel of certain "types" will influence the various personnel functions that have been discussed throughout this book.

Technological Developments

The changes in the composition of the labor force are largely the result of technological developments that have and are occurring at an unprecedented rate. Automation of many manufacturing processes has already resulted in a shift in the ranks of semiskilled workers from machining to assembly. A comparison of the 1950 and 1960 census employment data for the 25 largest industrial states shows that the number of assemblers in the fabricating industries in these states increased from 292,853 in 1950 to

Figure 27-4

**JOB OPPORTUNITIES GENERALLY WILL INCREASE
FASTEST IN OCCUPATIONS REQUIRING THE MOST
EDUCATION AND TRAINING. . . .**

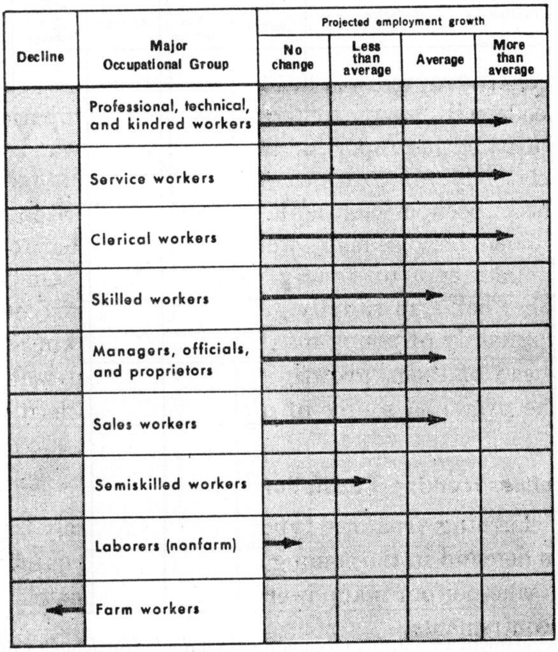

Decline	Major Occupational Group	Projected employment growth			
		No change	Less than average	Average	More than average
	Professional, technical, and kindred workers				→
	Service workers				→
	Clerical workers				→
	Skilled workers			→	
	Managers, officials, and proprietors				→
	Sales workers			→	
	Semiskilled workers		→		
	Laborers (nonfarm)	→			
←	Farm workers				

Source: U.S. Department of Labor, *Occupational Outlook Handbook*, 1966–1967 Edition, Bulletin 1450, p. 16.

463,355 in 1960 — an increase of 58 percent. In the same period the number of operative personnel increased from 855,564 to 952,716 — an increase of only 11 percent. Assembly appears to be the last frontier of automation, and progress is being made in that phase of industrial operations. The automotive and electronics industries have already accomplished varying degrees of automatic assembly on mass-production items.[4]

Automation not only affects the number of persons holding various types of jobs but is known to affect, in some degree, the policies and procedures established for the personnel program. Using opinions from 200 corporation executives concerning the effects of automation on personnel

---

[4]T. O. Prenting and M. D. Kilbridge, "Assembly: The Last Frontier of Automation," *Management Review*, Vol. 55, No. 2 (February, 1965), pp. 4–19.

policies and practices, Lipstreu and Reed made an exhaustive two-year study of one baking company that switched to an automated plant. The effects on personnel functions from selection to profit-sharing plans were studied; some of their hypotheses were confirmed, others were not. Since the findings are from only one company, they will not be discussed here. Such a study, however, points to the need for similar studies in other companies.[5]

Technological developments are affecting the office as well as the plant. Numerous clerical and computational tasks have been computerized, with appreciable effects on the nature of the work force. The computer has also revolutionized management techniques. For the first time, technical change in the form of the computer is displacing management personnel — and this is likely to be increasingly true at the middle levels of management.[6]

The electronic computer — hallmark of automation — has been accompanied on the business and industrial scene by the trend toward a "systems" approach. This means that all activities in an enterprise, such as production, warehousing, sales, finance, personnel, and purchasing, are ever more closely coordinated so that an organization can reach its goal with least effort at least cost. In many areas of business, this means drastic changes, which will have an impact upon the organizational structures and managerial responsibilities that are affected by the new computer technology. Myers believes that this should be one of the personnel man's key functions, yet in some firms the personnel department has scarcely been involved with the introduction of EDP, even though it has had a tremendous impact on personnel. Myers cites a study by Rico of 12 diverse companies in which he concluded:

> The personnel function played a sterile and inconsequential role in the management of change in the survey firms. The personnel department was not consulted, and generally had little or no idea of the organizational and manpower problems associated with computerization in their firms. Dr. Rico further found "no evidence that top management has concerned itself with anticipating changed manpower requirements under computerization."[7]

Effective personnel management demands that top management include a strong representation of individuals who are aware of the importance of the role of personnel in the total functioning of the organization and that these

---

[5]Otis Lipstreu and Kenneth A. Reed, "Automation's Impact on Personnel Administration: A Case Study," *Personnel*, Vol. 42, No. 1 (January–February, 1965), pp. 40–49.

[6]Charles A. Myers, "New Frontiers for Personnel Management," *Personnel*, Vol. 41, No. 3 (May–June, 1964), pp. 31–38; G. P. Shultz and T. L. Whisler (eds.), *Management Organization and the Computer* (Glencoe, New York: The Free Press, 1960).

[7]Charles A. Myers, *op. cit.*, and L. Rico, "The Dynamics of Industrial Innovation," *Industrial Management Review* (Fall, 1963), pp. 3–4.

personnel-oriented and trained individuals participate fully in the large-scale planning.

Social Forces

Personnel management is not only influenced by technological developments and by the changes in the job structure but also by various social forces, including those of an economic and political nature that provide the climate in which personnel activities are carried out. While it is beyond the scope of this chapter to give a detailed analysis of these social forces, the student of personnel management (in college and throughout his career) should be mindful of the larger society and its influences on the business organization. The general concern for employee welfare, for example, will continue to be an influential factor in determining personnel policies and practices. According to Ling, the first trend will likely lead to expanded SUB programs with higher payments and longer benefit periods. Also, vested pension systems will probably spread as an outgrowth of the "job property right" philosophy. Organized labor will also continue to press for protection against the hardships of technological change with such plans as a shorter workweek and a "sabbatical" — designed to raise the level of manufacturing employment.[8]

As a result of continuous training required to cope with automation, it is logical to assume that negotiated training benefits are to take hold in industry before long.[9] Such benefits, presumably, would accrue only to those who are employed and qualify for union membership. Many individuals in our nation, because of various social forces, would not share such benefits. In the *Manpower Report of the President*, it is emphasized that much remains to be done to achieve full opportunity for persons in the following categories:

1. *Unskilled workers* who, with almost double the national rate of unemployment, lack the training to develop their potential skills.
2. *Nonwhite workers*, who constitute 11 percent of our labor force, 20 percent of our unemployed, and nearly 25 percent of our long-term unemployed, suffer the double disadvantages of lower attainment and lingering discrimination.
3. *Young Americans*, who will swell our work force for many years to come, still experience triple the national unemployment rates.
4. *Farmworkers*, both operators and hired workers, remain the victims of high unemployment and underemployment.

---

[8]Cyril C. Ling, *The Management of Personnel Relations* (Homewood, Illinois: Richard D. Irwin, Inc., 1965), p. 490.

[9]George Bennett, "Unemployment, Automation and Labor-Management Relations," *Personnel Administration*, Vol. 27, No. 5 (September–October, 1964), pp. 22–23, 40.

5. *Workers in surplus labor areas,* such as Appalachia, can benefit only from more vigorous economic development in their home areas or from migration to centers of employment growth.[10]

As the opportunities are expanded for these individuals, the manpower resources of the country will be expanded. But industry and government, as well as citizens at large, will be required to participate in many ways if the needed opportunities are to be provided. The Manpower Development and Training Act of 1962, the Economic Opportunity Act of 1964, and Title VII of the Civil Rights Act of 1964, discussed in several of the preceding chapters, are steps in the direction of equalizing job opportunities for these disadvantaged groups. Each one of these laws affects industries and their personnel programs, requiring new policies and procedures in many of the functional areas of personnel management.

The Changing Job of the Personnel Manager

It is being recognized more and more that the work of the personnel manager of a company is as vital to the success of the organization as that of the line managers in such functional areas as production, finance, and sales that traditionally have received the primary attention of top management. For too long the personnel manager has been relegated to a subordinate position that gives him little voice in the extremely important area of manpower. This fact often has been the result of top management's attitude toward its employees and their role in the organization, but it is sometimes the result of the personnel manager's own inability to function as an executive. There is an increasing realization, therefore, that personnel managers must not only prepare themselves for performance of an executive quality but also be encouraged to play a more important role in business. Personnel executive, James J. Kennedy, has stated that:

> ... It is my conviction that organizations will not successfully survive the pace of current and future changing business conditions unless the personnel director functions on an executive level.
>
> The personnel director's contribution, although not easily measurable, has an important impact on a company's current success and future growth. As a specialist in the dynamic but complex "people" affairs of a business organization, the personnel director's responsibilities should be identified by commensurate organizational stature at the division as well as at the corporate level. He should always function in the perspective that people have been and will continue to be the dominant force of any organization. ...

---

[10]*Manpower Report of the President,* 1966.

The mission of the personnel director has evolved so that his charter reflects a dual role — a business manager and human relations manager.[11]

Later in the same article he points out that, in addition to a keen insight and skill in human matters, the present-day personnel director should be equipped with the same managerial talents identified with other successful senior-level executives.

It is quite possible that with the elevation of the personnel manager's job to a higher level within the company some of the major problems concerned with the utilization of personnel in the business enterprise may be handled more effectively. One of the major problems singled out by Argyris is the need to motivate human beings to strive to enlarge and express their full potentialities. It was observed in Chapter 12 that there is a vast untapped source of human potential. As self-realization increases, responsibility, commitment, competence, and a respect for oneself and others also tend to increase. These qualities are important sources of productiveness and effective leadership.[12]

Schaffer and Woodyatt voice the same warning when they advise that personnel executives must take advantage of the untapped resource of the individual's need for self-realization and that they must change their view of the personnel job.

> They must stop thinking of their task as that of making work and the workplace more pleasant, or making them appear to be more pleasant, and of making the worker more interested in his work.   Instead, they must begin regarding it as the job of helping management expect and demand more of all its people and of helping the people respond to the new expectations and demands.[13]

Finally, in addition to being concerned with the organization and its members, "the personnel executive will have to concern himself far more than before with the impact of the *external environment* on the management of the enterprise. There is no doubt that more will be demanded of tomorrow's personnel executive — in study, in planning, and in action."[14]

As the personnel manager attains increased status and is successful in attacking some of the broader and more significant problems of manpower management, it will be possible for him to make greater contributions to

---

[11]James J. Kennedy, "The Personnel Director's Changing Charter," *Personnel Journal*, Vol. 41, No. 8 (September, 1962), pp. 386–388.

[12]Chris Argyris, "A New Era in Personnel Relations," *Dun's Review and Modern Industry*, Vol. 79, No. 6 (June, 1962), pp. 40–51, 167–178.

[13]Robert H. Schaffer and Philip Woodyatt, "New Horizons for Personnel Management," *Personnel*, Vol. 39, No. 2 (March–April, 1962), pp. 42–51.

[14]Myers, *op. cit.*, p. 38.

the organization than he has made in the past. His success and his contributions will serve to challenge managerial and supervisory personnel at all levels in their roles as managers of personnel and will also stimulate individuals to consider personnel staff jobs as attractive opportunities for employment.

Personnel Management as a Career

Throughout this book an attempt has been made to clarify and to distinguish between the responsibilities of the line managers and supervisors and those of the personnel staff in the effective performance of the personnel functions. It is hoped that some interest concerning personnel work — in either a line or a staff capacity — has been stimulated by the discussions of its many phases. Some readers may even be giving serious thought to personnel work as a career and, therefore, desire further information about the available opportunities and how to prepare for them.

Career Opportunities in Personnel

It was observed earlier that the demand for personnel workers is expanding and will provide career opportunities for many individuals who are interested in this challenging type of work that offers a variety of jobs.

Types of personnel jobs. The various functions performed by the personnel department have already been discussed in detail. Among those personnel jobs included or implied in the discussions of preceding chapters are the following:

Chapter 2 — Systems and Procedures Analyst
Chapter 3 — Organizational and Planning Director
Chapter 4 — Job Analyst
Chapter 6 — Employment Interviewer
Chapter 6 — Employment Manager
Chapter 7 — Research Psychologist
Chapter 7 — Test Director
Chapter 8 — Training Director
Chapter 13 — Publications Editor
Chapter 16 — Employee Opinion Analyst
Chapter 16 — Employee Counselor
Chapter 19 — Labor Relations Director
Chapter 21 — Wage and Salary Administrator
Chapter 24 — Employee Benefits and Services Director
Chapter 24 — Recreation Director
Chapter 25 — Safety Director
Chapter 25 — Medical Director
Chapter 26 — Personnel Research Director

This listing of jobs includes those that are typically found in larger companies. In smaller companies there may be fewer personnel jobs with the result that a personnel staff worker is responsible for performing a wider variety of functions than if he were working for a larger company. There is also some relationship between the size of a company and the level at which a person without prior personnel experience is likely to find employment. Though there is no hard and fast rule, the job opportunities do vary with the size of the company and the organization of its personnel department.

The college graduate without full-time experience in personnel work who is employed by the small company or by a local branch of a larger company may find himself in the position of personnel manager charged with responsibility for handling most of the personnel functions, except perhaps those concerned with labor relations. If the same individual were employed by a medium-size company, he would not start at the personnel-manager level but would probably be placed in charge of nontechnical training, employee benefits, or some other phase of the personnel program that is not dependent upon a broad background of experience. On the other hand, if he were to be hired by a large company employing thousands of persons, his initial assignment more likely would be that of a job analyst, employment interviewer, psychological test administrator, or personnel technician. The last title is frequently used to cover a wide variety of functions including the collection, tabulation, and analysis of such data as test scores, exit interviews, and wages.

Employment opportunities. Opportunities for employment and advancement concern all persons who are choosing their lifework. The following predictions for personnel workers were reported in the *Occupational Outlook Handbook* (1966–67 edition) — a government publication widely used by vocational counselors and others who must have a sound basis for the information furnished to their clients:

> College graduates are expected to find many opportunities to enter personnel work through the mid-1970's. However, competition for beginning professional positions is likely to be keen in many parts of the country, and employment prospects will probably be best for college graduates who have specialized training in personnel administration. Opportunities for young people to advance to personnel positions from production, clerical, or subprofessional jobs will be limited.
>
> Employment in personnel work is expected to expand rapidly as the Nation's employment rises. More personnel workers will be needed to carry on recruiting, interviewing, and related activities. Also, many employers are recognizing the importance of good employee relations, and are depending more heavily on the services of trained personnel workers to achieve this.

Employment in some specialized areas of personnel work will rise faster than others. More people will probably be engaged in psychological testing; the need for labor relations experts to handle relations with unions will probably continue to increase; and the growth of employee services, safety programs, pension and other benefit plans, and personnel research is also likely to continue.[15]

This statement contains only predictions; however, since they come from a very reliable source, they have considerable value to one who is planning a career. These predictions should be checked from time to time against current trends and revised estimates of the employment situation.

The student in business should certainly consider employment opportunities in personnel work that exist outside industry. There are many opportunities in federal, state, and local governments. There are also various opportunities for those who desire to go into business for themselves as management or as labor relations consultants. In addition, a number of trained personnel workers are employed in colleges and universities, and there are some who are employed by labor organizations.

While the personnel department is responsible for coordinating personnel functions within the company and for recruitment, selection, wage and salary administration, and other specialized functions, line personnel are constantly engaging in personnel activities. The student who is interested in the daily face-to-face contacts with employees and finds the building of a working team a challenge should not overlook the possibilities of achieving his goals through a supervisory or managerial position. If he desires to move into a personnel staff job, he should endeavor to obtain some experience working in a line department in order that he may understand the types of problems that supervisors and employees in these departments may encounter.

Salaries and working conditions. Most students are interested in the financial opportunities in a career. Because of the changing conditions, it is not possible to quote figures on salaries that will be valid for a very long period of time. Current figures that are available, however, may be of some interest:

A national survey indicated that the average annual salary of job-analyst trainees employed in private industry was about $6,600 in early 1964; experienced job analysts averaged $10,200; directors of personnel who worked in companies employing between 250 and 750 workers averaged $9,700; directors of personnel in very large companies

---

[15]*Occupational Outlook Handbook*, 1966–67 Edition, United States Department of Labor, Bulletin No. 1215, pp. 40–41.

averaged $16,500; and some top personnel and industrial relations executives in very large corporations earned considerably more.

In the Federal Government, inexperienced graduates with bachelor's degrees started at $5,000 a year in early 1965; those with exceptionally good academic records or master's degrees began at $6,050; a few especially well-qualified master's degree holders received $7,220. Federal Government personnel workers with higher levels of administrative responsibility and several years of experience in the field were paid about $12,000; some in charge of personnel for major departments of the Federal Government earned $17,000 or more a year.

Employees in personnel offices generally work 35 to 40 hours a week. During a period of intensive recruitment or emergency, they may work much longer. As a rule, personnel workers are paid for holidays and vacations, and share in the same retirement plans and other employee benefits available to all professional employees in the organizations where they work.[16]

While the above figures are useful as guidelines, it should be realized that the level of the job, the size of the company, the nature of the business or industry, and its location are all factors that determine salaries.

Preparing for a Personnel Career

In addition to understanding the occupational world and its opportunities, it is equally important that the student understand himself — his abilities and aptitudes, his interests, and his personality characteristics. His professors, faculty adviser, or a vocational counselor may be depended upon to be of assistance in furthering his knowledge of the field of personnel work and in helping him to understand himself better. There is some advice of a more general nature, however, that may be of value to the student.

Academic training. Most of the personnel jobs listed earlier in this chapter usually require that a person have training or experience in order to qualify for them. In recent years college training has been emphasized, although many companies still prefer work experience as a prerequisite to assignment to the personnel department. In keeping with the growing professional nature of personnel work, specialized college courses in personnel management, supervision, labor relations, and other areas are being offered. The contributions of the fields mentioned in Chapter 1, such as psychology, sociology, law, statistics, economics, and industrial engineering, also cannot be overlooked. In fact, the personnel worker who has a broad point of view can usually work more effectively with the variety of backgrounds and interests that he finds among those with whom he comes into contact.

---

[16]*Ibid.* p. 41.

Activities outside of the classroom and the library can provide valuable experiences for the student who is interested in personnel work. In fact, many recruiters are as interested in the extracurricular activities of prospective applicants as they are in academic success. Positions of leadership in clubs, publication staffs, fraternities, and other organizations often provide the student with experiences that are comparable to those that he will find on the job. Participation in organizations directly connected with his occupational interest, such as a student chapter of the Society for the Advancement of Management, is especially valuable. During college and after graduation, participation in the local personnel association and similar professional organizations provides a means for exchanging ideas and for furthering the individual's progress as well as that of the profession.

Personal qualifications. The academic training that the prospective personnel worker acquires should provide him with the broad understandings and the special knowledge and skills needed for work in the field. His success, however, is dependent upon more than the training he has received and the knowledge and skills acquired. One of the most important qualifications is that the personnel worker possess good mental health. Other requirements are: a sense of humor, ability to tolerate frustrations, a flexible rather than a rigid approach to problems, ability to communicate with others, patience, and a high degree of objectivity toward other individuals. A permissive and understanding attitude toward human behavior and the ability to listen effectively are especially desirable. Although the individual should have some feeling for others, "liking people" or a "do-good" attitude is hardly a sufficient qualification for entering the personnel field.

Employment experiences. Employers not only attempt to make an analysis of the individual's personal characteristics and academic training but also usually look for employment experiences in his background that may be related to success in the personnel field. While each employer has different opinions on what experiences are most desirable, many of them believe that work experience at the operating level or experience in some type of leadership position in a military or some other organization can provide a good background for personnel work. Through this type of experience the individual has probably learned something about the problems of motivating personnel. It is also possible that he has developed some human relations skills that will make him more effective as a personnel worker.

The Challenge of Personnel Work

Personnel work may appear on the surface to be quite glamorous. The physical appearance of the personnel office is usually pleasant and relaxing. Personnel workers frequently appear to have fun while talking with applicants and employees and may appear not to be rushed, as are production workers who must meet a deadline. A more realistic picture, however, should be provided for the individual who is giving some thought to personnel work as a profession. By considering some of the frustrations and rewards, one may obtain a clearer picture of personnel work and recognize the challenge that lies in this type of work.

Frustrations of the personnel manager. At a personnel conference several hundred personnel executives were asked to complete a questionnaire covering many aspects of their careers including "gripes" about their work. At the top of the list were such complaints as "lack of management support" and "lack of cooperation of line personnel with the personnel department." Another important complaint was that "everyone from the janitor to the president of the company figures he is an expert in your field—but only you take the rap for composite bad guesses." Inability to measure results in concrete terms was another common source of frustration. Fear of getting fired because the personnel functions are usually the first to be curtailed in time of economic adversity, slow promotions, and low salaries in comparison to the heavy workload were other important sources of frustration reported.[17]

Rewards of the personnel manager. A reading of the reported gripes of the personnel executives who attended the AMA personnel conference might lead one to conclude that these individuals were ready to turn to any other type of work that might be available. It is interesting to note, however, that nine out of every ten respondents said that they intended to remain in the personnel field. One reason for this is perhaps that these individuals are reasonably successful in their work and feel that it is unwise to attempt to change. In most instances, however, this decision is probably a recognition of the satisfactions that arise out of the job.

If one were to talk with many individuals employed as personnel managers, he would undoubtedly find that the rewards and satisfactions of the job were many and that they varied with the individuals consulted. One of the major sources of satisfaction comes from playing an important part in helping employees realize their goals at the same time that the goals

---

[17]Edith Lynch, "The Personnel Man and His Job," *Personnel*, Vol. 32, No. 6 (May, 1956), pp. 487–497.

of management are being met. While some equipment may be used, the important role of the personnel worker in helping employees realize their goals and in performing other tasks often requires a high degree of personal skill. The field typically poses a variety of problems to be solved. As a result, personnel work is seldom dull or monotonous. The gratitude of an employee who was assisted in some way, the knowledge that an employee's performance and job satisfaction improved after a transfer to a more suitable job, and the progress of individuals whose talents were recognized by the personnel staff are but a few of the typical situations that make personnel work rewarding.

The challenge. An attempt has been made in this chapter to present the field of personnel management in business as accurately as possible. This type of work, like any other, has its rewards as well as its shortcomings. It should not be viewed through rose-colored glasses, nor should it be viewed with an undue pessimism. It is a type of work that presents a challenge to the individual.

The individual interested in personnel work would do well to explore its career possibilities further. In cases where the individual feels he needs to know more about himself, as well as the field of work, the assistance of a qualified vocational counselor is likely to prove helpful. Individuals in personnel jobs may also be consulted. The important thing is that the individual's decision be made only after careful evaluation of all available information.

Résumé

Personnel management in the future is likely to be even more dynamic than in the past. Technological developments have occurred at an increasingly faster pace, and the forces for rapid social change are clearly evident. As a result, the effective utilization of manpower in an individual company as well as in the total economy constitutes one of the major challenges of society. Those who are engaged in the many facets of personnel management must be prepared to meet the challenge. Today's corporate environment demands that the personnel functions be given the same status as the other major functional areas of the organization.

There are many career opportunities for the individual who is interested in personnel work, and much like any other work it has its desirable and undesirable qualities. It appeals to some individuals but not to others. The individual who feels that he has the required abilities and personality characteristics and whose interests appear to be grounded in reality rather than in wishful thinking should give careful consideration to a career in this field. If he aspires to move up the promotional ladder, he should recognize that success in staff personnel work requires that personnel managers be good leaders. Personnel managers, furthermore, must not only be able to lead their own employees but must also be able to train and to inspire all managerial and supervisory personnel in the organization to become better managers of personnel. The future of the field is dependent upon having more personnel workers who are able to provide that type of leadership.

DISCUSSION QUESTIONS AND PROBLEMS

1. Peter Drucker quotes a wit who said that the field of personnel administration "puts together and calls personnel management all those things that do not deal with the work of people and that are not management."
   a. What significance is there in this statement?
   b. How does this statement relate to the discussion in this chapter concerning the emerging role of the personnel manager?
2. It was observed that automation had affected a wide variety of jobs including those classified as office jobs. What predictions would you make for the automation of specific personnel management functions?
3. It is apparent that in the future the personnel executive will have to concern himself even more with the impact of the external environment on the management of the company. What are some of the external forces that will affect his work?
4. Make arrangements through your instructor to visit the personnel department of one or more local companies. Talk with the personnel manager and his assistants about their work, including its rewards and its frustrations. Compare their responses with the findings from the AMA survey reported in this chapter.
5. Study the descriptions of jobs in the personnel field that are listed in the *Dictionary of Occupational Titles.*
   a. What similarities do you find among these jobs? What differences?
   b. Make a list of your likes and dislikes in job tasks and compare them with the requirements of these jobs.
6. Interview a number of people who work for different companies. Ask them to give you their opinions of personnel management as it is carried on in their companies by the supervisory personnel and by the personnel department. Summarize your findings and comment on their implications for the training and supervision of personnel workers.
7. Some authorities predict that a personnel executive will need an advanced college degree in the years ahead. If you selected personnel management as a career and were planning to study beyond the bachelor's degree, in what

subjects would you specialize? Why? In what topical area would you probably write your thesis?

8. If you are interested in personnel work, what experiences could you have now that would be similar to those that you would be likely to find in a personnel job?

CASE 27-1

TOM MADISON'S CAREER

Tom Madison, the personnel director of a food processing plant employing 300 individuals, has been in his present job for four years and with the company for seven years. Upon graduation from college with an A.B. degree in business, he went to work with the company as a personnel assistant. Because of the expansion of the local plant and reorganization within the company, a separate personnel director's position was established, and many of the personnel activities formerly handled by a regional office were transferred to the branch plant. Tom was selected for that position and has been uniformly rated superior by his boss.

An investigation of Tom's records at the college where he obtained his bachelor's degree reveals that while in high school Tom was given a battery of tests, including an intelligence test and a vocational interest test. He attained an IQ of 125 on the California Short Form Intelligence Test and scored highest on the Persuasive and Social Service scales of the Kuder Preference Record.

One of Tom's teachers in junior college made these comments about him on a recommendation form:

> I knew him during the time that he attended Junior College and 10 years before that. He has a good personal appearance, an outgoing personality, is very energetic and hardworking. He has lots of initiative, is willing to accept responsibility, and is faithful at work. He is loyal to and cooperative with his employers. . . . Although married with 2 children, he has been able to support himself and his family and has obtained good grades in the process.

After completing junior college, Tom attended a four year college offering a degree in business administration. Tom enrolled in the program for this degree and was most successful as evidenced by the 3.4 average (on a 4.0 scale) at the time of his graduation. He was not only a good student but worked evenings and summers as a clerk in a large supermarket. Because of his employment, Tom was not able to participate as fully as he would have liked in extracurricular activities, but he did find time to participate in the campus chapter of the Society for the Advancement of Management.

About six months prior to graduation Tom prepared and assembled materials for his file at the college placement office so that he would be in a position for interviews with the various company representatives whom he would contact about employment and who would inquire of his competencies. At that time the head of the business department of the college wrote the following about Tom:

He has a pleasing personality and a marked ability to get along with people. He stands high in his classwork and is well regarded by his fellow-students for his ideas in business management and for his ability as a speaker. I believe he would do well in personnel work and supervision.

Tom, as we know, has done well in personnel work.

a. What are some of the factors in Tom's background that have probably contributed to his success in personnel management?

b. While his part-time employment prior to completing college did not include many different jobs, of what value was his experience as a store clerk?

c. How do the persuasive and social service interests which were revealed during high school testing influence his career? What role should tests play in the selection of an occupation?

d. What types of information should be assembled for a placement office file? What steps can the student take to make certain that the file represents him as fully and as accurately as possible?

CASE 27-2

PERSONNEL CAREERS*

During World War II thousands of young men who made application for training as bombardiers, navigators, and pilots in the U.S. Army Air Forces were administered a large battery of aptitude tests. As part of the test battery applicants were asked to complete a Biographical Data Blank that contained over 100 items and covered a wide range of activities.

In 1955 and 1956 Thorndike and Hagen obtained up-to-date information on a sample of over 10,000 of the men who had been tested in 1943. While the analysis of the aptitude scores for these 10,000 men in relation to their later careers provides the substance of the study, extensive analyses were also made of the responses to the items on the biographical data blank that had also been completed in 1943 — some 12 to 13 years prior to the analysis.

In the sample of 10,000+ men who were contacted by letter in 1955–56, survey results indicate that 66 of them were currently employed as personnel or employment managers. These 66 individuals were found to have a mean income of $609 and had been in personnel work for six years, on the average. An analysis of the responses to the Biographical Data Blank completed by these 66 individuals in 1943 reveals some interesting differences when their responses are compared with the total population of aviation cadets. Plus activities are those in which the group was significantly above the total cadet population in level of skill or frequency of participation. Three plus signs (+ + +) indicate that differences are highly significant, those with two plus signs (+ +) are of moderate significance, and those with one plus sign (+) are minimally significant.

The following biographical items were found to be significantly above the total cadet population to the degree of significance indicated by the plus sign.

---

*Adapted from data presented in Robert L. Thorndike and Elizabeth Hagen, *10,000 Careers* (New York: John Wiley & Sons, Inc., 1959). Reproduced with permission.

GENERAL FAMILY AND PERSONAL BACKGROUND

Many books in the home	+
Had some college education	+++
Father graduated from high school	++
Mother graduated from high school	++

SCHOOL SUBJECTS STUDIED AND DONE WELL

Dramatics	+
Foreign language	+
Public speaking	+++

ACTIVITIES DONE A NUMBER OF TIMES

Write essay or poem	+
Make a speech	+++

HOBBIES AND FREE-TIME ACTIVITIES

Dramatics	+++
Journalism, school paper	+++
Boy Scouts	+

WORK EXPERIENCES

Higher office work	+++
Instructor or leader	+
Entertainer	++

It should be recalled that these activities were checked off on the Biographical Data Blank completed some 12 to 13 years prior to contacting these individuals who are now employed as personnel or employment managers.

  a. As you look over the items listed above, what appear to be the basic characteristics required of persons engaging in these activities that were found to be significant?
  b. What use can the professor and student make of this information?
  c. While the sample is relatively small ($N = 66$), what advantages accrue from a study of this type?

SUGGESTED READINGS

Calvert, Robert J., and John E. Steele. *Planning Your Career.* New York: McGraw-Hill Book Company, Inc., 1963.

Ching, C. S. *Should You Go into Personnel Work?* (Pamphlet). New York: New York Life Insurance Company, 1955.

Chruden, Herbert J., and Arthur W. Sherman, Jr. *Readings in Personnel Management,* Second Edition. Cincinnati: South-Western Publishing Company, Inc., 1966. Chapters 1 and 8.

Golembiewski, Robert T. *Men, Management, and Morality.* New York: McGraw-Hill Book Company, 1965.

Ling, Cyril C. *The Management of Personnel Relations.* Homewood, Illinois: Richard D. Irwin Co., 1965.

Manpower Report of the President. Washington, D.C.: United States Government Printing Office. Published annually.

Schrader, Albert W., and George S. Odiorne (Editors). *Personnel Management . . . New Perspectives.* Ann Arbor: University of Michigan, School of Business Administration, Bureau of Industrial Relations, 1961.

Super, D. E. *The Psychology of Careers: An Introduction to Vocational Development.* New York: Harper & Brothers, 1957.

NAME INDEX

A

Abel, I. W., 498
Albright, Lewis E., 710
Allen, Louis A., 34, 54, 241, 612
Anderson, E. H., 60
Appley, Lawrence A., 220
Argyris, Chris, 56, 73, 222, 407–408, 489, 738

B

Baker, Alton W., 355, 359–360, 429, 474
Baker, Russell, 95
Bakke, E. Wight, 87
Barker, J. A., 687
Barkin, Solomon, 513
Bass, Bernard M., 154
Bassett, Glenn A., 160
Baumgartel, H. J., 400
Bavelas, Alex, 211, 213
Belasco, James A., 693
Belcher, David W., 554–555, 562, 568, 579, 604, 652
Bellows, Roger M., 155
Benge, Eugene, 555
Bennett, George, 736
Bernstein, Irving, 469
Bertotti, Joseph M., 179–180
Bingham, Walter Van Dyke, 23, 156
Bittner, Reign, 254
Black, James Menzies, 540
Blackett, Frank E., 687
Blake, Robert R., 237, 379–380
Block, J. R., 183
Boddewyn, J., 16
Booker, Gene S., 262
Boyce, Carroll W., 635
Brammer, Lawrence M., 431
Brody, Leon, 687
Brown, Wilfred, 603, 605
Buel, William D., 261
Bullock, Paul, 144
Burck, G., 316
Burns, Robert K., 102
Burtt, Harold E., 23, 316

C

Carson, Walter, Jr., 609
Cassell, Frank H., 204
Cassels, Louis, 427
Cattell, J. McKeen, 23
Chamberlin, T. C., 305
Chapanis, Alphonse, 685
Chase, Stuart, 346
Coch, Lester, 322, 394–395
Coleman, Charles J., 259
Comer, E. P., 261
Conover, Donald W., 685
Costello, Timothy W., 407
Couch, Peter D., 633
Cronbach, Lee J., 183

D

Davis, Harry E., 633
Davis, Keith, 76, 302, 327, 394
Davis, Louis E., 88
Dawis, Rene V., 147
Dennis, Wayne, 395
Dickson, William J., 55, 318, 390
Dolmatch, Theodore B., 207
Dooher, M. Joseph, 254
Drucker, Peter F., 26, 58, 258, 717–718
Dubin, Robert A., 90
Dunnette, Marvin D., 56, 212, 336
Dutton, Richard E., 681

E

Edwards, Allen E., 304
Eilbirt, Henry, 18
Elbing, Alvar O., Jr., 162, 174
Emery, David A., 314
England, George W., 147
Estep, M. Frances, 155
Ewen, Robert B., 311

F

Farson, Richard E., 307
Faunce, William A., 317
Fayol, Henri, 355
Felix, Robert H., 426
Finley, Robert E., 207
Flanagan, John C., 102, 175, 260–261
Fleishman, Edwin A., 361, 380–381, 459
Foegen, Joseph H., 444, 656–657, 662
French, J. R. P., Jr., 250, 322, 394–395
French, Seward H., Jr., 722
French, Wendell L., 162, 174

G

Gardner, B. B., 438
Gatza, James, 258–259
Gellerman, Saul W., 172
Gibbons, Charles C., 367
Gilman, W. H., 261
Glaser, Barney G., 402
Glennon, J. R., 710
Glickman, Albert S., 261
Gomberg, William, 173
Gompers, Samuel, 491–492
Goodacre, D. M., 171
Goode, Cecil E., 718–719
Gordon, Margaret S., 204
Gordon, Robert Aaron, 27
Gray, Robert D., 549, 704
Greene, Edward B., 172
Guion, Robert M., 170, 174, 186
Gwen, William B., Jr., 222

H

Habbe, Stephen, 262, 271, 441, 715
Hagen, Elizabeth, 748

SUBJECT INDEX